THE

CLASS-BOOK OF ETYMOLOGY,

DESIGNED

TO PROMOTE PRECISION IN THE USE,

AND

FACILITATE THE ACQUISITION OF A KNOWLEDGE

OF THE

ENGLISH LANGUAGE.

BY JAMES LYND,

PROFESSOR OF BELLES LETTRES IN DELAWARE COLLEGE.

REVISED STEREOTYPE EDITION.

PHILADELPHIA:
E. C. & J. BIDDLE, No. 6 SOUTH FIFTH ST.
1854.

Printed by T. K. & P. G. Collins.

PREFACE.

As the standard of education in our country has advanced, greater precision in the use of language has marked this progress, and increased attention has been paid to the study of the etymology of our language. To meet the demand, on the part of teachers, for works adapted to instruct in this branch of education, several publications have issued from the press within the past few years. On the merits of these, the compiler of this work does not design to comment. Believing that there was room for improvement, he undertook the compilation of the "Class-Book of Etymology," and now submits it to the examination of teachers.

In the introduction to this work, the nature and progress of language are briefly sketched; a concise account is given of the origin, composition, and development of the English language; and the use of Etymology is exhibited. It is not designed that this portion of the work should be committed to memory by the pupil; but a careful perusal of it will, it is believed, awaken an interest in his mind in regard to the subject he is about to study, and amply repay him for the time so devoted. As, however, many pupils would neglect to adopt the course here suggested, if it were left optional with them so to do, it is recommended to teachers, who may use this book, to require their classes to read the Introduction aloud, accompanying the exercise with such illustrations and questions relative to the subject as will further elucidate it, and leave no doubt that it is comprehended by the pupils.

Copious lists of Prefixes and Affixes compose the FIRST PART of the work. The SECOND PART consists principally of Latin and Greek words, together with a few from the French and other languages, arranged in alphabetical order, with upwards of seven thousand English words placed under their respective roots, and defined. Among the English words so arranged, only one of the various forms which a derivative may take is generally given : thus, under *Solar* is placed *console;* but *consoling, consoler, consolable, consolation,* and *consolatory,* are omitted. Again, under *Duco* is placed *inductive,* while *inductively, induction, inductor,* and *induct* are omitted. Those forms of the derivative thus omitted (and which may be found in Oswald's Etymological Dictionary) should be supplied by the pupil, as an oral exercise, which, it is believed, will be found of great advantage.

The THIRD PART, containing a copious list of words of Gothic origin, is a new feature in school text-books on Etymology: it is confidently recommended to teachers as an efficient means of exciting interest in the mind of the pupil engaged in this study.

The list of English Synonymes, constituting the FOURTH PART of the work, is unusually full, and will render efficient aid to the pupil in his efforts at composition.

The Key* to the Latin, Greek, and other Roots, contained in the Second Part, forms the concluding portion of this work. This will afford most important aid to the pupil in his various exercises on Etymology, and will enable him to analyze without difficulty the words met with in the course of his reading. Thus, should the word *strange* occur, the pupil, without the assistance of such a Key, would doubtless look for the root under the heading S, and look in vain, as the word is derived from *exterus,* outside, foreign. Again, suppose him to meet with *epoch* from *exis, sampler* from *exemplum,* or *hermit* from *eremos,* the same fruitless search would be made. In the case of compound words with several roots or several prefixes, difficulties equally as great would be presented. With the aid of the Key, these difficulties are entirely removed.

---

* This KEY having been prepared primarily for Oswald's Etymological Dictionary, from which the Second Part of the Class-Book of Etymology is abridged, will be found to explain the derivation of many more words than are contained in the Second Part of this work.

In regard to the mode of instructing from this book, little has been said, and this intentionally. Each teacher is acquainted with his own peculiar circumstances, and it is, therefore, presumed that he can adopt a system of exercises which will tend more to the improvement of his classes than would be likely to result from following any general directions which the author might give. It should, however, be borne in mind that, in the study of Etymology—more, perhaps, than in most others—the interest which the pupil may take in it depends, in a great degree, upon the manner in which the subject is presented; the inventive powers of the teacher should, therefore, be exerted in the contrivance of a variety of both oral and written exercises. For some valuable suggestions on this head, the reader is referred to the Introduction and Preface to Oswald's Etymological Dictionary, edited by J. M. Keagy.

In Part II. of this volume, many of the English derivatives have an ^{0} placed after them. This is designed to refer the pupil or teacher to the copious notes of Oswald's Etymological Dictionary, in which the definitions of scientific and technical terms, and the primitive or etymological meaning of many words will be found, the insertion of which in this volume its limits would not admit.

Every teacher using the First Book of Etymology, or the Class-Book of Etymology, as a text-book for his pupils, it is believed will find it advantageous to have in his school, for reference, at least one copy of Oswald's Etymological Dictionary.

PUBLISHERS' ADVERTISEMENT TO REVISED STEREOTYPE EDITION.

In the present "Revised Stereotype" edition, Part I., relative to Prefixes and Suffixes, has been re-written by Dr. Joseph Thomas, and is much more full than in the preceding editions of this work. The clearness and precision with which the various meanings of the Prefixes and Suffixes are here given will, the publishers feel assured, be an addition to the value of the work.

In accordance with Dr. Thomas's recommendation, the chapter on Derivation from the Latin through the French, which appears in "The First Book of Etymology" by Mr. Lynd, has been omitted in "The First Book of Etymology" by Dr. Thomas, on the basis of that by Mr. Lynd, and inserted as Part IV. of *this* volume, being specially adapted for the use of more advanced students.

GREEK ALPHABET.

Letter	Name	Sound	Letter	Name	Sound
Α α	Alpha	a	Ν ν	Nu	n
Β β ϐ	Beta	b	Ξ ξ	Xi	x
Γ γ	Gamma	g	Ο ο	Omicron	ŏ short
Δ δ	Delta	d	Π π	Pi	p
Ε ε	Epsilon	ĕ short	Ρ ρ	Rho	r
Ζ ζ	Zeta	z	Σ σ, final ς	Sigma	s
Η η	Eta	ē long	Τ τ	Tau	t
Θ ϑ θ	Theta	th	Υ υ	Upsilon	u or y
Ι ι	Iota	i	Φ φ	Phi	ph
Κ κ	Kappa	k* or c	Χ χ	Chi	ch
Λ λ	Lambda	l	Ψ ψ	Psi	ps
Μ μ	Mu	m	Ω ω	Omega	ō long

* Kappa and Upsilon are much more frequently changed into *c* and *y* in English, than into *k* and *u*: the latter is of very rare occurrence.

CLASS-BOOK OF ETYMOLOGY

INTRODUCTION.

Language is a collection of certain articulate sounds used as the signs of our ideas, or of certain written characters which represent those sounds. It has been much debated, whether language is of human or divine origin; that is, whether it was given by the Creator to the first of our race, who were thus enabled to converse with each other as soon as they were formed; or whether man was left to his own resources, and from its very rudest beginnings reared the whole fabric.

Those who advocate the former view of the subject, support their theory thus. "Mankind in the first ages were a wandering, scattered race, living upon the spontaneous fruits of the soil, or the flesh afforded by the chase. They were obliged to divide into small families, and each of these occupied an extensive tract of country. Their intercourse consequently must have been very rare, even if they had been inclined to associate. Under these circumstances, how could they agree upon any one set of sounds or words? Even if a few, who were brought together by accident or necessity, could succeed in determining upon certain signs, how could they impart them to the rest of the race, scattered thousands of miles around them? It is very reasonable to think that, prior to the establishment and spreading of language, men must have been congregated in large numbers; there must have been already con siderable progress towards the formation of society; and yet i seems almost impossible to conceive of society without speech—to conceive of men collecting together and co-operating in any enter prise, as long as they were incapable of communicating to one another their wants and desires. When to these considerations i added the fact, that there is an acknowledged resemblance between all languages in their construction and in some of their radical words, "how," say the upholders of this side of the question, "can we reject the conclusion that all languages have one common origin, and that language is the gift of the Deity?"

But, on the other hand, those who believe that language is the invention of man, advance the following arguments. "It is very improper, in human affairs, to attribute any results to the direct agency of God, except where we have undoubted evidence of the fact, or where it is obvious that the undertaking was such as to require the interference of omnipotence. The Creator made man, endowed him with physical, moral, and intellectual faculties, and placed him upon a world which his own hand had prepared, a world nicely adapted to the tastes, delights, wishes, and wants of man, and of which man was the destined lord; but that he did more than this will not be admitted, nor do the circumstances of the case require any such admission. The Almighty, at the formation of man, gave him certain capacities; but he did not give their development. The muscle was attached to the limb; but it was left to time and exercise to strengthen and mature it. So, too, the organs of speech were given, capable of a thousand varieties of articulation; but we cannot think that man was told which sounds to utter first. The work of the Deity was performed when he placed his creature thus gifted upon the earth: the rest was for the latter, operating under the laws that had been imposed upon him and all objects around him."

"As for the argument which attributes to language a divine origin, because of the analogy in the construction of all languages, however widely separated, and however different in other respects, it is of no force whatever, if we suppose mankind descended from a common pair; for then a language would have been formed, complete enough to account for this analogy, long before any separation of the primitive family would have taken place."

Much the greater number of philologists hold the latter theory, to which the compiler of this work also gives the preference. On this hypothesis, language, in the first age, must have been extremely rude. The wants and ideas of men were doubtless of the simplest kind, and were probably communicated by passionate cries, accompanied by such gestures and motions as would further their purpose. Thus, if one desired an object in the possession of another, he would go to him, and, pointing first to the object and then to himself, would utter some sound which, being repeated again and again, would gradually come to express the idea of giving or granting. Or, if one wished another to go with him anywhere, he would go to him and point in the direction he intended to take, accompanying it, as before, with some utterance which, in time, would be used as the sign of going or travelling. In this way many of the very common verbs might be formed.

In giving names to objects, or in the making of nouns, they would probably be governed by the nature of the object. To designate something soft and gentle, a liquid and musical sound would be used; while a harsh sound would be made to represent any thing rough and boisterous. In every language there are a great many words in which sound or motion is concerned; and, as it is easy for the voice to imitate the noise of external objects, these would constitute the beginnings of language. Illustrations of this may be seen in the following sentences: the wind *whistles;* the tempest *roars;* the wolf *howls;* the serpent *hisses;* the *crash* of falling timber; the stream *flows;* the hail *rattles*, &c.

We will suppose then a first language, rude and imperfect, indeed, but still sufficient to enable its possessors, in those early times, to communicate their simple wants and ideas. It is spoken by a small number of individuals, who compose a little family or tribe. Their dwellings are huts; their food is the wild berry, or the raw flesh of those animals they have been so fortunate as to capture; rough skins thrown gracelessly around their bodies serve them for clothing; their weapons are clubs and stones; they rise with the sun, and throw themselves upon the ground to rest as the light disappears; their knowledge is limited to the few objects around them, and even of the nature and properties of these they have but a vague notion—philosophy is not yet born; their sole object is to procure their daily sustenance, and protect themselves from the assaults of the wild beasts which meet them in every path; and the wide world, unexplored and uninhabited, except by the inferior orders of creation, lies open before them. Now, how, from such a commencement, have sprung so many distinct languages,—so dissimilar in their construction and in their words, and each comprising many different dialects,—as are now spoken throughout the world?

All the apparent difficulties of this subject will vanish upon considering the progress of society. As the numbers of the primitive family increased, the amount of food, which they could obtain in the neighborhood of their common lodging place, would be found insufficient; and, as they had nothing to attach them to a particular spot, a separation would take place, and a part of their body would go off to seek a new home. These would meet with new objects; new ideas would be formed; and this would give rise to new names.

At the same time, those left behind them would go on making continual additions to their stock of words; and here we see the first step in the development and variation of language. The change, however, would be very slight, as the discoveries of the one would be communicated to the other. But, in the course of time, the second family would find themselves obliged to send off a division to another spot; while the parent family, even prior to this, in all probability, have sent out a new colony. We now have four separate groups, and the same process which we traced before would continue. Both the new and the old settlements would invent new names, other habits would be formed, old customs would be modified, and, although there would yet be too much intercommunication to permit any extensive differences between their modes of speech, still a decided alteration would begin to be effected. Another period of time would elapse, a new separation would take place, and there would be eight families upon the earth. Upon the next separation, there would be sixteen; this would soon increase to thirty-two; and thus the race would go on multiplying and separating, each separation throwing them further and further from the parent stock, not only in regard to space, but also to manners, customs, and speech, until the whole world would be populated; and, in place of the primitive language, which could no longer be recognised, there would exist a multitude of new ones, altogether unlike it and each other.

Thus, the inhabitants of that part of western Asia, where Noah abode after the deluge, would be incapable of understanding those of Kamschatka, Northern or Western Europe, or Africa; and it is doubtful if the speech of Asia Minor would not be altogether unintelligible to them.

But we must take care that we do not fall into an error here. Although all the divisions of mankind, both those going off to form new colonies and those who remain, are represented as changing their language, yet it must not be thought that this change is identical either in kind or degree. Language is an index of the progress of society, and, as the latter advances or retrogrades, so will the former improve or degenerate. It is well known that mankind must have some fixed abode before civilization can commence, and as long as they lead a roving, migratory life, so long they will be mere savages. It follows, then, that those who in the early ages remained in the first locations, must have gradually improved; while those who were the pioneers of the new-made world continued in the same rude condition as in the beginning; so that, by the time the earth had been generally explored, the inhabitants of central Asia were enjoying the benefits of civilization, while those who occupied the borders of the earth lived in the same comfortless huts, and fed upon the same unpalatable food, that had covered and nourished their first ancestors.

The very same results were produced with regard to language. The one was copious, polished, and abounding with terms which showed that the human mind had awakened; the other had changed, to be sure, but it was only by the corruption or dropping of old words, and the addition of a few new ones; the language was as meager, and the ideas were as rude, as ever.

We have thus arrived at the first element in the diversification of language, and, for the sake of a name, we may call it *migration.* The whole world is now peopled; a thousand varieties of speech exist; *migration* can no longer affect language. What, then, is the next agent? Conquests. As national distinctions are formed disputes arise, and the weaker party must yield to the stronger. Then, as it is impossible to destroy a language without exterminating those who speak it, that of the conqueror must coalesce with that of the conquered to form a new one partaking of the properties of each. This would be a derivative language compounded of two original ones. After the lapse of time, when these nations had become assimilated, we may suppose a fresh conquest made by them. The results already noticed would ensue, and another derivative language would be formed, comprising three of the original languages. When we consider the number of conquests and reconquests that take place as society progresses, we will readily realize the efficiency of this second agent in revolutionizing speech. The remaining causes of the modification of language are comparatively unimportant, and only take place after civilization has made considerable progress. Of these may be mentioned commerce, which furnishes us with the names of offices, dignities, wares, and the terms of traffic, found in foreign countries; and the imitation and borrowing, by learned men, of the words and phrases of other tongues. From what has now been said, it will be seen that there is no great difficulty in believing that all the varieties of speech, now in existence, are the offspring of one common parent.

What this original language was, or the order in which others were derived from it, we are unable to ascertain. We are informed, in the Bible, that the deluge swept away all mankind but Noah and his family; and hence, at this period, the multiplication of languages, like the population of the world, was to begin anew. When we consider the longevity of our earliest ancestors, affording opportunities for men of different ages to mingle together, we cannot but believe that, from Adam down to Noah, the language first made use of underwent no material change. It was this primitive language, then, which Shem, Ham, and Japhet, the three sons of Noah, carried with them to the different parts of the earth which they were respectively to occupy. Shem and his descendants spread through Armenia, Persia, and the adjacent territories, into all the regions of Eastern Asia, forming the ground-work of the Armenian, the ancient Persian, the Sanscrit, the original Chinese, as well as all the languages having affinity to them. Ham and his posterity settled in Arabia, Abyssinia, and the remote parts of Africa, there giving rise to the old Egyptian, the Coptic, the Ethiopic, and their related tongues. Japhet and his offspring occupied Northern Asia, Asia Minor, Ionia, Greece, Italy, and ultimately the whole of Europe, giving birth to the old Pelasgic, the Gothic, the Celtic, and all their kindred dialects.

Of all the ancient languages, of which any knowledge remains, the Hebrew stands first. It is of undoubted antiquity, and is supposed to have experienced fewer alterations than any other. Our knowledge of it, too, is more ample. This is the same with the Phœnician, and other languages then spoken through Palestine and the neighboring countries as far as Syria, Mesopotamia, and Chaldea. Of the other early tongues, of those of Persia, Egypt, and Northern Asia, little or nothing is known. Through the medium of the old Pelasgic, the Hebrew, transplanted by the Phœnicians, became the parent of the Greek. The primitive Greek, in turn, gave origin to the Latin. While this process was going on, the Gothic and Celtic (the last two languages which we can notice at present) were founded. Both evidently appear to have been brought, at a remote period, from the regions bordering on the Caspian and Black Seas, by colonies passing northward and westward in search of a settlement. The languages at first may not have been dissimilar. The Gothic spread through the north of Europe, and gave birth to the Danish, the Swedish, German, and ancient Saxon. The Celtic diffused its dialects through France, Spain, and the British isles. We will have occasion to allude again to both these languages as we progress.

From our definition of language, it will be found to divide itself into spoken and written. The former addresses the ear, and enables us to communicate to those only who are before us, or, at best, within hearing; the latter addresses the eye, and through it our thoughts can be conveyed to those who are distant thousands of miles. The one consists of sounds, which represent ideas; the other comprises marks, or characters, which represent sounds. For a long time, mankind were obliged to content themselves with imparting their ideas to those immediately around them, or, when the occasion demanded that they should communicate with remote persons, their words were put into the mouth of a messenger; but, as society advanced and human relations multiplied, men became dissatisfied with this meager means of intercourse, and made the first step towards the invention of writing.

The first efforts of this kind were, no doubt, by pictures. In every age, mankind have found it easy to represent, by rude figures, the objects presented to their sight. Thus, to signify a battle, they would draw the figures of several men, with weapons in their hands, contending together. This picture-writing was, in fact, the only kind used in Mexico at the time of its discovery. It is very imperfect, however, only being capable of representing those objects and relations which are seen by the eye. Action or external event can be exhibited by it, but no accompanying words or intelligence of the producing causes can be conveyed.

To obviate, in a measure, these disadvantages, hieroglyphics were resorted to. These are symbols, which are made to stand for invisible objects, on account of the resemblance between such symbols and the objects. Thus, an eye was the hieroglyphical symbol of knowledge; a circle, of eternity, having neither beginning nor end; a lion, of strength and fortitude; a horse, of liberty; an ant, of wisdom, &c. These simple symbols were sometimes conjoined to form a new one, and represent a more complex idea. Thus, a serpent with a hawk's head denoted nature with God presiding over it. But from the arbitrary manner of choosing these hieroglyphics, and the imperfect method of putting them together, they must have served but very partially the purposes for which they were designed.

The next step in the progress of writing was to discard pictures and hieroglyphics, and to replace them by simple marks, each one of which should stand for a particular object. Many of these would consist of the hieroglyphical figures, so simplified as to facilitate the connecting of them in writing; and in the new characters to be formed they would undoubtedly pay some regard to the quality or form of the thing to be designated. Every character used in such writings, stands for a separate thing or idea, so that for every word there must be a corresponding mark. Under this system, the English language, instead of twenty-four signs, would require nearly one hundred thousand. Although this method of writing would be all-sufficient for the expression of every idea which might arise in the human mind, yet, on account of the great number of characters, it would require the effort of a lifetime perfectly to read and write them. Very few nations, then, would continue to labor under these disadvantages without making a vigorous effort to remove them.

It will be observed that, as yet, we have met with nothing which corresponds to our letters. The rude pictures first made use of, the hieroglyphics that succeeded them, and the arbitrary marks, were all the signs of things. The thought of inventing a system of marks, which should stand for *sounds*—themselves the spoken representatives of *things*, had not yet entered the minds of men. But, as the inconveniences of the old method of writing became more serious, men began to turn their attention to language, and they discovered that, notwithstanding the great number of words, the sounds which compose those words are very few, and, by representing each of these sounds by a distinct sign, that they could combine these signs in the written word, to correspond with the combination of the sounds in the spoken word, and thus obtain a complete written language without being encumbered with innumerable marks. The first result of this new reasoning was an alphabet of syllables. The distinct utterances, or syllables, of the language were classified, and a mark appropriated to each class. This would reduce the marks used in writing, within a much smaller compass than the number of words used in speaking. Still the number of characters would be very great, and reading and writing must have been attended with many difficulties. All these, however, at last vanished, when some one, more ingenious or more fortunate than the rest of his race, by closely analyzing the sounds made use of in speech, reduced them to a few simple elements. By affixing to these certain signs, which we call letters, an alphabet was formed, and writing made the easy and complete medium of communicating thought, which we now admire and enjoy.

Who invented the alphabet? This is a question, which, to our lasting regret, we cannot answer: even the nation of the inventor is the subject of dispute and uncertainty. Some look to Egypt, the earliest civilized kingdom, perhaps, and the great cultivator of art and science, for its origin; others would award this honour to Phœnicia, and, when we consider the *inventive* activity attendant upon commercial and mechanical pursuits, this award will not appear injudicious or unmerited. From the books of Moses, it appears that the alphabet must have been invented prior to his time. The belief among the ancients was, that letters were brought into Greece by Cadmus, a Phœnician, about 1500 B. C. The letters thus introduced were but sixteen in number, the rest having been added afterwards; and from these very letters, those, now in use by us, and many European nations, are derived.

Originally letters were written from the right hand to the left; for a time the Greeks wrote alternately from the right to the left, and from the left to the right; and, finally, the manner which we now follow, as more natural and easy, was adopted.

At first writing was only employed on important occasions, and pillars and tables of stone, or subsequently plates of the softer metals, as lead, were made use of. As writing became more common, lighter and more convenient articles were brought into service. In some countries leaves and the bark of certain trees were used; in others tablets of wood, covered with a thin coat of wax, on which impressions were made with an iron stylus; and in more modern times, parchment, prepared from the hides of animals, was the usual writing material. The cheap and convenient article which we now possess, paper, was invented no earlier than the fourteenth century.

We have thus taken a view of the nature and progress of language in general; it is time now to turn our attention in particular to our own language. The first accredited accounts of Britain are found in the commentaries of Julius Cæsar, who invaded this country about fifty-four years before the birth of Christ. The inhabitants were mere barbarians. From the resemblance which their customs, manners, language, religion, government, &c., bore to those of the neighboring people of Gaul, there can be no doubt that they were a part of the same family. That the primitive speech of these two regions was the same is undisputed. This speech, from a great tribe of people inhabiting Gaul, called Celtæ, was denominated the Celtic. We have already said, that this was one of the elementary languages, from which many of the modern languages of Europe were derived; and we now see that our own is of this number. The conquests of Cæsar and other Romans who came after him must, unquestionably, have made some impression on the language of the conquered. The country remained subject to Rome for more than four hundred years, during which time garrisons of those who used the Latin tongue were stationed in Gaul and in Britain; the young men of both these provinces were drafted into the Roman service, and many more resorted to the imperial city for an education. It is also clear that numbers of the higher classes were familiar with the Latin; and, indeed, there are traces of that language yet discoverable among the Welsh, the descendants of the ancient Britons. But, notwithstanding all these considerations, the great mass of the people continued to adhere firmly to their native tongue; and this would have still been the language of both France and England, if it had experienced no other changes than those occasioned by Roman invasion.

About four centuries, however, after the first occupation of England, the mighty empire of Rome began to decline. Every year left it diminished in strength, while the enemies that threatened it from without multiplied in numbers, so that it became necessary to withdraw the legions stationed in the extreme provinces—legions whose business had been to guard old conquests and add new ones to them, but whose services were now required to preserve the mistress of the world from the polluting grasp of barbarians. First, among those who were relieved of the presence of their intruders by these causes, were the Britons. But they were only freed from one disagreeable state to fall into another incomparably more unfortunate; for soon after the withdrawal of the Roman legions, the Saxons, a tribe from the north of Europe, inhabiting the country now called Denmark, or the shores of the Baltic, poured in upon their defenceless lands. It is said that they were at first invited over to assist the Britons in driving back the Picts and Scots, who occupied the northern part of the island, and were constantly ravaging the territory of their richer neighbors; and that after having accomplished this object, they turned their arms against those they had been called in to protect, and made themselves masters of the country. Be this account, however, as it may, one thing is certain, that, about A. D. 450, a band of Saxons made their appearance in England, and not only took possession of the whole of it, but entirely destroyed or expelled the former occupants. The flying Britons took refuge in Wales and Cornwall, where their language still exists—the purest specimen yet remaining of the primitive Celtic; and the language of the conquerors became that of England. Here was no affiliation of tongues, as in most cases would take place, no coalition of the speech of the conqueror with that of the conquered, to form a new one, partaking of the elements of both, but an entire expulsion of the latter and the mere substitu tion of the former. The Celtic language, then, as used by the original inhabitants of England, exerted so slight an influence upon the present English tongue, that, in tracing its composition, we must begin anew with the Saxon.

This is a dialect of the Gothic or Teutonic, which, it will be remembered, was represented as having progressed in very ancient times, from the western part of Asia to the north-western part of Europe. About the period of which we are now speaking, hordes of fierce, hardy warriors from this quarter poured down upon the southern parts of Europe, completely revolutionizing the government, the manners, and the language of the prior inhabitants, and imparting to them the form they now present. Among the foremost of these invaders were the Saxons, and through them our language is derived from the same stock as the German, the Dutch, the Danish, the Swedish, and the Swiss. The Saxon language was used in England, with no material alteration, till the time of William the Conqueror. A slight intermixture of Danish took place, in consequence of the irruptions of the Danes, which began with the ninth century, and were continued until, in the course of two hundred years, they gained entire possession of the kingdom. But as they were a kindred people, and only maintained their sway for a short time, the language was not extensively affected.

But, about the middle of the eleventh century, the English tongue was destined to undergo a radical and permanent change. In the year 1066, William, Duke of Normandy, in support of a right he claimed to the crown of England, landed upon its shores with a powerful force, and in the battle of Hastings, utterly defeated the army of the Saxons and killed their king. This placed him securely on the throne, and he began at once to parcel out the lands of the kingdom, and made vigorous efforts not only to impose upon the vanquished the customs and laws, but even the language of Normandy. It became the language of the court; all law proceedings were conducted in it; and the records of the government were clothed in the same foreign garb. All his efforts, however, were vain. The Saxon population was more numerous than the Norman, and finally prevailed; and, though many new words found their way into our language, the bulk of it, nevertheless, continued to be Saxon.

To be convinced of this, we have only to take up a few pages of different English authors, and mark the words not Saxon. In the following extracts, which have been taken at random, all such words are printed in *Italics*.

SHAKSPEARE.

To be, or not to be, that is the *question*;
Whether 'tis *nobler* in the mind to *suffer*
The stings and arrows of *outrageous fortune*,

Or to take *arms* against a sea of *troubles*,
And, by *opposing*, end them? To die, to sleep;
No more?—and by a sleep to say we end
The heartache and the thousand *natural* shocks
That flesh is heir to! 'twere a *consummation*
Devoutly to be wished.

ADDISON.

I was yesterday, about sunset, walking in the open fields, till the night *insensibly* fell upon me. I at first *amused* myself with all the richness and *variety* of *colours* which *appeared* in the western *parts* of heaven. In *proportion* as they *faded* away and went out, *several* stars and *planets appeared*, one after another, till the whole *firmament* was in a *glow*. The blueness of the *ether* was *exceedingly* heightened and enlivened by the *season* of the year.

YOUNG.

Let *Indians*, and the *gay*, like *Indians*, fond
Of feather'd *fopperies*, the sun *adore;*
Darkness has more *divinity* for me;
It strikes thought inward; it drives back the soul
To settle on herself, our *point supreme.*
There lies our *theatre:* there sits our *judge.*
Darkness the *curtain* drops o'er life's dull *scene:*
'Tis the kind hand of *Providence* stretch'd out
'Twixt man and *vanity;* 'tis *reason's reign*,
And *virtue's* too; these *tutelary* shades
Are man's *asylum* from the *tainted* throng.
Night is the good man's friend, and guardian too,
It no less *rescues virtue*, than *inspires.*

ROBERTSON.

This great *emperor*, in the *plenitude* of his *power*, and in *possession* of all the *honours* which can *flatter* the heart of man, took the *extraordinary resolution* to *resign* his kingdom, and to withdraw *entirely* from any *concern* in business or the *affairs* of this world, in *order* that he might spend the *remainder* of his days in *retirement* and *solitude*. *Diocletian* is *perhaps* the only *prince capable* of holding the *reins* of government, who ever *resigned* them from *deliberate* choice, and who *continued during* many years to *enjoy* the *tranquillity* of *retirement*, without fetching one *penitent* sigh, or casting back one look of *desire* towards the *power* or *dignity* which he had *abandoned.*

JOHNSON.

Of *genius*, that *power* which *constitutes* a *poet;* that *quality* without which *judgment* is cold, and knowledge is *inert;* that *energy* which *collects*, *combines*, *amplifies*, and *animates;* the *superiority* must, with some *hesitation*, be *allowed* to *Dryden*. It is not to be *inferred* that of this *poetical vigour Pope* had only a little, because *Dryden* had more; for every other writer since *Milton* must give *place* to *Pope;* and even of *Dryden* it must be said, that if he has brighter *paragraphs*, he has not better *poems.*

BYRON.

Ancient of days! *august Athena!* where,
Where are thy men of might—thy *grand* in soul?
Gone—glimmering through the dream of things that were.
First in the race that led to *glory's* goal,
They won, and passed away. Is this the whole?
A *school*-boy's tale—the wonder of an *hour!*
The warrior's weapon and the *sophist's stole*
Are sought in *vain*, and o'er each *mouldering* tower,
Dim with the mist of years, gray flits the shade of *power*.

The language which thus introduced into the English a new element, (represented in the foregoing quotations by the Italicised words,) was a mixture of Norman and French. The former was brought by a band of Normans, who, some two centuries before the conquest, had siezed upon and settled that part of France, afterwards called Normandy. Here they adopted, to a considerable extent, the words and idiom of the French, and their language became a compound of Norman (which was of the same stock as the Saxon) and French. The French language, on account of the long possession of the country by the Romans, was a kind of corrupted Latin, mingled with Celtic, until the invasions of the Franks and Normans, when it became a compound of the Teutonic dialect, and the former corrupted Latin. For this reason the French tongue has always borne a very close resemblance to the Latin; and to this tongue, or that portion of it introduced through the Norman, are we indebted for a great number of the words we now ascribe to Latin roots. This was the last violent modification the English language underwent. Subsequently it has been changed by the gradual efforts of the learned, and by the influence of those unnoticed circumstances which time brings along with it. A great many words have been transplanted by English authors directly from the Latin; a very large number of terms have been formed from the Greek by scientific men; and commerce has borrowed names from every trading nation on the globe. We will now present all the constituents of the English language, as it at present exists, in a condensed, tabular form:

1st. Saxon and Danish words of Teutonic and Gothic origin.

2d. British or Welsh, Cornish and Armoric, of Celtic origin.

3d. Norman, a mixture of French and Gothic.

4th. Latin, a language formed on the Celtic, Teutonic, and Hebrew.

5th. French, chiefly Latin corrupted, but with a mixture of Celtic.

6th. Greek, formed on Celtic, Teutonic, and Hebrew, with some Coptic.

7th. A few words directly from the Italian, Spanish, German, and other languages of the Continent.

8th. A few foreign words, introduced by commerce, or by political and literary intercourse.

We will close this brief account of our native language by presenting specimens of it at different periods, which will enable us to see clearly its changes, and mark the manner of its development. About the year 700, from the most ancient manuscript of the Saxon language, we find that the Lord's prayer ran thus:

"Uren fader thic arth in heofnas, sic gehalgud thin noma so cymeth thin ric, sic thin willa sue is in heofnas, and in eortho," &c.

This is not an exact copy from the old manuscript, the modern letters having been substituted for the Saxon. In the original it stands as follows:

"Vꞃen ꝼaꞇen ðic aꞃð ın Þeoꝼnaꞅ ꞅic ꝫehalꝫuð ðin noma, ꞇo cymeth thin ꞃic ꞅic thin ƿilla ꞅue ıꞅ ın Þeoꝼnaꞅ anð ın Eoꞃtho."

As this, however, would be altogether unintelligible to most readers, we have deemed it desirable to reduce all the extracts of this kind to the form first used.

The same part of the Lord's prayer, about two hundred years afterwards, was written thus: "Thue ur fader the eart on heofenum, si thin nama gehalgod; cume thin rice si thin willa on eorthan swa, swo on heofenum." It will be remembered that during this interval, between 700 and 900, the Danes had been pushing on their conquests in England. About the year 1160, the first part of the Lord's prayer was thus rendered in verse:

"Ure fader in heaven rich,
Thy name be halyed ever lich,
Thou bring us thy mechle blisse.
Als hit in heaven y doe,
Evar in yearth been it also."

The following is a quotation from a work of Sir John Mandeville, who wrote in the fourteenth century. "And I John Maundeville, knyghte aboveseyd, (alle thoughe I be unworthi) that departed from our contrees and passed the see, the zeer of grace 1322, that have passed manye londes and many yles and contrees, and cerched manye fulle straunge places, and have ben in manye a fulle gode honourable companye, and at manye a faire dede of armes, (alle be it that I dide none myself, for myn unable insuffisance) now I am comen hom (mawgree myself) to reste; for gowtes, artetykes, that me distreymen, tho diffynen the ende of my labour, azenst my will (God knowethe.) And thus takynge solace in my wretched reste, recordynge the tyme passed, I have fulfilled theise thinges and putte hem wryten in this boke, as it wolde come into my mynde, the zeer of grace 1356, in the 34 zeer that I departede from our contrees."

To this period is referred the rise of English poetry, and we will give an extract from Chaucer, which will illustrate, at the same time, the poetry and language of the nation.

"A knight ther was, and that a worthy man,
That fro the time that he first began

To ridin out, he lovid Chevalrie;
Trouth and honour, fredome and curtesy.
Full worthy was he in his lordis werre,
And thereto had he ridden nane more ferre
As well in Christendom, as in Hethness;
And evyr honoured for his worthiness."

About a century after this, Fortescue, Chief Justice in the reign of Henry VI., wrote the following: "Hyt may peraventure be marvelid by some men, why one Realme is a Lordshyp only *Royall*, and the Prynce thereof rulyth yt by his Law, callid *Jus Regale;* and another kyngdome is a Lordschip, *Royal* and *Politike*, and the Prince thereof rulyth by a Lawe, callyd *Jus Politicum et Regale;* sythen thes two Princes beth of egall Astate. To this dowte it may be answeryd in this manner; The first Institution of thes twoo Realmys, upon the Incorporation of them, is the Cause of this diversyte."

The following poem is a plaintive effusion of an unsuccessful lover. We give it entire, although it is rather long for our purposes, because of its poetical merit. It shows the condition of the language in the early part of the sixteenth century.

"My youthfull yeres are past,
My joyfull dayes are gone,
My lyfe it may not last,
My grave and I am one.
My myrth and joyes are fled,
And I a Man in wo,
Desirous to be ded,
My misciefe to forgo.
I burne and am a colde,
I freese amyddes the fyer,
I see she doth withholde
That is my honest desyre.
I see my helpe at hande,
I see my lyfe also,
I see where she doth stande
That is my deadly fo.
I see how she doth see,
And yet she will be blynd,
I see in helpyng me,
She sekes and will not fynde.
I see how she doth wrye,
When I begynne to mone,
I see when I come nye,
He fayne she would be gone.
I see what wil ye more,
She will me gladly kill,
And you shall see therfore
That she shall have her will.
I cannot live with stones,
It is too hard a foode,
I wil be dead at ones,
To do my Lady good."

The last specimen we will give is from the pen of Dr. Wilson, who was celebrated for the politeness of his style and the extent of his knowledge. He wrote about the year 1553.

"Pronunciation is an apt orderinge bothe of the voyce, countenaunce, and all the whole bodye, accordynge to the worthines of such woordes and mater as by speache are declared. The vse hereof is suche for anye one that liketh to haue prayse for tellynge his tale in open assemblie, that hauing a good tongue, and a comelye countenaunce, he shal be thought to passe all other that haue the like vtteraunce: though they haue muche better learning. The tongue geueth a certayne grace to euerye matter, and beautifieth the cause in like maner, as a swete soundynge lute muche setteth forthe a meane deuised ballade."

We have thus traced the English language from its earliest stage, in which it is unintelligible to the ordinary reader, to that in which it is at once recognised as our own speech, and, in fact, only differs from it in regard to orthography; we have also examined its structure and formation, showing the foreign tongues to which it has been indebted for its composition ; and the question that now naturally presents itself is, how can this language, thus compounded and developed, be most expeditiously, most pleasantly, and most thoroughly acquired? We answer, by an attentive study of its roots—by making ourselves acquainted with those foreign words (more particularly the Latin and Greek) which are the parents of our own words. Although it may be asserted that the basis of the language is Saxon, and literary extracts may be made to show that more than three-fourths of the words we use are of Saxon origin, yet we must not let this lead us into the idea that the other sources of our language are undeserving of our regard. The fact is, that the words from the Saxon are very little more numerous than those from the Latin and Greek, and the reason that a contrary opinion has been entertained is, that they are in very common use, and are more frequently repeated than the others. Beyond doubt they are the basis of our speech, and without them we would be unable to continue our intercourse with one another; but, at the same time, they are so simple, standing for the objects immediately around us, that we learn the meaning of most of them in our very childhood. They are acquired without any effort, and almost without our being aware of it.

But with the remaining words of our language it is very different. We do not meet with many of them in the nursery or in the play-ground. They are mostly compound words, and are used to represent complex or abstract ideas. We will give the following lists of words to illustrate what has just been said: *Yard, home, wolf, tool, world, gloom, mother, riddle, bellows, offspring, ask, lose, bleed, darken, forsake, overturn, cold, foremost, giddy, dumb, already, seldom, astray, besides, enough, wholly, indeed,* &c., may represent the Saxon element of the English tongue;

while the Latin element may be represented by *penalty, armistice, missile, abstinence, fragment, arson, regicide, supervision, conspiracy, anniversary, recantation, diction, ire, alien, impost, equinox, annihilate, err, dilute, soliloquize, audit, manacle, inimical, ocular, retributive, sonorous, eligible, malevolent, ultimate, predatory*, &c. To these may be added a few from the Greek: *Theme, axiom, symbol, skeptic, anarchy, hypocrite, symphony, diploma, analysis, tautology, epidemic, metaphysics, baptize, catechise, prophesy, metamorphose, astral, logical, hymeneal, arctic, graphic, nauseous, adamantine*, &c. It is evident, by a glance at each of these classes of words, that we need little assistance from books to learn those in the first; and it is equally evident that those in the two succeeding classes can only be mastered, with the usual helps, at least, after a long and weary effort, by reading good authors and mingling with the intelligent and learned.

But, it may be asked, are there not "expositors" and "dictionaries?" An abundance of them. But of what utility are they? No one ever made himself master of language by their instrumentality. The pupil commits a page of "definitions" to memory to-day, another to-morrow, and a month hence, in all probability, he will not remember five of the words on either page. Such books may answer for the purposes of reference; but to attempt to teach language by requiring their contents to be got by rote, is, to say the best of it, a very fruitless undertaking. Nor is this want of success to be wondered at. The bare definition of the word is given, without any reasons for the meaning attached to it, and without any attempt to furnish an associating principle, by which it may be impressed upon the mind of the learner.

It is very certain that one truth, accompanied by a reason, will be remembered where five truths not so accompanied will be forgotten. Upon this precept every judicious teacher will act, and in conformity with it every good school-book will be constructed. Among the works which have taken advantage of it—which have imparted, along with the instruction, reasons which shall render that instruction indelible—are those on the subject of etymology. Why should *igneous* mean *fiery; linguist, one who is learned in languages;* or *illiterate, one who is ignorant?* What is there in the form of these words, so analogous to their signification, that should prevent the pupil from confounding them, or from entirely forgetting them? Nothing, certainly. Now bring in the assistance of etymology. It informs the pupil that *igneous* is derived from the Latin word *ignis*, which means *fire*, and that *ous* is an English adjective termination expressing *full of*, or *consisting of;* and that *igneous* means *consisting of fire*, or *fiery*. It also informs him that *linguist* is formed from the Latin, *lingua*, a *tongue* or *language*, and *ist, one who*, and signifies *one who has studied many languages*. From the same source he will learn that *litera* is the Latin word for *letter;* that *il* is a prefix meaning *not*, and *ate* an adjective termination; and consequently that *illiterate* means, *not acquainted with letters, unlearned, ignorant.* The pupil now sees the full force of the definitions, and the next time he meets these words, the very images expressed by *ignis, lingua,* and *litera,* will rise vividly in his mind. If the student knows that *manus* signifies a *hand,* and that *manual* is the English adjective derived from it, he will be at no loss to understand such expressions as "*manual* operation," "the king's sign *manual*," &c. If he is aware, also, that *factum* means to make, he understands, at once, the meaning of *manufactures,* and can even see the hands of the operatives at work upon various articles.

There are some words in which the advantages of etymology in elucidating our language appear very conspicuously. *Impervious* is defined as *impenetrable, not to be passed through.* It is derived from *im, not; per, through; via, a way;* and *ous, having—not having a way through, not admitting a passage through.* When we read or hear, then, that glass is *impervious* to air; that oilcloth is *impervious* to water; that wood is *impervious* to light; the expressions are made clear to us by a knowledge of the etymology of the word. *Retaliate* is composed of *re, back,* and *talis, such,* or *the like,* and must then mean *to return such for such,* or *like for like.* The man was abused, and he *retaliated—returned like abuse.* Great Britain passed acts injurious to the commerce of the United States, and they *retaliated—passed acts injurious to British commerce.* The exact signification of *antepenultimate* is very likely to be forgotten from the mere definition; but, if the word is analyzed, and we learn that *ante* means *before; pene, almost;* and *ultimus, the last;* the word seems to acquire a tangibility which it had not before. In this way we might go on until a small vocabulary would grow up under our hands, illustrating the advantages of a knowledge of the Latin and Greek roots from which our words are derived, in enabling us to *comprehend* and *retain* them. But those which have been already given are amply sufficient for this purpose; and we will now proceed to show that this knowledge further assists us in the *use* of words.

There is a great difference among even good writers in this respect—in the delicate discrimination between those finer shades of meaning, which words are capable of assuming, and in the selection of the most apposite and forcible expressions. Almost without an exception, those authors who have adorned English literature have been classical scholars. They were masters of language. In their hands words acquired new meanings, and they could give them many different applications, which those unacquainted with their origin would be absolutely incapable of. Experience alone can make a person thoroughly conscious of the advantages of etymology in this respect; but we will render them in some degree evident by a few illustrations. *Meridian* is usually taken to signify "*a line drawn from north to south, which the sun touches at noon;*" yet the expressions, "I will be with you exactly at *meridian;*" or, "the *meridian* of his glory," are made use of by those acquainted with the etymology of the word. From *mercury* we have *mercurial*, which signifies *belonging to mercury;* but in the phrases a "*mercurial* nation," "*mercurial* habits," it has a signification very different from this, and one founded on its derivation. The usual acceptation of *immaculate* is *holy*, *sinless*, and is applied to the human race; yet a classical scholar would not hesitate to apply it to the surface of water, snow, paper, or any other surface that was *without spot*. *Advise* is ordinarily used as synonymous with *to counsel*, *to give advice;* its etymological signification, however, is *look to*, *see to*, consider; as,

> "*Advise*, if this be worth
> Attempting; or sit in darkness here
> Hatching vain empires."—MILTON.

Illustrations of this kind might be multiplied, but these are enough to corroborate the statement, that those who study the roots of our language have a great advantage over others, not only in the *comprehension*, but also in the *employment* of words.

There are two additional arguments in favor of the general introduction of the study of etymology. We have only time to name them. The first is, that it leads the mind of the student to analyze and synthesize, thus promoting two important processes of the mind; and, secondly, it is a very pleasant introduction to the study of the Latin and Greek languages: this, as a matter of course, only applies to those who anticipate acquiring a classical education.

In closing this introduction, we beg leave to recommend to the reader's notice the following paragraph, which contains some very appropriate hints with regard to the topics just discussed.

"Of the benefit of artificial language no one will ever think lightly who can use it: and without contesting the metaphorical proposition—that we think by the medium of words—we are at liberty to affirm, that—words are often used without thinking;—and that *much of education, as generally managed, has a strong tendency to produce such a habit*. Old as we are, we too sufficiently remember the hardships of attending to what we did not understand, and acquiring what we did not value . . . . . . we have vivid recollection of the heartlessness of storing up WORDS without IDEAS, and which we could not possibly imagine to be of any use but to furnish occasions for reproach and chastisement."—*Edinburgh Monthly Review*.

PRELIMINARY DEFINITIONS.

ETYMOLOGY is that science which explains the *true origin* and derivation of words, with the view to ascertain their *radical* or *primary* signification.

Etymology of the English language, treats of the *true origin* and *meaning* of English words.

English words are either *Primitive* or *Derivative.*

A *Primitive* word is not derived from any simpler word in the language; as, *sweet, tract.*

A *Derivative* word is formed from a *Primitive* word by adding or prefixing a syllable; as, *sweet*en, at*tract*, at*tract*ion.

The *Radical* or *Essential* part of a word is called a *Root;* as, *hope* in *hope*-ful; *clud*, in ex-*clude*, ex-*clus*-ion.

A *Root* is modified or restricted in sense by a *Prefix* or a *Suffix;* as, *fit*, *un*-fit, *not* fit; *anim*, *life*, anim-*ate*, *having* life, *in*-anim-*ate*, *not having* life.

A *Prefix* is a syllable or particle placed *before* a root to vary its sense; as, *un*, *not*, in *un*-seen, *not* seen; *ex*, *out*, in *ex*-clude, to shut *out.*

A *Suffix*, or *termination*, is a syllable *added* to the root to vary its signification; as, *ful*, in hope-*ful*, *full* of hope; *al*, in fin-*al*, *belonging to* the end.

In a few cases, however, the Prefix and Suffix do *not* affect the meaning of the Root; as, *un*, in *un*-loose; *dis*, in *dis*sever; *ate*, in medit*ate*, oper*ate*.

PREFIXES, AFFIXES,

AND

LATIN, GREEK, AND OTHER ROOTS

OF THE

ENGLISH LANGUAGE.

I. PREFIXES.

1. OF ENGLISH OR SAXON ORIGIN.

A, signifies *on, in, to,* or *at:* as, *a*foot′, *on* foot; *a*bed′, *in* bed; *a*field′, *to* the field; *a*far′, *at* a great distance.

Be, signifies *over;* to *cover with:* as, *be*daub′, to daub *over; be*dew′, to *cover with* dew.

En, signifies *in* or *into; to put into, in,* or *on; to make* or *make into:* as, *en*grave′, to grave *in* or *into; en*chain′, to *put into* chains; *en*throne′, to *put on* a throne; *en*act, to *make into* an act; *en*a′ble, to *make* able.

Em, for En, having the same signification as the preceding, is prefixed to words beginning with *b, m,* or *p:* as, *em*bot′tle, to *put into* a bottle; *em*mew′, to cage *in,* or put into a cage.

Fore, signifies *before* or *beforehand:* as, *fore*noon′, the part of the day *before* noon; *fore*see′, to see *beforehand.*

In and Im* are similar in signification to *en* and *em:* as, *in*close′, to close *in; in*sure′, to *make* sure; *im*bit′ter, to *make* bitter.

Mis, signifies *wrong* or *erroneous:* as, *mis*apply′, to apply *wrong,* or to an improper purpose; *mis*belief′, a *wrong* or *erroneous* belief.

Out, signifies *beyond,* or *more than,* denoting *excess* or *superiority:* as, *out*bid′, to bid *beyond* or *more than* another; *out*run′, to run *beyond,* to surpass in running.

Over, signifies *too, too much,* or *too great,* sometimes denoting *superiority:* as, *over*an′xious, *too* anxious; *over*bur′den, to burden *too much,* to impose *too great* a burden; *over*pow′er, to overcome by *superior* power.

Un, before a verb, signifies to *reverse the act of;* to *take off* or *deprive of:* as, *un*bind′, to *reverse the act of* binding, to loose; *un*crown′, to *reverse the act of* crowning, to *take off* the crown.

---

* For other significations of *in* and *im,* see Prefixes of Latin origin, page 22.

UN, before an adjective, signifies the *reverse* or *opposite of; not:* as, *un*holy, the *reverse* or *opposite of* holy; *un*able, *not* able.

UNDER, signifies *beneath; less than another; less than is proper* or *just:* as, *under*sheriff, one who is *beneath* or *under* the sheriff; *under*bid, to bid *less than another; under*value, to value *less than is proper* or *just.*

WITH, signifies *from; against:* as, *with*draw′, to draw *from* or away, to retire; *with*stand, to stand *against.*

2. OF LATIN ORIGIN.

A, signifies *from; off; away:* as, *a*vert′ (Verto), to turn *away*, to turn *from; a*vul′sion (Vello), a tearing *off* or *away.*

AB, another form of the preceding, has the same signification: as, *ab*duct′ (Duco), to take or carry *off; ab*erra′tion (Erro), a wandering *away.*

ABS, for A or AB, has the same signification: as, *abs*′ent (Ens), being *away; abs*tain′ (Teneo), to hold *from*, to refrain.

AD, signifies *to; by* or *near; on* or *upon;* and more rarely, *up; against; for; at:* as, *ad*apt′ (Apto), to fit *to; ad*ja′cent (Jaceo), lying *by* or *near.*

A, for AD, signification the same: as, *a*scend (Scando), to climb *up*, to rise; *a*sperse′ (Spergo), to sprinkle *upon;* hence, to stain or slander.

AC,* for AD, signification the same: as, *ac*cede′ (Cedo), to yield *to.*

AF, for AD, signifies the same: as, *af*flux′ (Fluo), a flowing *to; af*fu′sion (Fundo), a pouring *upon.*

AG, for AD, signifies the same: as, *ag*glu′tinate (Glutino), to glue *to*, to cause to adhere; *ag*gress′ (Gradior), to go *to* or *against.*

AL, for AD, signification the same: as, *al*lis′ion (Lædo), a dashing or striking *upon* or *against; al*locu′tion (Loquor), a speaking *to*, or address.

AN, for AD, signifies the same: as, *an*nex′ (Necto), to tie *to*, to join.

AP, for AD, signifies the same: as, *ap*pend′ (Pendo), to hang or join *to*, to affix.

AR, for AD, has the same signification: as, *ar*′rogate (Rogo), to ask or claim *for* (one's self); *ar*ro′sion (Rodo), a nibbling *at*, or gnawing.

AS, for AD, signifies the same: as, *as*similate′ (Similis), to make like *to; as*sist′ (Sisto), to stand *by*, to help.

AT, for AD, signification the same: as, *at*test′ (Testor), to bear witness *to.*

---

* It will be perceived that *ad* and several other prefixes change the final consonant so that it may correspond to the initial letter of the root to which it is joined. Thus, it becomes *ac* before a root beginning with *c; af*, before one beginning with *f*, and so on. In like manner, *con* becomes *col* before a root commencing with *l; cor*, before one beginning with *r*, &c. To this general rule, however, there are a number of exceptions.

AM, or AMB, (Gr. αμφι,) signifies *round* or *about:* as, *am'b*ient (Eo), going *round* or surrounding.

ANTE, signifies *before:* as, *ante*ce'dent (Cedo), going *before.*

CIRCUM, signifies *round* or *about:* as, *circum*nav'igate (Navigo), to sail *round.*

CIS, signifies *on this side of:* as, *cis'*alpine (Alpes), *on this side of* the Alps.*

CON, for CUM, signifies *together; with; altogether* or *entirely; the same with another*†: as *con'*catenate (Cateno), to link *together.*‡

CO, for CON, (prefixed to words beginning with a *vowel* or with *h,*) has the same signification: as, *co*e'qual; equal *with; co*here (Hæreo), to stick *together.*

COG,§ for CON, signifies the same: as, *cog'*nate (Nascor), born *together* or *with;* hence, related, allied.

COL, for CON, has the same signification: as *col*lect' (Lego), to gather *together.*

COM, for CON, (prefixed to words beginning with *b, m,* or *p,*) has the same signification: as, *com*bine' (Bini), to put two or more things *together.*

COR, for CON, signification the same: as *cor*rela'tion, relation *together,* or reciprocal relation.

CONTRA, signifies *against* or *contrary to:* as *contra*dict' (Dico), to speak *contrary to; contra*posi'tion (Pono), a placing *against* or opposite to.

COUNTER (from the French *contre*), for CONTRA: as, *counter*act' (Ago), to act *against.*

DE, signifies *down; from; off* or *away;* rarely, *about, concerning; Un* or *Dis*‖: as, *de*duce' (Duco), to lead or draw *from; de*fend', to strike or ward *off; de*ject' (Jacio), to cast *down; de*scribe' (Scribo), to write *about* or *concerning; de*stroy' (Struo), to *un*build or pull down, to put an end to, to annihilate.

DIS, (from the Italian or French,) signifies, before verbs, *to reverse the act of,* often denoting *privation:* before adjectives or nouns, the *reverse of; not:* as *dis*arm (Arma), to *un*arm, or *reverse the act of* arming, to *deprive* of arms; *dis*loy'al, *not* loyal; *dis*sat'isfied, *not* satisfied, the *reverse of* satisfied.

---

* Cisalpine and Transalpine are generally used with reference to *Rome.* Hence, Cisalpine signifies south of the Alps, i. e. between the Alps and Rome; Transalpine denotes the contrary side.

† See Note under the prefix *Con,* in Oswald's Etymological Dictionary, edition of 1852.

‡ For examples illustrating the other meanings of this prefix, see under its other forms, *Co, Cog, Col,* &c.

§ *Con* is changed to *Cog,* and *In* to *Ig,* before a few Latin words beginning with *n,* derived from Greek roots commencing with *g;* e. g. *cog*NATUS (NATUS being from the Greek γενητος), for *con*NATUS; *ig*NOSCO (NOSCO being derived from γινωσκω), for *in*NOSCO, &c.

‖ *De,* in some words derived from the French, has the same signification as *Dis* or *Un;* as *de*range (Fr. *déranger*), to *dis*arrange or put out of order; *de*tach, to *dis*-attach, to loosen, to separate. This signification of *De* in Latin words is rare.

DIS, in words derived directly from the Latin, signifies *apart; in different* or *opposite directions; differently**: as, *dis*pel′ (Pello), to drive *apart*, to scatter.

DI, for DIS, signifies the same: as, *di*vert′ (Verto), to turn *apart* or away.

DIF, for DIS: as *dif*fluent (Fluo), flowing *apart* or away.

EX, signifies *out* or *forth; beyond*†; *up; from* or *away:* as, *ex*clude′ (Claudo), to shut *out; ex*posi′tion (Pono), the act of setting *forth; ex*ceed′ (Cedo) to go *beyond; ex*tol′ (Tollo), to lift *up*, to exalt.

E, for EX, signifies the same: as, *e*ject′ (Jacio), to cast *out; e*m′a-nate (Mano), to flow *from.*

EF, for EX, has the same signification: as, *ef*fervesce′ (Fervesco), to boil *out* or over, to boil or bubble up; *ef*flux (Fluo), a flowing *out* or *forth.*

EXTRA, signifies *beyond* or *beyond the limits of:* as, *extra*mun′dane (Mundus), *beyond* the world; *extra*v′agant (Vagor), wandering or going *beyond* due limits.

IN, before verbs, participles and nouns, expressing the action of a verb, signifies *in; into; on* or *upon; against:* as *in*flux′ (Fluo), a flowing *in; in*fuse′ (Fundo), to pour *into* or *upon; in*vade′ (Vado), to go *against.*

IL, for IN, has the same signification: as, *il*lu′minate (Lumino), to shine *into* or *upon.*

IM, for IN, (used before *b*, *m*, and *p*,) signifies the same: as *im*bibe′ (Bibo), to drink *in*, to absorb; *im*port′, to carry or bring in or *into; im*pel′ (Pello), to drive *on; im*pend (Pendeo), to hang *upon* or over; *im*precate′ (Precor), to pray *against.*

IR, for IN, signifies the same: as, *ir*rup′tion (Rumpo), a breaking or bursting *into.*

IN, IG‡, IL, IM, and IR, before an adjective or noun, signifies *not; the reverse or opposite of; absence of:* as, *in*ac′tive (Ago), *not* active; *in*jus′tice (Justitia), the *opposite* of justice; *ig*no′ble (Nobilis), the *reverse* of noble; *il*le′gal (Lex), *not* legal; *ir*re-li′gion, the *absence of* religion, the *opposite of* religion.

INTER, signifies *between* or *among:* as, *inter*cede′ (Cedo), to go *between*, to mediate; *inter*mix′ (Misceo), to mix *among.*

INTRO, signifies *in* or *into; inward:* as, *intro*duce′ (Duco), to lead *in; intro*vert′ (Verto), to turn *inward.*

JUXTA, signifies *near to* or *by:* as, *juxta*position, a being placed *near* or next to.

---

* As *Con* generally implies "union," *Dis*, on the contrary, mostly signifies "separation" or "disunion." Thus, as *con*sent signifies to think *with* or agree with, *dis*sent signifies to think *apart* from, to differ in opinion or sentiment: *con*tribute means to give *together* or collect by giving; *dis*tribute signifies to give *apart* or to separate by giving.

† *Ex* often denotes "excess," or something beyond what is usual or proper.

‡ See Note § on the preceding page.

OB, signifies *against; before; in the way:* as, *ob*trude′ (Trudo,) to thrust *against; ob*struct′ (Struo), to build or place *against* or *in the way; ob′*ject (Jacio), something thrown or placed *before.*

OC, for OB, has the same signification: as, *oc*cur′ (Curro), to run *against* or *before*, to present (itself) before, to happen.

OF, for OB, signifies the same: as *of*fend′ (Fendo), literally to strike *against;* hence, to injure, to displease.

OP, for OB, has the same signification: as, *op*pose′ (Pono), to put or set *against*, to place (one's self) *against.*

PER,* signifies *through; thoroughly:* as, *per′*ambulate (Ambulo), to walk *through; per′*fect (Facio), made or done *thoroughly.*

POST, signifies *after:* as, *post*dilu′vian (Diluvium), *after* the flood.

PRE (Lat. præ), signifies *before* or *beforehand:* as *pre*cede′ (Cedo), to go *before; pre*dict′ (Dico), to tell *beforehand.*

PRETER (Lat. præter), signifies *beyond, past* or *by:* as, *preter*-nat′ural (Natura), *beyond* or more than natural; *pre′ter*ite (Eo), gone *past* or gone *by.*

PRO (προ), signifies *for* or *instead of; forward; out:* as, *pro*con′-sul (Consul), one who acts *for* (or *instead of*) a consul; *pro′*noun (Nomen), a word used *instead of* a noun; *pro*ceed′ (Cedo), to go *forward; pro*duce′ (Duco), to lead or bring *forth; pro*tract′ (Traho), to draw *out.*

RE, signifies *back; again* or *anew; against:* as, *re*cede′ (Cedo), to go *back; re*sume′ (Sumo), to take *again; re*sist′ (Sisto), to stand *against.*

RED, for RE, signifies the same, used chiefly before words beginning with a vowel: as, *re*deem′ (Emo), to buy *back*, to ransom; *red*in′tegrate (Integer), to make whole *again*, to restore.

RETRO, signifies *back* or *backwards:* as, *retro′*grade (Gradior), to go *back* or *backwards;* (adj.) going *backwards.*

SE, signifies *aside; apart; astray:* as, *se*cede′ (Cedo), to go *aside apart; se*duce′ (Duco), to lead *aside* or *astray.*

SEMI, (from Semis, a "half,") signifies *half; imperfectly:* as, *semi*an′nual (Annus), *half* yearly; *semi*fluid (Fluo), *imperfectly* fluid.

SINE, signifies *without:* as *sine′*cure (Cura), a situation or office *without* care or trouble.

SUB, signifies *under; up under; slightly:* as *sub*ja′cent (Jaceo), lying *under; sub*ac′id (Acidus), *slightly* acid.

SUC, for SUB, has the same signification: as, *suc*cumb′ (Cubo), to lie down or sink *under* a burden, to yield.

SUF, for SUB, signifies the same: as, *suf*fuse′ (Fundo), to pour or spread *under.*

---

* *Per* sometimes expresses *inversion* or doing *wrong.* Thus, *per*vert signifies to turn *through* (as a sleeve), to turn the wrong side out; *per*jury, *wrong* or false swearing; *per*fidy, *wrong*, bad, or false faith.

SUP, for SUB, signifies the same: as, *sup*port' (Porto), to bear *up under; sup*press' (Premo), to press *under*, to stifle, to subdue.

SUS, for SUB, or SURSUM, signifies *up:* as, *sus*pend' (Pendo), to hang *up*.

SUBTER, signifies *under; secretly:* as, *sub'ter*fuge (Fugio), a flying *under*, a secret escape.

SUPER, signifies *above* or *others; over; upon; very:* as, *super*add' (Do), to add *over* and *above; super*fine', fine *above others*, or above what is usual, *very* fine; *super*scribe' (Scribo), to write *upon*.

SUR (Fr. for Super), signifies *above* or *beyond; over; upon:* as, *sur*vive (Vivo), to live *above* or beyond another, to outlive; *sur*charge', to *over*charge; *sur*vey' (Video), to look *upon*.

TRANS, signifies *beyond; through; across* or *over; from one to another:* as, *trans*alpine' (Alpes), *beyond* the Alps; *trans*pa'rent (Pareo), appearing *through; trans*port' (Porto), to carry *across* (the sea), to carry away or excite beyond what is usual; *trans*fer' (Fero), to carry *from one to another*.

TRA, for TRANS, signifies the same: as, *tra*di'tion (Do), literally, a giving or handing *from one to another;* opinions handed down from parents to their children; *tra*mon'tane (Mons), *beyond* the mountains; hence, outlandish, extravagant.

ULTRA, signifies *beyond:* as, *ultra*mon'tane (Mons), *beyond* the mountains, tramontane.

3. OF GREEK ORIGIN.

A or AN (α, αν), signifies *without; Un; not:* as, *a*ceph'alous (Cephale), *without* a head; *an*om'alous (Homalos), *un*even, or *not* regular, irregular.

AMPHI,–AMBI (αμφι & ambo, Lat. *both*), signifies *both* or *double:* as, *amphi*b'ious (Bios), (capable of) living *both* on land and in water.

ANA (ανα), signifies *through* or *throughout; up; back; again:* as, *ana*l'ysis (Lysis), a loosening or separation *throughout*, a *re*solving into the original elements; *ana*t'omy (Tomos), a cutting *up*, the art of dissection, the science of animal structure.

ANTI (αντι), ANT before a vowel, signifies *against; opposite* or *opposed to:* as, *ant*arc'tic (Arctos), *against* or *opposite to* the arctic regions; *anti*repub'lican, *opposed to* republican institutions.

APO (απο), or AP, signifies *from; off; away:* as, *ap*he'lion (Helios), the point of a planet's orbit farthest *from* the sun; *apoc'*ope (Cope), a cutting *off* (or *away*) of the end of a word.

CATA (κατα), or CAT, signifies *down; against; relating to:* as, *cat*arrh' (Rheo), a flowing *down* or *de*fluxion; *cat'*aract, a dashing *down* or *against; cat*h'olic (Holos),* *relating to* the whole, universal.

---

* A title claimed by and given chiefly to the Church of Rome.

DIA (δια), or DI, signifies *through; apart; different:* as, *di*ær'esis (Æresis), a taking *apart,* a separation: *dia*m'eter (Metrum), the measure or distance *through.*

DYS (δυς), signifies *bad; difficult; diseased:* as, *dys*pep'sy (Peptos), *difficult* or *bad* digestion.

EC (εκ), or EX (εξ), before a *vowel* or *h,* signifies *out; from:* as, *ec*cen'tric (Centrum), going *out* or *from* the centre.

EN, or EM* (εν, εμ), signifies *in* or *upon:* as, *en*dem'ic (Demos), *in* or peculiar to a district or country; *em'*phasis (Phano), literally, a speaking *upon;* a particular force or stress of the voice laid *upon* (any word or sentence).

EPI (επι), or EP, signifies *upon; over; after; for:* as, *ep'i*demic (Demos), *upon* a whole people or country, general; *ep'i*logue (Logos), a speech or short poem spoken *after* a play, the *after* part or conclusion of a speech or discourse; *ep*hem'eral (Hemera), lasting *for* a day.

EU, or EV (ευ), signifies *good:* as, *eu*lo'gium, a *good* word, i. e. praise; *ev*an'gel (Angelos), *good* tidings, the gospel.

HYPER, (ὑπερ), signifies *above; over; beyond:* as, *hyper'*bole (Boleo), literally a shooting *above, over,* or *beyond* the mark, exaggeration.

HYPO (ὑπο), HYP, signifies *under:* as, *hyp*æ'thral (Æther), of or pertaining to something which is *under* the sky, i. e. exposed to the open air†.

META (μετα), or MET, signifies *after; beyond; from one to another:* as, *meta*phys'ics (Physis), that which is *after, beyond,* or higher than physics, the science of the mind; *metas'*tasis‡ (Stasis), a removal of a disease *from one* part to *another.*

PARA (παρα), or PAR, signifies *beside; like* or *similar;* rarely, *against:* as, *par'*allel (Allelon), *beside* one another; *par'*ody (Ode), a song or poem *like* or imitative of another; *para*dox (Doxa), something *against* or contrary to expectation, an apparent absurdity.

II. SUFFIXES.

ABLE, IBLE, BLE, (L.) denote *that may or can be; worthy to be; worthy of:* as, attain'*able* (Teneo), *that may be* attained; bla'm*able, that may be* blamed; *worthy of* blame; lau'd*able* (Laudo; Laus), *worthy to be* praised, or *worthy of* praise.

AC, (Gr.) signifies *of; pertaining to:* as, car'di*ac* (Cardia), *pertaining to* the heart; ele'gi*ac* (Elegia), *pertaining to* elegy.

---

* The *n* is changed to *m* before *b, m,* and *p,* as in Latin. See page 22.

† Applied to a building or temple without a roof.

‡ Literally a STANDING *from one to another:* GOING *from one to another* would imply continual change. *Metastasis* implies a single change, and after that a standing still.

ACEOUS, (L.) signifies *resembling* or *having the nature of; consisting of; y:* as, arena'*ceous* (Arena), *consisting of* sand; *resembling* sand; sand*y;* coria'*ceous* (Corium), *resembling* leather; leather*y;* foli*aceous* (Folium), *resembling* leaves; *consisting of* leaves; leaf*y*.

ACIOUS, (Latin *ax*)* signifies *very*, or *greatly; accustomed to* or *greatly addicted to; strongly:* as, auda'*cious* (Audeo), daring *much*, very daring; capa'*cious* (Capio); taking or containing *much;* menda'*cious* (Mentior), lying *much*, *greatly addicted to* lying; tena'*cious* (Teneo), holding *strongly* or firmly; holding fast to.

ACY, (L.) signifies *–ness; state of being; quality* or *attribute of office;* rarely, *–ing:* as, ac'cur*acy* (Cura), *the quality* or *attribute of being* accurate, accurate*ness;* celi'b*acy* (Cœlebs), the *state of being* unmarried; cu'r*acy* (Cura), the *office* of a curate; del'ic*acy* (Deliciæ), *the quality of being* delicate, delicate*ness*.

AGE, (L.) signifies *act of, –ing; state* or *condition of being; collection of*†; *allowance for:* as, mar'ri*age*, the *act of* marrying, the *state of being* married; bond'*age*, the *state of being* in bonds; fo'liage (Folium), a *collection of* leaves; peer'*age*, the *condition* or rank *of* a peer, the peers (of any country) *taken collectively;* wharf'*age*, an *allowance for* the use of a wharf.

AL, (L.) signifies *of; pertaining to; befitting; done* or *made by:* as, celes'ti*al* (Cœlum), *of* or *pertaining to* heaven; man'u*al* (Manus), *of* the hand, *done by* hand; mater'n*al* (Mater), *of* a mother, *befitting* a mother; paren't*al* (Parens), *of* a parent or parents.

AN, EAN, or IAN, (L.) in adjectives, signifies *of; pertaining to:* as, repub'lic*an* (Populus), *of* or *pertaining to* a republic; syl'v*an* (Sylva), *of* or *pertaining to* the woods.

AN, EAN, IAN, (L.) in nouns, denote *one who; one who belongs to; native inhabitant of:* as, ar'tis*an* (Ars), *one who* practises some art; Chris't*ian* (Christus), *one who belongs to* Christ,‡ a follower or disciple of Christ; Europe'*an* (Europa), a *native* or *inhabitant of* Europe.

ANCE, ANCY, ENCE, ENCY,§ (L.) signify the *act of; –ing; state of*

---

* This termination in Latin may be considered as an intensive form of the present active participle. Thus, *audax* seems to be equivalent to *audens multum*, "daring greatly;" *tenax*, to *tenens firmiter*, "holding firmly or fast," &c. &c.

† Instead of "*collection of*," it would be better in some instances to say "*taken or considered collectively*." Thus, *Foliage* may be defined as "leaves taken collectively;" *Herbage*, "herbs taken collectively," &c.

‡ See Mark ix. 41.

§ The terminations *Ance* and *Ancy*, *Ence* and *Ency* are more directly formed from the Latin *–antia* and *–entia:* e. g. *consonance* is from *consonantia; constancy*, from *constantia; vigilance*, from *vigilantia; impudence*, from *impudentia; innocence*, from *innocentia*, &c. As, however, there are a multitude of English nouns in *Ance, Ence*, &c., which have no corresponding Latin words in *–antia* or *–entia*, it is, perhaps, preferable, to refer at once to the present active participle in *–ans* or *–ens*, from which both the Latin and English nouns referred to, are ultimately derived. See note * on next page.

being; quality or *attribute of* (doing or being): as, accep'*tance* (Capio), the *act of* taking to (one's self) or *of* receiving, a receiv*ing;* assist'*ance* (Sisto), a stand*ing* by, aid; Con'st*ancy* (Sto), a stand*ing* together, or a standing firm, the *state* or *quality of being* constant; in'noc*ence* (Noceo), the *state* or *quality of being* harmless.

ANT, ENT, in nouns,* (L.) in nouns, signify *one who* or *the person that:* as, annu'it*ant* (Annus), *one who* receives an annuity; assis't*ant* (Sisto), *one who* stands by or assists; dis'put*ant* (Puto), *one who* disputes; a'g*ent* (Ago), *one who* acts (for another); stu'd*ent* (studeo), *one who* studies.

ANT, ENT, (L.) in adjectives, signify *-ing:* as, mil'it*ant* (Milito), fight*ing*, contend*ing;* pend*ent* (Pendeo; Pendens), hang*ing*.

AR,† signifies *in the form of; like, of, pertaining to; having:* as, acic'ul*ar* (Acus), *in the form of* a needle; an'gul*ar* (Angulus), *having* angles, *in the form of* an angle; an'nul*ar* (Annus), *in the form of* a ring.

AR, (Eng.) signifies *one who:* as, li'*ar*, *one who* lies.

ARD, (Eng.) denotes *one who has an habitual fault:* as, drunk'*ard*, *one who* gets drunk *habitually;* slug'g*ard*, *one who* is *habitually* sluggish or lazy.

ARIOUS, (L.) signifies *pertaining to:* as, greg*a'rious* (Grex), *pertaining to* flocks.

ARY, (L.) in nouns, signifies *one who;* the *thing that,* or *that which:* as, ad'vers*ary* (Adversus),‡ *one who* is against or opposed to; bound'*ary*, *that which* bounds; va'g*ary* (Vagor), a *thing* or thought *that* wanders, a whim. ARY, (L.) denotes the *place where* something is kept: as, li'br*ary* (Liber), the *place where* books are kept.

ARY, (L.) in adjectives, signifies *of,* or *pertaining to; of; by:* as, epis'tol*ary* (Epistola), *pertaining to* letters, *by* letters; hon'or*ary* (Honor), *for* honor, conferring honor.

ATE, (L.) signifies *office:* as, con'sul*ate* (Salio), the *office* of consul.

---

* The suffix *Ant* or *Ent*, both in nouns and adjectives, is derived from the termination of the present active participle in Latin. Hence, ASSIST*ant* literally signifies a person ASSIST*ing;* ASSAIL*ant*, a person ASSAIL*ing;* PEND*ant*, (from Pendeo), a HANG*ing* ornament, &c. Those acquainted with Latin will perceive that English words of this class, derived from Latin verbs of the first conjugation having the present participle in *ans*, will terminate in *ant:* those derived from the other three conjugations, which form the present participle in *ens*, will have *ent* for their terminal syllable, excepting a very few that come to us through the French, for a list of which see the new edition of Oswald's Etymological Dictionary, page 19.

† It will be perceived that adjectives of this class are usually formed from *diminutives.* Thus, *aciculus*, a "little needle," is the diminutive of *Acus; annulus*, a "little circle," a "ring," is the diminutive of *Annus*, a "circle," a "year," and so on. This circumstance does not seem generally to modify the signification of the adjectives so derived, euphony being apparently the only motive for forming them from the diminutive rather than from the primitive word.

‡ *Adversus*, though it has simply the signification of "against," and is therefore regarded as a preposition, is, in fact, a compound word, (from *ad* and *versus*,) signifying literally "turned to" or "turned against."

ATE, (L.) in nouns, signifies *one who:* as, leg'*ate* (Lego), *one who* is sent as ambassador.

ATE, (L.) in adjectives, signifies *having; -ed* or *-d:** as, for'tun*ate* (Fortuna), *having* fortune; illit'er*ate* (Litera), unletter*ed*, not acquainted with letters or literature, unlearned.

ATE, (L.) in verbs, signifies *to make; to give; to put; to take;* rarely *to have:* as, an'tiqu*ate* (Antiquus), *to make* ancient; depop'ul*ate* (Populus), *to take* the people from; incar'cer*ate* (Carcer), *to put* into prison; reg'ul*ate* (Regula), *to give* rules to.

ATIC, (L.) signifies *one who:* as, lu'n*atic* (Luna), *one who* is afflicted with lunacy.

CLE, CULE, ULE, (L.) signify *little; minute:* as, animal'*cule* (Animal), a *minute* animal; glob'*ule* (Globus), a *little* globe or ball.

DOM, (Lat. *dominium*, Sax. *dom*, Ger. *thum*,) signifies the *place in which dominion or jurisdiction is exercised; rank, quality* or *state:* as, duke'*dom* (Duco), the *place* or territory *in which* a duke *exercises jurisdiction*, the *rank* or *quality* of a duke; wis'*dom*, the *quality* or attribute of being wise.

EE, (Eng.) denotes *one to whom* something is done or given;† *one who:* as, absent*ee*' (Ens), *one who* is absent, one who absents himself; trus't*ee*, *one to whom* a trust is given.

EER, IER,‡ (Eng.) signifies *one who manages* or *has charge of; one who engages in* or *passes his time in:* as, chariot*eer*', *one who manages* or drives a chariot; mountain*eer*' (Mons), *one who passes his time* or lives on a mountain; mutin*eer*', *one who engages in* a mutiny.

EN, or N, (S.) in adjectives derived from nouns, signifies *made of; like:* as, bra'z*en*, *made of* brass, *like* brass.

EN, (S.) in verbs mostly derived from adjectives, signifies to *make:* as, dark'*en*, to *make* dark.

ENCE, ENCY. See ANCE, ANCY.

ENT. See ANT.

EOUS, (L.) signifies *consisting of; like: pertaining to; -y:* as, ig'n*eous*, *pertaining to* fire, *consisting of* fire, *like* fire, fiery.

ER, (Eng.) signifies *one who:* as, build'*er*, *one who* builds.

ESCENCE, (L.) signifies *state of growing* or *becoming; period of growing* or *becoming:* as, conval*es'cence* (Validus), the *state* or *period* of *growing* entirely strong.

ESCENT, (L.) signifies *growing* or *becoming; somewhat; ish:* as, rub*es'cent* (Ruber), *growing* red, *somewhat* red, redd*ish*.

ET. See LET.

ETIC, (G.) signifies *having:* as, path*et'ic* (Pathos), *having* feeling.

---

* The adjective suffix in *Ate* is usually derived from *atus*, the termination of the passive participle in Latin. Thus, CORPOR-O signifies I FORM INTO A BODY; CORPOR-*atus*, FORM-*ed* INTO A BODY.

† The suffix *Ee* is derived from the termination of the passive participle in French. Thus, DONN-er signifies to PRESENT; DONN-*ée*, PRESENT-*ed*, also a person PRESENT*ed* with any thing, or to whom any thing is presented.

‡ This suffix usually denotes one's employment.

Ety. See Ity.

Ey, (Eng.) signifies *consisting of:* as, clay'*ey*, *consisting of* clay.

Fic, (L.) signifies *making* or *causing:* as, horri*fic* (Horreo), *causing* horror.

Ful, (Eng.) signifies *full of:* as, hope'*ful*, *full of* hope.

Fy, (L.) signifies *to make:* as, for'ti*fy* (Fortis), *to make* strong.

Hood, Head, (S.) signify *state of being;* the *nature* or *distinguishing attributes of being:* as, child*hood*, *state of being* a child; God*head*, the *attributes* or *nature of* God, divinity.

Iac, (G.) signifies *one who:* as, ma'n*iac* (Mania), *one who* is mad.

Iac, (G.) signifies *belonging to:* as, demo'n*iac* (Demon), *belonging to* a demon.

Ible. See Able.

Ic, (G.) signifies *thing; art; science:* as, fab'r*ic* (Fabrico), the *thing* made; log'*ic* (Logos), the *science* of words.

Ic, (G.) signifies *one who:* as, crit'*ic* (Crites), *one who* judges.

Ic, Ical, (G.) signify *of: pertaining to; like:* as, angel'*ic* or angel'*ical* (Angello), *of* or *pertaining to* an angel, *like* an angel; hero'*ic* or hero'*ical* (Heros), *pertaining to* a hero, *like* a hero.

Ice, (L.) noun,* signifies *quality* or *attribute of being; –ness:* as, avar*ice* (Avarus), the *quality of being* avaricious, covetous*ness;* just*ice* (Justus, Justitia), just*ness*, the *quality* or *attribute of being* just.

Ician, denotes *one versed* or *skilled in*†*:* as, arith'met*ician* (Arithmos), *one versed in* arithmetic or the science of numbers; mus*i*'*cian* (Musa), *one versed* or *skilled in* music.

Icle, (L.) signifies *little:* as, par'*ticle* (Pars), a *little* part.

Ics, (G.) signifies the *science* or *art of:* as, econom'*ics* or œconom'*ics* (Œcos, and Nomos), the *science of* household affairs; tac'*tics* (Taxis), the *science* or *art* of military arrangement.

Id,‡ (L.) signifies *–ing:* as, fer'v*id* (Ferveo), burn*ing*, glow*ing*.

Ier. See Eer.

Ile, (L.) signifies *of, pertaining to; like; that may* or *can be easily:* as, do'c*ile* (Doceo), *that may be easily* taught; ju'ven*ile* (Juvenis), *of* or *pertaining to* youth.

Ine, (L.) signifies *one who:* as, ma'r*ine* (Mare), *one who* serves at sea.

Ine, signifies *of* or *pertaining to; like:* as, ca'n*ine* (Canis; Caninus), *pertaining to* dogs, like dogs; crys'tall*ine* (Crystallum, Crys-

---

* The termination in *Ice* (Latin *itia*), does not essentially differ in signification from that in *Ance* or *Ence* when denoting a "state or quality." The simple point of distinction between them is that the latter is derived from a Latin *participle present*, or adjective ending in *ens*, the former from an adjective in *us*.

† *Academician*, a "member of an academy," particularly a "member of the French Academy," appears to be the only exception among the words of this class.

‡ Adjectives of this termination are, with a very few exceptions, derived from Latin verbs in *eo*. The Latin *idus*, from which we form the suffix *Id*, is nearly similar in signification to the participial termination in *ans* or *ens;* e. g. SPLEND-*eo*, SPLEND-*ens* or SPLEND-*idus*, SHIN*ing;* TURG-eo, TURG-*ens*, or TURG-*idus*, SWELL-*ing*, &c.

tallinus), *of* crystal, *like* crystal; div*ine'* (Divus, Divinus), *pertaining to* God, *like* a god; fem'in*ine* (Femina, Femininus), *pertaining to* women, *like* a woman; ser'pent*ine* (Serpens, Serpentis, Serpentinus), *of* or *pertaining to* serpents, winding *like* a serpent.

ION,* (L.) signifies the *act of; -ing; state of being:* as, proba'*tion* (Probo), a try*ing* or prov*ing;* salva'*tion* (Salvus), the *act of* saving, the *state of being* safe or saved, eternal redemption.

IS, (G. L.) signifies *act of; state of:* as, syn'thes*is* (Thesis), *act of* putting together; cri'*sis* (Crites), the *state* or point of judging.

ISE. See IZE.

ISH, (Eng.) in adjectives, signifies *somewhat; of* or *belonging to; like:* as, black'*ish*, *somewhat* black; Span'*ish*, *of* or *belonging to* Spain; child'*ish*, *like* a child.

ISH, (L. Fr.) in verbs, signifies *to make:* as, fin'*ish* (Finis), *to make* an end of.

ISM, (G.) signifies *state* or *quality of being; an idiom; doctrine* or *doctrines of; -ing:* as, bar'bar*ism* (Barbarus), the *state of being* barbarous; Gal'lic*ism* (Gallicus, from Gallia), a French *idiom;* Cal'vin*ism*, the *doctrines of* Calvin.

IST, (G.) signifies *one who;* generally one who is engaged in some pursuit or study: as, ar't*ist* (Ars, Artis), *one who* practises an art.

ITE, (Eng.) signifies a *descendant of;* a *follower of* a *sectarian* or *party leader:* as, Amal'ek*ite*, a *descendant of* Amalek; Huss'*ite*, a *follower of* John Huss.

ITE, (L.) signifies *having* or *-ing:* as, defin'*ite* (Finis), *having* bounds; op'pos*ite* (Pono), oppos*ing*.

ITY, ETY, TY, signify *state* or *quality of being; -ness:* as, am'*ity* (Amo), the *state of being* friends, friendl*iness*, friend*ship;* (see the suffix *Ship*, page 32;) anti'qu*ity* (Antiquus), ancient*ness*, ancient times.

IVE, (L.) in nouns, signifies *one who; that which:* as, cap't*ive* (Capio), *one who* is taken; mo't*ive* (Moveo), *that which* moves or actuates.

IVE, (L.) in adjectives, denotes *having the power; disposed*, or *having the disposition; -ing:* as, ac't*ive* (Ago), *having the power* or *disposition to* act, act*ing;* adhe's*ive* (Hæreo), *having the power* (or quality) *of* sticking to; *having* a *tendency to* adhere.

IZE, or ISE, (Gr.) signifies *to make; to give;* to *act* or *do like:* as, fer'til*ize* (Fero), *to make* fertile; au'thor*ize* (Augeo), *to give* authority; crit'ic*ise* (Crites), *to act* the judge or critic.

KIN, (S.) signifies *little:* as, lamb'*kin*, a *little* lamb.

LESS,† (Eng.) denotes *free from; without:* as, care'*less*, *free from* care, *without* care.

---

* All the nouns of this very numerous class are derived from a corresponding Latin word in *io* (e. g. *expulsio*, EXPULSION-is; *probatio*, PROBATION-is, &c.), which is formed from the supine or passive participle, by changing *um* or *us* into *io*.

† From the Anglo-Saxon *leas* (German *los*), signifying "*loose*," "*free from*."

LET, ET, (S.) signify *little; young:* as, cyg'n*et* (Cygnus), a *young* swan; eye'*let*, literally a *little* eye, the hole or eye of a needle; mal'l*et*, a *little* mall.

LIKE, (Eng.) signifies *like* or *resembling:* as, child'*like*, *like* a child; God'*like*, *like* or *resembling* God.

LING, (Eng.) signifies *little; young:* as, found'*ling*, a *little* child found without parent or owner; gos'*ling*, a *little* or very *young* goose.

LY, (Eng.) in adjectives, signifies *like:* as, beast'*ly* (Bestia), *like* a beast.

LY, (Eng.) signifies *in a manner* or *way:* as, joy'ful*ly*, *in a* joyful *manner*.

MENT, (L.) denotes the *act of, –ing; state of being; that which:* as, accom'plish*ment*, the *act of* accomplishing, an accomplish*ing*, *state of being* accomplished; pay'*ment*, the *act of* paying, *that which* is paid.

MONY, (L.) signifies *state of being; quality of being; that which:* as, ac'ri*mony* (Acris), the *quality of being* sharp or acrid; mat'ri*mony* (Mater), the *state of being* a mother or wife, marriage; pat'ri*mony* (Pater), *that which* is inherited from a father.

OID, or OIDAL,* (G.) signifies *having* the *form* or *appearance of; resembling:* as, o'v*oid* or O'v*oidal* (ovum), *having the form of an* egg; va'riol*oid* (Variola), a disease *resembling* the small-pox.

NESS, (Eng.) signifies *state of being; quality* or *attribute of being:* as, bald'*ness*, the *state of being* bald; bold'*ness*, the *quality* or *attribute of being* bold.

OR,† (L.) signifies *one, who –er:* also, the *act of, –ing; sensation* or *emotion; that which causes* or *brings* sensation, &c.; *–ness:* as, au'dit*or* (Audio), *one who* hears, a hearer; col'*or*, a peculiar *sensation* in the eye, *that which causes* the sensation of color; fa'v*or* (Faveo), a favor*ing*, or the *act of* favoring, *that which causes* or *brings* favor; splen'd*or* (Splendeo), bright*ness*.

ORY, (L.) in nouns, signifies the *place* or *thing where:* as, ar'm*ory* (Arma), the *place where* arms are kept.

ORY, (L.) in adjectives, signifies *–ing; giving; making* or *causing; pertaining to:* as, ad'ulat*ory* (Adulor), flatter*ing*, *giving* flattery; am'at*ory* (Amo), *pertaining to* love or lovers, *causing* love.

OSE, (L.) signifies *full of:* as, joc*ose*' (Jocus), *full of* jokes.

OUS, (L.) signifies *full of; consisting of; like; –ing;* rarely, *having:* as, cartilag'in*ous* (Cartilago), *consisting of* cartilage, *like* cartilage; tim'or*ous* (Timeo), fear*ful*, fear*ing*.

RY, (Fr.) denotes the *state* or *quality of being;* the *art* or *practice*

---

* From the Greek *eidos*, "an appearance, or form."

† Words of this termination are purely Latin, and are, with scarcely an exception, derived from the supine or participle of the verb by changing *um* or *us* to *or*, *e. g.* ago, ACT-*um*, ACT-*or;* vinco, VICT-*um*, VICT-*or*.

of, *–ness;* the *place where;* things of a certain kind or class *taken collectively:* as, gal′lant*ry*, the *quality* or attribute *of being* gallant, gallant*ness*, nobleness, bravery; sla′ve*ry*, the *state of* a slave; brew′*ery*, the *place where* beer is brewed; cut′le*ry*, knives and other cutting instruments *taken collectively*, edged tools in general, also the *art* or business of a cutler.

SHIP, (Eng.), signifies *office of; state* or *relation of:* as, clerk′*ship* (Cleros), the *office of* clerk; friend′*ship*, the *state* or *relation of* a friend.

SOME,* (Eng.) signifies *full of; making* or *causing:* as, blithe′*some*, *full of* gayety, *causing* gayety or blitheness; wear′i*some*, *making* weary; *causing* weariness.

STER, (Eng.) signifies *one that:* as, song*ster*′, *one that* sings songs.

T,† (L.) denotes a *thing* done; *–ing:* as, gif*t*, a *thing* given; draf*t*, a draw*ing;* join*t*, a join*ing*.

TH, (S.) signifies *–ness;* the *act of; –ing; state of being; that which*‡*:* as, bread*th* (Sax. braed or bred), broad*ness;* grow*th*, a grow*ing*, or the *act of* growing, *that which* is grown, increase; weal*th* (Sax. welga or weleg), the *state of being* well off or rich, *that which* makes rich.

TUDE, or UDE, (L.) signifies *–ness:* as, al′ti*tude* (Altus), high*ness*, height; solic′i*tude* (solicitus), anxious*ness*, anxiety.

TY. See ITY.

ULE. See CLE.

ULENT, OLENT, or LENT, (L.) signifies *full of:* as, fraud′*ulent* (Fraus), *full of* fraud, deceitful, dishonest; pes′ti*lent* (Pestis), *full of* plague or pestilence, corrupt, troublesome; vi′*olent* (Vis), *full of* force or violence.

URE, (L.) denotes the *act of; –ing; state of being; that which:* as, cre′at*ure* (Creo), *that which* is created; cur′vat*ure* (Curvo), a bend*ing;* rap′t*ure* (Rapio), the *state of being* carried away (with joy); sei′*zure*, a seiz*ing*, the *act of* seizing.

WARD, (Eng.) signifies *towards:* as, home′*ward*, *towards* home.

Y, (Gr.) in nouns, signifies the *state* or *quality of being; –ing:* an′arch*y* (Arche), the *state of being* without government; lithog′raph*y*, engrav*ing* on stone.

Y, in adjectives, formed by adding this suffix to nouns, signifies *full of; consisting of; like:* as, rock*y*, *full of* rocks, *like* a rock; san′d*y*, *full of* sand, *consisting of* sand, *like* sand; spon′g*y* (Spongia), *like* a sponge, having the qualities of a sponge.

---

* From the Anglo-Saxon suffix *sum* (German *sam*), with the same signification as the above.

† This termination appears to be derived from an old form of the past participle, thus, gift, is something give*d* or give*n:* wef*t*, something weave*d* or wove*n*, &c.

‡ It also characterizes all the ordinal numbers *above* THREE; as FOUR*th*, FIF*th*, SIX*th*, HUNDRED*th*, THOUSAND*th*, &c.

PART II.

LATIN, GREEK AND OTHER ROOTS,

WITH THEIR ENGLISH DERIVATIVES.

GENERAL OBSERVATIONS.

PRONUNCIATION. The rules to be observed in the pronunciation of Latin and Greek, differ but slightly from those laid down for our own language. It is important, however, to bear in mind:

1. That every vowel or diphthong must be enunciated. Accordingly, *miles* is pronounced *mi-les; mare, mar-e; arche, arch-e; botane, botan-e.*

2. That the diphthongs *æ* and *œ* have the sound of *e*. *Ædes* is pronounced *Edes; ævum, evum; pœna, pena; fœdus, fedus.*

3. That *ch* is always sounded like *k*: as, *achos*, pronounced *akos; echeo, ekeo; chir, kir; chylos, kylos.*

4. That in the Latin *c* and *g* are hard before *a, o,* and *u,* and soft before *e* (*æ, œ*), *i* and *y*. *Calo* is pronounced *kalo; colo, kolo; cura, kura; cedo, sedo; civis, sivis.* In *Gallia, lego, gutta, the g* is sounded like the same letter in the English word *go;* in *gelu* and *gibbus,* like *g* in *giant*. In the Greek roots *c* (*χ*) and *g* are always sounded hard.

5. That dissyllables have the accent on the *first* syllable: *a'lo, a'ger, ca'nis.*

For the pronunciation of the roots from the French and other languages, we do not deem it necessary to make any provision. The roots of this character are so few, and, in regard to the French especially, all written instruction is so unserviceable, that, if the pupil feels any desire for such information, he must seek it in the proper books or from proper teachers.

In prosecuting the study of Etymology, it should be noticed that the form of the Latin or Greek word is subject to great variation, in order to express its number and case, or voice, mood, &c.; and, as our words are derived sometimes from one, and sometimes from another of these forms, two or more derivatives may differ very much in their appearance, although they spring from the same root. Thus, *core, courage,* and *encourage* come from *cor* (the *Nom.* of the Lat. for heart); while *accord, cordial,* and *discordant* come from *cordis* (the *Gen*). *Component* and *postpone* come from *pono* (*Ind. pres.*); *compose* and *position* from *positum* (*Supine*). In the same manner from *corpus* (*Nom.*), we have *corpse* and *corpuscle,* and from *corporis* (*Gen.*), *corporeal* and *incorporate;* from *ago* (*Ind. pres.*), *agent, cogent,* and *exigency,* and from *actum* (*Supine*), *action, actual,* and *exact.*

A slight modification in the form of the derivative arises from the change of *a* and *e* of the primitives into *i* in the compounds and derivatives. Thus, *teneo*, when it takes *con*, *per*, or any other prefix, becomes *contineo*, *pertineo*, and the corresponding English derivatives are *tenant*, *continent*, and *pertinent*. From *sapio* we have *sapid*, *sapient*, and *insipid*, *insipience*.

Academ-ia (ἀκαδημια), a grove near Athens where Plato taught philosophy.

ACAD'EMY, a place of instruction.
ACADEM'IC, relating to an academy.
ACAD'EMIST, a member of an academy.

Ace-o, to be sour or acid. **Acet-um,** vinegar.

ACES'CENT, tending to sourness.
ACE'TOUS, like vinegar.

Acerb-us, bitter, sour.

ACER'BITY, bitterness.
EXAC'ERBATE, to imbitter.

Acid-us, tart, sharp.

AC'ID, sour.
ACID'ULATE, to tinge with acid.
ANTIAC'ID, removing sourness.
SUBAC'ID, moderately acid.

Acou-o (ἀκουω), to hear.

ACOU'STICS, the science of sounds.
OTACOU'STIC, aiding the hearing.
POLYACOU'STIC, multiplying sounds.

Acr-is, sharp.

AC'RID, sharp.
AC'RITUDE, a bitter taste.
AC'RIMONY, sharpness, severity.

Acr-on (ἀκρον), end, summit.

ACROP'OLIS, the citadel.
ACROS'TIC, a kind of poem.

Acu-o, acut-um, to sharpen.

ACU'MEN, sharpness of intellect.
ACU'MINATED, ending in a point.
ACUTE', penetrating.

Adelph-os (ἀδελφος), a brother. PHILADEL'PHIA, brotherly love.

Adulat-um (*ab* **adulor**), to flatter.

ADULA'TOR, a flatterer.
ADULA'TION, flattery.

Aer (ἀηρ), the air.

A'ERIFORM, in the form of air.
A'EROLITE, a meteoric stone.
AEROL'OGY, a description of the air.
AEROM'ETRY, the measurement of the air.
A'ERONAUT, one who sails in the air.
AEROSTA'TION, aerial navigation.

Aeresis (αιρεσις), a taking.

APHÆR'ESIS, the taking away the first letter or syllable from a word.

DIÆR'ESIS, the mark [··] used to separate syllables.

Agger, a heap. EXAG'GERATE, to heighten; to magnify.

Agil-is, nimble.

AG'ILE, quick; active.

AGIL'ITY, nimbleness.

Agit-o, to drive, to stir.

AG'ITATE, to put in motion; to disturb.

COG'ITATE, to think.

EXCOG'ITATE, to think out; to contrive.

INCOG'ITATIVE, wanting the power of thought.

INCOG'ITANCY, wanting thought.

Ag-o, act-um, to do, to act.

ACT, to do, to perform.

AC'TIVE, busy; quick.

AC'TOR, a stage-player.

AC'TION, a deed; an operation.

AC'TUARY, a registrar or clerk.

AC'TUATE, to put in action.

A'GENT, a substitute; a factor.

CIRCUMNAV'IGATE, to sail round.

COACT', to act together.

CO'GENT, forcible.

COUNTERACT', to oppose; to hinder.

ENACT', to perform; to decree.

EXACT', strict; accurate.

EX'IGENCE, sudden occasion.

EXIGU'ITY, smallness.

INAC'TION, rest.

IN'DIGENT, poor, needy.

NAV'IGABLE, fit for the passage of vessels.

PROD'IGAL, a spendthrift.

REACT', to act again; to resist.

TRANSACT', to perform; to manage.

Agoge-us (αγωγευς), a leader.

DEM'AGOGUE, a leader of the populace.

PED'AGOGUE, a school-master.

SYN'AGOGUE, a Jewish church.

Agon (αγων), a combat.

AG'ONY, violent pain.

AG'ONIZE, to afflict with agony.

ANTAG'ONIST, an opponent; an enemy.

Ager, agri, a field.

AGRA'RIAN, relating to the field.

AGRES'TIC, relating to the country.

AG'RICULTURE, the art of cultivating the ground.

PER'EGRINATE, to travel.

PIL'GRIM, a traveller.

Alg-eo, to be cold.

AL'GID. cold.

ALGIF'IC, making cold.

Alg-os (ἀλγος), pain.

ANTAL'GIC, removing pain.
CARDIAL'GIA, heart-burn.
CEPHALAL'GIA, headache.
ODONTAL'GIA, toothache.
OTAL'GIA, ear-ache.

Ali-us, alien-us, another, foreign.

ABA'LIENATE, to make over to another.
A'LIEN, a foreigner.
A'LIAS, otherwise.
INA'LIENABLE, that cannot be transferred.

Allax-is (ἀλλαξις), a change.

PAR'ALLAX, a term in astronomy.
PARALLAC'TIC, pertaining to the parallax.

Allel-on (ἀλληλων), one another, each other.

PAR'ALLEL, equidistant at all points.
PARALLEL'OGRAM, a figure whose opposite sides are parallel.
PARALLELOPI'PED, a six-sided, solid figure, whose opposite sides are parallel.
UNPAR'ALLELED, unequalled; unmatched.

All-os (ἀλλος), another.

AL'LEGORY,° a figurative composition.
AL'LEGORIZE, to turn into allegory.
ALLEGOR'ICAL, not literal.

Al-o, alit-um, to nourish.

AL'IMENT, food; nourishment.
AL'IMONY, the allowance to a divorced woman.
AL'MONER, an officer who distributes alms.
ALMS, gifts to the poor.
COALESCE', to grow together; to unite.
COALITI'ON, union; league.

Alp-es, the Alps.

AL'PINE, pertaining to the Alps.
CISAL'PINE, on this side of the Alps.
TRANSAL'PINE, across the Alps.

Alpha (ἀλφα), the first letter in the Greek alphabet.

AL'PHABET, the letters of a language.
ALPHABET'ICAL, belonging to the alphabet.

Alter, another, change.

ADUL'TERATE, to debase.
AL'TER, to change.
UNAL'TERABLE, unchangeable.

Altern-us, by turns.

ALTER'NATE, by turns; in succession.
ALTER'NATIVE, a choice of two things.
ALTERCA'TION, a dispute.

Alt-us, high.

AL'TITUDE, height; elevation.
ALTIL'OQUENCE, lofty speech.
ALTIM'ETRY, the art of determining altitudes.
ALTIS'ONANT, high-sounding.
ALTIV'OLANT, flying high.
EXALT', to raise; to elevate.

Ambul-o, to walk.

AM'BLE, a gentle trot.
AMBULA'TION, the act of walking.
CIRCUMAM'BULATE, to walk around.
PERAM'BULATE, to walk through.

Amic-us, a friend.

AM'ITY, friendship.
AM'ICABLE, friendly; kind.
EN'EMY, a foe; an adversary.
EN'MITY, hatred.
INIM'ICAL, unfriendly; hostile.

Am-o, to love. *Amor*, love.

A'MIABLE, worthy of love.
AMOUR', an affair of love; an intrigue.
AM'ORIST, a lover; a gallant.
AM'OROUS, inclined to love.
AMATEUR', a lover of the fine arts.
AM'ATORY, relating to love.
ENAM'OR, to inflame with love.

Ampl-us, large.

AM'PLE, full; wide.
AM'PLY, largely; copiously.
AM'PLIFY, to enlarge; to exaggerate.
AMPLIFICA'TION, enlargement.
AM'PLITUDE, largeness; extent

Anem-os (ἄνεμος), the wind.

ANEMOG'RAPHY, a description of the wind.
ANEMOM'ETER, a wind-gauge.
ANEM'ONE, the wind-flower.
ANEM'OSCOPE, a machine to foretell the changes of the wind.

*Angel-lo** (ἀγγέλλω), to bring tidings.

AN'GEL, a celestial spirit.
ARCHAN'GEL, a chief angel.
EVAN'GELIST,° a writer or preacher of the gospel.
EVANGEL'ICAL, agreeable to the gospel.
EVAN'GELIZE, to teach the gospel.
GOS'PEL, the Christian revelation.

Ang-o (*anxi*), to vex.

AN'GUISH, intense pain.
AN'GER, resentment; rage.
AN'GRY, provoked; enraged.
ANXI'ETY, concern; solicitude.
ANX'IOUS, solicitous; concerned.

---

* γ or *g*, before γ *g*, κ *k*, χ *ch*, in Greek, sounds like '*ng*,' and accordingly in English, it assumes that *form*.

Angul-us, an angle.

AN'GLE, a corner.
AN'GULAR, having angles.
MULTAN'GULAR, many cornered.
OBTUSAN'GULAR, having obtuse angles.
OCTAN'GULAR, having eight angles.
PENTAN'GULAR, five cornered.
QUAD'RANGLE, a square.
REC'TANGLE, a right-angled parallelogram.
SEPTAN'GULAR, having seven angles.
SEXAN'GULAR, having six angles.
TRI'ANGLE, a figure of three angles.

Anim-a, wind, the vital air.

AN'IMAL, a living creature.
ANIMAL'CULE, a minute animal.
ANIMAL'ITY, animal existence.
AN'IMATE, to make alive.
EXAN'IMATE, lifeless; dead.
INAN'IMATE, void of life.
REAN'IMATE, to restore to life.
TRANSANIMA'TION, a passage of soul from one body to another.

Anim-us, the mind.

ANIMADVERT', to consider, to pass censure.
ANIMADVER'SION, reproof; censure.
ANIMOS'ITY, hatred; malignity.
EQUANIM'ITY, evenness of mind.
MAGNANIM'ITY, greatness of mind.
MAGNAN'IMOUS, brave; noble.
PUSILLANIM'ITY, cowardice.
UNANIM'ITY,° agreement.
UNAN'IMOUS, of one mind.

Ann-us, a year.

AN'NALS, yearly records.
AN'NALIST, a writer of annals.
ANNIVER'SARY, a stated day, coming once in every year.
A. M., AN'NO MUN'DI, in the year of the world.
A. D., AN'NO DOM'INI, in the year of our Lord.
AN'NUAL, yearly.
ANNU'ITY, a yearly allowance.
ANNU'ITANT, one who has an annuity.
BIEN'NIAL, in every two years.
CENTEN'NIAL, occurring every hundred years.
DECEN'NIAL, in every ten years.
MILLEN'NIUM, a thousand years.
OCTEN'NIAL, in every eighth year.
PEREN'NIAL, lasting through the year; perpetual.
QUADREN'NIAL, happening every four years.
SEPTEN'NIAL, happening every seven years.
SEXEN'NIAL, once in six years.
SUPERAN'NUATE, to impair by age.
TRIEN'NIAL, happening every third year.

Annul-us, a ring.

AN'NULAR, having the form of a ring.
AN'NULET, a little ring.
SEMIAN'NULAR, half round.

Anth-os (ἀνθος), a flower.

AN'THER, the tip of the stamen.
ANTHOL'OGY, a collection of flowers or poems.
EXANTHEM'ATOUS, efflorescent.
POLYAN'THUS, a plant with flowers in clusters.

Anthrop-os (ἀνθρωπος), a man.

ANTHROPOL'OGY, the doctrine of the anatomy of the human body.
ANTHROPOPH'AGI, man-eaters; cannibals.
CYNAN'THROPY, a madness in which men imitate dogs.
LYCAN'THROPY, a madness in which men imitate beasts.
MISAN'THROPY, hatred of mankind.
MIS'ANTHROPE, a hater of mankind.
PHILAN'THROPIST, one who loves mankind.
PHILANTHROP'IC, benevolent.

Antiqu-us, old or ancient.

AN'TIQUARY, one versed in antiquity.
ANTIQUA'RIAN, relating to antiquity.
AN'TIQUATE, to make obsolete.
ANTIQUE', ancient; of old fashion.
ANTIQ'UITY, old times.
AN'CIENT, old; antique.
AN'TIC, odd; fanciful.
AN'CESTOR, a forefather.
ANCES'TRAL, relating to ancestors.
AN'CESTRY, lineage; a series of ancestors.

Aperi-o, apert-um, to open.

APE'RIENT, gently purgative.
AP'ERTURE, an opening; a hole.

Apis, a bee. A'PIARY, a place where bees are kept.

Apt-us, fit, meet.

ADAPT', to fit; to adjust.
APT, fit; ready.
AP'TITUDE, fitness.
INAP'TITUDE, unfitness.
INEPT', trifling; foolish.

Aqua, water.

AQUAFOR'TIS, nitric acid.
AQUAVI'TÆ, spirit of wine.
AQUAT'IC, pertaining to water.
AQ'UEDUCT, a channel for water.
A'QUEOUS, watery.
TERRA'QUEOUS, composed of land and water.
SUBA'QUEOUS, lying under water.

Aquil-a, an eagle. AQ'UILINE, resembling an eagle; hooked.

Ar-o, to plough.

AR'ABLE, fit for tillage.
INAR'ABLE, not arable.

Arbiter, arbitr-i, an umpire or judge.

AR'BITER, a judge; an umpire.
ARBIT'RAMENT, will; award.
AR'BITRATE, to decide; to judge of.
AR'BITRARY, despotic; unlimited

Arbor, a tree.

AR'BORARY, belonging to trees.
AR'BORET, a small tree.
AR'BORIST, one who makes trees his study.
AR'BOR, a bower.

Arche (ἀρχη), the beginning; government.

AN'ARCH, an author of confusion.
ANTIMONAR'CHICAL, against monarchy.
ARCH, chief; principal; shrewd.
ARCHAIOL'OGY, knowledge of ancient things.
AR'CHAISM, an ancient phrase.
ARCHAN'GEL, a chief angel.
ARCHBISH'OP, the chief bishop.
ARCHDEA'CON, a church dignitary, next in rank to a bishop.
ARCHDUKE', a chief prince.
ARCHDUCH'ESS, the wife of an archduke.
ARCHPREL'ATE, the chief prelate.
AR'CHETYPE, the original; a model.
AR'CHITECT, a professor of the art of building; a builder.
AR'CHITECTURE, the art of building.
AR'CHITRAVE, the principal beam.
AR'CHIVES, ancient or public records.
CHIL'IARCH, a commander of a thousand men.
HEP'TARCHY, a sevenfold government.
HI'ERARCH, the chief of a sacred order.
MON'ARCH, a sovereign; a king.
OL'IGARCHY, a species of aristocracy.
PA'TRIARCH, a head of a family or church.
TE'TRARCH, a Roman governor.

Arct-os (ἀρκτος), a bear, the north.

ARC'TIC, northern; lying under the constellation called the Bear.
ANTARC'TIC, relating to the south pole.

Arc-us, a bow.

ARCH, a hollow structure, supported by its own curve.
ARCH'ER, he that shoots with a bow.

Ard-eo, ars-um, to burn.

AR'DENT, hot; passionate.
AR'DENCY, eagerness; heat.
AR'DOR, passion; zeal.
AR'SON, the crime of houseburning.

Ardu-us, high, steep. AR'DUOUS, difficult.

Aren-a, sand.

ARENA'CEOUS, sandy.
ARENOSE', full of sand.

Are-o, to be dry.

AR'EFY, to dry.
AREFAC'TION, a drying.
AR'ID, dry; parched.

Argent-um, silver. AR'GENT, silvery; white.

Argill-a, potter's clay. ARGILLA'CEOUS, clayey.

Arg-os (ἀργος), idle, inactive.

LETH'ARGY, drowsiness.
LETHAR'GIC, sluggish; dull.

Argu-o, to argue.

Ar'gue, to reason, to dispute.

Ar'gument, a reason alleged.

Aries, ariet-is, a ram.

A'ries, a sign of the zodiac.

Ari'etate, to butt like a ram.

Arist-os (ἀριστος), noblest, best.

Aristoc'racy, the government of the nobles.

Aris'tocrat, one who favors aristocracy.

Arithm-os (ἀριθμος), number.

Arith'mancy, a foretelling by numbers.

Arith'metic, the science of numbers.

Arithmetici'an, a master of arithmetic.

Log'arithms, a series of numbers in arithmetical progression.

Arm-a, arms.

Arm, to furnish with arms.

Arma'da, a fleet of war.

Armadil'lo, a four-footed animal of Brazil.

Ar'mament, a force equipped for war.

Armig'erous, bearing arms.

Armis'onous, sounding in arms.

Armip'otent, powerful in arms.

Ar'mistice, a cessation of hostilities; a truce.

Ar'mor, defensive arms.

Ar'mory, a place for arms.

Arms, weapons.

Ar'my, a large body of armed men.

Disarm', to deprive of weapons.

Aromat-a (ἀρωματα), spices.

Aromat'ics, spices; fragrant drugs.

Aromat'ic, spicy; fragrant.

Ar'omatize, to give a spicy taste.

Ars, art-is, art, skill.

Art, skill, cunning.

Ar'tifice, trick; fraud.

Artisan', a mechanic; a workman.

Art'ist, one skilled in any art.

Inartifici'al, plain; artless.

Inert', inactive; sluggish.

Unart'ful, without craft.

Arteri-a (ἀρτηρια), an artery.

Ar'tery, a blood vessel.

Arte'rial, relating to an artery.

Arteriot'omy, the letting of blood from an artery.

Articul-us, a little joint.

Ar'ticle, a part of speech; a single thing.

Artic'ulate, distinct; jointed.

Inartic'ulate, not distinct.

Arundo, arundin-is, a reed.

Arundina'ceous, of or like reeds.

Arundin'eous, full of reeds.

Asin-us, an ass.

As'inary, belonging to an ass.

As'inine, resembling an ass.

Ass, an animal of burden.

Asper, rough.

As'PERATE, to make rough.
ASPER'ITY, roughness, harshness.
ASPERIFO'LIOUS, having rough leaves.
EXAS'PERATE, to enrage; to vex.

Astr-on (ἄστρον), a star.

As'TERISK, mark [*] in printing.
As'TERISM, a constellation.
As'TRAL, starry.
ASTRIF'EROUS, bearing stars.
ASTROG'RAPHY, the describing of the stars.
As'TROLABE, an instrument for taking the altitude of stars.
ASTROL'OGY, the science of foretelling by the stars.
ASTROS'COPY, observation of the stars.
ASTRON'OMY, the science of the heavenly bodies.
DISAS'TER, misfortune; grief.

Atm-os (ἀτμος), vapor, air.

AT'MOSPHERE, the mass of air, &c., surrounding the earth.
ATMOSPHER'IC, pertaining to the atmosphere.

Atra, black.

ATRABILA'RIAN, affected with melancholy, or black bile.

Atrox, atroc-is, fierce, cruel.

ATRO'CIOUS, enormous; outrageous.
ATROC'ITY, great wickedness.

Audax, audac-is, daring.

AUDA'CIOUS, bold; impudent.
AUDAC'ITY, effrontery; boldness

Audi-o, audit-um, to hear.

AU'DIBLE, that can be heard.
AU'DIENCE, a hearing; an auditory.
AU'DIT, the hearing and settling of accounts.
AU'DITORY, those assembled to hear.
DISOBEY', to break commands.
INAU'DIBLE, not to be heard.
OBEY', to comply with commands.
OBE'DIENCE, compliance with commands.

Aug-eo, auct-um, to increase.

AUC'TION, a public sale of property, to the highest bidder.
AUGMENT', to increase.
AU'THOR, originator; maker.
AUTHOR'ITATIVE, having authority; positive.
AU'THORIZE, to give authority.

Augur, a soothsayer.

AU'GUR, to foretell; to predict.
AU'GURY, prediction by omens.
INAU'GURATE, to lead into office, with suitable ceremonies.

Aul-os (ἀυλος), a pipe.

HYDRAU'LICS,° the science of the force and motion of fluids.

Aur-is, the ear.

AU'RIST, one skilled in disorders of the ear.
AU'RICLE, the external ear.
AURIC'ULAR, told in secret.
AUSCULTA'TION, the act of listening to.

Aur-um, gold.

AURIF'EROUS, producing gold.
INAURA'TION, the act of gilding.

Auspici-um, soothsaying.

AU'SPICES, omens; protection.
INAUSPICI'OUS, unfavorable.

Auster-us, severe, rigid.

AUSTERE', severe, harsh.
AUSTER'ITY, severity; rigor.

Authent-eo (ἀυθεντεω), to authorize.

AUTHEN'TIC, genuine; true.
AUTHEN'TICATE, to prove by authority.
AUTHENTIC'ITY, authority; genuineness.

Aut-os (ἀυτος), one's self.

AUTOBIOG'RAPHY, biography of a person written by himself.
AU'TOCRAT, a sole ruler.
AU'TOGRAPH, one's own handwriting.
AUTOM'ATON, a self-moving machine.
AUTON'OMY, power of self-government.
AU'TOPSY, ocular demonstration.

Auxili-um, aid, help.

AUXIL'IAR, assisting.
AUXIL'IARY, a helper.

Avant, (Fr.) before, forward.

AVANT'GUARD, the van.
ADVANCE', to go forward.
ADVAN'TAGE, superiority; gain.
DISADVAN'TAGE, loss; injury.
VAN, the front of an army.
VANCOU'RIER, a light-armed soldier, who goes in advance.
VAN'TAGE, superiority.

Avid-us, greedy. AVID'ITY, eagerness; greediness.

Av-is, a bird.

AUSPICI'OUS, favorable.
A'VIARY, a place for birds.

Babel, (Heb.) confusion.

BA'BEL, confusion; disorder.
BAB'YLON, an ancient empire.

Bacc-a, a berry, a pearl.

BACCIF'EROUS, berry-bearing.
BACCIV'OROUS, eating berries.

Bacch-us, the god of wine.

BACCHANA'LIAN, relating to revelry.
BAC'CHANALS, drunken feasts.
BACCHAN'TES, the priests of Bacchus
DEBAUCH', to corrupt; to ruin.
DEBAUCHEE', a rake; a drunkard.
DEBAUCH'ERY, intemperance.

Balsam-on (βαλσαμον), fragrant ointment.

BALM, a plant.
BAL'SAM, a soothing ointment.
EMBALM', to preserve from decay.

Bapt-o (βαπτω), to dip, to wash.

ANABAP'TIST, one who rejects infant baptism, and maintains the necessity of rebaptization in an adult state.
BAPTIZE', to administer baptism
BAP'TISM, a Christian sacrament.
PÆDOBAP'TISM, the baptism of infants.

Barb-a, a beard.

BARB, the point that stands backward in an arrow.
BAR'BER, one who shaves the beard.

Barbar-us, rude, savage.

BAR'BAROUS, rude; uncivilized.
BARBA'RIAN, a savage.
BARBAR'IC, foreign; rude.
BAR'BARISM, inhumanity; ignorance of arts.
BARBAR'ITY, brutality.
BAR'BARIZE, to make barbarous.

Barre, (Fr.) a bar, a stop.

BAR, a long piece of wood or metal.
BARRICADE', to fortify.
BAR'RIER, a boundary; a stop.
BAR'RISTER, a counsellor at law.
EMBAR'RASS,° to perplex.
DISEMBAR'RASS, to free from embarrassment.

Bas-is (βασις), the base or foundation.

BASE, the bottom; mean; vile.
DEBASE', to degrade; to lower.

Bar-os (βαρος), weight.

BAROM'ETER, an instrument to measure the weight of the atmosphere.
BAROMET'RICAL, relating to a barometer.
BAR'OSCOPE, a sort of barometer.
BAR'YTONE, noting a grave, deep sound.

Basil-eus (βασιλευς), a king.

BAS'ILIC, a large hall; a magnificent church.
BASIL'ICON, an ointment.
BAS'ILISK, a serpent.

Beat-us, happy.

BEAT'IFY, to bless; to make happy.
BEATIF'IC, blissful.
BEAT'ITUDE, blessedness; perfect felicity.

Beau, belle (Fr.), fair, beautiful.

BEAU, a man of dress.
BEAU-MONDE', the gay world.
BEAU'TY, fairness; elegance.
BELLE, a gay young lady.
BELLES-LET'TRES, polite literature.
EMBEL'LISH, to adorn.

Bell-um, war.

BELLIG'ERENT, waging war.
BELLIP'OTENT, mighty in war.
REBEL', to rise against lawful authority.

Bene, good, well.

BENEDIC'TION, a blessing.
BENEFAC'TION, a benefit conferred.
BENEFAC'TOR, he who confers a benefit.
BEN'EFICE, a church living.
BENEF'ICENT, kind; doing good.
BENEFICI'AL, advantageous.
BENEFIC'IARY, a person benefited.
BEN'EFIT, kindness; advantage.
BENEV'OLENCE, good will; charity.
BEN'ISON, blessing.

Benign-us, kind, liberal.

BENIGN', kind; generous.
BENIG'NITY, actual kindness.

Beta (β), the second letter in the Greek alphabet.

AL'PHABET; the letters of a language.
ALPHABET'ICAL, pertaining to the alphabet.

Besti-a, a beast. BES'TIAL, like a beast; brutal.

Bibl-os (βιβλος), a book.

BI'BLE, the sacred Scriptures.
BIB'LICAL, relating to the Bible.
BIBLIOG'RAPHER, a man skilled in the knowledge of books.
BIBLIOP'OLIST, a bookseller.
BIBLIOTHE'CAL, belonging to a library.
BIBLIOMA'NIA, the rage for possessing scarce or curious books.

Bib-o, to drink.

BIBA'CIOUS, fond of drinking.
BIB'BER, a tippler; a sot.
BIB'ULOUS, absorbing.
IMBIBE', to drink in; to admit.

Bil-is, the bile.

BIL'IOUS, pertaining to the bile.
ANTIBIL'IOUS, remedying bilious disorders.
BILE, a yellow, bitter liquor, formed in the liver.

Bi-os (βιος), life,

AMPHIB'IOUS, living in two elements, air and water.
AUTOBIOG'RAPHY, biography of a person written by himself.
BIOG'RAPHY, an account of one's life.
CEN'OBITE, one of a religious order who lives in a community.

Blam-er (Fr.), to censure.

BLAME, to censure.
UNBLA'MABLE, not culpable.

Bin-i, two by two: ***Bis***, two, twice.

BICAP'SULAR, having two seed-vessels.
BICIP'ITAL, having two heads.
BICOR'NOUS, having two horns.
BICOR'PORAL, having two bodies.
BIDEN'TAL, having two teeth.

BIEN'NIAL, in every two years.
BIF'EROUS, bearing twice a year.
BI'FID, split in two.
BI'FOLD, twofold; double.
BI'FORM, having two forms.
BIFUR'CATED, having two forks.
BIG'AMY, the having two wives at once.
BIG'AMIST, one guilty of bigamy.
BILIN'GUOUS, speaking two tongues.
BI'NARY, two; double.
BINOC'ULAR, having two eyes.
BIP'AROUS, bringing forth two at a birth.
BI'PED, an animal with two feet.
BIPET'ALOUS, having two flower-leaves.
BIQUADRAT'IC, relating to the fourth power.
BIS'CUIT, a kind of bread.
BISECT', to divide into two equal parts.
BI'VALVE, having two valves.
COMBINE', to join together.

Bland-us, soothing, gentle.

BLAND, soft; mild.
BLAN'DISH, to smooth; to soften.

Blapt-o (βλαπτω), to injure.

BLASPHEME',° to speak impiously.
BLAS'PHEMY, impiety of speech.

Bole-o (βαλλω), to throw.

AMPHIBOL'OGY, ambiguous discourse.
DIABOL'ICAL,° devilish; atrocious.
EM'BLEM, a picture.
EMBLEMAT'IC, using emblems; allusive.
HYPER'BOLA, a section of a cone.
HYPER'BOLE,° an exaggeration.
PAR'ABLE, a similitude.
PARAB'OLA, one of the conic sections.
PARAB'OLOID, a paraboliform curve.
PROB'LEM,° a question proposed.
PROBLEMAT'ICAL, uncertain.
SYM'BOL, a sign; an emblem.

Bon-us, good.

BOUN'TY, liberality.
BOUN'TEOUS, liberal; kind.

Bore-as (βορεας), the north wind.

BO'REAS, the north wind.
HYPERBO'REAN, northern; cold.

Botan-e (βοτανη), an herb, a plant.

BOT'ANY, the science of plants.
BOTAN'ICAL, relating to plants.
BOT'ANIST, one skilled in plants.
BOTANOL'OGY, a discourse upon plants.

Brachi-um, an arm. BRACH'IAL, belonging to the arm.

Brach-ys (βραχυς), short.

BRACHYG'RAPHY, short-hand writing.

Brev-is, short, brief.

ABBRE'VIATE, to shorten.
ABRIDGE', to abbreviate.
BREV'IARY, an abridgment.
BREV'ITY, conciseness; shortness.
BRIEF, short; concise.

Brill-er (Fr.), to sparkle.

BRILL'IANT, shining; sparkling.
BRILL'IANCY, lustre; splendor.

Broch-e (βροχη), moisture.

EM'BROCATE, to moisten and rub a diseased part.

Bronch-os (βρονχος), the windpipe.

BRON'CHIAL, belonging to the bronchia or branches of the wind-pipe.
BRON'CHOCELE, a tumor in the throat.
BRONCHOT'OMY, incision of the wind-pipe.

Brut-us, brute, senseless.

BRUTE, senseless; rough.
BRU'TAL, like a brute.
BRU'TISH, bestial; ferocious.

Bull-a, a bubble in water.

BOIL, to bubble, from heat.
EBULLITI'ON, act of boiling.

Butyr-um, butter. BUTYRA'CEOUS, like butter.

Cac-os (κακος), bad, ill. CACOPH'ONY, a bad sound of words.

Cadaver, a dead body.

CADAV'EROUS, like a dead body; ghastly.

Cad-o, cas-um, to fall.

AC'CIDENT, casualty; chance.
CA'DENCE, the tone or sound.
CADU'CITY, tendency to fall.
CASCADE', a waterfall.
CASE, condition; state.
CAS'UAL, accidental.
CAS'UIST, one that studies and settles cases of conscience.
COINCIDE', to agree.
DECAY', to rot; to decline.
DECID'UOUS, falling; dying.
IN'CIDENT, an event.
OCCA'SION, to cause; to produce.
OC'CIDENT, the west.

Calamit-as, a misfortune.

CALAM'ITY, misfortune.
CALAM'ITOUS, full of woe.

Cæd-o, cæs-um, to cut, to kill.

CONCISE', brief; short.
DECIDE', to determine.
DECISI'ON, determination.
DECI'SIVE, conclusive; final.
DE'ICIDE, the murder of a god.
EXCISE', a tax.
FIL'ICIDE, the murder of a son.
FRAT'RICIDE, the murder of a brother.
HOM'ICIDE, manslaughter.
HOMICI'DAL, murderous.
INCISED', cut; made by cutting.
INCISI'ON, a cut; a gash.
INDECISI'ON, irresolution.
INFAN'TICIDE, the murder of an infant.
MAT'RICIDE, the murder of a mother.
PAR'RICIDE, the murder of a parent.
PRECISE', exact; strict.
PRECISI'AN, one very exact

PRECISI'ON, exactness.
REG'ICIDE, the murder of a king.
SOROR'ICIDE, the murder of a sister.
SU'ICIDE, self-murder.
TYRAN'NICIDE, the act of killing a tyrant.
VAT'ICIDE, the murder of a priest.

Calx, calc-is, limestone.

CALX, a powder made by burning, (as lime.)
CALCINE', to burn to a calx.
CALCINA'TION, the act of pulverizing by fire.
UNCAL'CINED, not burned to powder.

Calcul-us,° a small stone, a pebble.

CAL'CULATE, to compute; to reckon.
CAL'CULOUS, stony; gritty.
CAL'CULUS, a branch of mathematics.
INCAL'CULABLE, that cannot be calculated.

Cale-o, to be warm or hot. ***Calor,*** heat.

CAL'EFY, to grow hot.
CALEFAC'TION, the act of heating.
CAL'DRON, a pot; a boiler.
CAL'ID, hot; burning.
CALOR'IC, heat.
CALORIF'IC, causing heat.
INCALES'CENCE, a growing warm.
SCALD, to burn with a hot fluid.

Cal-os (καλος), beautiful. CALIG'RAPHY, beautiful writing.

Calumni-a, calumny.

CAL'UMNY, slander; false accusation.
CALUM'NIOUS, slanderous.
CALUM'NIATE, to slander.

Calypt-o (καλυπτω), to cover, to veil.

APOC'ALYPSE, revelation; a vision.
APOCALYP'TICAL, concerning revelation.

Camp-us, a plain; tents in the field.

CAMP, the place of an army.
CAMPAIGN', the time for which an army keeps the field.
CAMPES'TRAL, growing in fields.
CHAM'PAIGN, flat open country.
CHAMPAGNE', a kind of wine.
DECAMP', to shift a camp.
ENCAMP', to pitch tents; to halt.

Cande-o, to be white, to glow.

CAN'DOR, frankness; openness.
CAN'DID, fair; open.
CAN'DIDATE,* one proposed for office, or preferment.
CAN'DFNT, glowing with heat.
CAN'DLE, a light made of tallow, &c.
CHANDELIER', a branch for candles.
EXCANDES'CENCE, white heat.
INCEN'DIARY, one who maliciously sets houses, &c., on fire.
INCENSE', to enrage; to provoke.
INCEN'TIVE, a motive; a spur.

---

* Those who sought preferments among the Romans, were called *Candidati*, from a white robe (*toga candida*) worn by them, which was rendered shining (*candens*) by the art of the fuller.

Can-is, a dog.

CANINE', relating to the dog.
CANIC'ULAR, belonging to the dogstar.

Cano, cant-um, to sing.

AC'CENT, a stress of voice.
ACCENT'UATE, to mark or pronounce with accents.
CANT, affected manner of speech; slang.
CAN'TICLE, a song.
CAN'TO, a section of a poem.
CHANT, to sing.
CHARM, to bewitch; to delight.
DECANT', to pour off gently.
DESCANT', to sing; to discourse.
ENCHANT', to charm.
INCANTA'TION, an enchantment.
RECANT', to retract.
VATIC'INATE, to prophesy.

Canon (κανων), a rule.

CAN'ON, a rule; a law.
CAN'ONIZE, to declare one a saint.
UNCANON'ICAL, not agreeable to the canons.

Capi-o, capt-um, to take; to contain.

ACCEPT', to take; to receive.
ACCEPT'ABLE, grateful; pleasing.
ACCEPTA'TION, meaning.
ANTIC'IPATE, to take or do beforehand; to foretaste.
CA'PABLE, able; equal to.
CAPA'CIOUS, wide; large.
CAPAC'ITATE, to make capable.
CAP'TIOUS, apt to cavil.
CAP'TIVATE, to take prisoner.
CAP'TIVE, one taken in war.
CAP'TOR, he who takes prisoners.
CAP'TURE, a seizure; a prize.
CONCEIT', fancy; opinion.
CONCEIVE', to think.
CONCEP'TION, notion; thought.
DECEIVE', to cheat; to mislead.
DECEIT', fraud; a cheat.
DECEP'TION, act of deceiving.
EMAN'CIPATE, to free from servitude.
EXCEPT', to leave out.
IMPERCEP'TIBLE, not to be perceived.
INCA'PABLE, unable; unfit.
INCAPAC'ITY, inability.
INCEP'TIVE, beginning.
INCONCEIV'ABLE, not to be conceived.
INTERCEPT', to stop; to seize.
MAN'CIPLE, a steward.
MISCONCEP'TION, a false opinion.
MUNIC'IPAL, belonging to a corporation.
OC'CUPANCY, a holding.
OC'CUPY, to possess.
PARTIC'IPATE,° to share.
PAR'TICIPLE, a part of speech.
PERCEIVE', to see; to know.
PRE'CEPT, a rule; a mandate.
PRECONCEIVE', to imagine beforehand.
PREOC'CUPY, to occupy previously.
PRINCE, a sovereign; a ruler.
PRIN'CIPLE, cause; motive.
RECEIVE', to take; to admit.
RECEIPT', an acknowledgment for money paid.
RECEP'TACLE, that which receives or contains.
RECEP'TION, a receiving.
REC'IPE,* a medical prescription.
RECIP'IENT, a receiver.
SUSCEP'TIBLE, easily impressed or affected.

* This is the imperative mood of the Latin verb, *recipio.* In medical prescriptions written in Latin, it is the first word used—"*Recipe*" ("take"), &c

Capill-us, the hair.

CAP'ILLARY, like hair; minute.

CAPIL'LAMENT, a fine thread or fibre.

CAPILLA'CEOUS, hairy.

Caput, capit-is, the head.

BICIP'ITAL, having two heads.

CAP, a covering for the head.

CAP'ITAL,* chief; principal.

CAPITA'TION, counting by heads.

CAPIT'ULATE, to surrender on conditions.

CAP'TAIN, a chief commander.

CHAP'TER, a division of a book.

DECAP'ITATE, to behead.

OC'CIPUT, the hinder part of the head.

PREC'IPICE, a headlong steep.

PRECIP'ITANCE, rash haste.

RECAPIT'ULATE, to repeat.

Carbo, carbon-is, a coal.

CARBON'IC, containing carbon.

CAR'BUNCLE,° a gem; a tumor.

Carcer, a prison. INCAR'CERATE, to imprison.

Cardo, cardin-is, a hinge. CAR'DINAL,° chief; principal.

Cardi-a (καρδια), the heart.

CAR'DIAC, relating to the heart.

CARDIAL'GIA, the heart-burn.

PERICAR'DIUM, a membrane enclosing the heart.

Caro, carn-is, flesh.

CAR'NAGE, slaughter.

CAR'NAL, fleshly; lustful.

CARNA'TION, a flesh color.

CARNEL'ION, a precious stone.

CAR'NIVAL, a Catholic feast.

CARNIV'OROUS, flesh-eating.

CHAR'NEL, holding dead bodies.

INCAR'NATE, clothed with flesh.

Cartilag-o, cartilagin-is, a gristle, or tendon.

CAR'TILAGE, gristle.

CARTILAG'INOUS, gristly.

Car-us, dear, kind.

CARESS', to fondle.

CHER'ISH, to support; to nurse.

Castig-o, to chastise, to punish.

CAS'TIGATE, to chastise; to whip.

CHAS'TEN, to correct; to punish.

CHAS'TISEMENT, punishment.

Cast-us, pure, chaste.

CHASTE, pure; uncorrupt.

CHAS'TITY, purity.

IN'CEST, unnatural crime.

Caten-a, a chain.

CATENA'RIAN, relating to a chain.

CONCAT'ENATE, to link together.

---

* *Capital* crimes or punishments are those involving a loss of the *head*

Cavall-o, (Ital.) a horse.

CAV'ALCADE, a procession on horseback.
CAVALIER', an armed horseman.
CAV'ALRY, mounted troops.

Cav-us, hollow.

CAV'ITY, a hollow place.
CAV'ERN, a cave; a den.
CON'CAVE, hollow.
EX'CAVATE, to hollow out.

Caul-is, a stalk or stem.

CAULIF'EROUS, having a stalk.
CAUL'IFLOWER, a kind of cabbage.

Caus-a, a cause.

ACCUSE',° to charge with a crime.
CAUSE, reason; motive.
CAUSAL'ITY, the agency of a cause.
EXCUSE', to pardon; to remit.
INEXCU'SABLE, not to be excused.
RECU'SANT, refusing to conform

Caustic-os (καυστικος), burning.

CAUS'TIC, burning; corroding.
CAU'TELOUS, cautious; cunning.
CAU'TERIZE, to burn with a cautery.
CAU'TERY, an iron for burning.

Cautio, caution-is, caution.

CAU'TION, foresight; warning.
INCAU'TIOUS, unwary.
PRECAU'TION, previous care.

Cele (κηλη), a swelling.

BRON'CHOCELE, a tumor in the throat.

Ced-o, cess-um, to go, to yield.

AB'SCESS, a tumor filled with matter.
ACCEDE',° to assent; to agree.
ACCESS', approach; admission.
ANTECE'DENT, going before.
ANTECES'SOR, one who goes before.
CEASE, to leave off; to stop.
CEDE, to yield; to resign.
CESSI'ON, the act of yielding.
CONCEDE', to yield; to grant.
CONCESSI'ON, the act of granting.
DECEASE', death.
EXCEED', to go beyond; to excel.
EXCESS', superfluity.
INACCES'SIBLE, not to be approached.
INCES'SANT, unceasing.
INTERCEDE', to mediate.
INTERCESSI'ON, mediation.
PRECEDE', to go before.
PREDECES'SOR, one going before.
PROCEED', to go on; to advance.
PROC'ESS, a progress; a method.
RECEDE', to retreat.
RECESS', a place of retreat.
RETROCESSI'ON, a going back.
SECEDE', to withdraw from.
SECESSI'ON, the act of seceding.
SUCCEED', to follow; to prosper
SUCCESS', fortune; prosperity.
SUCCES'SIVE, following in order.
SUCCES'SOR, one that follows another.
SURCEASE', to be at an end.

Celebr-is, renowned.

CEL'EBRATE,° to praise; to extol. | CELEB'RITY, fame; renown.

Celer, swift.

ACCEL'ERATE, to hasten; to quicken. | CELER'ITY, rapidity; speed.

Cœlest-is (*ab* ***cœlum***), heavenly. CELES'TIAL, heavenly.

Cœleb-s, single, unmarried. CEL'IBACY, single life.

Cell-a, a cellar.

CELL, a small, close room.
CEL'LAR, a room under a house.
CEL'LULAR, consisting of little cells or cavities.

Cels-us, high.

CEL'SITUDE, height; elevation.
EXCEL', to outdo; to surpass.
EX'CELLENCE, purity; goodness.

Cel-o, to hide.

CONCEAL', to hide; to secrete. | INCONCEAL'ABLE, not to be hid.

Cens-oe, censum, to judge, to value, to blame.

CEN'SOR, an officer of Rome who corrected the manners of the people.
CENSO'RIOUS, apt to censure.
CEN'SURE, to blame; to condemn.
CEN'SUS, an enumeration of the people.

Centr-um (κεντρον), the centre.

CEN'TRE, the exact middle.
CEN'TRAL, relating to the centre.
CENTRIF'UGAL, flying from the centre.
CENTRIP'ETAL, tending to the centre.
CONCEN'TRIC, having one common centre.
CONCEN'TRATE, to bring together.
ECCENTRIC'ITY, irregularity.
GEOCEN'TRIC, having the earth for its centre.
HELIOCEN'TRIC, relating to the sun's centre.

Cent-um, a hundred.

CENT, a coin 100 of which=$1.
CEN'TURY, a hundred years.
CENTEN'NIAL, occurring every hundred years.
CENTIFO'LIOUS, having a hundred leaves.
CENTIL'OQUY, a hundred-fold discourse.
CEN'TIPEDE, an insect with many feet.
CEN'TUPLE, a hundred fold.
CENTU'RION, a Roman military officer, commanding 100 men.

Cephal-e (κεφαλη), the head.

ACEPH'ALOUS, without a head.
BICEPH'ALOUS, having two heads.
CEPHALAL'GIA, headache.
HYDROCEPH'ALUS, a dropsy in the head.

Cer-a, wax.

CE'RATE, an ointment of wax, oil, &c.
CERE, to cover with wax.
INSINCERE', not hearty; false.
SINCER'ITY,° honesty; purity; freedom from hypocrisy.

Cerebr-um, the brain.

CER'EBRUM, the brain.
CER'EBRAL, relating to the brain.

Ceremoni-a, a rite, a form.

CER'EMONY, outward rite.
CEREMO'NIOUS, civil; formal.

Cern-o, cret-um, to sift, to distinguish.

CONCERN', business; care.
DECREE', an edict; a law.
DECRE'TAL, a book of decrees.
DISCERN',° to descry; to judge.
DISCRETE', distinct; separate.
DISCRETI'ON,° prudence.
DISCRIM'INATE, to distinguish.
EX'CREMENT, a discharge from animal bodies.
INDISCER'NIBLE, not perceptible.
INDISCREET', imprudent.
INDISCRIM'INATE, not making any distinction.
SE'CRET,° concealed; private.
SECRETE', to hide; to conceal.
SEC'RETARY, one who writes for another.

Cert-o, to contend.

CONCERT',° to settle; to contrive.
DISCONCERT', to disturb.
PRECONCERT'ED, contrived beforehand.

Cert-us, certain, sure.

ASCERTAIN', to make certain.
CER'TAIN, sure; undoubted.
CER'TIFY, to assure.
CERTIF'ICATE, a testimony in writing.
CER'TITUDE, certainty.
UNCER'TAIN, doubtful.

Cerule-us, blue.

CERU'LEAN, sky-colored; blue.
CERULIF'IC, making blue.

Cet-us, a whale. CETA'CEOUS, of the whale kind.

Chalc-os (χαλκος), brass.

CHALCOG'RAPHY, the art of engraving on brass.

Chaos (χαος), confusion.

CHA'OS, a confused mass.
CHAOT'IC, confused; indigested.

Character (χαρακτηρ), a mark.

CHAR'ACTER, a mark; reputation.
CHARACTERIS'TIC, that which gives character.
CHAR'ACTERIZE, to give a character.

Charis, charit-os (χαρις), grace, joy.

CHAR'ITY, goodwill; alms.
CHAR'ITABLE, kind; bountiful.
EU'CHARIST,* the sacrament of the Lord's Supper.

Cheval (Fr.), a horse.

CHEVALIER', a knight; a gallant man.
CHIV'ALRY, knighthood; valor.

Chimæra (χιμαιρα), a fictitious monster.

CHIME'RA, a wild fancy.
CHIMER'ICAL, wild; fanciful.

Chir (χειρ), the hand.

CHIROG'RAPHY, hand-writing.
CHIROL'OGY, talking by signs.
CHIR'OMANCY, the art of foretelling by inspecting the hand.
SUR'GERY, the art of curing by manual operation.
CHIRUR'GEON, a surgeon.
SUR'GEON, a professor of surgery.

Chol-e (χολη,) bile.

CHOL'ERA, a bilious disease.
CHOL'ER, anger; rage.
CHOL'IC, pain in the bowels.
MEL'ANCHOLY,° sadness; dejection.

Chondr-os (χονδρος), the cartilage of the breast-bone.

HYPOCHON'DRIA,° melancholy; depression of spirits.

Chor-us, a company of singers.

CHOIR, a band of singers.
CHO'RAL, belonging to a choir.
CHOR'ISTER, a singer.
CHO'RUS, a number of singers.

Chord-a (χορδη), a gut, a string.

CHORD, the string of a musical instrument.
CLAR'ICHORD, a musical instrument,
CORD'AGE, a quantity of cords.
MON'OCHORD, an instrument of one string.
PEN'TACHORD, an instrument of five strings.

Christ-os (χριστος), the anointed.

AN'TICHRIST, an enemy to Christ.
CHRIST, the Saviour.
CHRIST'MAS, the festival of Christ's nativity.
CHRIS'TEN, to baptize and name.
CHRISM', consecrated oil.

Chron-os (χρονος), time.

ANACH'RONISM, an error in dates.
CHRON'IC, of long duration.
CHRON'ICLE, a register; a record.
CHRONOG'RAPHY, the description of past time.
CHRONOL'OGY, the science of computing time.
CHRONOM'ETER, an exact timepiece.
ISOCH'RONOUS, having the same length of time.
SYN'CHRONAL, happening at the same time.
SYN'CHRONIZE, to agree in time.

* Literally, the act of giving thanks; so called because it is an occasion of special and solemn thanksgiving to God for the gift of his son, Christ Jesus.

Chym-os (χυμος), juice.

AL'CHYMY, occult chemistry.
CHEM'ISTRY, the science of the nature and properties of bodies.
CHEM'ICAL, concerning chemistry.

Cib-us, meat, food. CIBA'RIOUS, relating to food.

Cicatrix, cicatric-is, a scar.

CIC'ATRICE, a scar; a mark.
CIC'ATRIZE, to heal a wound.

Cili-um, the eye-lids. CIL'IARY, relating to the eye-lids.

Cing-o, cinct-um, to bind.

CINC'TURE, a belt; a sash.
PRE'CINCT, a boundary.
SUCCINCT', concise; brought into small compass.

Cinis, cincr-is, ashes.

CIN'DER, a burnt mass.
INCIN'ERATE, to burn to ashes.

Circul-us, a ring.

CIR'CLE, a round plane with a line bounding it.
CIR'CULAR, round like a circle.
CIR'CULATE, to spread; to diffuse.
ENCIR'CLE, to surround.
SEM'ICIRCLE, a half circle.

Cit-o, citat-um, to call, to stir up.

CITE, to summon; to quote.
CONCITA'TION, a stirring up.
EXCITE', to rouse; to animate.
INCITE', to stir up; to urge on.
MISCITE', to quote wrong.
RECITE', to rehearse; to repeat.
RESUS'CITATE, to revive; to bring back to life.

Civ-is, a citizen.

CIT'Y, a large corporate town.
CIT'IZEN, an inhabitant of a city or state.
CIV'IC, relating to civil affairs or honors.
CIV'IL,° relating to the community; well-bred.
UNCIV'IL, impolite; rude.

Clam-o, clamat-um, to cry, to shout.

ACCLAIM', to give applause.
ACCLAMA'TION, a shout of applause.
CLAIM, to demand of right.
CLAM'OR, outcry; noise.
DECLAIM', to harangue.
DISCLAIM', to disown; to deny.
EXCLAIM', to cry out.
EXCLAMA'TION, vehement outcry.
IRRECLAIM'ABLE, not to be recalled.
PROCLAIM',° to publish.
PROCLAMA'TION, a public notice.
RECLAIM', to reform; to recall.

Clang-o, to make a shrill noise.

CLANG, to clatter; to rattle.
CLANG'OR, a loud, shrill noise.

Clar-us, clear.

CLAR'ICHORD, a musical instrument.
CLAR'IFY, to purify.
CLARIFICA'TION, the act of making clear.
CLAR'ION, a kind of trumpet.
CLAR'INET, an instrument of music.
CLEAR, bright; serene.
DECLARE', to make known.

Classi-is,° a fleet.

CLASS, a rank; a division.
CLAS'SIC, relating to authors of the first rank; elegant.
CLAS'SIFY, to arrange in classes.
CLASSIFICA'TION, a ranging into classes.

Claud-o, claus-um, to shut.

CLAUSE, a part of a sentence; a stipulation.
CLOIS'TER, a monastery.
CLOSE, end; cessation.
CLOS'ET, a small, private room.
CONCLUDE', to determine; to finish.
CONCLU'SION,° determination; close.
DISCLOSE', to reveal; to tell.
DISCLO'SURE, discovery.
ENCLOSE', to shut in; to surround.
EXCLUDE', to shut out; to debar.
EXCLU'SION, a shutting out.
INCLOS'URE, a space enclosed.
INCLUDE', to admit; to comprise.
INCONCLU'SIVE, not decisive.
PRECLUDE', to hinder or prevent.
RECLUSE', a solitary person.
SECLUDE', to shut up apart.

Clemens, clement-is, mild.

CLEM'ENCY, mercy; mildness.
INCLEM'ENT, severe; rough.

Cler-os (κληρος), a lot, a portion.

CLER'GY,* the body or order of divines.
CLER'ICAL, relating to the clergy.
CLERK, a secretary or bookkeeper.

Clin-o (κλινω), to bend; to lean.

CLIN'ICAL,† pertaining to a bed.
DECLEN'SION, fall; degeneracy.
DECLINE', to fail; to refuse.
DISINCLINE', to excite aversion.
INCLINE', to bend; to lean.
RECLINE', to lean back.

Cliv-us, a slope, an ascent.

ACCLIV'ITY, steepness upwards.
CLIFF, a steep rock.
DECLIV'ITY, gradual descent.
PROCLIV'ITY, tendency; proneness.

---

* So styled from the practice of heathen *priests*, who used to draw *lots*, either to ascertain the will of the Deity, or prognosticate future events. Formerly *clerk* was the usual term for a scholar; most situations of talent or trust being filled by the *clergy*.

† Clinical lectures—those given by professors of medicine at the bedside of a patient.

Codex, codic-is, the trunk of a tree; a roll; a will.

CODE, a collection of laws.

COD'ICIL, an addition to a will.

Colleg-a, a partner in office.

COL'LEAGUE, a partner; an associate.

COL'LEGE, an institution of learning.

Colo, cult-um, to till; to inhabit.

AG'RICULTURE, the art of cultivating the ground.

AUSCULTA'TION, the act of listening to.

COL'ONY,° a settlement.

CUL'TIVATE, to till; to improve.

CUL'TURE, cultivation; tillage.

Color, color, hue.

COL'OR, hue; tint.

DISCOL'OR, to stain.

Com-os (κωμος), a jovial meeting.

COM'EDY,° an amusing dramatic piece.

COM'IC, raising mirth.

ENCO'MIUM, praise; eulogy.

Comes, comit-is, a companion.

CONCOM'ITANT, going with.

COUNT, a title of nobility.

COUN'TY, a shire; a district.

Conch-a (κονχα), a shell.

CONCH, a marine shell.

CONCHOL'OGY, the science of shells.

Cone-o (κονεω), to manage; to serve another.

ARCHDEA'CON, a substitute for a bishop.

DEA'CON, a church officer.

DIAC'ONAL, relating to a deacon.

Con-os (κονος), a cone.

CON'IC, of the form of a cone.

CONIF'EROUS, bearing cones.

CO'NOID, a figure like a cone.

Concili-o, to make friends.

CONCIL'IATE, to win; to reconcile.

COUN'CIL, an assembly for consultation.

IRRECONCIL'ABLE, not to be reconciled.

REC'ONCILE, to adjust; to make friends again.

Contra, against, opposite to.

CON'TRARY, opposite; adverse.

CONTRAST', to place in opposition.

COUN'TER, contrary to.

COUNTERACT', to act contrary to.

Copi-a, plenty.

CO'PIOUS, plentiful; abundant.

CORNUCO'PIÆ, the horn of plenty.

Cope (κοπη), a cutting.

OS'TEOCOPE, pain in the bones.
APOC'OPE, an omission of the last syllable or letter of a word.
SYN'COPE, a contraction of a word.

Copula, a band.

COP'ULA, a connective.
COP'ULATE, to unite; to conjoin.
COUP'LE, two; a pair.
COUP'LET, two verses.

Coqu-o, coct-um, to boil; to digest; to ripen.

COC'TION, the act of boiling.
COOK, one who prepares victuals.
CONCOCT', to digest; to ripen.
DECOC'TION, a preparation made by boiling.
INCONCOCT'ED, not matured.

Cor, cord-is, the heart.

ACCORD',° to agree; to harmonize.
CON'CORD,° agreement; union.
COR'DIAL, warm; hearty.
CORE, the heart; the inner part.
COUR'AGE, bravery; valor.
DIS'CORD,° disagreement.
DISCOUR'AGE, to depress; to deter.
ENCOUR'AGE, to animate.
RECORD', to register.

Cori-um, a skin or hide.

CORIA'CEOUS, consisting of leather.
CUR'RIER, one who dresses leather.
EXCO'RIATE, to strip off the skin.

Corn-u, a horn.

BICORN'OUS, having two horns.
COR'NEA, the horny coat of the eye.
COR'NET, a musical instrument.
CORNU-CO'PIÆ, the horn of plenty.
TAURICOR'NOUS, having horns like a bull.
U'NICORN, a beast with one horn.

Coron-a, a crown.

CORONA'TION, the act of crowning.
COR'ONET, a little crown.
COR'OLLARY, a consequence.
CROWN, an ornament for a king's head.
UNCROWN', to deprive of a crown.

Corpus, corpor-is, a body.

BICOR'PORAL, having two bodies.
COR'PORAL, relating to the body.
CORPO'REAL, having a body; not spiritual.
CORPS', a body of soldiers.
COR'PULENCE, fulness of body.
COR'PUSCLE, a minute particle.
INCOR'PORATE, to embody.

Cortex, cortic-is, bark or rind.

DECOR'TICATE, to peel; to strip off the bark.
EXCORTICA'TION, the act of pulling off the bark.

Corusc-us, glittering.

CORUS'CANT, flashing.
CORUS'CATE, to glitter; to flash.

Cosm-os (κοσμος), order; ornament; the world.

COSMET'IC, beautifying.
COS'MICAL, relating to the world.
COSMOG'ONY, an account of the creation of the world.
COSMOG'RAPHY, the science of the general system of the world.
COSMOP'OLITE, a citizen of the world.
MI'CROCOSM, a little world.

Cost-a, a rib or side.

COS'TAL, belonging to the ribs.
INTERCOS'TAL, placed between the ribs.

Couvr-ir (Fr.), to cover, to hide.

COV'ER, to overspread.
COV'ERLET, the upper covering of a bed.
COV'ERT, a shelter; a defence.
DISCOV'ER, to reveal; make known.

Crani-um (κρανιον), the skull.

CRA'NIUM, the skull.
CRANIOL'OGY, the science of skulls.
PERICRA'NIUM, a membrane covering the skull.

Cras, to-morrow. PROCRAS'TINATE, to put off.

Crass-us, thick or gross.

CRAS'SITUDE, grossness; coarseness.
INCRAS'SATE, to thicken.

Crat-os (κρατος), power, government.

ARISTOC'RACY, the government of the nobles.
ARIS'TOCRAT, one who favors aristocracy.
AU'TOCRAT, a sole-ruler.
DEMOC'RACY, government by the people.
GYNEOC'RACY, female government.
THEOC'RACY, government directed by God.

Cred-o, credit-um, to believe, to trust.

ACCRED'ITED, allowed; believed.
CRE'DENCE, belief; credit.
CREDEN'DA, things to be believed.
CRE'DENT, believing.
CRED'IBLE, worthy of credit.
CRED'IT, belief; reputation.
CRED'ITOR, he to whom money is owed.
CREDU'LITY, inclination to believe.
CRED'ULOUS, apt to believe.
CREED, religious belief.
DISCRED'IT, to disgrace.
INCRED'IBLE, surpassing belief.

Crem-o, cremat-um, to burn.

CONCREMA'TION, a burning of things together.
CREMA'TION, the act of burning

Cre-o, creat-um, to create.

CREATE', to form; to cause.
CREA'TURE, a being created.
INCREATE', not created.
MISCREA'TED, deformed.
PRO'CREATE, to give birth.
REC'REANT, cowardly; false.
RECREA'TION, amusement; diversion.

Crep-o, crepit-um, to crackle.

CREP'ITATE, to make a crackling noise.
CREV'ICE, a crack; a cleft.
DECREP'IT, broken down by age.
DISCREP'ANCY, difference; contrariety.

Cresc-o, cret-um, to grow.

ACCRES'CENT, increasing.
ACCRE'TION, a growing to another; increase.
ACCRUE', to arise from.
CONCRE'TION, growth by a union of particles.
CONCRETE', grown together, into one mass.
CRES'CENT, the shape of the new moon.
DECREASE', to grow less.
DEC'REMENT, decrease; waste.
EXCRES'CENCE, a fleshy protuberance; a tumor.
INCREASE,' to make greater.
IN'CREMENT, matter added.
RECRUIT', to repair; to supply.

Cret-a, chalk. CRETA'CEOUS, chalky.

Crimen, crimin-is, a crime, an accusation.

CRIME, an offence; a great fault.
CRIM'INAL, faulty; guilty.
RECRIM'INATE, to retort a charge.

Crin-is, the hair. CRINIG'EROUS, overgrown with hair.

Crit-es (κριτης), a judge.

CRI'SIS, the deciding point.
CRITE'RION, a standard of judging.
CRIT'IC, a judge in literature or art.
CRIT'ICISE, to censure; to judge.
CRITIQUE', critical remarks.
HYPERCRIT'IC, one over critical.
HYPOC'RISY,° dissimulation.
HYP'OCRITE, a dissembler.

Croc-us (κροκος), saffron.

CRO'CUS, the name of a flower.
CROC'ODILE, an animal of the lizard tribe.

Crux, cruc-is, the cross.

CROSS, one straight body laid at right angles over another.
CRO'SIER, a bishop's staff.
CRU'CIAL, cross-wise.
CRU'CIBLE, a chemist's melting pot
CRU'CIFY, to nail to a cross.
CRU'CIFIX, a cross bearing an image of our Saviour.
CRU'CIFORM, shaped like a cross.
CRUCIG'EROUS, bearing the cross.
EXCRU'CIATE, to torture.

Crud-us, raw; cruel.

CRUDE, raw; undigested.
CRU'EL, inhuman; savage.

Crust-a, a crust.

CRUST, an outer coat; a case.
CRUSTA'CEOUS, shelly, with joints.
INCRUST', to cover with a crust.

Crystall-us (κρυσταλλος), congealed like ice.

CRYS'TAL, a regular, solid body.
CRYS'TALLINE, bright; clear.
CRYS'TALLIZE, to form into crystals.

Crypt-o (κρυπτω), to hide.

APOC'RYPHAL, of doubtful authority.
CRYPTOG'RAPHY, the art of writing in cipher.
CRYPTOG'AMY, concealed union.

Cub-o, cubit-um, to lie down.

ACCUM'BENT, leaning.
CUB, the young of a beast.
ENCUM'BER, to burden.
IN'CUBATE, to hatch.
IN'CUBUS, nightmare; a weight.
INCUM'BENT, resting upon.
PROCUM'BENT, lying down.
RECUM'BENCE, rest; repose.
SUCCUMB', to yield; to submit.
SUPERINCUM'BENT, resting on something else.

Culc-o, *for* **Calco**, to tread upon.

INCUL'CATE, to impress by admonitions.
KICK, to strike with the foot.

Culm-us, the top; a stalk of corn.

CULMIF'EROUS, producing stalks.
CUL'MINATE, to be vertical.

Culin-a, a kitchen. CU'LINARY, relating to cookery.

Culp-a, a fault, blame.

CUL'PABLE, guilty; blamable.
EXCUL'PATE, to excuse.

Cumul-o, to heap up.

ACCU'MULATE, to heap up.
CU'MULATIVE, heaped up.

Cune-us, a wedge.

CU'NEAL, relating to a wedge.
CU'NEIFORM, wedge-shaped.

Cupio, cupit-um, to desire. **Cupid-us**, eager.

CUPID'ITY, eager desire.
COV'ET, to wish for.

Cur-a, care.

AC'CURATE, exact; correct.
AC'CURACY, exactness.
CARE, solicitude; anxiety.
CURE, to heal; to restore health.
CU'RACY, the office of a curate.
CU'RATE, a parish priest.
CU'RIOUS, inquisitive; rare.
INAC'CURATE, not exact.

INCU'RIOUS, negligent.
INSECURE', not safe.
PROC'TOR, an advocate.
PROCURE', to obtain; to acquire.
PROX'Y,° a substitute.
SECU'RITY, safety.
SI'NECURE, an office of profit without employment.

Curr-o, curs-um, to run.

CAREER', a course; a race.
CAR'RY, to convey; to transport.
CON'COURSE,° a gathering.
CONCUR', to agree.
COU'RIER, a messenger sent in haste.
COURSE, career; progress.
CUR'RENT, common; popular.
CUR'RICLE, an open chaise with two wheels.
CUR'SORY, hasty; slight.
CU'RULE, belonging to a chariot.
DISCOURSE', conversation; speech.
EXCUR'SION, a ramble; a journey.
INCUR', to become liable to.
IN'TERCOURSE, communication.
OCCUR', to happen.
OCCUR'RENCE, an accidental event.
PRECUR'SOR, a forerunner.
RECOURSE', appeal to for help.
RECUR',° to rehappen; to return
SUC'COR,° to help; to relieve.
VAN-COU'RIER, a light armed sol dier sent before an army.

Curv-us, crooked, bent.

CUR'VATURE, crookedness.
CURVE, a bent line.
CURVILIN'EAR, composed of curved lines.
INCUR'VATE, to bend; to crook.

Cut-is, the skin.

CU'TICLE, the thin outer skin.
CUTA'NEOUS, affecting the skin.

Cuti-o, cuss-um, to shake.

CONCUSSI'ON, a striking together.
DISCUSS',° to debate.
PERCUSSI'ON, a stroke.
REPERCUSSI'ON, the act of driving back.

Coutume (Fr.), habit.

ACCUS'TOM, to habituate.
CUS'TOM, habit; usage.

Cycl-us (κυκλος), a circle.

CY'CLE, a period of time.
CY'CLOID, a kind of curve.
CYCLOM'ETRY, art of measuring cycles.
CYCLOPE'DIA, a circle of the arts and sciences.
ENCYC'LICAL, sent round.
ENCYCLOPE'DIA, see Cyclopedia
EP'ICYCLE, a little circle whose centre is in the circumference of a greater.

Cylindr-os (κυλινδρος), a roller.

CYL'INDER, a roller.
CYLIN'DRICAL, like a cylinder.
CYL'INDROID, a solid body resembling a cylinder.

Cyon, cyn-os (κυων, κυνος), a dog.

CYN'IC, snarling; satirical.

CYN'OSURE,* a constellation.

Dactyl-us (δακτυλος), a finger; a poetic measure.

DAC'TYLE, a poetic foot of one long syllable and two short ones.

DACTYLOL'OGY, the art of conversing by the hands.

Dam-ao (δαμαω), to tame.

AD'AMANT, a very hard stone.

ADAMAN'TINE, made of adamant.

DI'AMOND, the most valuable of gems.

Damn-um, loss, hurt.

CONDEMN', to find guilty; to blame.

DAM'AGE, loss; injury.

DAMN, to curse; to condemn.

DAM'NIFY, to injure.

INDEM'NIFY, to secure against loss.

INDEM'NITY, security from loss.

Debil-is, weak.

DEBIL'ITY, weakness; languor.

DEBIL'ITATE, to weaken.

Debit-us, a due.

DEBT, a sum due.

DEB'IT, to charge with debt.

DEBT'OR, one who is in debt.

INDEBT', to bind by debt.

Deca, decem (δεκα), ten.

DEAN,† one next to a bishop.

DEC'ACHORD, a musical instrument.

DEC'ADE, the sum of ten.

DEC'AGON, a plane figure having ten angles.

DEC'ALOGUE, the ten commandments.

DECEM'BER,‡ the twelfth month.

DECEM'VIRI, the ten governors of Rome.

DECEM'VIRATE, a government by ten rulers.

DEC'IMAL, numbered by ten.

DEC'IMATE, to take the tenth.

DECU'RION, a commander over ten.

DUODEC'IMO, having twelve leaves to a sheet.

Dech-omai (δεχομαι), to receive.

PAN'DECT, a digest of law.

SYNEC'DOCHE, a figure by which a part is taken for the whole, or the whole foı a part.

Decens, becoming.

DE'CENT, becoming; fit.

INDE'CENCY, want of modesty.

---

* *Literally*, the dog's tail. The north star. Figuratively, any thing that attracts general notice or admiration.

† So called, because he was anciently set over *ten* canons or prebendaries, at least in some cathedral churches.

‡ Formerly, March was taken as the first month, and consequently September would be the *seventh* month; October, the *eighth;* November, the *ninth* and December, the *tenth.*

Decor, grace, comeliness.

DECORA'TION, ornament.
DECO'RUM, propriety of conduct.
INDECO'ROUS, improper.

De-us, a god.

DE'IFY, to make a god of.
DE'ITY, the Divine Being.
DE'IST, one who believes in God but denies revelation.
DE'ODAND, a forfeit to God.
DIRE, dreadful; dismal.

Delici-æ, niceties.

DELICI'OUS, sweet; agreeable.
DEL'ICACY, softness; politeness.
DEL'ICATE, nice; soft.
INDEL'ICATE, wanting delicacy.

Demi, half. DEM'I-GOD, half a god.

Dem-os (δημος), the people.

DEM'AGOGUE, a popular leader.
DEM'OCRAT, one advocating government by the people.
ENDEM'IC,° peculiar to a place.
EPIDEM'IC,° a prevailing disease

Demon (δαιμων), a spirit.

DE'MON, a devil.
DEMONOL'OGY, a treatise on evil spirits.
PANDEMO'NIUM, the hall or council chamber of the fallen angels.

Dendr-on (δενδρον), a tree.

DENDROL'OGY, the natural history of trees.

Dens-us, thick, close.

CONDENSE', to compress.
DENSE', compact; thick.

Dens, dent-is, a tooth.

BIDEN'TAL, having two teeth.
DEN'TAL, belonging to the teeth.
DENTIC'ULATED, set with small teeth.
INDENT', to notch.
INDENT'URE,* a covenant.
LABIO-DEN'TAL, formed by the lips and teeth.
LINGUA-DEN'TAL, uttered by the tongue and teeth.
TRI'DENT, an instrument having three prongs.

Despot-es (δεσποτης), a master, a despot.

DES'POT, a cruel ruler.
DES'POTISM, absolute power.

Deterior, worse.

DETE'RIORATE, to impair; to grow worse.
DETERIORA'TION, the act of making worse.

---

* So called from the notches in the edge of the paper or parchment on which it is written.

Deuter-os (δευτερος), second.

DEUTEROG'AMY, a second marriage.
DEUTERON'OMY, the fifth book of Moses, or second of the law.

Dexter, right-handed.

AMBIDEX'TROUS, using either hand.
DEXTER'ITY, readiness.

Di-es, a day.

ANTEMERID'IAN, before noon.
DI'ARY, a daily account.
DIS'MAL, sorrowful; gloomy.
DIUR'NAL, daily.
MERID'IAN, noon; mid-day.
POSTMERID'IAN, afternoon.

Dic-o, dicat-um, to set apart; to show.

AB'DICATE, to resign.
DED'ICATE, to devote.
IN'DEX, a pointer.
IN'DICATE, to point out.
PREDIC'AMENT, condition; class.
PRED'ICATE, to affirm.

Dic-o, dict-um, to speak.

ADDICT', to devote.
BENEDIC'TION,° a blessing.
DIC'TATE, to give commands.
DIC'TION, style; language.
DIC'TIONARY, a book containing the words of a language explained, in alphabetical order.
ENDITE', to compose.
INDICT', to impeach; to accuse.
INTERDICT', to prohibit.
JURISDIC'TION, legal authority; extent of power.
MALEDIC'TION, a curse.
CONTRADICT', to gainsay.
PREDICT', to foretell; to foreshow.
VER'DICT, the decision of a jury.

Didasc-o (διδασκω), to teach. DIDAC'TIC, instructive.

Diet-a (διαιτα), diet, regimen.

DI'ET, food; regimen.
DIETET'IC, relating to food.

Digit-us, a finger.

DIG'IT, any number under ten; a twelfth part of the sun's or moon's diameter.
INDIG'ITATE, to point out.

Dign-us, worthy.

CONDIGN', merited.
DEIGN, to condescend.
DIG'NIFY, to exalt; to honor.
DIG'NITY, true honor; rank.
DISDAIN', to scorn.
INDIG'NANT, enraged.

Diluvi-um, the deluge.

ANTEDILU'VIAN, one that lived before the flood.
DEL'UGE, a flood.
POSTDILU'VIAN, after the flood.

Diploma (διπλωμα), a duplicate.

DIPLO'MA,° a paper conferring a literary honor.
DIPLO'MACY, negotiation.
DIPLO'MATIST, one versed in diplomacy.
DIPLOMAT'IC, respecting diplomacy.

Dis, Di (δις), two.

DILEM'MA, difficulty.
DIPH'THONG, a union of two vowels in one sound.
DISSEV'ER, to part in two.
DIS'SYLLABLE, a word of two syllables.

Discipul-us, a disciple.

DISCI'PLE, a follower.
DIS'CIPLINE, instruction; rule

Diuturn-us, long, lasting.

DIUTUR'NITY, length of duration.
DIUTUR'NAL, lasting.

Div-us, a god.

DIVINE', godlike; heavenly.
DIVIN'ITY, the Deity; theology.

Do, datum, to give.

ABDO'MEN, the lower belly.
ABDOM'INAL, relating to the abdomen.
ABSCOND', to hide one's self.
ADD', to join to.
ADDEN'DUM, a thing joined to another.
ADDITI'ON, the act of adding.
COMMAND', to govern; to order.
CONDITI'ON, quality; state.
DATE, a particular time.
DA'TUM, a truth admitted.
DEDITI'ON, a surrender.
DE'ODAND, a forfeit to God.
DONEE', one to whom any thing is given.
DO'NOR, a giver.
DONA'TION, a gift.
ED'IT, to superintend a publication.
MAN'DATE, a command.
PERDITI'ON, ruin; death.
REC'ONDITE, hidden; secret.
REDDITI'ON, a restitution.
SUBDUE', to crush; to conquer.
SUPERADD', to add over and above.

Doc-eo, doct-um, to teach.

DOC'ILE, easily taught.
DOCIL'ITY, aptness to be taught.
DOC'TOR,° the title of a learned man.
DOC'TRINE, a principle; a precept.
DOC'UMENT, a record.
INDOC'TRINATE, to instruct.

Dogma, dogmat-is, a tenet, an opinion.

DOG'MA, a settled principle.
DOGMAT'IC, positive; arrogant.
DOG'MATIST, one who teaches with an air of authority.

Dole-o, to grieve.

CONDOLE', to lament with others.
DOLE'FUL sorrowful.
DO'LOR, grief; complaint.
IN'DOLENCE, idleness.

Domin-us, a master.

DOMAIN', empire; estate.
DOM'INANT, prevailing; ruling.
DOMINEER', to rule with insolence.
DOMIN'ION, power; territory.
DON, a Spanish title.
A. D., AN'NO-DOM'INI, in the year of our Lord.
PREDOM'INANCE, superiority.
PREDOM'INATE, to prevail over the rest.

Dom-o, domit-um, to tame.

DAUNT, to intimidate.
INDOM'ITABLE, untamable.

Dom-us, a house.

DOME, a house; an arched roof.
DOMES'TIC, private; belonging to the house or family.
DOM'ICILE, a mansion; a residence.

Don-um, a gift.

DO'NOR, a giver; a bestower.
DONA'TION, a gift.
DON'ATIVE, a present.
DONEE', one who receives a gift.

Dorm-io, dormit-um, to sleep.

DOR'MANT, sleeping; concealed.
DOR'MITORY, a place to sleep in.

Dors-um, the back.

DOR'SAL, relating to the back.
ENDORSE', to write on the back.

Dos, dot-is, a dowry.

DO'TAL, relating to a dowry.
DOTA'TION, endowment.
ENDOW', to furnish; to enrich.

Dot-os (δοτος), given.

AN'ECDOTE,° a biographical incident.
AN'TIDOTE, a medicine that counteracts poison.
DOSE, a certain quantity of medicine.

Dox-a (δοξα), an opinion, glory.

DOXOL'OGY, words of glory to God.
HET'ERODOX,° not of sound doctrine.
OR'THODOXY, soundness in doctrine.
PAR'ADOX, an opinion apparently absurd.

Drama (δραμα), an action, a play.

DRA'MA, a poem suited for representation on the stage.
DRAMAT'IC, relating to plays.
DRAM'ATIST, a writer of plays.

Drom-os (δρομος), a running.

DROM'EDARY, a sort of camel.
PAL'INDROME, a word or sentence which is the same read forwards or backwards.
SYN'DROME, a concurrence.

Drus (δρυς), the oak-tree.

DRU'ID,*an ancient priest.
DRY'AD, a wood nymph.

Dubi-us, doubtful.

DOUBT, uncertainty of mind.
DU'BIOUS, doubtful.
DUBITA'TION, doubt; distrust.
INDU'BITABLE, not to be doubted.

Duc-o, duct-um, to bring, to lead.

ABDUC'TION, a taking away.
ADDUCE', to bring forward.
AQ'UEDUCT, a conveyance for water.
CIRCUMDUCT', to nullify; to cancel.
CONDUCE', to tend; to contribute.
CONDUCT', to lead; to manage.
CON'DUIT, a water pipe.
DEDUCE', to draw from; to infer.
DEDUC'TION, an inference.
DU'CAL, pertaining to a duke.
DUC'AT, a ducal coin.
DUCT, a canal; a passage.
DUC'TILE, flexile; pliable.
DUKE, a leader; a noble.
ED'UCATE, to bring up.
EDUCE', to bring out.
INDUCE', to lead; to persuade.
INDUCT', to bring in.
INTRODUCE', to usher in.
INTRODUC'TORY, serving to introduce.
MISCON'DUCT, ill behavior.
PRODUCE', to bring forth; to bear.
PRODUC'TIVE, capable of producing.
PROD'UCT, a thing produced.
RECONDUCT', to conduct again.
REDUCE', to diminish; to subdue.
REPRODUCE', to produce again.
SEDUCE', to entice; to corrupt.
SEDUC'TIVE, fitted to entice.
SUPERINDUCE', to bring in as an addition.
TRADUCE', to calumniate.
VEN'TIDUCT, a passage for the air.

Dulc-is, sweet to the taste.

DUL'CET, sweet; luscious.
DUL'CIFY, to sweeten.

Du-o (δυω), two.

DOUB'LE, twofold.
DU'AL, expressing the number two.
DU'EL, a combat between two.
DUET', an air for two performers.
DUODEC'IMO, having twelve leaves to a sheet.
DU'PLICATE, twofold.
DUPLIC'ITY, deceit.
REDU'PLICATE, to double again.

Dur-us, hard, solid, lasting.

DU'RABLE, lasting.
DU'RANCE, imprisonment.
DURA'TION, continuance.
ENDURE', to bear; to last.
IN'DURATE, to harden.
OB'DURATE, stubborn; harsh.

---

* The Druids, who were the priests of the ancient Gauls and Britons, performed worship under an oak tree.

Dynasti-a (δυναστεια), power.

DY'NASTY, a race of princes.

DYNAM'ICS, the science of moving powers.

Dys (δυς), weakness.

DYS'ENTERY, disease of the bowels.

DYSPEP'SY, difficulty of digestion.

DYS'PHONY, difficulty in speaking.

Ebri-us, drunk.

EBRI'ETY, drunkenness.

INE'BRIATE, to intoxicate.

INSOBRI'ETY,° drunkenness.

SOBRI'ETY, soberness.

Ech-eo (ἠχεω), to sound; to teach orally.

CAT'ECHISE, to question.

CATECHU'MEN, one yet in the rudiments of Christianity.

ECHOM'ETER, a kind of scale to measure the duration of sounds.

Ec-eo (οἰκεω), to dwell.

DI'OCESE, a bishop's jurisdiction.

DI'OCESAN, pertaining to a diocese.

ECON'OMY, frugality.

ECONOM'ICAL, frugal; thrifty.

Ed-es, *for* **Ædes**, a house.

ED'IFY,° to instruct; to improve.

ED'IFICE, a building.

Ed-o, to eat.

EDAC'ITY, desire for food.

ED'IBLE, fit to be eaten.

Edr-a (ἑδρα), a seat, a side.

CATHE'DRAL, the head church in a diocese.

POLYE'DRON, a figure having many sides.

Eg-eo, to need.

IN'DIGENCE, want; penury.

IN'DIGENT, poor; needy.

Ego, I. E'GOTIST, one who talks much of himself.

Egor-a, *for* **Agora**° (ἀγορα), a public place.

AL'LEGORY, a figurative discourse.

CAT'EGORY,* an order of ideas.

PANEGYR'IC, a eulogy.

Electr-um, amber.

ELEC'TRIC, relating to electricity.

ELECTRIC'ITY,° a subtile fluid diffused through most bodies and evolved by friction; first observed in amber.

ELECTROM'ETER, an electrical instrument.

ELEC'TRIFY, to communicate electricity to.

---

* *Category* (in Logic), a name for the *predicates* or *attributes* contained under any genus, which, according to the computation of Aristotle, are ten, viz.: *substance, quantity, quality, relation, acting, suffering, time, place, situation,* and *habit.*

Elegans, elegant-is, elegant.

EL'EGANT, pleasing; beautiful.
INEL'EGANCE, want of elegance.

Elegi-a (ἐλεγεια), a mournful poem.

EL'EGY, a dirge.
ELEGI'AC, mournful.

Elysi-um, elysium.

ELYS'IUM, the heaven of the heathens.
ELYS'IAN, exceedingly delightful.

Eme-o (ἐμεω), to vomit. EMET'IC, causing to vomit.

Em-o, empt-um, to buy.

EXEMPT', to free from.
PER'EMPTORY, absolute; positive.
PRE-EMP'TION, a right of buying before others.
PROMPT, quick; ready.
REDEEM', to ransom; to rescue.

Emul-us, *for* ***Æmulus,*** vying with.

EM'ULATE, to rival.
EM'ULOUS, rivalling.

En (ἑν), one. ENDEC'AGON, a figure of eleven sides.

Enigma, *for* ***Ænigma*** (αἰνιγμα), a riddle.

ENIG'MA, a riddle.
ENIGMAT'ICAL, obscure; dark.

Ens-is, a sword. EN'SIFORM, sword-shaped.

Ens, ent-is, being. ***Esse,*** to be.

AB'SENT,° not present.
ABSENTEE', he who is absent.
AB'SENCE, state of being away.
EN'TITY,° a real being.
ES'SENCE, the nature of any thing.
DISIN'TERESTED, without interest or partiality.
IN'TEREST, to concern; to affect.
MISREPRESENT', to represent falsely.
NON-EN'TITY, non-existence.
OMNIPRES'ENCE, presence everywhere.
PRES'ENT,° within sight; near.
QUINT'ESSENCE, the essential part.
REPRESENT', to describe.
UNESSEN'TIAL, not necessary.

Enter-on (ἐντερον), the bowels.

DYS'ENTERY, a disease of the bowels.
ENTERI'TIS, inflammation of the intestines.
MES'ENTERY, a membrane supporting the intestines.

Entom-on (ἐντομον), an insect.

ENTOMOL'OGY, the science which treats of insects.

Eo, it-um, to go.

AM'BIENT, surrounding.
AMBITI'ON,* desire of honor.
CIR'CUIT, extent round about.
CIRCUMAM'BIENT, surrounding.
IMPER'ISHABLE, not liable to perish.
INTRAN'SITIVE, not passing over upon an object.
O'BIT, decease.
OBIT'UARY, relating to a deceased person.
PER'ISH,° to die; to decay.
PRE'TOR, a chief judge in ancient Rome.
SEDITI'ON,° a popular outbreak.
TRAN'SIENT,° short; momentary.
TRAN'SIT, a passing over.

Epicur-us (ἐπίκουρος), a sensual philosopher.

EP'ICURE, one given to luxury.
EP'ICURISM, sensual enjoyment.

Ep-os (ἔπος), a word.

EP'IC, narrative; heroic.
ORTHO'EPY, the art of pronouncing words properly.
ORTHO'EPIST, one versed in orthoepy.

Eques, equit-is, a horseman.

EQUES'TRIAN, relating to horsemanship.
E'QUERY, a stable for horses.
EQUIP', to furnish; to dress.

Equ-us, for Æquus, equal, just.

AD'EQUATE, equal to.
COE'QUAL, of the same rank.
E'QUABLE, even; uniform.
E'QUALIZE, to make equal.
EQUANIM'ITY, composure.
EQUA'TION, a making equal.
EQUA'TOR, a great circle having the same poles as the earth.
EQUIAN'GULAR, having equal angles.
EQUIDIS'TANT, being at the same distance.
EQUILAT'ERAL, having all sides equal.
EQUILIB'RIUM, equality of weight.
E'QUINOX, the time of equal day and night.
E'QUIPOISE, equality of weight.
EQUIPON'DERATE, to be equal in weight.
EQ'UITY, justice; right.
EQUIV'ALENT, equal in value.
EQUIV'OCAL, ambiguous.
EQUIV'OCATE, to use doubtful expressions.
INAD'EQUACY, insufficiency.
INEQUAL'ITY, unevenness.
INIQ'UITY, injustice; sin.

Erc-eo,° *for Arceo,* to drive.

COERCE',° to restrain.
COER'CIVE, forcible.
EX'ERCISE, to employ; to train.
EXERCITA'TION, practice; essay.

* Those who sought honor or preferment among the Romans, endeavored to gain the favor of the people by every popular art, viz., by *going round* their houses, (*ambiendo*, ab *am* et *eo*,) by shaking hands, by addressing and naming them, &c.; hence *ambitio, ambition.*

Erem-os (ἔρημος), lonely, alone.

ER'EMITE, HER'MIT, one who lives in seclusion.

Erg-on (ἔργον), a work.

LIT'URGY, a formulary of public prayer.
SUR'GERY, a curing by manual operation.
CHIRUR'GEON, a surgeon.
EN'ERGY, force; vigor.
MET'ALLURGY, the art of working metals.

Err-o, to wander.

ABERRA'TION, a wandering away.
AR'RANT, bad in a high degree.
ERR, to stray; to mistake.
ERRA'TUM, an error in printing.
ERRAT'IC, wandering.
ERRO'NEOUS, incorrect.
ER'ROR, a mistake.

Estim-o, *for* **Æstimo,** to value.

ESTEEM', to value; to prize.
ESTIMA'TION, calculation; value.
INES'TIMABLE, invaluable.

Estu-o, *for* **Æstuo,** to boil. ES'TUARY, an arm of the sea.

Etern-us, *for* **Æternus,** without beginning, or end.

CO-ETER'NAL, equally eternal with another.
ETER'NIZE, to make eternal.

Ether, *for* **Æther,** the sky.

E'THER, a volatile fluid.
ETHE'REAL, celestial.

Eth-os (ἔθος), custom.

ETH'ICS, the doctrine or system of morality.
ETH'ICAL, relating to morals.

Ethn-os (ἔθνος), a people.

ETH'NICAL, relating to the human races.
ETHNOG'RAPHY, a description of nations or races.

Etymon (ἔτυμον), the true meaning of a word.

ETYMOL'OGY, the descent, or derivation of words.
ET'YMON, a root or primitive word.

Eu (ἐυ), well.

EULO'GIUM, praise; panegyric.
EU'LOGIZE, to commend; to praise.
EU'PHONY, agreeable sound.

Ev-um, *for* **Ævum,** life, time; an age.

COE'VAL, of the same age.
LONGEV'ITY, length of life.
PRIME'VAL, original; first.

Examen, examin-is, a balance.

EXAM'INE, to try; to question; to investigate.

Exempl-um, a copy.

EXAM'PLE, pattern; instance.
EXEM'PLAR, a model; a copy.
EXEM'PLIFY, to illustrate by example.
SAM'PLE, a specimen.

Ex-is (ἕξις), a state of mind or body.

CACH'EXY, ill state of body.
EP'OCH, a period; an era.

Exter-us, outward, foreign.

EXOT'IC, a foreign plant.
EXTE'RIOR, outward.
EXTER'NAL, exterior; visible.
EXTRA'NEOUS, not belonging to.
EXTREME', utmost; last.
EXTRIN'SIC, outward.
STRANGE, foreign; unusual.

Fabric-o, to make.

FAB'RIC, a building; an edifice.
FAB'RICATE, to form; to forge.
FAB'RILE, belonging to handicrafts.

Fabul-a, a feigned story.

FA'BLE, a feigned story.
FAB'ULOUS, feigned; forged.
CONFAB'ULATE, to talk together.

Facet-us, humorous. FACE'TIOUS, gay; witty.

Faci-es, the face.

DEFACE', to disfigure.
EFFACE', to blot out; to destroy.
FACE, the visage; the front.
FASH'ION, form; custom.
FEA'TURE, cast of the face.
SUPERFIC'IAL, shallow; being on the surface.
SUR'FACE, the outside.

Facil-is, easy.

DIF'FICULT, hard to be done; laborious.
FACIL'ITY, ease; readiness.
FACIL'ITATE, to make easy.

Faci-o, fact-um, to make; to do.

AFFECT', to act upon; to move.
AFFEC'TION, love; kindness.
AM'PLIFY, to enlarge; to extend.
AR'EFY, to dry.
AR'TIFICE, a trick; a fraud.
BEATIF'IC, blissful.
BENEFAC'TION, the act of conferring a benefit.
BEN'EFICE, a church living.
BEN'EFIT, advantage.
CALORIF'IC, causing heat.
CER'TIFY, to give evidence.
CERTIF'ICATE, a testimony in writing.
CLAR'IFY, to make clear.
CLAS'SIFY, to arrange in classes.
CO-EFFICI'ENT, co-operating.
CONFEC'TION, a sweetmeat.
COUN'TERFEIT, forged; fictitious.
CRU'CIFY, to nail to a cross.
DAM'NIFY, to injure.
DEFEAT', an overthrow.
DEFECT', a fault; a blemish.
DEFICI'ENT, wanting.
DEFIC'IT, want; deficiency.
DE'IFY, to make a god of.
DIG'NIFY, to exalt; to honor.
DISAFFEC'TED, unfriendly.
DISAFFEC'TION, dislike.
DISQUAL'IFY, to make unfit.
DISQUALIFICA'TION, incapacity
DIVER'SIFY, to make different

ED'IFY, to instruct; to improve.
ED'IFICE, a fabric; a building.
EFFECT',° result; consequence.
EFFICI'ENT, active; able.
EXEM'PLIFY, to illustrate by example.
FACT, a reality; a thing done.
FAC'TION, a party; a division.
FAC'TIOUS, turbulent.
FAC'TORY, a building where any article is manufactured.
FAL'SIFY, to make false.
FEA'SIBLE, that may be done.
FEAT, an action; an exploit.
FI'AT,° an order; a decree.
FOR'FEIT, a fine for an offence.
FOR'TIFY,° to strengthen.
FRIGORIF'IC, causing cold.
GLO'RIFY, to honor; to exalt.
GRAT'IFY, to indulge; to please.
GRATIFICA'TION, pleasure.
IG'NIFY, to form into fire.
IMPER'FECT, defective; frail.
INARTIFICI'AL, plain; artless.
INEF'FICACY, want of power.
INFEC'TIOUS, pestilential.
INFECT', to impart disease.
INOFFICI'OUS, not meddling.
INSIGNIF'ICANCE, want of meaning; unimportance.
INSUFFICI'ENT, inadequate.
LIQ'UEFY, to melt.
MAG'NIFY, to make great.
MALEFAC'TOR,° a criminal.
MANUFAC'TURE,° any thing made by art.
MOD'IFY, to shape; to alter.
MOL'LIFY, to soften; to assuage.
MOR'TIFY, to humble; to depress.
MUNIF'ICENT, liberal; generous.
NO'TIFY, to declare.
NOTIFICA'TION, the act of notifying.
NUL'LIFY, to make void.
OF'FICE, a place of business.
OFFICI'AL, pertaining to office.
OMNIF'IC, all-creating.
OR'IFICE, an opening to a cavity.
OS'SIFY, to change to bone.
PAC'IFY, to appease; to quiet.
PER'FECT, to finish; to complete.
PERSON'IFY, to change from a thing to a person.
PET'RIFY, to convert to stone.
PETRIFAC'TION, the act of turning to stone.
PRE'FECT, a governor.
PON'TIFF, a priest; the pope.
PROFICI'ENT, one skilled in a study or business.
PROF'IT, gain; advantage.
PROLIF'IC, productive.
PU'RIFY, to cleanse.
RAMIFICA'TION, a branching.
RAR'EFY, to make thin.
RAT'IFY, to confirm; to settle.
REC'TIFY, to make right.
REFEC'TORY, an eating room.
REFIT', to repair.
REVIV'IFY, to recall to life.
SAC'RIFICE, to destroy; to devote.
SANC'TIFY, to make holy.
SAT'ISFY, to content; to please.
SCAR'IFY, to make slight cuts.
SIG'NIFY, to declare; to mean.
SIGNIF'ICANCE, meaning; force.
SIM'PLIFY, to render simple.
SOMNIF'IC, causing sleep.
SONORIF'IC, producing sound.
SPEC'IFY, to mention particularly.
STRAT'IFY, to range in layers.
STUL'TIFY, to make foolish.
SUDORIF'IC, causing sweat.
SUFFICE', to supply; to satisfy.
TER'RIFY, to frighten.
TES'TIFY, to bear witness.
TOR'REFY, to dry by a fire.
TYP'IFY, to show in emblem.
VER'IFY, to prove true.
VER'SIFY, to make verse.
VIL'IFY, to debase; to abuse.
VIT'RIFY, to change into glass.

Falcat-us, bent like scythes.

DEFALCA'TION, abatement.
FAL'CHION, a short crooked sword.
FAL'CON, a hawk.
FAL'CONRY, the art of training hawks.

Fall-o, fals-um, to deceive.

FALSE, not true; not real.
FAL'LIBLE, liable to error.
FALSET'TO, a feigned voice.
FAL'SITY, an untruth.
FAL'LACY, deceitful argument.

Fam-a,* fame.

DEFAME', to slander.
FAME, celebrity; renown.
FA'MOUS, known; celebrated.
IN'FAMY, disgrace.

Fam-es, hunger.

FAM'ISH, to starve.
FAM'INE, scarcity of food.

Famili-a, a family.

FAMIL'IAR, easy in conversation; affable; well known.
FAM'ILY, the persons living in a house; a class.

Fantasi-a, *for* ***Phantasia*** (φαντασια), a vivid mental image.

FAN'CY, imagination; whim.
FANTAS'TIC, whimsical; odd.

Fan-um, a temple.

FANAT'IC,† an enthusiast.
FANE, a temple.
PROFANE,' without respect for sacred things; secular.

Fa-ri (ab For), to speak.

AF'FABLE, easy to be spoken to.
INEF'FABLE, unspeakable.
IN'FANT, a young child.
IN'FANCY, the first stage of life.
INFAN'TICIDE, the murder of an infant.
NEFA'RIOUS, wicked.
PREF'ACE, an introductory speech or writing.
PREF'ATORY, introductory.

Farin-a, meal, flour.

FARINA'CEOUS, consisting of meal or flour; mealy.

Fascin-um, enchantment, charm.

FAS'CINATE, to bewitch; to enchant.

---

* A heathen goddess, celebrated by the poets, who represented her, as having her palace in the air, and as possessing a vast number of eyes, ears, and tongues.

† *Fanatics*, those who passed their time in temples (*fana*), and being often seized with a kind of enthusiasm, as if inspired by the Divinity, showed wild and antic gestures: such as cutting and slashing their arms with knives, shaking their heads, &c.

The profane, those who were not initiated into the mysteries of *religion*, and therefore made to stand before or on the outside of the *temple*.

Fastidi-um, disgust.

FASTID'IOUS, apt to become disgusted; disdainful.

Fatig-o, to tire, to weary.

FATIGUE', to tire; to weary.

INDEFAT'IGABLE, not to be wearied; persevering.

Fat-um,° fate, destiny.

FATE, decree of destiny; destruction.

FATID'ICAL, prophetic; describing future events.

Fav-eo, to befriend. FA'VOR, kindness; regard.

Febr-is, a fever.

ANTIFE'BRILE, opposing fever.

FEB'RIFUGE, a medicine that mitigates fever.

FE'VER, a disease.

Fecund-us, *for* **Fœcundus**, fruitful.

FECUN'DITY, fruitfulness.

Fedus, *for* **Fœdus**, **feder-is**, a league.

CONFED'ERATE, one joined in a league.

CONFED'ERACY, a number of persons or states united by a league.

FED'ERAL, relating to a league.

FED'ERATIVE, securing union.

Felix, **felic-is**, happy.

FELIC'ITATE, to congratulate.

FELIC'ITY, happiness.

Femin-a, a woman, a female.

FEM'ININE, of the female sex.

EFFEM'INATE, womanish; soft.

Femur, **femor-is**, the thigh.

FEM'ORAL, relating to the thigh.

Fend-o, **fens-um**, to keep off, to strike.

DEFEND',° to protect.

DEFENCE', guard; security.

FEN'CING, practice in using a sword for defence.

FEN'DER, a utensil placed before the fire; any thing that defends.

INOFFEN'SIVE, harmless.

OFFEND',° to displease.

OFFENCE', crime; injury.

Fenestr-a, a window. FENES'TRAL, relating to a window.

Fer-a, a wild beast.

FEROC'ITY, cruelty; fierceness.

FIERCE, savage; furious.

Feri-o, to strike. INTERFERE', to interpose; to intermeddle.

Fer-o, to carry, to bear.

Alif'erous, having wings.
Circum'ference, the measure around the outside.
Confer', to converse; to consult.
Culmif'erous, producing stalks.
Defer', to put off; to delay.
Def'erence, regard; respect.
Dif'fer, to vary; to disagree.
Fer'ry, the passage over which ferry boats pass.
Fer'tile, fruitful; abundant.
Flammif'erous, producing flame.
Florif'erous, bearing flowers.
Frondif'erous, bearing leaves.
Indif'ference, impartiality; neglect; unconcern.
Infer', to deduce.
In'ference, a conclusion.
Insuf'ferable, not to be borne.
Lactif'erous, bearing milk.
Mammif'erous, having breasts.
Mellif'erous, productive of honey.
Metallif'erous, producing metals.
Misinfer', to draw a wrong inference.
Mortif'erous, fatal; deadly.
Nubif'erous, bringing clouds.
Of'fer, to present for acceptance or rejection.
Pestif'erous, destructive.
Pomif'erous, bearing apples.
Prefer', to regard more.
Prof'fer, to propose; to offer.
Refer', to direct to another for information or judgment.
Somnif'erous, causing sleep.
Stellif'erous, having stars.
Suf'fer, to undergo; to permit.
Transfer', to convey; to remove.
Vocif'erate, to make outcries.

Ferr-um, iron.

Ferru'ginous, partaking of iron.
Fer'rule, a metal ring at the end of a stick.

Ferul-a, a ferule.

Fer'ule, a rod used for correcting boys at school.

Ferv-eo, to grow hot.

Fer'vor, heat; zeal.
Fer'vent, hot; ardent.
Fer'vid, eager; zealous.

Fess-um, to own, to declare.

Confess', to acknowledge.
Confest', open; known.
Profess', to declare openly.

Festuc-a, a straw. Festu'cous, formed of straw.

Fest-um, a feast.

Fes'tal, befitting a feast.
Festiv'ity, gayety.

Fibr-a, a thread.

Fi'bre, a small thread.
Fi'brous, composed of fibres

Fid-es, faith, trust.

AFFI'ANCE, a marriage contract.
AFFIDA'VIT,* a declaration on oath.
BO'NA-FI'DE, in good faith.
CONFIDE', to trust in.
DEFY', to challenge; to dare.
DIF'FIDENT, distrustful.
FIDEL'ITY, faithfulness.
FIDU'CIAL, confident; having the nature of a trust.
IN'FIDEL, a disbeliever.
PER'FIDY,° breach of faith.

Figur-a, a figure.

CONFIG'URE, to dispose into any form.
DISFIG'URE, to deform; to deface.
EF'FIGY, image; likeness.
FIG'URE, shape; semblance.
PREFIG'URE, to foreshadow.

Fili-us, a son.

AFFIL'IATE, to adopt.
FIL'IAL, relating to a son.

Fil-um, a thread.

FILA'CEOUS, consisting of threads.
FIL'AMENT, a slender thread.
FIL'TER, to strain.
FILE, a line; a row.

Finance (Fr.), revenue.

FINANCE', income; revenue.
FINAN'CIAL, respecting finance.

Find-o, fiss-um, to cleave.

BI'FID, divided into two.
FIS'SURE, a cleft.

Fing-o, fict-um, to feign.

FEIGN, to invent; to pretend.
FIC'TION, a tale; an invention.
FICTITI'OUS, false; not real.

Fin-is, the end.

AFFIN'ITY,° relation by marriage.
CON'FINE, border; edge.
DEFINE', to explain; to describe.
DEF'INITE, certain; limited.
FI'NAL, ultimate; conclusive.
FIN'ISH, to perfect; to end.
INDEF'INITE, not limited.
IN'FINITE, boundless.
REFINE', to improve; to polish
SUPERFINE', eminently fine.

Firm-us, strong.

AFFIRM',° to declare positively.
CONFIRM', to establish; to strengthen.
DISAFFIRM', to contradict.
FIR'MAMENT, the sky.
INFIRM', weak; feeble.
INFIRM'ARY, an hospital.

---

* Literally, *he made faith to;* or, in the language of common law, *he made oath to*

Fisc-us, a bag.

CON'FISCATE,* to seize as a forfeit.
FIS'CAL, belonging to a public treasury.

Fix-us, fixed.

AFFIX',° to subjoin.
CRU'CIFIX, a cross bearing an image of our Saviour.
FIX'ITY, coherence of parts.
FIX'TURE, any thing fixed to a place or house.
INFIX,' to drive in; to set.
POST'FIX,° a syllable added.
PREFIX',° to fix at the beginning
TRANSFIX', to pierce through.

Flagiti-um, wickedness. FLAGITI'OUS, wicked; atrocious.

Flagr-o, to burn.

CONFLAGRA'TION, a general fire.
DEF'LAGRATE, to set fire to.
FLA'GRANT, burning; notorious.

Flamen, flamin-is, an ancient priest.

FLAMIN'ICAL, pertaining to a Roman Flamen.

Flamm-a, a flame.

FLAM'BEAU, a lighted torch.
FLAME, burning vapor; blaze.
INFLAME', to set on fire.
INFLAMMA'TION, a swelling and redness of an animal body, attended with heat.

Flat-us, a puff, a blast.

AFFLA'TUS, a light breath.
EFFLATE', to puff up.
FLAT'ULENT, windy; vain.
INFLATE', to puff up.

Flect-o, flex-um, to bend.

CIR'CUMFLEX, an accent denoting a long syllable. L. (^) Gr. (~).
DEFLEC'TION, a turning aside.
FLEX'IBLE, ductile; pliant.
FLEX'URE, a bending; a joint.
INFLECT', to bend; to turn.
REFLECT', to cast back; to think.

Fligo, flict-um, to beat, to strike.

AFFLICT', to pain; to grieve.
CON'FLICT, contest; struggle.
INFLICT', to lay on; to apply.

Flos, flor-is, a flower.

FLO'RA, the goddess of flowers.
FLO'RAL, relating to flowers.
FLOR'ID, flushed; brilliant.
FLO'RIST, a cultivator of flowers.

Fluctu-o, to rise in waves.

FLUC'TUATE, to move as waves.
FLUCTUA'TION, uncertainty.

---

* The *Fiscus* was originally a *hamper* or *bag*, in which the emperor's treasure was kept: hence, to confiscate a person's property is to put it into the *Fiscus* or treasury of the king.

Flu-o, flux-um, to flow.

AF'FLUENCE, riches; plenty.
AF'FLUX, a flowing to.
CIRCUM'FLUENT, flowing round.
CON'FLUENCE, a junction of streams.
EFFLU'VIA, minute particles always flying off from bodies.
EF'FLUX, a flowing out.
FLU'ENCY, smoothness of speech.
FLU'ID, any thing that flows.
FLUX'ION, a flowing.
IN'FLUENCE, to bias; to modify.
INFLUEN'TIAL, exerting influence.
IN'FLUX, the act of flowing in.
MELLIF'LUENT, sweetly flowing.
RE'FLUX, backward course; ebb.
RORIF'LUENT, flowing with dew.
SUPER'FLUOUS, unnecessary.

Foc-us, a point.

FO'CUS, the point where rays of light meet.
FO'CAL, belonging to the focus.

Foli-um, a leaf.

FOIL, leaf-metal.
FOLIA'CEOUS, consisting of leaves.
FO'LIAGE, a growth of leaves.
FO'LIO, a large book in which the paper is only once folded.
PORTFO'LIO, a case for loose leaves.
CINQUE'FOIL, five-leaved clover.
TRE'FOIL, three-leaved clover.

Fons, font-is, a source.

FONT, a baptismal vessel.
FOUN'TAIN, a well; a spring.

For-is, a door; abroad.

FOR'AGE, food for cattle.
FOR'EIGN, alien; remote.
FOR'FEIT, a fine for an offence.

Form-a, a form.

BI'FORM, having two forms.
CONFORM', to make like.
CRU'CIFORM, having the form of a cross.
DEFORM', to disfigure.
FORM, shape; figure.
FOR'MULA, a prescribed form.
INFORM', to instruct; to acquaint.
INFORMAL'ITY, absence of form.
MAM'MIFORM, having the shape of breasts.
MUL'TIFORM, having various shapes.
NONCONFOR'MITY, want of conformity.
PERFORM', to execute; to do.
REFORMA'TION, a growing better.
RET'IFORM, having the form of a net.
SCU'TIFORM, shaped like a shield.
TRANSFORM', to change the form.
TRI'FORM, of triple shape.
VER'MIFORM, having the shape of a worm.
U'NIFORM, even; regular.

Formid-o, fear, dread. FOR'MIDABLE, dreadful.

For-o, to bore.

IMPER'FORABLE, not to be bored through.
PER'FORATE, to pierce; to bore.

Fors, fort-is, chance, luck.

FORTU'ITOUS, accidental; casual.
FOR'TUNE, chance; wealth.
MISFOR'TUNE, calamity.
UNFOR'TUNATE, unlucky; unhappy.

Fort-is, strong, valiant.

COM'FORT,° support; consolation.
DEFORCE', to keep out of possession.
EF'FORT, exertion.
FORCE, to compel; to press.
FORT, a castle.
FORTE, that in which one excels.
FOR'TIFY, to strengthen.
FOR'TITUDE, courage; bravery.
FOR'TRESS, a strong-hold.
ENFORCE', to put in execution.

For-um,° a public place in Rome.

FOREN'SIC, belonging to courts of judicature.
FAIR, a stated market.

Foss-a, a ditch.

FOSSE, a ditch; a moat.
FOS'SIL, dug out of the earth.

Fragr-o, to smell sweetly. FRA'GRANCE, sweetness of smell.

Franc, Franche, (Fr.) free.

DISFRAN'CHISE, to deprive of privileges.
ENFRAN'CHISE, to liberate.
FRAN'CHISE, privilege; right.
FRANK, liberal; open.
FRANK'INCENSE, an odoriferous drug.
FRANK'LIN,° a freeholder.

Frang-o, fract-um, to break.

FRAC'TION, a part.
FRAC'TURE, a breach; a rupture.
FRAG'ILE, brittle; frail.
FRAIL, weak; infirm.
FRAIL'TY, weakness; infirmity.
INFRAC'TION, violation.
INFRAN'GIBLE, not to be broken.
INFRINGE', to violate; to break.
IRREF'RAGABLE, not to be confuted.
REFRACT', to break the course of rays of light.
REFRAN'GIBLE, capable of being refracted.

Frater, fratr-is, a brother.

CONFRATER'NITY, a brotherhood.
FRATER'NAL, brotherly.
FRAT'RICIDE, the murder of a brother.
FRATER'NIZE, to associate as brothers.

Fraus, fraud-is, fraud.

FRAUD, deceit.
DEFRAUD', to cheat.
FRAU'DULENCE, deceitfulness

Fren-um, for ***Frænum,*** a curb.

REFRAIN', to forbear; to abstain.

Frequens, frequent-is, frequent.

FREQUENT', to visit often.
INFRE'QUENCY, rareness.

Fric-o, frict-um, to rub.

DEN'TIFRICE, a powder for the teeth.
FRIC'TION, the act of rubbing.

Frig-us, frigor-is, cold.

FRIG'ID, cold; dull.
FRIGORIF'IC, causing cold.
REFRIG'ERATE, to cool.

Frivol-us, trifling.

FRIV'OLOUS, light; trifling.
FRIVOL'ITY, triflingness.

Frons, frond-is, a leaf. FRONDIF'EROUS, bearing leaves.

Frons, front-is, the forehead.

AFFRONT', to insult; to offend.
CONFRONT', to face; to oppose.
EFFRON'TERY, impudence.
FRONT, the face; the forepart.
FRONT'AL, relating to the forehead.
FRONT'LET, a band for the forehead.

Frug-es, fruit, (figuratively, thrifty).

FRU'GAL, thrifty; sparing.
FRUGIF'EROUS, bearing fruit.

Frument-um, corn.

FRUMENTA'CEOUS, made of grain.
FRUMENTA'TION, a general distribution of corn.

Fruor, fruit-us, to enjoy. ***Fruct-us,*** fruit.

FRUCTIF'EROUS, bearing fruit.
FRUC'TIFY, to make fruitful.
FRUIT, the produce of a tree or plant; profit.
FRUITI'ON, enjoyment; use.

Frustr-a, in vain. FRUS'TRATE, to balk; to make null.

Fugi-o, fugit-um, to flee.

CENTRIF'UGAL, flying from the centre.
FEB'RIFUGE, a cure for fever.
FUGAC'ITY, a flying away.
FU'GITIVE, unstable; fleeting.
REF'UGE, shelter; protection.
SUB'TERFUGE, a shift; an evasion.
VER'MIFUGE, medicine that expels worms.

Fulge-o, to shine.

EFFUL'GENCE, lustre; brightness.
FUL'GENT, shining; dazzling.
REFUL'GENCE, brightness.
REFUL'GENT, shining.

Fulmen, fulmin-is, lightning, thunder.

FUL'MINANT, thundering.
FUL'MINATE, to thunder.

Fum-us, smoke, fume.

FUME, to smoke; to be in a rage.
FU'MIGATE, to perfume; to smoke.
PERFUME', to scent.

Funct-us, discharged one's duty

FUNC'TION, office; power.
DEFUNCT', dead.

Fund-o, fus-um, to pour, to melt.

AFFU'SION, act of pouring upon.
CIRCUMFUSE', to pour round.
CONFOUND',° to mingle; to perplex.
CONFUSE', to confound; to mix.
DIFFUSE', to pour out; to spread.
EFFU'SION, a pouring out.
FUSE, to melt.
INFUSE', to pour into; to inspire
PROFUSE', lavish; prodigal.
REFUND',° to repay; to restore.
REFUSE', to deny; to decline.
REFU'SAL, a denial.
SUFFU'SION, an overspreading.
TRANSFUSE', to pour out of one into another.

Fund-us, the bottom.

FOUND,° to raise; to establish.
FOUN'DERY, a casting-house.
FOUNDA'TION, basis; origin.
FUNDAMEN'TAL, lying at the foundation.
PROFOUND',° deep; thorough.
PROFUND'ITY, depth.

Fung-us, a sponge.

FUN'GUS, an excrescence.
FUN'GOUS, spongy.

Fun-is, a rope.

FU'NICLE, a small cord.
FUNIC'ULAR, consisting of cord.
FUNAM'BULIST, a rope-dancer.

Funus, funer-is, a burial.

FU'NERAL, burial; interment.
FUNE'REAL, suiting a funeral.
FUNE'BRIAL, belonging to funerals.

Fur, a thief.

FURA'CIOUS, thievish.
FUR'TIVE, stolen.

Furc-a, a fork. BI'FURCATED, having two forks.

Furi-a, a madness.

FU'RIOUS, mad; raging.
FU'RY, rage; frenzy.
INFU'RIATE, to make furious.

Futil-is, trifling.

FU'TILE, trifling; worthless.
FUTIL'ITY, unimportance.

Fut-o, to blame; to disprove.

CONFUTE', to convict of error.
IRREFU'TABLE, not to be overthrown by argument.
REFUTE', to prove false.

Gala (Sp.), fine dress.

GA'LA, a festival.

GAL'LANT, brave ; gay.

Galax (γαλαξ), milk. GAL'AXY,° the milky-way.

Galli-a, ancient France.

GAL'LIC, French.

GAL'LICISM, a French idiom.

Galvani (It.),° Professor of Anatomy at Bologna.

GALVAN'IC, relating to galvanism.

GAL'VANISM, a species of electricity.

Gam-eo (γαμεω), to marry.

AMAL'GAMATE,° to mix or unite metals.

BIG'AMY, the crime of having two wives at once.

CRYPTOG'AMY, concealed union.

MONOG'AMIST, a disallower of second marriages.

POLYG'AMY, plurality of wives.

Garr-io, to prattle.

GAR'RULOUS, talkative.

GARRU'LITY, talkativeness.

Gaster, gastr-os (γαστηρ, γαστρος), the belly, or stomach.

GAS'TRIC, belonging to the stomach.

GASTRIL'OQUY, a speaking from the stomach.

Gazett-a, a gazette. GAZETTE',* a newspaper.

Ge (γῆ), the earth.

AP'OGEE,° greatest distance from the earth.

GEOCEN'TRIC, having the earth for its centre.

GEOG'RAPHY, a description of the earth's surface.

GEOL'OGY, the science of the structure of the earth.

GE'OMANCY, divination by figures or lines.

GEOM'ETRY,° the science of dimensions.

GEOPON'ICS, agriculture.

GEOS'COPY, knowledge of the soil, gained by inspection.

Gel-u, frost, ice.

CONGEAL', to freeze.

CONGELA'TION, a freezing.

GEL'ATINE, an animal substance resembling jelly.

GEL'ID, extremely cold.

JEL'LY, a kind of sweetmeat.

INCONGEAL'ABLE, that cannot be frozen.

Gemin-us, double.

GEM'INATE, to double.

GEM'INI, the Twins, Castor and Pollux, sign in the zodiac.

Gemm-a, a bud, a gem. GEM, a precious jewel.

---

* Gazetta is the name of a Venetian half-penny, which was the price of the first newspaper ever published. It was published at Venice, in the sixteenth century—a mere literary journal, in single sheets.

Genea (γενεα), a generation, a birth.

COSMOG'ONY, an account of the creation of the world.
GENEAL'OGY, an account of the succession of families.
GEN'ESIS, the first book of Scripture, treating of the creation of the world.
HETEROGE'NEOUS, dissimilar.
HOMOGE'NEAL, of the same kind.
HY'DROGEN,° a gas.
THEOG'ONY, the genealogy of the gods.
OX'YGEN,° a gas which generates acids.

Genu, the knee.

GENIC'ULATE, to joint or knot.
GENUFLEC'TION, the act of bending the knee.

Genus, gener-is, a race, a family.

CONGE'NIAL, kindred.
DEGEN'ERATE,° fallen; base.
DEGEN'ERACY, a growing worse.
DISINGEN'UOUS, unfair; artful.
ENGEN'DER, to beget; to produce.
GEN'DER, sex.
GEN'ERAL,° public; extensive.
GENERALIS'SIMO, the supreme commander.
GENER'IC, embracing the genus.
GEN'ERATE, to beget; to cause.
GEN'EROUS,° liberal; munificent.
GENEROS'ITY, liberality.
GE'NIAL,° cheerful; gay.
GE'NIUS, mental power.
GENTEEL', polite; elegant.
GEN'TILE, a pagan; a heathen.
GENTIL'ITY, dignity of birth.
GEN'TLE, soft; bland.
GEN'TRY, people of education and good breeding.
GEN'UINE,° not spurious; real.
GE'NUS, a class comprehending many species.
INGE'NIOUS,° witty; skilful.
INGEN'UOUS,° open; frank.
INGENU'ITY, wit; acuteness.
PRIMOGE'NIAL, first born.
PRIMOGEN'ITURE, state of being first born.
PROG'ENY, offspring; race.
PROGEN'ITOR, a forefather.
REGEN'ERATED, born anew.

Germen, germin-is, a sprout or shoot.

GER'MINATE, to sprout; to bud.

Ger-o, gest-um, to bear, to carry.

ALIG'EROUS, having wings.
BELLIG'ERENT, waging war.
CONGE'RIES, a mass of small bodies.
CONGES'TION, an accumulation of blood in a part of the body.
CORNIG'EROUS, horned.
CRINIG'EROUS, overgrown with hair.
DIGEST',° to arrange; to dissolve.
GESTA'TION, a bearing of young.
GESTIC'ULATE, to use gestures.
GES'TURE, action; posture.
INDIGEST'IBLE, not digestible.
LANIG'EROUS, bearing wool.
SUGGEST',° to hint; to intimate.
VICEGE'RENT,° a vicar; a substitute.

Gigas, gigant-is, a giant.

GI'ANT, a man of extraordinary size.

GIGAN'TIC, like a giant.

Glaci-es, ice.

CONGLA'CIATE, to turn to ice.

GLA'CIAL, icy; frozen.

GLA'CIERS, fields of ice and snow.

Gladi-us, a sword.

GLADIA'TOR, a sword player.

GLADIATO'RIAL, relating to sword-playing.

Glans, gland-is, a gland.

GLAND, a secretory organ of the human body.

GLANDIF'EROUS, bearing acorns.

GLAN'DULE, a small gland.

Gleb-a, a clod. GLEBE, turf; soil.

Glob-us, a globe, a round body.

CONGLO'BATE, to gather into a ball.

GLOBE, a sphere; a ball.

GLOB'ULE, a little globe.

Glom-us, glomer-is, a clue or ball.

CONGLOM'ERATE, gathered into a ball.

Glori-a, honor.

GLO'RY, praise; renown.

GLO'RIFY, to honor; to exalt.

INGLO'RIOUS, shameful.

Gloss-a (γλωσσα), the tongue.

EPIGLOT'TIS, a tongue-shaped cartilage over the opening into the wind-pipe.

GLOS'SARY, a dictionary of difficult words or phrases.

POL'YGLOT, in many languages.

Gluten, glutin-is, glue.

AGGLU'TINATE, to join; to glue to.

CONGLUTINA'TION, the act of uniting bodies.

GLUE, a cement.

GLU'TINOUS, gluey; viscous.

Glut-io, glutit-um, to swallow.

DEGLUTITI'ON, a swallowing.

GLUT'TON, one who eats to excess.

Glyph-o (γλυφω), to carve.

AN'AGLYPH, an ornament in sculpture.

HI'EROGLYPH, a symbolical character. (See Osw.Et D.p.179.)

Gnomon (γνωμων), a pointer, a thing that serves to make known.

GNOME, an imaginary being.
GNO'MON, the hand of a dial.
PATHOGNOMON'IC, indicating disease.
PHYSIOG'NOMY, the art of discovering the character by the features of the face.
PROGNOS'TIC, a sign by which a future event may be known.

Gnor-us *for* **Gnarus,** knowing.

IG'NORANCE, want of knowledge.
IGNORA'MUS, a foolish fellow.

Gon-ia (γωνια), an angle.

DIAG'ONAL, a line from angle to angle.
DEC'AGON, a plane figure having ten angles.
GONIOM'ETER, an instrument for measuring solid angles.
HEP'TAGON, a plane figure with seven angles.
OC'TAGON, a plane figure of eight angles.
PEN'TAGON, a plane figure of five angles.
POL'YGON, a figure of many angles.
TRIGONOM'ETRY, the art of measuring triangles.

Gourmand (Fr.), a glutton.

GOUR'MAND, a glutton.
GOR'MANDIZE, to eat to excess.

Gradi-or, gress-us, to go step by step.

AGGRESSI'ON, an attack.
CON'GRESS, a meeting of legislators.
DEGRADE',° to lower; to sink.
DEGRADA'TION, meanness of condition.
DEGREE', a rank; a step.
DIGRESS', to turn aside.
E'GRESS, a going out.
GRADE, rank; degree.
GRADA'TION, regular progress.
GRAD'UAL, advancing by steps.
GRAD'UATE,° to receive a degree.
INGRE'DIENT, a component part of any compound.
IN'GRESS, entrance.
PROGRESS', to proceed; to advance.
PROGRES'SIVE,° advancing.
RET'ROGRADE, going backwards.
RETROGRESSI'ON, the act of going backwards.
TRANSGRESS',° to violate; to break.

Gramen, gramin-is, grass.

GRAMIN'EOUS, grassy.
GRAMINIV'OROUS, eating grass.

Grand-is, grand.

AG'GRANDIZE, to make great; to enlarge.
GRAND, great; illustrious.
GRANDEE', a man of high rank.
GRAN'DEUR, state; splendor.
GRANDIL'OQUENCE, lofty speaking.

Gran-um, a grain of corn.

GRAIN, all kinds of corn; a minute particle.
GRAN'ARY, a storehouse for grain.
GRAN'ITE,° a hard stone.
GRANIV'OROUS, eating grain.
GRAN'ULE, a small grain.

GRAN'ULATE, to break into grains.

GRENADIER', a tall foot soldier, formerly a thrower of grenades.°

Graph-o (γραφω), to write.

AEROG'RAPHY, a description of the air.
AN'AGRAM,° the change of one word into another by the transposition of its letters.
ANEMOG'RAPHY, a description of the winds.
AP'OGRAPH, a copy; a transcript.
AUTOBIOG'RAPHY, biography of a person written by himself.
AU'TOGRAPH, one's own handwriting.
BIBLIOG'RAPHY, a history and description of books.
BIOG'RAPHY, an account of lives.
CALIG'RAPHY, beautiful writing.
CHALCOG'RAPHY, engraving in brass.
CHIR'OGRAPH,° a deed; a writing.
CHRONOG'RAPHY, a description of past time.
COSMOG'RAPHY, the science of the general system of the world.
CRYPTOG'RAPHY, the art of writing in cipher.
DI'AGRAM, a figure; a drawing.
ENGRAVE', to impress; to imprint; to cut with a graver.
EP'IGRAM,° a short witty poem.
EPIGRAMMAT'IC, like an epigram.
EP'IGRAPH, an inscription.
ETHNOG'RAPHY, a description of races.
GEOG'RAPHY, a description of the surface of the earth.

Gramm-a (γραμμα), a letter.

GRAM'MAR,° the science of language.
GRAPH'IC, well delineated.
HIEROG'RAPHY, sacred writing.
HOROG'RAPHY, an account of the hours.
LEXICOG'RAPHY, the writing of dictionaries.
LITHOG'RAPHY, the art of drawing on and printing from stone.
METALLOG'RAPHY, a description of metals.
ORTHOG'RAPHY, correct spelling.
PAN'TOGRAPH, a machine to copy drawings.
PAR'AGRAPH, a distinct part of a discourse, or writing.
PARALLEL'OGRAM, a quadrilateral figure.
POL'YGRAM, a figure having many lines.
STENOG'RAPHY, the art of writing in short hand.
TEL'EGRAPH, a machine for conveying intelligence to a distance by signals.
TOPOG'RAPHY, a description of a place.
TYPOG'RAPHY, the art of printing.
XYLOG'RAPHY, the art of engraving on wood.
ZOOG'RAPHY, a description of animals.

Grati-a, favor, gratitude.

AGREE', to concur; to assent.
AGREE'MENT, concord; compact.
CONGRAT'ULATE, to wish joy to.
DISAGREE'ABLE, unpleasing.
DISGRACE', to bring to shame.
GRACE, favor; kindness.
GRA'CIOUS, merciful; kind.
GRATE'FUL, thankful; pleasing.
GRAT'IFY, to indulge; to please.
GRA'TIS, for nothing.
GRAT'ITUDE, thankfulness.
GRATU'ITOUS, bestowed freely.
GRATU'ITY, a present.
IN'GRATE, ungrateful.
INGRA'TIATE, to put in favor.

Grav-is, heavy.

AG'GRAVATE, to make worse.
AGGRIEVE', to vex; to trouble.
GRAVE, solemn; serious.
GRAV'ITATE, to tend to the centre of the earth.
GRAV'ITY, weight; heaviness.
GRIEF, sorrow; trouble.
GRIEV'ANCE, an injury.

Grex, greg-is, a flock.

AG'GREGATE, the sum of many collected parts.
CON'GREGATE, to assemble.
CONGREGA'TION, an assembly.
EGRE'GIOUS,° remarkably bad.
GRE'GAL, belonging to a flock.
GREGA'RIOUS, flocking together.

Grus, gru-is, a crane.

CON'GRUENCE, agreement.
CONGRU'ITY,° consistency; fitness.
INCON'GRUOUS, unsuitable.

Guarant-ir, for Garantir (Fr.), to guard, to secure.

GUARANTEE', to secure performance.
WAR'RANT, to authorize.
WAR'RANTY, authority; security.

Guard-er, for Garder (Fr.), to keep, to watch.

GUARD, to protect; to defend.
GUAR'DIAN, a protector.
WARD, one who is under the care of a guardian.

Gubern-o, to govern.

GOV'ERN, to rule; to manage.
GUBERNATO'RIAL, relating to a governor.
MISGOV'ERNMENT, bad government.

Gust-us, a taste, a relish.

DEGUSTA'TION, a tasting.
DISGUST', aversion; dislike.
GUS'TO, relish; liking.

Guttur, the throat.

GUT'TER, a channel.
GUT'TURAL, belonging to the throat.

Gymn-os (γυμνος), naked.

GYMNOSPER'MOUS, having naked seeds.
GYMNA'SIUM, a place for athletic exercises.
GYMNAS'TIC,* pertaining to athletic exercises.
GYMNOS'OPHIST, an Indian philosopher. (see p. 168.)

---

* Among the ancients there were five kinds of gymnastic exercises: 1. running (*cursus*); 2. leaping (*saltus*); 3. boxing (*pugillatus*); 4. wrestling (*lucta*); and throwing the dart or quoit (*disci jactus*); hence called *certamen athleticum* or *gymnicum*, because they contended naked (γυμνοι), with nothing on but trousers or drawers.

Gyn-e (γυνη), a woman.

GY'NARCHY, female government.
GYNÆOC'RACY, government over which a female may preside.
MISOG'YNIST, a woman-hater.

Gyr-us (γυρος), a circle.

GYRA'TION, a whirling round.
GY'ROMANCY, divination by walking in a circle.

Hab-eo, habit-um, to have, to hold.

A'BLE, having strength.
ABIL'ITY, power; capacity.
COHAB'IT, to dwell together.
DEBT', a sum due.
DISA'BLE, to deprive of force.
ENA'BLE, to empower.
EXHIB'IT,° to show; to display.
HABIL'IMENT, dress; garment.
HAB'IT, custom; use.
HABITA'TION, a dwelling.
HABIT'UATE, to accustom.
INHAB'ITANT, a resident.
INHIB'IT, to hinder; to forbid.
PROHIB'IT,° to forbid; to restrain.

Her-eo, *for* **Hæreo, hæs-um,** to stick.

ADHERE', to stick to.
COHE'RENCE, connection.
COHE'SIVE, sticking.
HES'ITANCY, uncertainty; delay.
HES'ITATE, to delay; to pause.
INCOHE'RENT, unconnected.
INHE'RENT, existing in; innate.

Her-es, *for* **Hæres, hæred-is,** an heir.

COHEIR', a joint heir.
DISHER'ISON, a depriving of an inheritance.
DISINHER'IT, to deprive of an inheritance.
HEIR, one who inherits.
HER'ITABLE, capable of being inherited.
HER'ITAGE, the thing inherited.
HERED'ITARY, descending from father to son.
INHER'IT, to receive by descent.

Hal-o, to breathe.

ANHELA'TION,° panting.
EXHALE', to send out vapors.
EXHALA'TION, vapor, effluvia.
INHALE', to draw in with the breath.

Harmoni-a (ἁρμονια), harmony.

HAR'MONY, musical concord.
HARMON'IC, musical.
HAR'MONIZE, to agree.
HARMO'NIOUS, peaceful, musical.
INHARMON'ICAL, discordant.

Haust-um (*ab* **Haurio**), to draw.

EXHAUST', to drain.
INEXHAUS'TIBLE, not to be drained.

Hebes, hebet-is, blunt, dull.

HEB'ETATE, to dull; to blunt.
HEB'ETUDE, dulness; bluntness.

Hecaton (ἑκατον), a hundred.

HEC'ATOMB, a sacrifice of a hundred oxen.

Heli-os (ἥλιος), the sun.

APHE'LION,° the point most remote from the sun.
HELIOCEN'TRIC, relating to the sun's centre.
HELIOM'ETER, an instrument for measuring the diameter of the heavenly bodies.
HE'LIOSCOPE, a telescope for viewing the sun.
HE'LIOTROPE, a plant that turns to the sun.
PARHE'LION, a mock sun.
PERIHE'LION,° the point of a planet's orbit nearest the sun.

Hellen (Ἕλλην), a Greek.

HEL'LENIC, Grecian.
HEL'LENISM, a Greek idiom.
HEL'LENIST,° one skilled in the Greek language.

Hem-a (αἷμα), blood.

HEMOP'TYSIS, the spitting of blood.
HEM'ORRHAGE, a flow of blood.

Hemer-a (ἡμερα), a day.

EPHEM'ERAL, lasting a day.
EPHEM'ERIS,* an almanac.

Hemis-us (ἡμισυς), half.

HEM'ICYCLE, a half circle.
HEM'ISPHERE, half a globe.
HEM'ISTICH, half a poetic verse.

Hept-a (ἑπτα), seven.

HEP'TAGON, a plane figure with seven angles.
HEP'TACHORD, a system of seven musical notes.
HEP'TARCHY, a government by seven persons.
HEP'TATEUCH, the first seven books of the Old Testament.

Herb-a, an herb.

HERB, a plant.
HERBA'CEOUS, relating to herbs.
HER'BAGE, herbs; pasture.

Heres-is (αἱρεσις), an opinion.

HER'ESY,° error in religion.
HERE'SIARCH, a leader in heresy.
HER'ETIC, one guilty of heresy.

Hero-s (ἡρως), a hero.

HE'RO, a brave man.
HER'OISM, great bravery.

Heter-os (ἑτερος), other, dissimilar.

HET'ERARCHY, the government of an alien.
HET'ERODOXY, unsoundness of doctrine.
HETEROGE'NEOUS, dissimilar.

* *Ephemerides*, (the plural of Ephemeris,) astronomical tables, showing the present state of the heavens for every *day* at noon.

I

Hex (ἕξ), six.

HEX'AGON, a figure of six angles.
HEXAM'ETER, a verse of six feet.
HEXAMET'RICAL, consisting of hexameters.
HEXAN'GULAR, having six angles.

Hier-os (ἱερος), sacred.

HI'ERARCHY, ecclesiastical government.
HIEROGLYPH'IC,* a sacred character or symbol.
HIEROL'OGY, a discourse on sacred things.
HI'EROMANCY, divination by sacrifices.

Hilar-is, cheerful.

EXHIL'ARATE, to enliven.
HILAR'ITY, mirth; merriment.

Hipp-os (ἵππος), a horse.

HIPPOCEN'TAUR, a fabulous monster, half man and half horse.
HIPPOPOT'AMUS, the river-horse.
HIP'PODROME, a course for horse-races.
HIP'POGRIFF, a winged horse.

Histori-a (ἱστορια), history.

HIS'TORY, a narrative of past events.
HISTO'RIAN, a writer of history.
HISTOR'IC, relating to history.
HISTORIOG'RAPHY, business of a historian.

Histrio, histrion-is, a stage-player.

HISTRION'IC, theatrical.
HIS'TRIONISM, theatrical representation.

Hodie, to-day. HODIER'NAL, of this day.

Hol-os (ὅλος), the whole, all.

CATH'OLIC, universal; general.
CATHOL'ICISM, adherence to the Catholic church.

Homo, homin-is, a man.

HOM'ICIDE, manslaughter.
HU'MAN, belonging to mankind.
HUMANE'LY, kindly.
HU'MANIZE, to render susceptible of kind feelings.
INHUMAN'ITY, brutality.

Hom-os (ὁμος), like, equal.

HOMOGE'NEOUS, of the same kind.
HOMOL'OGOUS, proportiona to each other.

Honor, honor. ***Honest-us,*** honest.

DISHON'EST, wicked; fraudulent.
DISHON'OR, disgrace; shame.
HON'ESTY, justice; truth.
HON'ORARY, conferring honor.

---

* See the Introduction.

Hor-a, (ὥρα), an hour.

HO'RARY, relating to an hour.
HOR'OLOGE, an instrument that marks the hour.
HOR'OSCOPE, aspect of the planets at the hour of birth.
HOROM'ETRY, the art of measuring time.

Hor-os (ὅρος), a boundary.

APH'ORISM, a maxim; a precept.
APH'ORIST, a writer of maxims.
HORI'ZON, the line that bounds the view.

Horre-o, to be dreadful.

ABHOR', to detest; to loathe.
HOR'RIBLE, dreadful; shocking.
HOR'RID, hideous; frightful.
HORRIF'IC, causing horror.
HORRIS'ONOUS, sounding dreadfully.
HOR'ROR, dread; terror.

Hort-or, to exhort.

EXHORT', to incite; to advise.

Hort-us, a garden.

HOR'TICULTURE, the art of cultivating gardens.
HOR'TUS-SIC'CUS, a collection of dried plants.

Hospes, hospit-is, a host or guest.

HOS'PITABLE, kind to strangers.
HOS'PITAL, a building for the sick.
HOST, one who entertains another.
HOTEL,' an inn.
OST'LER, a man who takes care of horses.
INHOSPITAL'ITY, unkindness to strangers.

Host-is, an enemy.

HOST, an army; a multitude.
HOSTIL'ITY, open war.

Hum-eo, to be moist.

HUMEC'TATE, to wet; to moisten.
HU'MID, wet; moist.
HU'MOR, moisture of the body.
HU'MORIST, a jester; a wag

Humer-us, the shoulder. HU'MERAL, belonging to the shoulder.

Hum-us, the ground. **Humil-is,** low, poor.

HUMIL'IATE, to depress.
HUM'BLE, to crush; to subdue.
HUMIL'ITY, freedom from pride.
INHUME', to bury.
POST'HUMOUS, published after one's death.

Hydor (ὕδωρ), water.

CLEPSY'DRA, a water-clock.
HYDRAU'LICS, the science of the motion and force of fluids.
HYDROCEPH'ALUS, a dropsy in the head.

HY'DROGEN, a gas. (Osw.p.160.)
HYDROG'RAPHY, the art of measuring and describing the sea.
HY'DROMANCY, divination by water.
HY'DROMEL, a liquor formed of honey and water.
HYDROPHO'BIA, canine madness, in which there is a great dread of water.
DROP'SY,° a disease.
HYDROSTAT'ICS, the science of the weight and equilibrium of fluids.

Hygr-os, (ὑγρος), moist, wet.

HYGROM'ETER, an instrument to measure the degrees of moisture.
HY'GROSCOPE, an instrument to show the moisture of the air.

Hymen (ὑμην), the god of marriage.

HYMENE'AL, HYMENE'AN, pertaining to marriage.

Ichthys (ἰχθυς), a fish.

ICHTHYOPH'AGY, the practice of eating fish.

Icon (εἰκων), an image. ICON'OCLAST, a breaker of images.

Idea (ἰδεα), a mental image.

IDE'A, thought; notion.
IDE'ALIZE, to form ideas.

Idem, the same.

IDEN'TITY, sameness.
IDEN'TICAL, the same.
IDEN'TIFY, to prove the same.

Idi-os (ἰδιος), peculiar, private.

ID'IOCY, want of understanding.
IDIOP'ATHY, a primary disease.
ID'IOM, peculiarity of speech.
IDIOMAT'ICAL, containing an idiom.
IDIOSYN'CRASY, peculiar temperament.

Idol-um (εἰδωλον), an idol.

I'DOL, an image for worship.
IDOL'ATRY, image-worship.

Ign-is, fire.

IG'NEOUS, containing fire.
IGNIP'OTENT, ruling fire.
IG'NIS-FAT'UUS, a fiery meteor.
IG'NIFY, to form into fire.
IGNITE', to set on fire.
IGNITI'ON, the act of igniting.

Imag-o, an image.

IM'AGE, a picture; an idol.
IMAG'INE, to fancy; to conceive.

Imbecill-is, weak.

IM'BECILE, weak; feeble.
IMBECIL'ITY, weakness.

Imit-or, to copy or resemble.

IM'ITATE, to follow; to copy.
INIM'ITABLE, that cannot be imitated.

Imper-o, imperat-um, to command.

EM'PEROR,° a monarch.
EM'PIRE, the dominion of an emperor.
IMPER'ATIVE, commanding.
IMPE'RIAL, royal; regal.
IMPE'RIOUS, overbearing.

Indigen-a, the native of a place.

INDIG'ENOUS, native; produced in a country.

Industri-a, industry. INDUS'TRIOUS, diligent; laborious.

Infer-us, below.

INFE'RIOR, lower in place.
INFER'NAL, hellish.

Infest-us, hostile to. INFEST', to harass; to disturb.

Insul-a, an island.

IN'SULAR, belonging to an island.
IN'SULATE, to detach.
ISLE, an island.
PENIN'SULA, a piece of land almost surrounded by water.

Integer, entire.

IN'TEGER, a whole number.
IN'TEGRAL, whole; complete.
INTEG'RITY, honesty.
IN'TEGRATE, to make entire.
REDINTEGRA'TION, renovation; restoration.

Interpret-or, to explain.

INTER'PRET, to explain; to translate.

Intestin-a, the bowels.

INTES'TINAL, belonging to the intestines.
INTES'TINE, internal; inward.
INTES'TINES, the entrails.

Int-us, within.

INTE'RIOR, inner; inland.
INTER'NAL, inward.
IN'TIMATE, inmost; familiar.
IN'TIMACY, close familiarity.
INTIMA'TION, a hint.
INTRIN'SIC, internal; real.

Invit-o, invitat-um, to invite.

INVITE', to bid; to ask.
INVITA'TION, the act of inviting.
UNINVI'TED, not bidden.

Ir-a, anger. ***Irasc-or,*** to be angry.

DIRE,° dreadful; dismal.
IRE, anger; rage.
IRAS'CIBLE, prone to anger.
IR'RITABLE, easily provoked.
IR'RITATE, to tease; to fret.

Ironi-a (εἰρωνια), irony.

I'RONY, taunting speech.
IRON'ICAL, containing irony.

Is-os (ἴσος), equal.

ISOCH'RONOUS, performed in equal times
ISOS'CELES, having two sides equal, as a triangle.
ISOTHER'MAL, having equal heat.

Itali-a, Italy.

ITAL'IAN, a native of Italy.
ITAL'ICISE, to mark in italics.
ITAL'ICS, leaning letters, first used in Italy.

Iter-um, again.

ITERA'TION, repetition.
REIT'ERATE, to repeat again and again.

Iter, itiner-is, a journey.

ITIN'ERANT, travelling.
ITIN'ERARY, done on a journey.

Jac-eo, to lie.

ADJA'CENT, lying near.
CIRCUMJA'CENT, lying round.
INTERJA'CENT, lying between.
SUBJA'CENT, lying under.

Jac-io, jact-um, to throw.

AB'JECT, mean; vile.
AD'JECTIVE, a describing word.
CONJEC'TURE, a guess.
DEJEC'TION, lowness of spirits.
EJECT', to throw out; to expel.
EJAC'ULATE,° to utter abruptly.
INJECT', to throw in.
INTERJEC'TION, an exclamation.
MISCONJEC'TURE, a wrong guess.
OBJEC'TIVE, relating to the object.
PROJ'ECT, scheme; contrivance.
PROJEC'TILE, a body impelled forward.
REJECT', to cast off; to discard.
SUB'JECT, placed under.
TRAJECT', to throw through.

Janu-a, a gate, a door. JAN'ITOR, a door keeper.

Joc-us, a joke.

JOCOSE',° merry; waggish.
JOC'ULAR, sportive; merry.
JOC'UND, gay; lively.
JOKE, to jest; to frolic.

Jour (Fr.), a day.

ADJOURN', to put off; to defer.
JOUR'NAL, a diary.
JOUR'NEY,° travel by land.
SOJOURN', a temporary stay.

Jubil-um, a joyful shout.

JU'BILANT, shouting for joy.
JU'BILEE,° a season of joy.

Judic-o, judicat-um, to judge.

ADJUDGE', to pass a sentence.
ADJU'DICATE, to try and decide.
EXTRAJUDICI'AL, out of the ordinary judicial course.
INJU'DICABLE, not cognizable by a judge.
INJUDICI'OUS, unwise.
JUDGE, to discern; to decide.
JU'DICATURE, power of distributing justice.
JUDICI'AL, pertaining to courts of law.
JUDIC'IARY, the system of courts of justice.
MISJUDGE', to mistake.
PREJUDGE', to determine beforehand.
PREJU'DICATE, to prejudge.
PREJ'UDICE,° bias; injury.

Jugul-um, the throat. JU'GULAR, belonging to the throat.

Jug-um, a yoke.

CON'JUGAL, matrimonial.
CON'JUGATE, to inflect a verb.
SUBDUE',° to crush; to conquer.
SUBJUGA'TION, the act of subduing.

Jung-o, junct-um, to join.

ADJOIN', to join to.
AD'JUNCT,° something joined.
CONJOIN', to unite; to associate.
DISJOIN', to separate.
DISJUNC'TION, separation.
ENJOIN', to direct; to order.
INJUNC'TION, order; precept.
JOIN, to combine; to unite.
JUNC'TURE, union.
JUN'TO,° a cabal; a faction.
MISJOIN', to join unfitly.
REJOIN'DER, a reply; an answer.
SUBJOIN', to add to the end.
SUBJUNC'TIVE,° conditional.

Jupiter, Jov-is, the chief god of the Greeks and Romans.

JOL'LY, cheerful; free from care.
JO'VIAL,° gay; merry.

Jur-o, to swear.

ABJURE', to renounce upon oath.
ADJURE', to put upon oath.
CONJURE', to enjoin solemnly.
JU'ROR, one that serves on a jury.
JU'RY, twelve men sworn to render a true verdict.
NONJU'RING, refusing to swear.
PER'JURY, false swearing.

Jus, juris, law, right.

IN'JURE, to hurt; to wrong.
INJU'RIOUS, unjust; hurtful.
JURID'ICAL, used in courts of justice.
JURISDIC'TION, extent of power.
JURISPRU'DENCE, the science of law.
JU'RIST, one versed in the civil law.

Just-us, just.

ADJUST', to regulate.
INJUS'TICE, iniquity; wrong.
JUST, upright; honest.
JUSTIC'IARY, an administrator of justice.
JUS'TIFY, to free from fault.

Juven-is, young.

JU'VENILE, youthful.
JU'NIOR, one younger.

Juv-o, jut-um, to help.

AD'JUTANT, a major's aid.
AD'JUVANT, helpful; useful.
AID, to help; to assist.
COADJU'TOR, a fellow-helper

Lab-o (λαβω *for* λαμβανω), to take

As'trolabe, an instrument for taking the altitude of stars.
Dis'syllable, a word of two syllables.
Mon'osyllable, a word of one syllable.
Octosyl'lable, a word of eight syllables.
Pol'ysyllable, a word of many syllables.
Syl'lable, a letter or combination of letters uttered or taken together.
Syl'labus, a compendium.
Tris'yllable, a word of three syllables.

Labor, laps-us, to fall or glide.

Collapse', to fall together.
Elapse', to pass away.
Lapse, flow; fall.
Relapse', to slide back.

Labor, labor.

Elab'orate, finished with care.
Lab'oratory, a chemist's workroom.
La'bor, pains; toil.

Labyrinth-us, a maze.

Lab'yrinth, a place formed with inextricable windings.
Labyrin'thian, winding; perplexing.

Lac, lact-is, milk.

Ablac'tate, to wean from the breast.
Lac'tary, a dairy house.
Lac'teal, pertaining to milk.
Lactes'cence, milkiness.
Lactif'erous, bearing milk.

Lacer, torn.

Dilac'erate, to tear; to rend.
Lac'erable, that may be torn.

Lachrym-a, a tear.

Lach'rymal, generating tears.
Lach'rymary, containing tears.

Laconi-a, the country of the Spartans.

Lacon'ic, concise; brief.
Lac'onism, a pithy phrase.

Lament-or, to bewail. Lament', to bewail; to mourn.

Lamin-a, a thin plate.

Lam'ina, a thin plate.
Lam'inated, plated.
Lam'ellar, composed of thin scales.
Lam'ellated, covered with thin plates.

Lan-a, wool.

Lan'ifice, woollen manufacture.
Lanig'erous, bearing wool.

Langu-eo, to droop.

Lan'guid, faint; weak.
Lan'guish, to grow feeble.
Lan'guor, faintness; weakness.

La-os (λαος), the people.

LA'ITY, the people, as distinguished from the clergy.
LAY, not clerical; pertaining to the laity.

Lapis, lapid-is, a stone.

DILAPIDA'TION,° ruin; decay.
LAP'IDARY, a dealer in gems.
LAPIDES'CENT, turning to stone.
LAPIDIF'IC, forming stones.

Larg-us, big; liberal.

ENLARGE', to increase; to expand.
LAR'GESS, a gift; a bounty.

Lasciv-us, lewd. LASCIV'IOUS, lustful; wanton.

Lass-us, weary. LAS'SITUDE, weariness.

Late-o, to hide.

LAT'ITANCY, state of lying hid.
LA'TENT, hidden.

Latin-us, Latin.

LAT'INIST, one skilled in Latin.
LATIN'ITY, purity of Latin style

Latri-a (λατρεια), worship.

IDOL'ATER, a worshipper of idols; a pagan.

Latr-o, to bark. LA'TRANT, barking.

Lat-um (*ab* **fero**), to carry; to bring.

ABLA'TION, a taking away.
COLLATE', to compare things similar.
CORREL'ATIVE,° having a reciprocal relation.
DIL'ATORY,° tardy; slow.
ELA'TED, flushed with success.
LEG'ISLATE,° to enact laws.
MISRELATE', to relate falsely.
OBLA'TION, an offering.
PREL'ACY, the office of a prelate.
PREL'ATE,° a church dignitary.
RELATE', to tell; to recite.
REL'ATIVE, having relation.
SUPER'LATIVE, highest.
TRANSLA'TION, the act of interpreting into another language.
OB'LATE, flattened at the poles.

Latus, later-is, the side.

COLLAT'ERAL, from the side; not direct.
EQUILAT'ERAL of equal sides.
LAT'ERAL, belonging to the side.
MULTILAT'ERAL, of many sides.
QUADRILAT'ERAL, having four sides.
SEPTILAT'ERAL, having seven sides.
TRILAT'ERAL, having three sides.

Lat-us, broad.

DILATE', to extend; to widen.
DILATA'TION, expansion.
LAT'ITUDE, breadth; extent.
LATITUDINA'RIAN,° one not rigidly orthodox.

Laur-us, a laurel.

LAU'REATE, decked with laurel.
LAU'REL, an evergreen.

Laus, laud-is, praise.

ALLOW', to permit.
LAUD, to praise.
LAUD'ABLE, praise-worthy.
LAUD'ATORY, bestowing praise.

Lav-o, lot-um, to wash.

LAUN'DRESS, a washerwoman.
LA'VA, liquid and vitrified matter discharged by volcanoes.
LAVE, to wash; to bathe.
LAV'ATORY, a place for washing.
LO'TION, a medicinal wash.

Lax-us, loose.

LAX, loose; vague.
PROLIX'ITY, tediousness.
RELAX', to slacken; to remit.
RELAXA'TION, ease; remission.

Leg-o, legat-um, to send as an ambassador; to bequeath.

ALLEGE',° to affirm; to plead.
ALLEGA'TION, declaration; plea.
ALLE'GIANCE, the duty of a subject.
COL'LEAGUE, a partner.
COL'LEGE, a seminary of learning.
COLLE'GIAN, a member of a college.
DEL'EGATE, to send on an embassy.
LEG'ACY, a gift made by will.
LEGATEE', one who has a legacy.
LEG'ATE, the Pope's ambassador.

Leg-o, lect-um, to gather, to read; to choose.

COLLECT', to gather together.
DI'ALECT,° manner of expression.
DIALEC'TIC, argumentative.
DIL'IGENT, industrious; active.
ECLEC'TIC,* selecting.
ELEC'TION, choice.
ELEC'TORATE, the office of an elector.
EL'EGANCE, beauty, grace.
EL'IGIBLE, fit to be chosen.
ILLEG'IBLE, that cannot be read.
INEL'EGANT, not beautiful.
IN'TELLECT, understanding.
INTELLECTUAL'ITY, intellectual power.
INTEL'LIGENCE, information.
INTEL'LIGIBLE, that may be understood.
LEC'TURE,° a discourse.
LE'GEND,° a chronicle; a wild narrative.
LEG'IBLE, that may be read.
LE'GION,° a body of soldiers.
LEX'ICON,° a dictionary.
LEXICOG'RAPHY, the writing of dictionaries.
NEGLECT',° inattention; slight.
NEG'LIGENT, careless; heedless.
PREDILEC'TION, a liking beforehand.
PRE-ELECT', to choose beforehand.
PROLEGOM'ENA, introductory remarks.
RECOLLECT', to bring to mind.
RE-ELEC'TION, election a second time.
SELEC'TION, choice.

* *Eclectic*, literally, one who *gathers out;* one of those ancient philosophers, who, without attaching themselves to any particular sect, *gathered out* or *took from* any author or sect, what they judged good. One of a sect in the Christian church, called also modern *Platonics*, as considering the doctrine of Plato conformable to the spirit and genius of the Christian.

Len-is, gentle, soft, mild.

LE'NIENT, mild; soothing.
LEN'IFY, to assuage.
LEN'ITIVE, that which soothes.
LEN'ITY, mildness.

Lens, lent-is, lentil, a kind of pulse.

LENS,* a glass for diminishing or magnifying objects.
LENTIC'ULAR, having the form of a lens.
LEN'TIFORM, having the form of a lens.
LEN'TIL, a sort of pulse or pea.

Le-o, *or* ***Lin-o,*** to besmear, to blot.

DELE'TION, the act of blotting out.
DELETE'RIOUS, destructive.
INDEL'IBLE, that cannot be blotted out.

Leo, leon-is, a lion.

LE'ONINE, relating to a lion.
LI'ON, a fierce animal.

Lepr-a (λεπρα), leprosy.

LEP'ER, one infected with a leprosy.
LEP'ROSY, a loathsome disease of the skin.

Leps-is (λεψις), a taking or receiving.

CAT'ALEPSY,° a kind of apoplexy.
DILEM'MA,° a difficult, vexatious alternative.
EP'ILEPSY,° a convulsion.
EPILEP'TIC, convulsed.

Lethe (ληθη), forgetfulness.

LETHE'AN, causing forgetfulness.
LETH'ARGY, morbid sleepiness
LETHAR'GIC, sleepy by disease.

Leth-um, *or* ***Let-um,*** death

LE'THAL, deadly; mortal.
LETHIF'EROUS, bringing death.

Lev-o, levat-um, to lift up, to raise.

ALLE'VIATE, to ease; to soften.
EL'EVATE, to raise up.
IRREL'EVANT, not applicable.
LEAV'EN, a fermenting mixture.
LEVANT',† eastern; towards the rising sun.
LEV'EE,° a bank to prevent inundation.
LE'VER,° a mechanical power.
LEV'IABLE, capable of being levied.
LEV'Y, to raise; to collect.
LEV'ITY, lightness; vanity.
LIFT, to raise; to support.
REL'EVANT,° pertinent; suitable.
RELIEVE', to ease; to succor.
RELIEF', ease; assistance.

---

* *Lens*, a piece of glass or other transparent substance of the figure of a *lentil*, which either collects the rays of light into a point or disperses them, according to its form and the laws of refraction; such as a burning glass, or spectacle glass, or an object glass of a telescope. The *convex lens* converges the rays of light, and the *concave* disperses them.

† *Levant*, the countries around the Eastern end of the Mediterranean sea.

Lex, leg-is, a law or rule.

ILLE'GAL, contrary to law.
ILLEGIT'IMATE, contrary to law.
LAW, a rule of action.
LEGAL'ITY, lawfulness.
LE'GALIZE, to authorize.
LEG'ISLATE, to make laws.
LEGISLA'TURE, the power that makes laws.
LEGIT'IMACY, lawfulness of birth.
PRIV'ILEGE,° a peculiar advantage.
SAC'RILEGE,° a violation of things sacred.

Liber, libr-i, a book.

LI'BEL, to defame
LI'BRARY, an apartment for books.

Lib-o, to pour out. LIBA'TION, an offering made of wine.

Libr-a, a pound, a balance.

EQUILI'BRATE, to balance equally.
EQUILIB'RIUM, equality of weight.
LI'BRA, the Balance, the seventh sign in the zodiac.

Lice-o, licit-um, to be lawful. ***Licenti-a,*** license.

ILLIC'IT, unlawful.
LI'CENSE, permission; excess.
LICEN'TIATE, one who has a license.
LICEN'TIOUS, unrestrained.

Lici-o, licit-um, to draw, to allure.

ALLIC'IENCY, attraction.
ELIC'IT, to draw out.

Lido, lis-um, to hurt, to strike.

COLLISI'ON, a striking together.
ELISI'ON, a striking out.

Lieu (Fr.), place, stead.

LIEU, place; room.
LIEUTEN'ANCY, the office of a lieutenant.
LIEUTEN'ANT, a deputy.
PUR'LIEU,° border; district.

Lign-um, wood.

LIG'NEOUS, made of wood.
LIG'NIFORM, resembling wood.
LIG'NUM-VI'TÆ, a very hard wood.

Lig-o, ligat-um, to bind, to tie.

ALLIGA'TION, a tying together.
CIRCUMLIGA'TION, a binding round.
DISOBLIGE', to give offence to.
IRRELIGI'ON, impiety.
LEAGUE, a confederacy.
LI ABLE, subject.
LIEGE, a sovereign.
LIG'AMENT,° a tie; a ligature.
LIG'ATURE, a band; a cord.
OB'LIGATE, to bind by contract.
OB'LIGATORY, binding.
OBLIGE', to gratify; to compel.
RELIGI'ON, duty to God; piety.

Limen, limin-is, a threshold.

ELIM'INATE, to expel.
PRELIM'INARY, introductory.

Limes, limit-is, a path, a limit.

ILLIM'ITABLE, that cannot be limited.
LIM'IT, to confine; to restrain.
LIMITA'TION, a restriction.

Limpid-us, clear, transparent. LIM'PID, clear; pure.

Line-a, a line.

CURVILIN'EAR, composed of curved lines.
DELIN'EATE,° to describe; to sketch.
INTERLINE', to write between lines.
INTERLINEA'TION, the act of interlining.
LINE, a rank; a row.
LIN'EAL, descending in a line.
LIN'EAMENT, feature; outline.
LIN'EAGE,° race; progeny.
MULTILIN'EAL, having many lines.
RECTILIN'EAR, right-lined.

Lingu-a, the tongue, a language.

BILIN'GUOUS, having two tongues.
LIN'GO, language; speech.
LAN'GUAGE, human speech.
LIN'GUIST, one skilled in languages.
SUBLIN'GUAL, under the tongue.

Linqu-o, lict-um, to leave, to forsake.

DELIN'QUENT,° an offender.
DERELIC'TION, a forsaking.
REL'IC, something left.
REL'ICT, a widow.
RELIN'QUISH, to forsake; to quit.

Lip-o (λειπω), to leave out, to fail.

ECLIPSE',° obscuration.
ELLIP'SIS,° an omission.
ELLIP'TICAL, pertaining to an ellipsis.
LIPOTH'YMY,° a fainting fit.

Lique-o, to melt, to be liquid.

COL'LIQUATE, to dissolve; to melt.
COLLIQUEFAC'TION, a melting together.
LIQ'UEFY, to become liquid.
LIQ'UOR, any liquid.
LIQ'UIDATE, to clear away; to pay.

Lir-a, a furrow or ridge of land.

DELIR'IUM,° alienation of mind.
DELIR'IOUS, raving; doting

Lis, lit-is, strife; a lawsuit.

LIT'IGATE, to contest in law.
LITIGI'OUS, given to litigation.

Liter-a, a letter.

ALLITERA'TION, the beginning of several words in succession with the same letter.
ILLIT'ERATE, unlearned.
LET'TER, an alphabetic character.
LIT'ERAL, according to the letter.
LIT'ERARY, relating to letters.
LITERA'TI, men of learning.
LIT'ERATURE,° learning.
OBLIT'ERATE,° to rub out.

Lith-os (λιθος), a stone.

A'erolite, a meteoric stone.
Lith'arge,° the scum of lead.
Lithog'raphy, the art of drawing on and printing from stone.

Livr-er (Fr.), to give or deliver up.

Deliv'er, to set free.
Liv'ery,° a particular dress.

Loc-us, a place.

Col'locate, to place together.
Interloca'tion, a placing between.
Disloca'tion, the act of displacing; a putting out of joint.
Lo'cal, relating to place.
Lo'cate, to place; to fix.
Locomo'tion, the power of changing place.

Log-os (λογος), reason, a word, a discourse, science.

Anal'ogy,° correspondence.
Anthol'ogy, a collection of flowers or poems.
Apol'ogy, an excuse.
Apologet'ic, given as an excuse.
Ap'ologue,° a fable.
Astrol'ogy,° the practice of foretelling by the stars.
Cat'alogue, a list.
Chronol'ogy, the science of dates.
Chronolog'ical, relating to chronology.
Conchol'ogy, the science of shells.
Dec'alogue, the ten commandments.
Demonol'ogy, a treatise on evil spirits.
Di'alogue,° a conference.
Doxol'ogy, words of praise to God.
Ec'logue,° a pastoral poem.
El'ogy, praise.
Entomol'ogy, the science that treats of insects.
Ep'ilogue, the speech at the end of a play.
Etymol'ogy, derivation of words.
Eulo'gium, praise.
Eu'logize, to commend.
Geneal'ogy, a history of the descent of families.
Geneal'ogist, he who traces descents.
Geol'ogy, the science of the structure of the earth.
Homol'ogous, proportionate to each other.
Hor'ologe, an instrument that marks the hour.
Illog'ical, contrary to logic.
Log'arithms,* a series of numbers.

---

* "They are a series of artificial numbers, contrived for the expedition of calculation, and proceeding in an *arithmetical* proportion, as the numbers they answer to do in a *geometrical* one: for instance,

0 1 2 3 4 5 6 7 8 9
1 2 4 8 16 32 64 128 256 512.

When the numbers above, beginning with (0), and arithmetically proportional, are *logarithms*. The *addition* and *subtraction* of *logarithms* answers to the *multiplication* and *division* of the *numbers* they correspond with; and this saves an infinite deal of trouble. In like manner will the extraction of *roots* be performed by *dissecting* the *logarithms* of any numbers for the *square root*, and *trisecting* them for the *cube*, and so on."—*Hawis.*

LOG'IC,° the art of reasoning.
LOGOM'ACHY, a contention about words.
MARTYROL'OGY, a history of martyrs.
METEOROL'OGY, the science which treats of meteors.
MINERAL'OGY, the science of minerals.
MON'OLOGUE, a soliloquy.
MYTHOL'OGY,° a system of fables.
NECROL'OGY, a register of deaths.
NEOL'OGISM, new terms.
NEUROL'OGY, a description of the nerves.
ORNITHOL'OGY, the science of birds.
OSTEOL'OGY, a description of the bones.
PHILOL'OGY, grammatical learning; the study of language.
PHRASEOL'OGY, style; diction.
PROL'OGUE,° a preface.
PSYCHOL'OGY, the science which treats of the nature of the soul.
SYL'LOGISM,° a form of reasoning.
SYLLOGIS'TIC, relating to a syllogism.
TAUTOL'OGY, repetition of the same sense in different words.
THEOL'OGY, the science of God and divine things.
ZOOL'OGY, the science of animals.

Long-us, long.

ELON'GATE, to lengthen.
LONG, having length.
LONGANIM'ITY,° forbearance.
LONGEV'ITY, length of life.
LON'GITUDE, distance east or west.
OB'LONG, longer than broad.
PROLONGA'TION, the act of lengthening.

Loqu-or, locut-us, to speak.

ALLOCU'TION, the act of speaking to another.
ALTIL'OQUENCE, pompous speech.
CIRCUMLOCU'TION, a circuit of words.
COL'LOQUY, conversation.
COLLO'QUIAL, relating to common conversation.
ELOCU'TION, utterance; delivery.
EL'OQUENT, having the power of oratory.
GRANDIL'OQUENCE, lofty speaking.
INTERLOC'UTOR, one that talks with another.
LOQUAC'ITY, talkativeness.
MAGNIL'OQUENCE, swelling words.
MULTIL'OQUOUS, very talkative.
OB'LOQUY, blame; slander.
SOLIL'OQUY, a speech to one's self.
STULTIL'OQUENCE, foolish talk.
VENTRIL'OQUISM,* the act of speaking from the stomach.

Loy, or Loi, (Fr.) law.

DISLOY'ALTY, want of fidelity.
LOY'AL,° true; faithful.

Lubric-us, slippery, smooth.

LU'BRICATE, to make smooth.
LUBRIC'ITY, slipperiness.
LUBRIFAC'TION, a making smooth.

* The art of speaking so that the voice does not seem to come from the speaker, but from some one at a distance.

Luc-eo, to shine.

ELU'CIDATE,° to explain.
LU'CENT, shining; bright.
LUCID'ITY, splendor; clearness.
LU'CIFER,° the morning star.
PELLU'CID, clear; not opaque.
TRANSLU'CENT, transparent; clear.

Lucr-um, gain, profit.

LU'CRE, gain; profit.
LU'CRATIVE, profitable.

Luct-or, to struggle.

INELUC'TABLE, not to be overcome.
RELUC'TANCE,° unwillingness.

Lucubr-o, to study by candle-light.

LUCUBRA'TION, work or study by candle-light.

Ludo, lus-um, to play, to deceive.

ALLUDE',° to refer to.
ALLU'SION, a reference; a hint.
COLLU'SION,° deceitful agreement.
DELUDE', to beguile.
DELU'SIVE, deceptive.
ELUDE', to evade.
ELU'SORY, tending to elude.
ILLU'SION, false show; error.
LU'DICROUS, comical; sportive.
PREL'UDE, something introductory.

Lugubr-is, mournful.

LUC'TUAL, causing grief.
LUGU'BRIOUS, mournful.

Lumen, lumin-is, light.

ILLUME', to enlighten.
ILLUMINA'TION, a lighting up.
LU'MINOUS, shining; bright.
LU'MINARY, any body which gives light.
RELU'MINE, to light anew.

Lun-a, the moon.

INTERLU'NAR, belonging to the exact time of new-moon.
LU'NACY,* madness.
LU'NATIC, a madman.
LUNA'TION, a revolution of the moon.
LU'NAR, relating to the moon.
SEMILU'NAR, resembling half a moon.
SUB'LUNARY,° of this world.

Lu-o, lut-um, to wash away, or purge.

ABLU'TION,° the act of cleansing.
ALLU'VIAL,° added to land by the wash of water.
DILUTE',° to make thin or weak.
DIL'UENT, that which dilutes.
POLLUTE',° to defile; to taint.

Lure, *for* ***Leurre*** (Fr.), a decoy.

ALLURE', to entice.
LURE, an enticement.

---

* So called from a superstitious belief that the moon exerted an influence upon those who were insane.

Lustr-um,° a survey made every four years.

ILLUS'TRATE,° to explain.
ILLUS'TRIOUS, noble; eminent.
LUSTRA'TION,° purification.
LUS'TRE, splendor; renown.

Luxuri-a, luxury.

LUS'CIOUS, sweet; delicious.
LUX'URY, delicious fare.
LUXU'RIANT, very abundant.
LUXU'RIATE, to grow exuberantly.
LUXU'RIOUS, voluptuous.

Lymph-a, water.

LYMPH, a transparent fluid.
LYMPHAT'IC,° relating to lymph.

Lys-is (λυσις), a loosing.

ANTIPARALYT'IC, curing the palsy.
ANAL'YSIS, the separation of a compound body into its constituent parts.
AN'ALYZE, to make an analysis
PAL'SY,° a privation of motion.
PARALYT'IC, one struck by palsy.
PAR'ALYZE, to affect as with palsy.

Mace-o, to be lean or thin.

EMA'CIATE, to grow lean; to waste.
MAC'ERATE, to make lean.
MEA'GRE, lean; thin.

Machin-a, a machine, a device.

MACHINA'TION, artifice; plot.
MACHINE', a work of art; an engine.

Mach-omai (μαχομαι), to fight.

ALECTOROM'ACHY, cock-fighting.
LOGOM'ACHY, a contention about words.
NAU'MACHY, a mock sea-fight.
THEOM'ACHY,° a fight against the gods.

Macul-a, a stain or spot; a fault.

EMACULA'TION, a freeing from spots.
IMMAC'ULATE, spotless; pure.

Magister, magistr-i, a master.

MAGISTE'RIAL, lofty; proud.
MAG'ISTRACY, the office of a magistrate.
MAG'ISTRATE, a civil officer.
MAS'TER, one who controls.

Magnes, magnet-is, the loadstone.

MAG'NET,° the loadstone.
MAGNET'ICAL, attractive.
MAG'NETISM, the power of attraction.

Magn-us, great.

MAGNANIM'ITY, greatness of mind.
MAGNAN'IMOUS,° noble; brave.
MAGNIF'ICO, a grandee of Venice.
MAG'NIFY, to make greater.

MAGNIF'ICENT, grand; splendid.
MAG'NITUDE, size; greatness.
MAIN, principal; chief.
MAJ'ESTY, dignity; grandeur.
MAJES'TICAL, august; grand.
MA'JOR, greater; senior.
MAJOR'ITY, the greater number.

Mag-us, a diviner or enchanter.

MA'GI, wise men; eastern philosophers.
MAG'IC, enchantment.
MAGICI'AN, one skilled in magic.

Male, evil, ill.

DIS'MAL,° sorrowful; gloomy.
MALADMINISTRA'TION, bad management of affairs.
MALA-PROPOS',° unsuitably.
MALEDIC'TION, a curse.
MAL'CONTENT, one who is dissatisfied.
MALEFAC'TOR, a criminal.
MALEV'OLENCE, ill-will.
MALVERSA'TION, bad conduct.

Malign-us, envious, fatal to life.

MALIGN'ER, one who defames.
MALIG'NANT, pernicious; evil.
MALIG'NITY, violent hatred.

Maliti-a, deliberate mischief.

MAL'ICE, desire to injure.
MALICI'OUS, ill-disposed.

Malle-us, a hammer.

MAL'LET, a wooden hammer.
MAL'LEABLE, that may be spread by beating.

Mamm-a, a breast or pap.

MAM'MIFORM, having the shape of breasts.
MAM'MILLARY, belonging to the breasts.
MAMMIF'EROUS, having breasts.

Manci-a, *for* ***Mantia*** (μαντεια), a divining, prediction.

A'EROMANCY, the act of divining by the air.
ARITH'MANCY, a foretelling by numbers.
CHIR'OMANCY, the act of foretelling by inspecting the hand.
GE'OMANCY, divination by casting figures.
LITH'OMANCY, prediction by stones.
NEC'ROMANCY,° conjuration.
NECROMAN'TIC, relating to necromancy.
PYR'OMANCY, divination by fire.

Mand-o, mandat-um, to commit, to command.

COMMAND', to order; to lead.
COMMEND', to praise.
COMMENDA'TION, praise.
COUNTERMAND', to revoke a command.
DEMAND', a claim; a question.
MAN'DAMUS,* a kind of writ.

**Mandamus*, signifying *we command*, is the name of a command or writ issuing from the King's Bench in England, and in America from some of the higher courts, directed to any person, corporation, or inferior court, requiring them to do some act therein specified.—*Webster.*

MAN'DATE, a command.
REMAND', to send back.
RECOMMEND', to commend to another.

Mand-o, to chew, to eat.

MAN'DIBLE, the jaw.
MAS'TICATE, to chew

Mane-o, mans-um, to stay, to abide.

MAN'SION, a house; a residence.
PER'MANENCE, duration.
REMAIN', to continue; to endure.
REM'NANT, that which is left.

Mani-a (μανια), madness.

BIBLIOMA'NIA, a rage for possessing scarce and curious books.
MA'NIAC, mad; raving.
MA'NIA, madness.

Manifest-us, clear, evident.

MAN'IFEST, plain; open.
MANIFESTA'TION, discovery.
MANIFES'TO, a declaration.

Mano, manat-um, to flow. EM'ANATE, to issue from.

Man-us, the hand.

AMANUEN'SIS, a person who writes what another dictates.
EMAN'CIPATE,° to set free.
MAINTAIN', to preserve.
MAIN'TENANCE,° sustenance.
MAN'ACLE,° to shackle.
MAN'AGE,° to conduct.
MANCIPA'TION, slavery.
MAN'CIPLE,° a steward.
MANIPULA'TION,° a handling.
MANŒU'VRE,° skilful management.
MAN'UAL,° performed by hand.
MANUFAC'TURE, any thing made by art.
MANUMISSI'ON,° the act of giving liberty to slaves.
MANUMIT', to release from slavery.
MANURE',° to fertilize.
MAN'USCRIPT, a writing.
MISMAN'AGE, to manage ill.
PORTMAN'TEAU, a portable bag for clothes.

Mar-e, the sea.

MARINE', belonging to the sea.
MAR'INER, a seaman.
MAR'ITIME, near to the sea.
SUBMARINE', under the sea
TRANSMARINE', across the sea.
ULTRAMARINE', beyond the sea.

Margo, margin-is, a brink or edge.

MAR'GIN, the border; the edge.
MAR'GINAL, on the margin.

Marit-us, a husband.

AR'ITAL, pertaining to a husband.
MAR'RIAGE, wedlock.
MARIT'ICIDE, the murder of a husband.
MAR'RY, to unite in marriage.

Mars, mart-is, the god of war.

MARCH, to walk like soldiers.
MAR'TIAL, warlike.

Martyr (μαρτυρ), a witness, a martyr.

MAR'TYR, one put to death for adherence to a cause.
MAR'TYRDOM, the death of a martyr.
MARTYROL'OGY, a history of martyrs.
PROTOMAR'TYR, the first martyr.

Mascul-us, a male. MAS'CULINE, male ; manly.

Massacre, (Fr.) carnage, slaughter. MAS'SACRE, butchery.

Materi-a, matter.

IMMATE'RIAL, incorporeal.
MATE'RIALISM, the doctrine which denies the existence of spirit.
MATERIAL'ITY, material existence.
MATE'RIALIZE, to form into matter.

Mater, matr-is, a mother.

MATER'NAL, motherly.
MAT'RICIDE, the murder of a mother.
MATRIC'ULATE,° to admit to membership.
MA'TRON, an elderly woman.
MAT'RIMONY, marriage.

Mathem-a (μαθημα), learning.

MATHEMAT'ICAL, relating to mathematics.
MATHEMATICI'AN, one versed in mathematics.
MATHEMAT'ICS,° the science of quantity.
PHIL'OMATH, a lover of learning.
POLYM'ATHY, various knowledge.

Mat-os (ματος, ἀ μαω), a moving.

AUTOM'ATON, a self-moving machine.

Matur-us, ripe.

IMMATURE', not ripe.
MATU'RITY, ripeness.
MATURA'TION, the state of growing ripe.
PREMATURE', ripe too soon.

Maxim-um, the greatest.

MAX'IM, a general truth.
MAX'IMUM, the greatest quantity.

Mechan-ao (μηχαναω), to contrive, to invent.

IMMECHAN'ICAL, not according to the laws of mechanics.
MECHAN'ICS,° the science of motion.
MECHANICI'AN, a maker of machines.
MECH'ANISM, the construction of a machine.

Medi-us, middle.

IMME'DIATE, instant ; direct.
INTERME'DIATE, coming between.
MEDIA'TION, interposition.
MEDIA'TOR, an intercessor.
MEDIOC'RITY, middle rate.
MEDITERRA'NEAN, encircled with land.
ME'DIUM, the middle state.

Mede-or, to cure, to heal.

IMMED'ICABLE, incurable.
IRREME'DIABLE, not to be remedied.
MED'ICAL, relating to medicine.
MED'ICAMENT, any thing used in healing.
MED'ICINE, physic; a remedy.
REM'EDY, a cure; reparation.
REME'DIAL, affording remedy.

Medit-or, to muse, or think upon.

MEDITA'TION, deep thought.
PREMED'ITATE, to think before hand.

Mel, mell-is (μελι), honey.

HY'DROMEL, a liquor formed of honey and water.
MELLIF'EROUS, yielding honey.
MELLIF'LUENT, sweetly flowing.
MELLIFICA'TION, the making of honey.
OX'YMEL, a mixture of vinegar and honey.

Melan (μελαν), black, dark. MEL'ANCHOLY, sadness; dejection.

Melior, better.

AME'LIORATE, to improve.
MELIORA'TION, improvement.

Mel-os (μελος), a song or poem.

IMMELO'DIOUS, unmusical.
MEL'ODY,° sweetness of sound.
MEL'ODRAME, a drama containing songs.
PHILOME'LA,° the nightingale.

Membran-a, a membrane.

MEM'BRANE,° a thin, fibrous skin.
MEMBRANA'CEOUS, consisting of membranes.
MEMBRA'NIFORM, having the form of a membrane.

Memor, mindful.

COMMEM'ORATE, to hold in memory.
COMMEM'ORABLE, worthy of remembrance.
IMMEMO'RIAL, beyond memory.
MEMEN'TO,° a memorial.
MEMOIR', an account of transactions written from memory.
MEMORAN'DUM, a note to help the memory.
MEM'ORY, the faculty of recollecting.
MEMO'RIAL, serving to keep in memory.
MEN'TION, to speak of.
REMEM'BER, to bear in mind.
REMINIS'CENCE, recollection.

Men (μην), a month.

AL'MANAC, an annual calendar.
MENIS'CUS,° a sort of lens.
MOON, the orb of night.

Menage (Fr.), household; a collection of animals.

MENAG'ERY, a collection of animals.
ME'NIAL, a domestic servant.

Mend-a, a blemish; a mistake.

AMEND', to correct; to reform.
EMENDA'TION, correction.
EMEN'DATORY, improving.
MEND, to repair; to improve.

Mendic-us, a beggar.

MEN'DICANT, a beggar.
MENDIC'ITY, the state of begging.

Mens, ment-is, the mind.

COM'MENT, note; explanation.
COM'MENTARY, a writing to explain another.
COMMENTA'TOR, a writer of commentaries.
MEN'TAL, relating to the mind.
VE'HEMENCE, force; ardor.

Mensur-a, a measure. ***Meti-or***, to measure.

ADMEAS'UREMENT, the act of measuring.
COMMEN'SURATE, proportionate.
DIMEN'SION, bulk; extent.
IMMEAS'URABLE, not to be measured.
IMMENSE', unbounded; vast.
IMMEN'SITY, infinity; vastness.
INCOMMEN'SURABLE, having no common measure.
MEAS'URE, to compute quantity by a rule.
MENSURA'TION, the art of measuring.
METE, to measure.
ME'TER, a measurer.

Me-o, meat-um, to glide, to flow.

MEAN'DER,° to run with a winding course.
PER'MEABLE, that may be passed through.
PER'MEATE, to pass through.

Merci (Fr.), tenderness, goodness.

MER'CY, tenderness; pity.
UNMER'CIFUL, without pity.

Merc-or, to buy; to traffic.

COM'MERCE, trade; intercourse.
COMMER'CIAL, relating to commerce.
MER'CANTILE, trading.
MER'CENARY, a hireling.
MER'CER, one who sells silks.
MAR'KET, a place of sale.
MER'CHANDISE, things bought and sold.
MER'CHANT, a trader.
MER'CURY*, an ancient heathen deity.

Merg-o, mers-um, to plunge, to overwhelm.

EMERGE', to rise out of.
EMER'GENCY,° sudden occasion.
IMMERSE', to put under water.
MERGE, to sink.
SUBMERGE', to put under water.
SUBMER'SION, a drowning.

---

* He was the god of eloquence, the patron of merchants, the inventor of the lyre and harp, the protector of poets or men of genius, of musicians, wrestlers, &c., the conductor of departed ghosts to their proper mansions, and conveyed the messages of Jupiter and all the other gods.

Meridi-es, mid-day, noon; the south.

ANTEMERID'IAN, before noon.
MERID'IAN, noon; mid-day.
MERID'IONAL, southern.
POSTMERID'IAN, afternoon.

Merit-um (*ab* **Mereo**), to earn, or gain.

DEMER'IT, ill-desert; fault.
MER'IT, to deserve.
MERITO'RIOUS, deserving of reward.
UNMER'ITED, not merited.

Mes-os (μεσος), middle.

MES'ENTERY,° a membrane in the intestines.
MEZ'ZO, middle; mean; (a term in music.)

Metall-um (μεταλλον), a metal.

MET'AL,° a hard fossil substance.
METALLIF'EROUS, producing metals.
METALLOG'RAPHY, a description of metals.
MET'ALLOID, a substance resembling a metal.
MET'ALLURGY, the art of working metals.

Meteor-a (μετεωρα), flying luminous bodies in the air.

ME'TEOR, a shooting star.
METEOR'OLITE, a meteoric stone.
METEOROL'OGY, the science of the atmosphere and its phenomena.

Meter, metr-os (μητηρ, μητρος), a mother.

METROP'OLIS, the chief city.
METROPOL'ITAN, belonging to a metropolis.

Metr-um (μετρον), a measure.

ALTIM'ETRY,° the art of measuring heights.
ANEMOM'ETER, a wind-gauge.
BAROM'ETER,° an instrument to measure the weight of the atmosphere.
CHRONOM'ETER, a timepiece.
DIAM'ETER,° the measure through any thing.
DIAMET'RICAL, describing a diameter; direct.
GASOM'ETER, an instrument to measure gas.
GEOM'ETRY,° the science of dimensions.
GEOMETRICI'AN, one skilled in geometry.
HYGROM'ETER, an instrument to measure the degrees of moisture.
HEXAM'ETER, a verse of six feet.
ME'TER,° a measurer.
MICROM'ETER, an instrument to measure small spaces.
PENTAM'ETER, a verse of five feet.
PERIM'ETER, the bounding line of a figure.
PHOTOM'ETER, an instrument to measure light.
PYROM'ETER,° an instrument to measure heat.
SYM'METRY,° due proportion of parts.
SYMMET'RICAL, having symmetry.
THERMOM'ETER, an instrument to measure heat.
TRIGONOM'ETRY, the art of measuring triangles.

Micr-os (μικρος), little, small.

MI'CROCOSM,° a little world.
MICROM'ETER, an instrument to measure small spaces.
MI'CROSCOPE, an instrument for viewing the smallest objects.

Migr-o, migrat-um, to remove from one place to another.

EM'IGRANT, one who emigrates.
EM'IGRATE, to remove from a place.
IM'MIGRANT, one who immigrates.
IMMIGRA'TION, the act of coming into a new country.
MI'GRATE, to remove to another country.
TRANSMIGRA'TION, passage from one place to another.

Miles, milit-is, a soldier.

MIL'ITANT, fighting.
MIL'ITARY, relating to soldiers.
MIL'ITATE, to oppose.
MILIT'IA,° the enrolled soldiers.

Mille, a thousand.

MIL'FOIL, a plant; the yarrow.
MILLENA'RIAN, a believer in the millennium.
MILLEN'NIUM,° a thousand years.
MIL'LEPED, an insect having many feet.
MILLES'IMAL, thousandth.

Mim-us (μιμος), an imitator, a farce.

MIM'IC, a buffoon.
PAN'TOMIME, dumb show.

Min-æ, threats.

MEN'ACE, to threaten.
MINA'CIOUS, full of threats.

Min-eo, to jut out, to hang over.

EM'INENT, high; exalted.
IM'MINENT, threatening; impending.
PRE-EM'INENCE, superiority.
PROM'INENCE, distinction.
PROM'INENT, standing out.
SUPEREM'INENT, eminent in a high degree.

Mineral (Fr.), a mineral.

MIN'ERAL,° a hard fossil body.
MINERALIZA'TION, the act of converting into a mineral.
MINERAL'OGY, the science of minerals.

Minister, ministr-i, a servant, a helper.

ADMIN'ISTER, to supply.
ADMINISTRA'TION, the act of administering; dispensation.
MIN'ISTER,° a clergyman.
MIN'ISTRY, the body of ministers.
MINISTRA'TION, agency; service.

Minu-o, minut-um, to lessen.

COM'MINUTE, to pulverize.
DIMIN'ISH, to impair; to lessen.
DIMINU'TION, act of making less.
DIMIN'UTIVE, small; little.
INDIMIN'ISHABLE, that cannot be diminished.
MIN'IATURE, a picture less than the reality.
MIN'IMUM, the smallest quantity.

MIN'ION, a favorite; a small type.
MI'NOR,° one under age.
MINOR'ITY, the less number.
MIN'UEND, the number to be diminished.
MI'NUS, diminished by.
MINUTE', very small.

Mir-us, strange, wonderful.

AD'MIRABLE, worthy of being admired.
ADMIRE', to regard with wonder or esteem.
ADMIRA'TION, wonder; esteem.
MIR'ACLE,° a supernatural event
MIRAC'ULOUS, supernatural.
MIR'ROR, a looking-glass.

Misc-eo, mixt-um, to mix.

ADMIX'TURE, the substance mingled.
COMMIX', to mingle; to blend.
IMMIS'CIBLE, not capable of being mingled.
INTERMIX', to mingle together.
MIN'GLE, to mix; to join.
MIS'CELLANY, a collection of various things.
MIX, to put together.
MIX'TURE, a mixed mass.
PROMIS'CUOUS, mingled; confused.

Miser, wretched, pitiful.

COMMIS'ERATE, to compassionate; to pity.
MIS'ERABLE, wretched; helpless.
MI'SER, a person covetous to excess.
MIS'ERY, calamity; distress.

Mis-os (μισος), hatred, enmity.

MIS'ANTHROPE, a hater of mankind.
MISOG'AMY, hatred of marriage.
MISANTHROP'ICAL, hating mankind.
MISOG'YNIST, a woman hater.

Mitig-o, to make mild.

MIT'IGATE, to alleviate.
UNMIT'IGATED, not softened.

Mitt-o, miss-um, to send.

ADMISSI'ON, the act of admitting.
ADMIT', to receive; to allow.
ADMIT'TANCE, entrance.
COMMISSI'ON, a trust; a warrant.
COM'MISSARY, a delegate; a deputy.
COMMIT'MENT, the act of committing.
COMMIT'TEE,° persons selected to examine or manage any matter.
COM'PROMISE,° to adjust by concession.
DEMISE', death; decease.
DISMISSI'ON, discharge.
EM'ISSARY,° one sent on a secret mission; a spy.
EMISSI'ON, a sending out.
EMIT', to send forth.
INADMIS'SIBLE, not to be allowed.
INTERMISSI'ON,° cessation; pause.
INTERMIT'TENT, ceasing at intervals.
MANUMISSI'ON, the act of giving liberty to slaves

MANUMIT', to release from slavery.
MIS'SILE, that may be thrown.
MISSI'ON, a being sent.
MISSI'ONARY, one sent to propagate religion.
MIS'SIVE,° a letter sent.
OMIT', to leave out.
OMISSI'ON, neglect; failure.
PER'MIT,° a written permission.
PERMIS'SIVE, granting leave.
PREMISE', to state beforehand.
PROM'ISE,° a binding declaration.
PROM'ISSORY, containing a promise.
RE-ADMIT', to let in again.
RE-COMMIT', to commit anew.
REMISS',° slack; careless.
REMISSI'ON, abatement; pardon.
REMIT'TANCE, a sum sent back.
SUBMIS'SIVE, humble.
SUBMIT',° to resign; to yield.
SURMISE', a suspicion.
TRANSMISSI'ON, a sending over.
TRANSMIT', to send over.
UNREMIT'TED, not abated; incessant.

Mne-o**, for **Mnao (μναω), to remind.

AM'NESTY,° an act of general pardon.
MNEMON'ICS, the art of memory.

***Mod-us**,* a measure, a manner.

ACCOM'MODATE, to fit; to adjust.
COMMO'DIOUS, convenient.
COMMOD'ITY, interest; merchandise.
DISCOMMODE', to put to trouble.
IMMOD'ERATE,° excessive.
IMMOD'EST, wanting modesty.
INCOMMO'DIOUS, inconvenient.
MODE, method; form.
MOD'EL, a mould; a pattern.
MOD'ERATE, temperate; not violent.
MOD'ERN, late; recent.
MOD'ESTY, decency; diffidence.
MOD'ICUM, a small portion.
MOD'IFY, to shape; to soften.
MODIFICA'TION, the act of modifying.
MOOD, temper; disposition.
MOD'ULATE,° to vary sound.
REMOD'EL, to model anew.

***Mol-a**,*° a mill-stone.

EMOL'UMENT,° profit.
IM'MOLATE, to sacrifice.
MOL'ECULE, a minute particle.

***Molest-us**,* troublesome, teasing.

MOLEST', to trouble; to vex.
MOLESTA'TION, disturbance.

***Moli-or**,* to rear, to build.

DEMOL'ISH, to destroy.
DEMOLITI'ON, destruction.
MOLE, a spot; a mound.

***Moll-is**,* soft.

EMOL'LIENT, softening.
MOL'LIFY, to assuage; to quiet.
MOLLIFICA'TION, a softening.

***Moment-um**,* motion, force; a second.

MO'MENT, importance; an instant.
MOMEN'TOUS, weighty.
MOMEN'TUM,° force; impetus.
MO'MENTARY, lasting for a moment.

Mone-o, monit-um, to put in mind, to warn.

ADMON'ISH, to warn; to reprove.
ADMONITI'ON, gentle reproof.
ADMON'ITORY, admonishing.
MON'ITOR,° one who warns.
MON'UMENT, a memorial; a tomb.
PREMON'ITORY, giving warning beforehand.
SUM'MON,° to call; to cite.
SUM'MONS, a call of authority.

Mon-os (μονος), one, alone.

ANTIMONARCH'ICAL, against monarchy.
MON'AD, an atom.
MON'ARCH,° a sovereign.
MON'ASTERY, a convent.
MONAS'TIC, pertaining to monks.
MONK, one living in a monastery.
MONOC'EROS, the unicorn.
MON'OCHORD, an instrument of one string.
MONOC'ULAR, one-eyed.
MON'ODY, a poem sung by one person.
MONOG'AMY, marriage of one wife only.
MON'OLOGUE, a soliloquy.
MONOPET'ALOUS, having one leaf.
MONOP'OLIZE, to engross.
MONOSYL'LABLE, a word of one syllable.
MON'OTHEISM, belief in one God.
MONOT'ONY, sameness of sound.
MONOT'ONOUS, wanting variety.

Mons, mont-is, a high hill.

DISMOUNT', to alight from a horse.
MOUND, a heap or bank of earth.
MOUN'TAIN, a very large hill.
MOUN'TEBANK,° a quack.
PROM'ONTORY, a high land jutting into the sea.
REMOUNT', to mount again.
SURMOUNT', to rise above.
TANT'AMOUNT, equivalent.
ULTRAMON'TANE, beyond the mountains.

Monstr-o, to show, to declare.

DEMON'STRABLE, that may be demonstrated.
DEMON'STRATE, to show plainly.
MON'STER, something unnatural.
MON'STROUS, strange; shocking.
MUS'TER, to collect for review.
REMON'STRATE, to exhibit reasons against.
REMON'STRANCE, expostulation.

Morb-us, a disease.

MOR'BID, diseased; sickly.
MORBIF'IC, causing disease.

Mord-eo, mors-um, to bite.

MORDA'CIOUS, biting; acrid.
MOR'SEL, a mouthful.
REMORSE',° sorrow for a fault.

Moros-us, peevish. MOROSE', peevish; sullen.

Morph-e (μορφη), a form or figure.

AMORPH'OUS, shapeless.
METAMORPH'OSE, to change the form of.

Mors, mort-is, death.

IMMOR'TAL, exempt from death.
IMMOR'TALIZE, to make immortal.
MORTAL'ITY, death.
MORT'GAGE,° a pledge.
MORTIF'EROUS, fatal; deadly.
MOR'TIFY, to subdue; to humble.
MOR'TUARY, a burial place.
MUR'DER, to destroy.

Mos, mor-is, a custom, or manner.

ANTIMOR'ALIST, an opposer of morality.
DEMOR'ALIZE, to destroy the morals of.
IMMOR'AL, vicious.
MORAL'ITY, correctness of life.

Move-o, mot-um, to move.

COMMO'TION,° tumult; sedition.
EMO'TION, passion; excitement.
IMMOV'ABLE, fixed; firm.
LOCOMO'TION, the power of changing place.
MOB, a tumultuous crowd.
MOBIL'ITY, fickleness.
MO'TION, the act of changing place.
MO'TIVE, causing motion.
MOVE, to put in motion.
PROMOTE', to forward; to raise.
REMOTE', distant.
REMOVE', to put from its place.

Mult-us, many.

MULTAN'GULAR, many-cornered.
MULTIFA'RIOUS, having great variety.
MUL'TIFID, divided many times.
MUL'TIFORM, having various shapes.
MULTILAT'ERAL, having many sides.
MULTILIN'EAL, having many lines.
MUL'TIPLE, a number which exactly contains another several times.
MUL'TIPLEX, manifold.
MULTIPLICAND', the number to be multiplied.
MULTIPLICA'TION, the act of multiplying.
MUL'TIPLY, to increase in number.
MUL'TITUDE, a crowd or throng.

Mund-us, the world.

ANTEMUN'DANE, before the creation of the world.
EXTRAMUN'DANE, beyond the world.
MUN'DANE, belonging to this world.
SUPRAMUN'DANE, situated above the world.
ULTRAMUN'DANE, beyond the world.

Municipi-um, a free city.

MUNIC'IPAL,° belonging to a corporation or city.

Munio, munit-um, to fortify.

AMMUNITI'ON, military stores.
MUNITI'ON, materials for war.

Mun-us, muner-is, a gift, or present; an office; a portion.

COM'MON, an open, public ground.
COM'MONALTY, the common people.
COMMU'NION, intercourse.
COMMU'NITY,° the commonwealth.
COMMUNE', to talk together.
COMMUNICA'TION, conference.
EXCOMMU'NICATE, to eject from church membership.
IMMU'NITY, privilege.
INCOMMU'NICABLE, that cannot be imparted.
MUNIF'ICENT, liberal.
REMU'NERATE, to reward.

Murmur, a murmur.

MUR'MUR,° a low, shrill noise.
REMUR'MUR, to utter back in murmurs.

Mur-us, a wall.

IMMURE', to inclose; to confine.
MU'RAL,* pertaining to a wall.

Mus-a (μουσα), a muse, a poem.

AMUSE', to divert.
MUSE, to think.
MU'SIC, harmony; melody.
MUSE'UM,° a repository of curiosities.
MUSICI'AN, one skilled in music.

Muscul-us (*ab* ***Mus***), a muscle or sinew.

MOUSE, a little animal.
MUS'CLE, a fleshy fibre.
MUS'CULAR, relating to the muscles; strong.

Mutil-us, maimed.

MU'TILATE, to maim; to deface.
UNMU'TILATED, unmaimed.

Mut-o, mutat-um, to change.

COMMUTE', to exchange.
IMMU'TABLE, unchangeable.
MUTA'TION, change.
MU'TINY, to rise against authority.
MUTINEER', one guilty of mutiny.
MU'TINOUS, seditious.
PERMUTA'TION, exchange.
TRANSMUTE', to change to another nature.

Mut-us, dumb.

MUTE, dumb; speechless.
OBMUTES'CENCE, loss of speech.

Mutu-us, one another, each other.

MU'TUAL, reciprocal; each acting in return to the other.

Mys, my-os (μυς, μυος), a muscle of the body.

MYOG'RAPHY, a description of the muscles.
MYOL'OGY, the science of the muscles.

Myrias, myriad-os (μυριας), the number of ten thousand.

MYR'IAD, ten thousand; a very large number.

---

* The *corona muralis* or mural crown, among the ancient Romans, was a golden crown bestowed on him who first mounted the walls of a besieged place.

Myst-es (μυστης), hidden, secret.

MYS'TERY, something secret; an enigma.
MYSTE'RIOUS, full of mystery.
MYS'TIC, obscure; secret.
MYS'TICISM, the doctrine of the Mystics.

Myth-os (μυθος), a word, a fable.

MYTH'IC, fabulous.
MYTHOL'OGY, a system of fables.

Narc-e (ναρκη), numbness or torpidness.

NARCIS'SUS, the daffodil.
NARCO'SIS, stupefaction.
NARCOT'IC, soporific; causing sleep.

Narr-o, to narrate. NAR'RATE, to relate; to tell.

Nasc-or, nat-us, to be born, to spring.

COG'NATE, kindred; of the same stock.
IN'NATE, inborn.
NAS'CENT, coming into being.
NA'TAL, relating to one's birth.
NA'TION, a distinct people.
NATIONAL'ITY, state or character as a nation.
NA'TIONALIZE, to make a distinct nation of.
NA'TIVE, natural; original.
NATIV'ITY, birth.
NA'TURE, the universe.
NAT'URAL, produced by nature.
NAT'URALIST, one versed in the study of nature.
NAT'URALIZE, to invest with the privileges of a native citizen.
PRETERNAT'URAL, beyond what is natural.
RENAS'CENT, rising again into being.
SUBNAS'CENT, growing beneath.
SUPERNAT'URAL, above nature.
UNNAT'URALIZED, not made a citizen.

Nas-us, the nose.

NA'SAL, belonging to the nose.
NAS'ICORNOUS, having a horn on the nose.

Nat-o, natat-um, to swim.

NA'TANT, swimming.
NATA'TION, the act of swimming.
SUPERNA'TANT, swimming on the top.

Nause-a (ναυσια), sea-sickness.

NAU'SEA, loathing; sea-sickness.
NAU'SEOUS, loathsome; sickening.

Naut-a, a sailor, a mariner.

NAU'TICAL, relating to ships.
NAU'TILUS, a shell-fish that sails.

Nav-is (ναυς), a ship.

CIRCUMNAV'IGATE, to sail round.
CIRCUMNAV'IGABLE, that may be sailed round.
NA'VY, a fleet.
NAV'IGATE, to pass by ships.
RENAV'IGATE, to sail again.
UNNAV'IGABLE, not fit for the passage of vessels.

Ne, not.

NEC'ESSARY, needful.
NECES'SITATE, to make necessary.
NESCI'ENCE, ignorance.
NEFAND'OUS, not to be uttered.
NEFA'RIOUS, wicked.

Nebul-a (νεβος), a mist, a cloud.

NEB'ULA,° a thin cloud or mist.
NEB'ULOUS, misty; cloudy.

Necess-e (*ab* ***ne***, not, *and* ***cesso***, to give up), needful.

NECESSA'RIAN, an advocate for philosophical necessity.
NEC'ESSARIES, things needful.
NECES'SITY, compulsion; want.
NECES'SITOUS, needy.
UNNEC'ESSARY, not needed.

Necr-os (νεκρος), a dead body.

NECROL'OGY, a register of deaths.
NEC'ROMANCY, conjuration.

Nectar (νεκταρ), the drink of the gods.

NEC'TAR, the feigned drink of the gods.
NEC'TARINE, sweet as nectar.
NECTARIF'EROUS, producing nectar.
NEC'TARY, the melliferous part of a flower.

Nect-o, nex-um, to tie or bind, to knit.

ANNEX', to join to.
CONNECT', to join; to link.
CONNEC'TION, union; relation.
REANNEX', to annex again.
UNCONNEC'TED, not coherent

Neg, *for* *Nec*, neither, not.

NEGLECT', inattention; slight.
NEGO'TIABLE, that may be negotiated.
NEG'LIGENT, careless; heedless.
NEGO'TIATE, to transact business; to treat with.

Neg-o, negat-um, to deny, to refuse.

ABNEGA'TION, denial.
DENY', to contradict; to refuse.
NAY, no.
NEGA'TION, a denial.
NEG'ATIVE, implying denial.
REN'EGADE, a deserter.

Nemus, nemor-is, a grove. NEM'ORAL, relating to a grove.

Ne-os (νεος), new.

NEOL'OGY, a system of new words.
NE'OPHYTE,° a new convert; a novice.

Neur-on (νευρον), a nerve, a sinew.

APONEURO'SIS, expansion of a nerve.
EN'ERVATE,° to weaken.
NERVE, an organ of sensation.
NEURAL'GIA, a diseased state of the nerves.
NEUROL'OGY, a description of the nerves.
NEUROT'OMY, the dissection of the nerves.
UNNERV'ED, weak; feeble.

Neuter, neutr-um, neither.

NEU'TER, of neither party.
NEUTRAL'ITY, a neutral state.
NEU'TRALIZE, to render indifferent.

Nex, nec-is, death, destruction.

PERNICI'OUS, very hurtful; destructive.

Nic-e (νικη), victory. ARSE'NIC, a poisonous mineral substance.

Niger, nigr-um, black.

NE'GRO, one of the black race.
NIGRES'CENT, growing black.

Nihil, nothing.

ANNI'HILATE, to destroy.
NIHIL'ITY, nothingness.

Nitr-um, nitre or saltpetre.

NI'TRE, saltpetre.
NI'TRIC, composed of nitre.
NI'TROUS, impregnated with nitre.
NI'TROGEN, the elements of nitre.

Nive-o, to wink. CONNIVE', to wink at.

Noc-eo, to hurt. ***Noxi-us,*** hurtful.

IN'NOCENCE, purity; harmlessness.
INNOC'UOUS, harmless.
NOX'IOUS, hurtful.
NUI'SANCE, something offensive.
OBNOX'IOUS, subject; exposed; odious.

Nomen, nomin-is, a name.

BINO'MIAL, consisting of two members or terms.
DENOMINA'TION, a name; a class.
IG'NOMINY,°disgrace; shame.
MULTINO'MIAL, having many names or terms.
NAME, the term by which we call or distinguish things.
NO'MENCLATURE, a system of names.
NOM'INAL, not real; in name only.
NOM'INATE, to name; to propose.
PRO'NOUN, a word used instead of a noun.
TRINOM'INAL, containing three terms.

Nom-os (νομος), a law, a management.

ASTRON'OMY, the science of the heavenly bodies.
DEUTERON'OMY,* the fifth book of the Bible.
ECON'OMY,° frugality.
ECON'OMISE, to employ with economy.

Non, not.

NOLITI'ON, unwillingness.
NON'AGE, minority in age.
NONCONFORM'IST, one who does not conform.
NONDESCRIPT', not yet described.
NONEN'TITY, nonexistence.
NON'PLUS, a great difficulty.
NON'SENSE, unmeaning words.
NON'SUIT, stoppage of a suit at law.

---

* The *second* book of the law; from *deuteros*, second.

Nox, noct-is, night.

E'QUINOX, the time of equal day and night.
NOCTUR'NAL, nightly.
EQUINOC'TIAL, pertaining to the equinox.
NIGHT, the time of darkness.

Norm-a, a rule or square.

ENOR'MOUS, excessive.
NOR'MAL, according to rule.

Nosc-o, not-um, to know. ***Nobil-is,*** noble.

ACKNOWL'EDGE, to confess.
CONNOISSEUR',° a judge; a critic.
IGNO'BLE, of low birth.
KNOW, to perceive; to understand.
KNOWL'EDGE, learning; information.
NOBIL'ITY, dignity; rank.
N. B. NO'TA BE'NE, mark well.
NOTE, a mark; notice.
NO'TICE, to note; to heed.
NO'TIFY, to make known.
NO'TION, thought; idea.
NOTO'RIOUS,° publicly known.
PROTHON'OTARY, the head registrar.
REC'OGNIZE, to know again.
RECOGNITI'ON, the art of recognizing.
RECONNOI'TER, to examine; to survey.

Not-a, a mark.

ANNOTA'TION, a note; a comment.
DENOTE', to betoken.
NO'TABLE, memorable.
NO'TARY,° an officer who attests contracts and writings.
NOTA'TION, a mode of marking.
NO'TICE, observation.

Nov-us, new.

IN'NOVATE, to introduce novelties or change.
NEW, fresh; modern.
NOV'EL, new; unusual.
NOV'ELTY, newness; freshness.
NOV'ICE, one unskilled.
NOVIT'IATE, state of a novice.
RENEW', to make again.
RENOVA'TION, renewal.

Nub-es, a cloud. NUBIF'EROUS, bringing clouds.

Nub-o, nupt-um, to veil, to marry.

CONNU'BIAL, nuptial; matrimonial.
NUP'TIAL, relating to marriage

Nud-us, naked, bare.

DENUDE', to strip; to make bare.
NU'DITY, nakedness.

Nug-ae, trifles, toys.

NUGAC'ITY, trifling behavior.
NU'GATORY, trifling; futile.

Null-us, none, no one.

ANNUL', to abolish.
NULL, void; of no force.
NUL'LIFY, to make void.
NUL'LITY, nothingness.

Numer-us, a number.

ENU'MERATE, to reckon up singly.
EQUINU'MERANT, having the same number.
INNU'MERABLE, that cannot be numbered.
NUM'BER, to count; to reckon.
NU'MERAL, relating to number.
NUMERA'TION, art of numbering.
NUMER'ICAL, denoting number.
NU'MEROUS, many; not few.
SUPERNU'MERARY, above a stated number.

Nuncio, nunciat-um, to bring news, to tell.

ANNOUNCE', to publish.
ANNUNCIA'TION, the act of announcing.
DENOUNCE', to declare against.
DENUNCIA'TION, public threat.
ENUN'CIATE, to declare; to express.
INTERNUN'CIO, a messenger between two parties.
MISPRONOUNCE', to pronounce improperly.
NUN'CIO, an envoy from the pope.
PRONOUNCE', to speak; to utter.
PRONUNCIA'TION, mode of utterance.
RENOUNCE', to disown; to dis claim.
RENUNCIA'TION, a disowning.

Nu-o, to nod. INNUEN'DO,° an oblique hint.

Nutri-o, nutrit-um, to nourish, to suckle.

INNUTRITI'OUS, not nourishing.
NOUR'ISH, to support by food.
NURSE, a person who has the care of infants or sick persons.
NUR'TURE, to feed; to train.
NU'TRIMENT, nourishment; food.
NUTRITI'ON, the act or process of nourishing.

Nux, nuc-is, a nut.

NUCIF'EROUS, bearing nuts.
NU'CLEUS,° that about which matter is collected.

Oblivio, oblivion-is, forgetfulness.

OBLIV'ION,° forgetfulness.
OBLIV'IOUS, forgetful.

Obscen-us, *for* ***Obscœnus,*** immodest, unchaste.

OBSCENE', immodest; impure.
OBSCEN'ITY, impurity.

Obscur-us, obscure.

OBSCURE', dark; unknown.
OBSCU'RITY, darkness; privacy.

Occult-us, hidden, secret.

OCCULT',° secret; hidden.
OCCULTA'TION, the time that a star or planet is hid from our sight by another heavenly body.

Octo (ὀκτω), eight.

OC'TAGON, a plane figure of eight angles.
OCTAN'GULAR, having eight angles.
OCTO'BER, the tenth month. (p. 63.)
OCTA'VO, a book in which a sheet is folded into eight leaves.
OCTEN'NIAL, happening every eighth year.

Octogen-i, eighty.

OCTOGENA'RIAN, one who is eighty years of age.

Ocul-us, the eye.

BINOC'ULAR, having two eyes.
INOC'ULATE, to insert the eye or bud of one tree in another.
MULTOC'ULAR, having many eyes.
OC'ULIST, an eye-doctor.

Ode (ᾠδη), an ode, a hymn.

COM'EDY,° an amusing dramatic piece.
IL'IAD, a poem on Ilium or Troy.
MEL'ODY, sweetness of sound.
MON'ODY, a poem sung by one person.
ODE, a poem; a song.
PAL'INODE, a recantation.
PAR'ODY,° a humorous imitation.
PROS'ODY,° the laws of versification.
RHAP'SODY,° an irregular composition.
RHAP'SODIST, one who writes rhapsodies.
TRAG'EDY,* a dramatic representation.

Odi, I hate, or have hated.

O'DIOUS, hateful.
O'DIUM, hatred.

Odor, a scent or smell.

INO'DOROUS, wanting scent.
O'DORAMENT, a perfume.
ODORIF'EROUS, fragrant.
O'DOR, scent; fragrance.

Od-os (ὁδος), a road, a journey.

EP'ISODE,° incidental narrative.
IMMETHOD'ICAL, confused; without system.
METH'OD, a manner; a way.
PE'RIOD,° a circuit; an epoch.
SYN'OD,° a church assembly.

Odoys, odont-os (ὀδους, ὀδοντος), a tooth.

ODONTAL'GIA, the toothache.

Oid-os (ειδος), a form, a figure.

CO'NOID,° a figure like a cone.
MET'ALLOID,° a substance resembling a metal.
O'VOID, egg-shaped.
RHOM'BOID,° a figure like a rhomb.
SPHE'ROID, a body like a sphere.
VA'RIOLOID, a disease resembling the smallpox.

Ol-eo, to emit odor, to grow.

ABOL'ISH,° to annul; to repeal.
ABOLITI'ON, the act of abolishing.
ADOLES'CENCE, the age between childhood and manhood.
ADULT', one full grown.
OB'SOLETE, gone out of use.
OLFAC'TORY, having the sense of smelling.
RED'OLENT, diffusing odor.

---

* *Tragedy,* originally, a *song* or *poem* sung in honor of Bacchus, by a chorus of music, with dances and the sacrifice of a *goat.*

Olig-os (ὀλιγος), few. OL'IGARCHY, the government of a few.

Oliv-a (ἐλαια), olive. ***Ole-um,*** oil.

OIL, an unctuous matter.
OLEAG'INOUS, oily.
OL'IVE, a plant yielding oil.

Olymp-us ('Ολυμπος), a mountain of Macedonia.

OLYM'PIAD,* the four years from one celebration of the Olympic games to another.
OLYM'PIC, relating to games in Greece.

Omal-os (ὁμαλος), even, regular.

ANOM'ALY, irregularity; deviation from rule.
ANOM'ALOUS, irregular; out of rule.

Omen, omin-is, an omen.

ABOM'INATE,° to abhor; to detest.
ABOM'INABLE, hateful.
O'MEN, a sign; a prognostic.
OM'INOUS, foreboding.

Omn-is, all, every.

OMNIF'IC, all-creating.
OMNIPRES'ENT, present everywhere.
OMNIP'OTENT, almighty.
OMNISCI'ENCE, infinite wisdom.
OMNIV'OROUS, all-devouring.

Onom-a (ὀνομα), a name.

ANON'YMOUS, wanting a name.
METON'YMY,° a change of names.
PARON'YMOUS, resembling another word.
PATRONYM'IC, a name derived from a father.
SYN'ONYM, a word of the same meaning with another.

Onus, oner-is, a burden, or load.

EXON'ERATE, to disburden.
ON'EROUS, burdensome.

Opac-us, shady, dark.

OPAC'ITY, want of transparency.
OPAQUE', not transparent.

Oper-a; Opus, oper-is, work, labor.

CO-OP'ERATE, to labor jointly for the same end.
INOP'ERATIVE, not active.
MANŒU'VRE,° a skillful movement.
OP'ERA, a dramatic composition set to music.
OPERA'TION, agency; influence.
OPEROSE', laborious.
OPUS'CULE, a small work.

* These were solemn games among the ancient Greeks, dedicated to *Olympian* Jupiter, and celebrated once in four years at *Olympia,* a town in Greece, and constituting an important epoch in history and chronology. The first *Olympiad* commenced 775 years before the birth of Christ, and twenty-two years before the foundation of Rome. The computation by *Olympiads* ceased at the 364th *Olympiad,* in the year 410 of the Christian era.

Oph-is (ὀφις), a serpent.

OPHIOL'OGY, the science of serpents.

OPHIOPH'AGOUS, eating serpents.

Ophthalm-os (ὀφθαλμος), the eye.

OPHTHAL'MIC, relating to the eye.

OPHTHAL'MIA, a disease of the eyes.

Opin-or, to think, to imagine.

OPINE', to think.

OPIN'ION, judgment; notion.

OPIN'IONATED, obstinate in opinion.

Opt-o (ὀπτω), to see.

AU'TOPSY, ocular demonstration.

CATOP'TRICS, the science of the reflection of light.

CATOP'TRICAL, relating to catoptrics.

DIOP'TRICS, the science of the refraction of light.

DROP'SY, a collection of water in the body.

OP'TICS, the science of light and vision.

OPTICI'AN, one skilled in optics.

SYNOP'SIS, a general view.

Opt-o, optat-um, to wish, to choose.

ADOPT',° to receive as one's own.

OP'TATIVE, expressing a wish.

OP'TION, choice; preference.

Opulent-us, wealthy, rich.

INOP'ULENT, not wealthy.

OP'ULENCE, wealth; affluence.

Oram-a (ὁραμα), the thing seen.

DIORA'MA, a transparent painting showing the effect of light.

PANORA'MA,° a large circular painting.

Orb-is, a circle or globe.

EXOR'BITANT,° enormous; excessive.

ORB, a sphere; a wheel.

OR'BIT, a line described by a revolving planet.

ORBIC'ULAR, spherical.

Orc-os (ὁρκος), an oath. EX'ORCISE,° to expel evil spirits

Ord-o, ordin-is, order, arrangement, rank.

CO-OR'DINATE, holding the same rank.

DISOR'DER, to ruffle; to confuse.

EXTRAOR'DINARY,° remarkable.

INOR'DINATE,° immoderate.

INSUBORDINA'TION, disobedience; revolt.

ORDAIN',° to appoint; to decree.

OR'DINAL, noting order.

OR'DINANCE, a public law.

OR'DINARY, common; usual.

PREORDAIN', to ordain beforehand.

PRIMOR'DIAL, first in order; original.

SUBOR'DINATE, inferior; subject.

M

Organ-um (ὀργανον), an instrument.

DISOR'GANIZE, to dissolve union of parts.
OR'GAN,* a natural instrument.
ORGAN'ICAL, relating to organs.
OR'GANISM, an organical structure.
OR'GANIZE, to form; to construct.

Ori-or, ort-us, to rise, to spring. **Orig-o,** the beginning.

ABOR'TION, failure.
O'RIENT, the east.
ORIEN'TALIST, one versed in Oriental learning.
OR'IGIN, beginning; source.
ORIGINAL'ITY, the state of being original.
ORIG'INATE, to bring into being.

Ornis, ornith-os (ὀρνις, ὀρνιθος), a bird.

ORNITHOL'OGY, the science of birds.
ORNITH'OMANCY, augury; divination by birds.

Orn-o, ornat-um, to deck; or dress.

ADORN', to dress; to decorate.
OR'NAMENT, an embellishment.
OR'NATE, decorated.
SUBORN',° to procure to take a false oath.
SUBORNA'TION, the act of suborning.

Or-o, orat-um, to speak, to beg.

ADORE', to worship; to honor.
EX'ORABLE, that may be moved by entreaty.
INEX'ORABLE, not to be moved by entreaty.
OR'ACLE,† one famed for wisdom.
ORAC'ULAR, uttering oracles.
OR'ISON, a supplication.
O'RAL, delivered by mouth.
OR'ATOR, an eloquent speaker.
OR'IFICE, an opening to a cavity.
PERORA'TION,° the conclusion of an oration.

Orth-os (ὀρθος), erect, straight, right.

ORTHODROM'ICS, the art of sailing in the arc of some great circles.
OR'THOEPY, correct pronunciation.
OR'THODOX, sound in opinion.
ORTHOG'RAPHY, correct spelling.
ORTHOGRAPH'ICAL, relating to spelling.

Os, oss-is, a bone.

OS'SEOUS, bony.
OS'SIFY, to change to bone.
OSSIFICA'TION, the act of ossifying.
OSSIV'OROUS, devouring bones.

---

* *Organ*, a *natural instrument* of action or operation, or by which some process is carried on: thus, the muscles are *organs* of motion; the ears are *organs* of hearing; the eyes are *organs* of seeing; the tongue is the *organ* of speech, &c. A secretary of state is the *organ* of communication between the government and a foreign power.

† *Oracle*, among *Pagans*, the *answer* of a god or some person reputed to be a god, to an inquiry made respecting some affair of importance, usually some future event, as the success of an enterprize or battle. The *deity* who gave, or was supposed to give an answer to inquiries, as the *Delphic oracle*.

Oste-on, (ὀστέον), a bone.

OSTEOL'OGY, a description of the bones.

PERIOS'TEUM, a membrane covering the bones.

Oti-um, ease, retirement from business.

NEGO'TIATE, to transact business.

NEGOTIA'TION, a treaty of business.

DISEASE', distemper; malady.

EASE, quiet; facility.

Ouran-os (οὐρανος), heaven.

OURANOG'RAPHY, a description of the heavens.

Ous, ot-os (οὖς), the ear.

OTACOU'STIC, an instrument to assist hearing.

PAROT'ID, relating to glands situated below the ears.

Ov-um, an egg.

O'VAL, shaped like an egg.

O'VARY, the seat of eggs.

O'VOID, egg-shaped.

O'VIFORM, having the form of an egg.

OVIP'AROUS, producing eggs.

Oxy-s (ὀξυς), sharp, sour.

OX'YDIZE, to convert into an oxyde.

OXYDA'TION, the act of oxydizing.

OX'YDE,° a substance combined with oxygen.

OX'YGEN, a gas which generates acids.

OX'YMEL, a mixture of vinegar and honey.

PAR'OXYSM, temporary violence of a disease.

Pact-us, stipulated; agreed. **Pactiti-us,** made by agreement.

COM'PACT, a contract.

PACTITI'OUS, settled by agreement.

Pact-us, driven in, fixed.

COMPACT', firm; close.

IMPACT', to drive close.

Pag-us, a village.

PA'GAN,° a heathen; an idolater.

PA'GANISM, the worship of false gods.

Pais *or* **Pays** (Fr.), the country.

PEAS'ANT a rustic; a rural laborer.

Palati-um, a mount in Rome, where Augustus Cæsar resided.

PAL'ACE, a royal house.

PAL'ATINE,° invested with regal rights.

Palat-um, the taste, the palate.

PAL'ATE, the organ of taste.

PAL'ATABLE, pleasing to the taste.

Palin (παλιν), back, again.

PAL'INODE, a recantation or withdrawal of a former assertion.

PAL'INDROME,* a word or sentence that is the same when read *backwards* or *forwards.*

Pall-eo, to be pale.

PALE, dim; wan.

PAL'LID, pale; not bright.

PAL'LOR, paleness.

Palli-um, a cloak.

PALL, a covering for the dead.

PAL'LIATE,° to soften; to ease.

Palm-a, the palm of the hand; the palm-tree.

IMPALM', to grasp.

PALMET'TO, a species of the palm-tree.

PALMIF'EROUS, bearing palms.

PAL'MY, flourishing.

PAL'MISTRY, fortune-telling by the palm of the hand.

Palp-o, palpat-um, to touch gently or softly.

IMPAL'PABLE, not to be perceived by touch.

PAL'PABLE, that may be felt.

PAL'PITATE, to beat; to flutter.

Pand-o, pans-um, to open, to spread.

DISPAND', to spread abroad.

EXPAND', to spread; to open.

EXPANSE', wide extent.

EXPAN'SION, a spreading out.

Pan-is, bread.

PANA'DA, bread boiled in water, and sweetened.

PAN'NIER,° a basket carried on a horse.

PAN'TRY, an apartment for provisions.

Pann-us, cloth.

ACCOM'PANY, to go along with.

COM'PANY,° a band; a society.

COMPAN'ION, an associate.

IMPAN'NEL,° to enrol jurors.

PAN'NEL, a kind of rustic saddle.

Pap-as (παπας), a father.

ANTIPA'PAL, opposing popery.

PA'PACY, the office of the pope.

PA'PAL, popish.

POPE, the bishop of Rome.

POPE'DOM, papal jurisdiction.

PAPA', father.

Papill-a, a nipple, a pap.

PAP, food for infants.

PAP'ILLARY, relating to the nipple.

---

*As, *madam*, or "Roma tibi subito motibus ibit amor."

Papyr-us (παπυρος), an Egyptian aquatic plant.

PA'PER, a substance to write on, originally made of Papyrus.

Par, equal, like, match to.

COMPARE', to set side by side; to examine together.
COMPAR'ATIVE, estimated by comparison.
COMPEER', an equal.
DISPAR'AGE,° to cause disgrace.
DISPAR'ITY, inequality.
INCOM'PARABLE, beyond comparison.
NONPAREIL', matchless excellence.
PAIR, a couple.
PAR, state of equality.
PEER'AGE, the rank of a peer.
PEER'LESS, without an equal.

Pardonn-er (Fr.), to pardon.

PAR'DON, to forgive; to remit.
UNPAR'DONABLE, that cannot be pardoned.

Par-eo, parit-um, to appear.

APPEAR', to become visible.
APPA'RENT, visible; evident.
APPARITI'ON, a spectre; a ghost.
DISAPPEAR'ANCE, removal from sight.
TRANSPA'RENT, that can be seen through.

Par-io, part-um, to bring forth.

BIP'AROUS, bringing forth two at a birth.
O'VERT, open to view; public.
O'VERTURE, opening; proposal.
OVIP'AROUS, producing eggs.
PA'RENT, a father or mother.
PARTU'RIATE, to bring forth young.
VERMIP'AROUS, producing worms.

Parl-er (Fr.), to speak.

PAR'LANCE, discourse; talk.
PAR'LEY, a conference.
PAR'LIAMENT,° a supreme legislative council.
PAR'LOR, a room for the reception of company.
PAROLE', word of mouth.

Par-o, parat-um, to prepare.

APPARA'TUS, necessary instruments for any trade or art.
APPAR'EL, dress; clothing.
DISSEV'ER, to part in two.
EM'PEROR, a monarch.
EM'PIRE, the dominion of an emperor.
IMPER'ATIVE, commanding.
IMPE'RIAL, royal.
IMPE'RIOUS, haughty.
INSEP'ARABLE, not to be parted.
IRREP'ARABLE, not to be repaired.
PARADE', show; ostentation.
PREPAR'ATORY, introductory.
REPAIR', to restore; to amend.
REPARA'TION, amends.
SEP'ARABLE, that may be parted.
SEP'ARATE, to divide; to part.
SEV'ER, to force asunder.
SEV'ERAL, many; distinct.

Pars, part-is, a part, a portion.

APART′, at a distance.
APPOR′TION, to divide into just parts.
BIPAR′TITE, divided into two.
COMPART′, to mark out into parts.
COPAR′CENARY, joint inheritance.
COPART′NER, a joint partner.
DEPART′, to go away; to leave.
DEPAR′TURE, a going away.
DISPROPOR′TION, want of symmetry.
IMPART′, to give; to make known.
IMPAR′TIAL, equitable; just.
MISPROPOR′TION, to join without symmetry.
PAR′CEL,° a small bundle.
PARSE, to resolve by grammatical rules.
PART, a portion; a share.
PAR′TIAL, biased to one party.
PARTIC′IPATE, to partake.
PAR′TICIPLE, one of the parts of speech.
PAR′TICLE, a minute part.
PARTIC′ULAR, not general; distinct from others.
PAR′TISAN, an adherent.
PARTITI′ON, a division.
PART′NER, an associate.
PAR′TY, a faction.
POR′TION, a part; an allotment.
PROPOR′TION,° symmetry; size.
PROPOR′TIONATE, in proportion.
REPARTEE′, a witty reply.
TRIP′ARTITE, having three parts.

Parsimoni-a, frugality.

PAR′SIMONY, savingness.
PARSIMO′NIOUS, frugal; sparing.

Pas, pant-os; Pan (πας), all, whole.

PANACE′A, a universal medicine.
PAN′CREAS,° the sweetbread.
PAN′DECT,* a digest of law.
PANDEM′IC, incident to a whole people.
PANDEMO′NIUM, the great hall of the fallen angels.
PANEGYR′IC, a eulogy.
PAN′OPLY, complete armor.
PANORA′MA, a large circular painting.
PAN′THEISM, the doctrine that the universe is God.
PANTHE′ON, a temple dedicated to all the gods.
PAN′TOGRAPH, a machine to copy any sort of drawing or design.
PAN′TOMIME, a play in which only gesture and dumb show are used.
PASIG′RAPHY, a system of writing to be used by all nations.

Pasch-a (πασχα), the passover.

ANTEPAS′CHAL, before the time of Easter.
PAS′CHAL, relating to the passover.

Pasc-o, past-um, to feed.

AN′TEPAST, a foretaste.
PAS′TOR,° a clergyman.
PAS′TORAL, relating to shepherds.
PAS′TURE, land on which cattle graze.
REPAST′, a meal.

---

* *Pandect, all* the words, *all* the sayings. *Pandects*, in the plural, the digest or collection of civil or Roman law, made by order of the Emperor Justinian, and containing 534 decisions or judgments of lawyers, to which the emperor gave the force and authority of law. This compilation consists of fifty books forming the first parts of the civil law.

Pass-us, a pace, a step.

COM'PASS, grasp; space.
ENCOM'PASS, to surround.
OVERPASS', to cross; to omit.
PACE, to measure by steps.
PAS'SAGE, the act of passing; a journey.
PAS'SENGER, a traveller.
PASS'PORT, a permission of passage.
PAS'TIME, sport; amusement.
SURPASS', to excel; to exceed.
TRES'PASS,° an offence.

Pat-eo (πατεω), to tread, to walk.

PATROL', a guard.
PERIPATET'IC, a follower of Aristotle.
PERIPATET'ICISM,* the Peripatetic doctrine.

Pate-o, to be open. PAT'ENT,° an exclusive right.

Pater, patr-is (πατηρ), a father.

COMPA'TRIOT, one of the same country.
EXPA'TRIATE, to banish from one's country.
PAR'RICIDE, the murder of a parent.
PATER'NAL, fatherly; kind.
PA'TER-NOS'TER,° the Lord's prayer.
PATRICI'AN,° a nobleman.
PA'TRIARCH, the father and ruler of a family.
PAT'RIMONY, an inherited estate.
PA'TRIOT, a lover of his country.
PA'TRON,° a supporter.
PAT'RONIZE, to protect; to support.
PATRONYM'IC, a name derived from a father.

Path-os (παθος), feeling.

ANTIP'ATHY, aversion.
AP'ATHY, want of feeling.
APATHET'IC, without feeling.
PA'THOS, passion; warmth.
PATHOL'OGY, the science of diseases.
SYM'PATHY, fellow feeling.

Pati-or, pass-us, to suffer, to endure.

COMPASSI'ON,° pity; sympathy.
DISPASSI'ON, mental coolness.
IMPAS'SIBLE, incapable of suffering.
IMPASSI'ONED, strongly affected.
IMPA'TIENT, hasty; eager.
INCOMPASSI'ONATE, void of tenderness.
PASSI'ON,° anger; zeal.
PAS'SIVE,° unresisting.
PA'TIENCE, calm endurance.
UNIMPASSI'ONED, calm; unmoved.

Pauper, poor.

IMPOV'ERISH, to make poor.
PAU'PER, a poor person.
POOR, indigent; lean.
POV'ERTY, indigence; want.

---

* Aristotle was the founder of this sect of philosophers. They were called *peripatetics*, because their great teacher delivered his instructions, *walking up and down* the shaded paths of the Lyceum, a public grove at Athens.

Pax, pac-is, peace.

APPEASE', to quiet; to still.
PAC'IFY, to appease; to quiet.
PACIFICA'TION, the act of making peace.
PEACE, quiet; rest.

Pecc-o, to do wrong, to sin.

IMPEC'CABLE, not liable to sin.
PECCADIL'LO, a petty fault.
PEC'CANT, sinning; guilty.

Pect-us, pector-is, the breast.

EXPEC'TORATE, to eject from the breast.
PAR'APET, a wall breast-high.
PEC'TORAL, belonging to the breast.

Peculi-um, private property.

PECU'LIAR, particular; appropriate; belonging to.

Pecul-or, peculat-us, to steal public property.

PEC'ULATE, to embezzle.
PECULA'TION, embezzlement.

Pecuni-a, money. PECU'NIARY, relating to money.

Pedi-a (παιδεια), learning.

PED'AGOGUE, a schoolmaster.
PED'ANT, a man vain of low knowledge.
PED'ANTRY, vain show of learning.
PEDOBAP'TIST, one that holds to infant baptism.

Pelag-us, the sea.

ARCHIPEL'AGO, any sea which abounds in small islands.

Pell-o, pellat-um, to call, to name.

APPEAL', to refer to another tribunal.
APPEL'LANT, one that appeals.
APPELLA'TION, a name; a title.
REPEAL', to recall; to revoke.

Pell-o, puls-um, to drive, to strike.

APPULSE', a striking against.
COMPEL', to force; to oblige.
COMPUL'SORY, forcing.
COMPUL'SION, force; constraint.
DISPEL', to drive away.
EXPEL', to drive out.
EXPUL'SION, act of driving out.
IMPEL', to urge forward.
IM'PULSE, force given.
IMPUL'SIVE, causing to move.
PROPEL', to drive forward.
PROPUL'SION, the act of driving forward.
PULSE, the throbbing of the arteries.
PULSA'TION, a beating; a throbbing.
REPEL', to drive back.
REPULSE', a rejection.
REPUL'SIVE, driving off; forbidding.

Pend-eo, pens-um, to hang.

APPEND', to hang or join to.
APPEND'ANT, annexed to.
APPEND'IX, something appended.
DEPEND', to hang from; to rely.
DEPEND'ENCE, trust; reliance.
IMPEND', to hang over.
INDEPEND'ENT, free; not controlled.
PEND'ENT, hanging.
PEND'ULUM, a vibrating body.
PEN'SILE, suspended.
PERPENDIC'ULAR, directly down wards.
PREPENSE', preconceived.
PROPENS'ITY,° inclination.
SUSPEND', to hang; to interrupt.
SUSPENSE', uncertainty.
SUSPEN'SION, a hanging up.

Pend-o, pens-um, to weigh, to lay out.

COMPEND'IUM, an abridgment.
COM'PENSATE,° to requite.
DISPENS'ARY, the place where medicines are given to the poor.
DISPENSA'TION,° distribution.
DISPENSE', to deal out.
EXPEND', spend; to lay out.
EXPEND'ITURE, amount expended.
EXPENSE', cost; charges.
EXPENS'IVE, lavish; costly.
INDISPENS'ABLE, not to be omitted or spared.
PEN'SIVE, serious.
PEN'SION an annual allowance.
PEN'SIONARY, one who receives a pension.
REC'OMPENSE, a reward.
STI'PEND, wages; stated pay.

Pen-e, almost.

ANTEPENULT'IMATE, the last syllable but two.
PENIN'SULA, a piece of land almost surrounded by water.
PENUM'BRA, a partial shade.
PENULT', the last syllable of a word but one.

Penetr-o, penetrat-um, to pierce, or enter into.

IMPEN'ETRABLE, that cannot be penetrated.
PEN'ETRATE, to pierce; to enter.
PENETRA'TION, sagacity.

Penit-eo, *for* **_Pœniteo,_** to repent. **_Pœna,_** punishment.

IMPEN'ITENT,° obdurate.
PAIN, uneasy sensation.
PE'NAL, enacting punishment.
PEN'ALTY, punishment.
PEN'ANCE, voluntary suffering on account of sin.
PEN'ITENT, contrite for sin.
PENITEN'TIARY, a prison.
REPENT', to sorrow for sin.
SUBPŒ'NA, a writ commanding attendance at court.

Penn-a, a feather, a wing.

BIPEN'NATE, having two wings.
PEN, an instrument of writing.
PEN'NATE, winged.
PEN'NIFORM, quill-shaped.

Pent-e (πεντε), five.

PEN'TACHORD, a musical instrument with five strings.
PEN'TAGON, a plane figure with five angles.

PENTAM'ETER, a verse of five feet.
PENTAN'GULAR, five-cornered.
PEN'TATEUCH, the five books of Moses.
PEN'TECOST,* a Jewish feast.

Penuri-a, want, scarcity.

PEN'URY, extreme poverty.
PENU'RIOUS, sparing; scanty.

Pept-os (πεπτος), boiled, digested.

DYSPEP'SY, difficulty of digestion.
EUPEP'TIC, having good digestion.

Pericul-um, danger.

PER'IL, danger; hazard.
PER'ILOUS, full of peril.

Peri-or, perit-us, to try, to prove.

EXPER'IMENT, trial.
EXPE'RIENCE, to know by trial.
EXPERT',° skilful; prompt.
INEXPE'RIENCE, want of experience.
UNEXPERT', wanting skill.

Perpes, perpet-is, entire, never-ceasing.

PERPET'UAL, never-ceasing.
PERPET'UATE, to make perpetual.
PERPETU'ITY, duration to all futurity.

Persever-o, to persist. PERSEVERE', to persist, to continue.

Person-a, a mask used by players; a person.

IMPER'SONAL, not varied by person. (In grammar.)
PER'SONATE, to represent.
PER'SON, a human being.
PERSON'IFY, to change from a thing to a person.

Pes, ped-is, the foot, a foot.

BI'PED, a two-footed animal.
CAP-A-PIE,' from head to foot.
DECEM'PEDAL, ten feet in length.
EXPE'DIENT, device; means.
EX'PEDITE,° to facilitate.
EXPEDITI'OUS, quick.
IMPEDE',° to hinder.
IMPED'IMENT, hindrance.
INEXPE'DIENT, unfit; improper.
PED'ESTAL, the base of a pillar or statue.
PEDES'TRIAN, going on foot.
PED'ICLE,° the foot-stalk.
PED'IGREE,° lineage; descent.
PEDOM'ETER, an instrument for measuring distances by paces.
PEDUN'CLE, the stem of the flower and fruit.
PET'IOLE, a leaf-stalk.
QUAD'RUPED, a four-footed animal.
TRIP'EDAL, having three feet.

Pest-is, a plague, an infection.

ANTIPESTILEN'TIAL, efficacious against the plague.
PEST, a plague; an annoyance.
PESTIF'EROUS, noxious to health.
PES'TILENCE, a contagious distemper.

---

* *Pentecost*—so called because it was celebrated on the *fiftieth* day after the sixteenth of the month Nisan, which was the second day of the passover.

Petal-on (πεταλον), a flower leaf.

APET'ALOUS, without petals.
BIPET'ALOUS, having two petals.
PET'AL, a flower-leaf.
MONOPET'ALOUS, having but one petal.
POLYPET'ALOUS, having many petals.

Petit (Fr.), little, small.

PET'TIFOGGER, a petty lawyer.
PET'TY, small, little.

Pet-o, petit-um, to seek, to ask.

AP'PETITE,° desire; hunger.
CENTRIP'ETAL, tending to the centre.
COMPAT'IBLE,° consistent.
COMPETE', to rival.
COM'PETENCE, sufficiency.
COMPET'ITOR, a rival.
IM'PETUS,° force from motion.
IMPET'UOUS, violent; fierce.
INCOM'PETENT, not adequate.
PETITI'ON, entreaty.
REPEAT', to do again; to recite.
REPETEND', the number to be repeated.

Petr-a (πετρα), a rock, a stone.

PE'TER, a man's name.
PETRES'CENT, turning to stone.
PET'RIFY, to harden.
PETRIFAC'TION, the process of turning to stone.
SALTPE'TRE,° a mineral salt.

Petro, petrat-um, to commit. PER'PETRATE, to commit.

Petulans, petulant-is, saucy. PET'ULANT, fretful; saucy.

Phag-o (φαγω), to eat.

ANTHROPOPH'AGI, man-eaters; cannibals.
ICHTHYOPH'AGY, the practice of eating fish.
SARCOPH'AGUS,* a sort of stone coffin.

Phan-o, or *Phen-o* (φαινω), to appear; to show; to tell.

BLAS'PHEMY, impious language.
DIAPH'ANOUS, transparent.
EM'PHASIS, stress laid on a word or sentence.
EMPHAT'IC, forcible.
EPIPH'ANY,† the manifestation.
PHAN'TASM, a fancied appearance.
FANTAS'TIC, whimsical.
PHAN'TOM, an apparition.
FAN'CY,° imagination; whim.
PHÆ'TON,° a high open carriage.
PHASE, an appearance as of the moon.
PHENOM'ENON,° an appearance.
PROPH'ECY, a foretelling.
PROPH'ET, a foreteller.
PSEU'DO-PROPH'ET, a false prophet.
SYC'OPHANT,° a low flatterer.

---

* This word is derived from the name of a calcareous stone (λιθος σαρκοφαγος), anciently used by the Greeks, which decomposed the bodies deposited in it in a very short time.

† *Epiphany*, a Christian festival celebrated on 6th January, the 12th day after Christmas, in commemoration of the *appearance* of our Saviour to the wise men or philosophers of the east who came to adore him with presents; or of the *manifestation* of Christ to the Gentiles.

Pharmac-on (φαρμακον), a medicine or drug.

PHARMACEU'TIC, relating to pharmacy.
PHARMACOL'OGY, the knowledge of drugs.
PHARMACOP'OLIST, a druggist.
PHAR'MACY, the art of preparing medicines.

Pher-o (φερω), to carry, to bring.

MET'APHOR,° a short similitude.
METAPHOR'ICAL, figurative.
PERIPH'ERY,° circumference.
PHOS'PHORUS, a luminous substance.
PHOSPHORES'CENT, shining.

Phil-os (φιλος), a lover.

PHILADEL'PHIA, brotherly love.
PHILAN'THROPIST, one who loves mankind.
PHILOL'OGY,° the knowledge and study of language.
PHIL'OMATH, a lover of learning.
PHILOME'LA, the nightingale.
PHILOS'OPHY,° knowledge; the study of general laws.
PHILOS'OPHIZE, to reason.

Phlegm-a (φλεγμα), a burning; dulness.

ANTIPHLOGIS'TIC, counteracting inflammation.
PHLEGMAT'IC,° dull; cold.
PHLOGIS'TON, the principle of inflammability.

Phleps, phleb-os (φλεψ), a vein.

PHLEBOT'OMY, the art of blood-letting.

Phob-os (φοβος), fear, dread.

HYDROPHO'BIA, a dread of water; canine madness.

Phon-e (φωνη), a sound, a voice.

CACOPH'ONY, harshness of sound.
EU'PHONY, agreeable sound.
PHONOL'OGY, the science of sounds.
SYM'PHONY, harmony of sounds.

Phos, phot-os (φος), light, fire.

PHOS'PHOR, the morning star.
PHOSPHORES'CENCE, faint luminousness.
PHOTOM'ETER, an instrument to measure the intensity of light.

Phras-is (φρασις), a saying, a speech.

PAR'APHRASE, an explanation in other words.
PER'IPHRASE, circumlocution.
PHRASE, an expression; a short sentence.
PHRASEOL'OGY, style; diction.

Phren (φρην), the mind.

FRAN'TIC, PHRENET'IC, mad; raving.
FREN'ZY, madness.
PHRENOL'OGY, the science of the mind as connected with the brain.

Phtheg-ma (φθεγμα), a saying.

AP'OPHTHEGM, a remarkable saying.
APOTHEGMAT'ICAL, containing apothegms.
DIPH'THONG, a union of two vowels in one sound.
TRIPH'THONG, a union of three vowels in one sound.

Phyll-on (φυλλον), a leaf.

MONOPH'YLLOUS, having one leaf only.

Phys-is (φυσις), a bringing forth, nature.

EPIPH'YSIS,° a growing upon.
METAPHYS'ICS,° the science of mind.
NE'OPHYTE,° a new convert.
PHYSICI'AN, a professor of medicine.
PHYS'ICS, natural philosophy.
PHYS'ICAL, natural; not moral.
PHYSIOG'NOMY, the art of discovering the temper by the face.
PHYSIOL'OGY, the science of animals and plants.
SYM'PHYSIS,° a growing together.

Phyt-on (φυτον), a plant.

PHYTIV'OROUS, eating plants.
PHYTOG'RAPHY, a description of plants.
ZO'OPHYTE, a body partaking of the nature of both animal and vegetable.

Pignus, pignor-is, a pawn, a pledge.

IMPIG'NORATE, to pledge.
PAWN, something given as security.

Pil-o, pilat-um, to pillage, to rob.

COMPILE', to collect from various authors.
COMPILA'TION, a collection.
PIL'FER, to steal.
PIL'LAGE, plunder; spoil.

Ping-o, pict-um, to paint.

DEPICT', to paint; to describe.
PAINT, to describe; to color.
PICTS,* ancient inhabitants of Scotland.
PICTO'RIAL, containing pictures.
PIC'TURE, a painting.
PICTURESQUE', like a picture.
PIG'MENT, paint; color.

Pi-o, piat-um, to atone for.

EX'PIATE, to atone for.
EX'PIATORY, for atonement.
INEX'PIABLE, that cannot be atoned for.
PIAC'ULAR, expiatory.

Pirat-es (πειρατης), (*ab* **Peirao,** to try), a sea robber.

EM'PIRIC,° a quack.
EMPIR'ICISM, quackery.
PI'RACY, robbery on the sea.
PI'RATE, a sea robber.

---

* They were so called because they painted their bodies, to give them a formidable appearance to their enemies.

N

Pisc-is, a fish.

PIS'CARY, a privilege of fishing.
PIS'CATORY, relating to fishes.
PISCIV'OROUS, fish eating.

Pius, pious, religious. ***Piet-as***, piety.

IMPI'ETY, want of piety.
IM'PIOUS, wicked.
PI'OUS, godly; religious.
PI'ETIST,° one who professes great purity of life.

Plac-eo, to please.

COMPLA'CENCY, calm satisfaction.
COM'PLAISANT, pleasing in manners.
DISPLEASE', to make angry.
PLAC'ID, gentle; quiet.
PLEASE, to delight; to gratify.
PLEAS'ANT, gay; agreeable.
PLEAS'ANTRY, gayety; mirth.
PLEAS'URE, delight; choice.

Plac-o, to appease; to pacify.

IMPLA'CABLE, not to be appeased.

Plagi-um, a literary theft.

PLA'GIARY, a thief in literature.
PLA'GIARISM, literary theft.

Plan-e (πλανη), a wandering about.

PLAN'ET,° a wandering celestial body.
PLAN'ETARY, pertaining to the planets.

Plang-o, planct-um, to beat, to bemoan.

COMPLAIN', to murmur; to lament.
COMPLAINT', PLAINT, a lamentation; a murmuring.
PLAGUE, to infest; to tease.
PLAIN'TIFF,° he that commences a lawsuit.
PLAIN'TIVE, lamenting.

Plant-a, the sole of the foot; a plant.

DISPLANT', to pluck up.
IMPLANT', to insert; to engraft.
PLANT, any vegetable.
PLANTA'TION, a farm; a colony.
REPLANT', to plant anew.
SUPPLANT',° to displace.
TRANSPLANT', to move and plant in another place.

Plan-us, plain, smooth; evident.

COMPLANE', to level.
EXPLAIN', to expound; to make clear.
EXPLANA'TION, act of explaining.
PLAIN, flat; clear.
PLANE, to level; to smooth.

Plass-o (πλασσω), to smear, to form in clay.

CAT'APLASM, a poultice.
COSMOPLAS'TIC, forming the world.
PLAS'TIC, giving form.
PLAS'TER, lime to cover walls.

Plato, platon-is (Πλατων), an Athenian philosopher.

PLATON'IC, relating to Plato.
PLA'TONIST, a follower of Plato.

Plaud-o, plaus-um, to praise by clapping hands.

APPLAUD', to praise; to extol.
APPLAUSE', approbation.
EXPLODE', to drive out; to burst.
EXPLO'SION, a sudden bursting.
PLAU'DIT, loud praise.
PLAU'SIBLE,° specious; seemingly right.

Plebs, pleb-is, the common people. PLEBE'IAN, vulgar; low.

Plect-os (πληκτος), struck, seized.

AP'OPLEXY, a sudden loss of sense and the power of motion.
APOPLEC'TIC, relating to apoplexy.

Plen-us, full.

PLE'NARY, full; complete.
PLENIPOTEN'TIARY, a negotiator invested with full power.
PLEN'ITUDE, fulness; repletion
PLEN'TY, abundance.
REPLEN'ISH, to stock; to fill.

Ple-o, plet-um (πλεω), to fill.

ACCOM'PLISH, to execute; to finish.
COM'PLEMENT, full quantity.
COMPLETE', perfect; full.
COMPLE'TION, perfect state.
COM'PLIMENT,°an act of civility.
EX'PLETIVE, a word used to fill a vacancy.
IM'PLEMENT,°a tool; a utensil.
INCOMPLETE', not finished.
MAN'IPLE, a handful.
MANIPULA'TION, manual operation.
PLE'ONASM, a redundancy of words.
REPLETE', full.
SUP'PLEMENT, an addition.
SUP'PLETORY, supplying.
SUPPLY', to fill up; to furnish.

Pleur-a (πλευρα), the side, a rib.

PLEU'RISY,°an inflammation of the pleura.

Plic-o, plicat-um (πλεκω), to fold, to knit.

ACCOM'PLICE,° an associate in crime.
APPLY',°to put to; to suit to.
APPLI'ANCE, the thing applied.
AP'PLICABLE, suitable.
AP'PLICANT, he who applies.
APPLICA'TION, great industry.
COM'PLEX, intricate; entangled.
COMPLEX'ION, the color of the skin and features.
COM'PLICATE,°to entangle.
COMPLY', to yield to.
COMPLI'ANCE, submission.
DEC'UPLE, tenfold.
DISPLAY', to exhibit.
DOUB'LE, to make twice as great.
DU'PLICATE, double.
DUPLIC'ITY, deceit.
EXPLICA'TION, explanation.
EXPLIC'IT,°plain; clear.
IMPLY',°to express indirectly.
IMPLICA'TION, a tacit inference.
IMPLIC'IT, resting on; trusting.
INAP'PLICABLE, unfit.
INEX'PLICABLE, incapable of being explained.
MISAPPLY', to apply to wrong purposes.
MUL'TIPLE, a number which exactly contains another several times.
MUL'TIPLY, to make many fold.
MULTIPLICAND', the number to be multiplied.
MULTIPLIC'ITY, great variety.
PERPLEX',°to entangle; to vex.

PERPLEX'ITY, distraction of mind.
PLEX'US,* a net-work.
PLI'ABLE, flexible; pliant.
PLI'ANT, yielding; easily bent.
PLY, to work on closely.
PLI'ERS, small pincers.
QUAD'RUPLE, four-fold.
QUIN'TUPLE, five-fold.
REDU'PLICATE, to double.
REPLY', to answer.
REPLICA'TION, a reply.
SEX'TUPLE, six-fold.
SIM'PLE, plain; artless.
SIM'PLETON, a silly person.
SIMPLIC'ITY, plainness; singleness.
SIM'PLIFY, to render easy.
SUP'PLIANT,° a petitioner.
SUP'PLICATE, to implore.
SUP'PLICANT, entreating.
TRIP'LE, three-fold.
TREB'LE, to multiply by three.

Plor-o, plorat-um, to cry out, to wail.

DEPLORE', to bewail; to mourn.
DEPLO'RABLE, lamentable; sad.
EXPLORE', to search into.
EXPLORA'TION, examination.
IMPLORE', to entreat; to beg.
UNDEPLORED', not lamented.

Plum-a, a feather.

PLUME, a feather.
PLU'MAGE, feathers.

Plumb-um, lead, a leaden bullet.

PLUMB, a plummet.
PLUMBA'GO, black lead.
PLUMBIF'EROUS, yielding lead.
PLUM'MET, a weight of lead attached to a string.
PLUMB'ER, a worker in lead

Plus, plur-is, more.

NON'PLUS, to bring to a stand.
PLU'RAL, implying more than one.
PLUS, increased by; added to.
SUR'PLUS, that which remains over a certain quantity.

Plut-o, pluton-is, king of the infernal regions.

PLUTON'IC, relating to Pluto.
PLU'TONIST, one who believes that the earth was at first a melted mass.

Pluvi-a, rain.

PLU'VIAL, relating to rain.
PLUVIAM'ETER, a rain-gage.

Pneuma, pneumat-os (πνευμα), wind, breath, spirit.

PNEUMAT'ICS,° the science of the air, or gases.
PNEUMATOL'OGY, the doctrine of spiritual substances.

Poie-o (ποιεω), to make, to compose.

PO'EM, a metrical composition.
PO'ESY, poetry; verse.
PO'ET, a writer of poems.
UNPOET'ICAL, not proper to poetry.

Polem-os (πολεμος), war, a battle. POLEM'IC, a disputant.

---

* *Plexus*, in Anatomy, any union of vessels, nerves, or fibres, in the form of a net-work.

Pol-eo (πωλεω), to sell.

BIBLIOP'OLIST, a bookseller.
MONOP'OLY, exclusive sale.
MONOP'OLIZE, to engross.
PHARMACOP'OLIST, a druggist.

Pol-is (πολις), a city.

CONSTAN'TINOPLE, the city of Constantine.
COSMOP'OLITE, a citizen of the world.
IMPOL'ICY, imprudence.
IMPOLITE', rude; uncivil.
INTER'POLATE, to insert a spurious word or passage.
METROP'OLIS, the chief city.

Polio, polit-um, to polish.

POLICE', the government of a city.
POL'ISH, to smooth; to brighten.
POLITE', refined; genteel.
POLIT'ICAL, relating to politics.
POL'ITICS, the science of government.
POL'ITY, form of government.

Pollens, pollent-is, powerful.

EQUIPOL'LENT, having equal power.

Pol-us, the pole.

CIRCUMPO'LAR, round the pole.
POLAR'ITY, tendency to the pole.
POLE, the end of the earth's axis.

Poly (πολυ), many.

POLYANTH'OS, a plant which produces many flowers.
POLYG'AMY, a plurality of wives.
POL'YGLOT, having many languages.
POL'YGON, a figure having many angles.
POL'YGRAM, a figure having many lines.
POLYNE'SIA, a division of the earth, consisting of many isles.
POL'YPUS, a sea animal with many feet.
POLYSPERM'OUS, having many seeds.
POLYSYLLAB'IC, having many syllables.
POLYTECH'NIC, comprehending many arts.
POL'YTHEISM, the doctrine of a plurality of gods.

Pomp-a, a solemn procession.

POMP, show; parade.
POMPOS'ITY, ostentation.

Pom-um, an apple.

POM'ACE, the substance of apples or similar fruit ground.
POMEGRAN'ATE,° a kind of fruit.
POM'MEL,° a knob or ball.

Pond-us, ponder-is, weight.

COUN'TERPOISE, to balance; to equal.
EQUIPON'DERANCE, equality of weight.
IMPON'DERABLE, that cannot be weighed.
POISE, to weigh; to balance.
PON'DER,° to consider.
PON'DEROUS, heavy.
POUND, a weight.
PREPON'DERATE, to outweigh

Pon-o, posit-um, to put, or place.

Ap'posite,° fit; appropriate.
Ap'ropos, opportunely.
Compo'nent, forming part of a compound body.
Compose', to put together; to settle.
Compos'itor, one who sets types.
Com'post,° manure; any mixture.
Compo'sure, tranquillity.
Compound', to mingle; to adjust.
Decompose', to take apart.
Decompound', to decompose.
Depo'nent,° a witness on oath.
Depose', to put down; to divest.
Depos'it, to lodge; to place.
Depositi'on, the act of giving testimony on oath.
De'pot, a place of deposit.
Discompose', to disorder; to vex.
Dispo'sal, regulation; control.
Dispositi'on, temper of mind.
Expose', to lay open.
Expos'itor, an explainer.
Expo'sure, act of exposing.
Expound', to explain; to clear.
Impose', to lay on.
Impositi'on, constraint; cheat.
Im'post,° a tax; a toll.
Impos'tor,° a deceiver.
Indispose', to make unfit.
Interpose', to place between.
Malap'ropos, unsuitably.
Oppo'nent, an adversary.
Op'posite, adverse.
Positi'on, situation; place.
Pos'itive,° absolute; certain.
Post,° station; office.
Postpone', to put off; to delay.
Pos'ture, state; attitude.
Predispos'ed, previously inclined.
Prepositi'on, a part of speech.
Presuppose', to suppose beforehand.
Propo'sal, an offer.
Propositi'on, a thing proposed.
Propound', to offer; to exhibit.
Prov'ost, a chief officer.
Pur'pose, intention; design.
Recompose', to form anew.
Repose', to rest; to place.
Repos'itory, a place for laying up things.
Suppose', to imagine; to think.
Transpose', to put out of place.
Transpositi'on, the act of transposing.

Pons, pont-is, a bridge.

Pont'age, duty paid for repairing bridges.
Pont'iff,° a high-priest; the pope.
Pontif'ical, relating to the pontiff or pope.
Pontoon',° a boat used for making bridges.

Popul-us, the people. *Public-us,* public.

Depop'ulate, to deprive of inhabitants; to lay waste.
Dispeo'ple, to depopulate.
Peo'ple, a nation; persons.
Pop'ulace, the common people.
Pop'ular, pleasing to the people.
Popular'ity, the favor of the people.
Pop'ulous, full of inhabitants.
Popula'tion, the whole people of a country or place.
Pub'lic,° common; open.
Publica'tion, the act of publishing.
Public'ity, notoriety.
Pub'lish, to make known.
Repeo'ple, to people anew.
Repub'lic, a free state.

Porc-us, a hog.

POR'CINE, relating to swine.
POR'CUPINE, a kind of large hedgehog.
PORK, swine's flesh.
POR'PUS, the sea-hog.

Por-os (πορος), a passage or way.

EMPO'RIUM,° a place of commerce.
PORE, a small passage in the skin.
PO'ROUS, having pores.
POROS'ITY, the quality of having pores.

Porphyr-a (πορφυρα), purple. POR'PHYRY,° a kind of marble.

Porr-o, forth, farther.

PORTEND', to foretoken.
PORTENT', an omen of ill.

Porr-um, a leek, a scallion.

POR'RIDGE, a kind of broth.
POR'RINGER, a dish for soup.

Port-o, portat-um, to carry, to import.

COMPORT', to suit; to bear.
DEPORT'MENT, conduct; bearing.
EXPORT', to carry out.
IMPORT'ANT,° weighty; forcible.
IMPORT'ER, one who brings in goods from abroad.
IMPORTUNE',° to solicit earnestly.
IMPORT'UNACY, the act of importuning.
INOPPORTUNE', unseasonable.
INSUPPORT'ABLE, not to be endured.
OPPORTU'NITY, a fit place; occasion.
PORT, a harbor.
PORT'ABLE, that may be carried.
PORT'LY, bulky; swelling.
POR'TAL, a gate; a door.
PORTCUL'LIS,° a sort of drawbridge.
PORT-FO'LIO, a case for loose papers.
PORTMAN'TEAU, a portable bag for clothes.
RE-EXPORT', to export what has been imported.
REPORT', a rumor.
SUPPORT', to bear; to uphold.
TRANSPORTA'TION, conveyance.

Poss-e, pot-ui, to be able.

BELLIP'OTENT, mighty in war.
DISPOSSESS', to put out of possession.
IMPOS'SIBLE, that cannot be.
IM'POTENCE, want of power.
OMNIP'OTENCE, almighty power.
PLENIPOTEN'TIARY, a negotiator invested with full power.
POS'SE, an armed power.
POSSESSI'ON, property.
PO'TENT, powerful; strong.
PO'TENTATE, a monarch; a prince.
POW'ER, authority; force.
PREPOSSESSED', biased.
PUIS'SANT, forcible; potent.

Poster-us, after, that comes after.

POSTE'RIOR, later.
POSTER'ITY, succeeding generations.
POS'TERN,° a small gate; a door.
PREPOS'TEROUS, absurd; foolish

Postul-o, postulat-um, to ask.

EXPOS'TULATE, to remonstrate.
POSTULA'TUM, a thing required.

Potam-os (ποταμος), a river. HIPPOPOT'AMUS, the river-horse.

Pot-o, potat-um, to drink.

COM'POTATOR, a fellow-drinker.
PO'TION, a draught.

Pous, pod-os (πους ποδος), the foot, a foot.

ANTIP'ODES, those on the opposite side of the globe, whose feet are opposite to ours.
POL'YPUS, a sea animal with many feet.
TRI'POD,° a seat with three feet.

Pract-os (πρακτος), done. ***Pragma*** (πραγμα), a deed.

IMPRAC'TICABLE, that cannot be done.
MALEPRAC'TICE, evil doing.
PRAC'TICABLE, that can be done.
PRAC'TICE,° habit; use.
PRACTITI'ONER, he who is engaged in any art.
PRAGMAT'IC, impertinent; meddling.

Prav-us, crooked; wicked.

DEPRAVE', to corrupt; to debase.
DEPRAV'ITY, corruption.

Preci-um, *for* ***Prætium,*** a price, worth.

APPRAISE', to set a price upon.
APPRE'CIATE, to estimate.
DEPRECIA'TION, a falling in value.
PRAISE, to commend; to applaud.
PRECI'OUS, of great value.
PRICE, value; rate.
PRIZE, to value highly.

Prec-or, precat-us, to pray, to entreat.

DEP'RECABLE, to be deprecated.
DEP'RECATE, to pray against.
IMPRECA'TION, a curse.
PRAY, to supplicate.
PREACH,° to proclaim; to teach.
PRECA'RIOUS,° uncertain.

Pred-a, *for* ***Præda,*** prey, plunder.

DEP'REDATE, to rob; to pillage.
PRE'DAL, practising plunder.
PRED'ATORY, rapacious.
PREY, rapine; ravage.

Prehend-o, prehens-um, to take hold of, to seize.

APPREHEND', to seize; to fear.
APPREHEN'SION, seizure; fear.
APPREN'TICE, one bound to learn an art or trade.
APPRISE', to give notice.
COMPREHEND',° to include; to understand.
COMPREHEN'SIVE, capacious; full.
COMPRISE', to include.
EN'TERPRISE, an undertaking.
IMPREG'NABLE, not to be taken.
INCOMPREHEN'SIBLE, not to be understood.
IMPRIS'ON, to confine.
IRREPREHEN'SIBLE, blameless.
MISAPPREHEND', to misunderstand.
PREHEN'SILE, grasping.
PRENSA'TION, the act of seizing.
PRIS'ON, a place of confinement.
PRIZE,° reward; plunder.
REPREHEND',° to reprove.
REPREHEN'SION, reproof.
REPRI'SAL, a seizure in retaliation.
REPRIEVE', to respite.
SURPRISE',° to astonish.

Prem-o, press-um, to press.

COMPRESS', to press together.
DEPRESSI'ON, dejection.
EXPRESS', to utter; to press out.
EXPRESS'IVE, serving to express.
IMPRESS', to stamp; to fix deep.
IMPRESSI'ON, a stamp; influence.
IMPRIMA'TUR, a license to print.
IMPRINT', to press on.
INEXPRESS'IBLE, not to be told.
OPPRESS', to crush by severity.
PRESS, to squeeze; to urge.
PRINT, a mark made by types.
REPRESS', to subdue; to quell.
SUPPRESS', to put down.

Presbyter-os (πρεσβυτερος), older, a priest.

PRES'BYTERY, a body of elders.
PRESBYTE'RIAN, one who holds to church government by presbyters.

Prim-us, first. ***Princeps, princip-is,*** a prince.

IMPRI'MIS, in the first place.
PREM'IER, a prime minister.
PRIM, formal; precise.
PRI'MACY, the office of primate.
PRI'MARY, first; chief.
PRI'MATE, the chief ecclesiastic in a church.
PRIME, best; principal.
PRIM'ER, a child's first book.
PRIM'ITIVE, original.
PRIMOGEN'ITURE, state of being first-born of a family.
PRIN'CIPLE, fundamental truth; motive.
PRIMOR'DIAL, first in order.
PRINCE, a king's son.
PRIN'CIPAL, chief; essential.
PRINCIP'IA, first principles.
PRI'OR, former; anterior.
PRI'ORY, a convent.
PRIS'TINE, first; original.

Prism-a, prismat-os (πρισμα), a prism.

PRISM, an optical glass.
PRISMAT'IC, formed as a prism.
PRIS'MOID, a body having the shape of a prism.

Priv-us, single, one's own.

DEPRIVE', to take from.
PRI'VACY, secrecy; retirement.
PRI'VATE, secret; secluded.
PRIVA'TION, loss; absence.
PRIVATEER', a private ship of war.
PRIV'ILEGE, a peculiar benefit.
PRIV'Y, secret; private.

Prob-o, probat-um, to prove, to try.

APPROVE', to commend.
APPROBA'TION, act of approving.
DISAPPROVE', to censure.
DISPROVE', to prove false.
IMPROB'ABLE, unlikely.
IMPROB'ITY, dishonesty.
IMPROVE'MENT, a growing better.
PROB'ABLE, likely.
PRO'BATE, the proof of a will.
PROBA'TIONER, one upon trial.
PROBE, to search; to pierce.
PROB'ITY, honesty.
PROOF, evidence; test.
PROVE, to evince; to test.
REP'ROBATE, lost to virtue.
REPROVE', to blame; to chide.
REPROOF', open censure.

Probr-um, a shameful action; disgrace.

EX'PROBRATE, to upbraid.
OPPRO'BRIOUS, reproachful.

Prodigi-um, a prodigy.

PROD'IGY, a monster; a portent. | PRODIGI'OUS, vast; amazing.

Prol-es, an offspring or progeny. PROLIF'IC, fruitful.

Propag-o, a shoot, an offspring.

PROP'AGATE, to extend; to spread.
PROPAGAND'IST, one who zealously propagates any doctrines.

Prop-e, near; **Proxim-us,** nearest; next.

APPROX'IMATE, to draw near.
APPROACH', to go or come near to.
IRREPROACH'ABLE, free from blame.
PROPIN'QUITY, neighborhood.
PROPIT'IATE,° to conciliate.
PROPITI'OUS, favorable.
PROX'IMATE, next; nearest.
PROXIM'ITY, nearness.
REPROACH', to censure.

Propri-us, peculiar, one's own, fit.

APPRO'PRIATE, peculiar; fit.
APPROPRIA'TION, application to a particular purpose.
IMPROP'ER, unbecoming.
IMPROPRI'ETY, unfitness.
PROP'ER, natural; fit.
PROP'ERTY, an estate; goods.
PROPRI'ETARY, an owner.
PROPRI'ETY, fitness; justness.

Pros-a, prose.

PROSE, language without poetic measure.
PROSA'IC, belonging to prose.

Proselyt-os (προσηλυτος), one newly arrived.

PROS'ELYTE, a convert to a new opinion.
PROS'ELYTISM, zeal to make converts.

Prosper, successful.

PROS'PER, to thrive.
PROSPER'ITY, success; welfare.
UNPROS'PEROUS, not fortunate; wanting success.

Prote-us, a marine deity.

PRO'TEAN, like Proteus; able to change into different shapes.

Prot-os (πρωτος), first.

PROTHON'OTARY, the head registrar.
PRO'TOCOL,° the original copy.
PRO'TOTYPE, an exemplar; a model.

Pruri-o, to itch.

PRU'RIENCE, an itching desire.
PRURIG'ENOUS, tending to the itch.

Psalm-a (ψαλμα), a sacred song.

PSAL'MIST, a writer of psalms.
PSAL'MODY, a singing of psalms.
PSAL'TERY, a kind of harp.
PSALMOG'RAPHY, the art of writing psalms.

Pseud-os (ψευδος), falsehood.

PSEU'DOGRAPH, false writing.

PSEU'DO-PROPH'ET, a false prophet.

Psych-e (ψυχη), the breath, the soul.

METEMPSYCHO'SIS,* transmigration of souls.

PSYCHOL'OGY, the science which treats of the nature of the soul.

Ptom-a (πτωμα), a fall.

AS'YMPTOTE, a line approaching a curve, but never meeting it.

MON'OPTOTE,† a noun used only in one oblique case.

SYMP'TOM,° a token; an indication.

TRIP'TOTE, a noun used but in three cases.

Pty-o (πτυω), to spit. **Ptysm-a** (πτυσμα), spittle.

HEMOP'TYSIS, the spitting of blood.

PTYS'MAGOGUE, a medicine that promotes the flow of spittle.

Pud-eo, to be ashamed.

IM'PUDENT, saucy; shameless.

PUDIC'ITY, modesty, chastity.

REPU'DIATE, to put away; to reject.

Puer, a boy.

PU'ERILE, childish; trifling.

PUERIL'ITY, childishness.

Pugn-a, a fight, a battle.

EXPUGNA'TION, the act of taking by assault.

IMPUGN', to attack; to oppose.

INEXPUG'NABLE, not to be taken by assault.

OPPUGN', to oppose; to assault.

PU'GILISM, boxing.

PUGNA'CIOUS, fond of fighting.

REPUG'NANCE, opposition of mind.

Pull-us, a chick, a bud.

POUL'TRY, domestic fowls.

PUL'LET, a young hen.

Pulmo, pulmon-is, the lungs.

PUL'MONARY, belonging to the lungs.

Pulp-a, the pith or soft part of trees.

PULP, the soft part of fruit.

PULP'Y, soft; like pulp.

Pulvis, pulver-is, dust, power.

PUL'VERIZE, to reduce to dust or powder.

PULVER'ULENT, consisting of fine powder.

---

* Pythagoras, and his followers, held that after death, the *souls* ot men pass into other bodies; and this doctrine still prevails in some parts of Asia, particularly in India and China.

† Nouns, in the Latin language, have six cases: the Nominative, the Genitive, Dative, Accusative, Vocative, and Ablative. The first was called *Casus rectus*, the straight case, and the others *Casus obliqui*, the oblique cases, because they seem to *fall* or *lean* from the Nominative.

Pung-o, punct-um, to point, or prick.

COMPUNC'TION,° remorse.
EXPUNGE',° to rub out.
POIG'NANT, keen; severe.
POINT, to aim; to direct.
PON'IARD, a dagger.
POUNCE, to fall on and seize.
PUNCH, to perforate; to push.
PUNCTIL'IO, a nice point of exactness.
PUNC'TUAL, exact; precise.
PUNC'TUATE, to point off.
PUNC'TURE, a small prick; a point.
PUN'GENT, pricking; sharp.

Puni-o, punit-um, to punish.

IMPU'NITY, exemption from punishment.
PUN'ISH, to chastise.
PU'NITIVE, inflicting punishment.

Pup-a, a young child; the eye-ball.

PU'PIL, the apple of the eye; a scholar.
PUP'PET, a small image moved by wire.
PUP'PY, a whelp.

Purg-o, purgat-um, to make clean.

COMPURGA'TOR, one who bears witness to the innocence of another.
EXPURGE', to purge away.
EXPURGA'TION, act of cleansing.
PURGE, to clear; to cleanse.
PURG'ATIVE, a purging medicine.
PURG'ATORY, a place in which Papists suppose souls are purged from impurities.

Pur-us, pure, clean.

IMPURE', not pure; unholy.
PURE, chaste; clear; holy.
PU'RIFY, to make pure.
PU'RITAN, one of a sect professing to follow the pure word of God.
PU'RITY, innocence; chastity.

Pus, pur-is, the corrupt matter of sores.

DEP'URATE, to cleanse.
PU'RULENT, consisting of pus.
PUS'TULE, a pimple.
SUP'PURATE, to form matter.

Pusill-us, weak, little.

PUSILLANIM'ITY, cowardice; weakness of spirit.
PUSILLAN'IMOUS, cowardly; having little spirit.

Put-o, putat-um, to prune, to adjust accounts, to think.

ACCOUNT', reckoning.
AM'PUTATE, to cut off.
COMPUTE', to reckon; to calculate.
COUNT, to number.
DEPUTE', to send; to empower to act.
DEP'UTY, one that transacts business for another
DIS'COUNT,* a deduction.
DISPUTE', contest; controversy.
DISPUTA'TIOUS, inclined to dispute; cavilling.
DISREP'UTABLE, dishonorable.
IMPUTE', to attribute.
PU'TATIVE, supposed; reputed.
RECOUNT', to relate.
REPUTA'TION, credit; honor.

**Discount*, literally a *counting* back or from; a sum deducted from the principal for prompt or advanced payment.

Putr-is, rotten, fetid.

IMPUTRES'CIBLE, that cannot become putrid.
PUTRES'CENT, growing rotten.
PUTRID'ITY, rottenness. [rot.
PU'TREFY, to make rotten; to
PUTREFAC'TIVE, making rotten.

Pygme (πυγμη), the fist; as big as the fist.

PYGME'AN, small; little.
PIG'MY, a very little person.

Pyr, pyros (πυρ, πυρος), fire.

EMPYRE'AN, the highest heaven.
EMPYREUMAT'IC, having the smell or taste of burnt substances. [in a point.
PYR'AMID,° a solid figure, ending
PYRE, a funeral pile.
PYR'ITE, fire-stone.
PYROL'ATRY, fire-worship.
PYROLIG'NEOUS, obtained by the distillation of wood.
PYROL'OGY, a treatise on heat.
PYROM'ETER, an instrument to measure heat.
PYR'OMANCY, divination by fire.
PYROTECH'NICS, the art of making fireworks.

Pyrrho, Pyrrhon-is, the founder of the skeptics.

PYR'RHONISM, skepticism; universal doubt.

Quadr-a, a square. ***Quatuor***, four.

BIQUADRAT'IC, relating to the fourth power.
QUAD'RANGLE, a square.
QUAD'RANT,° a quarter of a circle.
QUADREN'NIAL, happening every four years. [sides.
QUADRILAT'ERAL, having four
QUADRILLE', a game at cards; a kind of dance in sets of four.
QUADROON', a person quarter-blooded.
QUAD'RUPED, a four-footed animal.
QUAD'RUPLE, fourfold.
QUADRU'PLICATE, to double twice.
QUAR'ANTINE,° the time that ships, suspected of infection, are prohibited from intercourse with the shore.
QUART, one-fourth of a gallon.
QUART'ER, to divide into four parts.
QUAT'RAIN, a stanza of four lines rhyming alternately.
SQUAD'RON,° part of a fleet.
SQUARE, a figure of four equal sides and four right angles.

Quær-o, quæsit-um, to ask, to obtain, to seek.

ACQUIRE',° to gain; to procure.
ACQUISITI'ON, the thing acquired.
CON'QUER, to gain by force.
CON'QUEST, victory; a subduing.
DISQUISITI'ON, a systematic investigation of a subject.
EX'QUISITE,° excellent; fine.
IN'QUEST, a judicial inquiry.
INQUIRE', to seek out.
INQUISITI'ON, search; trial.
INQUIS'ITIVE, curious.
INQUISITO'RIAL, relating to an inquisition or an inquisitor.
PER'QUISITE, a fee or gift of office. [tions.
QUE'RIST, one who asks ques-
QUE'RY, an inquiry; a doubt
QUEST, a search. [tions.
QUES'TION, to examine by ques
REQUEST', to ask; to solicit.
REQUIRE', to demand; to claim
REQ'UISITE, necessary.

Qual-is, of what kind or sort.

DISQUAL'IFY, to make unfit.
QUALIFICA'TION, fitness.
QUAL'IFY, to render fit.
QUAL'ITY, nature; property.

Quant-us, how great, how much.

QUAN'TITY, weight; a part.
QUAN'TUM, the amount required.

Quatio, quass-um, to shake. QUASH, to crush; to annul.

Quer-or, to complain, to bewail.

QUAR'REL, a brawl; a dispute.
QUERIMO'NIOUS, complaining.
QUER'ULOUSLY, in a complaining manner.

Quid, quod, what.

QUID'NUNC, one curious to know every thing; (what now?)
QUOD'LIBET, a nice point; (what you please.)

Quies, quiet-is, rest, ease.

ACQUIESCE', to quietly assent.
COY, modest; reserved.
DISQUI'ET, to make uneasy.
QUIES'CENT, resting.
QUI'ETUDE, rest; repose.
QUIE'TUS,° final discharge.
RE'QUIEM,° a hymn for the dead.

Quinque, five. ***Quint-us***, fifth.

QUINDECEM'VIR, one of fifteen men united in office.
QUINTES'SENCE, the best part.
QUIN'TUPLE, fivefold.

Quot, how many, so many.

AL'IQUOT,° exactly measuring.
QUO'RUM,° a competent number to transact business.
QUO'TA, a share.
QUO'TIENT, that which results on dividing one number by another.
QUOTID'IAN, a fever which returns daily.

Rabd-os (ῥαβδος), a rod, a wand.

RHAB'DOMANCY, divination by a rod.

Rabi-es, madness, rage.

RAB'ID, furious; mad.
RAVE, to be furious or mad.
REV'EL, a noisy feast.
REV'ELRY, mirth; festivity.

Racem-us, a bunch or cluster of grapes.

RACEMIF'EROUS, bearing clusters.
RAC'EMOUS, growing in clusters

Radi-us, the spoke of a wheel; a beam or ray.

BIRA'DIATE, having two rays.
IRRA'DIATE, to illumine.
RA'DIANCE, sparkling lustre.
RA'DIUS, the semi-diameter of a circle.
RAY, a beam of light.

Radix, radic-is, a root.

ERAD'ICATE, to root out.
RAD'ICAL, primitive; thorough.

Rad-o, ras-um, to shave, to scrape.

ABRADE', to rub off.
ABRA'SION, the act of rubbing off.
ERASE', to rub out.
RAZE, to overthrow from the foundation.
RA'ZOR, a tool for shaving.

Ram-us, a bough or branch.

RAMIFICA'TION, a branch; a division into branches.
RAM'IFY, to separate into branches.

Ranc-eo, to be stale, or strong scented.

RAN'CID, having a rank smell.
RAN'COR,° malice; enmity.
RANK, strong to the taste.
RAN'KLE,° to fester.

Rang (Fr.), a row, order.

ARRANGE', to put in order.
DERANGE', to disorder.
DISARRANGE'MENT, disorder.
RANGE, to place in a row.
RANK, a row; a class.

Rap-io, rapt-um, to snatch, to seize.

ENRAP'TURE,° to delight highly.
ENRAV'ISHED, enraptured.
RAP, a quick smart blow.
RAPA'CIOUS, given to plunder.
RAP'ID, quick; swift.
RA'PIER, a thrusting sword.
RAP'TURE, ecstasy; transport.
RAV'AGE, to lay waste; to sack.
RAV'ISH, to delight; to transport.

Rar-us, scarce, thin.

RARE, scarce; thin.
RAR'EFY, to make thin.
RAREFAC'TION, a making thin.
RAR'ITY, thinness; infrequency.

Rat-us, thinking, established.

IRRA'TIONAL, contrary to reason.
RATE, a fixed price; a degree.
RAT'IFY, to confirm; to settle.
RA'TIO, proportion.
RA'TION, a fixed allowance.
RATIOCINA'TION, the act of reasoning.
RATIONA'LE, a detail with reasons.
RATIONAL'ITY, reasonableness.
REA'SON, to argue rationally.

Recens, recent-is, new, fresh. RE'CENT, new; late.

Reciproc-us, alternate, mutual.

RECIP'ROCAL, done by each to the other.
RECIP'ROCATE, to interchange.
RECIPROC'ITY, mutual obligation.

Reg-o, to govern. ***Rect-us,*** straight. ***Regul-a,*** a rule.

CORRECT', right, accurate.
DIRECT',° to aim; to regulate.
DIREC'TION, aim; order.
ERECT',° to raise; to build.
INCORRECT', not exact; wrong.
INCOR'RIGIBLE, that cannot be corrected.
INDIRECT', not direct; not fair.
INTERREG'NUM, the time between two reigns.
IRREG'ULAR, not regular.
RECT'ANGLE, a right-angled parallelogram.
REC'TIFY, to make right.

RECTILIN'EAL, consisting of right lines.
REC'TITUDE, uprightness.
REC'TOR,° a minister of a parish.
RE'GAL, royal; kingly.
REGA'LIA, ensigns of royalty.
RE'GENT, a governor.
REG'ICIDE, murder of a king.
REG'IMEN, regulation of diet.
REG'IMENT,° a body of soldiers.
RE'GION,° a country; a tract.
REGULAR'ITY, conformity to rule
REGULA'TION, method; rule.
REIGN, to rule as a king.
RIGHT, equity; justice.
RULE, to govern; to control.

Rem-us, an oar.

TRI'REME, a galley with three tiers of oars on a side.

Rend-re (Fr.), to give back, to restore.

REN'DER, to return; to make.
REN'DEZVOUS,° a place appointed for a meeting.
RENDITI'ON, a rendering.
SURREN'DER, to deliver up.

Rept-um (*ab* **repo**), to creep.

REP'TILE, an animal that creeps.
SURREPTITI'OUS, done by stealth.

Res, a thing.

RE'AL, true; relating to things.
REAL'ITY, actual existence.
RE'ALIZE, to bring into being; to conceive of.

Ret-e, a net.

RET'ICULE, a small bag.
RETIC'ULATE, resembling net-work.
RET'IFORM, having the form of a net.
RET'INA,° one of the coats of the eye, like a net.

Rhapt-o (ῥαπτω), to sew, to unite.

RHAP'SODY,° an irregular composition.

Rhe-o (ῥεω), to flow, to speak.

CATARRH',° influenza.
DIARRHE'A, a flux; a purging.
HEM'ORRHAGE, a flux of blood.
RES'INOUS,° like resin.
RHET'ORIC, oratory.
RHEUM, a thin watery humor.

Rhin (ῥιν), the nose.

RHINOC'EROS, an animal with a horn on the nose.

Rhomb-os (ῥομβος), a rhomb.

RHOMB,° a quadrangular figure.
RHOM'BOID, a figure like a rhomb.

Rhythm-os (ῥυθμος), measured movement.

RHYME, to agree in sound.
RHYTHM,° metre; verse.
RYTH'MICAL, having proportion of sound.

Ride-o, ris-um, to laugh, to mock.

DERIDE', to laugh at; to mock.
DERISI'ON, contempt; scorn.
RID'ICULE, to expose to laughter.
RIS'IBLE, exciting laughter.

Rig-eo, to be cold or stiff.

RIG'ID, stiff; strict.
RIG'OR, severity.

Rig-o, rigat-um, to water a field.

IR'RIGATE, to water, as a garden.
IRRIG'UOUS, watery; moist.

Rit-us, a rite or ceremony.

RITE, a religious ceremony.
RIT'UAL, a book of religious ceremonies.

Riv-us, a river.

ARRIVE',° to come to; to reach.
CO-RI'VAL,° a competitor.
DERIVE', to deduce; to draw.
DERIVA'TION, act of deriving.
RI'VALRY, emulation.
RIV'ULET, a small river.

Robur, robor-is, an oak, strength.

CORROB'ORATE, to confirm.
ROBUST', strong; vigorous.

Rod-o, ros-um, to gnaw, to eat away.

CORRODE', to eat away by degrees.
CORRO'SION, the act of corroding.
ERO'SION, the act of eating away.

Rog-o, rogat-um, to ask, to request.

AB'ROGATE,° to repeal; to annul.
AR'ROGANT, assuming.
AR'ROGATE, to claim unduly.
DER'OGATE, to disparage.
DEROG'ATORY, detracting from.
INTER'ROGATE, to question.
INTERROG'ATIVE, denoting a question.
PREROG'ATIVE,° an exclusive privilege.
PROROGUE',° to protract.
SUPEREROG'ATORY, exceeding duty.
SUR'ROGATE, a deputy.

Rome (Ρωμη), strength; the capital of Italy.

ROME, a city of Italy.
RO'MANIZE, to convert to Romish opinions.
RO'MISH, relating to the church of Rome.
ROM'ULUS, the founder of Rome.

Ros, ror-is, dew.

RO'RAL, dewy.
RORIF'EROUS, producing dew.
RORIF'LUENT, flowing with dew.

Ros-a, a rose.

RO'SEATE, rosy; fragrant.
RO'SY, blooming; red.
RO'SARY, a string of beads on which prayers are counted.

Rostr-um, the beak of a bird: a pulpit.

BIROS'TRATE, having a double beak.
ROS'TRUM,° a platform from which orators harangue.

Rot-a, a wheel. ***Rotund-us***, round.

CIRCUMRO'TARY, whirling round.
ROTA'TION, a turning round.
ROTE, a mere repetition of words.
ROTUND', round; circular.
ROTUNDIFO'LIOUS, having round leaves.
ROUTINE', a round of business.

Roy, *for* **Roi** (Fr.), a king.

POME'ROY, a royal apple.
ROY'AL, kingly; regal.
VICE'ROY, a king's deputy governor.

Rub-er, rubri, red, ruddy.

ERUBES'CENCE, redness.
RU'BICUND, inclining to redness.
RU'BRICAL,° red.
RU'BY, a precious stone of a red color.

Ruct-us, a belch. ERUCTA'TION, the act of belching.

Rud-is, unwrought, rude.

ER'UDITE, learned.
ERUDITI'ON, learning.
RUDE, rough; coarse.
RU'DIMENT, a first principle.

Rug-a, a wrinkle.

COR'RUGATE, wrinkled.
RU'GOSE, full of wrinkles.

Ruin-a, a downfall, falling. RU'INOUS, pernicious; destructive.

Rumen, rumin-is, the cud. RU'MINATE,° to muse on.

Rumor, a common report. RU'MOR, a popular or flying report.

Rupt-um (*ab* **rumpo**), to break, to burst.

ABRUPT', broken off; sudden.
BANK'RUPT,° unable to pay.
CORRUPT',° to deprave; to debase.
CORRUP'TION, wickedness; depravity.
DISRUP'TURE, to rend; to sever.
ERUP'TIVE, bursting forth.
INCORRUPT'IBLE, incapable of corruption.
INTERRUPT',° to stop; to hinder.
IRRUP'TION, an inroad.
RUP'TURE, a breach.

Rus, rur-is, the country.

RU'RAL, relating to the country.
RUS'TIC, rude; plain; rural.
RUS'TICATE, to reside in the country.

Sabbat-um, rest, the Sabbath.

SABBATA'RIAN, one who observes the seventh day of the week as the Sabbath.
SAB'BATH, the day of rest.
SABBAT'ICAL, relating to the Sabbath.

Sacchar-um, sugar.

SAC'CHARINE, having the qualities of sugar.

Sacer, sacri, sacred, devoted.

CON'SECRATE, to make sacred.
DESECRA'TION, a profaning.
EX'ECRATE, to curse.
EX'ECRABLE, accursed.
OBSECRA'TION, an entreaty.
SACERDO'TAL, belonging to the priesthood.
SAC'RAMENT,° the Lord's supper
SA'CRED, holy; inviolable.
SAC'RIFICE, to destroy; to devote.
SAC'RILEGE, a violation of things sacred.
SAC'RISTY, the vestry room of a church.

Sagax, sagac-is, knowing, foreseeing.

Presage′, to forebode.
Saga′cious, discerning; acute.
Sagac′ity, acuteness.
Sage, wise; grave.

Sagitt-a, an arrow. Sag′ittal, belonging to an arrow.

Sal (ἅλς), salt, wit.

Sal′ad, raw herbs seasoned with salt, vinegar, &c.
Sal′ary,° a periodical payment for services.
Salif′erous, producing salt.
Saline′, briny.
Salt, the chloride of sodium.
Sauce, something to give relish to food.
Sau′cy, insolent; impudent.
Sau′sage, a composition of meat, seasoned with salt, &c.
Sea′son, to give a relish to.

Sal-io, salt-um, to leap, to jump.

Assail′, to fall upon; to attack.
Assault′, an attack.
Con′sul, a Roman magistrate.
Con′sulate, the office of consul.
Consult′,° to ask advice of.
Coun′sel, to advise.
Des′ultory,° roving; unconnected.
Dissil′ient, starting asunder.
Exult′,° to triumph.
In′sult,° a gross abuse.
Procon′sul, a Roman governor.
Result′,° consequence; effect.
Sa′lient, leaping; bounding.
Sal′ly,° to issue out.
Sal′mon, a leaping fish.
Salt′ant, dancing.
Salta′tion, a jumping.

Saliv-a, spittle

Sal′ivate, to purge by the salival glands.
Sal′ivary, relating to spittle.

Salus, salut-is, safety, health. ***Salv-us,*** unhurt.

Insalu′brious, unhealthy.
Safe, free from danger.
Salu′brity, wholesomeness.
Sal′utary, healthful; safe.
Salute′, to greet; to hail.
Salu′tatory, containing salutations.
Saluta′tion, a greeting.
Salv′age, a recompense for saving goods from a wreck.
Salva′tion, a deliverance from injury.
Salve, an ointment.
Sal′vo,° a reservation; excuse.
Save, to preserve; to spare.

Sanct-us, holy, sacred.

Saint, a person eminent for piety.
Sanc′tify, to make holy.
Sanc′timony, holiness.
Sanc′tion, confirmation.
Sanc′tus, a chant beginning with Holy.
Sanc′tity, godliness.
Sanc′tuary, a temple.

Sanguis, sanguin-is, blood.

Consanguin′ity, relation by blood.
Cous′in, a kinsman.
Sanguif′erous, conveying blood.
Ensan′guine, to smear with gore.
San′guinary, cruel; bloody.
San′guine,° warm; ardent.

San-us, sound, whole.

INSANE', mad; distracted.
SAN'ATIVE, tending to heal.
SAN'ITY, soundness of mind.
SOUND, whole; healthy.

Sapi-o, to savor, to know.

INSIP'ID, tasteless; flat.
SAP'ID, having flavor.
SA'PIENCE, wisdom.
SA'VOR, odor; taste.

Sapo, sapon-is, soap.

SOAP, a substance used in washing.
SAPONA'CEOUS, soapy.

Sarx, sarc-os, (σαρξ, σαρκος), flesh.

ANASAR'CA,° a species of dropsy.
SAR'CASM,° a keen reproach.
SARCAS'TIC, keen; severe.
SARCOPH'AGUS, a sort of stone coffin, (See note p. 137.)

Satelles, satellit-is, a lifeguard, an attendant.

SAT'ELLITE, a small planet revolving round a larger.

Satir-a, a satire.

SAT'IRE,° a censorious poem.
SAT'IRIST, one who writes satires.

Satis, enough, sufficient.

DISSATISFAC'TION, discontent.
INSA'TIABLE, not to be satisfied.
INSATI'ETY, want of satiety.
INSAT'URABLE, not to be saturated.
SATE, to glut; to pall.
SAT'ISFY, to content; to please.
SAT'URATE, to impregnate fully.
SUPERSAT'URATE, to saturate to excess.

Saturn-us,° an ancient heathen deity.

SATURNA'LIAN,° sportive; loose.
SAT'URNINE,° gloomy; grave.
SAT'URDAY, the last day of the week, (Saturn's day.)

Sax-um, a stone or rock.

SAX'IFRAGE, a medicine which dissolves stone.

Scal-a, a ladder, a stair.

ESCALADE', the act of scaling walls.
SCALE, to climb; to mount.

Scalen-os (σκαληνος), uneven, unequal.

SCALENE', having unequal sides.

Scandal-on (σκανδαλον), a cause of offence.

SCAN'DAL, an offence; a reproach.
SCAN'DALOUS, shameful; vile.

Scand-o, scans-um, to go, to mount.

ASCEND', to move upwards.
ASCENT', an eminence.
CONDESCEND', to stoop; to submit.

ASCEN'SION, the act of ascending.

CONDESCEN'SION, a voluntary stooping from dignity.

DESCEND', to go down.

DESCENT', declivity; progress downward.

REASCEN'SION, a mounting up again.

SCAN,° to examine nicely.

SCAND'ENT, climbing.

TRANSCEND'ENT, pre-eminent.

Scapul-a, the shoulder-blade, the shoulder.

INTERSCAP'ULAR, between the shoulders.

SCAP'ULAR, relating to the shoulder.

Scariph-os (σκαριφος), a pointed instrument.

SCAR'IFY, to let blood by cutting the skin.

SCARIFICA'TOR, an instrument for scarifying.

Scel-os, (σκελος), the leg. ISOS'CELES, having two sides equal.

Scen-a (σκηνη), the stage, a representation.

SCENE, an appearance.

SCE'NERY, a collection of scenes.

SCENOG'RAPHY, the art of perspective.

Scept-omai (σκεπτομαι), to look about; to doubt.

SCEP'TIC, a doubter; an infidel.

SCEP'TICISM, doubt; infidelity.

Schem-a (σχημα), a design, a project.

SCHEME, a plan; a project.

SCHEM'IST, one who makes schemes.

Schism-a (σχισμα), division or separation in the church.

SCHISM, a division in a church or society.

SCHISMAT'IC, one guilty of schism.

Schol-a (σχολη), a school.

SCHOL'AR, a man of letters.

SCHOLAS'TIC, an adherent of *the schools*.

SCHO'LIAST, a commentator.

SCHO'LIUM, an explanatory note.

SCHOOL, a place of education.

Sci-a (σκια), a shadow.

AMPHIS'CII,° people who inhabit the torrid zone, whose shadows fall both ways.

ANTIS'CII,° people on different sides of the equator, whose shadows at noon fall opposite ways.

SCIAG'RAPHY,° the art of sketching.

SCIOM'ACHY, a battle with a shadow.

Scind-o, sciss-um, to cut.

RESCIND', to revoke.

SCIS'SORS, small shears.

Scintill-a, a spark of fire.

SCIN'TILLATE, to emit sparks.

SCINTILLA'TION, the act of throwing off sparks.

Scio, to know. ***Sciens, scient-is,*** knowing.

CON'SCIENCE, the knowledge of right and wrong.
CONSCIEN'TIOUS, regulated by conscience.
CON'SCIOUS, knowing; perceiving.
NESCI'ENCE, ignorance.
OMNISCI'ENT, all-knowing.
PRE'SCIENCE, fore-knowledge.
SCI'ENCE,° knowledge.
SCIENTIF'IC, relating to science.
SCI'OLIST, a pretender to science.
UNCON'SCIONABLE, unjust; unreasonable.

Scop-eo (σκοπεω), to look, to observe narrowly.

ANEM'OSCOPE, a weather-vane.
ARCHBISH'OP, the principal of the bishops.
BAR'OSCOPE, a sort of barometer.
BISH'OPRIC, the diocese of a bishop.
EPIS'COPACY, a government by [bishops.
SCOPE, aim; intention.
HE'LIOSCOPE, a telescope for viewing the sun.
HY'GROSCOPE, an instrument to show the moisture of the air.
MI'CROSCOPE, an instrument for viewing the smallest objects.
TEL'ESCOPE, a glass used for distant views.

Scopt-o (σκοπτω), to gibe, to deride.

SCOFF, to mock; to deride.
SCOFF'ER, one who scoffs.

Scorbut-um, the scurvy.

SCORBU'TIC, ill with scurvy.
SCUR'VY, scabbed; vile.

Scori-a, dross, the refuse of metal.

SCORIA'CEOUS, resembling dross.
SCO'RIFY, to reduce to dross.

Scrib-o, script-um, to write.

ANTISCRIP'TURAL, contrary to scripture.
ASCRIBE',° to attribute.
ASCRIP'TION, the act of ascribing.
CIRCUMSCRIBE', to bound, to limit.
CIRCUMSCRIP'TION, a limiting.
CON'SCRIPT, one enrolled for the army.
DESCRIBE', to give an account of.
ESCRITOIR', a box with implements for writing.
INDESCRI'BABLE, that cannot be described.
INSCRIBE', to write on.
INSCRIP'TION, a title; an address.
MAN'USCRIPT, a book or paper written, not printed.
NONDESCRIPT', not yet described.
PRESCRIBE',° to set down; to order.
PRESCRIP'TION, a medical receipt.
PROSCRIBE',* to condemn; to denounce.
PROSCRIP'TIVE, denouncing.
RE'SCRIPT,° an edict or answer of an emperor.
SCRIB'BLE, to write carelessly.
SCRIBE,° a writer; a notary.
SCRIP,° a small writing.
SCRIP'TURE, a writing; the Bible.

---

* The sense of this word originated in the Roman practice of *writing* the names of persons doomed to death, and posting the list in public.

SUBSCRIBE′,° to sign; to attest.
SUBSCRIP′TION, the act of subscribing.
SUPERSCRIBE′, to write on the outside.
SUPERSCRIP′TION, a writing on the outside.
TRANSCRIBE′, to copy; to write from.
TRAN′SCRIPT, a copy.

Scrupul-us, a scruple, a doubt.

SCRU′PLE, a weight of twenty grains; a doubt.
SCRU′PULOUS, careful; cautious.

Scrut-or, to seek, to trace out.

INSCRU′TABLE, unsearchable.
SCRU′TINIZE, to search.
SCRU′TINY, examination; search.

Sculpo, sculpt-um, to carve

SCULP′TOR, a carver of stone or wood.
SCULP′TURE, the art of carving.

Scurr-a, a scoffer, a buffoon.

SCURRIL′ITY,° abusive language.
SCUR′RILOUS, abusive; vulgar.

Scut-um, a shield, a defence.

ESCUTCH′EONED, having a scutcheon.
SCU′TAGE,° an old English tax.
SCUTCH′EON, a shield on which a coat of arms is represented.
SCU′TIFORM, shaped like a shield.

Saison (Fr.), one of the four parts of the year.

SEA′SON, time; occasion.
UNSEA′SONABLE, ill-timed.

Seb-um, tallow, fat. SEBA′CEOUS, relating to tallow.

Sec-o, sect-um, to cut.

BISECT′, to divide into two equal parts.
BISEG′MENT, a half segment.
DISSECT′, to cut in pieces.
DISSEC′TION, act of dissecting.
IN′SECT,° a small creeping animal.
INSECTIV′OROUS, eating insects.
INTERSECT′, to cut mutually.
SAW, an instrument to cut with.
SE′CANT, a line cutting another.
SECT, a division; a party.
SEC′TARY, one of a sect.
SEC′TION, a part; a division.
SECT′OR, a part of a circle between two radii and the arc.
SEG′MENT, a part cut off.
TRISECT′, to divide into three equal parts.
VENESEC′TION, blood-letting.

Secul-um, the world, an age. SEC′ULAR, not spiritual; worldly

Secund-us, a second in number or order.

SEC′OND, to support, to assist.
SEC′ONDARY, subordinate.

Secret-us, hidden, retired.

EX-SEC′RETARY, one who has retired from the office of secretary.
SE′CRET, hidden; concealed.
SEC′RETARY,° one who writes for another.

Sedat-us, calm, peaceful.

SEDATE', calm; quiet.
SED'ATIVE, assuaging.

Sed-eo, sess-um, to sit.

ASSESS',° to value.
ASSID'UOUS,° constant in application.
ASSIZE',° a kind of court of law.
BESIEGE', to hem in; to beset.
CONSID'ER,° to study; to ponder.
CONSID'ERATE, thoughtful.
DISPOSSESS', to put out of possession.
INCONSID'ERABLE, unimportant.
INSID'IOUS,° treacherous.
OBSESSI'ON, the act of besieging.
OBSID'IONAL, belonging to a siege.
POSSESS',° to enjoy; to own.
PREPOSSESSI'ON, preconceived opinion.
PRESIDE', to be set over; to direct.
PRES'IDENCY, the office of president.
PRESID'IARY, relating to a garrison.
REPOSSESS', to possess again.
RESIDE',° to live in a place.
RES'IDENT, one who resides.
RES'IDUE, that which is left.
SEDAN',° a portable chair.
SED'ENTARY, sitting; inactive.
SED'IMENT, that which settles at the bottom.
SED'ULOUS,° diligent.
SESSI'ON, a sitting.
SIEGE, the act of besetting a fortified place.
SUBSIDE',° to sink away.
SUBSID'IARY, assisting.
SUB'SIDIZE, to furnish with money and arms.
SUPERSEDE',° to set aside.

Selen-e (σεληνη), the moon.

PARASELENE', a mock moon.
SELENOG'RAPHY, a description of the moon.

Semen, semin-is, seed.

DISSEMINA'TION,° a scattering.
SEM'INAL, belonging to seed.
SEM'INARY,° a nursery; a school.
SEMINIF'IC, productive of seed.

Semi (ἡμι), half.

SEMIAN'NUAL, half yearly.
SEMIAN'NULAR, half round.
SEM'ICIRCLE, a half circle.
SEM'ICOLON, a punctuation mark.
SEMIDIAM'ETER, half a diameter.
SEMILU'NAR, resembling half a moon.
SEM'IMETAL, a half metal.
SEMIPELLU'CID, imperfectly transparent.
SEM'IQUAVER, half a quaver.
SEM'IVOWEL, an imperfect consonant.

Semper, always.

SEMPERVI'RENT, evergreen.
SEMPITERN'AL, everlasting.

Senex, sen-is, an old man.

SEIGN'IOR, a lord; a title.
SEIGN'IORY, a lordship.
SEN'ATE,* a body of senators.
SENES'CENCE, a growing old.
SENIL'ITY, old age.
SIRE, a father.

---

* This was so called, because it originally consisted of the *oldest* members of the state.

Sent-io, sens-um, to feel, to think.

ASSENT',° the act of agreeing to.
CONSENT', to yield; to agree.
CONSENTA'NEOUS, accordant.
DISSENT', to differ in opinion.
DISSEN'SION, strife; quarrel.
DISSEN'TIENT, disagreeing.
INSENS'ATE, stupid; foolish.
NON'SENSE, unmeaning language.
PRESENT'IMENT, apprehension of something future.
RESENT', to take as an affront.
SCENT, smell; odor.
SENSA'TION, perception by the senses.
SENSE, perception; meaning.
SENSO'RIUM, the seat of sense.
SENS'UAL, pleasing the senses.
SEN'TIENT, having perception.
SEN'TENCE, to judge; to condemn.
SENTEN'TIOUS,° pithy; pointed.
SEN'TIMENT,° thought; opinion.
SENT'INEL, a soldier on guard.

Sep-o (σηπω), to corrupt, to make putrid.

ANTISEP'TIC, counteracting putrefaction.

Septem, seven.

SEPTAN'GULAR, having seven angles, (See p. 63.)
SEPTEM'BER, the ninth month.
SEV'EN, one more than six.
SEPTEN'NIAL, lasting seven years.
SEPTILAT'ERAL, having seven sides.

Sepulchr-um, a grave.

SEP'ULCHRE, a grave; a tomb.
SEP'ULTURE, interment; burial.

Septuagint-a, seventy.

SEPTUAG'ENARY, consisting of seventy.
SEP'TUAGINT,* the Greek version of the Old Testament.

Sequ-or, secut-us, to follow.

CONSEC'UTIVE, following in regular order.
CON'SEQUENT, following as an effect.
CONSEQUEN'TIAL, conclusive; pompous.
ENSUE', to follow.
EX'ECUTE,° to carry into effect.
OB'SEQUIES, funeral rites.
OBSE'QUIOUS, servilely obedient.
PER'SECUTE, to pursue with malignity.
PURSUE', to chase; to follow.
PROS'ECUTE,° to carry on; to continue.
PURSUIT', act of pursuing.
PUR'SUIVANT, a state messenger.
SEQUA'CIOUS, following.
SE'QUEL, what follows.
SE'QUENCE, succession; a following.
SUB'SEQUENT, coming after.
SUE, to prosecute by law.
SUIT, a petition; a set.
SUITE, retinue; company.

---

* So called, because it was the work of *seventy*, or rather of *seventy-two* interpreters. This translation from the Hebrew, is supposed to have been made in the reign, and by the order of Ptolemy Philadelphus, king of Egypt, about two hundred and seventy, or two hundred and eighty years before the birth of Christ.

Seren-us, clear, fair, calm.

SERENADE′,° music performed at night in the open air.
SERENE′, calm; placid.
SEREN′ITY, calmness; peace.

Serp-o, to creep.

SER′PENTINE, winding like a serpent.
SER′PENT, a creeping animal.

Serr-a, a saw.

SER′RATE, indented like the edge of a saw.
SER′RATURE, an indenture like the teeth of a saw.

Sert-um (*ab* ***Sero***), to knit, to join in discourse.

ASSERT′, to maintain; to affirm.
DESERT′, to abandon.
DISSERTA′TION, a discourse; a treatise.
EXERT′, to put forth.
INSERT′, to set in or among.
REASSERT′, to assert anew.
REINSERT′, to insert again.
SE′RIES, a succession of things.
SER′MON, a religious discourse.

Serv-io, servit-um, to serve, to obey.

DESERVE′, to be worthy; to merit.
DISSERV′ICE, injury; mischief.
SER′GEANT, an officer in the army.
SERVE, to assist; to wait on.
SERV′ILE, slavish; dependant.
SERV′ITOR, an attendant.
SERV′ITUDE, slavery.
SUBSERVE′, to serve as an instrument.
UNSERV′ICEABLE, useless.

Serv-o, servat-um, to keep, to save.

CON′SERVE, a sweet-meat.
CONSERV′ATIVE, opposing injury.
INOBSERV′ANT, not taking notice.
OBSERVE′, to watch; to keep.
OBSERVA′TION, the act of observing.
PRESERVE′, to keep; to save.
RESERVE′,°to hold back.
RESERVOIR′, a place where any thing is stored; a cistern.
SERV′ANT, a menial; a dependant.

Set-a, a bristle.

SETA′CEOUS, bristly.
SE′TIFORM, formed like a bristle.

Sever-us, severe.

SEVERE′, sharp; harsh.
SEVER′ITY, cruelty; harshness.

Sex, six.

SEN′ARY, containing six.
SENOC′ULAR, having six eyes.
SEXAGENA′RIAN, one aged sixty.
SEXAGES′IMAL, sixtieth.
SEXAN′GULAR, having six angles.
SEXEN′NIAL, in six years.
SEX′TUPLE, six-fold.
SIX, twice three.

Sex-us, sex.

BISEX'OUS, consisting of both sexes.
SEX'UAL, belonging to sex.
SEX, the distinction between male and female.

Sibil-us, a hissing.

SIB'ILANT, hissing.
SIBILA'TION, a hissing sound.

Sicc-o, to dry.

DES'ICCATE, to dry up.
SIC'CITY, want of moisture.
HOR'TUS-SIC'CUS, a collection of dried plants.

Sidus, sider-is, a star.

CONSID'ER, to deliberate; to think of.
DESIRE', a request; a wish.
DESIDERA'TUM, something needed.
SIDE'REAL, relating to the stars.

Sign-um, a mark or sign.

ASSIGN', to mark out; to appoint.
ASSIGN'MENT, a making over.
CONSIGN', to transfer; to commit.
DESIGN', a scheme; a purpose.
DES'IGNATE, to point out.
INSIG'NIA, marks of office or honor.
INSIGNIF'ICANT, wanting meaning; unimportant.
PRESIG'NIFY, to signify beforehand.
RESIGN', to give up; to yield.
REASSIGN', to assign again.
SIGN, a mark; a token.
SIG'NAL, a sign to give notice.
SIG'NALIZE, to render memorable.
SIG'NATURE, a stamp; a mark.
SIGNIFICA'TION, meaning.
UNDESIGN'ED, not intended.

Sil-co, to be still.

SI'LENCE, stillness; quiet.
SI'LENT, mute; noiseless.

Silex, silic-is, a flint-stone.

SILICIF'EROUS, bearing flint.
SIL'ICIFY, to turn into flint.
SILICI'OUS, flinty; stony.

Siliqu-a, a seed vessel or pod.

MULTISIL'IQUOUS, having many pods.
SIL'IQUOUS, having a pod.

Silv-a, a wood, a grove.

SAV'AGE, wild; uncivilized.
SIL'VAN, woody.
PENNSYLVA'NIA, the groves of Penn; one of the U. S. of N.A.

Simil-is, like, resembling.

ASSIM'ILATE, to make like to.
DISSEM'BLE, to hide under false appearance.
DISSIMIL'ITUDE, want of resemblance.
DISSIM'ILAR, unlike.
DISSIMULA'TION, hypocrisy.
FAC-SIM'ILE, an exact copy.
SIM'ILAR, like; uniform.

SIM'ILE,° a comparison.
SIMIL'ITUDE, resemblance.
SIM'ULATE, to feign; to pretend.
VERISIMIL'ITUDE, likelihood.

Simoni-a, simony.

SIM'ONY,* the crime of trafficking in church preferments.
SIMONI'ACAL, relating to simony.

Simul, together. SIMULTA'NEOUS, at the same time.

Singul-us, one, not double.

SIN'GLE, one; alone.
SIN'GULAR, particular; odd.

Sinister, sinistr-i, on the left hand; bad.

SIN'ISTER, unfair; corrupt.
SIN'ISTROUS, perverse; absurd.

Sinus, the bosom, a bay, a bend.

INSIN'UATE,° to hint; to introduce slowly and artfully.
SI'NUS, a bay.
SINUOS'ITY, a bending in and out.

Sip-o, to throw, to cast.

DIS'SIPATE,° to scatter; to disperse.
UNDIS'SIPATED, not scattered; not dispersed.

Sist-o, to stand, to stop.

ASSIST',° to help.
CO-EXIST', to exist together.
CONSIST',° to be composed of.
CONSIST'ORY, an assembly of prelates.
DESIST', to cease from; to stop.
EXIST',° to have being.
INCONSIST'ENT, incompatible.
INSIST', to stand upon; to urge.
IRRESIST'IBLE, superior to opposition.
NONEXIST'ENCE, negation of being.
PERSIST',° to persevere.
PRE-EXIST', to exist before.
RESIST',° to make opposition.

Sit-os (σιτος), bread. PAR'ASITE,° a low, mercenary flatterer.

Situs, place.

SITE, local position.
SITUA'TION, place; state.

Soci-o, to join.

ASSO'CIATE, a partner; a companion.
CONSO'CIATE, to unite; to join.
SO'CIABLE,° familiar; friendly.
SO'CIAL, relating to society.
SOCI'ETY, a collection of persons.

Sol, the sun.

IN'SOLATE, to dry in the sun.
SO'LAR, belonging to the sun.
SOL'STICE,° the tropical point.

Solec-os (σολοιχος), one who speaks incorrectly.

SOL'ECISM,° impropriety in language.
SOLECIST'ICAL, not correct; incongruous.

---

* This is supposed to be derived from *Simon* Magus, who wished to purchase the power of conferring the Holy Spirit. Acts viii.

Solemn-is, solemn.

SOL'EMN, grave ; serious.

SOL'EMNIZE, to make solemn.

Sol-eo, to be accustomed.

IN'SOLENCE, haughtiness ; impudence.

IN'SOLENT,° haughty ; contemptuous.

Solicit-us, anxious, uneasy.

SOLIC'IT,° to importune ; to intreat.

SOLICITA'TION, entreaty.

SOLIC'ITOUS, anxious ; concerned.

SOLIC'ITUDE, anxiety ; concern.

Solid-us, firm, hard.

CONSOL'IDATE, to unite into a solid mass.

INSOLID'ITY, want of solidity.

SOL'DIER,° a warrior.

SOL'DER, to unite with metallic cement.

SOLID'IFY, to make solid.

SOLID'ITY, hardness ; firmness.

Sol-or, to cheer, to comfort.

CONSOLE', to comfort ; to cheer.

DISCON'SOLATE, hopeless ; sorrowful.

INCONSO'LABLE, not to be comforted.

SOL'ACE, ease ; comfort.

Sol-us, alone.

DES'OLATE, without inhabitants ; laid waste.

SOLE, single ; alone.

SOLIL'OQUY, a speech to one's self.

SOL'ITARY, retired ; alone.

SOL'ITUDE, loneliness.

Solv-o, solut-um, to loose, to free, to melt.

ABSOLVE', to clear ; to acquit.

AB'SOLUTE, complete ; positive.

ABSOLU'TION, acquittal ; remission.

DISSOLVE', to melt ; to loose.

DIS'SOLUTE, loose ; debauched.

INSOL'UBLE, not to be dissolved.

INSOL'VENT, unable to pay.

INDIS'SOLUBLE, that cannot be separated.

IRRES'OLUTE, wavering ; not determined.

REDISSOLVE', to dissolve again

RESOLVE',° to determine.

RESOLU'TION, firmness.

SOLVE,° to explain.

SOLV'ENCY, ability to pay.

Somn-us, sleep.

SOMNAM'BULIST, one who walks in his sleep.

SOMNIF'EROUS, causing sleep.

SOM'NOLENT, sleepy ; drowsy.

Son-us, a sound.

ALTIS'ONANT, high-sounding.

CON'SONANCE, agreement.

DIS'SONANT, harsh ; discordant.

INCON'SONANT, not consistent.

RESOUND', to send back sound.

SON'NET, a small poem.

SONIF'EROUS, producing sound.

SONO'ROUS, loud sounding.

SOUND, a noise.

Soph-ia (σοφια), wisdom.

GYMNOS'OPHIST,* an Indian philosopher.
PHILOS'OPHY, knowledge; the study of first principles.
SOPH'ISM, a fallacious argument.
SOPH'ISTRY, fallacious reasoning.
UNSOPHIS'TICATED, not acquainted with evil; pure.

Sopor, sleep.

SOPORIF'IC, causing sleep.
SOPORIF'EROUS, inducing sleep.

Sorb-eo, sorpt-um, to suck up.

ABSORB', to suck up.
ABSORP'TION, a sucking up.

Soror, a sister. SOROR'ICIDE, the murder of a sister.

Sors, sort-is, lot, kind.

ASSORT', to arrange; to select.
CON'SORT, a companion; a wife or husband.
RESORT', to betake; to turn to.
SORT, a kind; a species.
SORTIE', an issuing out; a sally.
SORT'ILEGE, the drawing of lots.
SORTITI'ON, appointment by lot.

Sparg-o, spars-um, to scatter.

ASPERSE', to bespatter with calumnies.
DISPERSE', to scatter.
INTERSPERSE', to scatter between.
SPARSE, thinly scattered.

Spasm-a (σπασμα), a convulsion, a drawing.

ANTISPASMOD'IC, preventing convulsions.
SPASM, a violent contraction.
EPISPAS'TIC,° drawing; blistering.
SPASMOD'IC, convulsive.

Spati-um, space.

EXPA'TIATE, to enlarge upon; to move at large.
SPACE, room; extension.
SPA'CIOUS, wide; roomy.

Speci-o, spect-um, to look. **Speci-es**, a sort.

AS'PECT, look; appearance.
AUS'PICE,° influence; favor.
AUSPICI'OUS, favorable.
CIR'CUMSPECT,° watchful; cautious.
CONSPIC'UOUS,° in full view.
DES'PICABLE, contemptible; worthless.
DESPISE',° to scorn; to contemn.
DESPITE', malice; defiance.
DISRESPECT', want of regard; rudeness.
ESPECI'AL, special; particular.
ESPY', to see; to discover.
EXPECT', to look for.
EXPECT'ANT, looking for.
INSPECT', to look into; to examine.

* The *Gymnosophists*—so called from their going with bare feet, or with little clothing—lived on wild productions of the earth. They never drank wine, nor married. Some of them travelled about, and practised physic. They believed the immortality and transmigration of the soul, and placed the chief happiness of man in a contempt of the goods of fortune, and of the pleasures of sense.

IRRESPECT'IVE, without regard to.
PERSPECT'IVE,° the art of representing scenes on a plain surface.
PERSPICA'CIOUS, quick-sighted.
PERSPICU'ITY,° clearness.
PROS'PECT, sight; appearance.
REINSPECT', to examine anew.
RESPECT',° regard; honor.
RETROSPECT'IVE, looking backwards.
SPECIF'IC, limited; peculiar.
SPEC'IMEN, a sample.
SPE'CIOUS, plausible; showy.
SPEC'TACLE, a show; a sight.
SPECTA'TOR, a looker-on.
SPEC'TRE, an apparition.
SPEC'ULUM, a mirror.
SPEC'ULATE,° to meditate; to theorize.
SUSPECT',° to mistrust; to doubt.
SUSPICI'ON, act of suspecting.

Sperm-a (σπερμα), seed.

AC'ROSPIRE, a sprout of a seed.
GYMNOSPERM'OUS, having naked seeds.
POLYSPERM'OUS, having many seeds.
MONOSPERM'OUS, having one seed.

Sper-o, to hope.

DESPAIR', to be without hope.
DESPERA'DO, a reckless villain.
DES'PERATE, hopeless.
PROSPER'ITY, success; fortune.
PROS'PER,° to succeed; to flourish.
UNPROS'PEROUS, not prosperous.

Spher-a, for Sphæra (σφαιρα), a sphere or globe.

AT'MOSPHERE, the air surrounding the earth.
SEMISPHER'ICAL, belonging to a half sphere.
SPHERIC'ITY, roundness.
SPHE'ROID,° a body like a sphere.
SPHER'ULE, a little globe.

Spic-a, an ear of corn, a spike.

SPI'CATE, having a spike, or ear.
SPIKE, a long nail.

Spin-a, a thorn; the spine.

SPINE, the back-bone.
SPINIF'EROUS, bearing thorns.
SPI'NOUS, thorny; relating to the back-bone.

Spir-o, spirat-um, to breathe.

ASPIRE', to desire ardently.
AS'PIRATE, to pronounce with full breath.
CONSPIRE', to concert; to plot.
CONSPIR'ACY, a plot; treason.
CONSPIR'ATOR, one who plots.
DISPIR'IT, to discourage.
EXPIRE',° to die.
INSPIRE', to breathe into.
INSPIR'IT, to animate.
PERSPIRE', to emit by the pores.
REINSPIRE', to inspire anew.
RESPIRE',° to breathe.
SPIR'IT, the soul; the life.
SPIR'ITUAL, belonging to the spirit.
SPIR'ITUALIZE, to refine.
SPRITE, a spirit.
SUSPIRA'TION, a sigh.
TRANSPIRE', to pass out; to become known.

Spiss-us, thick.

INSPIS'SATE, to thicken.

SPISS'ITUDE, thickness.

Splen (σπλην), the spleen.

ANTISPLEN'ETIC, curing diseases of the spleen.

SPLEEN,° spite; ill-humor.

Splend-eo, to shine.

RESPLEN'DENT, bright; shining.

SPLEN'DID, showy; magnificent.

SPLEN'DOR, lustre; pomp.

TRANSPLEN'DENCY, great splendor.

Spoli-um, booty.

DESPOIL', to rob; to strip.

SPOIL, plunder; pillage.

SPOLIA'TION, the act of taking away.

Spond-eo, spons-um, to promise.

CORRESPOND', to suit; to answer.

DESPOND',° to despair.

DESPOND'ENT, despairing.

ESPOUSE', to wed; to betroth.

IRRESPONS'IBLE, not bound to answer.

RESPOND', to answer; to reply.

RESPONSE', answer.

RESPONS'IBLE, accountable.

RESPONS'IVE, replying.

SPON'SOR, one who promises for another.

SPOUSE, a husband or wife.

Spontane-us, voluntary.

SPONTANE'ITY, self-agency.

SPONTA'NEOUS, acting of itself.

Squal-eo, to be filthy.

SQUAL'ID, foul; dirty.

SQUA'LOR, foulness; filth.

Squam-a, a scale of a fish.

SQUAMIG'EROUS, bearing scales.

SQUA'MOUS, scaly.

Stagn-um, standing water

STAG'NANT, standing; not flowing.

STAG'NATE, to cease to move.

Stann-um, tin.

STAN'NARY, a tin mine.

STAN'NIC, relating to tin.

Stas-is (στασις), a standing, a weighing.

APOS'TASY, departure from one's profession.

APOS'TATIZE, to forsake one's faith or religion.

EC'STASY,° rapture; enthusiasm.

ECSTAT'IC, rapturous.

HYDROSTAT'ICS, the science of the weight, motion, and equilibrium of fluids.

SYS'TEM,° regular method.

UNSYSTEMAT'IC, without system.

Stegan-os (στεγανος), concealed.

STEGANOG'RAPHY, the art of writing in secret characters.

Stell-a, a star.

CONSTELLA'TION, a cluster of stars.
INTERSTEL'LAR, between the stars.
STEL'LATE, like a star.
STELLIF'EROUS, having stars.
STEL'LIFORM, in the form of a star.

Stell-o (στελλω), to send.

APOS'TLE,° a messenger.
DIAS'TOLE,° the dilatation of the heart.
EPIS'TLE, a letter sent.
PERISTAL'TIC, spiral; worm-like.
SYS'TOLE,° the contraction of the heart.

Sten-os (στενος), short.

STENOG'RAPHY, the art of writing in shorthand.

Stere-os (στερεος), solid.

STEREOG'RAPHY, the art of drawing the forms of solid bodies on a plane.
STEREOM'ETRY, the art of measuring solids.
STER'EOTYPE,° solid type.

Steril-is, barren.

STER'ILE, barren; unfruitful.
STERIL'ITY, barrenness.

Stern-o, strat-um, to cast down, to lay flat.

CONSTERNA'TION, great terror; amazement.
PROS'TRATE, lying flat.
STRA'TUM, a bed; a layer.
STRAT'IFY, to arrange in layers.
STRATIFICA'TION, arrangement in layers.

Stich-os (στιχος), a row, a line, a verse.

ACROS'TIC,° a kind of poem.
DIS'TICH, a couplet.
HEM'ISTICH, half a verse.
MON'OSTICH, a single verse.

Stigma, stigmat-os (στιγμα), a mark of infamy.

STIG'MA, a blot; a reproach.
STIG'MATIZE, to disgrace; to censure.

Stig-o, to prick, to spur.

IN'STIGATE, to provoke; to set on.
INSTIGA'TOR, one who instigates.

Still-a, a drop.

DISTILL', to drop; to extract spirit.
DISTILL'ERY, a place for distilling.
INSTILL', to infuse by drops; to teach slowly.
STILL, a vessel for distillation.

Stimul-us, a spur.

STIM'ULATE, to urge; to animate.
STIM'ULUS, that which excites.

Stingu-o, stinct-um, to mark, to thrust.

CONTRADISTIN'GUISH, to distinguish by opposite qualities.
CONTRADISTINC'TION, distinction by opposite qualities.

DISTIN'GUISH,° to mark difference; to make eminent.
DISTINCT', different; clear.
EXTIN'GUISH, to quench; to destroy.
EXTINCT', put out; destroyed.
INDISTINCT', not plain; confused.
INEXTIN'GUISHABLE, unquenchable.
INSTINCT'IVE,° natural; intuitive.

Stin-o (obs.), to fix.

DES'TINE, to doom; to appoint.
DESTINA'TION, purpose; end.
OB'STINATE, stubborn.
PREDES'TINE, to foredoom.
PREDESTINA'TION, the act of ordaining beforehand.

Stipendi-um, wages.

STI'PEND, settled pay; pension.
STIPEN'DIARY, a pensioner.

Stip-o, stipat-um, to stuff.

CON'STIPATE, to thicken; to stop up.
COS'TIVE, bound in body.

Stipul-a, a straw.

STIP'ULATE,° to bargain; to settle terms.
STIPULA'TION, the act of stipulating; a contract.

Stirps, stirp-is, a root or stem.

EX'TIRPATE, to root out; to destroy.
EXTIRPA'TION, a rooting out; total destruction.

St-o, stat-um, to stand, to set.

AR'MISTICE, a short truce.
ARREST', to stop; to seize.
CIR'CUMSTANCE,° event; condition.
CIRCUMSTAN'TIAL, incidental; particular.
CON'STABLE,° a police officer.
CON'STANT, fixed; unvaried.
CON'STITUTE, to establish; to form.
CONSTITU'TION,° the fundamental laws of a nation or society.
CONTRAST',° to place in opposition.
DESTITU'TION, want; poverty.
DIS'TANT,° remote; not near.
EQUIDIS'TANT, at the same distance.
ESTAB'LISH, to settle firmly.
EX'TANT,° in being; not suppressed.
IN'STANCE,° example; urgency.
IN'STANT, pressing; urgent.
INSTANTA'NEOUS, immediate.
IN'STITUTE, to establish.
INSUBSTAN'TIAL, not real.
IN'TERSTICE,° narrow space between things.
INTERSTITI'AL, containing interstices.
OB'STACLE, a hinderance.
PRIEST,° a sacred officer.
PROS'TITUTE, to debase.
REINSTATE', to put again in possession.
REST,° repose; quiet.
RESTITU'TION, a giving back.
SOL'STICE, the tropical point.
STAM'EN, the fixed, firm part of a body which gives it strength.
STAND, to be erect; to remain fixed.
STAND'ARD,° an ensign of war; a test.
STATE,° rank; condition.
STAT'ICS, that branch of mechanics which treats of bodies at rest.

STA'TION, situation ; position.
STA'TIONARY, fixed.
STATIS'TICS,° statement of the strength and resources of nations.
STAT'UE, a standing image.
SUB'STANCE, being ; body.
SUBSTAN'TIAL, real ; material.
SUB'STANTIVE, having separate existence.
SUB'STITUTE, to put in place of another.
SUPERSTITI'ON,° false religion.
TRANSUBSTAN'TIATE, to change to another substance.

Sto-a (στοα), a portico.

STO'IC,° an ancient philosopher.
STO'ICISM, the doctrines of the Stoics.

Stor-o, *for* Stauro, to give or bring.

RESTORE', to give back.
RESTORA'TION, a giving back.

Strangul-o, to choke.

STRAN'GLE, to choke ; to suffocate.
STRANGULA'TION, the act of strangling.

Strat-os (στρατος), an army.

STRAT'AGEM, a military artifice.
STRATOC'RACY, a military government.

Strep-o, to make a noise. OBSTREP'EROUS, noisy ; clamorous.

String-o, strict-um, to bind, to contract.

ASTRING'ENT, binding ; contracting.
CONSTRIC'TION, a contraction.
CONSTRAIN', to compel.
RESTRAINT', hinderance of the will.
RESTRICT', to limit ; to confine.
STRAIN, to make violent efforts.
STRICT, exact ; severe.
STRICT'URE, a contraction ; critical censure.
UNCONSTRAINED', voluntary.

Strophe (στροφη), a turning round.

APOS'TROPHE,° a figure of speech; an address.
APOS'TROPHIZE, to address by an apostrophe.
CATAS'TROPHE,° an unfortunate accident ; a final event.

Stru-o, struct-um, to build.

CON'STRUE,° to interpret ; to explain.
CONSTRUCT', to build ; to form.
DESTROY', to ruin ; to pull down.
DESTRUC'TION, the act of destroying.
INDESTRUC'TIBLE, not to be destroyed.
INSTRUCT', to teach ; to inform.
IN'STRUMENT, a tool ; a means.
MISCON'STRUE, to interpret wrong.
MISCONSTRUC'TION, wrong interpretation.
OBSTRUCT', to oppose ; to hinder.
SUPERSTRUC'TURE, that part of the building above the foundation.
UNINSTRUCT'IVE, not imparting knowledge.

Stud-eo, to study.

STU'DENT, a scholar.
STU'DIOUS, given to study.
STUD'Y, to learn; to consider attentively.

Stult-us, foolish.

STULTIL'OQUENCE, foolish talk.
STUL'TIFY, to make foolish.

Stup-eo, to be dull, to astonish.

STUPEN'DOUS, amazing; wonderful.
STU'PEFY, to make stupid.
STUPEFAC'TION, insensibility; dullness.
STU'PID, dull; senseless.

Styl-os (στυλος), a column or pillar; a style.

STYLE, manner of writing or speaking.
STY'LIFORM, shaped like the stylos or pen of the ancients.

Styx,° styg-is, a fountain of Arcadia.

STYG'IAN, hellish, infernal.

Suad-eo, suas-um, to advise.

ASSUAGE', to appease; to ease.
ASSUA'SIVE, mitigating.
DISSUADE', to advise from.
DISSUA'SION, the act of dissuading.
PERSUADE', to influence by argument or entreaty.
PERSUA'SIVE, having power to persuade.
SUA'SION, the act of persuading.

Suav-is, sweet.

SUAV'ITY, sweetness; softness.
SWEET, not sour; agreeable.

Sublim-is, high; exalted.

SUBLIME', lofty; grand.
SUBLIM'ITY, grandeur.
SUB'LIMATE, to refine.

Subtil-is, fine, cunning,

SUB'TILE, acute; artful.
SUBT'LETY, artifice; slyness.
SUB'TILIZE, to make thin.
SUPERSUBT'LE, over subtle.

Sud-o, to sweat.

EXUDE', to sweat out.
SUDORIF'IC, causing sweat.
SWEAT, moisture from the skin.
TRANSUDE', to sweat through.

Sueo, suet-um, to be accustomed.

AS'SUETUDE, custom; use.
DES'UETUDE, disuse; neglect.

Suffragi-um, a vote; assistance.

SUF'FRAGE, a vote.
SUF'FRAGAN, an assistant bishop.

Sug-o, suct-um, to suck or draw in.

SUCK, to draw into the mouth.
SUCK'LE, to nurse at the breast.
SUC'TION, the act of sucking.
SUC'CULENT, juicy; moist

Sui, of one's self.

SU'ICIDE, self-murder.

SUICI'DAL, self-destroying.

Sulphur, brimstone.

SULPHU'REOUS, resembling sulphur.

SULPHU'RIC, consisting of sulphur.

Summ-a, the whole.

CON'SUMMATE, complete; finished.

SUM, the amount.

SUM'MARY, a compendium.

SUM'MIT, the top; the utmost height.

Sum-o, sumpt-um, to take.

ASSUME', to arrogate; to take.

ASSUMP'SIT,° a promise, (law term.)

CONSUME', to waste slowly.

CONSUMP'TION, a disease; waste.

INCONSU'MABLE, not to be wasted.

PRESUME',° to suppose.

PRESUMP'TUOUS, arrogant; confident.

PRESUMP'TIVE, supposed.

REASSUME', to take again.

RESUME', to take back; to recommence.

SUMP'TUARY, relating to expense

SUMP'TUOUS, expensive.

UNASSU'MING, not arrogant; modest.

Super, above; high.

INSU'PERABLE, invincible; insurmountable.

SOV'EREIGN, supreme; chief.

SUPERCIL'IOUS,° haughty; overbearing.

SUPERB', grand; magnificent.

SUPER'LATIVE, highest.

SUPERN'AL, relating to things above.

SUPREME', highest in authority.

Supin-us, reclining.

SU'PINE, lying with the face upwards; indolent.

Surg-o, surrect-um, to rise.

INSUR'GENT,° a rebel.

INSURREC'TION,° a rebellion.

SOURCE, origin; first cause.

SURGE, a large wave.

Syc-os (συκος), a fig.

SYC'AMORE, a kind of fig-tree.

SYC'OPHANT,° a mean flatterer.

Tabern-a, a tent; an inn.

TAB'ERNACLE,° a temporary dwelling.

TAV'ERN, an inn; a public house.

Tabul-a, a board, a table.

TA'BLE, an article of furniture.

TAB'ULAR, in the form of a table.

TAB'LET, a flat surface for writing.

Taceo, tacit-um, to be silent.

TAC'IT, silent; implied.

TACITURN'ITY, habitual silence.

Tact-os (τακτος), put in order.

EU'TAXY, established order.
SYN'TAX, the construction of sentences.
SYNTAC'TIC, relating to syntax.
TAC'TICS,° the art of directing movements in war.

Taill-er (Fr.), to cut, to deal.

DETAIL', a minute account.
ENTAIL', to settle the descent of an estate.
RE'TAIL, sale by small quantities.
TAI'LOR, one who cuts out men's clothes.

Tal-is, such; like for like.

RETAL'IATE, to return like for like.
TA'LION, the law of retaliation.
TAL'LY, to fit; to suit.

Tang-o, tact-um, to touch.

ATTAIN',° to gain; to reach to.
CON'TACT, touch; close union.
CONTA'GION, propagation of disease by touch; infection.
CONTIGU'ITY, actual contact.
CONTIN'GENT, accidental; casual.
ENTIRE', whole; unbroken.
INCONTIG'UOUS, not touching.
IN'TEGER,° a whole number.
IN'TEGRATE, to form one whole.
IN'TEGRAL, whole; not fractional.
INTEG'RITY, honesty; purity.
REDIN'TEGRATE, restored; made whole.
TACT, touch; peculiar skill.
TAN'GENT,° a line touching a curve.
TAN'GIBLE, that can be touched or taken hold of.

Taph-os (ταφος), a tomb.

CEN'OTAPH, a monument for one buried elsewhere.
EP'ITAPH, an inscription upon a tomb.

Tard-us, slow.

RETARD', to delay; to hinder.
TAR'DY, slow; not swift.

Tartar-us, hell. TARTA'REAN, belonging to hell.

Tast-er, for Tater (Fr.), to try by the mouth, to feel.

DISTASTE', dislike; aversion.
TASTE, to perceive and distinguish by the palate.

Taur-us, a bull.

TAUR'US, the second sign in the zodiac.
TAUR'ICORNOUS, having horns like a bull.

Taut-os (ταυτος), the same.

TAUTOL'OGY, repetition of the same words, or the same sense in different words.
TAUTOLOG'ICAL, containing tautology.

Tax-o, to tax.

TAX, a charge for the use of the state.
TAXA'TION, the act of imposing taxes.

Techn-e (τεχνη), an art or science.

POLYTECH'NIC, embracing many arts.
PYR'OTECHNY, the art of making fireworks.
TECH'NICAL, belonging to art.
TECHNOL'OGY, a discourse upon the arts.

Tect-on (τεκτων), an artist, a fabricator.

AR'CHITECTURE, the science of building.
AR'CHITECT, a builder; a former.

Tedi-um, *for* ***Tœdium,*** weariness, disgust.

TE'DIOUS, wearying; irksome.
TE'DIUM, irksomeness.

Teg-o, tect-um, to cover.

DETECT', to discover.
INTEG'UMENT,° a covering.
PROTECT', to defend; to cover.
PROTECT'ORATE, government by a protector.

Tel-os (τελος), the end, distance.

TEL'EGRAPH, a machine for conveying intelligence to a distance by signals.
TEL'ESCOPE, an instrument for viewing distant objects.

Temer-e, rashly. TEMER'ITY, rashness.

Temn-o, tempt-um, to scorn.

CONTEMN', to despise; to slight.
CONTEMPT', disregard; scorn.

Temper-o, to temper, to regulate.

ATTEM'PER, to soften; to regulate.
DISTEM'PER,° disease.
TEM'PER, disposition.
TEM'PERANCE, moderation.
TEM'PERATE, moderate.
TEM'PERAMENT, native constitution.
TEM'PERATURE, state as regards heat or cold.

Tempus, tempor-is, time.

CONTEM'PORARY, one who lives in the same age with another.
CONTEMPORA'NEOUS, existing at the same time.
EXTEM'PORE,° without premeditation.
INTEMPEST'IVE, untimely.
TEM'PEST,° a violent storm.
TEM'PORAL,° relating to time.
TEM'PORARY, lasting for a time.
TEM'PORIZE, to yield to circumstances.
TENSE, an inflection of verbs to denote time.
TIME, the measure of duration.

Tend-o, tens-um, to stretch.

ATTEND',° to regard; to wait on.
ATTEN'TION,° regard; care.
COEXTEND', to extend equally.
CONTEND', to strive; to struggle.
CONTEN'TION, strife; emulation.
DISTEND', to stretch; to expand.
DISTEN'TION, the act of stretching.
EXTEND', to reach; to spread.
EXTEN'SIVE, large; wide spread

EXTENT′, size; compass.
INTEND′,° to mean; to design.
INTENSE′,° strained; ardent.
INTENS′ITY, ardor; violence.
INTENT′, purpose.
OSTEN′SIBLE, plausible; seeming.
OSTENTA′TION, vain display.
PORTEND′, to foretoken.
PORTENT′, an omen; a prodigy.
PRETEND′,° to feign.
PRETENSE′, a feigning.
SUBTEND′, to extend under.
SUPERINTEND′, to direct; to overlook.
TEND, to aim at; to contribute.
TEND′ENCY,° direction; course.
TEN′DON, a sinew; a cord.
TEN′DRIL, a spiral shoot of a plant.
TENSE, stiff; stretched.
TEN′SION, tightness.
TEN′SOR, that which stretches.
TENT,° a portable dwelling.
UNINTEN′TIONAL, not designed.
UNOSTENTA′TIOUS, not making display.

Ten-eo, tent-um, to hold.

ABSTAIN′, to keep from.
ABSTE′MIOUS, temperate; sober.
AB′STINENT, refraining.
APPERTAIN′, to belong; to relate.
APPUR′TENANCE, an appendage.
CONTAIN′, to hold; to comprise.
CONTENT′,° satisfied.
CON′TINENCE, restraint upon passion.
CONTIN′UE, to remain; to last.
CONTIN′UAL, incessant.
CONTINU′ITY, unbroken connection.
COUN′TENANCE,° features; look.
DETAIN′, to keep back.
DETEN′TION, confinement; restraint.
DISCONTENT′ED, uneasy; dissatisfied.
DISCONTIN′UANCE, cessation.
DISCOUN′TENANCE, to discourage; to abash.
ENTERTAIN′, to harbor; to amuse.
IMPER′TINENCE, rudeness; insolence.
LIEUTEN′ANT, an officer who acts in the absence of a superior.
MAINTAIN′,° to support; to persist in.
MAL-CONTENT′, one dissatisfied.
OBTAIN′, to gain; to acquire.
PERTAIN′, to belong to.
PERTINA′CIOUS,° obstinate; stubborn.
PER′TINENT, to the purpose.
RETAIN′, to keep; to reserve.
RETEN′TIVE, having the power to retain.
RET′INUE, a train of attendants.
SUSTAIN′, to support; to prop.
SUS′TENANCE, support.
TENA′CIOUS, holding fast.
TEN′ANT, an occupier of a house or lands.
TEN′EMENT,° a house; an abode.
TEN′ET,° an opinion; a principle.
TEN′OR, a part in music.
TEN′URE, a holding.
UNTEN′ABLE, not to be held or maintained.

Tent-o, tentat-um, to try.

ATTEMPT′, a trial; an effort.
TEMPT′, to solicit; to entice.
TENT′ATIVE, trying; essaying.

Tenu-is, thin.

ATTEN'UATE, to make thin.
TENU'ITY, thinness.
EXTEN'UATE,° to lessen; to palliate.

Tepe-o, to be warm.

TEP'EFY, to make warm.
TEP'ID, lukewarm.

Terg-eo, *or* ***Tergo***, ***ters-um***, to wipe.

DETERG'ENT, cleansing.
TERSE, neat; well-finished.

Terg-um, the back.

TER'GIVERSATE, to shift; to practice evasion.

Termin-us, a limit, end.

CONTERM'INOUS, having a common boundary.
DETERM'INE, to resolve; to fix.
DETERM'INATE, fixed; definite.
EXTERM'INATE, to destroy.
INDETERM'INATE, not defined.
INTER'MINABLE, having no end.
PREDETERM'INE, to resolve previously.
TERM, boundary; condition; a word or expression.
TERM'INATE, to close; to end.
TERMINOL'OGY, a treatise on terms.

Tern-us, threefold; ***Terti-us***, three.

TERN'ARY, consisting of three.
THIRD, the ordinal of three.
TER'TIAN, occurring every other day.

Tero, ***trit-um***, to rub, to wear by rubbing.

ATTRITI'ON, a rubbing.
CON'TRITE,° sorrowful; penitent.
DET'RIMENT,° loss; damage.
DETRI'TUS, matter worn off.
TRITE, worn out; common.
TRIT'URATE, to rub or grind to a fine powder.

Terr-a, the earth.

DISINTER', to take out of the earth.
FRONTIER', the border of a country.
INTER', to bury in the earth.
MEDITERRA'NEAN, encircled with land.
TER'RACE, a raised bank of earth; a flat roof.
TERRA'QUEOUS, composed of land and water.
TERRES'TRIAL, earthly.
TER'RIER, a small dog that hunts under ground.
TER'RITORY, a tract of land.

Terr-eo, to make afraid.

DETER',° to hinder; to discourage.
TER'ROR, extreme fear.
TER'RIFY, to frighten.
TERRIF'IC, causing fear.

Test-a, a shell; an earthen pot.

TEST,° a trial; a standard.
TESTA'CEOUS, composed of shells.

Test-is, a witness.

ATTEST′, to bear witness.
CON′TEST, dispute; struggle.
DETESTA′TION, abhorrence.
INCONTEST′ABLE, not to be disputed.
INTEST′ATE, dying without having made a will.
OBTEST′, to beseech; to call to witness.
PROTEST′,° to declare against.
PROT′ESTANT, one who protests.
TEST′AMENT, a will.
TESTA′TOR, one who makes a will.
TEST′IFY, to witness; to give evidence.
TESTIMO′NIAL, a certificate.
TEST′IMONY,° a declaration; evidence.

Tetr-a, *for* ***Tessares*** (τετρα), four.

TET′RACHORD, a series of four sounds.
TETRAM′ETER, a verse consisting of four feet.
TET′RARCH,° a Roman governor.
TES′SELATED, formed into squares.

Teuch-os (τευχος), a vessel; a book.

PEN′TATEUCH, the five books of Moses.

Text-us, woven.

CON′TEXT,° the connected passages.
PRE′TEXT, pretence; feigned motive.
TEXT, a passage upon which a discourse is made.
TEXT′URE, the thing woven; the quality of that which is woven.

Thanat-os (θανατος), death. EUTHAN′ASY, easy death.

Theatr-um (θεατρον), a theatre.

AMPHITHE′ATRE,° a theatre of circular form.
THE′ATRE, a place of action or exhibition.

Thec-e (θηκη), a place of deposit.

APOTH′ECARY, one who sells drugs.
BIBLIOTH′ECAL, pertaining to a library.

Theor-os (θεωρος), a beholder, a speculator.

THE′OREM,° a proposition to be demonstrated.
THE′ORY, speculation.
THEORET′IC, speculative; not practical.
THE′ORIZE, to form theories.

The-os (θεος), a god.

APOTHE′OSIS,° deification.
A′THEIST, one who denies the existence of a God.
ENTHU′SIASM,° violence of passion.
PAN′THEIST, one who confounds God with the universe.
MON′OTHEISM, belief in one God.
THEOC′RACY, government directed by God.
THEOG′ONY, the generation of the gods.
THEOL′OGY, the science of God and divine things.

Therm-os (θερμος), warm.

ISOTHERM'AL, having equal heat.
THER'MAL, pertaining to heat.
THERMOM'ETER, a measurer of heat.
THER'MOSCOPE, a thermometer.

Thesis (θεσις), a placing or putting.

ANATH'EMA,° ecclesiastical curse.
ANTITH'ESIS,° opposition of words or sentiment.
EP'ITHET, a descriptive word.
HYPOTH'ECATE,° to pawn; to pledge.
PAREN'THESIS, a sentence or clause within another.
HYPOTH'ESIS, a supposition.
SYN'THESIS,° a putting together; combination.
SYNTHET'ICAL, relating to synthesis.
THEME,° a subject.
THE'SIS,° a position; a proposition advanced.

Thron-us (θρονος), a throne.

DETHRONE', to deprive of royal power.
ENTHRONE', to put on a throne.
THRONE, a king's seat of state.

Thus, thur-is, incense.

THURIF'EROUS, bearing frankincense.
THURIFICA'TION, the act of burning incense.

Tim-eo, to fear.

INTIM'IDATE, to make fearful.
TIM'ID, fearful.
TIM'OROUS, cowardly.

Ting-o, tinct-um (τεγγω), to dip, to paint, to stain.

ATTAIN'DER,° the act of attainting.
ATTAINT', to corrupt; to find guilty of treason.
TAINT, corruption; blemish.
TINCT'URE, a liquid containing the principal qualities of some substance.
TINGE, to infuse or impregnate slightly.
TINT, a dye; a slight coloring.

Titill-o, to tickle.

TIT'ILLATE, to tickle.
TITILLA'TION, a tickling.

Titul-us, title, inscription.

ENTI'TLE,° to give a claim.
TI'TLE, an appellation of honor; a claim of right.
TIT'ULAR, relating to a title.
UNTI'TLED, having no title.

Toler-o, tolerat-um, to bear, to suffer.

INTOL'ERABLE, that cannot be borne.
INTOL'ERANCE, want of toleration
TOL'ERANT, enduring; permitting.
TOLERA'TION, allowance of that which is not approved.

Toll-o, to raise.

EXTOL', to praise; to exalt.
TOLL, a tax; a charge for passing.

Tom-os (τομος), a cutting.

ANAT'OMY, the art of dissecting.
AT'OM, an indivisible particle.
ENTOMOL'OGY, a treatise upon insects.
EPIT'OME, an abridgment; a compendium.
GASTROT'OMY, a cutting into the abdomen.
PHLEBOT'OMY, the art of bleeding.
TRACHEOT'OMY, a cutting into the windpipe.

Ton-os (τονος), a stretching, a sound.

ASTON'ISH, to surprise; to amaze.
ASTOUND', to strike dumb.
ATTUNE', to put in tune.
DET'ONATE, to explode.
HYPOT'ENUSE,° the longest side of a right-angled triangle.
INTONA'TION, manner of sounding.
MONOT'ONY, uniformity of tone or sound.
THUN'DER, the report which follows lightning.
TONE, tension; vigor; sound.
TON'IC, increasing tension or vigor; imparting tone.
TUNE, sound; note; harmony.

Top-os (τοπος), a place.

TOPOG'RAPHY, a description of a place.
TOP'IC, a subject of discourse.

Torp-eo, to benumb; to be stiff.

TORPE'DO, an electric fish.
TOR'PID, numbed; sluggish.
TOR'PITUDE, sluggishness.
TOR'POR, numbness.

Torre-o, to dry, to parch.

TOR'REFY, to dry by fire.
TORREFAC'TION, a drying by fire.
TOR'RENT, a rapid stream.
TOR'RID, parched; dried.

Tort-um (*ab* ***Torqueo***), to twist; to writhe.

CONTORT', to writhe.
DISTOR'TION, a twisting out of shape.
EXTOR'TION,° illegal exaction.
RETORT', to throw back a censure or objection.
TOR'MENT, extreme pain.
TOR'SEL, something twisted.
TOR'TIOUS, wrongful.
TORT'UOUS, twisted; crooked.
TORT'URE, agony.
UNDISTORT'ED, not perverted.

Tot-us, whole, all.

FACTO'TUM, one who can perform all kinds of service.
SURTOUT',° an overcoat.
TO'TAL, the whole.

Toxic-um, poison.

INTOX'ICATE,° to make drunk.
TOXICOL'OGY, a discourse on poisons.

Trache-a, the windpipe.

TRACHEOT'OMY, a cutting into the windpipe.
TRA'CHEA, the windpipe.

Trad-o, tradit-um, to deliver, to hand down.

TRADITI'ON, oral account handed down from age to age.
TRAI'TOR, one who betrays trust.
TRAD'ITIVE, transmitted from age to age.

Tragedi-a, for Tragœdia, a tragedy.

TRAG'EDY, dramatic representation of a fatal action.
TRAG'IC, mournful; fatal.
TRAGICOM'IC, half tragic and half comic.

Trah-o, tract-um, to draw.

ABSTRACT',° to draw from.
ABSTRAC'TION, absence of mind.
ATTRACT', to draw to; to allure.
ATTRACT'IVE, engaging.
BETRAY', to give up treacherously.
CONTRACT', to draw together.
DETRACT', to take from.
DISTRACT',° to draw apart; to separate; to perplex.
DRAG, to draw along.
EXTRACT', to draw out.
INTRACT'ABLE, stubborn; unmanageable.
POR'TRAIT,° a likeness.
PORTRAY',° to delineate.
PROTRACT',° to prolong.
RETRACT', to draw or take back.
SUBTRACT', to deduct.
TRACE, a mark left by any thing passing; a vestige.
TRACK,° a foot-print; a path.
TRACT, a region; a small treatise.
TRADE, commerce; traffic.
TRAIL, to draw along on the ground.
TRAIN, something drawn along.
TRAIT, a feature; a line
TREAT, to use; to discuss
TREAT'ISE,° a discourse; an essay.
TREAT'Y, a contract; a league.

Tranquill-us, calm, peaceful.

TRAN'QUIL, calm; peaceful.
TRAN'QUILLIZE, to soothe; to compose.

Trapezium (τραπέζιον), a figure with four unequal sides.

TRAPE'ZIUM, a plane figure with four unequal sides, and none of them parallel.
TRAPE'ZOID, a solid figure with four sides and none of them parallel.

Travail (Fr.), labor.

TRAV'AIL, labor; toil.
TRAV'EL,° to journey; to pass.

Trem-o, to shake.

TREM'BLE, to shake; to quiver.
TREMEN'DOUS, terrible; dreadful.
TRE'MOR, a trembling.
TREM'ULOUS, shaking; quivering.

Trepid-us, trembling.

INTREP'ID, fearless; daring.
TREPIDA'TION, fear; tremor.

Tres, tri-a (τρεις, τρια), three.

TREB'LE, threefold.
TRE'FOIL, three-leaved clover.
TRI'AD, the union of three.
TRIAN'DER, a plant having three stamens.
TRI'ANGLE, a figure having three angles.
TRICHOT'OMY, division into three parts.
TRICOR'PORAL, having three bodies.
TRI'DENT,° an instrument having three prongs.
TRIEN'NIAL, happening every three years.
TRIF'ID, divided into three.
TRI'FLE,° a thing of little value.
TRIGONOM'ETRY, the art of measuring triangles.
TRILAT'ERAL, having three sides.
TRIM'ETER, a verse of three feet.
TRIN'ITY, a union of three in one.
TRINO'MIAL, in mathematics, a root of three terms or parts.
TRI'O, a part in music for three performers.
TRIP'ARTITE, having three corresponding parts.
TRIPH'THONG, a union of three vowels in one sound.
TRIP'LE, threefold.
TRI'POD,° a three-legged stool.
TRI'REME, a galley with three benches of oars on a side.
TRISECT', divided into three parts.
TRIS'YLLABLE, a word of three syllables.
TRIUM'VIR, one of three men united in office.
TRI'UNE, three in one.
TRIV'IAL,° trifling; worthless.

Trib-us, a tribe.

TRIBE, a distinct body of people.
TRIBU'NAL, a court of justice.
TRIB'UNE,° a Roman officer.
TRIBUNITI'AL, relating to a tribune.

Tribut-um (*ab* ***Tribuo***), to give.

ATTRIB'UTE, to ascribe.
CONTRIB'UTE, to give in common with others.
DISTRIBU'TION, a giving to several.
RETRIB'UTIVE, repaying.
TRIB'UTE, a tax paid to a conqueror.
TRIB'UTARY, paying tribute.

Tric-æ (θριξ, τριχος), an impediment.

EX'TRICATE, to free from.
INEX'TRICABLE, that cannot be disentangled.
IN'TRICACY, complexity.
INTRIGUE', a plot; an amour.
TRICK, a sly fraud.

Triumph-us, triumph. TRIUMPH'ANT, exulting.

Trop-os (τροπος), a turning.

HE'LIOTROPE, a plant that turns to the sun.
TROPE,° a figure of speech which changes a word from its ordinary meaning.
TROP'IC,° the point at which the sun appears to turn again towards the north or from it.
TRO'PHY, a monument of victory.

Trouv-er (Fr.), to find.

CONTRIVE', to plan; to invent.
CONTRI'VANCE, a plan; a scheme.
IRRETRIE'VABLE, not to be recovered.
RETRIEVE', to repair; to regain.

Trud-o, trus-um, to thrust, to push.

ABSTRUSE′,° concealed; obscure.
DETRUDE′, to thrust down.
EXTRUDE′, to thrust off.
INTRUDE′, to thrust one's self in; to encroach.
INTRU′SION, the act of intruding.
OBTRUDE′, to thrust in or on.
INTRU′SIVE, entering without invitation.
OBTRU′SIVE, bold; intrusive.
PROTRUDE′, to thrust forward.
PROTRU′SION, a thrusting forward.
UNOBTRU′SIVE, not forward; modest.

Trunc-o, truncat-um, to lop, to cut off.

DETRUN′CATE, to cut off; to lop.
OBTRUNCA′TION, a cutting off.
TRUNC′ATE, maimed; cut off short.
TRUN′CHEON, a short staff; a club.
TRUNK, the main body of any thing; a chest.

Trux, truc-is, fierce.

TRU′CULENCE, fierceness.
TRU′CULENT, fierce; cruel.

Tuber, a swelling.

PROTU′BERANCE, a prominence; a swelling.
TU′BER, a knob in roots.
TU′BERCLE, a little tumor.

Tub-us, a pipe or tube.

TUBE, a long hollow vessel.
TU′BULAR, resembling a tube.
TU′BULIFORM, in the shape of a tube.

Tue-or, tuit-us, to keep, to protect; to see.

INTU′ITIVE, seen instantly by the mind.
TUITI′ON, instruction.
TU′TELAGE, guardianship; care.
TU′TELAR, protecting.
TU′TOR, a teacher; a guardian.

Tume-o, to swell.

CONTUMA′CIOUS,° stubborn.
CON′TUMELY,° rudeness; insolence.
ENTOMB′, to put into a tomb.
INTUMES′CENCE, a swollen state.
TOMB,° a grave; a burial place.
TUM′BLE, to fall; to roll about.
TU′MEFY, to swell.
TU′MID, swollen; pompous.
TU′MOR, a swelling.
TU′MULT,° a commotion.
TUMULT′UARY, disorderly.

Tund-o, tus-um, to beat, to bruise, to blunt.

CONTUND′, to beat; to bruise.
CONTU′SION, a bruise.
OBTUSAN′GULAR, having obtuse angles.
OBTUSE′, dull; blunted.

Turb-a, a crowd, confusion.

DISTURB′, to disquiet.
IMPERTURB′ABLE, not to be disturbed.
PERTURBA′TION, disquiet; mental agitation.
TROUB′LE, perplexity.
TUR′BID, muddy; not clear
TUR′BULENT, tumultuous.
TUR′MOIL, tumult; trouble.

Turg-eo, to swell.

TURGES'CENCE, inflation; bombast.
TUR'GID, bloated; swollen; bombastic.

Typ-us (τυπος), a type, a mark.

AN'TITYPE, the model of a type.
STER'EOTYPE, solid type.
TYP'ICAL, symbolical.
TYPE, an emblem; a printing letter.
TYPOG'RAPHY, the art of printing.

Tyrann-us (τυραννος), a despot.

TY'RANT, a cruel ruler.
TYRAN'NIC, relating to a tyrant.
TYRAN'NICIDE, the murder of a tyrant.

Uber, fertile.

EXU'BERANT, abundant.
U'BERTY, fruitfulness.

Ubi, where. UBIQ'UITY, a being everywhere at the same time.

Ulcus, ulcer-is, a sore.

UL'CER, a running sore.
UL'CERATE, to turn to an ulcer.

Ultim-us, last.

ANTEPENULT', the last syllable but two.
OUT'RAGE, wanton injury.
ULTE'RIOR, further.
PE'NULT, the last syllable but one.
UL'TIMATE, final; last.
ULTIMA'TUM, a final proposition.

Umbr-a, a shadow, or shade.

PENUM'BRA, an imperfect shade.
UM'BRAGE, offence.
UMBRA'GEOUS, shady.
UMBREL'LA, a screen or shade carried in the hand.

Und-o, undat-um, to rise in waves.

ABOUND', to be in great plenty.
ABUND'ANT, plentiful.
INUNDA'TION, a flood.
REDOUND', to conduce; to result.
REDUND'ANCY, superfluity.
SUPERABOUND', to be very abundant.
SUPERABUND'ANT, very plentiful.
UN'DULATE, to wave; to vibrate.
UN'DULATORY, moving like waves.

Ungu-o, unct-um, to anoint.

UNC'TION, an anointing.
UNC'TUOUS, oily.
UN'GUENT, ointment.
OINT'MENT, a salve.
ANOINT', to rub with oil.

Un-us, one, alone.

DISU'NION, separation.
RE-UNITE', to join again.
TRIUNE', three in one.
UNAN'IMOUS, of one mind.
U'NICORN, a beast with one horn
U'NIFORM, even; regular.
U'NION, concord; conjunction
UNIQUE', sole; peculiar.

U'NISON, agreement; harmony.
U'NIT, a single thing.
UNITE', to concur; to join.
UNIVALV'ULAR, having one valve.
UNIVERS'ITY, a universal school in which all branches of learning are taught.
U'NIVERSE, the whole system of things.

Uran-os (οὐρανος), heaven.

URANOG'RAPHY, a description of the heavens.
URANOL'OGY, a discourse on the heavens.

Urbs, a city.

SUB'URBS, the outpart of a city.
URBAN'ITY, politeness.

Urg-eo, to press on.

URGE, to press; to solicit.
UR'GENT, pressing; earnest.
UR'GENCY, pressure; earnest solicitation.

Ust-um (*ab* ***Uro***), to burn.

COMBUS'TION, a burning.
INCOMBUST'IBLE, not to be burned

Ut-or, usus, to use.

ABUSE', to make an ill use of.
DISUSE', to cease to use.
INUTIL'ITY, uselessness.
MISU'SAGE, ill use.
PERUSE',°to read.
USE, to employ.
U'SAGE, custom; treatment.
U'SUAL, ordinary.
U'SUFRUCT,° temporary use.
U'SURY,°illegal interest.
USU'RIOUS, practising usury.
USURPA'TION, illegal seizure.
UTEN'SIL, a vessel; an instrument.

Uxor, a wife.

UXOR'ICIDE, murder of a wife.
UXO'RIOUS, fond of a wife.

Vacc-a, a cow.

VAC'CINE, belonging to a cow.
VAC'CINATE, to inoculate with vaccine matter.

Vac-o, vacat-um, to be empty.

EVAC'UATE, to quit; to leave.
VA'CANT, empty.
VACA'TION, recess; leisure.
VAC'UUM, empty space.
VACU'ITY, emptiness.

Vacill-o, to waver.

FIC'KLE, wavering; changing.
VAC'ILLATE, to wavei.

Vad-o, vas-um, to go.

EVADE', to avoid; to escape.
EVA'SIVE, avoiding; eluding.
INVADE',°to attack; to assail.
INVA'SION, a hostile entrance.
PERVADE', to pass through.
VADE-ME'CUM,° a manual.
WADE, to walk through water

Vag-us, a wandering.

EXTRAV'AGANT,° prodigal; wasteful; excessive.
VAG'ABOND, an idle fellow.
VAGA'RY, a whim; a wild freak.
VA'GRANT, an idle wanderer.
VAGUE, uncertain; unsettled.

Val-eo, to be well or strong, to be worth.

AVAIL,' to be of use.
CONVALES'CENT, improving in health.
COUNTERVAIL', to bàlance.
EQUIV'ALENT, equal in value.
IN'VALID, a sick person.
INVAL'IDATE, to weaken.
PREVAIL', to overcome; to be general.
INVAL'UABLE, extremely precious.
PREV'ALENCE, influence; predominance.
VALEDIC'TION, a farewell.
VALETUDINA'RIAN, weakly; sickly.
VALID'ITY, strength.
VAL'OR, personal bravery.
VAL'UE, worth; price.

Vall-um, a fence.

CIRCUMVALLA'TION, a wall round a place; a rampart.
IN'TERVAL, space between places.
WALL, a work of stone or brick to enclose or defend a place.

Valv-æ, folding-doors.

BIVALV'ULAR, having two valves.
TRIVALV'ULAR, having three valves.
VALVE, a folding-door.
VALV'ULE, a small valve.

Van-us, vain, empty, boastful.

EVANES'CENT, vanishing.
VAIN, empty; worthless.
VAN'ISH, to disappear.
VAN'ITY, idle show.
VAUNT, to boast.

Vapor, steam; fume.

EVAP'ORATE, to disperse in vapors.
VAPORIF'IC, converting into vapor.
VA'POR, fume; steam.
VAPORIZA'TION, the artificial formation of vapor.

Varico, varicat-um, to straddle, to shuffle.

PREVAR'ICATE, to evade the truth; to shuffle.
PREVARICA'TION, the act of prevaricating.

Variol-æ, small pimples.

VA'RIOLOID, a disease resembling the small-pox.
VARI'OLOUS, pertaining to the small-pox.

Vari-us, diverse, changeable.

INVA'RIABLE, unchangeable.
VA'RY, to change.
VA'RIANCE, dissension.
VA'RIEGATE, to diversify.
VARI'ETY, change; diversity

Vas, a vessel.

EXTRAV'ASATED, forced out of its proper vessels.
VASE, a vessel.
VAS'CULAR, full of vessels.
VES'SEL, a cask or utensil for holding liquids.

Vast-us, large, desert.

DEV'ASTATE, to ravage.
DEVASTA'TION, a laying waste.
VAST, large; great.
WASTE, a desolate country.

Vates, vatis, a prophet.

VAT'ICIDE, the murder of a prophet.
VATIC'INATE, to prophesy.

Veget-o, to grow.

VEG'ETABLE, a plant.
VEG'ETATE, to grow, as plants.

Veh-o, vect-um, to carry.

CON'VEX, rising in a spherical form.
CONVEY', to carry; to send.
CONVEY'ANCE, that which conveys.
INVEIGH', to censure.
INVEC'TIVE, angry abuse.
VE'HEMENCE, ardor; violence.
VE'HICLE, a carriage.
VET'ERINARY,° pertaining to farriery.
VEX, to trouble; to irritate.
VEXA'TIOUS, troublesome.
WEIGH, to ascertain the weight.

Vell-o, vuls-um, to pull; to pluck.

AVUL'SION, a rending.
CONVULSE', to give violent motion to.
REVEL', to draw back.
REVUL'SION, a drawing back.
VELLICA'TION, a twitching.

Vel-o, to cover, to conceal.

DEVEL'OPMENT, an unfolding.
ENVEL'OP, to enfold.
REVEAL', to disclose.
REVELA'TION, discovery; disclosure.
VEIL, to hide; to cover.
UNVEIL'ED, open to view.

Velox, veloc-is, swift. VELOC'ITY, swiftness.

Ven-a, a vein.

VEIN, a tube for the blood.
VENESEC'TION,° blood-letting.

Vend-o, vendit-um, to sell.

VENDUE', a public sale.
VENT, utterance; sale.

Ven-or, to hunt.

VEN'ARY, relating to hunting.
VEN'ISON,° the flesh of deer.

Venen-um, poison.

ENVEN'OM, to poison.
VENEFICI'AL, acting by poison.
VEN'OM, poison.
VEN'OMOUS, poisonous.

Vener-or, to adore, to reverence.

VEN'ERATE, to reverence.
VEN'ERABLE, worthy of reverence.

Ven-io, vent-um, to come, to go.

ADVENE', to come to.
AD'VENT, a coming.
ADVENTITI'OUS,° accidental.
ADVENT'URE, an enterprise; a risk.
AV'ENUE, a passage.
CIRCUMVENT',° to deceive; to cheat.
CONTRAVENE', to oppose; to baffle.
CONVENE', to assemble.
CONVE'NIENT, suitable; fit.
CON'VENT, a nunnery; a monastery.
CONVENT'ICLE, a meeting for worship.
CONVEN'TION, an assembly.
EVENT'UAL,° ultimate.
EVENT'UATE, to come to an end.
INCONVE'NIENCE, unfitness; disadvantage.
INTERVENE', to come between.
INVENT',° to discover; to feign.
IN'VENTORY, an account of goods.
PERADVENT'URE, perhaps.
PREVENT',° to hinder; to obstruct.
RECONVENE', to assemble again.
REV'ENUE,° income of a state.
SUPERVENE', to come as an addition; to happen to.
VENT, an aperture; a hole.
VENT'UROUS, daring; bold.

Venter, ventr-is, the belly.

VEN'TER, the belly.
VEN'TRICLE, a small cavity in an animal body.
VENTRIL'OQUISM,° the art of speaking from the stomach.

Vent-us, the wind.

VEN'TIDUCT, a passage for air.
VEN'TILATE, to cause a free circulation of air.

Ver, the spring. VER'NAL, belonging to spring.

Verber-o, verberat-um, to beat.

REVER'BERATE,° to resound.
VERBERA'TION, a beating.

Verb-um, a word.

AD'VERB, a part of speech.
PROV'ERB,° a maxim.
VERB'IAGE,° empty discourse.
VERBOSE', full of words.

Verd-is, *for* ***Viridis,*** green.

VER'DANT, flourishing; green.
VER'DEROR, an officer who has charge of the king's forests.
VER'DIGRIS, rust of copper.
VERD'URE, freshness of vegetation; greenness.

Vere-or, to fear, to reverence.

IRREV'ERENT, wanting respect.
REVERE', to respect highly.
REV'ERENCE, respect mingled with awe.
REV'EREND, worthy of reverence.
REVEREN'TIAL expressing or feeling reverence.
VERECUND'ITY, modesty.

Verg-o, to tend.

DIVERG′ENT, receding; separating.
CONVERGE′, to tend to one point.
VERGE, to tend; to incline.

Verm-is, a worm.

VERMEOL′OGY, a treatise upon worms.
VERMICEL′LI, a paste in the form of worms.
VERMIC′ULAR, resembling worms.
VERM′IFORM, in the shape of a worm.
VERMIL′ION, a bright red color; formerly the cochineal.
VERM′IFUGE, a medicine to destroy worms.
VERM′IN, noxious animals, insects, &c.
VERMIP′AROUS, producing worms.
VERMIV′OROUS, devouring worms.
WORM, an insect that crawls.

Vert-o, vers-um, to turn.

ADVERT′, to turn to.
AD′VERSE, opposite; hostile.
ADVERS′ITY,° misfortune; calamity.
ADVERTISE′, to publish a notice.
ANIMADVER′SION, censure.
ANNIVERS′ARY, a stated day coming once in every year.
AVERT′, to turn away.
AVER′SION, dislike.
CON′TROVERT,° to dispute.
CON′TROVERSY, disputation.
CONVERT′IBLE, susceptible of change.
CON′VERSANT, familiar.
CONVERSE′, to discourse with.
DIVERT′, to please; to turn off.
DIVER′TISEMENT, pleasure; delight.
DIVERS′ITY, variety; difference.
DIVERS′IFY, to vary.
DIVORCE′, legal dissolution of marriage.
INADVERT′ENT, negligent; inattentive.
INCONTROVERT′IBLE, not to be disputed.
INVERT′, to turn upside down.
INVER′SION, the act of inverting.
IRREVERS′IBLE, not to be recalled.
MALVERSA′TION, evil practice.
PERVERSE′,° cross; stubborn.
PERVERT′, to distort.
RECONVERT′, to convert anew.
RET′ROVERT, to turn back.
RETROVER′SION, the act of turning back.
REVERT′, to turn back.
REVERSE′, to repeal; to put in an opposite direction.
REVER′SION, a turning or falling back.
SUBVERT′, to overthrow; to ruin.
TERGIVERSA′TION, evasion: change.
TRANSVERSE′, lying across.
TRAV′ERSE, to cross; to pass over.
U′NIVERSE, the whole system of things.
UNIVERS′ALISM, the doctrine that all men will be saved.
UNIVERS′ITY, a universal school in which all branches of learning are taught.
VERS′ATILE, changing; turning with ease from one thing to another.
VERSE, a poetical line; a short division of any composition.
VER′SIFY, to make verse.
VERSIFICA′TION, the art of making verses.
VER′SION, a translation.
VERT′EX, the top; the point over head.
VERT′ICAL, overhead.
VERT′IGO,° giddiness.
VOR′TEX, a whirlpool.

Ver-us, true.

AVER', to declare positively.
VERAC'ITY, truth.
VER'DICT, the decision of a jury.
VER'IFY, to prove true.
VERISIM'ILAR, probable; likely.
VERISIMIL'ITUDE, resemblance to truth.
VER'ITY, truth.
VER'ILY, certainly; truly.

Vestigi-um, a footstep.

INVEST'IGATE,° to search into.
VES'TIGE, a trace; a mark.

Vest-is, clothing.

DIVEST', to strip; to deprive.
INVEST'ITURE, the act of giving possession.
INVEST', to clothe; to confer.
VEST, an outer garment.
VEST'URE, a garment; a robe.

Vet-o, to forbid. VE'TO,° a prohibition.

Vetus, veter-is, old.

INVET'ERATE, old; long established.
VET'ERAN,° an old soldier.

Vi-a, a way.

CON'VOY,° an attendance for defence.
DE'VIATE, to wander; to err.
EN'VOY,° a public messenger.
IMPER'VIOUS, impenetrable.
IN'VOICE, a catalogue of merchandise sent away.
OB'VIATE,° to remove; to prevent.
OB'VIOUS, plain; evident.
PER'VIOUS, admitting passage.
PRE'VIOUS, antecedent; prior.
TRI'FLE,° a thing of little value.
TRIV'IAL,° worthless; trifling.
VI'ADUCT, a structure supporting a passage way.
WAY, a road; a passage.

Vibr-o, vibrat-um, to swing.

VI'BRATE, to move to and fro.
VI'BRATORY, causing vibration.

Vic-is, a change, in stead.

VIC'AR, a substitute.
VICA'RIOUS, acting for another.
VICEGE'RENT, a deputy.
VICE'ROY, a king's deputy governor.
VICIS'SITUDE, change; revolution.
VIS'COUNT,° a degree of nobility next below an earl.

Vicin-us, neighboring.

VICIN'ITY, proximity.
VIC'INAGE, neighborhood.

Vid-eo, vis-um, to see.

ADVICE', counsel.
ADVI'SABLE, expedient; fit.
EN'VY,° hatred of another for his success, or excellence.
EV'IDENT, plain; apparent.
IMPROV'IDENT, wasteful; careless.
IMPRU'DENCE, indiscretion.
INVID'IOUS, exciting envy.
INVIS'IBLE, not to be seen.

JURISPRU'DENCE, the science of law.
PROVIDE', to supply; to prepare.
PROV'ENDER, food for cattle.
PROV'IDENCE, foresight.
PROVIDEN'TIAL, effected by Providence.
PROVISI'ON, victuals; food.
PROVI'SO, a condition.
PRU'DENCE,° practical wisdom.
PURVEY', to provide; to procure.
RESURVEY', to survey anew.
REVIEW', a critical examination.
REVISE', to re-examine.
REVIS'IT, to visit again.
SUPERVISE', to overlook.
SURVEY', to view; to oversee.
VIEW, prospect.
VIDEL'ICET, to wit; namely.
VIS'AGE, look; countenance.
VIS'IBLE, that may be seen.
VISI'ON, sight.
VIS'IT, to go to see.
VIS'OR, a mask.
VIS'TA, a view; a prospect.

Vidu-o, to deprive of, to part.

AVOID', to shun.
DEVICE', contrivance; design.
DEVOID', empty; free from.
DIVIDE', to separate.
DIV'IDEND, a share.
DIVISI'ON, act of dividing.
INDIVID'UAL, a single person.
INDIVIS'IBLE, that cannot be divided.
SUBDIVIDE', to divide a part into more parts.
SUBDIVISI'ON, the division of a part.
VOID, empty; unoccupied.
WID'OW, a woman whose husband is dead.

Vigil, watchful.

VIG'IL, a watch.
VIG'ILANCE, watchfulness.

Vigor, strength.

INVIG'ORATE, to strengthen.
VIG'OR, force; energy.
VIG'OROUS, full of strength.

Vil-is, of small price; base.

REVILE', to reproach; to abuse.
VILIFICA'TION, the act of vilifying.
VIL'IPEND, to treat with contempt.

Vill-a, a country seat.

VIL'LA, a country seat.
VIL'LAGE, a collection of houses

Villan-us, a villain.

VIL'LAIN, a wicked person.
VIL'LANY, wickedness; crime.

Vinc-o, vict-um, to conquer.

CONVINCE',° to satisfy by evidence.
CONVICT', to prove guilty.
EVINCE', to make evident.
EVIC'TION, dispossession, (in law.)
INVIN'CIBLE, unconquerable.
PERVICAC'ITY, obstinacy.
PROV'INCE,° a subject country, a division of a country.
VAN'QUISH, to conquer.
VIC'TIM, one who is sacrificed; prey.
VIC'TORY, conquest; triumph.

Vindex, vindic-is, an avenger.

AVENGE',°to punish for an injury.
REVENGE', to return an injury.
VINDIC'TIVE, revengeful.
VIN'DICATE, to justify; to support.
VENGE'ANCE, recompense of evil.

Vin-um (οἶνος), wine.

VINE, the plant that bears the grape.
VI'NOUS, having the qualities of wine.
VIN'EGAR,°an acid liquor.
VINT'AGE, the time of gathering grapes; the crop of grapes.
VIN'TRY, a place where wine is sold.

Viol-o, violat-um, to injure.

INVI'OLABLE, not to be profaned or broken.
INVI'OLATE, unbroken.
VI'OLATE, to injure; to profane; to break.
VI'OLENCE, force; outrage.

Vir, a man.

DECEM'VIR, one of ten men united in office.
VIRA'GO,°a turbulent woman.
TRIUM'VIRATE, a coalition of three men.
VI'RILE, manly; bold.

Virgo, virgin-is, a virgin.

VIR'GIN, maidenly; pure.

Virtus, bravery; power.

VIR'TUE, moral goodness.
VIR'TUAL, in effect; real.
VIRTUO'SO, one skilled in the fine arts.

Vir-us, poison.

VIR'ULENCE, malignity.
VIR'ULENT, venomous; bitter.

Visc-um, glue.

VISCID'ITY, glutinousness.
VIS'COUS, glutinous; sticky.

Visc-us, viscer-is, an entrail.

EVIS'CERATE, to take out the entrails.
VIS'CERAL, relating to the entrails.

Viti-um, vice.

VICE, depravity; wickedness.
VICI'OUS, wicked; sinful.
VIT'IATE, to deprave; to spoil.

Vit-o, to shun.

INEV'ITABLE, that cannot be avoided.
INEV'ITABLY, surely; unavoidably.

Vitr-um, glass.

VIT'REOUS, resembling glass.
VIT'RIFY, to change into glass.
VIT'RIOL,°copperas.
VIT'RIFORM, having the form of glass.

Vitupero, vituperat-um, to blame.

Vitu'perate, to blame; to censure.

Viv-o, vict-um, to live.

Conviv'ial, gay; jovial.
Revive', to live again; to arouse.
Reviv'ify, to recall to life.
Survive', to outlive.
Vi'and,° an article of food.
Vict'uals,° food; provisions.
Vi'tal, necessary to life.
Vivac'ity, liveliness.
Viv'id, sprightly; active.
Vivifica'tion, the act of giving life.
Viv'ify, to animate.

Voc-o, vocat-um, to call.

Ad'vocate, an intercessor; a pleader.
Avoca'tion,° the business which calls aside.
Avouch', to affirm; to declare.
Convoca'tion, an assembly.
Convoke', to call together.
Equiv'ocal, ambiguous; doubtful.
Equiv'ocate, to use doubtful expressions.
Evoke', to call forth.
Invoke', to implore; to pray to.
Irrev'ocable, not to be recalled.
Invoca'tion, a calling upon solemnly or in prayer.
Provoca'tion, a cause of anger.
Provoke',° to enrage; to offend.
Revoca'tion, a recalling.
Unequiv'ocal, not equivocal.
Vocab'ulary, a list of words.
Vo'cal, relating to the voice.
Vocif'erate, to make outcries.
Voice, sound from the mouth; an opinion.
Vouch,° to bear witness.
Vow'el, a simple sound.

Vol-o, volat-um, to fly.

Altiv'olant, flying high.
Vo'lant, flying; active.
Vol'atile,° gay; lively.
Vol'ley,° a flight of shot.

Vol-o, volit-um, to wish, to will.

Benev'olent, kind; wishing well.
Invol'untary, not willing.
Malev'olence, ill will.
Voliti'on, the act or power of willing.
Vol'untary, willing; of choice.
Volunteer', a voluntary soldier.

Volupt-as, pleasure.

Volup'tuary, a man given up to pleasure.
Volup'tuous, indulging to excess in pleasure.

Volv-o, volut-um, to roll.

Circumvolu'tion, a rolling round.
Con'volute, rolled together.
Evolve', to open; to unroll.
Evolu'tion, act of unfolding; a displaying.
Involve', to envelop; to entangle.
Involu'tion, act of infolding.
Revolt',° to throw off subjection; to shock.
Revolu'tion, rotation; thorough change.
Revolu'tionize, to produce a revolution.
Revolve', to roll round.
Vol'uble, rolling; fluent.

VOL'UME,° a book; a roll.
VOLU'MINOUS, consisting of many volumes.
WAL'LOW, to roll in mire.

Vomit-o, to vomit.

IGNIV'OMOUS, vomiting fire.
VOM'IT, to throw up from the stomach.

Vor-o, to eat, to devour.

CARNIV'OROUS, eating flesh.
DEVOUR', to eat up greedily.
GRANIV'OROUS, eating grain.
HERBIV'OROUS, feeding on herbage.
INSECTIV'OROUS, eating insects.
OMNIV'OROUS, eating all things.
OSSIV'OROUS, devouring bones.
PISCIV'OROUS, eating fish.
VERMIV'OROUS, feeding on worms.
VORAC'ITY, greediness.

Vot-um, a vow.

AVOW', to declare openly.
DEVOTE', to dedicate; to set apart.
DEVO'TION,° piety; affection.
DEVOUT',° earnest; sincere.
VO'TARY, one devoted or addicted.
VOTE, suffrage; a ballot.
VO'TIVE, given by vow.
VOW, a solemn promise.

Vulcan-us, the god of fire.

VOLCA'NO, a burning mountain.
VOLCAN'IC, relating to a volcano.

Vulg-us, the common people.

DIVULGE', to make public.
PROMULGA'TION, publication; exhibition.
PROMULGE', to publish.
VUL'GAR, unrefined; rude.
VUL'GATE,° an ancient Latin version of the Bible.

Vulnus, vulner-is, a wound.

INVUL'NERABLE, not to be wounded.
VUL'NERARY, useful in the cure of wounds.

Zel-os (ζηλος), zeal.

ZEAL, earnestness; warmth.
ZEAL'OT, a person full of zeal.

Zo-on (ζωον), an animal.

ZO'DIAC,° a broad circle in the heavens.
ZOOG'RAPHY, a description of animals.
ZOOL'OGY, the science of animals.
ZO'OPHYTE, a body which partakes of the nature of both vegetables and animals.
ZOOT'OMY, dissection of the bodies of beasts.

PART III.

WORDS PRINCIPALLY OF GOTHIC ORIGIN.

It is somewhat surprising that, in the works of Etymology in general, and particularly those from the American press, no notice has been taken of the Gothic roots; and when we remember that, at least, one-half of our words owe their origin to these, we can scarcely deem a work worthy of the title of "An Etymology of the English Language," which altogether omits the consideration of them. For the purpose of obviating an objection to the "Class-Book of Etymology," which such an omission would fairly call forth, the following collection has been made. It will be seen that the words are traced not only to one language, but their connection with most of the principal dialects of Gothic origin is pointed out. Not only the corresponding word from the old Saxon is given, but also, in many cases, those from the German, Scotch, Dutch, Icelandic, and even from the original Gothic. The lists of prepositions, conjunctions, and adverbs, prefixed, will be found to afford much instruction and interest to the youthful philologist.

PREPOSITIONS—PRINCIPALLY FROM THE SAXON.

About—from *boda*, extremity or boundary. Some derive this word from *bout* (French), an end.

Above, upon, up, over. *Ufa* (Anglo-Saxon), high; *ufera*, over or upper; *ufemæst*, uppermost. *Auf* (German), *boven* (Dutch).

Against—*gein sta* (Gothic), standing opposite.

Along—on length.

Amid—*on middian*, in the middle.

Among—*mængan*, to mix.

Around—from *round*.

At—*ad* (Latin), to.

Athwart—*thweorian*, to wrest or twist.

Bating—*abattre* (French), to beat down.

By (Saxon)—*be*, the imperative of *beon*, to be.

Before, behind, below, beneath, besides, between—made up of the imperative *be* and *hind*, *low*, *neath*, *sides*, *twain*.

Betwixt—from the imperative *be* and *twos* (Gothic), two.

But—from *beon-utan*, to be out.

Down—from *dufen*, to dip.

For—from *fairina* (Gothic), cause.

From—from *frum*, beginning, original, source, author.

Figs come *from* Turkey; figs come *beginning* Turkey.

In—connected with *inna*, a cave. An *inn*, a house of reception.

Near—from the Anglo-Saxon adjective *nih*, the comparative of which forms *near*, and the superlative *next*.
Of—from *afora*, progeny.
On—*on* (Gothic).
Out—*ut* (Gothic). This word may be traced in many formations, thus —utter, oust, jut, put, butt, &c.
Since—from *sithan* (Gothic), after that. According to Tooke, *sithan* or *sithence* means seen and thenceforward.
Through—from *dauro* (Gothic), a door.
Till—compounded of *to* and *while*.
To—as *from* denotes beginning, *to* denotes, according to Tooke, termination, and is derived from the Gothic substantive *tani*, act, effect. The Latin *ad*, to, is derived by Tooke, on the same principle, from *actum*, the past participle of *agere*, to act.
Towards—from *wardian*, to look at.
Under—from *on-neder*, or *nether*.
With—from *withan*, to join.

CONJUNCTIONS.

Also—*all* and *so*.
And—from *anad*, the imperative of *anan*, to give.
As—Tooke makes this word an article, meaning *it*, *that*, or *which*.
But—the imperative of *botan*, to boot, to superadd.
Because—from *be* and *cause*.
Either—*aithwar*, *eitt-twar* (Gothic), one of two. *Or* and *other* probably connected with it.
Else—from *alesan*, to dismiss.
If—from *gif*, imperative of *gifan*, to give. This is Tooke's derivation by others it has been traced from a Gothic root, signifying *even*.
Lest—from *lesan*, to dismiss.
Since—from *seon*, to see.
Still—from *stellan*, to put.
So—from the Gothic article *sa* or *so*, signifying *it* or *that*.
That—from *thean*, to get, to take, or to assume.
Then, and the article *the*—also from *thean*.
Though—from *thaf*, the past participle of *thafian*, to allow.
Yet—from *get*, the past participle of *getan*, to get.

ADVERBS.

Asunder—*sondrian*, to separate; *sand*, what is separated.
Astray—from *to stray*.
Awry—from *writhan*, to writhe.
Enough—*genaeg* (Dutch), from *genoegen*, to content.
Lief—from *lufian*, to love.
Farewell—from *faran*, to go, and *well*.

"So on he *fares*, and to the border comes of Eden."—MILTON.

Halt—from *healdan*, to hold.
Lo—imperative of *look*.
Perhaps—by or through *haps*.
Aloft, or loft—*lyft* (Saxon), the air.
Ought—*wiht* (Saxon), a point or jot; *a whit*, or one whit.
Nought—*na wiht*.
More—connected, according to Tooke, with a *mow* or *heap*.

Rather—from *rath* (Saxon), soon; comparative, *rather*, sooner.

I had *rather* go myself; I had *sooner* go myself.

Quickly—from *cwic*, alive. "The *quick* and the dead."
Alone—all-one. *Only*, one-like.
Anon—in one; in one instant.

GENERAL VOCABULARY.

Abode—from *bidan* (Saxon), to bide. Some derive this word from *but* or *bit* (Arabic or Persian), to pass the night.
Acorn—*aecern* (Saxon), oak-corn.
Acre—a measure of ground; *æcer* (Saxon), *acker* (German).
Adder—a venomous reptile; from *ættrene* (Saxon), *natter* (German).
Addle—rotten; from *ata* (Gothic), to defile.
Ail—from *adlian* (Saxon), to be sick.
Ague—from *agis* (Gothic), fear, trembling; *ajur* (Icelandic).
Ajar—leaning to one side; *jadur* (Gothic), aside.
Ale—probably from *aelan* (Saxon), to burn, that which inflames. It is remarkable that the Greek word *zuthos*, a drink made from barley, should be derived from *aithos*, heat.
Allow—to permit; from *lofian* (Saxon), to praise; *allouer* (French), from *laudo* (Latin), to praise.
Aloof—all off.
Ambush—lying in wait; among *bushes; bois* (French), a wood.
Amount—to *mount to.*
Angle—to fish with a *hook; angeln* (German); from *angel*, a hook.
Anneal—to temper glass or metal; *anælan* (Saxon); from *el*, *eld* (Gothic), fire.
Answer—a reply; *andswer* (Gothic), *antwoord* (Belgic), counter-speech.
Atone—to make *at one*, according to some; *una* (Gothic), favour; *aduno* (Latin), to unite.
Awe—fear; *aga* (Gothic), *oga* (Saxon), *awe* (Danish).
Awn—a covering or hull: *hauln* (Gothic), *hüllen* (German), to cover.
Bait—to feed; from *bitan* (Saxon), to bite; hence, *to batten. To bait* also means to put food in the way for the purpose of tempting.
Baking—from *bak* (Gothic), fire, signifies to harden at the fire; hence, *beacon*, a signal originally by fire.
Bale—to throw out water from a ship. *Baile* (French), *balga* (Swedish), a pail.
Band—a tie; from *bind;* hence, *bond*, *bound*, *bunch*, *bundle*, and *bent*, a kind of grass used for *binding*.
Bandy—crooked; from *to bend.* It signifies also a crooked bat for striking a ball; hence, to *bandy* words, to throw back.
Bargain—*borgian* (Saxon), to lend, *to borrow; berga* (Gothic), to secure. Some derive *borough* from *borh* (Saxon), a pledge—the members of a borough being pledged to each other.
Bark—*bergen* (German), to save, to hide. *Harbour*, a place of shelter; from the same.
Baron—a lord; from *bar* (old German), a man; *ver* (Icelandic), *vir* (Latin).

Barter—exchange; from *braetan* (Gothic), to change.
Bask—to lie in the sun. *Basa*, *bada* (Gothic), heat, connected with *bake*. From the same word, *bath*, which signified originally *hot water*.
Bead—a small globe of glass, &c.; *boed* (Saxon), prayer. The number of prayers were counted by *beads*.
Beaker—a cup with a *beak*; *becher* (German), a cup.
Beef—from *bœuf* (French), an ox.
Begin—*gynnan* (Saxon), to go in; compounded of *ga-inna*.
Behave—from *to have*, signifying to possess one's self; hence, also, *behove*, to be proper.
Bequeath—to leave by will; *cwæthan* (Saxon), to say; hence, also, *quoth*.
Berry—from *to bear*.
Bet—*wed* (Saxon), a pledge; hence, *wager*; hence, also, to *wed*, to pledge love.
Bier—from *to bear*; what the dead are *borne* on; hence, also, *barrow*.
Bit—from *to bite*. In the same way, *morceau* in French, from *mordre*; hence, also, *bitter*.
Blank and bleach—from *blæcan* (Saxon), to fade. *Blanc* (French), white; hence, *blankets*.
Blend—to mix; *bland* (Gothic), many; hence, *blunder*, confusion. These words have also been derived from *blind*.
Bless—to wish happy; *blithsian* (Saxon), to make *blithe*.
Boast—*bogan* (Saxon), to use a bow, to boast. A person who vaunts is said to draw a long bow. *Jactare* (Latin), to shoot, has the same extension of meaning.
Book—derived, according to some, from *beech*; the beech-tree being used as paper by the Goths. Others derive it from *bugan*, to bend or fold; referring to the folded leaves of the parchment.
Boon—a favour, a prayer; *bon* (Icelandic), *ben* (Saxon).
Boor—a clown; *beorman* (Saxon), a cultivator; *bauer* (German), *beoran*, to bear.
Boot—a covering for the leg; *bottes* (Welsh), a shoe; *botte* (French).
Booth—a stall; *bude* (Saxon), a dwelling; hence, *bude* (Saxon), from *bwa* (Gothic), to build; hence, also, the termination *buttle* in the names of places.
Bread—what is made of *brayed* or ground corn.
Break—connected with this word are *bray*, *breach*, &c. A *brook*, a rivulet, a *broken* stream. *Bracken*, a fern, according to Skinner, what *breaks* easily.
Brown—connected with *to burn*; hence, *brand*, to mark with fire; *brindled*, variegated by fire; and *brandy* (*branntwein*, German), burnt wine. A *brand*, a *flaming* sword; to *brandish*, to waive a *brand*, or sword.
Brogue—*bro-aeg* (Welsh), country speech.
Brunt—vehemence; *brennen* (German), to burn.
Bulk—*bolg* (Gothic); hence, *big*, *bulge*.
Burden—a load, from *to bear*.
Burganet—armour for the head; *beorgan* (Saxon), to defend, and *heafoa*, the head.
Bury—to hide; *beorgan* (Saxon), *bergen* (German), to protect, to conceal. *A barrow*, a tumulus where the dead have been interred; or from *berg* (German), a hill. *To burrow*, to make holes in the ground.
But—end, mark; *but* (Swedish), *butt* (Teutonic), *bout* (French).

Butler—*boutillier* (French), one who has the charge of *bottles*.
Butterfly—*buter-flege* (Saxon); *but* (Gothic), large, and *flege*, fly.
Bye—good-bye; *good be with you*.
Cajole—*goela* (Gothic), fraud; hence, *gull*, *guile*, and *wile*.
Chase—pursuit after game; *jaga* (Gothic), *jagen* (German), to hunt; or rather from *chasse* (French), which is traced to *calco* (Latin), I trample on.
Cheapen—to ask the price; *ceap* (Saxon), a bargain; *koop* (Dutch); hence, *chapman; kauf* (German), purchase; *coup* (Scotch), exchange.
Churl—*ceorl* (Saxon), a boor; *eorl*, noble; *ceorle*, plebeian; hence, also, *carle; kerl* (German), a man, a fellow.
Churn—from *cyrran* (Saxon), to turn; *kehren* (German).
Clamber—from *to climb; clifwa* (Swedish), to climb, to go up a *cliff; klimmen* (German).
Clammy—wet; *klem* (Belgic), wet clay.
Clasp—from *clyppan* (Saxon), to embrace; *clespe* (Dutch); hence, *to clip*, to bound; and the secondary meaning, to cut off, to divide.
Cleave—to split, to adhere; *clifian* (Saxon), kleben (German,) to adhere; hence, *cliff*, a division or fissure of the rock; *claw*, a division of the foot; *club*, a division of expenditure; and *clover*, from its cloven leaves.
Clever—*glagur* (Icelandic), sharp-eyed; hence, *gleg* (Scotch), quick.
Clock—from *cleccian* (Saxon), to strike; hence, *to clock*, to hatch chickens, from the noise made by the hen.
Cloth—*clad* (Saxon); from *lod* (Icelandic), wool; *kleiden* (German), to clothe.
Coal—from *aelan* (Saxon), to burn.
Cope—to contend; *comp* (Saxon), a contest; *kampf* (German).
Cow—to terrify; *oga* (Saxon), fear.
Craft—cunning, knowledge; *cræft* (Saxon), *kraft* (German), power. There seems to be a natural association between knowledge and power. (See *King*.)
Cramp—*kram* (Gothic), *krumm* (German), crooked. *Cramps*—in Scotland, a piece of sharp iron attached by a strap to the shoe, to prevent sliding on the ice.
Craven—one who meanly *craves* his life, a coward.
Craze—*krachen* (German), to break or crack; *crazed*, or *crack*-brained.
Creek—*crecca* (Saxon), *kreek* (Belgic), an inlet of the sea; from *crook*.
Creep—*creopan* (Saxon), *kriechen* (German), to creep; hence, *crawl* and *cringe;* hence, also, *cripple*, one who creeps.
Crew—a ship's company; *cread* (Saxon); hence, *crowd*.
Crock—an earthen pot; *crocca* (Saxon), *krug* (German); hence, *cruise; cruisgin* (Irish), a small pot.
Crony—a confidant; *kronen* (Teutonic), to whisper.
Crotchet—a mark in music; from *croche* (French), a hook.
Crumb—*krumm* (German,) crooked, bent; hence, *to crumple*.
Cuff—*gauf* (Teutonic), the fist; a blow with the hand.
Cunning—skill, craft; *kunna* (Gothic), *cnawan* (Saxon), *kennen* (German), to know; *to ken* (old English and Scotch).
Curmudgeon—a miser; from *karg* (German), parsimonious, and *mod*, the mind.
Dairy—from *dey*, old English for milk.
Daisy—*daege's ege* (Saxon), day's eye.
Dale—a vale; *dale* (Gothic), *dal* (Swedish), *thal* (German), *dol* (Welsh).

Dally—*dahlen* (German), to trifle. Some connect this word with *dwell.*

Dangle—to hang loosely; from *hang.*

Darling—from *dear* and *ling*, diminutive.

Dawn—from *dæg* (Saxon), day, to become day; *tagen* (German), from *tag*, day.

Decoy—from *koi* (Dutch), a cage; *a decoy duck*, a duck in a cage, which induces others to go in.

Deal—from *dæl* (Saxon), *theil* (German), a part; *dælan* (Saxon), *theilen* (German), to divide; hence, *to deal*, to sell in parts.

Denizen—a freeman; from *dinas* (Welsh), a city, and *sydd* (Welsh), free.

Dye—to tinge; *deagan* (Saxon), to colour.

Diet—a meeting; *thiot-mat* (Gothic), the national meeting.

Dight—to arrange or *deck; decan* (Saxon), *decken* (German), to cover; hence, *dizen.* Hence, the *deck* of a vessel. Connected with this, *theccan* (Saxon), to cover, to *thatch.*

Dike—a mound; from *to dig.*

Dine—*dægnan* (old Saxon); from *day;* to take the *day-meal.*

Dint—a blow, a mark; from *dencgan* (Saxon), to knock; *to ding* (Scotch). Tooke traces it to *din*, noise.

Dolt—from *dull.*

Door—*dauro* (Gothic), *thür* (German), *duru* (Saxon), *thura* (Greek).

Doughty—from *dihtig* (Saxon), arranged, prepared; or from *duguth* (Saxon), *tugend* (German), riches, power; *tüchtig* (German), able.

Doze—to slumber; *dasa* (Swedish); hence, *daze* (Scotch), to be stupid.

Drag—*dragan* (Saxon), *dreggen* (German), *trekken* (Belgic); hence, a *track-boat.*

Draught—a drink; from *draw.*

Draughts—a game, in which *moves* or *drawings* are made; hence, a *draught*, a sketch or *drawing.*

Dray—a thing *drawn.*

Dread—*roed* (Danish), *red* (Scotch), afraid; from *offraedd* (Gothic), greatly affrighted.

Dream—*drauma* (Gothic), *traum* (German).

Drear—*traurig* (German), mournful.

Drench—from *to drink.*

Dribble and drip—from *drop.*

Drill—*thirlian* (Saxon), *drillen* (German), to bore; hence, *drill*, military exercise.

Droll—comical; *drôle* (French).

Drown—connected with *drink.*

Drudge—from *to drag.*

Dub—to strike; *dubban* (Saxon), signifies to create or name, from the ceremony of *striking* the candidate for knightship with a sword.

Dun—to crave clamorously; from *din*, noise.

Dunce—*dumeriss* (Swedish), dull understanding; *dumm* (German), dull, stupid.

Dusk—*dancks* (Gothic), *düster* (German), *du* (Welsh), dark.

Dwindle—*dwinan* (Saxon), to pine; *to dwine* (Scotch).

Earl—from *oera* (Gothic), *ehre* (German), honour.

Earn—*earnan* (Saxon), *ernten* (German), to reap, to gather.

Earth—soil; *erde* (German), *eard* (Saxon), *yird* (Scotch).

Elbow—*elbogen, bogan* (Saxon), a bending; *bogen* (German).

Elope—to run away; *loopen* (Belgic), *hleopan* (Saxon), to run; hence, *leap*.

Entangle—to implicate; may be derived, as Dr. Jameson suggests, from *tangle*, long sea-weed, from *tengia* (Icelandic), to join. *Teino* (Greek), to extend.

Errand—*ærend* (Saxon); from *ara* (Gothic), to employ.

Essay—a trial; *essayer* (French), to try.

Etch—from *etzan* (German), *to eat*, to mark with aquafortis.

Evil—according to some, from *uwell* (Gothic), meaning not well, *uebel* (German); others deduce it from *chebel* (Hebrew), pain.

Fault, and faulter—from *fail; fehlen* (German), to fail; *fehl*, wrong.

Fardel—a burden; *fardeau* (French), *fero* (Latin), I carry.

Fare—to go; *faran* (Saxon), hence, *fare*, passage-money.

Farewell—*go on well; faran* (Saxon), to go.

Feather—*fæther* (Saxon), *feder* (German).

Fellow—a partner; *felag* (Gothic); *fe*, goods, and *lag*, society. *Fe* in the northern languages denoted cattle or money; in the same way *pecus* (Latin), cattle, is connected with *pecunia*, money.

Fell—a rocky hill; *fioell* (Swedish), a ridge of mountains; *fels* (German), a rock.

Felon—from *fel* (Gothic), a fault.

Fen—a marsh, a bog; *fenn* (Saxon), clay.

Feodal or feudal—from *fe*, property, and *audal* (Gothic); *udal* (Scottish), full possession. *Udal* and *allodial* are connected, applying to lands that were not subject to a superior lord like the *feudal*.

Ferry—*fere* (Saxon), *fähre* (German), a passage over a river or firth; *farja* (Swedish), a boat; *ferge* (German), a ferryman.

Fetter—to chain the feet; from *feet*.

Feud—a quarrel; from *fian* (Saxon), to hate.

Field—cultivated ground, a meadow; *feld* (German); from *fla* (Gothic), flat; but Tooke makes out a field to be a place where the trees are cut down, or *felled*.

Fiend—a foe, a devil; from *fian* (Saxon), to hate. *Feind* (German), an enemy, the devil.

Fife—*pfeifen* (German), to whistle, to pipe.

Fifty—*five tens*.

Fight—to contend, or battle; *vigan* (Gothic), *fechten* (German). *Vixen* is by some derived from the first; also *vie*, to contend.

Film—a thin skin; from *fell*, a hide or skin.

Finance—from *feing* (Gothic), fine, payment.

Find—to discover, to feel; *finna* (Gothic), *finden* (German) *findan* (Saxon).

Fine—not coarse; *thyn*, *fin* (Gothic), *fein* (German); connected with these, *dünn* (German), *thin*.

Finger, fangs—from *fangen* (Saxon), taken; *fangen* (German), to catch. *Finger* (German).

Fire—*fyr* (Icelandic), *feuer* (German), *fyr* (Saxon), *feu* (French), *pyr* (Greek).

Fist—*fast* (Gothic), *faust* (German); the hand *fast*.

Flake—a *flock* of snow or wool; *flage* (Swedish), a fragment.

Flatter—from *flat*, smooth; *fletzen* (Teutonic), to flatter; *to fleitch* (Scotch).

Flaw—a break—*flage* (Gothic), a fragment.

Flax—*fleax* (Saxon), *flachs* (German).

Fleet—a navy; *flota* (Gothic), to float.

Flesh—*flaesc* (Saxon), *fleish* (German).
Flit—to remove; originally from *float*, to remove by water.
Flood—that which *flows; fluth* (German).
Floor—the bottom of a room; from *fla* (Gothic), flat, *flur* (German).
Flounder—a flat fish; from *fla* (Gothic), *flat*.
Flush—from *to flow; fliessen* (German).
Fly—*fliega* (Gothic), *fliegen* (German), *fleogan* (Saxon).
Fodder—from *food*.
Folk—people, nation; *volk* (German); *folgia* (Gothic), *folgen* (German), to *follow* or associate.
Forefend—from *fore* and *fend*, to take previous means of defence.
Forget—from *for*, negative, and *geta* (Gothic), to heed.
Forlorn—lost, destitute; *lora* (Swedish), loss; *verloren* (German).
Forsake—from *for*, not, and *seek;* not to seek, to desert.
Forswear—from *for*, not, and *swear;* to swear falsely; *verschwören* (German).
Fortnight—*fourteen nights*.
Forty—*four tens*.
Fowl—*fugel* (Saxon); from *fleogan*, to fly.
Fox—an animal remarkable for cunning; *foxa* (Icelandic), to deceive, *ffug* (Welsh), deceit.
Freight—to load a vessel; *fracht* (German).
Friend—*freond* (Saxon), *freund* (German); from *freon* (Saxon), *freien* (German), to free, to love.
Frolic—from *fro* (Gothic), *froh* (German), joyful.
Fuel—material for burning; *feu* (French), *focus* (Latin), fire.
Fulsome—from *foul*.
Fun—merriment; *unna* (Gothic), to please.
Furlough—leave of absence; *furleif*, *orlof* (Gothic), for leave.
Furze—a prickly shrub; probably from *fire*, as this and other shrubs were used for ovens.
Gab—idle talk; *gaber* (old French), to laugh at; *gabban* (Saxon), to trifle; hence, *gibe*, *jabber*, *gibberish*, &c.
Gad—to run about like an animal stung by the *gad-fly*.
Gad—a sting; hence, *goad; gadda* (Icelandic), to sting.
Gain—advantage; *agan* (Saxon), to obtain. This verb, and the verb of motion, *gan*, to go, and *anan*, to give, form the infinitives of most of the Saxon verbs; thus, *deal-an*, to give a deal or part, *care-an*, to have care, *bidd-an* (from *bidde-gan*), to go to pray.
Gallop—to move by leaps; *laupo* (Gothic), to leap; *gallopiren* (German), to gallop.
Gaol—*goilo* (Italian); from *caveola* (Latin), a cage; hence, *jail; geol* (Welsh.)
Garden—what is enclosed or *guarded; gyrdan* (Saxon), to enclose, *to gird*.
Garlic—a plant: from *geir* (Gothic), a spear, and *lauk* (Teutonic and German), a leek, *Geir-man* (Icelandic), the man of the javelin; *ed-gar*, a happy weapon; *ethal-gar*, a noble weapon.
Garret—originally a watch-tower; *guerite* (French), *warte* (German); from *wara* (Gothic), to defend, to observe; hence, also, *garrison*.
Gas—inflammable vapour; *asa* (Gothic), to burn.
Gate—derived by some from *gata*, to hold, but in all probability from the verb *to go*.
Gather—to bring *together*.
Gauge—to measure; from *gaule* (French), a rod; *gaial* (Arm).

Gaunt—lean; *gewoned* (Saxon), wanting; hence, *to wane.*

Gay—cheerful; *gae* (Arm.), *gai* (French).

Gazelle—an Arabian deer; *gaz* (Hebrew), a goat, and *al*, a deer.

Ghost—spirit, breath, the soul of one deceased; *gast* (Swedish), *geist* (German).

Gibe—to mock; *gabban* (Saxon), to mock.

Gild—to cover with *gold.*

Gills—the openings at the neck of a fish; *gil* (Gothic), a fissure; hence *glen.*

Gin—a liquor; contraction of *Geneva; genevre* (French), juniper.

Gin—a snare; according to some, a contraction of *engine.*

Girl—a young woman; *goila* (Gothic), diminutive of *karla*, a woman; feminine of *carl*, a man.

Gist—the substance or spirit of any thing; *geist* (German), spirit.

Glare—*gler* (Gothic), clear; hence, *glow* and *glory.*

Glance—a quick view; from *to glow;* hence, *glent* (Scottish), and *glee*, an oblique view.

Gleam—a coruscation; connected with *gloom, loom,* and *glimmer*—all signifying an unsteady light. *Gloamin* (Scotch), the evening twilight.

Glee—a song; *glig* (Saxon), music.

Glide—to go gently; *glidan* (Saxon), *gleiten* (German), *glisser* (French).

Glove—*glof* (Icelandic); from *to cleave.*

Gold—*gall* (Gothic), *goelen* (Saxon), yellow.

Good—connected with *God; aud* (Gothic), power. *Good* originally means furious, brave in battle; bravery in savage times being the principal virtue; so, *virtue*, from *vis* (Latin), strength. *Goths*, brave warriors.

Gooseberry—from *gehos* (Saxon), rough, and *berry.*

Gossip—a sponsor in baptism; from *gud* (Gothic), religious, and *sib*, a relation. In Scotland, persons are said to be *sib* when they are relatives.

Grape—fruit of the vine; *grappe* (French), *traube* (German), cluster; *trauen* (German), to unite; hence, *groupe* (French).

Grapple—to lay hold of; from *graff* (Gothic), the hand; hence, *gripe, grasp; griffe* (French), a finger or claw. *To grope—to gripe* or *feel* one's way.

Grass—*groes* (Saxon), *gras* (German), that which *grows.*

Grave—to dig; *grafan* (Saxon), *graben* (German); hence, *groove.*

Graze—to eat *grass.*

Green—*groen* (Teutonic), that which is in a *growing* state; *gro* (Gothic), to increase; hence, *great.*

Greet—to salute; *grithan* (Saxon), to give peace. *To greet* (Scotch), to weep; *greitan* (Gothic), *gredare* (Italian), to weep.

Greyhound—from *grey* (Gothic), a dog; *greyhound* (Saxon).

Grim—frightful; *grim* (Saxon), *grimm* (German), furious; *grim* (Celtic), war.

Grimace—distortion from affectation; from *gryma* (Icelandic), a mask; hence, *to begrime*, to sully.

Grind—to reduce to powder; *grunn* (Gothic), a stone. *To grin—to grind* or set the teeth.

Grisly—*graus* (Teutonic), horror.

Grist—corn to be *ground;* the fee paid to the miller.

Groat—a coin; so named from its *great* size.

Grocer—one who deals in spices; from *grus* (Gothic), aromatics; hence, *kraut* (German), vegetables, spicery.

Groom—from *guma* (Gothic and Saxon), a man, a servant; a bride*groom*, a bride's-man.
Grove—a walk shaded by trees; *gro-hof* (Gothic), a growing cover.—*Thomson.*
Grovel—*grufla* (Gothic); connected with *crawl.*
Ground—the earth; perhaps from *grun* (Teutonic), green.
Grub—from *greben* (German), to dig; hence, *groove.*
Guerdon—recompense; *werd* (Gothic), value, worth; *guiderdone* (Italian), *guerdon* (French), a reward.
Guest—*giest* (Gothic), *gast* (German), *gest* (Saxon), one receiving hospitality; from *gista* (Icelandic), to take food.
Guild—a society; from *gild* (Saxon), contribution; hence, *yield* and *guilt*, originally fine, punishment.
Gulf—a whirlpool; *gol* (Swedish), *gaul* (Icelandic).
Gull—to trick; *goela* (Gothic), to entice; hence, *cajole, guile,* and *wile.*
Gun—derived by Tooke from *gynian* (Saxon), to gape, to yawn; *gähnen* (German), gaunt.
Habergeon—armour to defend the neck; *halz* (Gothic and German), the neck, and *bergen*, to cover.
Haft—the handle of a tool; that by which it is *hav'd* or held.
Haggard—withered; from *hag*, a witch.
Haggle—to bargain tediously; *haecklen* (Teutonic).
Hail—frozen drops of rain; *hragel* (Gothic), *hagel* (German), *hagal* (Saxon).
Hale—healthy; *heil* (Gothic and German), *hal* (Saxon); hence, *whole, heal, health, holy.*
Halt—*halta* (Gothic), *halten* (German), to hold.
Hamlet—from *ham*, a home or village, and *little; a little village.*
Hamper—a basket used for carriage; supposed to be *handpannier.*
Handkerchief—a kerchief used in the *hand.*
Happy—from *hap*, luck; good luck.
Harangue—a speech: from *hringan* (Saxon), to sound.
Harbour—literally, a place for soldiers; from *here* (Saxon), an army, and *beorgan* (Saxon), to defend.
Hare—an animal that *hears* quickly; in the same way *lagos* (Greek), from *ous*, the ear.
Hare-brained—from *hwera* (Gothic), to whirl, and brain; giddy-headed. Some connect it with *hare*—an animal which is vulgarly said to be periodically mad.
Harvest—*hærfest* (Saxon); according to some, the feast of the *Herth* (the earth), a deity of the ancient Germans; according to others, from *ar* (Gothic), the year, and *vest*, food, the produce of the year; *herbst* (German).
Haste—speed; *hast* (Gothic, German, and Swedish).
Hat—what covers the *head; hut* (German).
Hate—malice; *hata* (Gothic), *hass* (German), *hate* (Saxon); from *hat* (Saxon), hot.
Have—to possess; *hava* (Gothic), *haben* (German), *habeo* (Latin).
Haven—a harbour; *hafn* (Gothic), *hafen* (German), *havre* (French).
Haw—an inclosure, a hedge; *hag* (German), an inclosed meadow, *haugh* (Scotch), *augh* (Gaelic). The name *Hague*, the capital of Holland, is derived from these roots. The Dutch pronounce it like the guttural *haugh* of the Scotch.
Hawthorn—a thorn employed in making *haws*, or hedges.

Hay—grass cut and dried; *hau* (Gothic), *heg* (Saxon), *heu* (German); from *hauga* (Gothic), *hauen* (German), to cut; hence, *hew* and *hoe*.

Head—the top, the chief; *haufd* (Gothic), *heafd* (Saxon), *haupt* (German), *caput* (Latin); hence, *heave, heavy, heaven.*

Hear—to perceive by the *ear; heyra* (Gothic), *hören* (German), *hyran* (Saxon).

Heart—*herda* (Sanscrit), *hearta* (Gothic), *hertz* (German).

Hearth—a fire-place; *heorth* (Saxon), *herd* (German); perhaps from *haurga* (Moeso-Gothic), a fire.

Heat—warmth; *heit* (Gothic), *hitze* (German), *heat* (Saxon), *hit* (Hebrew), fire, the sun.

Heathen—perhaps from *heid* (Gothic), a forest; *heide* (German), heath; *heiden* (German), heathen.

Heed—attention; perhaps from *hug* (Gothic), the mind; *hüten* (German), to observe, to take *heed.*

Heinous—hateful; *haine* (French), hatred.

Heirloom—what descends to an *heir; loma* (Saxon), a utensil. *Loom* is still used in Scotland for the kitchen utensils.

Hell—originally, the grave; from *hyla* (Gothic), to cover; whence, *hull*, a cover, *helmet*, a covering for the head, and *helm*, that which protects or governs a vessel.

Help—aid; *hialp* (Gothic,) *hülfe* (German), *help* (Saxon).

Herd—a guard; a flock; *herd* (Gothic), *herde* (German), *heord* (Saxon); connected with these, *her* (Gothic), *heer* (German), an army. *Herring* has also been connected with these, as it appears in herds, or *hoards.*

Hight—named, called; *heissen* (German), to distinguish by a name, to call.

Hill—an eminence; *hal, hangel* (Gothic), *hügel* (German), *hyl* (Saxon); from *hilan* (Saxon), to conceal; hence, also, *hole.*

Hilt—what is *held.*

Hoard—a treasure; *hirda* (Gothic), to guard.

Hollow—from *hole.*

Home—*haim* (Gothic), *heim* (German), *ham* (Saxon); from *heima* (old German), to cover.

Hood—a covering for the *head.*

Hope—*hapa* (Gothic), *hoffen* (German), *hopian* (Saxon).

Horse—from *ras* (Gothic), speed; from the same word may come *rash*, impetuous, *rush*, to go with force, and a *rush*, what rushes up.

Hover—to hang *over.*

Hound—a dog for chase; *hund* (Gothic and German); hence, *hunt.*

Huge—high; *hoeg* (Swedish), *heah* (Saxon), *hoch* (German), high, vast. The Scotch word *howe*, signifying a knoll, has been derived from the same.

Hurst—in names, means a *forest.*

Husband—from *house* and *bua* (Gothic), to conduct.

Husbandman—a farmer; supposed to be one *bound* to a house or farm, a *bond*-man.

Iron—a metal; *iarn* (Gothic), *iren* (Saxon), *hiarn* (Welsh), *eisen* (German).

Island—*eyland* (Gothic), *ealand* (Saxon); from *ea*, water, and *land.*

Ivy—from *upa* (Saxon), up, what climbs up; *ifig* (Saxon), *epheu* (German).

Jaundice—a distemper accompanied by a yellowness of the skin; *gut* (Gothic), *geolew* (Saxon), *jaune* (French), yellow.

Jaw—the bone which *chews* or *chaws; kau* (Teutonic).
Jet—to shoot out; *jetter* (French), to throw; from *jacto* (Latin).
Juggle—*jongler* (French), *giocolare* (Italian), to play mountebank tricks; from *jocus* (Latin), a jest.
Jumble—to mix confusedly; *schommeln, wommelen* (Belgic).
Keel—the lowest timber of a ship; *kiol* (Gothic), *kiel* (German).
Kerchief—*couvre chef* (French), to cover the head.
Kidnap—to steal children; from *kind* (German), a child, and *nab.*
Kill—perhaps from *kilia* (Gothic), to hurt, or from *cwellan* (Saxon), to kill or quell.
Kin—kindred—*kyn* (Gothic).
Kind—indulgent; the tenderness shown for one of our own *kind.*
King—a monarch; *kong* (Gothic), *kung*, (Swedish), *cyning* (Saxon), *könig* (German); derived by some from *kun, kyn* (Gothic), a nation, people. It may, perhaps, be as naturally allied with *können* (German), to be able, to know, *to ken;* hence, our auxiliary *can.*
Kirk—*kyrk* (Gothic), *kirche* (German); sometimes derived from *kuriou-oikos* (Greek), the house of the Lord.
Knack—from *to know; knabe* (German), a boy, a servant.
Knave—a rogue; *knecht* (German), servant, slave.
Knead—*knya* (Gothic), *kneten* (German), *cnoedan* (Saxon); from *kno* (Gothic), the fist, the hand folded.
Knife—*knifa* (Gothic), *kneif* (German), *cnif* (Saxon), *canif* (French).
Knight—*knecht* (German); originally, an inferior, one inferior to a baronet.
Knit—to make by *knots.*
Knot—*knutt* (Gothic), *knoten* (German), *cnotta* (Saxon).
Lack—to suffer want; *lecan* (Saxon), to diminish; hence, *inlake* (Scotch), to fall off in quantity or measure.
Lackey—footboy; from *lacken* (Gothic), to run, or *lega* (Gothic), to hire.
Lad—*laed* (Teutonic), *ladig* (Swedish); perhaps from *lausa* (Gothic), loose, one unmarried; hence, *lass.*
Ladder—*leid* (Gothic), a way, and *ra* (Gothic), a range; *loedra* (Saxon), *leiter* (German); from *leiten*, to lead; hence, mill-*lead*, the artificial canal *led* to a mill.
Lady—*lafda* (Gothic), *hlaefdiga* (Saxon), *hleof*, high. According to some, from *hlaf* (Gothic), bread, and *dian*, to serve; as the mistress used to distribute the bread to the domestics.
Landscape—*landschape* (Belgic), a portion of land in a particular *shape* or form.
Lank—from *lean.*
Lash—*laschen* (German), to beat.
Laugh—*hloeja* (Gothic), *hlihan* (Saxon), *lachen* (German), (Scotch).
Law—statute, edict; *la, lag* (Gothic), what is *laid* down; *loi* (French), *lex* (Latin). *Alloy*—a mixture proportioned by *law.*
Lay—to place, to put down; *loega* (Gothic), *legen* (German), *legan* (Saxon).
Lay—a song; *liod* (Gothic), *lied* (Belgic), a song or ballad; *laut* (German), sound; hence, *loud* and *lute.*
Lazy—*losk* (Gothic), *lässig* (German), perhaps from *leisa* (Gothic), to loose.
Lead—a heavy metal; from *load.*
Leap—*laup* (Gothic), *hleapan* (Saxon), *laufen* (German), to run.

Leech—a small water-serpent; from *laecken* (Teutonic), to diminish.
Left-hand—literally, that which is *left*, not used. *Link* (German), has in the same way been traced to *linquo* (Latin), to leave, and *sinister* (Latin), to *sino*, to let alone.
Leman—a sweetheart; *lieb* (German), beloved, and *man*.
Lend—to grant; *loena* (Gothic), *lehnen* (German), *to lean*, to lend.
Let—*lia* (Gothic), *lassen* (German), *lætan* (Saxon), *laisser* (French); hence, *lease*.
Lick—to strike; *lag* (Icelandic), a stroke.
Lie—a falsehood; *lygi* (Gothic), *lüge* (German), *lig* (Saxon); from *lœ* (Gothic), fraud.
Lief—*lieben* (German), to love, to like; *lieber*, rather, sooner.
Life—*lif*, *lib* (Gothic), *leben* (German), *luf* (Saxon).
Lift—to raise into the air, literally; *lyft* (Saxon), *luft* (German), the air; the *lift* (Scotch), *lugu* (Gothic), air; hence, *lungs*. *Lofty*, what is *lifted* up.
Like—*lyk* (Gothic) *gleich* (German), *lic* (Saxon).
Limb—*litha* (Gothic), to bend; hence, *limber* and *lithe*, *lith* (Saxon), *lith* (Scotch), a joint, used also as a verb, signifying *to put out of joint*.
Limp—to walk *lame*.
Linger—to stay *long*.
Links—*lyck* (Gothic), *loenk* (Icelandic), *lenken* (German), to bend.
Lip—*lub* (Persic), *lub* (Hindostanee), *lippe* (Saxon and German) *labium* (Latin).
Listen—to give attention; *hlistan* (Saxon), *lauschen* (German), to listen.
Loaf—*lef*, *hlaif* (Gothic), *hlaf* (Saxon), *læib* (German); from *lofa* (Gothic), to raise up, *hlifian* (Saxon), to raise. *Hlafmæsse* (Saxon), loaf-mass or feast; hence, *Lammas*.
Lock—to shut; *luka* (Icelandic), *lucan* (Saxon). A *lock* of hair, hair clustered. *Lock* (Scotch), a quantity.
Loiter—to be *late*; *lat* (Suevo-Gothic), slow; hence, *lout*.
Love—affection; *luib* (Gothic), *luva* (Saxon), *liebe* (German), *lief* (Belgic).
Luck—chance, good fortune; *lucka* (Gothic), *glück* (German).
Lug—to drag; *lugga* (Suevo-Gothic), to draw.
Lure—a bait; *luder* (Swedish and German), carion, bait; *lura* (Spanish), flesh. On the same principle, *appas* (French), a charm, has been traced from *pasco* (Latin), to feed.
Lurk—*lura* (Swedish), *lauern* (German), to lie in wait.
Mad—disordered in mind; *mod* (Saxon), the mind, also passion.
Maid—a young woman; *may* (Gothic), *mai*, *mægd* (Saxon), *magd* (German).
Main—powerful; *mage* (Saxon); from *meiga* (Gothic), to be able, *macht* (German), might, power; hence, *might*, *may*, *make*; *machen* (German), to make.
Man—*man* (Gothic and Swedish), *mann* (German); connected with *magn* (Gothic), strength; in the same way, *vir* (Latin), a man, with *vis*, strength.
Manger—a trough to *eat* out of; *manger* (French), to eat; *mando* (Latin), to chew; *mounch* (old English and Scotch), to chew.
Mangle—to mutilate; *manga* (Gothic), *mangeln* (German).
March—the limit of a county: *mark* (Gothic and German); hence, *marquis*, one who takes care of the *marches*.
March—a *marked* or measured movement.

Market—*markt* (German), from *mark*, an assignation; *tryst* (Scotch), an *appointed* place of meeting, is used to signify a *market*; from *to trust*. Some connect *market* with *mercor* (Latin), to buy.

Master—the chief; *maestur* (Gothic); from *mæst* (Saxon), greatest; *meister* (German).

Mastiff—perhaps from *maest* (Gothic), greatest, and *tiffe* (Teutonic), a dog.

Maw—the stomach; *maga* (Gothic), *magen* (German); hence, *mawkish.*

Mayor—the chief magistrate; from *major* (Latin), greater; or *maer* (Gothic), *mehr* (Teutonic), *mare* (Saxon), more or greater.

Meadow—a field of grass; *mæd* (Saxon); *mähen* (German), to mow.

Meal—*melo* (Saxon), *mehl* (German); from *malu* (Icelandic), *molo* (Latin), to grind.

Mean—*midan* (Gothic), *mittel* (German), *medium* (Latin), *moyen* (French), something in the middle, or between, to effect a purpose. *Middle*, from *mid-deal*, the mid share; *midla* (Icelandic), to divide, to interpose; hence, *meddle.*

Mean—low, vulgar; *mæne* (Saxon), *gemein* (German); from *menge* (German), great number; hence, *mengen*, to mix; hence, *many* and *among.*

Measles—from *maser* (German), a spot.

Meet—*mota* (Gothic), *metan* (Saxon), *gemote* (Saxon), meeting, and the place where a meeting was held. *Mote-hills*, hills of meeting; *written agemot*, meeting of wise men.

Mesh—the space between the threads of a net; *meis* (Gothic), *masche* (German), *max* (Saxon); from *meisa* (Gothic), to divide.

Mettle—*muthvol* (German), full of courage; *muth*, courage, and *voll*, full.

Milk—*miolk* (Gothic), *milch* (German), *milc* (Saxon); hence, *milt*, the sperm of a fish.

Mind—*mod*, *minne* (Gothic), *gemynd* (Saxon); *inna* (Gothic), to hold internally.

Mince—to make small; *minska* (Swedish), *minuo* (Latin), I lessen.

Mire—*myra* (Gothic), *moder* (German), mud; hence, *mud.*

Miss—to go from the mark; *missa* (Gothic), *missen* (German), *missian* (Saxon). *Mis*, the prefix, derived from this word; perhaps a *mist*, a fog, is also derived from this.

Moan—*mænan* (Saxon), to express grief; the same Saxon word signifies *to mean, to think;* the Saxon word also signifies *to remember*, in the same way as *to mind* (Scotch).

Month—derived from *moon.*

Mood—disposition of mind; *moody*, haughty, pensive; *mod* (Saxon), *muth* (German), mind, heart, passion; hence, *mad.* In the same way, *frenzy*, from *phren* (Greek), the mind.

Moon—*mana* (Gothic), *mona* (Saxon), *mond* (German,) *mene* (Greek). *Moon* has been derived from *mana* (Gothic), to admonish, as the northern nations were superstitiously swayed by the appearances of that luminary.

Morning—*morgan* (Gothic), *morgen* (German and Saxon). The *morn*, in Scotland, signifies the morrow. *Morning* is derived by Tooke from *myrran* (Saxon), to scatter.

Most—*mest* (Gothic), *mæst* (Saxon), *meist* (German).

Moth—*moth* (Saxon), *motte* (German); from *meida* (Gothic), to divide, as *insect* is derived from *seco* (Latin), to cut.

Mother—*mata* (Sanscrit), *moder* (Gothic), *mutter* (German), *modor* (Saxon), *mater* (Latin), *métér* (Greek).

Mould—earth; *mold* (Gothic), *molde* (Saxon), *mull* (German); from *mala* (Gothic), to beat small; hence, *mules* (Scotch), the earth of the grave. Connected with these, *meal, mill; mola* (Latin).
Mound—a fence; *mund* (Gothic), defence; *mundian* (Saxon); to defend; *mund* (Icelandic), a hand.
Mouth—*mun* (Gothic), *mund* (German,) *muth* (Saxon), *munds* (Scotch), perhaps from *in* (Gothic), an entrance. Like *os* (Latin), *mun* (Gothic) also signified the countenance.
Much—*mitt* (Gothic), *michel* (old German), *mycel* (Saxon); hence, *mickle* (Scotch).
Murder—*maurther* (Gothic), *morth* (Saxon), *mord* (German), *meurtre* (French).
Mutton—the flesh of sheep; *mouton* (French), a sheep.
Nag—a horse; from *hnægan* (Saxon), to neigh.
Nail—a pin, the corneous substance on the toes and fingers; *nagle* (Gothic), *nagel* (German), *nægel* (Saxon).
Naked—*naken* (Gothic), *nackend* (German), *nacod* (Saxon), *noeth* (Welsh).
Name—*nam* (Gothic, Persic, and Sanscrit), to tell.
Nap—to take a short sleep; *hnæppian* (Saxon); perhaps from *hnigan* (Saxon), *neigen* (German), to nod, to bend; hence, also, *knee.*
Narrow—from *near; nahe* (German), *nigh*, or near.
Neat—small and handsome; *natid* (Gothic), *nett* (German), *nitidus* (Latin); hence, *natty.*
Need—exigence, want; *naud* (Gothic), *noth* (German), *neod* (Saxon).
Needle—*nadel* (German), *nædl* (Saxon).
Neighbour—from *neah*, near, and *bur* (Saxon), a bower, cottage; *bua* (Gothic), to dwell.
Neither—*not either.*
Ness—a point of land running into the sea, a *nose* of land; *näsa* (Swedish), *nese* (Saxon), *nase* (German).
Net—*net* (Icelandic), *netz* (German), *net* (Saxon), what is *knit* or *knotted.*
Nettle—*nässla* (Swedish), *nessel* (German), *netele* (Saxon), from *el* (Gothic), fire; thus, *urtica* (Latin), from *uro* (Latin), to burn.
New—*nawa* (Sanscrit), *nou* (Persic), *nava* (Hindostanee), *neos* (Greek), *novus* (Latin), *ny* (Gothic and Swedish), *neu* (German), *niwe* (Saxon).
Night—*not* (Gothic), *nacht* (German), *niht* (Saxon), *nuks* (Greek), *nox* (Latin).
Nightingale—from *night*, and *gala* (Swedish and Icelandic), to sing; *galan* (Saxon); connected with this, *gellen* (German), to sound; whence *yell*, and perhaps *gale; gulgul* (Sanscrit), *bulbul* (Persic).
Nim—to filch; *nema* (Gothic), *nehmen* (German), *niman* (Saxon), to take away; hence, also, *nimble*, catching quick. *To benumb*, to take away the senses, from the same root.
Nine—*niun* (Gothic), *neun* (German), *nigon* (Saxon).
Nose—the protuberance on the face; *nasa* (Sanscrit), *naus nef* (Gothic), *nase* (German), *nēse* (Saxon), *nasus* (Latin), *nez* (French); hence, *ozle, snaffle, snarl, sneeze, snore, snout, snuff.*
Not—*neit* (Gothic), *nicht* (German), *nate* (Saxon.)
Now—*nu* (Gothic and Saxon), *nun* (German), *nun* (Greek), *nunc* (Latin).
Nut—a gland, the fruit of a tree; *nuss* (German), *hnut* (Saxon), *nux* (Latin), *noix* (French).

Oak—*ek* (Gothic), *eiche* (German); *ac* (Saxon), like the Latin word *robur*, signifying also strength; connected with *ecan* (Saxon), to increase, *to eke*.

Oath—*aith* (Gothic), *eid* (German), *ath* (Saxon), *æ* (Saxon), law; from *æ* (Gothic), always; thus denoting what has continued till it became a law; *aei* (Greek), always; *aye* (English).

Odd—singular; *udda* (Swedish); perhaps from *eit*, *ein* (Gothic), one.

Old—*alda* (Gothic), *alt* (German), *eald* (Saxon); *eildens* (Scottish), equals in age; *yldan* (Saxon), to put off, *to yield*.

One—*ein* (German), *æn* (Saxon). Only—*ænlic* (Saxon), one-like. Any —*ænig* (Saxon).

Open—*open* (Gothic), *offen* (German), *open* (Saxon), to lift *off* or *up*.

Orchard—a garden; *aurtigards* (Gothic), *ortgeard* (Saxon); from *wyrt*, an herb, and *geard*, a garden.

Ordeal—a trial of innocence by fire or water; *ordeil* (Gothic), *urtheil* (German), *ordæl* (Saxon); from *or*, without, and *dael*, a part or separation, judgment without distinction of persons.

Otherwise—*other ways; weise* (German), *wisi* (Saxon), wise, manner.

Outrage—extreme violence; meaning, according to some, *utter rage*, or violence. Thomson derives it from *oultrage* (French), *oltraggio* (Italian); from *ultra agere* (Latin), to drive beyond.

Owe—to be indebted to; *aga* (Gothic), *agan* (Saxon). *Eigen* (German), own, peculiar.

Pace—from *pas* (French), a step.

Pad—a foot-path; used also as a verb, to travel gently, to rob on *foot*. A *foot-pad* is therefore a redundancy; *path* (Saxon), *pfad* (German); *pedd* (Celtic), a foot.

Pageant—a show; from *pæcan* (Saxon), to deceive; hence, according to Tooke, *page*, an attendant, as servants were frequently addressed as *knaves*, &c.

Pain—*pin* (Saxon), *pein* (German). *Pœna* (Latin), *poiné* (Greek), punishment.

Pallet—a bed of *straw*, a mean bed; *paille* (French), *paglia* (Italian), straw. *Pad*, a saddle stuffed with *straw; paga* (Spanish), straw.

Palter—to deceive; *pultar*, *baldar* (Spanish), *fallo* (Latin).

Paltry—mean; from *paltor* (Gothic), rags; hence, *pelting* (English), pitiful, and *peltrie* (Scotch), trash.

Parcel—a small bundle; from *part*.

Parboil—to boil in *part*.

Pare—to trim; *parer* (French), to deck, to make ready; hence, *parry; paro* (Latin).

Parlour—literally, a room for conversation; from *parler* (French), to speak; hence, also, *parliament*.

Parse—from *part;* to resolve a sentence into *parts*.

Pastime—an amusement; what *passes* the *time* agreeably.

Passover—a sacrifice; so named from God's *passing over* the habitations of the Israelites.

Pear—*pera* (Icelandic), *birn* (German), *poire* (French), *pera* (Saxon), *peren* (Welsh), from *per*, sweet.

Peck—a measure; from *poki* (Icelandic), *pack* (old German), *pocca* (Saxon), a bag; hence, *poke*, *pouch*, *pocket*, and *poche* (French).

To peck—from *to pick*; *picken* (German), *pycan* (Saxon)

To peer—to come just in sight; contracted from *to appear*.

To pelt—derived by Johnson from *pellet*, a little ball or bullet; *pila* (Latin), a ball; hence, *pill*.

Pen—a fold; *pyndan* (Saxon), to inclose; hence, a *pound*, a *pinfold*, and the verb *to poind*, signifying to distrain, to seize on, or *inclose as a surety*. *Pfandan* (German), to seize or distrain; hence, *pawn*. *Pond* is by some connected with *pyndan*.

Pent—*penned up*.

Perhaps—from *per* (Latin), through or by, and *haps*.

Perry—a drink from *pears*.

Pert—perhaps a contraction of *impertinent*.

Pet—a lamb taken into the house and much made of; hence, any creature that is indulged. Jameson says that it may be from *pete* (Teutonic), a little god-daughter. It is more probably from *petit* (French), small.

Pet—slight passion; derived by Johnson from *despit* (French).

Pie—a bird; *pie* (French), *pica* (Latin); hence, *pied*, party-coloured.

Pit—connected with *put* (Dutch), a well; *pfutze* (German), a puddle; *pittr* (Icelandic), a well; *puits* (French), *puteus* (Latin), *put* (Sanscrit).

Plaid—perhaps from *pleth* (Welsh), a fold. *Plico* (Latin), I fold; hence, *plait*, to fold. *Pli* (French), a fold, wrinkle, habit; hence, *to ply, to apply*, &c.

Plan—something which makes *plain*; connected with *platt*, (German), flat, plain; hence, *plate*, and a *plot* or *plat* of ground, meaning a smooth piece of ground; hence, *plot*, according to some, the plan or basis of a conspiracy.

Plea—the act of pleading; according to some, from *plaider* (French), to plead; according to others, from *pleo* (Saxon), quarrel, debate.

Plight—*pligt* (Swedish), *pflicht* (German), a duty or pledge; *pliht* (Saxon), *pligt* (Danish), duty, penance; *plicht* (Scottish), obligation in a disagreeable matter; hence, *to plight*, to bind one's self; *verpflichten* (German), to oblige.

Plough—*plog* (Gothic), *pflug* (German).

Pluck—*luka* (Swedish), to draw; *pflücken* (German), *plocka* (Icelandic), *plukken* (Dutch).

Plump—with a sudden motion; from *plomp* (Teutonic), leaden; *plumbum* (Latin), lead. *Plump*—round or fat; might at first be employed to signify what was solid or heavy.

Poach—literally, to carry off in a *poke* or bag; *poche* (French), a bag.

To poke—to search for with a long instrument; perhaps from *paak* (Gothic), a staff; connected with this *pauken* (German), to beat, and *paik* (Scotch), a blow.

Pool—*pol* (Swedish), *pfuhl* (German).

Poulterer—one who sells fowls; *poule* (French), a hen.

Pound *pund* (Icelandic), *pfund* (German), *pund* (Saxon); connected, perhaps, with *pyndan*, to inclose, a certain measure or weight; hence, a *pound*, a *pinfold*, a place in which beasts are inclosed, and *to poind*, a Scotch law-term, literally to shut up or retain any thing as a security, to distrain.

Pout—to express anger by *putting out* the lip.

Praise—*prisa* (Gothic), *preis* (German), price, praise; *pretium* (Latin).

Prance—to move in a showy way; *prangen* (German), to glitter, to parade; hence, *prank*, frolic.

Prate, and Prattle—to talk childishly; *prata* (Swedish), *praten* (Dutch), *phradzo* (Greek), to speak.

Pride—*præte* (Saxon), *prydad* (Swedish), adorned; hence, *pretty*, and *prude*, an over nice woman. *Prætt* (Saxon), craft or subtlety, may be connected with this.

Prim—affectedly nice; *prampera* (Suevo-Gothic), to walk loftily; according to some, a contraction of *primitive*.

Primrose—the rose that appears *first*; *primus* (Latin), first.

Prong—a fork; *prionn* (Icelandic), *pren* (Danish), the point of a graving tool; *prion* (Saxon); hence, *to print*, and the Scotch word *prin*, a pin.

Prop—*por appuis* (French), for support.

Prove—*prova* (Gothic), *proben* (German), to try, to taste; *prie* (Scotch), to taste.

Prowl—to rove about in search of a thing; according to some, a corruption of *patrol*; but referred by others, with more probability, to *proie* (French), prey, and *aller*, to go, thus signifying to go in search of prey.

Pry—to look carefully into; perhaps from *to prove*.

Pucker—to contract into folds; perhaps from *poke*, a bag or pocket.

Puddle—a pool; *poel* (Teutonic), a pool; *pfuhl* (German), *puteus* (Latin), a well.

Pug—a kind name for a monkey, a playful appellation; *piga* (Swedish), *pika* (Icelandic), a virgin; *piga* (Saxon), a little maid.

Puny—petty, inconsiderable; *puis né* (French), since born; applied to an inferior order of judges in England. *Punye* (Scotch), a small body of men, is derived by Jameson from *poignée* (French), a handful; *pugnus* (Latin), a fist.

Pun—to use the same word in different senses; perhaps from *punian* (Saxon), to beat, bray, or pound; or from *pungo* (Latin), I pierce, I point.

Purchase—to buy, to obtain with labour, to acquire; derived from *pourchasse* (French), and meaning originally what was procured by the *chasse* or *chase*.

Purge—to make *pure*; *pur* (German), pure, merely; or from *purgo* (Latin), I purify, which has been traced to *pur* (Greek), fire.

Purl—to flow with a gentle noise; *byrla* (Gothic), to pour out liquor.

Purloin—to take by theft; derived by Skinner from *pour* and *loin* (French), far, meaning to put *far* away.

Purse—*posi* (Icelandic), a little bag; *puse* (Saxon), a purse. The Scotch word *pose*, a secret hoard of money, has been derived from these by some; others trace it to *positus* (Latin), placed.

Purse—to draw the mouth together like a *purse*.

Pursy—short-breathed and fat; *borstigh* (Teutonic), asthmatic; from *borste*, the breast, the seat of the lungs. Some might ally this word with *purse*, distended like a *purse*.

Push—*pousser* (French).

Quack—a pretender, one who *noises* his own fame; *quaken* (German), to cry, to quack; *quacksalber* (Teutonic), a crier of salves.

Quagmire—a shaking bog; *quatio* (Latin), *wagian* (Saxon), to shake; hence, *wag*.

Quail—to languish; *quälen* (German), to occasion pain.

Quake—to shake; *quakaeln* (Teutonic), *cwacian* (Saxon), *quatio* (Latin).

Quakers—a sect of religionists so named from the *tremblings* which they at times exhibited.

Qualm—a sudden fit of sickness; *cwælm* (Saxon), death; hence, *quell*, to crush, to subdue, originally to kill.

Quandary—a doubt or difficulty; *qu'en diraije* (French), literally, what shall I say of it. Thomson derives it from *draga tweon* (Saxon), the agitation of doubt.

Quarry—a stone-mine; so called from the stones being *squared* when taken out of a quarry; *quarré* (French), square; *quatuor* (Latin), four.

Quash—to crush; *quæsa* (Swedish), to shake; *cwysan* (Saxon), to crush, *to squeeze.*

Quaver—to shake; from *wagian* (Saxon), to move, to wag; hence, *quiver.*

Queen—the wife of a king; *quens* (Gothic), *kwinna* (Icelandic), *cwen* (Saxon), a wife.

Queer—odd, strange; *quer* (German), opposite, cross; *thweor* (Saxon); hence, *thwart.*

Quench—*acwencan* (Saxon), to put out.

Quick—living, swift; *cuik* (Teutonic), *quick* (German), *cwic* (Saxon).

Quill—a feather; *kiel* (German), the offset of a bulbous plant, the keel of a ship, a quill; connected by others with *calamus* (Latin).

Quirk—a subtlety; perhaps from *quer* (German), opposite, cross.

Quiver—a *cover* for armour; *couvrir* (French), to cover.

Quoth—said; *cwithan* (Gothic), *cwæthan* (Saxon), to say.

Quote—to cite what another *quoth* or said; some derive it from *quota,* share or part, and others from *cite, cito* (Latin), to call. Thomson derives it from *côté* (French), the side, making it a side or marginal note.

Race—contest in running; *resa* (Gothic), a course by land or water. *Race,* signifying the origin of a family, is given as from *radix* (Latin), a root.

Rack—an instrument of torture; *racka* (Swedish), to reach or extend; *reichen* (German), to reach; *recken* (German), to extend; hence also *stretch; strecken* (German).

Racy—strong, pungent; *rasa* (Gothic), to be carried with great force; *ras* (Icelandic), precipitancy in words, &c.; connected with these, *rush, rash,* &c. Others connect it with *radix* (Latin), the root, de noting tasting of the root or soil.

Rafter—*raeftræ* (Gothic), a roof-tree; *ræfter* (Saxon).

Ragged—torn; *recken* (German), to extend.

Rail—to scold; *ralla* (Swedish), *ræga* (Icelandic), *rügen* (German), *wregan* (Saxon), to accuse.

Raiment—from *to array;* which is derived from *ra* (Gothic), a line, order; *rada* (Icelandic), to put in order; hence, *reihe* (German), a *row; rue* (French), a *row* of houses, a street. From the same root, *range, rank.*

Rain—what *runs* or flows; *rægn* (Saxon), *regen* (German).

Rake—*raka* (Gothic), *rawan* (Saxon), *rechen* (German), to scrape, to live dissolutely.

Rally—to bring together, to *re-ally.*

Ramble—perhaps from *to roam,* to wander

Ram—to drive with force like a *ram; ram* (Gothic), strong.

Rampant—overgrowing restraint; *rempend* (Saxon); connected by some with *ramper* (French), *repo* (Latin), to creep. In heraldry, animals creeping up or rearing are said to be *rampant. To romp,* is connected with these words.

Random—want of direction, hazard; *randun* (Saxon), *randon* (French), a *running down.*

Rank—strong, fruitful; *rank* (German and Danish), *ranc* (Saxon), slender, high-grown, tall.

T 2

Ransack—to plunder; from *ran* (Gothic), plunder, and *sækia* (Gothic), to seek.

Ransom—a price paid for liberty; according to some, a variation of *redemption*; according to others, from *ran* (Gothic), plunder, and *sona* (Gothic), to appease.

Rant—bombast, senseless vociferation; perhaps from *ran* (Icelandic), a song; in the same way, *cant*, from *cano* (Latin), to sing. In Scotland, a *ranting* fellow is a merry, roaring fellow, and a *rant* is a merry song.

Rap—a quick smart blow; *rapp* (German and Gothic), quick; *frapper* (French), to strike.

Rasp—to rub off; *raspeln* (German), *rasper* (French), *raspare* (Italian). Some connect these with *rado* (Latin), to scrape.

Rate—to chide; *rethe* (Saxon), savage, austere; *wred* (Swedish), *reider* (Icelandic), angry; connected with these, *wrath*.

Rather—sooner; comparative of *rath* (Saxon), soon; *rad* (Gothic), direct, prompt; hence, *ready*.

Raw—not cooked, crude; *ra* (Gothic), *hreaw* (Saxon), *roh* and *rauh* (German), *rough*.

Reach—to stretch; *ræcan* (Saxon), *reichen* (German).

Reach—to vomit; *hræca* (Icelandic), *hreæn* (Saxon); hence, *wreck*, and *wrack*, what is vomited forth by the sea.

Ream—a parcel of paper; supposed to be from *ream* (Saxon), *riemen* (German), *reim* (Icelandic), a thong or strap.

Reap—to cut down corn when it is *ripe*; *ripe* is connected with *to rip*, to separate, to tear, as fruits are torn up when *ripe*; hence, *ripple*.

Reave—to rob; *hrifsna* (Icelandic), *reafian* (Saxon), *rauben* (German), *ravir* (French); hence, *bereave* and *reft*; hence, *to rob*, *to rove*, and *ruffian*.

Rebuke—to reprimand; derived by some from *re* and *bouche* (French), the mouth; *reboucher*, to stop the mouth. Others derive it from *repugno* (Latin), to resist.

Reck—to care for or regard; *rækia* (Gothic), *recan* (Saxon); *geruhen* (German), to condescend.

Reckon—to count, to consider; *recan* (Saxon), *rechnen* (German); derived by some from *reege* (old Saxon), a series or chain, from the ancient mode of calculating with small balls attached to a string.

Red—*rudher* (Sanscrit), *raudr* (Icelandic), *rhudd* (Welsh), *roth* (German), *rutilus* (Latin), *read* (Saxon), *rouge* (French), *roda* (Greek). *Rob Roy*, Rob the *red*.

Reed—a small cane; *raus* (Gothic), *rieth* (German), *hreod* (Saxon); hence, a *rush*, and *rash* (Scotch).

Reek (old English), vapour; *reik* (Gothic), *rauch* (German), *rec* (Saxon); hence, *reek* (Scotch), smoke, and *rook* (Scotch), mist.

Reel—to stagger; connected with *roll*.

Regale—to entertain in a *regal* or kingly way; or perhaps from *galan* (Saxon), to enchant.

Rehearse—to relate aloud; to *hear* one *saying*.

Release—to set free; *erlaesa* (Gothic), to set loose.

Relish—taste; *lécher* (French), to lick; *relécher*, to lick again.

Rely—to *lie* on, to depend on.

Rend—to tear; *raena* (Icelandic), to snatch, to spoil; hence, perhaps, *renard*, a fox; *trennen* (German), to divide.

Rest—repose; *roi* (Gothic), *rest* (Saxon), *rast* (German); hence, *restiff* unwilling to move; *resto* (Latin), to stand against, to resist.

Reverie—dreaming; from *to rave; rabies* (Latin), madness.

Reward—from *re*, back, and *worth;* to give back the worth.

Rhyme—measure or consonance of verse; from *riman* (Saxon), to number; *rythmus* (Latin), *ruthmas* (Greek).

Rib—derived by some from *reif*, a hoop, from its bending shape; *rif* (Icelandic), *ref* (Swedish), *rippe* (German).

Riband, or ribbon—perhaps connected with *band;* originally something to bind with.

Rich—*rikr* (Icelandic), powerful; *reich* (German), *ryk* (Dutch), *riche* (French), *ric* (Saxon). The termination *ric*, denotes dominion or power; bishop-*ric*, the dominion of a bishop; ala-*ric*, all-powerful. Connected with this word, *rex* (Latin), *roi* (French), *re* (Italian), *rey* (Spanish), a king; and *raj* (Sanscrit), government.

Rick—a heap; *hreika* (Gothic), to heap up; *hrauk* (Icelandic), *hreac* (Saxon), a heap; hence, *ridge*, and *rig* (Scotch).

Rid—to free; *rida* (Gothic), *radda* (Swedish), *retten* (German), *hreddan* (Saxon).

Ride—*reidu* (Gothic), *ridan* (Saxon), *reiten* (German). *Rheda*, (Latin), a chariot.

Rife—plentiful; perhaps connected with *to rive;* or connected with *reif* (German), ripe, mature.

Rifle—to rob; from *to reave.*

Rifle—a gun with a grooved barrel; derived by Thomson from *ræfla* (Swedish), to groove.

Right—justice, law; *rett* (Gothic), *recht* (German), *reht* (Saxon), *droit* (French); in many languages signifying *straight.*

Rim—a border; *raund* (Icelandic), *rand* (German), a border; hence, *rind*, a husk; perhaps connected with these, *round.*

Ring—a circle; *hring* (Saxon), *ring* (German).

Rinse—to wash, to cleanse; *hrein* (Gothic), *rein* (German), clean.

Riot—*noisy* debauchery; *rauta* (Icelandic), to roar like a wild beast, to rage.

Road—from *to ride;* a place *ridden* on.

Roam—to wander, to go at *room; raumen* (German), to remove, to clear away, to make *room* for; hence, also, *roum* (Scotch), to make way for.

Roan-tree—the mountain ash; from *runa* (Gothic), incantation, as it was often made use of in magical arts.

Robe—a long vest; connected with *hraf* (Saxon), a *roof* or covering; hence, *rauba* (barbarous Latin), *robe* (French).

Rock—a mass of stone; *roch* (Armoric), *roche* (French), *rupes* (Latin), *rōks* (Greek), from *ressō* (Greek), to break; *hruse* (Saxon), perhaps from *reosan* (Saxon), to rush or fall.

To rock—to shake; *rücken* (German), to move.

Rood—the cross; *rod* (Gothic and Saxon), from *roda* (Icelandic), an image; crosses being once used with an image of Christ upon them.

Roost—a place for hens; derived by some from *to rest;* by others connected with *roste* (Gothic), the highest part of a building.

Root—the part from which a plant springs; *rot* (Gothic), *wyrt* (Saxon), *ridza* (Greek), *radix* (Latin).

Rope—a thick cord; *rep* (Gothic), *rap* (Saxon), *reif* (German); connected with these, *to reef*, to bind together.

Round—circular; *rand* (Swedish, Danish, and German), a border, extremity. Bosworth connects this word with *to run*, designating, in its primitive sense, the quick motion of a body round its axis.

Rouse—to stir up; connected with *rise* and *raise.*

Rout—a clamorous multitude; *rauta* (Icelandic), to rage.

Rout—a defeat; from *ruptus* (Latin), broken.

Row—to impel with oars; *rodr* (Icelandic), *rudern* (German), *rowan* (Saxon), hence, *rudder*.

Rub—to make a friction; *reiben* (German).

Ruddy—connected with *red*.

Rue—to repent; *reuen* (German), *hreowan* (Saxon); perhaps connected with *hreow* (Saxon), raw, cruel; denoting the repentance which follows acts of cruelty; hence, *ruth*, pity.

Ruffle—to make *rough*.

Rumour—noise, report; *hream* (Saxon), sound; *ruhmen* (German), to praise.

Run—to flow; *renna* (Gothic and Swedish), *rennan* (Saxon), *rinnen* (German), *ruo* (Latin); from this, *rain*, and *runnet*, juice which makes milk *run* together.

Rye—*rocken* (German), *rug* (Danish), *rige* (Saxon); from *rih* (Saxon), hairy, rough.

Saddle—*sadel* (Swedish), *sattel* (German), *selle* (French); from *to sit*.

Saffron—a yellow flower; *zufran* (Arabic), yellow.

Sail—a canvas sheet; *segel* (German, Swedish, and Saxon); perhaps connected with *sæl* (Saxon), a rope.

Sake—cause, account; *sache* (German), *sacu* (Saxon); originally signifying, like *ding* (German), thing, wrangling. Some connect it with *to seek*; thus, for his *sake*, means for what he would *seek* or desire.

Saloon—a hall; *sal* (Icelandic), *saal* (German), *sal* (Saxon); from *saljan* (Mœso-Gothic), to entertain; *Upsal*, a town in Sweden; the high court.

Salt—connected, in various languages, with *sea*.

Same—like, together; *saman* (Gothic), *samne* (Saxon), *gesammt* (German); hence also *some*, a number together, and *to sum*; *somnian* (Saxon), *sammeln* (German), to gather together; *simul* (Latin), together.

Sand—stone reduced to small particles; *sand* (German, Swedish, Saxon); *syndrian* (Saxon), to divide or sunder; *sinder* (Scotch).

Sap—juice; *saft* (German), *sæp* (Saxon).

Saw—an instrument for separating; *sag* (Swedish), *säge* (German), *saga* (Saxon), *sierra* (Spanish); from *sega* (Gothic), to cut; *seco* (Latin), to cut.

Say—to speak, to tell, to teach; *saga* (Gothic), *sagen* (German), *secgan* (Saxon); hence, *saw*, a wise saying.

Scale—a balance; from *shell*, shells being used for measuring.

Scamper—to fly off, to decamp; *schampen* (Teutonic), to slip aside; whence, says Dr. Jamieson, *escamper* (French), to escape; others have it from *ex campo* (Latin).

Scanty—bare, scarce; *skemta* (Icelandic), to divide; others from *scindo* (Latin), to cut.

Scar—a rock; *skaer* (Icelandic), a rock; from *skera*, to cut; *scyran* (Saxon), to divide; hence, *share*, *shire*, *shore*, *score*, *scar* (a cut), *shear*, *shred*, a share; the word *sheer*, complete, may be allied with these, as *decided* is with *cæsus* (Latin), cut.

Scare—to take fright; *skiar* (Icelandic), afraid; applied to the horse when it is *shy*; *shy* and *skittish* from the same root.

Scate, or skate—an iron to slide with; *sked* (Swedish), *skoeite* (Dutch); from *skiuta* (Gothic); hence, also, *to shoot* (English), and *schiessen* (German), which, as well as *sceotan* (Saxon), signifies *to discharge*; hence, to pay one's *shot*.

Scold—to blame; connected with *scyld* (Saxon), *schuld* (German), guilt, fault.

Scoop—to hollow; *scopa* (Gothic), a vessel; *schaff* (Frankic), a hollow vessel, *skaptein* (Greek), to excavate; *scapha* (Latin), a *skiff; skep* (Scotch), a case for a bee-hive.

Scorch—to dry up; connected with *searian* (Saxon), to dry; hence, *sear*, and *sere*.

Scour—to cleanse; *skura* (Gothic), *scheuern* (German), *scheur* (German), a shed or barn.

Scowl—to look askant or sullen; *skoela* (Gothic), *schielen* (German).

Scramble—to climb up by the hands; from *hram* (Gothic), a hand.

Scrap—small pieces, scrapings; from *to scrape;* which may be connected with *scrob* (Saxon), a shrub or scrog; *schrapen* (German), to scrape; hence, *scrub*, a mean fellow; a *scrip*, a bag for holding *scraps*.

Scratch—to tear with the nails; connected with *scrape; kratzen* (German); *schreiben* (German), to write; hence, *scrawl* and *scribble*, to write badly; *scribo* (Latin), to write.

Screech and scream—to cry out in affright; *skria* (Gothic); hence, *schrecken* (German), to terrify. *Shreck-horn*, the peak of terror.

Screen—to protect; *scrin* (Saxon), *schrein* (German), a box or *shrine;* from *skia* (Gothic), to protect. *Screen* has also been derived from *secerno* (Latin), to keep apart.

Scuffle—confused fighting; connected with *shove; skiufa* (Gothic), *schuppen* (German), to shove; hence, perhaps, *scoff*.

Scull, or skull—of the same origin with *shell; hirnschale* (German), the brain-shell. Some have derived shell, a cup, from *skull*, as our forefathers made cups of the skulls of their enemies. But these words, with the following, are all traceable to *skia* (Gothic), to protect or cover—*scale, scalp, sconce, shell, shield, shieling, shelter, shaw, shade, screen, shrine, shirt, skin, sky, skirmish* (to fight under cover), *sham, shoe, scuttle*.

Scum—froth, that which rises to the top; *schaum* (German), *schiuma* (Italian), *écume* (French); from *skia* (Gothic), to cover; hence, *skim*, to touch the top lightly.

Scurf—a scab; *hreof* (Saxon), rough; hence, *scurvy*.

Scuttle—to make holes in a ship; to make it open like a basket or *scuttle*.

Sea—the ocean; *sae* (Gothic and Saxon), *see* (German), *zee* (Dutch); from *ae* (Gothic), water. *Aa* or *ae*, according to etymologists, denotes continuance, extent; *aei* (Greek), from its combination of vowels, expresses always, or eternity; and, on the same principle, *ae* (Saxon), a law, a custom which has been long continued.

Seam—a joining; *saum* (German), connected with *to sew*.

Seat—a chair, residence; *set* (Gothic), *saet* (Saxon), *sitz* (German); connected with this, *to set*, to place, *setzen* (German); *sitte* (German), means custom, morals.

See—to perceive by the eye; *sia* (Gothic), *seon* (Saxon), *sehen* (German); derived from *eye;* hence, a *seer*, a prophet.

Seed—what is *sown; soed* (Gothic), *sæd* (Saxon), *saat* (German).

Seek—to look for; *secan* (Saxon), *suchen* (German); derived from *auge* (German), the eye.

Seldom—rarely; *sealdn* (Gothic), *seldan* (Saxon), *selten* (German); according to some, from *seld* (Saxon), rare, and *when*.

Send—to despatch; *senda* (Gothic), *sendan* (Saxon), *sind* (old German), a way.

Seneschal—one who has the charge of a household; *skalk* (Gothic), a minister or servant; *schalk* (German), a rogue, and *senis* (Latin), old. Such names as rogue and servant, come to be applied indifferently by a common pleasantry. A *marshal*, or *mareskalk*, from *mere* (Teutonic), a horse, and *skalk*, signifying one who has the superintendence of the horse.

Shabby—bare, *shaving* close; *scafen* (Saxon), to shave; *schaben* (German), to rub. *To scuff* (Scotch), to touch lightly, is connected by Jamieson with *to shove;* it seems naturally connected with *scafen.*

Shackle—chains for prisoners; *sceacul* (Saxon), *schauel* (Dutch), a link of a chain, what *shakes;* the *shackle-bone* (Scotch), signifies the wrist-bone, by which prisoners were chained. This is a humiliating word, and must have arisen from the frequency of tyrannical imprisonment in Scotland in early times.

Shaft—a pole or spear, handle or arrow; *schaft* (German), *sceaft* (Saxon), *sagitta* (Latin), an arrow; *shebat* (Hebrew), to extend.

Shagreen—a preparation of shark's skin resembling a file; *sagry* (Arabic), *chagrain* (French); hence, *to chagreen*, or *shagreen*, to irritate.

Shake—to agitate, to tremble; *skoeka* (Gothic), *sceacan* (Saxon), *schütteln* (German.)

Shall—*sollen* (German), *sceal* (Saxon), signify originally *to owe; schuld* (German), punishment, debt.

Shambles—stalls where butchers expose their meat; *scamel* (Saxon), *schämel* (German), a stool or bench.

Shame—the feeling of disgrace; from *skam* (Gothic), to blush; *scham* (German), *sceamn* (Saxon).

Shape—to make, form; *skapa* (Gothic and Swedish), *scyppan* (Saxon), *schaffen* (German); hence, *ship*, a vessel, and the termination *ship* (English), *schaft* (German).

Share—to part, to divide; *skoera* (Gothic), *sceran* or *scyran* (Saxon); hence, *shore*, *shire*, *shears*, *score*, plough*share*, *scar*, *sherd*, *short.*

Sharp—*scharf* (German), *scearf* (Saxon); hence, *carve.*

Shatter—from *scheiden* (German), to cut or separate; *scæth* (Saxon), a *sheath.*

Sheaf—a bundle of corn, what is *shoved* together; *schaub* (High German); *sceaf* (Saxon); or it may be a portion, from *skyfa* (Gothic), *schyfen* (Belgic), to cut.

Sheen—brightness; *schein* (German).

Sheer—clear, unmixed; *skir* (Gothic), *scir* (Saxon), from *sciran* (Saxon), to separate; *schier* (German), almost.

Sheet—any thing broad; *skaut* (Gothic), *sceat* (Saxon), a garment; from *sceotan* (Saxon), to cast forth.

Shelf—a board to lay things on, a bank in the sea; *scelf* (Saxon), to separate in laminæ; *schelffe* (Teutonic), a scale; perhaps from *skilia* (Icelandic), to separate; some refer *shallow* and *shoal* to shelf.

Shelter—from *to shield.* (See Skull.)

Shepherd—a *sheep-herd.*

Sherbet—sugar, acid, and water mixed; *shurbut* (Hindostanee); hence, *shrub.*

Sheriff—the *shire-reeve*, or steward; from *shire* and *gerefd* (Saxon), a companion, a governor.

Shield—*skiald* (Gothic), *scyld* (Saxon), *schild* (German. (See Skull.)

Shilling—a coin; from *skilia* (Gothic), to divide; small money: some derive it from *shield*, from the impression of a shield upon some coins

Shiver—to shake or tremble; *schauer* (German), a shivering fit, a shower.

Shoal—from *sceole* (Saxon), a multitude, a *school; skelea* (Icelandic), to divide, a separate company.

Shock—connected with *shake*.

Shop—a place where articles are *shaped* or made.

Short—not long; from *scyran* (Saxon), to cut; *curtus* (Latin), *court* (French), *kurtz* (German), short.

Shove—to push; *skiufa* (Gothic), *scufan* (Saxon), *schieben* (German).

Shoulder—*sculder* (Saxon), *schulter* (German), *skiolldr* (Icelandic), a shield; supposed to be from *skia* (Gothic), to protect or cover.

Shout—a sound *shot* out; some connect it with *tauta* (Gothic), *theotan* (Saxon).

Show—to exhibit to view; *sceawean* (Saxon), *schauen* (German), to see, to look at; *auge* (German), the eye.

Shrew—a clamorous, contentious woman; supposed to be from *syrwan* (Saxon), to ensnare; the word *shrewd* is said to have the same origin.

Shrive—to receive confession; *scrifan* (Saxon); according to some, from *scribo* (Latin), to write, as the priests were wont to give a written prescription as to the course of penance; others take it from *skyra* (Gothic), to explain.

Shrink—to draw together; *rynka* (Gothic), *wrinclian* (Saxon), *runtzeln* (German), to wrinkle.

Shroud—a cover, a winding-sheet; *scrydan* (Saxon), to clothe; from *skraut* (Icelandic), pomp.

Shrug—to draw up the *back; ryka* (Gothic), *hric* (Saxon), *rücken* (German), the back or *ridge*.

Shun—to avoid; *scunian* (Saxon), *scheuen* (German), *eschew* (English).

Sick—afflicted with disease; *seoc* (Saxon), *siech* (German); connected with *to sigh*.

Side—the part of the body fortified by the ribs, a party; *sida* (Icelandic and Swedish), *seite* (German), *side* (Saxon), *sid* (Saxon), broad. In the same way, *latus* (Latin), the side; from *latus* (Latin), broad; *platus* (Greek), broad.

Sieve—what *sifts; sia* (Icelandic), *sieb* (German), *sife* (Saxon).

Sight—*siene* (Saxon), *gesicht* (German), sight, countenance.

Sign—token, standard; *zeichen* (German), *segen* (Saxon).

Silk—*silke* (Swedish), *seolc* (Saxon), *silk* (Persian), a thread.

Silly—poor, miserable; derived by some from *saelig* (Saxon), fortunate, simple; by others from *salig* (Gothic), poor.

Sin—an act against the laws of God; *synd* (Gothic), *sünde* (German), *syn* (Saxon), *sons* (Latin), guilty; *sinein* (Greek), to hurt.

Sinew—a tendon; *sehne* (German), *sinu* (Saxon), *senon* (Scotch).

Singe—to scorch; from *to sing*, on account of the singing noise attending *scorching;* it has also been connected with *ignis* (Latin), fire.

Sink—to fall down; *sigguan* (Gothic), *sencan* (Saxon), *sinken* (German).

Sip—*to sup* by small draughts; *saufen* (German), to drink immoderately. This word, in the northern languages, is confined to drinking; by an extension of meaning, it signifies the evening meal. The word is formed from the sound which accompanies the *sucking up* of liquors; hence, *soupe*, and *souper* (French), to eat the evening meal.

Sir, lord—the word of respect in address; from *sihor* (Gothic), lord, which is connected with *sig*, victory. It has also, like *sire*, a father.

or term of respect, been connected with *senior* (Latin), older; whence, *seigneur* (French), *signor* (Italian). *Sar* (Hebrew), a prince.

Sirloin—*surlonge* (French), above the loin; according to others, a title given to the loin of beef by one of our kings in a fit of good humour.

Sirname, or surname—a name in addition to another; *sur* (French), *super* (Latin), upon.

Sister—a woman born of the same parents; *syster* (Gothic), *schwester* (German), *swuster* (Saxon), *soror* (Latin).

Sketch—to draw the outline; from *scitan* (Saxon), to cast forth; others connect it with *schatten* (German), a shadow.

Skiff—a small light boat; *schiff* (German), *scapha* (Latin).

Skill—discernment; from *ska* (Gothic), division, a seeing of things asunder; *scylan* (Saxon), to divide. The same idea of division is observable in the word discernment, from *cerno* (Latin), to see, and *dis*, asunder.

Skim—to take off the *scum*.

Skipper—the master of a ship; a *shipper*; *scyp* (Saxon), a ship.

Slake—to allay thirst; *slokna* (Gothic); from *læka* (Gothic), *leccan* (Saxon), to wet, to moisten.

Slander—false invective; connected by some with *to sully* or *slur*; by others with the word *scandal*; and by Dr. Jamieson with *kland* (Gothic), infamy.

Slant—to go in a side way; *slenta* (Icelandic), to slip, *slind*, the side.

Slate—a kind of stone in laminæ; from *to slit*.

Slay—to kill; *slaga* (Gothic), to strike; *schlagen* (German), *slean* (Saxon), *slaighim* (Irish); hence, *slaughter*; also a *sledge*-hammer. *Slean* (Saxon), also signifies *to cast*, *to throw*; hence, according to Tooke, *sleet*.

Slave—one without liberty; from *Sclavonia*, the inhabitants of which were enslaved by the Venetians.

Sledge—a carriage without wheels; that which *slides*.

Sleek—smooth, shining; *schlicht* (German), plain, smooth; figuratively denoting cunning, deceitful. *Schlich* (German), trick; hence, *sleight* of hand, and *sly*.

Sleep—*slaep* (Saxon), *schlaf* (German); from *slap* or *slack* (Gothic), remiss, loose.

Sleeve—a cover for the arms; from *slefan* (Saxon), to put on, to clothe. "To laugh in one's *sleeve*," to laugh concealedly, covering the countenance with the sleeve.

Slender—thin; *klen* (Gothic), *klein* (German), small, thin; *slinder* (Belgic); connected by others with *schlange* (German), a serpent; *schlingen* (German), to wreath.

Slight—small; according to some, from *schlecht* (German), mean, plain; figuratively ignoble, of no account; others, from *light*, to make *light* of.

Slink—to sneak, to steal out of the way; *slincan* (Saxon), *schleichen* (German), to creep.

Slip—to slide; *slaepa* (Gothic), to creep; *slipan* (Saxon), *schlüpfen* (German.) A slipper, a shoe into which the foot *slips*, or goes easily; hence, a *slope*, a smooth descent.

Sloth—idleness; connected with *slow*. A *sloven*, a *slow* person; *to slouch*, to walk *slowly*; a *slug*, a *slow*-creeping snail; hence, *sluggard*.

Sluice—a floodgate; from *schliessen* (German), to shut; *sluyse* (Dutch), *escluse* (French). *Claudo* (Latin), to shut.

Slur—to sully; from *slorig* (Teutonic), nasty.

Slut—*slodder* (Teutonic), filthy; hence, also, *slattern*, and *to slotter* (Scotch). Tooke connects *slut* with *slow*.

Sly—cunning; *slaegur* (Icelandic), *verschlagen* (German), from *schlagen*, to turn; *slith* (Saxon), slippery.

Smack—taste; *smaec* (Saxon), *schmacke* (German); connected, perhaps, with *smoke*.

Small—*sma* (Gothic and Swedish), *schmal* (German), *smael* (Saxon); hence, *smack*, a *small* vessel; *smile*, a *small* laugh (from *sma* and *le*, Gothic, laughter); *smatter*, a *small* quantity; and *smash*, to break in *small* pieces; hence *melt*, and *smelt*.

Smell—odour; some derive it from *melt*; others connect it with *smack*; and Skinner from *smoel* (Dutch), warm, as smells are increased by heat.

Smelt—to *melt* ore so as to extract the metal; from *to melt*; *schmeltsen* (German), to melt, to make small.

Smith—literally, one who *smites*, one who works in iron; originally, an artist in general; from *smithan* (Saxon), *schmiden* (German), to beat, to strike; hence perhaps *smooth*, what is beaten down; *smethe* (Saxon), *schmeidig* (German), soft, pliant.

Smoke—*smic* (Saxon), *schmauch* (German).

Smother—to suffocate; *smoran* (Saxon), *schmoren* (German), *smore* (Scotch); hence, *smoulder*, to burn chokingly.

Smuggle—to import without paying duty; *smugan* (Saxon), to creep; *schmiegen* (German), to bend; *smuigen* (Dutch), to eat secretly; *smouster* (Scotch).

Smut—a spot, obscenity; *smitta* (Saxon), *schmutz* (German), a spot; *smitta* (Gothic), to infect; hence, *smittle* (old English), and *smit* (Scotch), to infect.

Snack—a part or share; *schneiden* (German), to cut, to go *snacks*, to be partners; hence also *snag*, a sharp protuberance.

Sneak—to crawl, to creep slyly; *snican* (Saxon), hence *snake* and *snail*; hence also *snug*, concealed, safe, comfortable.

Sneer—contempt expressed by drawing up the *nose*; *snuyte* (Teutonic), the nose; connected with this, *snort*, *snore*, *snout*, *snarl*. *To snare*, *to noose*, may have the same origin.

Snow—*sno* (Swedish), *snior* (Icelandic), *schnee* (German), *snaw* (Saxon), *sneachd* (Celtic), *sneg* (Slavonic), *nix* (Latin).

Soak—perhaps connected with *to suck*; *sucan* (Saxon), *saugen* (German), to suck.

Soap—*sape* (Saxon), *seife* (German), *sapa* (Icelandic), *sebon* (Welsh); derived, according to some, from *sebum* (Latin), tallow—soap being composed of tallow and ashes.

Soft—mild, not hard; connected by some with *saft* (Gothic), sap.

Soil—to sully; *sula* (Gothic), *sudeln* (German), *souiller* (French).

Song—from *son* (Saxon), a sound.

Sooth—truth; *soth* (Saxon). *Forsooth*, for truth.

Sordid—base, filthy; commonly supposed to be from *sordidus* (Latin), mean; but referred by some to *saur* (Icelandic), filthy. The word *sorry*, signifying contemptible, has been derived from *saur*; but it may come from *sorrow*, in the same way as *pitiful* from *pity*.

Sorrow—care, anxiety; *saurgan* (Gothic), *sorge* (German), *sorg* (Saxon). *Sar* (Saxon and Icelandic), a wound; hence, a *sore*. The adverb *sore*, it has been remarked, means, in old English, intensely; but there is little doubt that it has been originally connected with *sore*, meaning painful. Intensatives in our own day are frequently taken from adjectives denoting pain.

Soul—the immortal part; *saiwala* (Gothic), *seele* (German), *saul* (Saxon); signifying originally life.
Sound—entire, whole; *sund* (Saxon), *gesund* (German).
South—the direction opposite the north; *sud* (German), *sud* (French), *suth* (Saxon); according to Tooke, from *seothan* (Saxon), to seethe, connected with *sinda* (Gothic), and *sieden* (German), to be hot.
Sow—to cast seed into the ground; *saian* (Gothic), *säen* (German), *sawan* (Saxon).
Span—the measure of the hand extended; *spanne* (German), from *spanna* (Gothic), to draw out; hence, *spin*.
Spangle—a locket, any thing sparkling; *spange* (Saxon and German), from *spannan* (Saxon), to span or clasp.
Spar—to shut, to close; *sperren* (German), *sparran* (Saxon); hence, *to spar*, to keep out an adversary's blows.
Sparrow—*sparwa* (Gothic), *sperling* (German), *speara* (Saxon); supposed by some to be connected with *spreka* (Gothic), to speak, from its incessant chirping.
Spatter—to besprinkle; from *spit*; hence, *spat*, *spatterdashes*, and *speck*; also *sputter*, to speak confusedly.
Speak—*spreka* (Gothic), *spekia* (Icelandic), *sprechen* (German), *sprecan* (Saxon).
Spearmint—a kind of mint growing in a *spear* form.
Speed—to make haste; *sputan* (German), *spedan* (Saxon), *speudein* (Greek).
Spell—originally a speech, mystic words or charms; *spial* (Icelandic), discourse. *Spell*, to divide a word, has been derived from *spalten* (German), to divide, connected with *splita* (Icelandic), to tear; hence, *split* and *splinter*. *Spell*, a turn of work, a word common among sailors, is derived from *spelian* (Saxon), to supply another's place, to act; *spielen* (German), to act or play.*
Spider—according to some, a *spinner*; derived by others from *spy*, and *dor* (Saxon), a stingless bee, thus signifying the insect that watches the fly; others have it *spin-atter*, from *spin*, and *atter* (Saxon), poison.
Spill—to shed; from *spillan* (Saxon), *spillen* (German), to destroy, to deprive of; *spoil*, to ravage, is from *spolio* (Latin).
Spoon—perhaps from *spann* (Icelandic), a corn measure; *spannan* (Saxon), to extend, span, or measure.
Sport—play, diversion; from *spott* (Icelandic), a make-game; *spott* (German), mockery, derision.
Sprain—an extension of the ligaments; from *springan* (Saxon), to spring, to bud; *springen* (German), to leap; hence, the *spring*, the season of *springing*; a *spring*, water *springing* out; *sprout*, *sprig*, *spurt*, *sprit*, and *spriet* (Dutch), a spear. A *stripling* or *springald*, from *spritan* (Saxon), to sprout (by a metathesis).
Spruce—trim, nice; *spraeg* (Swedish), beautiful.
Spurn—to drive away with the foot; *spur* (Gothic), the foot; hence, according to some, a *spur*. From the same root, *spüren* (German), and *spyrian* (Saxon), to trace by the footstep.
Squander—*schänden* (German), *scendan* (Saxon), to destroy, *to shend*. *Squander* has also been made a variation of *wander*.
Squeeze—to press; *cwysan* (Saxon), to crush, to quash.
Squint—to look obliquely; *scyle-eyed* (Saxon), squint-eyed, or *skelly*-

---

* Hence, *bon-spiel*, a term employed for a game on the ice in Scotland.

eyed (Scotch).. *Ska* (Icelandic), signifies oblique or transverse, and has passed into the composition of many words in the northern languages.

Squire, and esquire—an attendant on a knight, his armour-bearer; from *escu* (French), *scutum* (Latin), a shield. The title *esquire*, formerly limited to certain ranks, is now given by courtesy to all who are, in the common acceptation, gentlemen.

Stag—derived by Tooke from *stigan* (Saxon), *steigen* (German), to ascend; and named from its lofty head. From the same root, *stage*, an elevated place; *stæger* (Saxon), a *stair; storey*, a set of stairs; and *stigel* (Saxon), a stile. Others refer *stag* to *steggr* (Icelandic), the male of wild beasts.

Stale—long kept; perhaps connected with *stellen* (Teutonic), to place; connected with this, *stall.* Others refer these words to *sto* (Latin), a stand. *Stabulum* (Latin), a stall or stable.

Stale—a decoy; from *stælan* (Saxon), to steal.

Stalk—from *to steal;* originally, meant *to go stealthily*, to walk slowly, and, by a natural extension of meaning, to walk loftily.

Stand—*standan* (Gothic), *stehen* (German), *standan* (Saxon), *stare* (Latin and Italian), *staein* (Greek).

Staple—a settled mart; this, with *stay*, *stead*, *stern*, *stiff*, *stilt*, and many other words, obviously connected with *to stand* in various languages.

Star—*stairno* (Gothic), *stern* (German), *steorra* (Saxon), *steorn* (Gaelic), *astrum* (Latin), *aster* (Greek), *stareh* (Persian). This word has been derived by northern scholars from *to steer*, ships being guided by the *stars.* The *stern*, the hinder part, where the vessel is *steered. Steoran* (Saxon), to govern, to reprove; hence, *stern*, reproving, severe.

Stare—to look fixedly; from *to stand.*

Stark—stiff, strong; *sterkr* (Icelandic), *stark* (German), *stearc* (Saxon); hence, *starch*, that which *stiffens.*

Start—to move suddenly; *styran* (Saxon), to move, *to stir; stören* (German), to trouble; hence, *storm* and *stream.*

Starve—to perish with hunger or cold; *steorfan* (Saxon), and *sterben*, (German), to die.

Steak—a slice of flesh broiled; derived by some from *to stick;* a piece roasted on a point; by others from *stycke* (Swedish), *stück* (German), a part or piece.

Steal—to take by theft; *stela* (Icelandic), *stehlen* (German), *stelan* (Saxon); connected with *still;* to take in a *still* or quiet way.

Steam—vapour; *stoom* (Dutch), *dampf* (German), *stem* (Saxon).

Steep—an ascent; *stepan* (Saxon), to raise; hence, *step* and *steeple.*

Step-child—literally, one deprived of its father or mother; *stepan* (Saxon), to bereave. A *step-mother*, a mother to a child bereaved. By others, it is made to be one in the *stead* or place of another; and Johnson refers it simply to *step*, one *stepping* into the place of another.

Steward—an overseer; from *stow* (Saxon), a place or mansion, and *weard* (Saxon), a warder or guard.

Stint—to limit; *stunta* (Icelandic), *stent* (Scotch), a limited or appointed task; *stound* (old English), a small space of time; hence, also, *stunted.*

Stirrup—from *stigan* (Saxon), to ascend, and *rap* (Saxon), a cord; literally, *a cord to ascend by.*

Stithy—a smith's anvil; from *stith* (Saxon), strong.

Stone—*stain* (Gothic), *sten* (Swedish), *stein* (German), *stan* (Saxon).

Storm—a tempest (Gothic, Swedish, and Saxon), *sturm* (German), *stoirm* (Irish); *styran* (Saxon), *stören* (German), to stir, move.

Stout—strong; sometimes derived from *stautan* (Gothic), to strike; hence, *stot*, a young bull.

Straight—not crooked; from *streccan* (Saxon), *strecken* (German), to stretch; thus denoting what is *stretched out. Strait*, narrow; from *estroit* (old French).

Strand—the margin of the sea; *rand* (German), border, extremity; hence, the *Strand* in London, which lies along the Thames.

Stray—scattered; connected with *straw;* hence, also, *stroll*, and *straggle*, and *strawberry*, as this plant is *strewed* here and there at distances.

Streak—a line of colour different from that of the ground; *strica* (Saxon), *strich* (German), a stroke or line; from *streichen* (German), to draw; connected with these *stroke* and *strike.*

Stream—a running water; *straumr* (Icelandic), *strom* (German), *ystrym* (Welsh).

Street—*stræt* (Saxon), *strasse* (German), *strada* (Italian and Spanish), *stratum* (Latin); connected by some with *tretten* (German), to *tread.*

Strong—*straung* (Icelandic), severe; *strang* (Saxon), *strenge* (German); connected by some with *stringo* (Latin), to grasp hard; hence, *strangle*, and *strain. String*, a rope, connected with these.

Strife—contention, contest; *strith* (Saxon), *streit* (German).

Strip—to deprive of covering; *streifen* (German), to take off the bark; hence, perhaps, *stripe*, as a variety of colour is produced by peeling the bark, and *stripe*, a blow, from the variety of colour produced; hence, also, a *strip*, a narrow shred, and *strap*, a narrow slip of leather.

Strut—to walk in a stately way; *strotzen* (German).

Stubborn—according to some *stout-born;* obstinate by nature; connected by others with *stub*, a trunk.

Stuff—any matter or body; *stoffe* (Teutonic and Dutch), matter; *estoffe* (old French). *To stuff*, to fill with matter.

Stump—a trunk; *stompen* (Danish), to lop. *To stump*, to walk about heavily.

Stun—to confound; *stunian* (Saxon), *staunen* (German), to be astonished; derived by Serenius from *duna* (Icelandic), to thunder. In the same way, *attono* (Latin), to astonish, from *tono* (Latin), to thunder.

Sturdy—hardy, obstinate; *stuer* (Teutonic), *stern. Stor* (Saxon), great, vast; hence, *store*, a large number, an accumulation.

Sultry—hot; connected with *sweltan* (Saxon), to die; *swaelta* (Gothic), to perish by hunger; *suilizon* (old German), to perish by heat; hence, *swelter*, to be pained with heat.

Summer—the warm season; *sumar* (Gothic), *sumer* (Saxon), *sommer* (German), related to *sun.*

Sun—*sunno* (Gothic), *sunne* (Saxon), *sonne* (German); derived by Wachter from *sana* (Arabic), to shine.

Sunder—to separate; *sundria* (Gothic), *syndrian* (Saxon), *sondrian* (German). *Sondern* (German), but. Cinder, *sinder* (Saxon), what flies off from iron when beaten on an anvil. *Sundry*, several.

Sure—certain; *sicher* (German), *sicker* (Scotch), *sur* (French), *securus* (Latin).

Surly—ill-natured; from *sour.*

Swaddle—to clothe; connected with *swad*, an old English word signifying a pea-cod; both from *swethan* (Saxon), to clothe.

Swagger—to bluster; from *swegan* (Saxon), to sound, to make a noise.

Swain—a young man, a pastoral youth; *swan* (Saxon), a herdsman.

Swallow—to devour; *schwelgen* (German), to carouse, to *swill; schwalg* (German), the throat. The bird *swallow* might seem connected with this word, but Serenius derives it from *swale* (Gothic), a roof, as swallows build in the roofs of houses.

Sward—*sweard* (Saxon); *schwarte* (German), the skin of bacon, the surface of the ground.

Swarm—a multitude; *swearm* (Saxon), *schwarm* (German).

Sway—to wield, to poise; *swiga* (Gothic), to bend; *schweben* (German), to move. *To swing*, is connected with the first. A *switch—swaig* (Gothic), a bending rod.

Swear—to call a higher power to witness for the truth; *swerian* (Saxon), *schwören* (German). Many derivations are given of this word; some connect it with *wahr* (German), true.

Sweat—*swat* (Saxon), *schweiss* (German), sweat, blood; connected with *wet.*

Sweepstakes—*stakes*, or forfeits, are so called when they are all *swept* or carried off by one.

Sweet—*swet* (Saxon), *süss* (German), *soave* (Italian), *swad* (Sanscrit).

Swell—to grow bigger; *swellan* (Saxon), *schwellen* (German).

Swerve—to deviate, to wander; *swerven* (Belgic), to wander; perhaps from *swoerfwa* (Gothic), to whirl.

Sweep—to carry off rapidly; *swapan* (Saxon), *schweifen* (German); hence, also, *swift.*

Swim—*swimman* (Saxon), *schwimmen* (German); hence, *to swoon.*

Tack—to fasten; *attacher* (French), to attach, to arrest; from *toucher* (French), *tango* (Latin), to touch; connected with *to take.*

Tackle—the ropes of a ship; some have it from *tacel* (Welsh), an arrow; *tacclan* (Welsh), the ornaments of a ship. It might be simply referred to be the *tackings* of a ship, what is *attached* to it. Some connect *to tack*, to turn a ship, with the *tackle* of the vessel.

Tadpole—a young frog; from *tad* (Saxon), a frog, and *pole*, the head.

Tailor—one who cuts out and shapes; *tailler* (French), to cut; hence, *tallage*, a tax, a *share* of a man's substance; hence, also, *tally*, a stick *cut* so as to correspond with another stick, used in keeping accounts; hence, *to tally*, to agree; *to detail*, *detailler* (French), to relate minutely; *to retail*, to sell in small lots.

Take—*taka* (Icelandic), to take; *tango* (Latin), *I touch;* connected with these *tongs*, what touches or takes.

Tale—from to tell; *zählen* (German), *tellan* (Saxon), to relate, to number. In this last sense, *tell* (English), is frequently used; hence, *toll*, according to some. *Talk* is connected with *to tell.*

Tan—to embrown by the sun; *tan* (Celtic), fire. *Tendan* (Saxon), to kindle; hence, *tinder.*

Tap—to strike gently with the tip or top; *taper*, what comes to a top; *tippet*, what is worn high on the *tip* of the shoulders; *typpi* (Icelandic), the top.

Tar—probably connected with *tear;* a *tarpauling*, from *tar*, and *pall*, a cover.

Tariff—*tarif* (Arabic), a detail, a tax.

Tart—sour; *teart* (Saxon), sharp, severe.

Tatter—*to-teran*, to tear to pieces.

Taunt—to reproach; from *teon* (Saxon), to accuse. The same word in many of the northern languages, as well as in Saxon, signifies *to draw, to tug, to tow;* hence, *tau* (German), and *tow* (Scotch), a rope, and the English *tow.*

Teach—to instruct; *tögen* (Teutonic), *zeigen* (German), *tæcan* (Saxon), to show, direct; derived from *ataugian* (Gothic), which is made up of *at*, to, and *augo* (Gothic), the eye.

Tear—*tagr* (Gothic), *thräne* (German), *tear* (Saxon), *dear* (Irish), *dakrus* (Greek).

Tear—to rend; *tairan* (Gothic), *teran* (Saxon), *zehren* (German), *tara* (Swedish), to consume.

Tease—to unravel wool; from *tæsan* (Saxon), to pluck, to gather.

Ten—derived by Tooke from *tina* (Saxon), to inclose as numeration closes with ten; by others, from *tyna* (Icelandic), to number, in allusion to the natural mode of counting on the fingers. On the same principle, the German *zehen*, and Latin *decem*, have been traced to *taihend*, both hands, or the ten fingers; from *ten* comes *tithe*, the tenth part assigned to the church.

Termagant—tumultuous; used also as a noun to signify a turbulent woman; from *tir*, an Anglo-Saxon prefix denoting eminence, and *maga* (Saxon), powerful.

Tester—a sixpence; from *teste* (French), a head, on account of a head being impressed on it; *testy*, headstrong, fretful, is by some traced to *teste*.

Thane—a nobleman, literally a servant of the king; from *thenian* (Saxon), to serve; *thiena* (Icelandic), *dienen* (German), to serve; *ich dien*, I serve, motto of the Prince of Wales, formerly of the King of Bohemia, who fought and fell at the battle of Cressy, where Edward the Black Prince distinguished himself.

Thief—*theof* (Saxon), *dieb* (German).

Thin—not thick; *thyn* (Saxon), *dünn* (German), *tenuis* (Latin); *dehnen* (German), *tendo* (Latin), *teino* (Greek), to extend.

Thing—whatever is; *ding* (German), signifying, in the northern languages, discourse, judgment, controversy, council; *stor-thing*, the Norwegian parliament; it has the same meaning in old Scotch; derived from *thun* (Gothic), to make. *Thing*, a council, is connected by some with *tinga* (Gothic), to speak, as *parliament* is with *parler* (French), to speak; from *tinga*, to speak, some derive *tongue; zunge* (German).

Think—to have ideas; *thankan* (Gothic), *thencan* (Saxon), *denken* (German).

Thrash—to beat corn, to drub; *threskia* (Icelandic), *dreschen* (German), *therscan* (Saxon); connected by some with *to tread*, in allusion to the oldest mode of thrashing.

Thread—literally, what is *thrown* or twisted; *thrawan* (Saxon), signifies not merely to throw, but to twist. In this last sense, it is retained in the Scotch word *thraw; draht* (German), thread, from *drehen*, to twist.

Thrive—to prosper; supposed to be from *throa* (Icelandic), to increase.

Throat—*drossel* (German), *throte* (Saxon), *strozza* (Italian), *strupe* (Swedish).

Throe—agony; *throwran* (Saxon), *trauren* (German), to be driven, to suffer pain.

Throng—a crowd; from *thringan* (Saxon), *dringen* (German), to press.

Thumb—*daumen* (German), *thuma* (Saxon); *tum* (Swedish), an inch.

Thunder—*dynr* (Icelandic), *donner* (German), *duner* (Saxon); connected with *din*.

Tide—time, season, the alternate ebb and flow of the sea; *tid* (Danish and Swedish), *zeit* (German), time; *tidy*, orderly, from tide; but *tidy*, meaning trig, has been derived from *tidig* (Gothic), beautiful.

Tie—to bind; *tigan* (Saxon); hence, *tight*.

Timber—wood for building; *zimmern* (German), *timbrian* (Saxon), to build.

Time—measure of duration; *timi* (Icelandic), *tim* (Gaelic), *tempus* (Latin), *temps* (French), *tempo* (Italian).

Ting, tingle, and tinkle—words imitative of a particular sound; hence, a *tinker*, from the noise which he makes when working.

Tire—to grow weary; *teorian* (Saxon), *zehren* (German), to waste; *türa* (Swedish), to consume; hence, *tare*, a weed in corn.

Toil—from *tilian* (Saxon), to labour, *to till*; a *tool*, an instrument of labour.

Tooth—*tunthus* (Gothic), *zahn* (German), *toth* (Saxon), *dens* (Latin), *dent* (French).

Toss—to throw with the hand; *tasse* (Suevo-Gothic), the hand.

Tough—flexible, not easily injured; *teon* (Saxon), to pull, *to tow*; *zahe* (German), from *ziehen*, to pull.

Town—literally, a place fenced in, a fortified place; from *tynan* (Saxon), to inclose; *tuun* (Teutonic), *tuin* (Dutch), a hedge, a garden; *zaun* (German), a hedge. A *tun*, an inclosure for fluids.

Toy—a plaything, literally something dressed or adorned; from *tooijen* (Belgic), to adorn.

Trace—mark left by any thing passing; *treccia* (Italian); connected with *trechein* (Greek), to run, or *trahere* (Latin), to draw; *trekken* (Belgic), *tragen* (German), to draw; hence, *train*, to draw, to educate, &c.

Trail—to draw along the ground; *trailler* (French); perhaps from *trahere* (Latin), *treylen* (Belgic), to draw; *trachle* (Scotch), to trail, to overwork.

Trample—to tread under foot; *trampa* (Gothic), *trampen* (Belgic).

Trap—to ensnare, *to trepan*; *treppan* (Saxon), *etrappen* (German), *attrapper* (French), to catch.

Trash—refuse; supposed to be from *to trash*, to cut, and signifying originally the loppings of trees.

Treachery—breach of faith; derived from *tricher* (French), *triegen* (German), to deceive; hence, also, *trick*. *Treachery* is also traced to *trado* (Latin), to betray.

Trench—to cut; *trancher* (French), a *trench*, a cut.

Trice—in a trice; from *thrice*; before one can count *three*.

Trickle—to fall in drops; connected with *tregill* (Icelandic), a channel, tears forming a channel in the cheek; connected also with *trilla* (Swedish), to roll.

Trim—to put in order; *trymian* (Saxon); it signifies also to suit one's self to opposite parties.

Troll—from *trallen* (Dutch), to roll.

Trot—a frequentative of *to tread*; hence, also, *trudge*.

Trouble—from *tribulan* (Saxon), *tribulieren* (German), to bruise, to vex; connected with *tribula* (Latin), a flail; *turbo* (Latin), to disturb.

Trout—*truht* (Saxon), *truite* (French), *truta* (Latin).

Truck—to exchange, to traffic; *troquer* (French). This word has been connected with *trochaō* (Greek), to wheel, signifying to bandy about; from the same Greek root, a *truckle*, or *truckle*-bed, one that runs on wheels; and *to truckle*, to go under, to be subservient to, has been derived from *truckle*, as this kind of bed, it is said, is under another bed.

Trump—a winning card; connected by some with *triumph;* but *trumph* (Swedish) has the same meaning, and is connected with *trumpha*, to play at cards, to deceive; hence, *tromper* (French), *trompen* (Teutonic), *trump* (English), to deceive.

Trundle—to roll; *trendel* (Saxon), a sphere. The river *Trent*, from its circuitous course, has been connected with this word.

Truth—from *treowian* (Saxon), *trauan* (Gothic), to confide; *trauen* (German), to marry, to confide; hence, *trust* and *tryst* (Scotch), an appointed place of meeting, a place where parties *trust* to meet; hence, also, *truce*, a *reliance* on a temporary suspension of hostilities.

Try—*trier* (French), has been connected with *tur* (Hebrew), to stretch, to show the power. The word *truth* may be connected with *try*.

Tuck—to gather up; *tucken* (German), to press.

Tumble—*tummeln* (German), *tumbian* (Saxon), *tomber* (French), to fall.

Turf—*torf* (Swedish and German), *tourbe* (French); from *torfa* (Gothic); to dig.

Tweak—to pinch; *twiccian* (Saxon), *zwicken* (German), to pinch with pincers.

Twelve—from *twalif* (Mœso-Gothic), compounded of *twa*, two, and *laib*, the residue or *lave* (Scotch), denoting the two fingers more than the *ten*.

Twenty—from *twain* and *tig* (Gothic), ten, two tens.

Twilight—from *tweo* (Saxon), doubt, which is connected with *two*, and light.

Twin—from *two;* hence, also, *to twine*, *to twist*, *to twin* (Scotch), to separate.

Twinkle—to sparkle; *twinclean* (Saxon), *blinken* (German), to shine.

Twit—to sneer, to reproach; *idweit* (Gothic), reproach; *wite* (Saxon); affliction, torture, a fine.

Ugly—horrible; from *oga* (Saxon and Icelandic), to fear.

Umber—dark; from *Umbria*, in Italy, whence the earth which produced a dark coloring matter was brought.

Us—*uns* (Gothic and German).

Usher—to introduce; *huis* (French), a door.

Vampire—*vampur* (German), a blood-sucker.

Van—the front of an army; *avant* (French), before; hence, *to vaunt*, to set one's self before others; *vanter* (French), to boast.

Veal—from *veau* (French), a calf; *vitellus* (Latin); hence, *vellum*, the skin of a calf dressed for writing on.

Veer—to turn about; *wirren* (German), *huera* (Gothic), to whirl.

Wag—a cheat, an impostor; *wægan* (Saxon), to deceive.

Wallet—a bag; from *weallian* (Saxon), to travel, a traveller's bag.

Wallop—to boil; from *weallan* (Saxon), to spring up; hence, *well*.

Walnut—from *walh* (Saxon), a stranger, and *nut*, signifying a foreign nut.

Wan—pale; from *wann* (Saxon), deficient, a want of colour; connected with this, *wana* (Saxon), deficiency, want; *wahn* (German), empty; and *wanian* (Saxon). This last, with *weinen* (German), and *whine* (English), may be connected.

Wanton—unrestrained, free; from *want* and *teon* (Saxon), to draw, to train, one untrained.

Wassail—a liquor, revelry; from *wæs hal* (Saxon), be whole, your health.

Weal—happiness, prosperity; *wohl* (German), *wela* (Saxon), signifying also *well.*

Weather—the temperature of the air; *weder* (Saxon), *wetter* (German), *Athar* (Gaelic), *aither* (Greek), the air.

Ween—to think, to imagine; *wenan* (Saxon), *wahnen* (German), to mean, imagine.

Weep—to lament; *wepan* (Saxon); from *wop* (Saxon), a cry or bewailing; hence, *whoop.*

Weird—skilled in witchcraft; from *wyrd* (Saxon), fate, which is derived from *word;* literally, what is spoken or decreed by God. In the same way, *fatum* (Latin), from *fari,* to speak.

Welcome—from *well* and *come.*

Wend—to go, to turn; *wendan* (Saxon), *wenden* (German), to change. *Went,* the past tense of go, is the real past of *to wend.*

Whale—*hwæl* (Saxon), *wallfisch* (German), *wald* (Saxon), *gewalt* (German), power. *To wield,* connected with these.

Wharf—a harbour or quay; *hwoorf* (Saxon), *hwarf* (Swedish), *huerfa* (Gothic), to throw out; in the same way *jettee* (French), from *jetter* (French), *jacto* (Latin), to throw.

Whelm—to cover by throwing something over another; *hilma* (Icelandic), to cover.

Whet—to sharpen; *hwettan* (Saxon), *wetzen* (German), *hwæt* (Saxon), sharp; hence, *whittle* (old English), a knife.

Whisk—to move quickly, to brush; *wischen* (German), to wipe; hence, also, *whisker.*

Whist—a game at cards, so called from *hist* or *whist;* interjections demanding silence, as silence and attention are necessary in this game.

Wife, a woman that has a husband; in Saxon and Scotch, also a woman; *wif* (Saxon), *weib* (German). This word has been traced to *weave,* weaving being at one time the occupation of females; in the same way, a *spinster,* a young woman, literally one who *spins.*

Wight—a person, a being; *wiht* (Saxon); as an adjective, it signifies powerful, and is derived from *wigan* (Saxon), to fight.

Wile—craft; *wile* (Saxon), *villa* (Icelandic), error.

Will—*wille* (German), *wella* (Saxon), *wilgo* (Swedish), *dill* (Gaelic), *wolia* (Slavonic), *volo* (Latin), *vouloir* (French), *boulomai* (Greek), to will.

Wind—a movement of the air; *wind* (German, Saxon, Dutch, and Swedish), *waien* (Gothic), *wehen* (German), to blow; *ventus* (Latin), the wind; *to winnow,* to separate by means of the *wind.*

Winsome—pleasant, merry; from *wyn* (Saxon), *wonne* (German), pleasure.

Wiseacre—one wise in his own conceit; *weissager* (German), a wise sayer.

Wish—to desire; *wiscan* (Saxon), *wünschen* (German); perhaps from *wonne* (German), pleasure.

Wit—mind, understanding; *witan* (Saxon), *wissen* (German), *to wot,* to know. A *witness,* one who makes known; *witan* (Saxon), signifies also to blame; hence, *wite* (old English and Scotch), blame.

Witch—from *wiccian* (Saxon), to use incantation; *wice* (Saxon), the mountain ash or rowan-tree, so named from its magical use.

Withe—a tie; *withan* (Gothic), to join; *weide* (German), *withig* (Saxon), a willow-tree. *Withers,* the joining of the shoulder-bones at the bottom of the neck and mane.

Woman—*wifman* (Saxon); literally, a *wife-man.*
Won—to dwell, to live (old English and Scotch), *wohnen* (German), *wunian* (Saxon); hence, *wont*, to remain, to continue, to be accustomed.
Wonder—admiration; *wunder* (German), *wundor* (Saxon); perhaps connected with *wander*.
Wool—the fleece of sheep; *wolle* (German), *wull* (Saxon), *ull* (Swedish and Icelandic).
Word—a single part of speech; *waurd* (Gothic), *wort* (German), *ord* (Swedish and Icelandic), *wartha* (Sanscrit).
Work—labour; *werk* (German), *weore* (Saxon); in some of the northern dialects, it signifies pain. A *wright*, one who works.
World—the earth; *woruld* (Saxon), *wereld* (Dutch), *welt* (German), has been traced to *wer* (Icelandic), a man, and old, signifying natural age.
Worm—*waurm* (Gothic), *wyrm* (Saxon), *wurm* (German), *vermis* (Latin).
Worry—to tear; *wurgen* (old Saxon), to suffocate; *worg* (German), an obstruction in the throat.
Worse—*wairs* (Gothic), *verri* (Icelandic), *wyrse* (Saxon); perhaps connected with *wear*. In the same way, *deterior* (Latin), worse, from *tero*, to rub, to wear.
Worship—honour, a title of honour; literally, worth, and *ship*, a termination denoting dignity.
Worsted—woollen yarn; from *Worsted*, a town in Norfolk famous for the woollen manufacture.
Wort—an herb, a plant; *wyrt* (Saxon), *wurze* (German), spices.
Worth—price, value; *weorth* (Saxon), *würde* (German), dignity; *weorthan* (Saxon), *werden* (German), *wairthan* (Gothic), to be, to become.
Wrangle—to contend perversely; connected perhaps with wrong; *wræng* (Swedish), perverse.
Wrath—anger; *reidi* (Icelandic), *ira* (Latin), *eris* (Greek), anger; see *rate*.
Wreak—to avenge; *rächen* (German), *wrikan* (Gothic), *wrecan* (Saxon); hence, according to some, *wretch*; but *wræc* (Saxon), exiled, wretched, seems connected with *wracian* (Saxon), to reject; hence, *wreck*.
Wreathe—to twist; *writhan* (Saxon), to twist; hence, *writhe*.
Wrench—to wrest; from *wringan* (Saxon), *ringen* (German), to *wring*; hence, *wrong*, what is out of the right path, what is crooked.
Wrest—to twist, to take by force; *wræstan* (Saxon); from *wræst* (Saxon), powerful. *Wrist* and *wrestle* connected with these.
Wriggle—to move with short twists; *wrigan* (Saxon), to move; hence, *wry*.
Yard—what is *guarded* or *girded*.
Yclept—*beclyped*, from *clypian* (Saxon), to call, and *be* changed into *y*, the common adjunct of the imperfects.
Year—*jer* (Gothic), *jahr* (German), *gear* (Saxon); hence, *yore*, a long time.
Yest—foam; *yst* (Saxon), a tempest.
Yesterday—*gyrstan dæg*, *gestern* (German), *yestreen* (Scotch).
Yield—from *gildan* (Saxon), to pay.
Yoke—a bond; *geoc* (Saxon), *joch* (German), *jugum* (Latin).
Young—not old; *geong* (Saxon), *jung* (German), *ung* (Swedish).

PART IV.

DERIVATION FROM THE LATIN THROUGH THE FRENCH.

As most of the English words of Latin origin are derived through the French, it is both interesting and important to trace the changes which the Latin words underwent in their transition to French. Without some attention to this subject, it will be difficult to appreciate the connection between many English words and the Latin roots to which they are referred.

Almost all Latin words, in passing into the French, were modified by *apocope*, or the loss of their final syllable; many by *syn cope*, or the loss of their middle syllable; and the *commutation*, *addition*, and *transposition* of letters, occasioned various other differences in the derivative words.

I.

In the following list, the consonants, *c*, *g*, *d*, or *t*, when preceded and followed by a vowel, are dropped; and, as usual, the final syllable is rejected.

Latin.		French.	English.
Publi*c*are,	(publiare,)	publier,	to publish.
Pre*c*ari,	(preari,)	prier,	to pray.
Dupli*c*are,	(dupliare,)	doubler,	to double.
Dene*g*are,	(deneare,)	denier,	to deny.
Alli*g*are,	(alliare,)	allier,	to ally.
Pli*c*are,	(pliare,)	plier,	to ply.
Fri*g*ere,	(friere,)	frire,	to fry.
Desi*d*erare,	(desierare,)	desirer,	to desire.
Invi*d*ere,	(inviere,)	envier,	to envy.
Do*t*are,	(doare,)	douer,	to endow.
Mari*t*are,	(mariare,)	marier,	to marry.
Peri*c*ulum,	(periulum,)	peril,	peril.
Foeni*c*ulum,	(foeniulum,)	fenouil	fennel.
Cuni*c*ulum,	(cuniulum,)	connil,	a cony.
O*c*ulus,	(oulus,)	œil,	an eye.
Se*c*urus,	(seurus,)	sur,	sure.
Te*g*ula,	(teula,)	tuile,	a tile.
Re*g*ula,	(reula,)	——	a rule.
Re*g*ina,	(reina,)	reine,	——
Sa*g*ena,	(saena,)	seine,	a seine.
Fra*g*ilis,	(frailis,)	frêle,	frail.
Inte*g*er,	(inteer,)	entière,	entire.
Cru*d*elis,	(cruelis,)	cruel,	cruel.
Vo*c*alis,	(voalis,)	voyelle,	a vowel

Latin.		French.	English.
Le*g*alis,	(lealis,)	loyal,	loyal.
Re*g*alis,	(realis,)	royal,	royal.
Ro*t*ula,	(roula,)	rouelle,	rowel, roll.
Ro*t*undus,	(roundus,)	rond,	round.
Arma*t*ura,	(armaura,)	armure,	armor.
Ra*d*ius,	(raius,)	rayon,	a ray.
Me*d*ius,	(meius,)	moyen,	a mean.

*** This *syncope* is observable, also, in the modern proper names of towns, rivers, places, and persons; as in TRENT, from *Tridentum*, by apocope of *um*, (*Trident*) and syncope of *d* (*Trient*); YORK, from *Eboracum*, (E-*b*-orac, *Eorac*;) RHONE, from *Rhodanus*, (Rho-*d*-an, *Rhoan*;) the LOIRE, from (Li-*g*-er) *Ligeris*; the MARRO, from *Me-t-aurus*; AUSTIN, from (A-*g*-ustin) *Augustinus*; BENNET, from (Bene-*d*-it, Bene-*d*-ict) *Benedictinus*, &c.

II.

CHANGE OF VOWELS AND DIPHTHONGS.

A is changed into E and A I.*

Latin.	French.	English.
Arm*a*re,	arm*e*r,	to arm.
Ador*a*re,	ador*e*r,	to adore.
Cit*a*re,	cit*e*r,	to cite.
Err*a*re,	err*e*r,	to err.
Sign*a*re,	sign*e*r,	to sign.
S*a*l,	s*e*l,	salt.
N*a*sus,	n*e*z,	the nose.
Gr*a*num,	gr*ai*n,	grain.
Rom*a*nus,	Rom*ai*n,	Roman.
Hum*a*nus,	hum*ai*n,	human.

E is changed into A, I, and OI.

*E*mendare,	*a*mender,	to amend.
Retinēre,	reten*i*r,	to retain.
Pallēre,	pal*i*r,	to be pale.
Prevalēre,	preval*oi*r,	to prevail.
Condolēre,	condoul*oi*r,	to condole.
M*e*,	m*oi*,	me.
T*e*,	t*oi*,	thee.

I is changed into E, AI, and EI.

*I*ntrare.	*e*ntrer,	to enter.
*I*nvidēre,	*e*nvier,	to envy.
N*i*ger,	n*e*gre,	negro.
Car*i*na, *s*.	car*e*ner, *v*.	to careen.

* The interchange of vowels is so frequent, and so obvious, that it is almost unnecessary to adduce examples. Thus, in our own language, we have B*a*nd, B*i*nd, B*o*nd, B*u*ndle, B*ou*nd; S*i*ng, S*a*ng, S*u*ng, S*o*ng; L*o*ng, L*e*ngth; Br*oa*d, Br*ea*dth, &c.

Latin.	French.	English.
D*i*gnari,	d*a*igner,	to deign.
*I*ns*i*gne,	*e*ns*ei*gne,	an ensign
Cons*i*lium,	con*s*eil,	counsel.
Dom*i*nium,	dom*a*in,	domain.

O changed into OU, EU, and OI.

Pr*o*bare,	pr*ou*ver,	to prove.
Dem*o*rari,	dem*eu*rer,	to demur.
Amor,	am*ou*r,	amor.
H*o*ra,	h*eu*re,	an hour.
S*o*lus,	s*eu*l,	sole.
F*o*lium,	f*oi*l,	foil (leaf.)

U changed into O, OI, and OU.

Ann*u*nciare,	ann*o*ncer,	to announce
Ab*u*ndare,	ab*o*nder,	to abound.
F*u*ndare,	f*o*nder,	to found.
*U*ngere,	*oi*ndre,*	to anoint.
*U*ncia,	*o*nce,	an ounce.
M*u*sca,	m*ou*sse,	moss.
Cr*u*x,	cr*oi*x,	cross.

COMMUTATION OF CONSONANTS.

Interchange of B, P, F, and V.

Deli*b*erare,	deli*v*rer,	to deliver.
Gu*b*ernare,	gou*v*erner,	to govern.
Pro*b*are,	prou*v*er,	to prove.
Du*p*licare,	dou*b*ler,	to double.
Se*p*arare,	se*v*rer,	to sever.
Recu*p*erare,	recou*v*rer,	to recover.
Reci*p*ere,	rece*v*oir,	to receive.
Coö*p*erire,	cou*v*rir,	to COVER.
Canna*b*is,	cane*v*as,	canvass.
Fe*b*ris,	fiè*v*re,	fever.
Li*b*ra,	li*v*re,	livre.
Ver*b*ena,	ver*v*eine,	vervain.
Dia*b*olus,	dia*b*le,	de*v*il.
*F*i*b*er,	*b*ie*v*re,	a beaver.
Ne*p*os,	ne*v*eu,	a nephew.
A*p*rilis,	A*v*ril,	April.
Sa*p*or,	sa*v*eur,	savour.
Pau*p*ertas,	pau*v*reté,	poverty.
Pau*p*er,	pau*v*re,	poor.
*V*ara,	*b*arre,	a bar.
Vannus,	*v*an,	*f*an.
Bre*v*is,	bre*f*,	brief.

* *Oindre.* See below, for the change of *g* into *d*.

Interchange of B, V, and G *soft*.

Latin.	French	English.
Ra*b*ies,	ra*g*e,	rage.
Ti*b*ia,	ti*g*e,	——
Lum*b*us,	lon*g*e,	the loin.
Ru*b*eus,	rou*g*e,	rouge.
Abbre*v*iare,	abre*g*er,	to ABRIDGE.*
Suble*v*are,	soula*g*er,	——
Dilu*v*ium,	delu*g*e,	deluge.
Ca*v*ea,	ca*g*e,	a cage.
Reple*g*ium,	reple*v*in,	replevin.
Ser*v*iente,†	ser*g*ent,	a sergeant.
Ni*v*e,	nie*g*e,	——
Sal*v*ia,	sau*g*e,	sage.
*V*espa, (*guespe*,)	*g*uêpe,	a wasp.
*V*astare, (*gaster*,)	*g*âter,	to waste
In *g*yro,	en*v*iron,	environs

Interchange of C *hard*, G *hard*, Q and K.

Lo*c*are,	lo*g*er,	to LODGE.
A*c*er,	ai*g*re,	eager.
Ala*c*er,	alle*g*ro,	allegro.
Ma*c*er,	mai*g*re,	meagre.
*C*rassus,	*g*ros,	gross.
*C*rypta.	*g*rotte,	a grot.
Fi*c*us,	fi*g*ue,	a fig.
Su*g*ere,	su*c*er,	to suck.
*Q*uadrare,	*c*adrer,	to square.
A*q*uila,	ai*g*le,	an eagle.

C changed into CH,‡

Cantare,	*ch*anter,	to chant.
Carmen,	*ch*arme,	a charm.
Castus,	*ch*aste,	chaste,
Camera,	*ch*ambre,	chamber.
Carrus,	*ch*ar,	car, chariot

Interchange of C *soft*, S, and T.

Pla*c*ens,	plai*s*ant,	pleasing.
Ra*c*emus,	rai*s*in,	a raisin.
Ra*t*ione,	rai*s*on,	reason.
Po*t*ione,	poi*s*on,	poison.

* *Abridge.* In this, and in several other words borrowed from the French, *d* has been inserted before *g* to strengthen the sound; as in to *lodge*, from *loger*; *judge*, from *juger*; *budge*, from *bouger*; *budget*, from *bougette*; and *pledge*, from *pleige*. Hence the disposition to pronounce, and sometimes to write, the words *allege* and *oblige*, alledge, oblidge.

† *Serviente*, ablative of serviens. (See Observation III.)

‡ Hence we derive CHEST from *cista*; CHEESE from *caseus*: and from our own word *care*, CHARY and CHARILY, i. e., *careful* and *carefully*.

Latin.	French.	English.
Fac*t*ione,	façon,	fashion.
Lec*t*ione,	leçon,	lesson.
Gra*t*ia,	grace,	grace.
Distan*t*ia,	distance,	distance.

Interchange of D and G.

Latin.	French.	English.
Jun*g*ere,	join*d*re,	to join.
Tin*g*ere,	tein*d*re,	to tinge.
Pin*g*ere,	pein*d*re,	to paint.
Man*d*ere,	man*g*er,	to munch.
Ro*d*ere,	ron*g*er,	——
Se*d*e,	sie*g*e,	siege.
Ju*d*ice,	ju*g*e,	judge.
Diurnalis,*	journal,	a journal
Sta*d*ium, (*estage*,)	etage,	a stage.

Interchange of L, M, N, R.

Latin.	French.	English.
Chartu*l*a,	chartre,	a chapter.
Capitu*lu*m,	chapit*r*e,	a chapter.
Titu*l*us,	tit*r*e,	a title.
U*l*mus,	*or*me,	the elm.
Tempo*r*a,	tempes,	the temp*l*es.
Turtu*r*,	tourt*r*e,	turt*l*e.
G*r*anum, *s*.	g*l*aner,	to GLEAN.
F*r*agrare,	f*l*airer,	——
Pere*g*rinus,	pé*l*erin,	pilgrim.
*M*atta,	*n*atte,	a mat.
*M*appa,	*n*appe,	napkin.
Pu*m*ice,	po*n*ce,	pumice-stone.
Pampi*n*us,	pamp*r*e,	pamper ?
Diaco*n*us,	diac*r*e,	a deacon.
Tympa*n*um,	timb*r*e,	timbre*l*.
Cophi*n*us,	cof*f*re,	a coffer and coffin.

The frequent substitution of the vowel U for the consonant L deserves particular notice.

Latin.	French.	English.
So*l*idare,	so*u*der,	to SODER or solder.
Sa*l*vare,	sa*u*ver,	to save.
Abso*l*vere,	absoudre,	to absolve.
Ba*l*samum,	ba*û*me,	balm.
A*l*tare,	a*u*tel,	an altar.
Falsus,	fa*ux*,†	false.

---

* *Diurnalis*, L., giornăll, It., *j*ournal, F.

† Hence the formation of the plural number of French nouns ending in *al* or *ail;* which, with a few exceptions, pass into *aux*. Hence, also, such changes as Nouve*lle*, Nouve*au*, Be*l*, Bea*u*, &c.; and, in our language, Emb*ell*ish and *Beau*tify. In several English words, as in *Walk*, *Talk*, *Chalk*, *Balk*, this letter, though it is still retained, is pronounced exactly like *u*. See the word PIANO, in which *i* has taken the place of *l*.

Latin.	French.	English.
A*l*tus,	ha*u*t,	high.
U*l*tra,	outre,	OUT.
Penici*ll*us,	pincea*u*,	a pencil.
A*l*ter,	a*u*tre,	OTHER.
	T changed into D.	
Arcua*t*um,	arca*d*e,	arcade.
Para*t*um,	para*d*e,	parade.
Grana*t*um,	grena*d*e,	grenade.
Ca*t*ena,	ca*d*enas,	——
Renegatus,	renéga*t*,	renega*d*e.
Charta,	car*t*e,	car*d*.
Sali*t*um,	sala*d*e,	sala*d*e.
Arma*t*a,	arma*d*a,*	armada.
	Interchange of X, S, Z.	
No*x*a,	noi*s*e,	noise.
Co*x*a,	cui*ss*e,	cuisse.
A*x*is,	e*ssi*eu,	axis.
E*x*ire,	issue,	to issue.
Te*x*tus,	ti*ss*u,	tissue.
Nasus,	nez,	the nose.
Oryza,	ri*s*,	rice.

EXAMPLES OF LETTERS INSERTED.

	B inserted.	
Numerare,	nom*b*rer,	to number.
Cumulare,	com*b*ler,	to accumulate.
Simulare,	sem*b*ler,	to seem.
Tremulare,	trem*b*ler,	to tremble.
Camera,	*ch*ambre,	a chamber.
Humilis,	hum*b*le,	humble.
	D inserted.	
Cinere,†	cen*d*re,	a cinder.
Sicera,	ci*d*re,	cider.
Genere (*gendre*),	genre,	gen*d*er.
Pulvere,	pou*d*re,	pow*d*er.
	G inserted.	
Hispania,	Espa*g*ne,	Spain.
Britannia,	Breta*g*ne,	Britain.

* *Armada.* It is almost unnecessary to remark that this word is properly Spanish, in which language the change of *d* into *t* is very frequent; as in Pe*d*ro, from *Petro;* Pa*d*re, from *Patre;* Trini*d*a*d*a, from *Trinitate.*—But we need not go farther than our own language for examples of the change of *d* into *t;* as bereaved, bereav'd, *bereft:* weaved, weav'd, *weft;* cleaved, cleav'd, *cleft;* gived, giv'd, *gift,* &c. The change of *v* into its kindred letter *f* is also exemplified by these words.

† The ablative case.

Latin.	French.	English.
Campaneus,	campagne,	campaign.
Montanus,	montagne,	mountain.
Linea,	lignea,	a line.
Vinea,	vigne,	a vine.
Linum,	ligne,	linen.
Simia,	singe,	———
Granum,	grange,	GRANGE.
Somnium,	songe,	———
Damnum,	danger,	DANGER.
Vindemia,	vendange,	vintage.

EXAMPLES OF LETTERS PREFIXED.

E prefixed.

This letter was very frequently prefixed to French-Latin words commencing with *s*.

Latin.	French.	English.
Sperare,	esperer,	———
Spicare (*espier*),	*é*pier,*	to spire.
Specere,	*é*pier,	to SPY.
Status,	*é*tat,	estate.
Species,	espèce,	species.
Spiritus,	esprit,	sprite.
Scriptorium,	*é*critoire,	scrutoire.
Schola,	*é*cole,	school.
Studium,	*é*tude,	study.
Stola,	*é*tole,	a stole.
Stomachus,	*é*stomac,	stomach.

H prefixed.

Latin.	French.	English.
U*l*ulare,	*hur*ler,	to howl.
Audire,	ouir,	to *h*ear.
Oleum,	*h*uile,	oil.
Octo,	*h*uit,	eight.
Ostrea (*huistre*),	huitre,	an oyster.
Ostiarius,	huissier,	an usher.
Ascia,	*h*ache (hachette),	a hatchet.
Aula,	*h*alle,	a hall.

III.

It is necessary to observe, that it is from the *ablative* case that French-Latin nouns are generally formed.

EXAMPLES.

Latin.	French.	English.
Bos, *bove*,	bœu*f*,†	beef.
Calix, *calice*,	calice,	a chalice.

* *Epier.* In this, and in most of the French words which follow, the *s* has been dropped. For the elision of the middle consonant, see Observation I.

† For the commutation of *b*, *f*, and *v*, see above.

Latin.	French.	English.
Ars, *arte*,	art,	art.
Ebur, *ebore*,	*i*v*o*ire,	ivory.
Ratio, *ratione*,	raison,	reason.

IV.

Latin verbs became French generally by *apocope*, or the omission of the final letter.

EXAMPLES.

Latin.	French.	English.
Armare,*	armer,	to arm.
Errare,	errer,	to err.
Damnare,	damner,	to damn.
Taxare,	taxer,	to tax.
Admirari,	admirer,	to admire.
Assignare,	assigner,	to assign.
Prohibēre,	prohiber,	to prohibit.
Abhorrēre,	abhorrer,	to abhor.
Absorbēre,	absorber,	to absorb.
Accedĕre,	acceder,	to accede.
Assistĕre,	assister,	to assist.
Arguĕre,	arguer,	to argue.
Finire,	finir,	to finish.
Punire,	punir,	to punish.
Consentire,	consentir,	to consent.

Many French-Latin verbs are formed differently; but their irregularities may, in general, be explained by the preceding principles. Thus, from DEBERE, by dropping the final letter, and changing *b* into *v*, we have *dever*, which becomes dev*oi*r by the same analogy as *moi* from *me*, *toi* from *te*, &c. Thus, also, VALERE (valer), *valoir*. HABERE (ha*b*er, ha*v*er, aver), *avoir*, to HAVE, the asperate being restored. ASSIDERE (assi*d*er, assier), *asseoir*. VIDERE (vi*d*er, vier), *voir*. SAPERE (sa*p*er, sa*v*er), *savoir*. DECĬDERE (decider, decier, de*ch*ier), *déchoir*. SOLVERE (so*l*ver, sou*v*er), *soudre*. AUDIRE (au*d*ir, auir), *ouir*, to HEAR, the asperate being prefixed.

* In Latin verbs of the first conjugation, the *a* before *re* was changed into *e*. See above.

PART V.

ENGLISH SYNONYMES.

ABAN'DON—desert', forsake'; leave, give up, cast off, quit; renounce', resign', relinq'uish, reject', surren'der, ab'dicate, yield, cede, concede', forego'. *See* Give *up*, Leave, Cast *back*.

ABAN'DONED—rep'robate, prof'ligate, corrupt', depra'ved, viti'ated, vici'ous, wick'ed; lorn, forlorn', left, forsa'ken, desert'ed, help'less, des'titute, lost, des'perate, hope'less; out'cast, cast off. *See* Wicked, Hopeless, Loose.

ABASE'—depress', cast down, debase', disgrace', lo'wer, make low; hum'ble, humil'iate, reduce'. *See* Lower, Disgrace, Humble.

ABHOR'—hate, detest', abom'inate, lothe. *See* Disgust.

ABIDE'—stay, contin'ue, remain'; endure', last. *See* Stay, Lasting.

ABIL'ITY—capac'ity, capabil'ity, ca'pableness, clev'erness, com'petence, com'petency, ad'equacy, ad'equateness, suffici'ency, effici'ency; skill, tact, address', dexter'ity; ge'nius, tal'ent, fac'ulty, pow'er. *See* Power.

A'BLE—ca'pable, com'petent, ad'equate, suffici'ent, effici'ent, qual'ified, skil'ful, clev'er, expert', adroit', dex'trous; pow'erful, strong, vig'orous. *See* Powerful, Active, Clever, Strong, Inadequate.

ABODE'—habita'tion, dwell'ing, res'idence, dom'icil, house; *for a short time*, vis'it, so'journ, so'journing. *See* House.

ABOUND'ING—suffici'ent, co'pious, abund'ant, overflo'wing, am'ple, plent'iful, plen'teous, fer'tile; prevail'ing, prev'alent; exu'berant. *See* Fruitful, Enough, Generous, Excess, Large.

ABRIDGE'—abbre'viate, compress', epit'omize, condense', contract'; reduce', curtail', shor'ten. *See* Take.

ABRIDGE'MENT—compend'ium, com'pend, ab'stract, synop'sis, epit'omê, sum'mary, abbrevia'tion; contrac'tion, diminu'tion, reduc'tion. *See* Shorter.

ABRUPT'—sud'den, unloo'ked for, unexpect'ed, unforeseen'; rough, rude, coarse; une'ven, rug'ged; steep, crag'gy, precip'itous; unconnect'ed. *See* Bold, Sudden.

ABSTAIN'—refrain', forbear', withhold', desist', discontin'ue, hold off, cease, stop. *See* Keep, Leave.

ABSTAI'NING—ab'stinent, abste'mious, so'ber, tem'perate, mod'erate. *See* Sober.

ABU'SE—scurril'ity, invect'ive, vitupera'tion, oppro'brium, in'sult, in'solence, reproach'.

ABUSE'—revile', reproach', vil'ify, vitu'perate, insult'; scur'rilize, inveigh' against, declaim', upbraid', chide, scan'dalize; ill-use', deceive', impose' on. *See* Chide, Gibe, Beguile, Misuse, Injure, Reproach, Deceive.

ABU'SIVE—oppro'brious, scur'rilous, insult'ing, in'solent, scan'dalous, reproach'ful, vitu'perative, offens'ive, inju'rious. *See* Hurtful.

AC'CENT—em'phasis, stress.

ACCIDENT'AL—fortu'itous; cas'ual, contin'gent, incident'al, adventi'tious, adsciti'tious, append'ant, annex'ed, non-essen'tial. *See* Additional.

ACCOM'PANYING—attend'ing, go'ing with, concom'itant, connect'ed, conjoin'ed, concur'rent, collat'eral. *See* Connected.

ACCOM'PLICE—ac'cessory, abet'tor, confrère, col'league, part'ner, asso'ciate, compan'ion; ally', confed'erate, assist'ant. *See* Companion.

ACCOM'PLISH—effect', effect'uate, do, achieve', ex'ecute, perform', complete', re'alize, fulfil'. *See* Do, Perfect, Bring *about*, Compass.

ACCOM'PLISHMENT—perform'ance, ecu'tion, achieve'ment, effectua'tion, fulfil'ment, comple'tion, realiza'tion; acquisiti'on, acquire'ment, attain'ment. *See* Performance, Completion, Work.

ACCOM'PLISHMENTS—refine'ments, embel'lishments, el'egancies; endow'ments; qualifica'tions, attain'ments, acqui'rements. *See* Qualification.

ACCORD'ANT—agree'ing with, concord'ant, con'sonant, consist'ent, con'gruous, compat'ible, conform'able, agree'able, suit'able. *See* Agreeable, Suitable, Answerable to.

ACCOUNT'—descrip'tion, rela'tion, explana'tion, narra'tion, nar'rative, his'tory, sto'ry, reci'tal, detail'. *See* Chronicle, Memoir.

ACCOUNT'ABLE—respons'ible, an'swerable, ame'nable, sub'ject to, obnoxi'ous, li'able. *See* Answerable, Subject.

ACCUSE'—impeach', indict', charge; arrai'gn; impute' to, attrib'ute to. *See* Lay, Count.

AC'ID—*See* Sour.

ACQUAINT'—apprise', commu'nicate, inform'; disclose', reveal'; make famil'iar. *See* Make known, Tell.

ACQUA'INTANCE — friend, asso'ciate, compan'ion; famil'iar, in'timate. *See* Companion, Intimacy, Familiarity.

ACQUIES'CENCE—qui'et assent', resigna'tion, submissi'on; endu'rance, pa'tience; consent', assent', compli'ance; accord'ance, agree'ment. *See* Agreement, Approbation, Agree to.

ACT *between*—interpose', intercede'; me'diate, interme'diate; med'dle, intermed'dle, interfere'. *See* Interrupt.

ACT'IVE—expert', dex'trous, adroit', alert', vig'orous, stren'uous, ag'ile, nim'ble, brisk, live'ly, an'imated, spright'ly, quick, prompt, read'y; indus'trious, dil'igent, assid'uous, sed'ulous; prac'tical, op'erative. *See* Lively, Quick, Ready, Diligent, Able, Effect *producing*.

ACT'UAL—real, true, authent'ic, cer'tain, gen'uine, pos'itive; incontest'ible, unques'tionable, irref'ragable, irrefu'table, undoubt'ed, indu'bitable. *See* Doubted, *not to be*, Certain, Genuine, Positive.

ADDITI'ON—something add'ed, addit'ament; accessi'on, in'crease, aug'ment, augmenta'tion, accre'tion; append'ix, append'age, sup'plement; annexa'tion; adden'da. *See* Increase.

ADDITI'ONAL—supplement'al, supplement'ary, adventiti'ous, adsciti'ous, supernu'merary, superve'nient; add'ed, superadd'ed, append'ed, append'ant, annex'ed, affix'ed, attach'ed. *See* Accidental.

ADDUCE'—cite, quote. *See* Call.

ADORN'—*See* Beautify.

ADVANCE'MENT—progressi'on, prog'ress; prefer'ment, promo'tion; profici'ency, improve'ment; for'wardness. *See* Improvement.

AD'VERSARY—oppo'nent, antag'onist, oppo'ser, com'batant, Sa'tan, foe, en'emy.

ADVICE'—coun'sel, informa'tion, instruc'tion; no'tice, intel'ligence; delibera'tion, consulta'tion. *See* Caution, Knowledge.

AFFECT'ING—mov'ing, touch'ing, pathet'ic, ten'der; exciting the passions or affections; impress'ive; pit'iable. *See* Pitiable.

AFFEC'TION—attach'ment, fond'ness, kind'ness, devo'tion, devo'tedness; regard', love. *See* Kindness, Attachment.

AFFEC'TIONATE—lov'ing, kind, fond, warm, ten'der. *See* Warm, Kind, Loving, Hearty.

AFFRONT'—in'sult, indig'nity, out'rage; provoca'tion, irrita'tion, exaspera'tion; ill-treat'ment, abu'se. *See* Injury, Offend, Abuse.

AFFRONT'ING—insult'ing, provo'king, ir'ritating, exas'perating, ag'gravating; apt to affront'; pet'ulant, hast'y, ir'ritable. *See* Impertinent, Invidious.

AFRAID'—tim'id, tim'orous, fear'ful; pusillan'imous, das'tardly, cow'ardly. *See* Fearful, Cowardice.

AFRAID' *be*—ap'prehend, fear, dread. *See* Fear.

AGITA'TION — commo'tion, striv'ing; disturb'ance, perturba'tion, excite'ment; emo'tion, trepida'tion, tre'mor; discussi'on. *See* Fear, Stir, Trouble, Trembling.

AGREE *to*—comply', accede', consent', assent', acquiesce', approve', accord', conform'. *See* Approve.

AGREE *with*—har'monize, be consist'ent, acquiesce', coincide', concur'.

AGREE'ABLE — pleas'ant, pleas'ing, grat'ifying, delight'ful, delect'able; ac'ceptable, grate'ful, wel'come; accord'ant. *See* Accordant, Becoming, Suitable, Amiable, Grateful.

AGREE'ABLE *not*—inconsist'ent, incon'gruous, incompat'ible, unsuit'able, discord'ant, incohe'rent.

AGREE'MENT — accord'ance, concur'rence, u'nion, u'nison, har'mony; con'tract, cov'enant, conven'tion, com'pact, bar'gain, stipula'tion, truce, peace, treat'y. *See* Acquiescence, Concord, League, Bargain, Disagreement, Arrangement, Communion.

AID—*See* Assist.

AIM—pur'pose, pur'port, inten'tion, design', ob'ject, end, tend'ency, drift, scope; wish, aspira'tion, desire'. *See* Direction, Desire, End, Object, Meaning.

AIM—strive to hit a mark; direct', point, lev'el; aspire' to, pretend to; endeav′our, seek. *See* Seek, Wish *for*.

ALL—*See* Whole.

ALLAY′—calm, qui′et, tran′quillize, soothe, compose′, appease′, sof′ten, relieve′, alle′viate, mit′igate, abate′, dimin′ish, assuage′. *See* Ease, Lessen, Soft, Still.

ALLI′ANCE—connex′ion, affin′ity, league, confed′eracy, treat′y, com′pact; combina′tion. *See* League, Company.

ALLOW′—suf′fer, permit′, tol′erate; concede′, admit′, grant. *See* Grant, Give, Suffer, Support, Own.

ALLU′RE—*See* Tempt.

ALMIGHT′Y—all-pow′erful, omnip′otent. *See* All, Able, Powerful.

ALONE′—*See* One, Single.

ALONE′—sol′itary, des′olate, des′ert, forlo′rn, reti′red, remote′, sole, sin′gle, lone′ly, on′ly. *See* Lonely, Desolate, Solitary.

AL′WAYS—incess′antly, ev′er, perpet′ually, contin′ually, con′stantly; unchange′ably, immu′tably, unal′terably, irre′vocably. *See* Changeable.

AMENDS′—compensa′tion, repara′tion, restitu′tion, requit′al, atone′ment, satisfac′tion. *See* Restoring, Satisfaction, Pay.

AMENDS′ *make*—compens′ate, rec′ompense, remu′nerate, reward′; repair′, sat′isfy, requite′, atone′. *See* Expiate, Reward, Satisfy.

A′MIABLE—love′ly, sweet, gen′tle, kind, soft, oblig′ing; pleas′ing, charm′ing, fas′cinating, enchant′ing, accom′plished, attract′ive, prepossess′ing, engag′ing, agree′able, delight′ful, ad′mirable. *See* Obliging, Charm, Agreeable.

AMU′SING—divert′ing, entertain′ing, beguil′ing, in′teresting, sport′ive, rec′reating; droll, com′ical, com′ic, lu′dicrous, far′cical, ridic′ulous. *See* Laughable, Odd, Sport, Beguile.

AN′CESTOR—progen′itor, forefa′ther, predeces′sor. *See* Old.

AN′CIENT—*See* Old.

ANG′ER—wrath, resent′ment, dudg′eon, ire, irrita′tion, irritabil′ity, indigna′tion, exaspera′tion, excite′ment, displea′sure, disapproba′tion; cho′ler, rage, passi′on, spleen. *See* Displeasure, Rage, Malice.

ANG′ER—incense′, ir′ritate, enrage′, exas′perate, heat, kin′dle, enkin′dle, inflame′, fire, incite′, stim′ulate, provoke′, excite′. *See* Displease, Burn, Stir, Heighten.

AN′GRY—ir′ritated, incens′ed, exas′perated, vex′ed, excit′ed; iras′cible, ire′ful, wroth, chol′eric, passi′onate, hot, hast′y, impet′uous; inflam′ed, red; ra′ging, fu′rious, tumult′uous, provok′ed. *See* Hot, Fretful, Cross, Passionate, Hasty, Tumultuous.

AN′IMATE—enli′ven, quick′en, invig′orate, inspire′, exhil′arate; in′stigate, incite′, inspir′it, embol′den, encour′age, impel′, stim′ulate, urge, move, act′uate. *See* Cheer, Quicken, Encourage, Move, Stir.

ANNUL′ *laws or rules*—do away with, make void, nul′lify, disannul′, can′cel, ab′rogate, abol′ish, repeal′, revoke′, recall′. *See* Call *back*, Overrule.

AN′SWERABLE—account′able, respons′ible, ame′nable, li′able. *See* Accountable, Subject.

AN′SWERABLE for *be*—guarantee′, war′rant, secure′, be respons′ible or account′able, be surety or security for, pledge, vouch for. *See* Pledge, Security.

ANTIC′IPATE—precede′, prevent′, forestal′, prepossess′, foretaste′, prejudge′, forerun′. *See* Prevent, Go.

APH′ORISM—max′im, ax′iom, ap′ophthegm, say′ing, ad′age, prov′erb, saw, bye′-word. *See* Say, Speech.

APPEAL′—refer′, submit′; call on, invoke′. *See* Refer, Call.

APPEAR′ *make*—man′ifest, demon′strate, evince′; reveal′, display′, discov′er; seem, look. *See* Discover, Look.

APPEAR′ANCE—phenom′enon, scene, sem′blance, show, fig′ure, form, seem′ing, like′ness, resem′blance, air, look, man′ner, as′pect; mien, deport′ment, gait; verisimil′itude, probabil′ity, like′lihood; plausibil′ity, spe′ciousness. *See* Form, Aspect, Attitude, Likeness, Show, Ghost.

APPEAS′ED *not to be*—impla′cable, inex′orable, unappeas′able, relent′less, unrelent′ing. *See* Unrelenting, Deadly.

APPLY′—lay on; use, employ′, adhib′it, put, refer′; ded′icate, devote′, assign′, allot′, appor′tion; suit, agree′; make request′, solic′it, have recourse′, betake′. *See* Refer, Dedicate, Assign, Ask.

APPOINT′—ordain′, or′der, depute, prescrib′e, fix, devote′, allot′, con′stitute, in′stitute, provide′, appor′tion, assign′, par′cel. *See* Ordain, Assign, Fix.

APPROACH′—approx′imate, draw nigh, come near, draw near. *See* Draw, Near.

APPROVE′—*See* Praise.

APPROBA′TION—approv′al, consent′, assent′, acquies′cence, concur′rence. *See* Praise, Acquiescence, Leave

AR′BITER—*See* Judge

Ar'bitrary—depend'ing on will or discretion, despot'ic, tyran'nical, impe'rious, per'emptory, pos'itive; ab'solute, unlim'ited, unrestrain'ed, unrestrict'ed, op'tional, discreti'onary. *See* Despotic, Positive.

Ar'gue—*See* Think.

Ar'gue—dispute', re'ason, debate', contend', discuss', al'tercate, con'trovert, ques'tion; prove, evince'; expos'tulate, remon'strate. *See* Reason.

Ar'gument—dispute', re'asoning, debate', conten'tion, discussi'on, alterca'tion, disputa'tion, con'troversy, con'test, re'ason, proof, allega'tion, ev'idence; remon'strance, expostula'tion. *See* Proof, Reason, Dissertation.

Arm—*See* Covering.

Arrange'ment—sym'metry, propor'tion, adjust'ment, adapta'tion; har'mony, agree'ment, accord'ance. *See* Order, Disposition, Agreement.

Art *without*—art'less, guile'less, ingen'uous, can'did, o'pen, frank; unaffect'ed, nat'ural. *See* Open, Fair.

Art *made by*—artifici'al, factiti'ous; feign'ed, fictiti'ous. *See* Forged.

Ascend'—*See* Mount.

Asham'ed—*See* Modest.

Asham'ed *make*—abash', shame, confound', confuse', disgrace'. *See* Disgrace, Shame.

Ask—request, solic'it, entreat', beg, petiti'on, require', claim, crave, demand'. *See* Invite, Beg, Apply.

Ask *questions*—ques'tion, inter'rogate, inquire'.

As'pect—mien, air, physiog'nomy, appear'ance. *See* Appearance, Look.

Asperse'—accuse' false'ly, slan'der, defame', calum'niate, detract', vil'ify, scand'alize. *See* Slander, Disgrace.

Assem'bly—*See* Company, Council.

Assert'—vin'dicate, just'ify, maintain', aver', affirm', positively, defend'. *See* Declare, Clear.

Assign'—allot', appoint', grant, desig'nate, fix, spec'ify; make over, transfer', a'lienate; allege', show, bring for'ward, advance', adduce', state; devote', appor'tion. appro'priate, set apart'. *See* Appoint, Ordain, Set *apart*.

Assist'—aid. suc'cour, relieve', help; conduce', contrib'ute, min'ister, admin'ister. *See* Help, Minister, Support, Oblige.

Assume' *falsely*—ar'rogate; usurp'; affect', pretend'.

Atone'—*See* Expiate.

Attach'ment—adhe'rence, adhe'sion; fond'ness, affec'tion, love, regard', esteem', inclina'tion, addic'tion; fidel'ity, faith. *See* Affection, Stick.

Attack'—fall upon, assail', assault', impugn', oppose'. *See* Incursion, Onset.

Attempt'—ef'fort, endeav'our, tri'al, exper'iment, es'say; en'terprise, un'dertaking. *See* Essay, Try, Dare.

Atten'tion—stretch'ing to, applica'tion, stud'y, devo'tion, assidu'ity, dil'igence; civil'ity, court'esy. *See* Diligence, Civility, Politeness.

At'titude—positi'on, fig'ure, pos'ture; ac'tion, gest'ure, gesticula'tion. *See* Appearance, Form.

Audac'ity—bold'ness, hard'ihood, im'pudence, in'solence, effront'ery. *See* Impudence, Bold.

Au'thor—*See* Writer.

Auth'orize—give author'ity, empow'er; authent'icate; instruct', direct', give a right. *See* Invest, Instruct.

Av'arice—love of money, avarici'ousness, cov'etousness, cupid'ity. *See* Desire.

Averse'—back'ward, unwill'ing, loth, reluct'ant. *See* Unwilling.

Avoid'—*See* Shun.

Awa'ken—wa'ken, rouse, arouse', incite', excite', stir up, provoke', stim'ulate. *See* Stir, Move.

Aware'—con'scious, appri'zed; watch'ful, vig'ilant, guard'ed, cau'tious, attent'ive, wa'ry. *See* Wary, Watchful.

Awk'ward—clum'sy, unnat'ural, uncouth', clown'ish, unpol'ished, unto'ward, unhand'y, inconven'ient, bung'ling, unread'y; inel'egant, unpolite', ungrace'ful. *See* Blunt, Barbarous, Polite, Countryman.

Axe—*See* Weapon.

B.

Back'ward—*See* Averse.

Back'ward *go*—ret'rograde, retrocede', retreat', retire', recede'. *See* Go.

Bad—*See* Malicious, Wicked.

Baf'fle—balk, frus'trate, thwart, foil, disappoint'. *See* Put *down*, Defeat.

Band—*See* Tie.

Band—shack'le, fet'ter, man'acle, col'lar, chain, bond, tie, band'age; com'pany, soci'ety, associa'tion, coaliti'on, league, confed'eracy; gang; crew. *See* Company, League, Tie.

Bane—pest, plague; poi'son, ru'in. *See* Hurt.

Ban'ish—*See* Exile.

Ban'ishment—ex'ile, transporta'tion, deporta'tion, expatria'tion, os'tracism; proscrip′tion, out′lawry, expul′sion. *See* Exile.

BARBAROUS—unciv′ilized, rude, sav′age, vandal′ic, unlet′tered, illit′erate, untu′tored, ig′norant, barba′rian; cru′el, fero′cious, inhu′man, inhospit′able. *See* Cruel, Bloody, Ignorant, Awkward.

BARE—uncov′ered, na′ked, rude, detect′ed; des′titute, poor, in′digent, em′pty, unfurn′ished, defici′ent, scant, scant′y; plain, sim′ple, unadorn′ed. *See* Naked, Poor.

BAR′GAIN—*See* Agreement, League, Condition.

BAR′GAIN—nego′tiate, treat with; agree′, stip′ulate, contract′, cov′enant, capit′ulate. *See* Agree, League.

BAR′REN—ster′ile, effete′, unfruit′ful, unproduct′ive, ar′id. *See* Idle, Poor.

BAS′TARD—illegit′imate, nat′ural; spu′rious, not gen′uine, false, supposititi′ous, adul′terate. *See* Spurious, Genuine *not.*

BAT′TLE—fight, con′flict, com′bat, du′el, con′test, conten′tion, encoun′ter, strug′gle, engage′ment, ac′tion, rencoun′ter. *See* Fight, Argument, War.

BEAM—ray, gleam, glit′ter. *See* Shine.

BEAR *bring forth*—*See* Breed.

BEAR—suf′fer, support′, endure′, tol′erate, sustain′, un′dergo, be pa′tient; car′ry, convey′, transport′; bring forth, produce′, beget′. *See* Suffer, Passive, Support, Beget, Produce.

BEAST′LY—bru′tal, bru′tish, bes′tial; sens′ual, irrati′onal; coarse, fil′thy. *See* Brutal.

BEAT—*See* Bruise.

BEAT—strike, hit, thrash; break, ham′mer, bruise, pul′verise; defeat′, con′quer, van′quish, subdue′, overcome′, overthrow′, overpow′er, smite, afflict′. *See* Palpitate, Bruise, Overcome, Defeat.

BEAU′TIFUL—beau′teous, pret′ty, hand′some, el′egant, fair, grace′ful, fine; dec′orated, or′namented, embel′lished, or′nate, deck′ed, adorn′ed; love′ly, charm′ing, attract′ive. *See* Fair, Charming, Amiable, Nice.

BEAU′TIFY—adorn′, dec′orate, embel′lish, deck, bedeck′, enam′el, array′, attire′, dress, grace, or′nament, embroid′er; gild, pol′ish, refine′, smooth, furb′ish, burn′ish. *See* Dress, Invest.

BECOM′ING—de′cent, befit′ting, suit′able, fit, meet; agree′able, grace′ful, come′ly. *See* Fit, Meet, Suitable, Polite.

BEFIT′TING—*See* Becoming.

BEG—sup′plicate, beseech′, implore′, entreat′, crave, pray, petiti′on. *See* Ask, Wish *for*, Entreaty.

BEGET′—*See* Breed, Cause.

BEGIN′—commence′, take rise, orig′inate; en′ter on, start, resume′. *See* Found, Origin, Preface, Introduce.

BEGUILE′—delude′, deceive′, impose′ on; elude′; pass pleas′ingly, divert′, amuse′, entertain′. *See* Deceive, Cheat. Amusing.

BEHA′VIOUR—con′duct, deme′anor, deport′ment, car′riage, port, man′ners, address′. *See* Manners, Aspect, Appearance.

BEHEAD′—decap′itate, de′collate, guillotin′. *See* Kill, Head.

BEHOLD′—*See* Look.

BELIEF′—faith, cre′dence, cred′it, trust, con′fidence; creed. *See* Confidence, Hope, Faithfulness, Unbelief.

BEMOAN′—*See* Mourn.

BEND—*See* Incline, Crooked.

BEN′EFIT—prof′it, ser′vice, use, avail′; good, advan′tage, bless′ing, fa′vour confer′red. *See* Privilege, Use, Good, Interest, Gain.

BENT—flex′ure, flex′ion, curv′ity; bi′as, inclina′tion, dispositi′on, tend′ency, drift, scope, turn, direc′tion, propens′ity; prepossessi′on, in′fluence, sway. *See* Disposition, Direction, Humor, Course, Crooked.

BEQUEATH′—*See* Will.

BETO′KEN—sig′nify, portend′, au′gur, presage′, forebode′, predict′, foreshow′, denote′. *See* Denote, Bear, Foretell, Omen.

BET′TER—mel′iorate, amel′iorate, amend′, emend′, improve′; rect′ify, correct′, reform′; advance′, support′. *See* Correct, Improvement.

BEWAIL′—*See* Grieve.

BEWARE′—*See* Aware, Wary.

BID—call, invite′, ask, sum′mon; command′, or′der, direct′; of′fer, propose′; denounce′, threat′en. *See* Call, Offer, Invite, Ask.

BIG—great, large, bulk′y, huge; protu′berant, preg′nant; full, fraught; swel′led, tu′mid, inflat′ed; haught′y, proud. *See* Great, Large, Greatness, Full, Swell, Bombastic.

BIG′NESS *of body*—cor′pulence, cor′pulency, lust′iness, flesh′iness, gross′ness; fat′ness, obes′ity, coarse′ness, bulk, size. *See* Size, Greatness, Fatness.

BILE—*See* Anger.

BIND—*See* Tie.

BIRTH—*See* Beget.

BIT′TER—*See* Sour.

BLACK—*See* Dark.

BLAME—*See* Censure, Reproach.

BLAME—cen′sure, upbraid′, reproach′, condem′n, reprehend′, chide, reprove′, disapprove′. *See* Reproach, Chide, Fault, Culpable.

BLAME′LESS—incul′pable, unblam′able, irreproach′able, irreprehens′ible, irreprov′able, in′nocent, guilt′less; unblem′ished, spot′less, fault′less, immac′ulate, unspot′ted. *See* Stain, Blemish, Culpable.

BLAZE—glare, flare, flame; irra′diate, illume′, illu′mine, illu′minate, emblaze′, bla′zon, pub′lish. *See* Gleam, Shine, Publish.

BLEM′ISH — stain, spot, flaw, tint, speck, scar; imperfec′tion, fault, defect′; stig′ma, reproach′, disgrace′, taint, deform′ity, tur′pitude. *See* Stain, Fault, Blame, Disgrace, Reproach.

BLESS—*See* Happiness.

BLOCK′HEAD — stup′id fel′low, dolt, thick-skull, clod′poll, clod′pate, clod′hopper, num′skull, dunse, dul′lard, bull′head, lub′bard, lub′ber, drone, slug′gard, id′ler, boob′y, los′el, scound′rel. *See* Countryman, Villain.

BLOOD′Y — san′guinary; mur′derous, cru′el, sav′age, bar′barous. *See* Cruel, Barbarous, Skill.

BLOT—*See* Stain, Blemish, Expunge.

BLUNT—*See* Dull.

BLUNT — obtuse′, dull, not sharp, point′less, edge′less; plain, unceremo′nious, unciv′il, rude, unpol′ished, unpolite′, rough, inel′egant, indel′icate, abrupt′, coarse. *See* Awkward, Dull, Polite.

BOAST′ER — vaunt′er, braggado′cio, brag′gart, brag′ger, bra′vo, puf′fer, rod′omont, rodomont′adist, rodomonta′dor, blust′erer, bul′ly, swag′gerer. *See* Vaunting.

BOIL—seethe, bub′ble, effervesce′. *See* Hot.

BOLD —da′ring, coura′geous, brave, intrep′id, fear′less, undaunt′ed, daunt′less; con′fident, not tim′orous; auda′cious, in′solent, contuma′cious, im′pudent, rude, for′ward, barefa′ced, shame′less; licen′tious; steep, abrupt′. *See* Determined, Foolhardy, Brave, Impertinent, Courage.

BOMBAST′IC — bom′bast, inflat′ed, pomp′ous, swel′led, tu′mid, tur′gid, high-sound′ing, hyperbol′ical, grandil′oquent, magnil′oquent. *See* Big, Swell.

BOND′AGE—*See* Liberty *being deprived of*.

BOR′DER—*See* Brink, Edge.

BORN—*See* Beget.

BOUND—lim′it, restrict′, qual′ify, restrain′, confine′, circumscribe′; end, term′inate. *See* End, Qualify, Confine, Limited.

BOUND *back*—rebound′, recoil′; resound′, reverb′erate, ech′o. *See* Cast *back*, Sound.

BOUNDS—lim′its, bor′ders, bound′aries, fron′tiers, con′fines, march′es; extent′, restric′tions. *See* Limited, End, Edge.

BOUN′TY — liberal′ity, munif′icence, benef′icence, generos′ity, benev′olence, benig′nity, kind′ness; abund′ance, profu′sion. *See* Good, Kindness, Generous.

BRACE′LET—*See* Covering.

BRAVE—coura′geous, bold, da′ring, intrep′id, undaunt′ed, fear′less, gal′lant, val′orous, val′iant, hero′ic, magnan′imous. *See* Bold, Courage.

BREAK—*See* Overcome, Fail, Violation, Incursion.

BREATHE—*See* Spirit.

BREED—gen′erate, hatch, engen′der, produce′, occa′sion, cause, orig′inate; ed′ucate, instruct′; bring up, nurse, fos′ter. *See* Cause, Fruitful, Race, Foster.

BRIEF—short, concise′, lacon′ic, succinct′, sum′mary, compend′ious. *See* Short.

BRIGHT—shin′ing, lu′cid, splen′did, bril′liant, lu′minous, spark′ling, an′imated; glos′sy, glis′tering; lim′pid, transpic′uous, translu′cent, clear, transpa′rent; ev′ident, mani′fest; resplen′dent, lus′trous, illus′trious, glo′rious, irra′diated, illum′inated; burn′ished, furb′ished, pol′ished. *See* Shine, Strong, Clear, Transparent.

BRING *about*—effect′, bring to pass, accom′plish, perform′, effec′tuate, achieve′, fulfil′, attain′, do, cause to be, produce′. *See* Accomplish, Do, Performance, Effect.

BRINK—mar′gin, edge, verge, bor′der, bank; brim, rim; coast, shore, beach, side. *See* Edge.

BRISK′NESS — live′liness, vivac′ity, quick′ness, spright′liness, gay′ety, efferves′cence; alac′rity, cheer′fulness, alert′ness, assidu′ity; read′iness, promp′titude, activ′ity, agil′ity. *See* Quickness, Lively, Cheerfulness.

BROAD—*See* Large.

BROAD′NESS—breadth, lat′itude, extent′, wide′ness, width. *See* Wide.

BROKEN *easily*—brit′tle, frag′ile, frail, weak, slight, fran′gible. *See* Weak.

BROTH′EL—*See* Lewd.

BRUISE—crush or man′gle with blows, contuse′; pound, break, man′gle, crush, beat, pul′verise. *See* Beat.

BRU'TAL—beast'ial, bru'tish, sav'age, cru'el, inhu'man, fero'cious, unfeel'ing, bar'barous, mer'ciless, sens'ual, irrati'onal, sense'less. *See* Beastly, Cruel.
BRUTE—*See* Brutal.
BUB'BLE—*See* Boil.
BUCK'LER—*See* Covering.
BUD—put forth, sprout, germ'inate, shoot.
BUILD—*See* Found, House, Instruct.
BUILD'ING—struc'ture, ed'ifice, fab'ric, erec'tion, construc'tion, pile, shed, house. *See* House, Fabric.
BURD'EN—*See* Weight.
BURD'EN — load, weight, bur'then; freight, car'go. *See* Freight.
BURN—*See* Hot, Anger.
BUR'Y — inter', entomb', depos'it a corpse, inhume', inhu'mate; hide, conceal', overwhelm', cov'er. *See* Unbury, Hide.
BUS'INESS—voca'tion, avoca'tion, cal'ling, professi'on, trade, art, employ'ment, occupa'tion, engage'ment, of'fice, dut'y; mat'ter, concern', affair', point, sub'ject. *See* Office, Trade.
BUT'CHER—*See* Kill, Destruction.
BUY—*See* Trade, Redeem.

C.

CAJOLE'—flat'ter, ad'ulate, com'pliment, praise, fawn, whee'dle, coax, soothe, delude', hu'mor, induce', persuade'. *See* Fawn, Flatter, Deceive.
CALL *back what one has said or written* —retract', recall', disavow', recant', revoke', reverse'; abjure', forswear'; reject', renounce', deny'; countermand', contradict'; rescind', repeal', ab'rogate, abol'ish, annul', disannul', nul'lify. *See* Recall, Disown, Annul.
CALL *out*—evoke'; vocif'erate, ut'ter, cry, exclaim', ejac'ulate. *See* Utter, Cry.
CALL *together*—convoke', convene'; sum'mon, cite, collect', gath'er, assem'ble, mus'ter, con'gregate, amass', accu'mulate. *See* Gather.
CAL'LING *together*—convoca'tion, congrega'tion, assem'bly, gath'ering; par'liament, con'gress, di'et, conven'tion, convent'icle, sessi'on, pres'bytery, syn'od, san'hedrim, sen'ate, coun'cil cham'ber, con'ference, meet'ing, com'pany. *See* Council, Interview, Collection.
CALM—serene', unruf'fled, plac'id, sedate', gen'tle, bland, mild, qui'et, cool, collect'ed, peace'ful, hal'cyon, compo'sed, still, unmov'ed, undisturb'ed, tran'quil. *See* Gentle, Even. Silence.
CARE—concern', anxi'ety, solic'itude; heed, cau'tion, circumspec'tion, wa'riness, atten'tion, regard'; charge, o'versight, man'agement, direc'tion, econ'omy; troub'le, perplex'ity. *See* Trouble, Caution, Look, Oversight, Thought.
CARE'FUL—an'xious, solic'itous, cau'tious, wa'ry, mind'ful, heed'ful, atten'tive, intent', observ'ant, cir'cumspect, prov'ident, pru'dent, watch'ful, vig'ilant, dil'igent, assid'uous, sed'ulous, elab'orate. *See* Thoughtful, Wary.
CARE'LESS — heed'less, thought'less, neg'ligent, unthink'ing, inattent'ive, regard'less, unmind'ful, neglect'ful, unsolic'itous, improv'ident, remiss', list'less, reck'less, incau'tious, inconsid'erate, inadvert'ent, unconcern'ed; hast'y, slight, cur'sory, des'ultory, superfici'al, loose, immethod'ical; ro'ving, wa'vering. *See* Indifferent, Lazy, Hasty, Loose.
CAR'RIAGE—char'iot, coach, cur'ricle, ve'hicle, car, om'nibus, phae'ton, drosk'y, so'ciable, gig, cart, wag'on.
CASH—*See* Money.
CAST — throw, fling, hurl, drive, thrust, push, sling, jerk. *See* Send, Throw.
CAST *down* — deject'ed, depress'ed, griev'ed, discour'aged, disheart'ened, humil'iated. *See* Sad, Dull.
CAST *back* or *off*—reject', retort', ech'o, reverb'erate, rebound', report', reflect', rebuff'; desert'; forsake', aban'don, renounce'. *See* Bound *back*, Abandon.
CAT'ALOGUE—list, reg'ister, mus'ter, roll, record'; scroll, sched'ule. *See* Chronicle, Enlist, Nomenclature.
CATCH'ING—seiz'ure, cap'tion, cap'ture; apprehen'sion, arrest'. *See* Take, Seize.
CATH'OLIC—*See* Whole, All.
CAUSE—produce', effect', bring into exist'ence, create', occa'sion, engen'der, gen'erate, breed, induce'; mo'tive, incite'ment, induce'ment, rea'son. *See* Do, Breed, Effect, Induce, Occasion, Origin.
CAU'TION — care, concern', regard', care'fulness, circumspec'tion, prudence, solic'itude, wa'riness, watch'fulness, vig'ilance; no'tice, advice, warn'ing, admoniti'on. *See* Care, Warning.
CAVE—*See* Opening.
CAV'IL — carp, cen'sure, catch at, quar'rel, object', evade'; contest',

dispute′. *See* Censure, Object, Quarrel, Shift.

Cav′il—*See* Jest, Trick.

Ceas′ing—cessa′tion, truce, leav′ing off, discontin′uance, vaca′tion, intermissi′on, pause. *See* Rest, Agreement.

Cen′sure—*See* Blame, Cavil.

Cer′tain—sure, infal′lible, secure′, doubt′less. *See* Actual, Doubted *not to be.*

Chain—*See* Band, Covering, Linking *together.*

Chance — luck, cas′ualty, fortu′ity, for′tune, ac′cident, in′cident, occur′rence, event′, contin′gency, adven′ture, haz′ard. *See* Fortune, Luck, Event, Occasion, Danger.

Change — al′ter, va′ry; exchange′, sub′stitute, commute′; recip′rocate, interchange′, bar′ter, truck, traf′fic. *See* Interchange, Trade; Wave.

Change′able — va′riable, mu′table, fick′le, incon′stant, vers′atile, unstead′y, irres′olute, wa′vering, uncer′tain, veer′ing. *See* Undetermined, Always, Lightness.

Char′acter—mark, fig′ure; reputa′tion, repute′, estima′tion; descrip′tion, account′, representa′tion; per′son; sort, class, spe′cies, kind. *See* Mark, Fame, Sort.

Charge—*See* Office.

Char′ity — love, affec′tion; alms; benev′olence, benef′icence; kind′ness, good′ness, benig′nity, gra′ciousness, tend′erness. *See* Kindness, Mercy, Favour.

Charm—*See* Amiable.

Chaste—*See* Modest.

Chaste′ness—chas′tity, con′tinence; mod′esty, pu′rity, vir′tue. *See* Honesty.

Chastise′—*See* Punish.

Cheat — decep′tion, finesse′, fraud, delu′sion, impos′ture, impositi′on, trick, ar′tifice, deceit′, guile, cun′ning, craft, sleight, strat′agem. *See* Hypocrisy, Trick, Cunning.

Check—restrain′, repress′, curb, control′, inhib′it, stop, hin′der. *See* Chide, Put *down,* Keep, Hinder, Damp, Forbid.

Cheer — glad′den, exhil′arate, an′imate, enli′ven, viv′ify, revive′, inspir′it, quick′en, com′fort, encour′age, invig′orate; incite′, excite′, stim′ulate, rouse. *See* Gladden, Animate, Comfort, Encourage, Quicken.

Cheer′fulness—gay′ety, live′liness, vivac′ity, mer′riment, mirth, spright′liness, blithe′someness, alac′rity, jol′lity, jocund′ity. *See* Mirth, Pleasure, Briskness.

Chide—scold at, reprove′, rep′rimand, rebuke′, reprehend′, upbraid′, reproach′. *See* Blame, Abuse, Check, Disgrace, Censure, Gibe.

Chil′dren—off′spring, prog′eny, iss′ue, poster′ity, descend′ants. *See* Offspring, Issue.

Choice—elec′tion, selec′tion, op′tion, pref′erence; *of two things,* altern′ative. *See* Will, Means.

Choke—*See* Kill.

Choose—*See* Wish.

Chron′icles—an′nals, arch′ives, rec′ords. *See* Chronicle.

Chron′icle—his′tory, reg′ister, rec′ord, memoir′, nar′rative, trav′els. *See* Account, Memoir, Catalogue, Story.

Cinder—*See* Ashes.

Civil′ity — civil beha′viour, good′-breeding, polite′ness, urban′ity, cour′tesy, cour′teousness, complaisance′, affabil′ity. *See* Politeness, Attention.

Civiliza′tion—refine′ment, cul′ture, cultiva′tion, reclama′tion. *See* Education, Improvement.

Class—rank, or′der, degree′, grade, stand′ing. *See* Kind, Order, Sort.

Clear—transpa′rent, translu′cent, lu′cid, translu′cid, diaph′anous, pellu′cid, lim′pid, pure, unmix′ed; o′pen; serene′, uncloud′ed, lu′minous, unobscu′red; sharp, perspica′cious; in′nocent, unspot′ted, irreproach′able; unprepossess′ed, unpreoc′cupied, impar′tial; unentan′gled, unperplex′ed, unembar′rassed, free; lib′erated, freed, acquit′ted. *See* Transparent, Bright, Open, Free.

Clear—plain, appa′rent, ev′ident, undoubt′ed, indu′bitable, indis′putable, undeni′able, man′ifest, vis′ible, unobscure′, ob′vious, o′pen, conspic′uous, distinct′, perspic′uous, express′, explic′it. *See* Explanatory, Discernible.

Clear — pu′rify, clar′ify, cleanse, purge; lib′erate, ex′tricate, disembar′rass, disentan′gle, disengage′, evolve′; elu′cidate, illume′, illu′mine, illu′minate, illus′trate; excul′pate, exon′erate, absolve′, acquit′, par′don, discharge′, relieve′; just′ify, vin′dicate. *See* Free, Assert, Shine, Explain, Discharge, Forgive.

Cler′gyman—ecclesias′tic, min′ister, pas′tor, pres′byter, pope, car′dinal, archbish′op, bish′op, arch′dean, dean, rect′or, vic′ar, cu′rate. *See* Ecclesiastic, Minister.

Clev′er—expert′, dex′trous, adroit, read′y, skil′ful, expe′rienced; intel′ligent. *See* Able, Ready, Intellectual.

CLIMB—*See* Go.
CLOAK—mask, veil, blind, cov′er, disguise′, pretext′, pretense′, excuse′. *See* Cover, Gloss, Excuse, Pretense.
CLOSE—*See* Thick, Surround, Narrow.
CLOTHE—*See* Invest.
CLOTHES—gar′ments, appar′el, dress, cloth′ing, attire′, array′, vest′ments, ves′ture, rai′ment, robes, garb, hab′its, habil′iments, cov′erings. *See* Dress, Covering, Beautify.
COARSE—*See* Thick.
COAT—*See* Covering.
COIN—*See* Money.
COLD—*See* Insensibility.
COLLEC′TION—gath′ering, mus′ter, assem′blage, assem′bly, group, crowd, congrega′tion; contribu′tion. *See* Crowd, Company, Calling *together.*
COL′OR—hue, tint, tinge, dye; false show, pretense′, pretext′, guise, sem′blance. *See* Paint, Stain, Pretense, Cloak, Show.
COMBINE′—unite′, *or* join two or more things, link closely, join, unite′, coalesce′, asso′ciate, league, confed′erate, band. *See* Plot, League.
COME—*See* Go.
COM′FORT — strength′en, invig′orate, console′, cheer, sol′ace, an′imate, glad′den, revive′, encour′age, support′. *See* Animate, Cheer, Encourage.
COMMAND′—man′date, or′der, injunc′tion, pre′cept, charge, behest′; e′dict; bull. *See* Order, Precept, Decree.
COMMAND′ING—magiste′rial, imper′ative, impe′rious, author′itative, dictato′rial, haught′y; ar′rogant, assu′ming; overbear′ing, domineer′ing. *See* Proud.
COMMENT′—com′mentary, annota′tion, note, explana′tion, expositi′on, elucida′tion, no′tice, remark′. *See* Remark, Explanation.
COM′MON—or′dinary, vul′gar, gen′eral, pub′lic, univers′al, fre′quent, us′ual; not no′ble, not respect′ed, not distin′guished, low, mean; pros′titute, lewd. *See* Public, Universal, Mean, Gross, Lewd.
COMMU′NION—fel′lowship, in′tercourse, con′verse, associati′on, soci′ety, in′terchange; agree′ment, con′cord, alli′ance. *See* Interchange, Agreement, Concord, Speech.
COMPAN′ION — asso′ciate, compeer′, e′qual, com′rade, con′sort, part′ner, fel′low, mate, confed′erate, ally′, accom′plice; coadju′tor, col′league. *See* Acquaintance, Follower, Accomplice.
COM′PANY — collec′tion, associa′tion, corpora′tion, soci′ety, part′nership, commu′nity; alli′ance, confed′eracy, combina′tion, u′nion, league, coaliti′on; congrega′tion, assem′bly, assem′blage, crowd, group, crew, gang, troop. *See* Collection, Party, Council, Band, Crowd.
COMPAR′ISON — sim′ilē, simil′itude, similar′ity, like′ness; propor′tion. *See* Likeness.
COM′PASS—surround′, envi′ron, encom′pass, incir′cle, inclose′, invest′, besiege′, beleag′uer; obtain′, attain to, procure′, accom′plish; pur′pose, intend′, imag′ine, plot, contrive′. *See* Invest, Surround, Contrive, Accomplish, Embrace.
COMPASSI′ON—*See* Feeling.
COMPEN′DIUM—*See* Abridgment.
COMPLAIN′—*See* Grieve, Mourn.
COMPLAIN′ING *always* — quer′ulous, querimo′nious, discontent′ed, dissat′isfied, peev′ish, fret′ful, ill-hum′oured, test′y, pet′ulant, ir′ritable, cap′tious. *See* Cross, Fretful, Angry.
COMPLE′TION — consumma′tion, perfec′tion, achieve′ment, accom′plishment, fulfil′ment, attain′ment. *See* Accomplishment, Performance.
COMPRESS′—condense′, press, squeeze, crowd. *See* Abridge, Squeeze.
CONCEAL′—*See* Hide.
CONCEIT′—concep′tion, ide′a, thought, im′age; no′tion, imagina′tion, opin′ion, fan′cy, freak, whim, mag′got. *See* Whim, Pride, Thought, Vain, Opinion.
CON′CORD — har′mony, agree′ment, peace, u′nion, u′nity; har′mony, mel′ody. *See* Agreement, Peace.
CONDITI′ON—term, stipula′tion, ar′ticle, provi′so, provisi′on. *See* Situation, State, Bargain.
CON′FIDENCE—trust, reli′ance, hope, assu′rance, depend′ence. *See* Belief, Hope, Trust.
CONFINE′—bound, lim′it, circumscribe′, shut up, inclose′, impris′on, stint, restrain′, restrict′. *See* Bound, Liberty *deprived of.*
CONFU′SED—disor′dered, derang′ed, in distinct′, indiscrim′inate; involv′ed, in′tricate. *See* Intricacy, Entangle, Order *put out of*, Promiscuous Crowd.
CONFU′SION—*See* Medley.
CONNECT′ED—join′ed, conjoin′ed, link-ed, uni′ted; rela′ted, rel′ative, rel′evant; contig′uous, adjoin′ing; consec′utive, consequen′tial; alli′ed, confed′erate. *See* Accompanying.
CON′QUER—*See* Overcome.
CONSTIT′UENT—compo′nent, essent′ial,

element'al, intrin'sic. *See* Necessary, Intrinsic, Formal, Important.

Consult'—advise' with, seek coun'sel; delib'erate, consid'er, submit' to, refer' to. *See* Refer.

Contain'—hold, comprehend', comprise', embrace', include', inclose'. *See* Hold, Embrace.

Contemp'tible—deserving contempt', des'picable, mean, vile, base, pal'try, pit'iful. *See* Mean, Disdain.

Contin'ue *in a course*—persevere', pursue', pros'ecute, persist'.

Con'trary—op'posite, reverse', ad'verse, contradict'ory, inconsist'ent, repug'nant, inim'ical. *See* Against, Opposite.

Contrive'—devise', plan, scheme, invent'; mach'inate, plot, colleague', concert', man'age. *See* Design, Discover, Invent, Make.

Con'tumely—contemp'tuousness, in'solence, contempt', contempt'uous lan'guage; rude'ness, ob'loquy, reproach'. *See* Disdain, Disgrace, Slander.

Conviv'ial—fest'al, fest'ival, fest'ive, so'cial, so'ciable, jov'ial. *See* Merry.

Cool—refrig'erate, refresh'. *See* Refresh, Cold.

Cop'y—*See* Imitate.

Correct'—set right; prop'er, right, up'right, hon'est, just, ac'curate, exact', fault'less, nice, precise', punc'tual, punctil'ious, strict, scrup'ulous. *See* Right, Particular, Honesty, Nice.

Correspond'ent — an'swerable to, conform'able, agree'able, suit'able, adap'ted. *See* Accordant.

Corrupt'—pu'trid, rot'ten, spoil'ed, taint'ed, viti'ated, unsound', deprav'ed, debas'ed, impure', wick'ed, sin'ful; not gen'uine. *See* Rotten, Wicked.

Corrupt'—become pu'trid, pu'trify, rot; viti'ate, deprave', infect', defile', pollute', contam'inate, taint, adul'terate, debase', sophis'ticate; waste, spoil, consume'; pervert', fals'ify; bribe; entice', allure'. *See* Rot, Stain, Worse *make*, Waste.

Cot'tage—Cot, Cabin. *See* House.

Coun'cil — assem'bly, par'liament, con'gress, di'et, sen'ate, san'hedrim, cor'tes; sessi'on, pres'bytery, syn'od, gen'eral assem'bly; consist'ory, col'lege. *See* Calling *together*.

Count—num'ber, reck'on, compute', es'timate, rate, cal'culate; ascribe', impute', charge; esteem', account', think, judge, consid'er, repute', hold. *See* Reckon, Accuse, Lay, Value, Think.

Coun'tryman—rus'tic, peas'ant, far'mer, hus'bandman, agricul'turist, cul'tivator, lab'orer, vil'lager, cot'tager, cot'ter; swain, hind, clown, plough'man, churl, boor, bump'kin, lout. *See* Blockhead, Coxcomb, Awkward.

Cour'age—bra'very, intrepid'ity, resolu'tion, for'titude, her'oism, bold'ness, fear'lessness, val'our, firm'ness, dar'ing, coura'geousness, spir'it, gal'lantry. *See* Bold, Brave.

Course—run'ning, flow'ing, pas'sing, race, career', pas'sage, voy'age, road, route; se'ries, successi'on, or'der, turn, class, train, chain, concatena'tion, string, link, consecu'tion; sys'tem; man'ner, way, mode, meth'od, line, deport'ment; bent, propens'ity, will. *See* Order, Proceeding, Stream, Way, Bent.

Cov'enant—*See* Bargain, Alliance.

Cov'er—*See* Cloak, Hide.

Cov'ered *with*—Y. *See* Full.

Cov'ering—cov'er, cov'ercle, cov'erlet, lid; shel'ter, defense', protec'tion, cov'ert; pavil'ion; vail, coat, tu'nic, capuch'in; cloth'ing, rai'ment, dress, gar'ment, har'ness, ar'mor, tack'le, tack'ling, coat of mail, pan'oply, cap à pie, casque, hel'met, mor'ion, head-piece, vi'sor, mask, hab'ergeon, cuirass', breast'plate, brace'let, gaunt'let, buck'ler, tar'get, shield, greaves, shoe. *See* Clothes, Dress.

Cov'et—*See* Desire, Wish.

Cow'ardice—timid'ity, pusillanim'ity, cow'ardliness, das'tardliness, das'tardness, tim'orousness, poltroon'ery; fear, apprehen'sion, dread. *See* Fear, Afraid.

Cox'comb—vain showy fellow, fop, gay trifling man, macaro'ni, frib'ble, fin'ical fellow. *See* Blockhead, Fool.

Crane—*See* Bird.

Cred'it—*See* Trust.

Crime—*See* Blame, Sin, Wicked, Debt.

Crook'ed—bent, curv'ed, curv'ing, incurv'ated, bow'ed, aq'uiline, hook'ed; oblique', wind'ing, aw'ry, asquint'; de'vious, fro'ward, perverse'; disfig'ured, deform'ed. *See* Bent, Winding, Obstinate, Disfigure, Twist.

Cross—transverse', oblique', falling athwart'; ad'verse, op'posite, obstruct'ing; perverse', intract'able; con'trary, contradict'ory; perplex'ing; pee'vish, fret'ful, cyn'ical, ill-humored, sour, morose', sur'ly, snap'pish, crust'y; vexa'tious, fro'ward, unto'ward, pet'ulant, cap'tious, ir'ritable, an'gry, splen'etic, test'y, crab'-bed, ill-tem'pered; interchang'ed. *See* Fretful, Angry, Ill-tempered, Pain.

CROSS—pass over; thwart, obstruct', hin'der, stop, embar'rass, perplex', oppose', retard', impede', counteract', contravene'; clash with, interfere' with, be inconsist'ent with. *See* Hinder, Puzzle, Entangle.

CROWD—collec'tion, mul'titude, con'-course, assem'blage, assem'bly, congrega'tion, throng, group, clus'ter, swarm. *See* Collection, Company.

CRU'EL—inhu'man, mer'ciless, unmer'-ciful, pit'iless, unrelent'ing, relent'-less, ruth'less, sav'age, fierce, fero'-cious, bar'barous, hard'hearted, bru'-tal, inex'orable. *See* Brutal, Barbarous, Hard-hearted, Hardened, Unrelenting.

CRUM'BLE—*See* Break.

CRY—*See* Call *out*, Noise, Loud, Jingle.

CUL'PABLE—deserv'ing blame, blame'-able, cen'surable, reprehens'ible, reprov'able, reproach'able, faul'ty; sin'ful, crim'inal, immo'ral. *See* Blame, Fault.

CUL'TIVATE—*See* Countryman.

CUN'NING—(know'ledge, skill, dexter'-ity, *obs.*); art, ar'tifice, art'fulness, craft, craf'tiness, cun'ningness, sub'-tilty, duplic'ity, deceit', deceit'fulness, fraud, fal'lacy, cheat, fraud'ulency, treach'ery, trick'ery, strat'agem; *in law*, trick, device', collu'sion, shift, co'vin. *See* Cheat, Falsehood, Trick, Story.

CUN'NING—(know'ing, skil'ful, expe'-rienced, well-instruct'ed, dex'terous, cu'rious, inge'nious, *obs.*); art'ful, craf'ty, sly, shrewd, astute', pen'e-trating, design'ing, wi'ly, arch, sub'-tile, subt'le, deceit'ful, trick'ish. *See* Sly, Deceitful.

CURB—*See* Check.

CUS'TODY—keep'ing, guard'ing, guard, care, watch, inspec'tion; impris'on-ment, confine'ment, incarcera'tion, restraint'; defense', preserva'tion, secur'ity. *See* Liberty *being deprived of*.

CUS'TOM—com'mon use, u'sage, hab'it, fash'ion; prac'tice, way, man'ner; prescrip'tion. *See* Use, Way, Tax.

CUT *off*—rescind', abscind', sev'er, prune, lop; sep'arate, remove', take away', am'putate; destroy', extirp'-ate; interrupt', intercept'; end, fin'-ish; prevent', preclude', shut out. *See* Separate, Part, Maim.

D.

DAG'GER—*See* Weapon.

DAIN'TY—nice, delici'ous, sa'voury, pal'atable, squeam'ish, fastid'ious. del'icate, rare, luxu'rious; scrup'u-lous; el'egant, ten'der, soft, pure, neat. *See* Nice, Soft.

DAMP—mois'ten, make hu'mid, humec'tate, wet, wat'er; chill, cool, dead'en, depress', deject', abate'; weak'en, make dull; check, restrain', make lan'guid, discour'age, dishear'ten, dispir'it. *See* Humor, Check, Lower.

DAN'GER—per'il, haz'ard, risk, jeop'-ardy, ven'ture. *See* Chance.

DARE—have cour'age, be bold, ven'-ture, presume'; chal'lenge, provoke', defy', brave, set at defi'ance. *See* Attempt, Brave.

DARK—*See* Gloom, Dull.

DARK'NESS—ab'sence of light, obscur'-ity, opaqu'eness, opac'ity, nebulos'-ity, cloud'iness, tenebros'ity, dim'-ness, dusk, dusk'ishness, eclipse', gloom, gloom'iness, shade, mist'i-ness, dis'malness, myste'riousness, inex'plicableness; ig'norance; se'-crecy, priv'acy; hell; calam'ities, perplex'ities, troub'le, distress'. *See* Gloom, Trouble, Dull.

DART—*See* Cast, Throw.

DASH—*See* Strike.

DAUB—*See* Blot, Stain.

DAY—*See* Time.

DE'ACON—*See* Clergyman.

DEAD—life'less, deceas'ed, defunct', inan'imate; deep, sound; still, moti'onless; emp'ty, va'cant; unemploy'ed, use'less, unprof'itable; dull, inac'tive; gloom'y; frig'id, cold, unan'imated, unaffect'ing, *used of prayers;* taste'less, vap'id, spir'it-less, *used of liquors*. *See* Lifeless, Inanimate, Dull, Flat.

DEAD'LY—mor'tal, fa'tal, le'thal, life-destroy'ing, delete'rious, destruct'-ive, pois'onous; impla'cable, inex'-orable, malig'nant. *See* Mortal, Unrelenting.

DEAL—*See* Trade.

DEATH—*See* Perish.

DEBT—obliga'tion, due, liabil'ity, claim, right; *in Scripture*, sin, tres'pass, transgres'sion, guilt, crime. *See* Obligation, Right, Sin.

DECEIT'FUL—deceiv'ing, mislead'ing, insnar'ing, beguil'ing, cheat'ing. pu'nic, falla'cious, delu'sive, illu'-sive, illu'sory, fraud'ulent, trick'ish, elu'sive, coun'terfeit; sim'ulating.

feign'ing, pretend'ing. *See* Cunning, Sly, Corrupt, Spurious.

DECEIVE'—mislead', cause to err, impose' on, delude', coz'en, beguile', cajole', cheat; frus'trate, disappoint'. *See* Cajole, Abuse, Cheat.

DECI'DER *of disputes*—um'pire, ar'biter, ar'bitrator.

DECK—*See* Beautify.

DECLARE'—*See* Tell.

DECLARE'—make known, tell explic'itly; exhib it, man'ifest; proclaim', pub'lish, promul'gate, announce'; assert', aver', affirm'; assev'erate, protest'. *See* Profess, Discover, Publish, Show.

DECLINE'—*See* Waste, Droop.

DECREE' — e'dict, law, or'der, command', man'date, or'dinance, procla-ma'tion, rule, prohibiti'on; decisi'on, judg'ment, sen'tence, adjudica'tion; pur'pose, determina'tion. *See* Command, Order, Judgment, Rule.

DED'ICATE—*See* Set *apart*, Apply.

DEED—*See* Performance.

DEFAME'—*See* Slander.

DEFEAT'—frus'trate, disappoint', foil, balk, thwart, baf'fle, ren'der null and void; disconcert', derange', unset'tle; overcome'. *See* Beat, Baffle, Overcome.

DEFECT'IVE—want'ing, defici'ent, imper'fect; fault'y, bad, blame'able. *See* Culpable, Bad.

DEFEND'—*See* Protect.

DEFENSE'—excuse', apol'ogy, plea, justifica'tion, vindica'tion. *See* Covering, Excuse, Pretense, Fence.

DEF'INITE — lim'ited, bound'ed, determ'inate; pos'itive, cer'tain, fix'ed, precise', exact'; defi'ning, lim'iting. *See* Limited, Settled.

DELAY'—put off, prolong', defer', postpone', protract', prorogue'. procras'tinate; length'en, contin'ue; retard', stop, hin'der, detain', restrain'. *See* Prorogue, Hinder, Keep, Pause, Stay, Loiter.

DELIV'ER—*See* Give *up*.

DEL'UGE—*See* Water.

DENOTE' — mark, sig'nify, express', show, in'dicate, imply'. *See* Betoken, Mean, Mark.

DENSE—thick, close, compact', heav'y. *See* Thick, Close, Tight.

DENY'—*See* Call *back*.

DEPRAV'ITY — corrup'tion, deprava'tion, wic'kedness, vice, prof'ligacy, crime, sin. *See* Iniquity, Crime, Debt.

DESCRIBE'—depict', delin'eate, rep'resent, mark, explain', define', recount'. *See* Explain, Relate, Write.

DESERT'—*See* Alone, Desolate.

DESIGN'—plan, representa'tion, sketch; contri'vance, proj'ect, plan, scheme; pur'pose, pur'port, inten'tion, aim. *See* Intention, Aim, Plan.

DESIGN'—delin'eate, sketch, form an out'line; pur'pose, intend', mean; project', scheme, plan, mach'inate, plot, colleague', contrive'. *See* Mean, Invent, Plot, Plan, Contrive.

DESIRE'—*See* Wish, Hope, Avarice, Lust.

DES'OLATE — devast'ated, laid waste, neglect'ed, destroy'ed; sol'itary, des'ert, void, bar'ren; waste, drear'y, drear, uninhab'ited, sad, mel'ancholy, gloom'y, des'titute, lone'ly, lone; desert'ed of God, afflict'ed, depriv'ed of com'fort. *See* Abandoned, Alone, Lonely.

DESPAIR' — hope'lessness, hope'less state despera'tion, despair'ing; despond'ency. *See* Lowness, Hopeless.

DESPISE'—*See* Disdain, Contumely.

DESPISE'—disdain', contem'n, scorn, slight, disregard', neglect'. *See* Disdain, Neglect.

DES'POT—*See* King.

DESPOT'IC—ar'bitrary, ab'solute, self-willed, supreme', independ'ent, uncontrol'led, unlim'ited, unrestrict'ed; tyran'nical. *See* Arbitrary.

DES'TINY—state appoint'ed *or* predeterm'ined, ul'timate fate; fate, neces'sity, lot, doom, appoint'ment. *See* Necessity, Ordain, Fix.

DESTROY'—*See* Build, Waste.

DESTRUC'TION *great*—slau'ghter, car'nage, but'chery, mas'sacre, hav'oc, mur'der, trucida'tion. *See* Waste, Kill, Slaughter, Hurt.

DETERM'INED—end'ed, conclu'ded, deci'ded, lim'ited, fix'ed, set'tled, resolv'ed, direct'ed; res'olute, bold, firm, stead'y, per'emptory, deci'sive. *See* Bold, Firm, Ordain, Undetermined.

DEV'IL—*See* Enemy, Adversary.

DEVOTE'—*See* Set *apart*.

DEVOUR'—*See* Swallow.

DIC'TION — phraseol'ogy, word'ing, style, expressi'on, man'ner of expressi'on. *See* Language, Speech.

DIC'TIONARY — lex'icon, vocab'ulary, nomencla'ture, gloss'ary. *See* Nomenclature.

DIE—*See* Death.

DIF'FERENCE—distinc'tion, discrimina'tion, disagree'ment, dissimilar'ity, varia'tion, vari'ety, divers'ity, dissimil'itude, dispar'ity, inequal'ity, contrari'ety; dispute', va'riance, debate', conten'tion, quar'rel, con'troversy, dissen'sion, dis'cord. *See* Disagreement, Quarrel.

DIF'FERENT—*See* Unlike.

DIF'FICULT—not e'asy, hard to do, labo'rious, elab'orate, ar'duous; unaccom'modating, rig'id, austere'. *See* Severe.

DIF'FICULTY (*opposed to easiness or facility*)—hard'ship, lab'or, toil; perplex'ity, embar'rassment, troub'le; imped'iment, ob'stacle, obstruc'tion, oppositi'on, hin'derance, let. *See* Hinderance, Obstacle, Trouble, Ease.

DIL'IGENCE—*See* Attention.

DIL'IGENT—assid'uous, sed'ulous, attent'ive, indus'trious, care'ful, labo'rious, persever'ing, con'stant, ac'tive. *See* Active.

DIREC'TION—aim; course, line; or'der, con'duct, man'agement, dispo'sal, administra'tion, gui'dance, superintend'ence, supervisi'on; address', superscrip'tion. *See* Bent, Aim, Lead, Show.

DISAGREE'MENT—dif'ference, divisi'on, dissen'sion, dis'cord, va'riance, strife, quar'rel; unsuit'ableness. *See* Agreement, Difference, Quarrel.

DISCERN'IBLE—percep'tible, vis'ible, discrim'inable, distin'guishable, discov'erable, ascertain'able; man'ifest, ob'vious, appa'rent, ev'ident. *See* Clear, See.

DISCHARGE'—*See* Do, Pay, Receipt, Clear.

DISCI'PLE—adhe'rent, fol'lower, par'tisan; learn'er, schol'ar. *See* Follower, Scholar.

DIS'CIPLINE—train'ing, educa'tion, instruc'tion, cultiva'tion and improve'ment; correct'ness, or'der, control', restraint', gov'ernment, rule; subjec'tion; correc'tion, chast'isement, pun'ishment. *See* Education, Order, Improvement, Punish.

DISCOURSE'—*See* Speech, Dissertation.

DISCOV'ER—*See* Find *out*, Appear *make*.

DISCOV'ER—find out, invent', contrive', design', devise'; ascertain', detect'; uncov'er, lay open, disclose', show, make vis'ible, reveal', make known, divulge', man'ifest, declare', expose'; espy'. *See* Contrive, Invent, Declare, Publish, Show.

DISDAIN'—contempt', contemp'tuousness, scorn; haught'iness, hauteur', ar'rogance; indigna'tion. *See* Contumely, Despise, Contemptible.

DISEASE'—*See* Illness, Sick.

DISFIG'URE—deform', deface', change to a worse form, mar, impair', injure the form of. *See* Injure, Crooked, Form, Order *put out of*.

DISGRACE'—disfa'vour, disesteem', discred'it, dishon'or, disrepute', disreputa'tion, scan'dal, reproach', ig'nominy, shame, in'famy; o'dium, ob'loquy, oppro'brium. *See* Ashamed, Slander, Contumely, Lower, Shameful, Stain, Blemish.

DISGUST'—disrel'ish, distaste', disinclina'tion, dislike'; aver'sion, repug'nance, antip'athy, o'dium, offens'iveness, ha'tred; loth'ing, nau'sea, nau'seousness. *See* Nausea, Hatred, Displeasure, Disgrace.

DISOWN'—disclaim', disavow', not to own, not to allow', deny'; renounce', reject'; recant', abjure', retract'. *See* Call *back*.

DISPEL'—drive asun'der, disperse', dis'sipate, ban'ish, scat'ter. *See* Scatter, Spread *abroad*.

DISPLEASE'—dissat'isfy, annoy', tease, vex, offend', an'ger, ir'ritate, wor'ry, provoke'. *See* Anger, Offend, Worry.

DISPLEAS'URE—dissatisfac'tion, disapproba'tion, dislike', distaste', vexa'tion, indigna'tion, offense', chagrin', mortifica'tion, an'ger, annoy'ance. *See* Anger, Disgust, Enmity.

DISPOSITI'ON—dispo'sal, or'der, meth'od, distribu'tion, arrange'ment, adjust'ment; nat'ural fit'ness or tend'ency; inclina'tion, bent, bi'as, propens'ity, propen'sion; tem'per, frame, mood, hu'mor. *See* Order, Arrangement, Humor, Bent.

DISSERTA'TION—treat'ise, es'say, disquisiti'on, discus'sion, discourse'. *See* Argument, Essay.

DISTIN'GUISH—make or ascertain' dif'ference, discrim'inate, sep'arate, discern', spec'ify; make em'inent or known, sig'nalize. *See* Perceive, Separate, Find *out*.

DIS'TRICT—divisi'on, cir'cuit, por'tion, allot'ment; quar'ter, tract, re'gion, ter'ritory, coun'try. *See* Part, Country, Kingdom, Dominion.

DIVINE'—*See* Clergyman.

DO—perform', effect', effect'uate, bring to pass, ex'ecute, carry into effect', accom'plish, achieve', prac'tice; exert'; discharge', convey'; fin'ish, transact'. *See* Accom'plish, Bring *about*, Make, Effect, Finish.

DO *a crime*—commit', effect', per'petrate.

DOC'TOR—*See* Scholar.

DOC'TRINE—whatever is taught; prin'ciple, truth, positi'on; dog'ma, ten'et; pos'tulate; max'im. *See* Truth.

DOLE'FUL—sor'rowful, express'ing grief, mourn'ful, mel'ancholy, sad, afflict'ed, rue'ful, woe'ful, pit'iful, pit'eous, dis'mal, gloom'y. *See* Dull, Sad, Pitiable, Melancholy.

DOMIN'ION—sov'ereign or supreme' author'ity, rule, sway, author'ity, control', pow'er; reign, em'pire, sov'ereignty, gov'ernment; ter'ritory, region, coun′try, dis′trict; an order of angels. *See* Government, Kingdom, District.

Dote—*See* Madness.

Doubt—*See* Difficulty.

Doub′ted *not to be*—indis′putable, incontrovert′ible, incontest′able, indu′bitable, unques′tionable, undeni′able, irrefu′table, irref′ragable, doubt′less, ques′tionless, ev′ident, cer′tain. *See* Certain, Sure, Actual.

Doze—slum′ber, nap, be drow′sy, sleep ligh′tly; stu′pify.

Draw *back*—retire′, recede′, retreat′, withdraw′; *out* or *from*, extract′, extort′, exact′; derive′, deduce′; abstract′.

Dread—*See* Fear, Fright, Terrify.

Dream—*See* Sleep.

Dregs—sed′iment, lees, grounds, fec′ulence, fe′ces, waste or worth′less matter, dross, sco′ria, fil′ings, rust, sweep′ings, refuse′, scum, rec′rement. *See* Remains.

Dress—appar′el, attire′, hab′it, suit, clothes, array′. *See* Clothes, Covering, Formality, Beautify.

Drink—bev′erage, liq′uor, tip′ple; po′tion, draught, dose.

Drive—*See* Force.

Droop—sink or hang down, lan′guish, pine, fail, sink, decline′, fade, faint, grow weak, be dispir′ited. *See* Faint, Weaken.

Dross—*See* Remains.

Drunk—drunk′en, intox′icated, ine′briated, crap′ulous, intem′perate; drench′ed, sat′urated with moisture or liquor; tip′sy, fud′dled, tip′pled. *See* Intoxication, Luxury.

Dru′id—*See* Priest.

Dry′ness—ar′idness, arid′ity, sic′city, drought, thirst; bar′renness, jejune′ness, want of ornament *or* pathos; want of feeling or sensibility. *See* Insensibility.

Dull—stu′pid, dolt′ish, block′ish, slow of understanding; heav′y, slug′gish, without life, spirit, *or* motion, vap′id, insens′ate, insens′ible, insip′id, flat, phlegmat′ic, sleep′y, drows′y; sat′urnine; sad, mel′ancholy, dis′mal, gloom′y, deject′ed, dispir′ited, cheer′less; gross, clog′gy; not bright, cloud′ed, tarn′ished, dim, obscure′, not viv′id, cloud′y, o′vercast, not clear; blunt, obtuse′. *See* Sad, Doleful, Flat, Lifeless, Dead, Lonely, Pale.

Dumb—mute, si′lent, not speak′ing, speech′less, tac′iturn; tac′it. *See* Silent.

Dwell—inhab′it, reside′, live, abide′; remain′, stay, rest, contin′ue; *for a time*, vis′it, so′journn, lodge. *See* Abide, Stay.

E.

E′agerness—ardent desire, animated zeal, vehement longing, avid′ity; ar′dour, ar′dency, zeal, heat, warmth, ferv′ency, ve′hemence, impetuos′ity; for′wardness, read′iness, prompt′ness. *See* Zeal, Greediness, Heat Warmth, Quickness.

Ease—facil′ity, e′asiness, light′ness; qui′et, rest. *See* Quiet, Difficulty.

Ease *or* Calm—free from pain, &c., relieve′, mit′igate, alle′viate, assuage′, allay′; calm, appease′, pac′ify, soothe, compose′, tran′quillize, qui′et, still. *See* Calm, Quiet, Allay.

Eat—*See* Swallow.

Eccen′tric—de′viating, anom′alous, irreg′ular; depart′ing, wan′dering, roam′ing, ro′ving. *See* Odd, Wander.

Ecclesias′tic — theolo′gian, divine′, priest, cler′gyman, prel′ate, &c. *See* Clergyman, Divine.

Edge—mar′gin, brink, bor′der, brim, verge, rim, extrem′ity; sharp′ness, ac′rimony, keen′ness, intense′ness. *See* Brink, Bounds, Sharpness.

Ed′ify—*See* Build.

Educa′tion—the bringing up, instruc′tion, train′ing; forma′tion, tuiti′on, nur′ture, breed′ing, informa′tion. *See* Instruct, Improvement, Discipline.

Effect′—what is produc′ed, con′sequence, result′, event′, is′sue; pur′pose, intent′; util′ity, prof′it, advan′tage; real′ity, fact; force, valid′ity; *effects*, goods, mov′ables personal estate. *See* Issue, Goods, Make, Bring *about*, Operation.

Effect′ *producing*—effect′ive, effici′ent, effect′ual, effica′cious, op′erative, act′ive, cau′sing to be, product′ive; a′ble, pow′erful. *See* Make, Active, Able, Powerful.

Ef′figy—im′age, like′ness, pic′ture, resem′blance, representa′tion, simil′itude, por′trait, fig′ure, make. *See* Form, Likeness.

El′der—*See* Old.

El′ement—*See* Constituent.

Em′blem—inlay′, mosa′ic work; type, sym′bol, fig′ure, allusive picture, painted enigma, typical designation, representa′tion, allu′sion. *See* Figure, Mark.

Embrace′—take, clasp *or* inclose in the arms, press, hug, gripe; seize eagerly, lay hold on, receive *or* take willingly; comprehend′, include′ *or* take in; comprise′, inclose′, com′pass, encom′pass, contain′, encir′cle;

salute′, &c. *See* Take, Kiss, Contain, Compass.

EMP′TY *space*—vac′uum, vacu′ity, void, chasm. *See* Void.

EM′ULOUS—*See* Jealousy.

ENCOUR′AGE—give courage to, coun′tenance, sanc′tion, abet′, fos′ter, support′, cher′ish; embold′en, an′imate, inspire′, incite′, in′stigate, inspir′it, urge, impel′. *See* Animate, Cheer, Foster, Protect, Strengthen, Support.

END—*See* Finish.

END — extreme′, point, extrem′ity, lim′it, termina′tion, close, conclu′sion, ul′timate state; fin′ish, con′sequence, is′sue, result′; ultimate point, ob′ject intend′ed, scope, aim, drift. *See* Aim, Bound, Intention, Issue.

END *without*—end′less, eter′nal, everlast′ing, sempitern′al, in′finite, interm′inable, perpet′ual, contin′ual, incess′ant; bound′less, illim′itable, unlim′ited. *See* Unbounded, Bounds, Immense.

ENDOW′—gift, indue′, invest′, supply′ with, furn′ish, imbue′. *See* Invest.

EN′EMY—*See* Adversary, Inimical.

ENGROSS′—seize in the gross, take the whole, engage wholly, absorb′, monop′olize, appro′priate. *See* Swallow up.

ENJOY′MENT—fruiti′on, pleas′ure, satisfac′tion, gratifica′tion, agree′able sensa′tions, delight′, delecta′tion; possessi′on, oc′cupancy. *See* Pleasure, Sport.

ENLIGHT′EN—make light, shed light on, supply with light; light′en, illume′, illu′mine, illu′minate; give light to, give clearer views, instruct′. *See* Light, Instruct.

ENLIST′—enroll′, enter in a list, reg′ister, record′, chron′icle; recruit′. *See* Catalogue.

ENLI′VEN—an′imate, cheer, exhil′arate. *See* Animate, Cheer.

EN′MITY—unfriendly disposition, ill′-will, malev′olence, animos′ity, ha′tred, malig′nity, hostil′ity, ran′cour, mal′ice, aver′sion, displea′sure. *See* Displeasure, Hatred, Anger, Envy, Malice, Spite.

ENOUGH′ — suffici′ency; abun′dance, plent′y; com′petence, com′petency, ad′equacy. *See* Abounding.

ENTANG′LE—twist, entwine′, im′plicate, infold′, inwrap′, involve′, perplex′, embar′rass, distract′, com′plicate, in′tricate, puz′zle, bewild′er; insnare′, catch, trepan′, entrap′, illaq′ueate. *See* Twist, Cross, Grieve, Puzzle, Intricacy, Confused.

ENTHU′SIAST—person of ardent zeal, zeal′ot, fanat′ic, visi′onary; big′ot. *See* Warm.

ENTIRE′—*See* Whole.

EN′TRAILS—*See* Bowels.

ENTREAT′—beseech′, sup′plicate, importune′, exhort′, implore′. *See* Beg, Ask, Pray, Encourage.

ENTREAT′Y — urgent prayer, earnest petition, pray′er, supplica′tion, petiti′on, request′, solicita′tion, suit, exhorta′tion, persua′sion. *See* Petition, Beg, Pray.

EN′VY—malev′olence, ill′-will, mal′ice, malig′nity, pique, grudge; suspici′on, jeal′ousy, public o′dium, ill-repute′, invid′iousness; ri′valry, emula′tion, competiti′on. *See* Enmity, Malice, Spite.

E′QUAL—same, e′ven, u′niform, not va′riable, e′quable; just, eq′uitable, right; ad′equate, propor′tionate, commens′urate, equiv′alent, com′petent, meet. *See* Able, Suitable, Fair, Like, Even, Inadequate.

ERECT′—*See* Right.

ESPOUS′ED—engaged in marriage, betroth′ed, affi′anced, contract′ed, mar′ried, wed′ded; embrac′ed. *See* Marriage.

ESPY′—see, discern′, detect′, discov′er, perceive′, descry′. *See* Perceive, Look.

ES′SAY—tract, treat′ise; essay′, trial, &c. *See* Dissertation, Attempt, Try.

ESTEEM′—*See* Value, Reckon.

ETERN′AL—*See* Lasting.

E′VEN—lev′el, smooth, not rough, flat, plain; u′niform, e′qual, calm, e′quable. *See* Equal, Calm.

EVENT′—*See* Chance.

EV′ERY—*See* All, Whole.

EV′IDENCE—proof, test′imony, attesta′tion; vouch′er, certif′icate, depositi′on. *See* Prove, Proof.

E′VIL—*See* Ill, Bad, Wicked.

EXAM′PLE — pat′tern, mod′el, par′adigm, cop′y, prec′edent, for′mer in′stance, exem′plar, orig′inal, arch′etype, in′stance, ex′emplary person; sam′ple, spec′imen. *See* Copy, Likeness.

EXCESS′—more than enough′, super′flousness; superflu′ity, redund′ancy; exu′berance, superabund′ance. *See* Extravagance, Much *too*.

EXCUR′SION—ram′bling; expediti′on, journ′ey, trip, tour, jaunt, ram′ble *See* Ramble.

EXCUSE′ — apol′ogy, plea, defense′ pretense′, pretext′. *See* Defense, Cloak, Covering.

EXHORT′—*See* Encourage, Entreat.

EXILE′—ban′ish, expa′triate, expel′, proscribe′. *See* Banishment.

EXPENSE′—money expended, cost, charge, price; dear′ness, cost′liness, expens′iveness. *See* Lavish.

EXPENS′IVE—cost′ly, sump′tuous, val-uable, dear; given to expense′, ex-trav′agant, lav′ish, prod′igal, pro-fuse′; lib′eral, gen′erous. *See* Spend, Lavish, Waste.

EXPE′RIENCE—*See* Trial.

EXPERT′—dex′trous, skil′ful, read′y. *See* Ready.

EX′PIATE—atone′ for, sat′isfy, propiti′-ate; compens′ate, requite′. *See* Amends *make*, Satisfy.

EXPLAIN′—make plain, expound′, il-lus′trate, ex′plicate, unfold′, elu′ci-date, illu′minate, inter′pret, describe′, define′, solve. *See* Describe, Clear, Relate, Unfold.

EXPLANA′TION—expositi′on, illustra′-tion, interpreta′tion, explica′tion, definiti′on, descrip′tion, elucida′tion, solu′tion. *See* Comment.

EXPLAN′ATORY—serving to explain′, exeget′ical, expos′itory, descrip′tive, illus′trative, elu′cidatory; explic′it, express′; circumstan′tial, minute′. *See* Clear.

EXPUNGE′—efface′, blot out, oblit′e-rate, erase′, rase, can′cel.

EXTRAV′AGANCE—wand′ering beyond lim′its, prodigal′ity, profu′sion, pro-fuse′ness, excess′; irregular′ity, wild′ness, prepost′erousness, mons-tros′ity. *See* Excess, Waste, Lavish.

EXTREM′ITY—*See* End.

F.

FA′BLE—*See* Story.

FAB′RIC—frame, struc′ture, build′ing, ed′ifice; tex′ture, context′ure, web, work′manship. *See* Building, House.

FAC′TION—jun′to, clique, cabal′, part′y, coterie′; tu′mult, dis′cord, dissen′-sion. *See* Quarrelling, Party, Plot.

FADE—*See* Droop.

FAIL—*See* Weakness, Fault, Miscar-riage.

FAIL′URE—fail′ing, defic′ience, cessa-tion of supply, total defect; omissi′on, non-perform′ance; decay′, defect′; bank′ruptcy, break′ing in estate, break′ing, insol′vency.

FAINT—weak, fee′ble, lan′guid, ex-haust′ed, low; not bright; not loud, low; imper′fect, not strik′ing; cow′-ardly, tim′orous; not vig′orous, not act′ive; deject′ed, depress′ed, dis-pir′ited. *See* Weak, Droop, Low.

FAIR—clear, beau′tiful, hand′some; clear, not cloud′y; o′pen, frank, hon′est; e′qual, just, eq′uitable, right, reas′onable, upright′; hon′orable, mild; civ′il, pleas′ing, not harsh. *See* Beautiful, Clear, Art *without*, Equal, Open, Reasonable.

FAITH—*See* Trust.

FAITH′FULNESS—fidel′ity, fe′alty, loy′-alty, trust′iness, hon′esty, firm ad-he′rence, strict perform′ance; truth, verac′ity. *See* Belief, Truth, Honesty.

FAITH′LESS—unbeliev′ing, not believ-ing; perfid′ious, treach′erous, pu′nic, disloy′al, unfaith′ful, neglect′ful; false. *See* Deceitful, Unfaithfulness.

FALL—*See* Tumble.

FALSE—*See* Deceive, Genuine *not*.

FALSE′HOOD—untruth′, fabrica′tion, fic′-tion, fals′ity, lie, fib; mendac′ity; deceit′, fraud, fal′lacy, duplic′ity, doub′le-deal′ing, false′ness, coun′ter-feit, impos′ture. *See* Cheat, Cun-ning, Invent, Lie, Story.

FAME—public report *or* ru′mor; celeb′-rity, renown′; reputa′tion, cred′it, esteem′, hon′or; ru′mor, report′. *See* Character, Respect, Hearsay, Name.

FAM′ILY—*See* House.

FAMIL′IAR—acquaint′ed with, con′ver-sant, vers′ed in; af′fable, free, so′-ciable. *See* Free.

FAMILIAR′ITY—in′timate acquain′-tance, in′timacy, affabil′ity, sociabil′-ity, cour′tesy, free′dom. *See* Free-dom, Acquaintance, Intimacy.

FA′MOUS—renown′ed, cel′ebrated, much talk′ed of and prais′ed, illus′-trious, distin′guished, em′inent; con-spic′uous; ex′cellent, transcend′ent. *See* Noted.

FAN′CIFUL—full of fan′cies or wild im′-ages, fantas′tical, whim′sical, ide′al, visi′onary, chimer′ical, caprici′ous, hu′morsome, freak′ish; imag′inative. *See* Odd, Imaginary.

FAN′CY—*See* Think.

FARCE—*See* Sport.

FAS′TEN—make fast, lock, bolt, bar, secure′, fix; join to, affix′, attach′, append′, annex′, conjoin′, adjoin′, subjoin′; adhere′, cohere′, stick. *See* Fix, Join.

FATE—*See* Destiny.

FATNESS—obes′ity, obese′ness, flesh′-iness, cor′pulency, gross′ness, coarse′-ness; unc′tuousness, sli′miness, rich′-ness, fertil′ity, fruit′fulness. *See* Bigness, Lusty.

FAULT—*See* Blame.

FAULT—er′ring, fail′ing, er′ror, mis-take′, blun′der, defect′, blem′ish, imperfec′tion, slight offense′, foib′le, weak′ness, frail′ty. *See* Mistake, Blemish, Weakness, Culpable.

FA′VOR—kind regard′, kind′ness, coun-tenance, friend′ly dispositi′on, grace, kind act *or* office, benef′icence, benev′olence, good′-will, len′ity; leave, par′don; advan′tage, conve′nience; support′, defense′, vindica′tion. *See* Kindness, Charity, Support.

Fawn—coax, wheed′le, cajole′, soothe, hu′mor, flat′ter meanly, blan′dish, court servilely, cringe and bow to gain favor. *See* Flatter, Cajole.

Fear—apprehen′sion, alarm′, dread, ter′ror, fright, pan′ic, consterna′tion; anxi′ety, solic′itude; slav′ish dread; fil′ial fear, reveren′tial fear, awe, rev′erence, venera′tion; law and word of God. *See* Cowardice, Afraid, Dread, Fright, Terrify, Trembling, Jealousy.

Fear′ful—full of fear, apprehen′sive, afraid′, tim′id, tim′orous, want′ing cour′age; impress′ing fear, fright′ful, dread′ful, tremend′ous, ter′rible, terrif′ic, for′midable, hor′rible, hor′rid, horrif′ic. *See* Afraid, Formidable, Ghastly.

Feast—ban′quet, regale′, sump′tuous entertain′ment, rich repast′, delici′ous meal, carous′al, treat; fes′tival, hol′iday. *See* Luxury.

Fee′ble—*See* Weak.

Feed—*See* Nourish.

Feel′ing—sensa′tion, sense; sensibil′ity, susceptibil′ity; excite′ment, emo′tion; path′os, tend′erness, concern′. *See* Sense, Kindness.

Feel′ing *want of*—ap′athy, &c. *See* Insensibility.

Feign—*See* Forged.

Fel′low-helper—coadju′tor, assist′ant; col′league, part′ner. *See* Share.

Fence—wall, hedge, ditch, bank, &c.; guard, secur′ity, defense′; fens′ing. *See* Ditch, Defense, Guard.

Fe′ver—*See* Hot.

Fierce—*See* Cruel.

Fig′ure—*See* Form.

Fig′ure *of speech*—trope, met′aphor, al′legory, meton′ymy, synec′dochē, i′rony, &c. *See* Speech, Emblem.

Find *out*—discov′er, invent′, detect′, ascertain′; unrid′dle, solve; descry′, discern′, discrim′inate, distin′guish. *See* Discover, Invent, Distinguish.

Fine—mulct, amerce′, confis′cate; pecu′niary pun′ishment, mulct, amerce′ment, pen′alty, for′feit, for′feiture, confisca′tion. *See* Punish, Pay.

Fin′ish—complete′, per′fect, accom′plish, conclude′, end, ter′minate, close. *See* Do, Perfect.

Firm—fix′ed, compact′, hard, sol′id, sclerot′ic, sta′ble, stead′y; con′stant, unsha′ken, res′olute; strong, robust′, sturdy. *See* Determined, Solid, Strong.

Fit—suit′able, conve′nient, meet, becom′ing, expe′dient, prop′er, apt; qual′ified. *See* Able, Becoming, Suitable, Meet, Necessary.

Fit—adapt′, suit, accom′modate, fur′nish, adjust′, propor′tion; qual′ify, prepare′, fit out, furn′ish, equip′, accou′tre. *See* Qualify.

Fix—make stable, set immov′ably, des′tine, estab′lish, set′tle, confirm′, ingraft′, implant′; resolve′, determ′ine, lim′it; appoint′, in′stitute; make fast, fas′ten, secure′, attach′; place stead′ily, direct′. *See* Settle, Appoint, Assign, Ordain, Fasten.

Flat—smooth; lev′el, horizont′al; pros′trate, fal′len; taste′less, stale, vap′id, insip′id, dead; inan′imate, life′less, inert′; dull, unan′imated, frig′id; deject′ed, spir′itless, depress′ed; unpleas′ing; per′emptory, ab′solute, pos′itive, down′right; not sharp or shrill, not acute′; low, dull. *See* Dull, Inanimate, Lifeless, Taste, Positive, Low.

Flat′ter—ad′ulate, fawn, blan′dish, compliment′, soothe, please, grat′ify, gloze, wheed′le, coax. *See* Fawn, Cajole.

Flay—skin, exco′riate, strip off the skin, gall, rub or wear off the skin, abrade′.

Fleet—*See* Ship.

Flirt—pert hussy, jilt, coquette′.

Flood—*See* Water.

Flour′ish—grow luxu′riantly, thrive, pros′per, succeed′. *See* Prosper.

Flow—*See* Issue, Overflow.

Flut′ter—move or flap the wings rapidly, hov′er; pal′pitate, vi′brate, un′dulate, pant. *See* Palpitate.

Fold—*See* Entangle.

Fol′lower—adhe′rent, par′tisan, depend′ent, vas′sal, retain′er, im′itator; disci′ple, schol′ar, lear′ner; pursu′er; succes′sor; attend′ant, compan′ion, asso′ciate. *See* Disciple, Companion, Scholar, Villain.

Fol′ly—weak′ness of in′tellect, imbecil′ity of mind, want of understand′ing; non′sense, fool′ery, sil′liness, inan′ity, irrational′ity, unreas′onableness; trif′ling, pueril′ity; weak′ness, vacu′ity. *See* Madness, Weakness.

Food—di′et, reg′imen; meat, al′iment, vic′tuals, provis′ion, eat′ables, ed′ibles, fare, main′tenance; *for beasts*, prov′ender, fod′der, lit′ter; pas′ture, pas′turage. *See* Livelihood.

Fool—nat′ural, id′iot, driv′eller, sim′pleton, chang′ling, trif′ler. *See* Coxcomb, Mimic, Blockhead.

Fool-hard′y—daring without judgment, rash, precip′itate, hast′y, foolishly bold, incau′tious, dar′ing, advent′urous, vent′uresome, vent′urous. *See* Bold, Hasty.

Fool′ish—void of understanding *or* sound judgment, weak in in′tellect; unwise′, impru′dent; sim′ple, sil′ly, irrati′onal, vain, trif′ling; ridic′ulous, absurd′, prepos′terous, unreas′onable, des′picable; wick′ed, sin′ful. *See* Weak, Vain, Insensible, Wicked, Impertinent.

Forbid′—prohib′it, interdict′, bid not to do, proscribe′, inhib′it; restrain′, check, oppose′, hin′der, obstruct′; deny′, gainsay′, contradict′. *See* Gainsay, Keep, Check, Hinder.

Force—compel′, coerce′, constrain′, oblige′, neces′sitate; enforce′, urge, press, drive, impel′; storm, assault′; exact′, extort′. *See* Oblige, Make.

Force—strength, active power, pow′er, vig′or, might, en′ergy; vi′olence, compuls′ory power, coer′cion, compul′sion, obliga′tion, constraint′, des′tiny, neces′sity; moment′um *or* quantity of power produced by the action of one body on another; virt′ue, ef′ficacy; valid′ity, power to bind or hold; strength or power for war, ar′mament, troops, ar′my, na′vy; *phys′ical force*, or force of material bodies; *mor′al force*, or power of acting on or influencing the mind; *mechan′ical force*, or power that belongs to bodies at rest or in motion,—as pressure, tension, &c. *See* Power, Obligation, Oblige.

For′eign—*See* Outward, Abroad.

Fore′sight—fore′thought, premedita′tion, fore′cast; pres′cience, foreknowl′edge, prognostica′tion; prov′ident care; previous contrivance. *See* Before, Knowledge.

Foretel′—*See* Betoken, Know.

Forg′ed—ham′mered, beat′en, made; coun′terfeit, feign′ed, false, fictiti′ous, invent′ed, fab′ricated, dissem′bled, fram′ed, untrue′, base. *See* Falsehood, Genuine *not*, Art *made by*, Invent.

Forgive′—*See* Clear, Excuse.

Forlorn′—*See* Alone, Solitary.

Form—shape, fig′ure, mould, configura′tion, conforma′tion, construc′tion; man′ner, dispositi′on; mod′el, pat′tern, draught; beau′ty, el′egance, splend′or, dig′nity; regular′ity, meth′od, or′der; empty show, external appearance, sem′blance; stated method, established practice, rit′ual, proscribed mode, rite, cer′emony, observ′ance, fashi′on. *See* Appearance, Attitude, Way, Make, Effigy, Order.

Form—shape, mould, fashi′on, mod′el, mod′ify; scheme, plan, contrive′, invent′; arrange′, combine′; make, frame, cause to be, create′, produce′, compose′, con′stitute, construct′, compile′, estab′lish; enact′, ordain′. *See* Plan, Invent, Make, Ordain.

For′mal—according to form, reg′ular, method′ical; precise′, ceremo′nious, exact′, stiff, express′; extern′al, constit′uent, essen′tial, prop′er. *See* Regular, Constituent.

Formal′ity—practice *or* observance of forms, external appear′ance, cer′emony, mode, meth′od, sys′tem, or′der, rule, precisi′on, deco′rum, de′cency, seem′liness; mode of dress, hab′it, robe. *See* System, Order, Dress.

For′midable—exciting fear *or* apprehension, impressing dread, appal′ling, terrif′ic, ter′rible, deter′ring, tremend′ous, hor′rible, fright′ful, shock′ing. *See* Fearful, Ghastly, Hideous.

Forsake′—*See* Leave, Abandon.

For′tunate—luck′y, success′ful, pros′perous, hap′py; propiti′ous, auspici′ous. *See* Lucky, Happy.

For′tune—chance, haz′ard, ac′cident, luck; success′, event′; chance of life, means of living, wealth; estate′, possessi′ons; large estate, great wealth; futur′ity, des′tiny, fate, doom, lot. *See* Chance, Misfortune, Riches, Destiny,

Fos′ter — feed, nour′ish, support′, bring up; cher′ish, har′bor, indulge′, encour′age. *See* Breed, Encourage, Harbor, Nourish.

Found—lay the basis, set, set′tle, place, estab′lish, fix; in′stitute, begin′, orig′inate; rest, ground; build, construct′, rear, erect′. *See* Settle, Fix, Begin, Build.

Foun′tain—*See* Spring.

Frame—*See* Make.

Fraud—*See* Cheat, Deceitful.

Free—disengage′, disentan′gle, rid, strip, clear; set at liberty, lib′erate, enfran′chise, eman′cipate, res′cue, release′, relieve′, manumit′, loose, save, preserve′, deliv′er, exempt′. *See* Clear, Redeem, Liberty *being deprived of*.

Free—being at liberty, unconstrain′ed, unrestrain′ed, unconfin′ed, permit′ted, allow′ed; o′pen, can′did, frank, ingen′uous, unreserv′ed; lib′eral, gen′erous, bount′iful, munif′icent, not parsimo′nious; gratu′itous; famil′iar, e′asy; clear, exempt′, guilt′less, in′nocent. *See* Open, Clear, Generous, Ready.

Free′dom — lib′erty, independ′ence, unrestraint′; exemp′tion, priv′ilege, immu′nity, fran′chise; frank′ness, bold′ness; familiar′ity; li′cense, improper familiar′ity; libera′tion, emancipa'tion, release', enfranchise'-ment. *See* Privilege, Liberty *being deprived of*, Familiarity.

FREIGHT — car'go, bur'den, load, la'ding, transporta'tion of goods; ship's hire. *See* Burden, Ship.

FRET'FUL — ill-hu'mored, peev'ish, test'y, easily ir'ritated, splen'etic, an'gry, pet'ulent, cap'tious. *See* Cross, Angry, Complaining *always*.

FRIGHT — fright'en, ter'rify, scare, alarm', daunt, dismay', intim'idate; dishear'ten, discour'age, deter'. *See* Fear, Terrify, Dread.

FROL'IC—wild prank, flight of lev'ity, or gai'ety and mirth, game, jest, joke, gam'bol, fun. *See* Jest, Sport, Whim.

FRUIT'FUL — fer'tile, prolif'ic, preg'-nant, fe'cund, gen'erating, product'-ive, abund'ant, plent'iful, plent'eous. *See* Abounding, Breed.

FURY—*See* Madness.

G.

GAIN—get, win, earn, re'alize, obtain', acquire', procure', receive'; reach, attain' to, arrive' at;—gain, prof'it, in'terest, advan'tage, emol'ument, lu'cre, ben'efit. *See* Prosper, Profitable, Benefit.

GAINSAY'—contradict', oppose', deny', forbid', con'trovert, dispute'. *See* Forbid, Object.

GALL—*See* Anger, Spite.

GAP—o'pening, breach, break; av'e-nue, pas'sage, way; chasm, ap'er-ture, cleft, hia'tus; defect', flaw. *See* Opening, Way.

GATH'ER—*See* Calling *together*, Collection, Council.

GAY—mer'ry, air'y, jo'vial, spor'tive, frol'icsome; fine, show'y, fashi'ona-ble, styl'ish, gal'lant; dis'sipated, prof'ligate. *See* Merry, Showy.

GEN'ERATE—*See* Breed.

GEN'EROUS—well'born, no'ble, hon'or-able, magnan'imous; lib'eral, be-nign', benef'icent, bount'iful, boun'-teous, munif'icent, free to give; strong, full of spirit; full, overflow'-ing, abun'dant; *overmuch*, profuse', prod'igal, extrav'agant. *See* Free, Abounding, Strong, Full, Bounty.

GENTEEL'—polite', well'bred, easy and graceful, gen'tlemanly, gen'tleman-like, ur'bane, cour'teous, pol'ished, refin'ed, el'egant. *See* Polite.

GEN'TLE—*See* Calm, Soft, Kind.

GEN'UINE—na'tive, re'al, authen'tic, nat'ural, true, pure, not spu'rious; unadul'terated, unalloy'ed, unso-phis'ticated, unpollu'ted, pure, un-mix'ed, uncontam'inated. *See* Actual, Intrinsic, Sincere.

GEN'UINE *not*—spu'rious, unre'al, un-true', suppositi'ous, sophis'ticated, contam'inated, pollu'ted, viti'ated, corrup'ted, adul'terated, adul'terine. *See* Forged, Spurious, Bastard, Vain.

GHAST'LY—like a ghost, pale, dis'mal, death'like, cadav'erous, wan, grim, fright'ful, hid'eous, appall'ing, hor'-rible, shock'ing. *See* Fearful, Formidable, Hideous.

GHOST—spec'tre, appariti'on, phan'-tom, visi'on, hobgob'lin, fair'y, fay, elf, de'mon, evil spirit, dev'il. *See* Vision, Appearance.

GI'ANT—*See* Great.

GIBE—reproach', sneer, deride', taunt, scoff, rail at, flout, fleer, jeer. *See* Reproach, Abuse, Jest, Laugh at.

GIFT—dona'tion, don'ative, benefac'-tion, pres'ent, gratu'ity; reward', bribe; pow'er, fac'ulty, tal'ent, en-dow'ment; *by will*, leg'acy, bequest'; devise'. *See* Reward, Power.

GIM'BLET—*See* Bore.

GIRD—*See* Surround, Tie.

GIVE—bestow', confer', impart', com-mu'nicate, present', grant, allow', transmit', deliv'er; afford', supply', furn'ish; produce', show, exhib'it; ren'der, pronounce', yield, resign'; *back*, restore', return'. *See* Grant, Allow, Give up, Offer.

GIVE *up*—deliv'er, consign', cease, leave, resign', quit, yield, surren'der, relin'quish, cede, concede', aban'don, addict', devote'; renounce', ab'dicate, forego'; forsake', desert'. *See* Leave, Abandon, Lay.

GLAD—grat'ified, hap'py, pleas'ed, de-light'ed, rejoic'ed, exhil'arated; cheer'ful, joy'ous, joy'ful, exhil'arat-ing, exciting joy. *See* Happy, Merry, Lively.

GLAD'DEN—make glad, cheer, please, grat'ify, exhil'arate, delight', rejoice'. *See* Cheer, Rejoice.

GLANCE—glimpse, quick view, short transitory look, peep. *See* Look.

GLEAM—shoot of light, glim'mer, beam, ray; bright'ness, splen'dor. *See* Beam, Blaze, View, Shine.

GLIDE—*See* Fall.

GLOOM—obscur'ity, partial *or* total darkness, thick shade, cloud'iness, heav'iness, dul'ness, mel'ancholy, sad'ness, as'pect of sorrow, sul'len-ness. *See* Darkness, Dull, Lonely.

GLORY—*See* Honor.

GLOSS—make smooth and shining, varn'ish, cov'er; pal'liate, cover with excuse, exten'uate, les'sen. *See* Cloak, Lessen

GLOW—*See* Warm, Hot.

GNAW—*See* Eat.

GO—move, pass, flow, walk, trav'el, jour'ney, depart'; *up*, ascend', mount, rise; *forward*, advance', proceed', for'ward, promote'; *before*, precede', prevent', antic'ipate; *beyond*, transgress', exceed', surpass', excel', transcend'; *back*, recede', return', retreat', withdraw', retire, ret'rograde, ret'rocede; *in* or *on*, invade', encroach', intrench'. *See* Move, Ramble, Wander, Anticipate, Proceeding, Intrude.

GOAD—*See* Stir.

GOD'LIKE—resembling God, divine', superhu'man; heav'enly, celes'tial. *See* Heavenly.

GOD'LY—ho'ly, sanc'tified, right'eous, pi'ous, religi'ous, devout', sanctimo'nious. *See* Spiritual, Heavenly, Holy, Religion.

GO'ING *before*—prece'ding, forego'ing, antece'dent, pre'vious, ante'rior, pri'or, for'mer. *See* Introductory, Priority.

GOOD—ben'efit, in'terest, advan'tage, emol'ument, prof'it; wel'fare, prosper'ity; vir'tue, right'eousness. *See* Interest, Benefit, Kindness, Bounty.

GOODS—mov'ables, effects', chat'tels, fur'niture, personal estate; wares, mer'chandise, commod'ities, stock. *See* Stock, Merchandise, Property.

GORE—*See* Blood.

GOV'ERN—*See* Master.

GOV'ERNMENT—direc'tion, regula'tion, rule, control', sat'rapy, jurisdic'tion, restraint', man'agement, pow'er, domin'ion, sov'ereignty; administra'tion, constitu'tion, min'istry; em'pire, king'dom, state; executive power. *See* Dominion, Kingdom.

GRACE—*See* Mercy, Kindness, Becoming, Beautify.

GRAND—great, illus'trious, splen'did, magnif'icent, no'ble, dig'nified, el'evated, sublime', loft'y, exalt'ed, majes'tic, magiste'rial, state'ly, pomp'ous, august'. *See* Majestic, Great, High, Showy.

GRANT—admit', allow', yield, concede'; give, bestow', confer'; permit'; transfer', convey'. *See* Give, Allow, Suffer.

GRATE'FUL — thank'ful, impress'ed, mind'ful; agree'able, pleas'ing, ac'ceptable, grat'ifying, pleas'ant, wel'come; delic'ious. *See* Agreeable.

GRAT'ITUDE—thank'fulness, grate'fulness; thanks, acknowl'edgments. *See* Pleasure.

GRAVE—low, depres'sed; sol'emn; so'ber, se'rious, sedate'; plain, not gay, not show'y; impor'tant, momen'tous, weight'y. *See* Low, Sober, Severe, Important.

GREAT—*See* Grand, Large.

GREAT'NESS—*of size*, mag'nitude; bulk; cor'pulence; *of mind*, magnanim'ity; *of rank*, maj'esty; *of number*, major'ity; *of show* or *state*, magnif'icence, gran'deur. *See* Bigness, Size, Fatness, Large.

GREAT *or* GREATER *make*—mag'nify, enlarge', am'plify, exag'gerate, augment', ag'grandize; extol', exalt', el'evate. *See* Larger *make*, Praise, Heighten.

GREED'INESS—keenness of ap'petite, rav'enousness, glut'tony, vorac'ity, vora'ciousness, rapac'ity, rapa'ciousness; ardent desire, avid'ity, e'agerness. *See* Eagerness, Rapacious, Eat.

GRIEF—sor'row, regret', lamenta'tion, weep'ing, mourn'ing, afflic'tion, pain. *See* Pain, Repentance.

GRIEVE—mourn, bewail', bemoan', lament', complain', weep, sor'row, cry; afflict', wound, hurt, move, concern', distress', troub'le, perplex', vex, disqui'et; *for*, deplore', bewail', bemoan', &c.; *with another*, condole', sym'pathize. *See* Mourn, Complain, Hurt, Entangle.

GROSS—thick, bulk'y; fat, cor'pulent; coarse, rude, rough; indel'icate, mean, vul'gar, impure', unrefin'ed, inde'cent, obscene', improp'er, inappro'priate, unseem'ly, unbecom'ing, shame'ful; large, enor'mous, great; dense; unatten'uated; stup'id, dull; whole, entire'. *See* Thick, Common, Mean, Fatness.

GROW—*See* Spring.

GUARANTEE'—*See* Answerable *for*.

GUARD—*See* Security, Keep.

GUESS—*See* Think.

GUIDE—*See* Lead, Instruct.

GUILE—*See* Cheat.

H.

HAB'IT—*See* Dress, Custom.

HAM'MER—*See* Beat.

HAND'SOME—el'egant, nice, beau'tiful. *See* Beautiful, Nice.

HAP'PEN—*See* Chance.

HAP'PINESS—beat'itude, felic'ity, bliss, bles'sedness; wel'fare, prosper'ity, success'. *See* Prosper.

HAP'PY—*See* Glad, Fortunate.

HAR'BOR—ha'ven, port, bay, in'let, asy'lum, shel'ter, lodg'ing.

HAR'BOR—shel'ter, secure, secrete', receive', lodge; entertain', cher'ish, fos'ter, indulge'. *See* Hide, Protect, Foster.

HARD—*See* Solid.

HAR'DENED—made hard, in'durated, inu'red; ob'durate, cal'lous, impen'etrable, ob'stinate, unfeel'ing, insens'ible, impen'itent; remorse'less. *See* Insensible, Cruel.

HARD-HEART'ED—cru'el, pit'iless, mer'ciless, unfeel'ing, inhu'man, inex'orable, unmer'ciful. *See* Cruel, Unrelenting.

HARM—See Hurt.

HARM'LESS—not hurt'ful *or* inju'rious, innoc'uous, innox'ious, inoffens'ive, unoffend'ing; in'nocent, not guilt'y; unhurt', undam'aged, unin'jured. *See* Stain *without*.

HAS'TEN—make haste, haste, ex'pedite, speed, despatch', hur'ry, press, drive *or* urge forward, push on, precip'itate, accel'erate. *See* Quicken.

HAS'TY—quick, speed'y, hur'ried; e'ager, precip'itate, rash; cur'sory, slight; ir'ritable, iras'cible, passi'onate. *See* Quick, Careless, Foolhardy, Rashness, Angry, Tumultuous.

HATE'FUL—exciting great dislike', aver'sion *or* disgust', o'dious, abom'inable, detest'able, ex'ecrable; malig'nant, malev'olent. *See* Malicious.

HA'TRED—great dislike' *or* aver'sion, hate, en'mity, ran'cor, malev'olence, mal'ice, abhor'rence, detesta'tion, aver'sion, repug'nance, antip'athy, dislike'. *See* Enmity, Malice, Spite, Envy.

HAUGHT'Y—*See* Proud, Commanding.

HEAD—*See* Behead, Master.

HEAP—*See* Collection, Crowd.

HEAR—lis'ten, hear'ken, overhear', attend', heed, mark, observe', no'tice, regard', obey'; learn, be told. *See* Mark, Notice.

HEAR'SAY—common talk, ru'mor, report', fame, gos'sip, mere *or* idle talk. *See* Talk, Fame.

HEART'Y—from the heart, cor'dial, sincere', warm, zeal'ous; sound, strong, health'y. *See* Warm, Affectionate, Zealous.

HEAT—*See* Warm, Hot, Anger.

HEAV'ENLY—celes'tial; angel'ic, angel'ical, spir'itual, sublime', divine', supremely ex'cellent, superhu'man, supernat'ural, preternat'ural. *See* Godlike, Godly, Holy.

HEIGHT *of any thing*—cri'sis, ac'mé; cli'max, sum'mit, top, point, a'pex. *See* Top.

HEIGHT'EN—raise higher, lift, raise, el'evate, exalt'; advance', improve', mel'iorate, increase'; ag'gravate, exas'perate, ir'ritate, inflame', excite'. *See* Greater *make*, Lift, Anger.

HEL'MET—*See* Covering.

HELP—*See* Assist.

HER'ETIC—schismat'ic, secta'rian, sect'ary, skep'tic, in'fidel, unbelie'ver, disbelie'ver, pa'gan, heath'en.

HE'RO—*See* Brave.

HID'DEN—*See* Secret.

HIDE—keep secret, conceal', abscond', disguise', shel'ter, secrete', cov'er, screen, dissem'ble. *See* Harbor, Protect, Bury, Cover.

HID'EOUS—fright'ful, terrif'ic, ug'ly, hor'rible, hor'rid, dread'ful, shock'ing, detest'able. *See* Ghastly, Formidable.

HIGH—tall, el'evated, al'pine, loft'y, exalt'ed, rais'ed; no'ble, magnan'imous; aspir'ing, proud. *See* Proud, Grand, Majestic.

HIN'DER—stop, interrupt', intercept', obstruct', impede', prevent', oppose', thwart, embar'rass; retard', delay'. *See* Oppose, Check, Delay, Interrupt, Prevent, Stay.

HIN'DERANCE—let, imped'iment, ob'stacle, obstruc'tion, retard'ing, delay', oppositi'on, dif'ficulty. *See* Difficulty, Let, Obstacle.

HINT—suggest', in'timate, insin'uate, refer to, allude to, glance at—*a hint*, innuen'do. *See* Refer.

HIRE—*See* Pay.

HIS'TORY—*See* Chronicles.

HOLD—*See* Contain, Keep.

HO'LINESS—sanc'tity, sanc'titude, pi'ety, devo'tion, devout'ness, god'liness, right'eousness; sa'credness. *See* Religion.

HO'LY—whole, entire', per'fect; pure, immac'ulate; sanc'tified, pi'ous, devout', religi'ous; hal'lowed, con'secrated, sa'cred, divine'. *See* Whole, Godly, Heavenly, Spiritual.

HON'ESTY—integ'rity, prob'ity, rec'titude, up'rightness, jus'tice, pur'ity, sincer'ity, verac'ity, vir'tue; eq'uity, fair'ness, cand'or, truth, hon'or. *See* Justice, Chasteness, Truth, Uprightness, Faithfulness, Correct.

HON'OR—*See* Praise.

HON'OR—revere', respect', rev'erence, ven'erate, dig'nify, exalt', glor'ify, render glorious. *See* Respect.

HOPE—expecta'tion, wish, desire', anticipa'tion; opin'ion, belief', trust, depend'ence, reli'ance, con'fidence. *See* Wish, Belief, Confidence.

HOPE'LESS—without hope, des'perate, irretriev'able, irreme'diable, irrecov'erable, lost, gone, aban'doned; despair'ing, despon'dent. *See* Abandoned, Wicked, Despair.

HOT—cal'id, ferv'id, ferv'ent, ar'dent, burn'ing, fe'verish, sul'try, fi'ery, pip'ing; exci'ted, exas'perated, vi'olent, fu'rious, impet'uous, passi'onate, ir'ritable; e'ager, ve'hement, zeal′ous, an′imated, brisk, keen; ac′rid, bi′ting, stim′ulating, pun′gent. *See* Intense, Boil, Heat, Angry, Passionate, Warm, Keen.

HOUSE—habita′tion, res′idence, dwel′ling, abode′, cot′tage, vil′la, cot, hut, hov′el, cab′in, wig′wam, shed; man′sion, manse, mes′suage, ten′ement, ed′ifice, build′ing; tem′ple, church, mon′astery, col′lege, pal′ace; manner of living, the table; fam′ily, house′hold, an′cestors, lin′eage, race, dyn′asty, stock, tribe; delib′erative *or* legisla′tive body of men. *See* Building, Abode, Race, Stock.

HUE—*See* Color.

HUM′BLE—near the ground, low; low′ly, mod′est, meek, submis′sive; unpresum′ing, unpretend′ing, unassum′ing, unaspir′ing. *See* Low, Obedient.

HUM′BLE—make low, humil′iate, abase′, reduce′, low′er, bring down, debase′, degrade′, disgrace′, deject′; crush, break, subdue′; mor′tify; make lowly, make meek and submissive to the divine will; humble one's self, repent′, make contrite′. *See* Abase, Lower, Lessen.

HU′MOR—mois′ture, flu′id; turn of mind, tem′per, dispositi′on, mood, frame, turn, tend′ency, bent, bi′as; freak, whim, mag′got, caprice′; wit, sat′ire, burl′esque, drol′lery, fun, pleas′antry, jocular′ity, comical′ity. *See* Damp, Disposition, Bent.

HURT—*See* Injury, Grieve, Maim.

HURT—wound, bruise; det′riment, dam′age, loss, in′jury, disadvan′tage, harm, mis′chief, bane, prej′udice, deteriora′tion, deprav′ity, deprava′tion, corrup′tion, vitia′tion. *See* Bane, Destruction, Injury.

HURT′FUL—inju′rious, mis′chievous, pernici′ous, detriment′al, prejudici′al, bane′ful, pestilen′tial, harm′ful, destruc′tive, no′cent, nox′ious, nois′ome, insalu′brious, unwhole′some. *See* Inimical, Injure, Abusive.

HYPOC′RISY—simula′tion, dissimula′tion; disguise′, deceit′, insincer′ity, false appear′ance. *See* Cheat.

I.

I′DLE—doing nothing, unemploy′ed, unoc′cupied, inact′ive, leis′ure, va′cant; use′less, ineffect′ual, vain, friv′olous, trif′ling; unprof′itable, bar′ren, unfruit′ful. *See* Lazy, Vain, Trifling, Barren.

IG′NORANT—not knowing, uninstruct′ed, uninform′ed, untaught′, unenlight′ened, unlearn′ed, illit′erate, unlet′tered; unacquaint′ed, unappris′ed. *See* Barbarous, Wise.

ILL—*See* Bad, Wicked, Sick, Malicious.

ILL′NESS—indispositi′on, disease′, mal′ady, distem′per, disor′der, sick′ness; wick′edness, iniq′uity. *See* Invalid, Sick.

ILL-TEM′PERED—sour, morose′, crab′bed, peev′ish, pet′ulant. *See* Cross, Fretful.

IMAG′INARY—ide′al, fan′cied, visi′onary, uto′pian, not re′al. *See* Fanciful.

IM′ITATE—ape, mim′ic, mock, per′sonate, feign, coun′terfeit. *See* Mimic.

IMME′DIATELY—in′stantly, pres′ently, direct′ly, instant′er.

IMMENSE′—unlim′ited, unbound′ed, immeas′urable, in′finite, bound′less; vast, very great, huge, very large, prodigi′ous, mon′strous. *See* End *without*, Large.

IMMOD′ERATE—exceeding just *or* u′sual bounds, exces′sive, inor′dinate, intem′perate, extrav′agant, unreas′onble, egre′gious, unrestrain′ed, unbounded, unlim′ited. *See* Immense.

IMPERT′INENT—not pertaining to the matter in hand, irrel′evant; rude, im′pudent, intru′sive, med′dling, sau′cy, in′solent; trif′ling, fool′ish. *See* Bold, Foolish, Officious, Impudence, Affronting.

IMPORT′—*See* Mean, Bear.

IMPORT′ANCE—con′sequence, weight, mo′ment, signif′icance, signif′icancy, avail′. *See* Moment.

IMPORT′ANT—bearing on *or* to, weight′y, moment′ous, of con′sequence, significant, consequen′tial, mate′rial, essen′tial, for′cible, driv′ing. *See* Grave, Constituent, Pressing.

IMPORTUNE′—request with urgency, press, urge, tease. *See* Plague, Force.

IMPRESS′—imprint′, stamp, print, mark; fix on the mind, incul′cate, instil′, infuse′, ingraft′, implant′, engrave′. *See* Mark.

IMPROVE′MENT—advance′ment, prog′ress, advan′tage, meliora′tion, amend′ment, refor′mation, reform′; edifica′tion, instruc′tion; emenda′tion, correc′tion; good use *or* employment, applica′tion. *See* Advancement, Better, Education, Civilization.

IM′PUDENCE—shame′lessness, immod′esty, indel′icacy, inde′cency; assu′rance, effron′tery, boldness with contempt of others, audac′ity, hard′ihood, bold′ness, con′fidence, in′solence, imper′tinence. *See* Audacity, Shameless, Impertinent.

INAD′EQUATE—not equal to, insuffici′ent, incom′petent, incap′able, una′ble, ineffici′ent, une′qual, par′tial, incomplete′, defec′tive. *See* Equal, Able.

INAN′IMATE—not having life, life′less, exan′imate, dead. *See* Flat, Dull, Dead, Lifeless.

IN′CENSE—*See* Burn.

INCLINE′—*See* Lean.

INCOMMODE′—put to inconvenience, give trouble to, molest′, troub′le, annoy′, vex, har′ass, disturb′. *See* Trouble.

IN′CREASE — augmenta′tion, additi′on, accessi′on, growing larger, enlarge′ment, exten′sion, aggrandise′ment, in′crement; prof′it, in′terest; prog′eny, is′sue, off′spring, prod′uce. *See* Added *something*, Larger *make or grow*, Offspring.

INCUR′SION — running into; in′road, irrup′tion, inva′sion, attack′; expediti′on. *See* Attack, Battle, Run.

IN′DICATE—*See* Show.

INDIF′FERENT — neu′tral, care′less, heed′less, regard′less, unconcern′ed. *See* Careless, Insensible.

INDIVID′UAL—not divided *or* not to be divided, sin′gle, one, iden′tical, partic′ular, sep′arate, distinct′, undivi′ded, ab′stract. *See* Particular, Same, Separate.

INDUCE′—bring on, produce′, cause; persuade′, prevail on, in′fluence, bi′as; incite′, move, in′stigate, act′uate, impel′; infer′. *See* Invite, Lead, Move, Tempt.

INFATUA′TION—hallucina′tion, stupefac′tion. *See* Intoxication, Destiny, Mistake.

INFEC′TION—contamina′tion, taint, pollu′tion, poi′son, vitia′tion, defile′ment; conta′gion. *See* Pest, Plague.

INFE′RIOR—low′er, sec′ondary, subor′dinate, subserv′ient. *See* Servant.

IN′FIDEL—unbeliev′er. *See* Heretic.

IN′FLUENCE—flowing in, into, *or* on, pow′er, cred′it, fa′vor; control′, direc′tion. *See* Power, Lead.

INGE′NIOUS—skil′ful, invent′ive, clev′er, imag′inative, wit′ty. *See* Intellectual, Sharp.

INGRA′TIATE—insin′uate, recommend′, concil′iate, propit′iate. *See* Hint, Favour.

INIM′ICAL—unfriend′ly, hos′tile, ad′verse; hurt′ful, con′trary, ap′posite, repug′nant. *See* Hurtful, Opposite.

INIQ′UITY — unright′eousness, injus′tice, nefa′riousness, sin, crime, wick′edness, irreligi′on, profan′ity, impi′ety, deprav′ity. *See* Injury, Depravity, Misdeed, Unjust.

IN′JURE—hurt, wound; wrong, impair′, weak′en, dam′age, make worse, dete′riorate, dimin′ish, less′en; tarn′ish, slan′der, vi′olate; grieve; *the form*, disfig′ure, deform′, deface′. *See* Disfigure, Maim, Hurt, Abuse, Offend, Worse *make*.

IN′JURY—wrong, dam′age, loss, hurt, harm, mis′chief, det′riment, out′rage, deteriora′tion, injus′tice, e′vil, ill, unfair′ness, iniq′uity; in′sult, affront′. *See* Hurt, Iniquity, Affront, Violation.

INSENSIBIL′ITY—want of sensibil′ity, unfeel′ingness, ap′athy, indif′ference, insusceptibil′ity, torpid′ity, cold′ness, cal′lousness, unconcern′, disregard′, dull′ness, stupid′ity, tor′por. *See* Feeling, Dryness.

INSENS′IBLE—that cannot be felt *or* perceived, impercep′tible, insens′ate, apathet′ic, insuscep′tible, tor′pid, stu′pid, dull, fool′ish; indif′ferent, unconcern′ed, regard′less. *See* Hardened, Dull, Foolish.

INSTRUCT′—teach, inform the mind, ed′ify, ed′ucate; direct′, enjoin′, persuade′, admon′ish, command′, inform′, advise′, give notice to. *See* Guide, Show, Education, Authority *give*, Enlighten, Build.

IN′STRUMENT—tool; dupe, gud′geon.

INSURREC′TION—rising against civil *or* political authority, sediti′on, rebel′lion, revolt′, ri′sing, commo′tion, mu′tiny. *See* Tumult.

INTELLECT′UAL — men′tal, tal′ented, gift′ed, clev′er, invent′ive, imag′inative, ide′al. *See* Ingenious, Spiritual, Mind.

INTENSE′—strain′ed, stretch′ed; very close, raised to a high degree, vi′olent, ve′hement; very severe *or* keen, extreme′; ar′dent, ferv′ent. *See* Hot, Zealous, Warm.

INTEN′TION—stretching *or* bending of the mind towards an object, close applica′tion, ear′nestness; design′, pur′pose, pur′port, im′port, mean′ing, intent′, intend′ment, view, aim, drift, end, ob′ject, scope. *See* Aim, End, Design, Mean, Meaning.

INTERCEDE′—plead in favor of. *See* Act *between*.

INTERCHANGE′—mutual change, exchange′, commuta′tion, permuta′tion, bar′ter, reciproc′ity. *See* Change, Communion, Trade.

IN′TEREST—concern′, regard′, advan′tage, good benefit; in′fluence; share, por′tion, part, participa′tion; pre′mium for the use of money. *See* Relate, Benefit, Care, Good, Part.

INTER′PRET—*See* Explain.

INTERRUPT′—break in upon, stop, hin′-

der, disturb′; interfere′; divide′, sep′arate, break continu′ity, rescind′, disjoin′, disconnect′. *See* Hinder, Prevent, Act *between*, Separate, Order *put out of*.

IN′TERVIEW—mutual view *or* sight, meet′ing, con′ference, communica′tion, oral discussi′on, consulta′tion, conven′tion, par′ley. *See* Calling *together*, Speech.

IN′TIMACY—close familiar′ity *or* friend′ship, fel′lowship, acquain′tance, familiar′ity. *See* Acquaintance, Familiarity.

INTOXICA′TION—drun′kenness, inebri′ety, ebri′ety, inebria′tion, tip′siness; infatua′tion. *See* Drunk, Infatuation.

IN′TRICACY — perplex′ity, perplex′edness, complex′ity, complica′tion, involu′tion, entang′lement, confu′sion; maze, lab′yrinth, mean′der. *See* Confused.

IN′TRICATE—entang′led, involv′ed, intwin′ed, com′plicated, perplex′ed, com′plex. *See* Confused, Entangle.

INTRIGUE′—*See* Plot.

INTRIN′SIC—intrin′sical, in′ward, intern′al, in′nate, true, gen′uine, re′al, essen′tial, inhe′rent. *See* Genuine, Constituent.

INTRODUCE′—lead or bring in, ush′er in, present′, prepare′; begin′, open to notice; pref′ace, premise′. *See* Begin, Preface.

INTRODUC′TORY—serving to introduce′, prepar′atory, init′iatory, prelim′inary, pref′atory, proe′mial, prelu′sive, prelu′sory, pre′vious, antece′dent, prefix′ed. *See* Going *before*, Preface.

INTRUDE′—thrust one's self in, obtrude′, come, go in or enter uninvi′ted, or unwel′comed; *unlawfully*, encroach′, infringe′, invade′, intrench′. *See* Go.

INVAL′ID—weak, fee′ble, of no force, weight, *or* cog′ency, infirm′, debil′itated, sick, unwell′, ill, indispo′sed; *in law*, having no force, effect *or* ef′ficacy, null, void:—*In′valid*, a person weak and infirm, sick′ly *or* indisposed, valetudina′rian. *See* Illness, Sick, Weak.

INVENT′—come on by making, find out by making, devise′, contrive′; fab′ricate, forge, feign; discov′er. *See* Contrive, Discover, Find *out*, Lie.

INVEST′—clothe, dress, array′, adorn′; clothe with office *or* author′ity, endow′, endue′, au′thorize; inclose′, surround′, besiege′. *See* Beautify, Authority *give*, Endow, Compass, Surround.

INVID′IOUS—looking on with an evil eye, en′vious, malig′nant, spite′ful, ran′corous, likely to incur ill-will *or* hatred, *or* provoke envy, offens′ive, provo′king, ir′ritating. *See* Malicious, Affronting.

INVITE′—bid, call, ask, sum′mon; allure′, draw to, attract′, tempt to come. *See* Ask, Bid, Call, Induce.

IN′WARD—*See* Intrinsic.

ISS′UE—passing *or* flowing out, e′gress, out′let; sending out; event′, con′sequence, effect′, result′, end, up′shot; prog′eny, child *or* children. *See* Effect, End, Children, Offspring.

ISS′UE—pass *or* flow out, em′anate, spring, result′, proceed′, arise′, emerge′, flow, go out, rush out.

J.

JEAL′OUSY—suspici′on, fear, apprehen′sion, cau′tion, vig′ilance; ri′valry, en′vy; indigna′tion. *See* Fear.

JEST—gibe, jeer, sneer, scoff, mock, taunt; joke, fun, trick, game, sport, rid′icule, laught′er, laugh′ing-stock, spor′tiveness, face′tiousness, jocular′ity. *See* Frolic, Sport, Mirth, Gibe.

JIN′GLE—clink, ring, rat′tle, jan′gle, clang; crack′le, decrep′itate. *See* Sound.

JOC′ULAR—jocose′, wag′gish, mer′ry, given to jest′ing, face′tious; spor′tive, not se′rious. *See* Merry, Lively.

JOIN—*See* Tie.

JOINT *out of*—disjoint′ed, dis′located, dismem′bered, disuni′ted; unconnect′ed, incohe′rent.

JOUR′NEY—*See* Excursion.

JO′VIAL—*See* Merry.

JOY *to profess*—congrat′ulate, grat′ulate, felic′itate; greet, com′pliment. *See* Rejoice.

JOY *excessive*—ec′stacy, rap′ture, tran′sport, exulta′tion. *See* Pleasure.

JUDGE—*See* Decider.

JUDG′MENT — discern′ment, penetra′tion, discrimina′tion, sagac′ity, intel′ligence, discre′tion, pru′dence; determina′tion, decisi′on, sen′tence, award′, adjudica′tion; opin′ion, no′tion. *See* Decree. Sense, Sharpness. Thought, Understanding, Rule.

JUST—*See* Right, Reasonable.

JUS′TICE—law, legal′ity, right; eq′uity, impartial′ity; retribu′tion; hon′esty, integ′rity. *See* Honesty, Law, Correct, Unjust.

K.

KEEN—e′ager, ve′hement; sharp, severe′, pier′cing, pen′etrating; bit′ter, acrimo′nious. *See* Severe, Sharp, Eagerness.

KEEP—hold, detain′, retain′, possess′, occupy, reserve′; preserve′, save; protect′, defend′, guard; sustain′, maintain′, board, support′; tend, have the care of, feed, pas′ture; prac′tice, do, perform′, observe′, fulfil′, obey′; *back*, reserve′, retain′, withhold′; *in*, conceal′, restrain′, curb; *from*, abstain′, refrain′, restrain′; forbear′, desist′; *up*, maintain′, contin′ue, hinder from ceasing. *See* Do, Occupy, Maintain, Leave, Abstain, Delay.

KILL—deprive of life, mur′der, assas′sinate, slay, mas′sacre, put to death, slaught′er, but′cher, destroy′. *See* Destruction, Waste, Behead.

KIN—relation by birth, consanguin′ity, relation by marriage, affin′ity; rel′atives, kin′dred; kin′sman, rela′tion, rel′ative. *See* Relationship.

KIND—spe′cies, sort, class, ge′nus; or′der, set, rank. *See* Sort, Character, Order.

KIND—mild, ten′der, bland, indul′gent; clem′ent, gen′tle, compassi′onate, meek, benign′, benig′nant, gen′erous, benev′olent, good; court′eous, civ′il, civ′ilized, oblig′ing, com′plaisant, af′fable; gra′cious, le′nient, humane′. *See* Affectionate, Loving, Merciful, Obliging, Soft.

KIND′NESS—good′-will, benev′olence, benef′icence, benig′nity, tend′erness, human′ity; generos′ity, liberal′ity, good′ness; cour′tesy, polite′ness, urban′ity, civil′ity, complaisance′, affabil′ity, fa′vor. *See* Bounty, Charity, Affection, Mercy, Favor.

KING—*See* Majestic, Prince.

KING′DOM—realm, state, ter′ritory, coun′try; em′pire; na′tion, inhab′itants *or* popula′tion; *in natural history*, divisi′on; re′gion, tract; reign of the Messi′ah, heaven; gov′ernment, rule, sov′ereignty, supreme administra′tion. *See* Government, Dominion, Country.

KISS—touch with the lips, salute′, embrace′, touch gent′ly, caress′. *See* Embrace.

KNIT—*See* Tie.

KNOT—*See* Tie.

KNOW—*See* Understand, Wise.

KNOW′LEDGE—learn′ing, eruditi′on, let′ters, sci′ence; wis′dom, skill; acquain′tance, no′tice; informa′tion; *of all things*, omnis′cience. *See* Learning, Foresight.

L.

LA′BOR—*See* Work.

LAMENT′—*See* Grieve.

LAN′GUAGE—hu′man speech, ton′gue, speech; di′alect, id′iom; sol′ecism; dic′tion, phraseol′ogy, express′ion. *See* Speech.

LARGE—big, great, huge, of great size, spa′cious, wide, room′y, capa′cious, extens′ive, comprehens′ive, co′pious, am′ple, abun′dant, plent′iful, diffu′sive, broad, extend′ed, lib′eral. *See* Big, Immense, Abounding, Roomy, Great, Size.

LAR′GER *make*—mag′nify, augment′, enlarge′, increase′, ag′grandize, extend′. *See* Great *make*, Increase.

LAST′ING—contin′uing, endur′ing, remain′ing; du′rable, per′manent, diuturn′al; invet′erate. *See* Abide, Stay.

LAUGH *at*—rid′icule, ban′ter, ral′ly, deride′, mock, fleer, grin, leer, scoff, gibe, jeer. *See* Gibe, Scoff, Reproach.

LAUGH′ABLE—exciting laughter *or* mer′riment, ris′ible, lu′dicrous, ridic′ulous, com′ic, com′ical, spor′tive, odd, droll, burlesque′, mirth′ful. *See* Jocular, Amusing, Odd, Ridicule.

LAV′ISH—prod′igal, waste′ful, wan′ton, profuse′, extrav′agant. *See* Waste, Spend, Extravagance, Expense.

LAW—*See* Decree, Order, Command, Justice.

LAY *hold of*—grasp, catch, snatch, seize, gripe, fas′ten on, clutch; *open*, o′pen, make bare, uncov′er, show, expose′, reveal′; spread out, dilate′, expand′, extend′; *down*, depos′it, resign′, give up, quit, relin′quish, surren′der, of′fer, advance′; *up*, hoard, store, treas′ure, repos′it, provide′, pre′viously; *out*, expend′, plan, dispose in order, exert′; *to*, charge upon, impute′, set to the account of, attrib′ute. *See* Seize, Swell, Place, Catching, Show, Spread, Give, Count, Reckon, Accuse.

LA′ZY—slug′gish, in′dolent, sloth′ful, i′dle, list′less, inert′, inac′tive, supine′; slow. *See* Careless, Idle, Slow, Dull.

LEAD—guide, conduct′, direct′; *away*, abduce′, draw, entice′, allure′, attract′, decoy′, seduce′; induce′, persuade′, prevail on, in′fluence, bias, incline′. *See* Induce, Guide, Tempt, Lean.

LEAGUE—confed′eracy, alli′ance, national com′pact, cov′enant, truce, combina′tion, coaliti′on, u′nion. *See* Alliance, Combine, Band.

LEAN—wanting flesh, me′agre, not fat, thin, atten′uated, wast′ed, ema′ciated; not rich, des′titute, bare, bar′ren, jejune′. *See* Bare, Thin.

LEAN—incline′, propend′, tend toward bend. *See* Bend.

LEARN—*See* Scholar, Hear.

LEARN'ING—eruditi'on, let'ters, sci'ence, lit'erature, acquired knowledge, art. *See* Knowledge.

LEAVE—*See* Remains.

LEAVE—permissi'on, allow'ance, li'cense, lib'erty, consent', approv'al, assent'; *a taking*, farewell', valedic'tion, adieu', part'ing. *See* Approbation, Let.

LEAVE—withdraw', depart' from, quit; forsake', desert', aban'don, relin'quish; bequeath', give by will; *off*, desist', withhold', discontin'ue, refrain', forbear', hold, cease, stop; *out*, omit', pass by, neglect'. *See* Abandon, Give *up*, Ceasing, Keep, Abstain.

LES'SEN—make less, dimin'ish, reduce', decrease', abate', liq'uidate; pal'liate, exten'uate; *in value* or *worth*, depre'ciate, underval'ue, der'ogate, dete'riorate, dispar'age, detract', decry', traduce', degrade', low'er; *become* less, abate', decrease', dimin'ish, shrink; subside'. *See* Lower, Gloss, Humble, Slacken, Allay.

LET—*See* Hinderance.

LET—permit', suf'fer, allow', give leave *or* power; lease, demise'; retard', hin'der, impede'. *See* Allow, Hinderance, Leave.

LEWD—*See* Lust, Loose.

LIB'ERTY *being deprived of*—restraint', confine'ment, impris'onment, incarcera'tion, captiv'ity, bon'dage, thral'dom, slav'ery, serv'itude, enslave'ment. *See* Custody, Privilege, Freedom, Confine.

LIE *or* LEAN—*See* Lean.

LIE—false'hood, untruth', mendac'ity, fabrica'tion, fic'tion, fib, inven'tion. *See* Falsehood.

LIFE—vital'ity, live'liness, spright'liness, vivac'ity, viva'ciousness, anima'tion, spir'it. *See* Lightness *of manner*, Spirit, Warmth, Animate.

LIFE'LESS—deprived of life, dead, des'titute of life, inan'imate, exan'imate; dull, heav'y, inac'tive, vap'id; tor'pid. *See* Dead, Dull, Inanimate, Flat.

LIFT—el'evate, raise, erect', exalt', elate'. *See* Heighten.

LIGHT—*See* Enlighten.

LIGHT'NESS *of manner*—lev'ity, gid'diness, gay'ety, unstead'iness, incon'stancy, change'ableness, mutabil'ity, van'ity, freak, flight'iness, volatil'ity, buoy'ancy, elastic'ity, anima'tion, vivac'ity, viva'ciousness; wan'tonness, lewd'ness, unchast'ity. *See* Life, Whim, Changeable, Loose.

LIKE—alike', iden'tical, e'qual, sim'ilar, u'niform, resem'bling; prob'able, like'ly. *See* Equal, Same.

LIKE'NESS—resem'blance, similar'ity, form, external appearance; simil'itude, sim'ilē; representa'tion, cop'y, coun'terpart; im'age, pic'ture, ef'figy, stat'ue. *See* Comparison, Effigy, Example, Appearance.

LIM'IT—*See* Bound.

LIM'ITED—bound'ed, fi'nite, term'inable, determ'inate, circumscrib'ed, restrain'ed, confin'ed, restrict'ed; qual'ified; nar'row. *See* Definite, Narrow, Bound.

LINE—*See* Mark.

LINK'ING *together*—connec'tion, concatena'tion, succes'sion, consecu'tion, chain, train, se'ries. *See* Follow, Chain.

LIS'TEN—*See* Hear.

LIVE'LIHOOD—means of living, support of life, liv'ing, subsist'ence, main'tenance, sus'tenance, sustenta'tion, support'. *See* Food, Living.

LIVE'LY—brisk, vig'orous, viva'cious, an'imated, spir'ited, spright'ly, spor'tive, blithe, mer'ry, cheer'ful, mirth'ful, joc'und, gay, air'y; hu'morous, face'tious, wit'ty, joc'ular, jocose'; strong, energet'ic. *See* Active, Gay, Merry, Jocular, Quick, Spirit.

LIV'ING *ecclesiastical*—ben'efice, vic'arage, par'sonage, rec'tory; incum'bency; prefer'ment, endow'ment. *See* Livelihood.

LIV'ING *in the same age with another*—coe'val, of the same age, of equal age, coeta'neous; *at the same time*, contem'porary *or* cotem'porary, contempora'neous, coexist'ent. *See* Time.

LOAD—*See* Burden.

LOFT'Y—*See* High, Great.

LOIT'ER—lin'ger, move slowly *or* idly, lag, stay behind, delay', be dil'atory, spend time idly, saun'ter. *See* Delay.

LONE'LY—sol'itary, reti'red, seques'tered, seclu'ded, ascet'ic, lone, lone'some, unfrequent'ed, desert'ed, dull, gloom'y. *See* Dull, Alone, Desolate.

LOOK—*See* Appearance.

LOOK—see, behold', view, eye, glance, peep, observe'; appear', seem; face, front; *after*, attend', tend, take care of; *for*, expect', seek, search; *into*, inspect', observe', exam'ine, consid'er; *on*, regard', esteem', consid'er, view, conceive of, think, be a mere spectator. *See* Glance, Appear, Search, Care.

LOOK'ER-ON—behold'er, specta'tor, observ'er.

LOOSE—unbound', unti'ed, unsew'ed; not tight *or* close, not dense *or* compact'; not concise', lax, not precise *or* exact', vague, indeterm'inate, remiss′; unconnect′ed, ram′bling; dis′-solute, saturna′lian, wan′ton, lewd, lust′ful, unrestrain′ed, unchaste′, li-cen′tious, lax. *See* Abandoned, Lust, Careless, Lightness.

Lop—*See* Cut *off*, Maim.

Lord—*See* Master.

Lord's Supper—commu′nion, sac′ra-ment, eu′charist.

Loss—dam′age, det′riment. *See* In-jury, Hurt.

Lot—*See* Chance, Clergy.

Loud—having a great sound, high-sound′ing, altis′onant, obstrep′erous, strep′erous, nois′y, clam′orous, vo-cif′erous, ve′hement, tur′bulent, tu-mul′tuous, blus′tering; emphat′ical, impres′sive. *See* Tumultuous, Noise.

Love—*See* Affection.

Love *inclined to*—am′orous, fond, do′-ting, lov′ing; *in love*, enam′ored, smit′ten; *relating to*, am′atory, ama-to′rial, amato′rious. *See* Loving.

Lov′er—one who loves, woo′er, suit′-or, sweet′heart, beau, swain; ama-teur′.

Lov′ing—enam′ored, am′orous; fond, affec′tionate, attach′ed. *See* Affec-tionate, Kind.

Low—not high, hum′ble; deep; de-ject′ed, depress′ed; mean, ab′ject, grov′elling, base, dishon′orable; fee′-ble, weak, exhaust′ed; mod′erate; plain, sim′ple, as *diet*. *See* Humble, Grave, Weak, Faint, Flat.

Low′er—cause to descend, let down, take *or* bring down, reduce′, hum′-ble, disgrace′, humil′iate, degrade′, debase′, abase′, depress′. *See* Hum-ble, Abase, Lessen, Damp.

Low′liness—freedom from pride, hu-mil′ity, hum′bleness, self-abase′-ment, mod′esty, unworth′iness, pen′-itence, submissi′on, submis′siveness. *See* Humble.

Low′ness *of spirits*—dejec′tion, depres-si′on, despond′ency, mel′ancholy, hypochon′dria, low-spir′itedness; *in rank* or *state*, humilia′tion, degrada′-tion, debase′ment, abase′ment, re-duc′tion. *See* Despair, Disgrace.

Luck—*See* Chance.

Luck′y—for′tunate, success′ful, pros′-perous, fa′vourable. *See* Fortunate.

Lure—*See* Tempt, Induce, Entangle.

Lust—longing desire, desire′, passi′on, concupis′cence, lust′ing, carnal ap′-petite, unlawful desire, lasci′vious-ness, sala′ciousness, salac′ity, lech′-erousness, lech′ery, lubric′ity, incon′-tinence, incon′tinency, unchas′tity, evil propensity, depraved affections and desires. *See* Desire, Loose.

Lust′y—fat, cor′pulent, stout, robust′, vig′orous, health′ful, able of body; bulk′y, large. *See* Fatness, Strong.

Lux′ury—free *or* extravagant indul-gence in the pleasures of the table, volup′tuousness, sensual′ity; ep′icu-rism, sensual enjoyments; dain′ty, delicious food *or* drink; any thing delightful to the senses. *See* Glut, Drunk, Pleasure, Feast.

M.

Machine′—*See* Instrument.

Mad—*See* Foolish.

Mad′ness—disorder of the intellect *or* reason, distrac′tion, derange′ment, insan′ity, insane′ness, lun′acy, delir′-ium, ma′nia, phren′zy *or* fren′zy, fran′ticness, mental aberration; ex-treme folly, headstrong passion and rashness; wildness of passion, rage, fu′ry. *See* Folly, Rage, Possession.

Maim—deprive of the use of a limb, lame, crip′ple, man′gle, mu′tilate, in′jure, hurt. *See* Mangle, Cut *off*, Injure, Hurt.

Maintain′—assert′, vin′dicate. *See* Keep, Support.

Majes′tic—august′, state′ly, dig′ni-fied, magnif′icent, grand, splen′did, pomp′ous, el′evated, loft′y; prince′-ly, roy′al, re′gal, king′ly, no′ble; magiste′rial. *See* Grand, High, Great.

Make — constrain′, compel′; form, fashi′on, mold, contrive′, cause to exist, produce′, create′, compose′, con′stitute, construct′, estab′lish; do, perform′, ex′ecute, effect′, cause; raise, gain, collect′; *over*, transfer′, convey′, assign′, a′lienate; *out*, learn, discov′er, obtain′, prove, evince′, find *or* supply. *See* Force, Form, Contrive, Do.

Mal′ice—extreme enmity, ran′cor, malev′olence, malig′nity, malig′-nancy, spite, grudge, pique, ill′-will. *See* Enmity, Hatred, Envy, Spite.

Malici′ous—harboring ill-will *or* en-mity, malev′olent, malig′nant, ma-lign′, evilmind′ed, e′vil, wic′ked, fiend′ish, fiend′like, diabol′ical, in-fern′al, hell′ish, styg′ian, dev′ilish, spite′ful. *See* Hateful, Wicked, Invidious.

Man′gle—lac′erate, tear, rend, mu′ti-late, maim. *See* Maim, Worry.

Man′ner—*See* Appearance, System, Way.

Man′ners—mor′als, hab′its; beha′-viour. *See* Custom, Behaviour, Civility.

Man′y—man′ifold, mul′tiform, sev′e-ral, di′vers, sun′dry, va′rious, nu′-merous.

MAR'GIN —*See* Brink, Edge.
MARK — line, incisi'on, impressi'on, print, stamp; note, sign, sym'ptom, indica'tion, to'ken; trace, ves'tige, foot'step, foot'print, track; *of disgrace*, brand, stig'ma, badge. *See* Character, Emblem.
MARK—draw a visible line, stamp, impress', print, imprint'; note, no'tice, observe', remark'; heed, attend', regard'. *See* Impress, Hear, Denote.
MAR'KET—*See* Trade.
MAR'RIAGE — mat'rimony, wed'lock; nup'tials, wed'ding; *relating to*, connu'bial, con'jugal, matrimo'nial, nup'tial, hyme'neal, hyme'nean. *See* Espoused, Relationship.
MAR'TIAL—war'like, mil'itary, sol'dier-like, brave, given to war; suited to battle.
MASK—*See* Cloak.
MASS—*See* Medley.
MAS'TER — possess'or, propri'etor, own'er; ru'ler, direct'or, gov'ernor, head, chief, prin'cipal, supe'rior, control'ler, lord; teach'er, tu'tor, instruct'or, precep'tor, profess'or. *See* Chief, Scholar.
MAX'IM—*See* Aphorism.
MAZE—*See* Intricacy.
MEAN—wanting dignity, low, vul'gar, low minded, base, spir'itless, contemp'tible, des'picable; of little value, hum'ble, poor; sor'did, mi'serly, penu'rious, nig'gardly. *See* Low, Gross, Contemptible, Poor, Saving, Sneaking, Miserly, Sorry.
MEAN—have in mind *or* view, intend', pur'pose, design', con'template; sig'nify, in'dicate, ex'press', imply', import', denote'. *See* Design, Denote, Betoken.
MEAN'ING—significa'tion, signif'icance, im'port, sense, intend'ment, inten'tion, tend'ency, aim, pur'pose. *See* Intention, Aim, Sense.
MEANS, *instrument of effecting any purpose*—in'come, rev'enue, resour'ces, sub'stance, estate'; or'gan; *that offer*, expe'dient, altern'ative, resource', me'dium; moy'en. *See* Way, Choice, Medium.
MECHAN'IC—artisan', ar'tist, artif'icer, op'erative, work'man, journ'eyman.
MED'ITATE—*See* Think.
ME'DIUM—mid'dle, mean; medioc'rity, mod'erateness, modera'tion, tem'perateness, tem'perance. *See* Way, Means, Mildness.
MED'LEY—mingled and confused mass, mix'ture, confu'sion, mass, hotch'potch, heteroge'neousness, divers'ity, vari'ety, miscel'lany.
MEET—fit, prepar'ed, suit'able, prop'er, qual'ified, conve'nient, adap'ted. *See* Fit.
MEET—come together, come face to face, confront', encoun'ter, come in con'tact, join; come to, find, light on, receive'; assem'ble, con'gregate, collect', concen'trate, group, mus'ter, imbod'y. *See* Call *together*, Collection, Crowd, Find.
MEL'ANCHOLY—*See* Sad, Doleful.
MEMOIR'—personal history, life, personal narrative *or* chronicle, his'tory, nar'rative, narra'tion, chron'icle, written account, register of facts, reci'tal. *See* Chronicle, Story, History.
MER'CENARY—that may be hired or sold, ve'nal, hire'ling, hired, pur'chased, sold; greedy of gain, mean, selfish. *See* Mean.
MER'CHANDISE—*See* Goods, Trade, Buy.
MER'CIFUL—having *or* exercising mer'cy, clem'ent, compassi'onate, humane', ten'der, le'nient, benign', benig'nant, indul'gent, not cru'el, pit'iful. *See* Kind, Mildness.
MER'CY—*See* Grace.
MER'CY—grace; benev'olence, tend'erness, mild'ness, pit'y *or* compassi'on, or clem'ency exercised towards offenders; clem'ency, len'ity, len'iency, human'ity, benig'nity, compassi'on, pit'y. *See* Kindness, Pity, Mildness.
MER'RY—gay and noisy, jo'vial, exhil'arated, cheer'ful, mirth'ful, joy'ful, joy'ous, spright'ly, live'ly, gay, viva'cious, blithe, blithe'some, joc'und, spor'tive, fes'tive, conviv'ial, so'cial, so'ciable. *See* Convivial, Lively, Glad, Gay, Jocular, Cheerfulness.
MES'SAGE—verbal *or* written notice sent, er'rand, missi'on, commissi'on, em'bassy, despatch', communica'tion, man'date, or'der. *See* Order, Command.
MILD—*See* Kind, Merciful.
MILD'NESS — soft'ness, gen'tleness, suav'ity, placid'ity, bland'ness, tend'erness, mer'cy, clem'ency; mod'erateness. *See* Mercy, Kindness, Peace, Medium.
MIM'IC — im'itator, buffoon', za'ny, mer'ryan'drew, jes'ter, mount'ebank, fool. *See* Fool, Blockhead, Coxcomb, Imitate.
MIND—*See* Intellectual, Thoughtful.
MIN'GLE—*See* Mix.
MIN'ISTER—chief ser'vant, a'gent, of'ficer, offici'al, mag'istrate, del'egate, ambass'ador, en'voy; pas'tor. *See* Clergyman, Servant, Assist.
MIRTH—social mer'riment, hilar'ity, noisy gayety, jol'lity, jol'liness, jo-

cose′ness, jocular′ity, jocund′ity, joc′undness, festiv′ity, jovial′ity, convivial′ity, social′ity, sociabil′ity; joy, glad′ness, cheer′fulness. *See* Cheerfulness, Joy, Pleasure, Jest, Sport.

MISCAR′RIAGE—fai′lure, mishap′; ill con′duct, evil *or* improper beha′vior, misbeha′vior; abor′tion, untimely birth. *See* Behavior, Misdeed.

MISDEED′—evil deed, wicked action, fault, transgressi′on, tres′pass, offense′, misbeha′vior, crime. *See* Miscarriage, Fault, Iniquity.

MI′SER—extremely covetous person, sordid wretch, avaricious fellow, very parsimonious creature, curmudg′eon, nig′gard, churl. *See* Money.

MI′SERLY—very covetous, avarici′ous, sor′did, nig′gardly, nar′row, parsimo′nious, mean, churl′ish, curmudg′eonly. *See* Mean, Narrow.

MISFOR′TUNE—ill-fortune, ill-luck, advers′ity, calam′ity, disas′ter, afflic′tion, distress′, mischance′, evil *or* cross ac′cident, mishap′, misadven′ture. *See* Trouble, Fortune.

MISTAKE′—er′ror, misconcep′tion, misunderstand′ing; slip, hallucina′tion, fault; ac′cident. *See* Fault, Oversight, Deceive.

MISUSE′—ill-use, use ill *or* improperly, use to a bad purpose, wrong, in′jure; abuse′, treat ill. *See* Abuse, Injure.

MIX—*See* Medley.

MOB—*See* Crowd.

MOCK—*See* Laugh at.

MOD′EST—restrained by a sense of propriety, not forward *or* bold, not presump′tuous *or* ar′rogant, not boast′ful, bash′ful, dif′fident, reserv′ed; not loose, not lewd, chaste, pure, ves′tal, vir′tuous; mod′erate, not exces′sive *or* extreme′, not extrav′agant. *See* Pure, Chasteness, Loose, Shameless.

MOIST—*See* Soak.

MO′MENT—sec′ond, in′stant; import′ance, &c. *See* Importance, Transitory.

MON′EY—coin, stamped metal, gold, sil′ver, cop′per, cash; spe′cie, bank notes *or* bills, finance′, exchequ′er.

MO′RALS—*See* Manners.

MOR′TAL—subject to death, destined to die; dead′ly, fa′tal, causing death, bringing death; hu′man, terres′trial, earth′ly, mun′dane; per′ishable, fleet′ing, evanes′cent. *See* Deadly, Transitory.

MOUNT—*See* Go.

MOURN—*See* Grieve.

MOUTH—*See* Speech.

MOVE—*See* Go, Stir.

MOVE—impel′, car′ry, convey′, draw; excite′, affect′, touch pathetically, ag′itate, rouse, incite′, in′stigate, prompt, stir, act′uate, urge, persuade′, induce′, prevail on. *See* Induce, Animate, Stir, Shake, Go, Awaken.

MOVE *round*—revolve′, circumvolve′, turn, circumgy′rate, cir′culate; wheel, whirl, twirl, twist, reel. *See* Twist, Surround.

MUCH *too*—excess′, exu′berance. *Se* Excess, Luxuriance.

MUR′DER—*See* Kill.

MUT′UAL—*See* Return *like for like*.

N.

NA′KED—not covered, bare, nude, uncov′ered, uncloth′ed, undress′ed; unarm′ed, defense′less, o′pen, expo′sed; plain, ev′ident, undisguis′ed. *See* Bare, Open.

NAME—appella′tion, appel′lative, ti′tle, denomina′tion, designa′tion; reputa′tion, repute′, char′acter. cred′it, estima′tion; renown′, fame, hon′or, celeb′rity, em′inence, praise, distinc′tion; remem′brance, mem′ory; author′ity, behalf′, part; appearance only, sound only, not reality. *See* Fame, Praise.

NAME—call, give name to, denom′inate, enti′tle, char′acterize, style, term, desig′nate, nom′inate. *See* Call.

NAR′ROW—of little breadth, not wide *or* broad, strait, confin′ed, lim′ited, contract′ed, cov′etous, not lib′eral *or* boun′tiful; close, near, ac′curate, scrut′inizing. *See* Miserly, Limited.

NAT′URAL—implanted by nature, in′born, in′nate, ingen′erate, in′bred; inhe′rent; na′tive, indig′enous. *See* Born.

NAU′SEA—sea-sick′ness, sick′ness, qualm, lo′thing, disgust′, squeam′ishness. *See* Disgust, Sick.

NEAR—*See* Neighborhood, Narrow.

NEC′ESSARY—that must be, that cannot be otherwise, essen′tial, indispens′able, req′uisite, need′ful, fit; expe′dient, desir′able; want′ed, requir′ed; unavoid′able. *See* Fit, Constituent.

NECES′SITY—what must be; irresistible power, compulsive force; want, need, occa′sion, require′ment, indispens′ableness; extreme in′digence, pinching pov′erty, pressing need, distress′, ex′igency, emer′gency; unavoid′ableness, inev′itableness. *See* Destiny, Poorness, Want, Occasion Trouble, Obligation.

NEED—*See* Necessity.

NEE′DLE—*See* Sharp.

NEGLECT′—omiss′ion, forbearance to do, inadvert′ence, o′versight; neg′ligence, inatten′tion, care′lessness, disregard′, remiss′ness, indif′ference, reck′lessness, ap′athy, unconcern. *See* Oversight, Apathy.

NEGLECT′—omit′; forbear to do *or* use; slight, contemn′, disregard′, not to notice. *See* Despise, Shun.

NEI′GHBORHOOD—a place near, vicin′ity, vic′inage, proxim′ity, adja′cency. *See* Near, Nigh.

NERVE—*See* Strong.

NET—*See* Snare.

NEWS—ti′dings, recent account, fresh informa′tion, intel′ligence.

NICE—soft, del′icate, ten′der, daint′y, sweet, fine, delici′ous; ac′curate, exact′, precise′, method′ical, correct′, partic′ular, scrup′ulous, distin′guishing. *See* Dainty, Correct, Squeamish, Luxury.

NIGH—*See* Neighborhood.

NIGHT—*See* Darkness.

NO′BLE—*See* Generous, Great.

NOBIL′ITY—noblesse′, no′blemen, no′bles, aristoc′racy, ol′igarchy, bar′ons, patrici′ans, lords, peers, grandees′, op′timacy; dig′nity, gran′deur. *See* Grand, Greatness, Government.

NOISE—*See* Sound, Jingle.

NOISE—sound, mur′mur, creak; cry, out′cry, clam′or, vocifera′tion. *See* Cry, Loud.

NOMENCLA′TURE—list *or* cat′alogue of words, vocab′ulary, sched′ule, &c. *See* Dictionary, Catalogue.

NO′TED—set down in writing; observ′ed, no′ticed, noto′rious; remark′able, conspic′uous, em′inent, fa′mous, cel′ebrated, distin′guished, renown′ed, illus′trious, extraor′dinary. *See* Famous.

NOT′ICE—observe′, see, regard′, attend′, heed, mind, remark′, men′tion, mark, note. *See* Mark, Perceive, Hear.

NOUR′ISH—nur′ture, cher′ish, fos′ter, support′, maintain′, encour′age; ed′ucate, instruct′. *See* Support, Foster.

NOV′ICE—*See* Ignorant.

NUMB—benum′bed, deprived of sensation, tor′pid, chill, mo′tionless, stu′pified.

NUM′BER—*See* Count.

O.

OBE′DIENT—disposed to obey, submis′sive, obse′quious, compli′ant, hum′ble, tract′able, doc′ile, dut′iful, respect′ful. *See* Humble.

OBJECT′—oppose′, except to, gainsay′, deny′, controvert′, dissent′. *See* Oppose, Gainsay Cavil, Aim, Refuse.

OBLIGA′TION — du′ty; compul′sion, force, coer′cion, neces′sity. *See* Debt, Force, Necessity.

OBLIGE′—ob′ligate, engage′, constrain′, compel′, bind, do a favour to, fa′vour, serve, assist′, please, grat′ify. *See* Force, Please, Assist.

OBLIG′ING — bind′ing, constrain′ing, compel′ling; kind, complaisant′, cour′teous, civ′il, af′fable. *See* Kind, Amiable, Officious.

OBLIQUE′—*See* Crooked.

OB′STACLE — what opposes, what stands in the way, obstruc′tion, hin′derance, let, imped′iment. *See* Difficulty, Hinderance, Let.

OB′STINACY—fixedness in opinion *or* resolution, stub′bornness, pertinac′ity, persist′ence, persist′ency, inflexibil′ity, con′tumacy, perverse′ness, refract′oriness, intract′ibleness, ob′durateness, ob′duracy.

OB′STINATE—fixed in opinion *or* resolution, stub′born, inflex′ible, refract′ory, contuma′cious, pertina′cious, perverse′, ob′durate, unyield′ing, res′olute, opin′iated, head′strong, head′y. *See* Crooked, Unwilling, Averse.

OCCA′SION — fal′ling, hap′pening *or* coming to, occur′rence, cas′ualty, in′cident; opportun′ity, conve′nience, favourable time, sea′son *or* cir′cumstances; incident′al need, cas′ual ex′igency, neces′sity, need. *See* Cause, Necessity, Chance.

OC′CUPY—take possession; keep in possession, possess′, hold *or* keep for use; take up, cov′er *or* fill; employ′, use; maintain′; invest′. *See* Keep, Maintain, Possession.

ODD—not even *or* equal; sin′gular, extraor′dinary, strange, eccen′tric, irreg′ular, anom′alous, partic′ular, uncom′mon; fantas′tic, fantas′tical, whim′sical, com′ic, com′ical, droll, queer, lu′dicrous, fun′ny, laugh′able, burlesque′. *See* Fanciful, Amusing, Laughable, Eccentric.

ODE—*See* Sing.

OFFEND′—displease′, make angry, vex, affront′, insult′, mor′tify, shock, wound; pain, annoy′, in′jure; transgress′, tres′pass, vi′olate. *See* Displease, Affront, Injure.

OFFEND′ER—one who offends, vi′olator, transgres′sor, tres′passer, crim′inal, malefact′or, fel′on; cul′prit, delin′quent, default′er. *See* Crime.

OF′FER—bring in the way, bring to *or* before, present′, prof′fer, give, bestow′, exhib′it, tend′er; sac′rifice, im′molate; bid, propose′. *See* Give Kill, Bid.

OF′FERING—sac′rifice, obla′tion; presenta'tion, tend'er; *a burnt*, hol'o-caust.

OF'FICE—dut'y, charge, trust, func'-tion, place, post, situa'tion, sta'tion, rank, bus'iness, employ'ment, occu-pa'tion, a'gency. *See* State, Situa-tion.

OFFICI'OUS—kind, oblig'ing; exces-sively forward in kindness; act'ive, bus'y med'dling, intermed'dling, in-tru'sive, imper'tinent, impor'tunate. *See* Obliging, Active, Impertinent.

OFF'SPRING—child *or* children, de-scend'ant *or* descend'ants, prog'eny, young, iss'ue; propaga'tion, gene-ra'tion; produc'tion. *See* Children, Issue, Increase.

OF'TEN—oft, fre'quently, many times, not seldom, not rarely, repeat'edly, con'stantly, contin'ually.

OINT'MENT—*See* Perfume.

OLD—advanced far in years *or* life, a'ged; decay'ed, not new *or* fresh; an'cient, antique', old'en; el'derly, se'nile; an'tiquated, old-fashi'oned, ob'solete. *See* Ancient, Ancestor.

O'MEN—*See* Foretell.

ONE—*See* Alone.

ON'SET—rushing *or* setting upon, vio-lent attack, attack', charge, assault', encoun'ter, storm'ing. *See* Attack, Battle.

O'PEN—*See* Spread.

O'PEN *and free*—ingen'uous, frank, fair, cand'id, sincere', free from re-serve, disguise, equivocation *or* dis-simulation, unreserv'ed, undis-guis'ed, undissem'bling, art'less; commu'nicative. *See* Free, Fair, Art *without*, Clear.

O'PENING—breach, gap, ap'erture, cleft, rent, crack, crev'ice, fis'sure, cran'ny, chink, slit, chasm; cav'ity, cave, cav'ern, grot'to, den; or'ifice, hole, perfora'tion, bore, pore; av'e-nue, pas'sage, way, en'trance, dawn, first appearance *or* visibleness. *See* Gap, Way.

OPERA'TION—work'ing, proc'ess, a'gency, ac'tion, effect'; manipula'-tion; move'ment. *See* Work, Pro-ceeding, Effect.

OPIN'ION—sen'timent, ide'a, no'tion, judg'ment, settled persua'sion. *See* Thought, Judgment, Conceit.

OPPOSE'—put *or* set against, act against, resist', withstand', com'bat, oppugn', gainsay', con'trovert, con-tradict', deny', object' to, except' to. *See* Hinder, Gainsay, Object, Refuse.

OP'POSITE—*See* Cross, Inimical.

ORDAIN'—set, set'tle, estab'lish, in'-stitute, con'stitute, appoint', decree', or'der, prescribe'; adjudge', adju'di-cate. *See* Appoint, Fix, Destiny, Form.

OR'DER—regular disposition *or* me-thodical arrangement, regular'ity, rule, meth'od, sys'tem, settled mode; rank, degree', class, divisi'on, spe'cies; se'ries, successi'on, conse-cu'tion, consec'utiveness; religious fratern'ity; regular government *or* discipline. *See* Command, Decree, Arrangement, Order, System, Kind, Course, Discipline, Formality, Mes-sage.

OR'DER—reg'ulate, meth'odize, put in order, sys'temize, adjust', dispose', digest', class, clas'sify, range, rank, arrange'; direct', command'. *See* Command, Class.

OR'DER *put out of*—disor'der, break order, derange', confuse', disar-range', disturb', perplex', confound', displace', unset'tle, ruf'fle, discom-pose', interrupt'; *change the*, invert'; reverse'. *See* Unsettle, Disfigure, Interrupt, Confused.

OR'DERLY—reg'ular, method'ical, sys-temat'ic; well reg'ulated, not tu-mul'tuous; not unru'ly, peace'able. *See* Regular.

OR'IGIN—first existence, orig'inal, commence'ment, begin'ning, rise, source, first cause, foun'tainhead, descent'; grounds, founda'tion, base, ba'sis; ru'diments, el'ements; prim'itive, et'ymon, etymol'ogy. *See* Begin, Cause, Rise.

OUT'RAGE—*See* Affront.

OUT'WARD—out'er, extern'al, exte'rior, extrin'sic, adventiti'ous; extra'-neous; *in theology*, carn'al, flesh'ly, corpo'real, not spiritual. *See* Abroad.

OUTWEIGH'—exceed in weight, over-bal'ance, prepond'erate; exceed in value, influence, *or* importance. *See* Go.

OVERBEAR'—bear down, overpow'er, subdue', oppress', overwhelm', sup-press'. *See* Conquer, Overcome.

OVERCOME'—con'quer, van'quish, sub-due', sub'jugate, overpow'er, sup-press'; surmount', get the better of. *See* Beat, Defeat, Overbear.

OVERFLOW'—flow over, inun'date, cover with waters, del'uge, over-whelm', cov'er. *See* Flow, Over-bear, Water.

OVERRULE'—influence *or* control by predominant power, dispense' with, supersede', annul', reject'. *See* An-nul, Refuse.

O'VERSIGHT—superintend'ence, watch ful care, supervisi'on, inspec'tion; mistake', overlook'ing, omissi'on, er'ror inadvert'ence, inatten'tion, sight, ac'cident. *See* Care, Mistake, Neglect.

OWN—acknowl'edge. avow', confess', not to deny, admit', rec'ognize. *See* Recognize, Profess, Allow.

P.

PACE—step, gait, stride; am'ble. *See* Step.

PAIN—uneasy sensation, une'asiness, distress', suf'fering; an'guish, ag'ony, tor'ture, pang, tor'ment; disqui'etude, anxi'ety, solic'itude, grief, sor'row, remorse', compunc'tion; *pains*, labor, work, toil. *See* Grief, Trouble, Bear, Repentance, Work.

PAINT—form a figure *or* likeness in colors, depict', represent', delin'eate, col'or, besmear', sketch, describe'. *See* Color, Stain.

PAL'ACE—*See* House.

PAL'ATE—*See* Taste.

PALE—white *or* whitish, fair, wan, cadav'erous, pall'id, ghast'ly, deficient in color, not ruddy; not bright, not shining, dim. *See* Dull, Ghastly.

PAL'PITATE—beat gently, beat, flut'ter, pant, heave, gasp. *See* Beat Flutter.

PARCH—*See* Burn, Hot.

PAR'DON—*See* Forgive.

PART—por'tion, piece, frag'ment, share, divisi'on, sec'tion, spe'cies, sort, class, mem'ber; concern', in'terest; side, part'y, fac'tion; *parts*, qual'ities, pow'ers, fac'ulties, accom'plishments; quar'ters, re'gions, dis'tricts. *See* Party, Rate, Interest, District.

PART—divide', par'cel, sep'arate, break, sev'er, disunite'. *See* Separate, Cut *off*.

PARTIC'ULAR—not gen'eral, individ'ual, distinct', sin'gle, minute'; speci'al, especi'al, pecu'liar, exclu'sive, specif'ic, prin'cipal, chief; odd, sin'gular. *See* Correct, Odd.

PART'Y—*See* Company, Faction, Plot.

PART'Y—fac'tion, clique, set, cabal', junt'o; side, com'pany. *See* Company, Faction, Plot.

PASS—*See* Go, Way.

PASSED *or* PIERCED *not to be*—impass'able, impen'etrable, imper'vious.

PASSI'ONATE—iras'cible, chol'eric, an'gry, ir'ritable, hast'y, impet'uous; highly excited, ve'hement, warm; an'imated. *See* Angry, Hasty, Hot.

PAS'SIVE—suf'fering, endu'ring, pa'tient, resign'ed; submis'sive, unresist'ing, not opposing, quies'cent; unmov'ed, unprovok'ed. *See* Sufferance, Peaceable.

PAT'TERN—*See* Copy, Example.

PAUSE—make a short stop, stop, cease, intermit', delay', wait, forbear; *in uncertainty*, demur', hes'itate, delib'erate, wav'er, fluct'uate. *See* Delay, Waver.

PAWN—*See* Pledge.

PAY—compensa'tion, rec'ompense, reward', remunera'tion, equiv'alent, wa'ges, sal'ary, allow'ance, sti'pend, hire. *See* Amends.

PEACE—qui'et, tranquill'ity, calm, calm'ness, qui'etness, ease, repose', rest, peace'fulness, seren'ity, still'ness, peace'ableness, mild'ness. *See* Quiet, Mildness, Concord, Calm.

PEACE'ABLE—tran'quil, qui'et, undisturb'ed, unag'itated, calm, serene', peace'ful, mild, still, pacif'ic. *See* Calm, Passive.

PECU'LIAR—*See* Particular.

PEER—*See* Nobility, Equal.

PEE'VISH—*See* Fretful.

PEN'ALTY—*See* Fine.

PEN'CIL—*See* Paint.

PERCEIVE'—*See* See.

PERCEIVE'—know by the senses, feel, see, discern', distin'guish, know, understand', no'tice, regard', observe'. *See* Distinguish, Notice, Espy.

PER'FECT—bring to perfection, complete', fin'ish, con'summate, fulfil', accom'plish, achieve'. *See* Finish, Accomplish, Bring *about*.

PERFORM'ANCE—execu'tion, comple'tion, do'ing, ac'tion, act, deed, thing done; compositi'on, written book; *of some note*, exploit, achieve'ment, feat, hero'ic act, deed of renown, great *or* noble achievement. *See* Accomplishment, Production, Work, Thing *done*.

PER'FUME—*See* Smell.

PER'ISH—die, lose life, expire; with'er, fade, decay', waste away, pine. *See* Die, Dead, Wasting.

PERPLEX'—*See* Entangle, Worry.

PEST—plague, pest'ilence, epidem'ic, infec'tion, bane, wor'rying, nu'isance, annoy'ance. *See* Infection.

PETITI'ON—request', supplica'tion, pray'er, suit, entreat'y, solicita'tion. *See* Entreaty, Beg.

PILE—*See* Heap.

PI'OUS—*See* Godly.

PITH—*See* Strength.

PIT'IABLE—exciting pity, pit'eous, pit'iful, mis'erable, dole'ful, woe'ful, rue'ful. *See* Doleful, Unhappy.

PIT'Y—commisera'tion, compassi'on, fel'low-suf'fering, sym'pathy, condo'lence, mer'cy, human'ity. *See* Feeling, Mercy.

PLACE—spot, site, positi'on, situa'tion, sta'tion; rank, or'der; seat, res'idence, man'sion; of'fice, employ' ment; cal'ling, occupa'tion, condition; ground, room, stead; por'tion. *See* Office, Situation.

PLACE—put, set, lay, locate', posite', depos'it, repos'it; appoint', induct', estab'lish, fix; invest', lend'. *See* Order, Fix, Lay.

PLAGUE—*See* Pest.

PLAGUE—infest with disease, &c.; vex, tease, har'ass, troub'le, embar'rass, annoy', molest', torment', tor'ture, tant'alize, importune'. *See* Worry, Weary, Importune.

PLAIN—*See* Clear.

PLAN—draught, form: scheme, proj'ect, design', device', contri'vance, strat'agem. *See* Design, Invent, Plot.

PLEAS'URE—joy, delight', gratifica'tion, lux'ury, enjoy'ment, com'fort, delecta'tion, agreeable sensations *or* emotions; will, choice, pur'pose, inten'tion, command'; fa'vor. *See* Enjoyment, Gratitude, Mirth, Joy, Satisfaction, Luxury, Sport.

PLEASURE *one given to*—volup'tuary, ep'icure, sens'ualist. *See* Luxury.

PLEDGE—pawn, sure'ty, host'age, secur'ity, mort'gage, cau'tion. *See* Security.

PLEDGE—*See* Answerable *for*.

PLENT'Y—*See* Enough.

PLOT—conspir'acy, intrigue', confed'eracy, combina'tion, cabal', junt'o, part'y clique, set, coaliti'on; device', machina'tion, contri'vance, scheme, strat'agem. *See* Design, Contrive, Party, Plan, Combine.

PLOW—*See* Till.

PLUN'DER—pil'lage, rap'ine, prey, boot'y, spoil; ru'in, rav'age, waste. *See* Rapacious, Waste.

POI'SON—*See* Deadly.

POL'ISH—*See* Beautify.

POLITE'—pol'ished, refin'ed, well-bred', el'egant, grace'ful; court'eous, complaisant', oblig'ing, civ'il, urbane', af'fable, genteel', deferen'tial. *See* Genteel, Awkward, Becoming.

POLITE'NESS—polish *or* elegance of manners, gentil'ity, good-breed'ing, good-man'ners, refine'ment, civil'ity, court'eousness, cour'tesy, urban'ity, affabil'ity, complaisance', obliging attentions. *See* Civility, Attention.

POMP—splendid procession, magnif'icence, parade', splend'or, grand'eur, state. *See* Procession, Show, Grand.

POOR—need'y, in'digent, des'titute, neces'sitous, distress'ed; bar'ren, mean, jejune'; depress'ed, low, deject'ed; *in spirit*, hum'ble, contrite', abased in one's own sight by a sense of guilt. *See* Bare, Barren, Mean, Sorry.

POOR'NESS—destitu'tion, in'digence, pov'erty, want, need, distress', neces'sity, ex'igency; mean'ness, low'ness; bar'renness, steril'ity. *See* Necessity, Want.

POP'PY—*See* Sleep.

PORE—*See* Opening.

POR'TER—*See* Bear.

POR'TION—*See* Part.

POS'ITIVE—set, laid down, express'ed, direct', explic'it; ab'solute, real, express', per'emptory, ar'bitrary, despot'ic, dogmat'ical, con'fident. *See* Actual, Arbitrary, Flat.

POSSESSI'ON—oc'cupancy, occupa'tion, ten'ure, ten'ancy; thing possessed, land, estate', goods, &c.; mad'ness, lu'nacy. *See* Occupy, Goods, Madness.

POUR—*See* Melt, Flow.

POW'ER—abil'ity, strength, po'tency, force, en'ergy, capac'ity, capabil'ity, pu'issance, co'gency, ef'ficacy, effica'ciousness, effici'ency; in'fluence; command', rule, sway, author'ity, right of governing, domin'ion, domina'tion, ascend'ancy; *royal*, roy'alty, scep'tre, crown. *See* Ability, Force, Influence, Dominion, Gift.

POW'ER *want of*—inabil'ity, disabil'ity, im'potence, im'potency, weak'ness, incapac'ity, inef'ficacy, ineffici'ency, insuffici'ency, inad'equacy, incom'petency, imbecil'ity. *See* Weakness.

POW'ERFUL—might'y, po'tent, strong, pu'issant, for'cible, effica'cious, influen'tial, co'gent, energet'ic, ve'hement, emphat'ic, intense'. *See* Effect *producing*, Prevailing, Strong, Able, Almighty.

PRAISE—commenda'tion, approba'tion, applause', enco'mium, eu'logy, panegyr'ic. *See* Approbation, Name.

PRAISE—commend', approve', applaud', laud, extol', mag'nify, glo'rify, eu'logise, pan'egyrise, do honor to. *See* Great *make*.

PRAISE'WORTHY—deserving praise, commend'able, laud'able, approv'ed.

PRAT'TLE—*See* Talk.

PRAY—*See* Beg, Entreat, Entreaty, Petition.

PRE'CEPT—command', rule, doc'trine, max'im, prin'ciple. *See* Command, Order.

PREF'ACE—introduc'tion, pro'em, prelim'inary, prel'ude. *See* Introductory, Introduce.

PRES'ENT—*See* Gift, Reward, Give.

PRESERVE'—*See* Keep, Free.

PRESS—*See* Embrace, Force.

PRESS'ING—urging with force *or* weight, squeez'ing, constrain'ing, crowd'ing, embrac'ing, distres'sing, for'cing; ur'gent, impor'tunate, emer'gent. *See* Important, Squeeze.

PRETENSE'—false appearance, pretext', excuse', delu'sion, impos'ture. *See* Color, Defense, Cloak.

PRET'TY—*See* Beautiful.

PREVAIL'ING—gaining advantage, superiority *or* victory, having effect, persuading, succeed'ing; predom'inant, prev'alent, superior in power, effica'cious; most general, epidem'ic, epidem'ical. *See* Powerful.

PREVENT'—go before, precede', antic'ipate; hin'der, obstruct', intercept', impede', ob'viate, preclude'. *See* Anticipate, Go, Hinder, Interrupt.

PREY—*See* Plunder.

PRICE—*See* Value, Sell.

PRICK—*See* Stir.

PRIDE—inordinate self-esteem, self-conceit', conceit', ar'rogance, haught'iness, hauteur', presum'ption, assum'ption, in'solence, van'ity; splendid show, ostenta'tion. *See* Conceit, Proud, Show.

PRIEST—*See* Ecclesiastic.

PRINCE—sov'ereign, mon'arch, po'tentate, king, em'peror, chief, ruler.

PRIOR'ITY—prece'dence, pre-em'inence, pref'erence. *See* Going *before.*

PRIS'ON—*See* Liberty *being deprived of.*

PRI'VATE—*See* Secret.

PRIV'ILEGE—immun'ity, exem'ption; ben'efit, advant'age, fa'vor, prerog'ative, right, claim, lib'erty. *See* Freedom, Benefit.

PROCEED'ING—proc'ess, proce'dure, move'ment, course, prog'ress, progressi'on; affair', mat'ter, concern', transac'tion, suit, meas'ure, step. *See* Course, Operation, Go.

PROCESSI'ON—cav'alcade, tri'umph, ova'tion; train, ret'inue, suite. *See* Pomp, Victory.

PROCLAIM'—*See* Publish.

PRODUCE'—*See* Beget.

PRODUC'TION—that which is produced, prod'uce, prod'uct; perform'ance, compositi'on, work. *See* Performance, Offspring.

PROFESS'—make open declaration of, avow', acknowl'edge, declare', assev'erate. *See* Declare, Own.

PROF'IT—*See* Gain.

PROF'ITABLE—yielding *or* bringing profit *or* gain, gain'ful, lu'crative; benefici'al, use'ful, advanta'geous. *See* Gain, Use.

PROJ'ECT—*See* Plan, Design.

PROMIS'CUOUS—min'gled, mix'ed, confu'sed, undistin'guished, indiscrim'inate, com'mon. *See* Mix, Confused, Common.

PROM'ISE—binding declaration, assur'ance, guarantee', engage'ment, undertak'ing. *See* Warrant.

PROOF—tri'al, es'say, exper'iment, test; demonstra'tion, convic'tion, satisfac'tion; test'imony, attesta'tion, ev'idence, certifica'tion; firm'ness, hard'ness, impenetrabil'ity. *See* Evidence, Trial.

PROP'ERTY—qual'ity, at'tribute; wealth, possessi'ons, paraphérna'lia. *See* Quality, Goods, Riches.

PROPH'ESY—*See* Foretell.

PROROGUE'—protract', prolong', defer', adjourn', delay', postpone'. *See* Delay.

PROS'PER—fa'vor, render successful; be successful, succeed'; grow, increase', thrive, make gain. *See* Gain, Favor, Increase, Flourish, Happiness.

PROTECT'—cov'er, shield, defend', guard, preserve', secure', support', har'bor, shel'ter, fos'ter, cher'ish, coun'tenance, pat'ronise, encour'age, sanc'tion. *See* Covering, Defend, Harbor, Foster, Encourage.

PROTEC'TION *place for*—asy'lum, sanc'tuary; shel'ter, defense' ref'uge, retreat'. *See* Defense, Security.

PROUD—having inordinate self-esteem, self-conceited, conceit'ed, vain, ar'rogant, haught'y, supercil'ious, assum'ing, in'solent; dar'ing, presump'tuous; grand, loft'y, splend'id, magnif'icent; ostenta'tious. *See* High, Grand, Pride.

Prove—try, test; evince', estab'lish, ascertain', ver'ify, demon'strate, man'ifest; cer'tify, attest', ev'idence. *See* Evidence, Proof.

PROVIDE'—procure beforehand, get, furn'ish, supply'. *See* Give.

PRU'DENT—*See* Wise.

PRUNE—*See* Cut *off.*

PRY'ING—inspecting closely, inquis'itive, scru'tinizing, search'ing, cu'rious. *See* Search.

PUB'LIC, PUB'LISH—*See* Common.

PUB'LISH—make known, divulge', disclose', promul'gate, proclaim', discov'er, expose', declare', reveal', impart', commu'nicate. *See* Discover, Public, Declare, Spread, Utter, Blaze.

PUFF—*See* Swell.

PULL—*See* Draw, Tear.

PUN'ISH—*See* Discipline, Fine.

PURGE—*See* Clean.

PURSE—*See* Money.

PUSH—*See* Drive.

PUT—*See* Place.

PUT *down*—baf'fle, repress', crush, quell, suppress', subdue', reduce', restrain'; degrade', deprive', depose'; confute', si'lence. *See* Baffle, Check, Delay.

PUZ'ZLE—perplex', embar'rass, put to a stand, grav'el, confound'; bewil'der, entan'gle. *See* Cross, Entangle, Worry.

Q.

QUACK—em'piric, char'latan, mount'ebank.

QUAKE—*See* Shake, Fear.

QUALIFICA'TION — endow'ment, acquire'ment; legal *or* requisite power; modifica'tion, restric'tion, limita'tion. *See* Accomplishment, Endow.

QUAL'IFY—fit for, furnish with; mod'erate, mod'ulate, tem'per, hu'mor, restrain', lim'it, mod'ify, reg'ulate. *See* Fit, Bound.

QUAL'ITY—*See* Property.

QUAR'REL—wran'gle, scold, petty fight, scuf'fle, dispute', con'test, conten'tion, brawl, broil, jar, jan'gle, alterca'tion, tu'mult, feud, fray, affray', va'riance, dif'ference, disagree'ment, breach. *See* Difference, Disagreement, Tumult, Insurrection.

QUAR'RELLING—conten'tion, dispute', disputa'tion, cav'iling, dis'cord, dissen'sion, strife, fac'tion, con'troversy, alterca'tion, wran'gling, debate', va'riance, dif'ference, disagree'ment. *See* Difference, Quarrel, Faction.

QUES'TION—*See* Ask, Search.

QUICK—alive', liv'ing; swift, hast'y; speed'y, prompt, expediti'ous, read'y; act'ive, nim'ble, ag'ile, brisk, vig'orous, live'ly, viva'cious. *See* Hasty, Active, Lively, Ready, Sharp.

QUICK'EN—make alive, viv'ify, revive', resus'citate; has'ten, accel'erate, ex'pedite, despatch'; shar'pen, stim'ulate, incite'; cheer, reinvig'orate. *See* Animate, Cheer, Hasten.

QUICK'NESS—speed, veloc'ity, swift'ness, celer'ity, fleet'ness, rapid'ity, rap'idness, nim'bleness, brisk'ness, alert'ness; expediti'on, despatch'; activ'ity, prompt'ness, agil'ity, dexter'ity; acute'ness, keen sensibility; sharp'ness, pun'gency; *of intellect*, acute'ness, sharp'ness, sagac'ity, penetra'tion, acu'men, shrewd'ness. *See* Briskness, Sharpness, Eagerness.

QUI'ET—rest, repose', still'ness, peace, ease, tranquil'lity, calm, qui'etness. *See* Peace, Ease, Still, Silence, Subside.

QUOTE—*See* Adduce.

R.

RACE—run'ning, rapid course *or* motion, course, prog'ress, move'ment; breed; lin'eage, fam'ily, house, descent', stock, dyn'asty, genera'tion. *See* Course, House, Breed, Stock.

RAGE—violent anger, passi'on, fu'ry, excite'ment, extreme violence; enthu'siasm; extreme eagerness *or* passion. *See* Madness, Anger, Boil.

RAISE—*See* Lift.

RAM'BLE—rove, wan'der, stroll, range, walk, ride *or* sail at random. *See* Excursion, Stray, Go, Wander.

RANK—*See* Order.

RAPA'CIOUS—given to plunder, seizing by force, greedy on seizing, rav'enous, vora'cious, greed'y, devour'ing. *See* Plunder, Greediness.

RARE — uncom'mon, not frequent, scarce, sin'gular, choice, prec'ious, unusually excellent, incom'parable, unique'; thin, por'ous, not dense; nearly raw, imperfectly roasted *or* boiled. *See* Uncommon, Thin.

RASH—*See* Foolhardy.

RASH'NESS—temer'ity, precip'itance, precip'itancy, precipita'tion, hast'iness. *See* Hasty.

RATE—propor'tion, stand'ard, ra'tio, quo'ta, degree'; price, amount'; tax, sum. *See* Tax, Value, Count, Part.

RAVE—*See* Madness.

RAW—*See* Rare.

RAY—*See* Beam.

READ—*See* Collect.

READ'Y—quick, apt, prompt, not hesitating; acute'; expert', dex'trous; prepar'ed, fit'ted; wil'ling, free, cheer'ful, dispos'ed; being at the point, near, not distant; e'asy, fac'ile, opportune', short. *See* Quick, Active, Clever, Free, Sharp, Briskness.

RE'ASONABLE — rati'onal, eq'uitable, just, fair; not immod'erate, mod'erate, tol'erable, not exces'sive. *See* Fair, Just.

REBEL'LIOUS—sediti'ous, mu'tinous. *See* Tumultuous.

RECALL'—revoke', repeal'. *See* Call *back*.

RECAL'LED, REGAIN'ED *or* REM'EDIED *not to be*—irrev'ocable, irretriev'able, irrevers'ible, irrecov'erable, irrep'arable, incur'able, irreme'diable. *See* Call *back*, Recover.

RECEIPT'—act of receiving, accep'tance, accepta'tion, recep'tion; discharge', acquit'tance; rec'ipē, pre'script, prescrip'tion. *See* Take, Pay.

RECK′ON—count, num′ber, compute′, cal′culate, es′timate; esteem′, account′, repute′. *See* Count, Pay.
REC′OGNISE—remem′ber, no′tice, recollect′. *See* Own, Mark.
RECOV′ER—get *or* obtain what was lost, regain′, retrieve′; restore′, repair′, recruit′. *See* Recalled *not to be*, Redeem.
REDEEM′—purchase back, ran′som, lib′erate, relieve′, res′cue, affranch′ise, manumit′, recov′er, deliver from, save; compens′ate, make amends for. *See* Free, Buy, Recover.
REDRESS′—relief′, rem′edy, deliverance from wrong, in′jury *or* oppression; repara′tion. *See* Cure.
REDUND′ANT—*See* Abounding.
REFER′—relate′, regard′, respect′; appeal′, apply′; allude′, glance at, hint; direct′; reduce′. *See* Relate, Appeal, Hint, Apply, Consult.
REFRESH′—cool, allay heat; reinvig′orate, give new strength to, revive′, ren′ovate, renew′. *See* Cool, Animate.
REF′UGE—*See* Protection.
REFUSE′—reject′, deny′ decline′, oppose′, repel′, rebuff′, object′. *See* Object, Oppose, Overrule, Remains.
REGARD′—*See* Respect, Interest.
REG′ULAR—*See* Rule.
REG′ULAR—conformed to a rule, methyod′ical, systemat′ic, or′derly, exact′, period′ical. *See* Orderly, Formal.
REIGN—*See* Govern.
REJOICE′—make joyful, gladden, exhil′arate; exult′, joy; grat′ulate, congrat′ulate, felic′itate. *See* Joy, Gladden.
RELATE′—tell, recite′, rehearse′, repeat′, narrate′, recount′, recapit′ulate, detail′, enum′erate; refer′, concern′, respect′, regard′, appertain′, in′terest, affect′. *See* Tell, Explain, Describe, Refer.
RELA′TIONSHIP — kin′dred, rela′tion, alli′ance; affin′ity, consanguin′ity. *See* Kin, Marriage.
RELIGI′ON—god′liness, pi′ety, devo′tion, sanc′tity; sys′tem of faith and worship. *See* Holiness.
REMAIN′—*See* Dwell.
REMAINS′—that which is left, leav′ings, rasp′ings, scrap′ings, rel′ics, rem′nant, remain′der, res′idue, ref′use, sco′ria, dross; dead body, corpse, car′cass. *See* Dregs.
REMARK′—no′tice, observa′tion, annota′tion, note, com′ment, com′mentary. *See* Comment, Explanation.
REMEM′BER—*See* Recognize.
RENOWN′—*See* Fame.
REPEAT′—*See* Seek.
REPENT′ANCE—sor′row, pain, grief, regret′, pen′itence, contriti′on, compunc′tion, remorse′. *See* Pain, Grief.
REPORT′—*See* Fame.
REPLY′ *smart or witty*—repartee′, retort′.
REPROACH′—cen′sure, find fault with, chide, reprove′, upbraid′, cast in the teeth, scold, rail, brawl, rate. *See* Blame, Abuse, Disgrace, Gibe.
RESPECT′—regard′, atten′tion, def′erence, considera′tion, esteem′, estima′tion, hon′or; venera′tion, rev′erence. *See* Honor, Refer.
RESPECT′—hold in respect *or* estimation, esteem′, val′ue, regard′, relate to; ven′erate, revere′, rev′erence. *See* Refer, Value, Honor.
REST—*Ser* Ceasing.
RESTOR′ING *or* RETURN′ING *the act of*—restora′tion, renditi′on, restitu′tion, retribu′tion. *See* Amends.
RETURN′ *of like for like*—retalia′tion, requit′al, reciproca′tion, reciproc′ity, mutual′ity, alterna′tion. *See* Each, Other.
REWARD′ — remunera′tion, rec′ompense, compensa′tion, requit′al, satisfac′tion, amends′, guer′don; bribe; pun′ishment. *See* Amends, Satisfaction, Gift.
RICH′ES—wealth, op′ulence, af′fluence, possessi′ons, mam′mon, sub′stance. *See* Possession, Fortune.
RID′ICULE — contemptuous laughter, derisi′on, burlesque′; sat′ire, i′rony, sar′casm. *See* Censure, Laughable.
RIGHT—straight; just, eq′uitable, fair, hon′est; fit, prop′er, suit′able, becom′ing; law′ful; true; correct′; not left. *See* Fair, Fit, Correct.
RIG′ID—*See* Severe.
RING—*See* Surround, Jingle.
RISE—*See* Go, Issue, Origin.
RITE—*See* Form.
RIV′ER—*See* Water.
ROAD—*See* Way.
ROLL—*See* Catalogue.
ROOM—space, com′pass, extent′, place, stead; apart′ment, cham′ber. *See* Place.
ROOM′Y—spa′cious, large, wide, capa′cious. *See* Large, Immense.
ROT—pu′trefy, corrupt′, decay′. *See* Corrupt.
ROT′TEN—pu′trid, pu′trefied, ca′rious, decay′ed, corrupt′; unsound′, defect′ive, treach′erous, deceit′ful; fet′id, stink′ing, ran′cid, ill-smelling *See* Corrupt, Deceitful.
ROUSE—*See* Stir.
RUDE—*See* Barbarous, Impertinent.
RULE—*See* Precept, Order, Decree.
RUN—*See* Course.

S.

Sa'cred—*See* Holy.

Sad—sor'rowful, mel'ancholy, mourn'ful, dull, down'cast, deject'ed, depress'ed, cheer'less, dole'ful, trist, gloom'y. *See* Dull, Doleful, Mourn, Cast *down*.

Safe—*See* Sure.

Salute'—saluta'tion, greet'ing. *See* Kiss.

Same—*See* Equal, One, Individual.

Sanc'tion—*See* Fix, Ordain.

Satisfac'tion—content'ment, repose of mind; convic'tion; pleas'ure, gratifica'tion; amends', rec'ompense, compensa'tion, indemnifica'tion, atone'ment; pay'ment, discharge'. *See* Pleasure, Amends, Reward.

Sat'isfy—suffice', content', grat'ify, please; pay to content, rec'ompense, indem'nify; free from doubt, suspense *or* uncertainty; convince'; pay, discharge'. *See* Amends *make*, Pay.

Sau'cy—*See* Fretful.

Save—*See* Free, Redeem.

Sav'ing—preserv'ing, spar'ing, fru'gal, not lav'ish, econom'ical, thrift'y, parsimo'nious, except'ing. *See* Mean.

Saw—*See* Cut.

Say—*See* Speech, Tell, Aphorism.

Scale—*See* Climb.

Scarce—*See* Rare.

Scar'city — scarce'ness, defici'ency, pen'ury, dearth, fam'ine; rare'ness, infre'quency. *See* Want.

Scat'ter—*See* Spread, Dispel.

Scent—*See* Smell.

Schol'ar—learn'er, pu'pil, disci'ple, ty'ro; man of letters, doct'or. *See* Follower, Master.

Sci'ence—*See* Knowledge.

Scoff—*See* Laugh *at*, Disdain.

Scope—*See* Aim.

Scroll—*See* Catalogue.

Scrup'le—*See* Doubt.

Sculp'ture—*See* Carve.

Sea—o'cean, main, deep, wave, bil'low, surge. *See* Wave.

Se'aman—se'afarer, sail'or, mar'iner, tar, marine', sea-sol'dier; sea-rob'ber, pi'rate, sea-freeboot'er.

Search—seek'ing, looking for, scrut'iny, investiga'tion, inqui'ry, examina'tion, research', rum'mage, quest, inquest', pursuit'. *See* Prying.

Search—look over *or* through, explore', rum'mage, exam'ine, scrut'inize, inves'tigate, inquire', seek for, probe, pry. *See* Look.

Se'cret — hid, hid'den, conceal'ed, clandes'tine, unreveal'ed, occult', unseen', priv'ate, unknown', seclud'ed, la'tent, myste'rious, mys'tic, *See* Hide.

Sect—*See* Heretic.

Secur'ity — protec'tion, guard, defen'se, palla'dium, guarantee', fence, safe'ty, cer'tainty, depos'it, pledge, mort'gage. *See* Guard, Sure, Protection, Pledge.

Sed'iment—*See* Dregs.

See—*See* Look.

Seek—*See* Look.

Seize—*See* Take, Catching.

Sell—*See* Buy, Merchandise, Trade.

Send—throw, cast, thrust, impel', drive, cause to go *or* pass, commissi'on; *away*, dismiss', discard', discharge', despatch', cause to depart; *forth* or *out*, produce', put *or* bring forth, emit', exhale'; *on a special commission*, depute', del'egate. *See* Cast, Throw.

Sense—sensa'tion, percep'tion, apprehen'sion, discern'ment, judg'ment, fac'ulty, in'tellect, re'ason, understand'ing; con'sciousness, convic'tion; mean'ing, im'port, significa'tion. *See* Feeling, Judgment, Understanding, Meaning.

Sep'arate—divided from, disjoin'ed, disconnect'ed, unconnect'ed, not united, distinct', dif'ferent, detach'ed, disunit'ed, apart', asund'er. *See* Part, Unlike, Individual.

Sep'arate—disunite', divide', sev'er, part, sund'er, disconnect', detach', disjoin', disengage'. *See* Part, Cut *off*, Distinguish, Interrupt.

Serene'—*See* Calm.

Ser'mon—*See* Speech, Dissertation.

Serv'ant—*See* Minister.

Serv'ant—one who serves, domes'tic, me'nial, drudge; help, assist'ant; *in Scripture*, slave, bond'man, one used as an instrument. *See* Minister, Inferior, Instrument.

Set—*See* Fix, Appoint.

Set *apart*'—ded'icate, devote'; con'secrate, hal'low, sanc'tify. *See* Apply.

Set'tle—make permanent, fix, estab'lish, determ'ine, corrob'orate, confirm'; mar'ry; adjust', compose', tran'quillize; reg'ulate, arrange'; col'onize; liq'uidate, balance *or* pay. *See* Fix, Found, Still, Pay.

Severe'—rig'id, harsh, stern, austere, not mild *or* indulgent, strict, hard, rig'orous; grave, so'ber, sedate'; afflic'tive, distress'ing, sharp, vi'olent; bi'ting, extreme'; exact', crit'ical, nice. *See* Rigid, Sharp, Difficult, Grave.

Shade—*See* Darkness, Dull.

Shake — ag'itate, move, trem'ble,

shud′der, shiv′er, quiv′er, quake, tot′ter. *See* Trembling, Move.

SHAME—*See* Disgrace.

SHAME′FUL—what brings shame *or* disgrace, scand′alous, disgrace′ful, in′famous, oppro′brious, ignomin′ious, injurious to reputation. *See* Disgrace.

SHAME′LESS—destitute of shame, wanting modesty, im′pudent, bra′zen-faced, immod′est, auda′cious, insensible to disgrace; inde′cent, indel′icate. *See* Impudence, Modest.

SHAPE—*See* Form.

SNARE—*See* Part.

SHARP—keen, acute′, not blunt, not obtuse; discern′ing, pen′etrating, saga′cious, shrewd, quick, wit′ty, inge′nious; sour, ac′id, pier′cing, shrill; severe′, harsh, rig′id, cru′el, bit′ing, sarcast′ic, taunt′ing, satir′ical; fierce, ar′dent, fi′ery, vi′olent; keen, severe′, pun′gent, pain′ful, prick′ing, piq′uant. *See* Keen, Quick, Active, Severe, Ready.

SHARP′NESS—keen′ness, acid′ity, sour′ness, ac′rimony, pun′gency, pain′fulness; acute′ness, penetra′tion, shrewd′ness, sagac′ity, discern′ment, quick′ness, ingenu′ity; keen′ness, edge, sever′ity. *See* Sourness, Quickness, Judgment, Edge.

SHIELD—*See* Covering.

SHIFT—change, turn′ing; expe′dient, ref′uge, resource′, altern′ative; fraud, art′ifice, chicane′, eva′sion, sub′terfuge, trick, turn. *See* Cheat, Trick.

SHINE—*See* Light.

SHINE—emit rays of light, ra′diate, give light, beam, glit′ter, corus′cate, glis′ten, gleam, glare, spark′le. *See* Gleam, Blaze, Bright.

SHOOT—*See* Sprout, Bud.

SHORE—*See* Brink, Edge.

SHOR′TER *made*—shor′tened, abridg′ed, abbre′viated, epit′omized, condens′ed, contract′ed, curtail′ed, les′sened, dimin′ished. *See* Brief, Abridgment.

SHOUT—*See* Call.

SHOW—spect′acle, exhibiti′on, sight, representa′tion; ostenta′tion, parade′, display′, array′, pomp; appear′ance, sem′blance, seem′ing, spe′ciousness, plausibil′ity. *See* Pomp, Appearance, Color.

SHOW—exhib′it, present′, display′; make to know, direct′, point out, in′dicate, man′ifest, prove, inform′, instruct′, teach, explain′; disclose′, discov′er, bestow′, confer′, afford′. *See* Instruct, Discover, Declare, Direction.

SHOW′Y—making a great show, ostenta′tious, splend′id, fine, gay, gaud′y, glar′ing, pomp′ous, sump′tuous, grand, magnif′icent, state′ly. *See* Gay, Grand, Vain.

SHUD′DER—*See* Shake, Fear.

SHUF′FLE—prevar′icate, equiv′ocate, evade′, quib′ble, cav′il, sophis′ticate.

SHUN—avoid′, keep clear of, eschew′; evade′, escape′, elude′; decline′, neglect′. *See* Neglect.

SHUT—*See* Close, Surround.

SHY—fearful of near approach, coy, reserv′ed, not familiar; cau′tious, war′y, care′ful; suspici′ous, jeal′ous. *See* Careful, Jealousy.

SICK—sick′ly, ill, diseas′ed, mor′bid; disgust′ed. *See* Illness, Invalid.

SIDE—*See* Edge.

SIFT—*See* Separate, Judge.

SIGHT—*See* See, Look.

SIGN—*See* Mark.

SI′LENCE—taciturn′ity; still′ness, calm′ness, qui′et, calm, repose′, cessa′tion; dum′bness, mute′ness. *See* Calm, Quiet, Still.

SI′LENT—*See* Calm, Dumb.

SIL′VER—*See* Money.

SIM′PLE—*See* Bare.

SIN—*See* Wicked, Crime, Violation, Debt, Depravity.

SINCERE′—real, unfeign′ed, gen′uine, true, hon′est, undissem′bling, up′right, uncorrupt′; unvarn′ished, plain; frank. *See* Genuine, Honesty.

SIN′GLE—*See* Alone, Particular.

SITUA′TION—positi′on, seat, loca′tion, site, state, conditi′on, predic′ament, plight, case; place, of′fice. *See* Place, Condition, State, Office.

SIZE—bulk, big′ness, mag′nitude, great′ness, extent′. *See* Bigness, Fatness, Greatness.

SKILL—*See* Ability.

SKIN—*See* Flay.

SLACK′EN—slack, make less tense, tight *or* severe, relax′, remit′; mit′igate, dimin′ish, abate′, low′er, relieve′, unbend′. *See* Lessen, Lower.

SLAN′DER—defama′tion, detrac′tion, scand′al, cal′umny, backbit′ing, asper′sion; disgrace′, reproach′, disreputa′tion, ill′name. *See* Disgrace, Contumely, Asperse.

SLAUGHT′ER—mas′sacre, carn′age, but′chery, mur′dering. *See* Destruction, Kill.

SLAVE—*See* Liberty *being deprived of.*

SLEEP—*See* Doze.

SLEEP′Y—drow′sy, lethar′gic, inclined to sleep; causing *or* inducing sleep, soporif′ic, soporif′erous, narcot′ic, o′piate, dor′mitive, somnif′ic, somnif′erous, an′odyne, sed′ative, compos′ing. *See* Dose.

SLEN′DER—*See* Thin.

SLIP—*See* Deceive, Mistake.

SLOW—tard′y, dil′atory, slug′gish, te′dious. *See* Lazy, Dull.

SLY′—cun′ning, deceit′ful, art′ful, insid′ious, craft′y, wi′ly, circumvent′ive, sub′tle, sub′tile. *See* Cunning, Deceitful.

SMELL—*See* Sweet-smelling.

SMOOTH—*See* Soft, Beautify.

SNAKE—*See* Serpent.

SNARE—*See* Entangle.

SNARL′ING—growl′ing, grum′bling angrily, cyn′ical, snap′pish, wasp′ish.

SNATCH—*See* Seize.

SNEAK′ING—creeping away slily, stealing away; crouch′ing, cring′ing, ser′vile, obse′quious, mean, pit′iful; meanly parsimo′nious, cov′etous, nig′gardly. *See* Mean, Miserly.

SOAK—steep, imbrue′, mac′erate, imbue′, wet, mois′ten, drench.

SO′BER—tem′perate; stead′y, se′rious, sol′emn, grave. *See* Abstaining, Grave.

SOFT—easily yielding to pressure, easily to be bent *or* led, flex′ible, sup′ple, lithe, lim′ber, flac′cid, pli′ant, yield′ing, duct′ile, pli′able, compli′ant, tract′able, doc′ile; mal′leable; gen′tle, mild, meek, kind, civ′il; smooth, flow′ing; e′asy, qui′et. *See* Kind, Dainty, Allay, Ease, Weak.

SOIL—*See* Stain.

SOLE—*See* Alone.

SOL′EMN—*See* Grave.

SOL′ID—hard, firm, compact′, sta′ble, strong, mas′sive; real, substan′tial, sound, val′id, true, just; entire′, whole. *See* Firm, Strong, Thick.

SOL′ITARY—living alone, des′olate. *See* Alone, Desolate, Lonely.

SOPH′ISTRY—fallacious reasoning, chicane′, chica′nery, soph′ism, fal′lacy. *See* Falsehood.

SOR′RY—griev′ed, pain′ed, afflict′ed, affect′ed, hurt, mort′ified, vex′ed, chagrin′ed; poor, mean, vile, worth′less. *See* Mean, Poor, Grieve.

SORT—*See* Kind, Character.

SOUL—*See* Spirit, Mind.

SOUND—*See* Jingle, Bound *back*.

SOUND—*See* Whole.

SOUR—*See* Sharp.

SOUR′NESS—acid′ity, ac′idness, tart′ness, sharp′ness; *of manner*, asper′ity, harsh′ness, ac′rimony. *See* Sharpness.

SOURCE—*See* Origin.

SPAR′ING—*See* Saving.

SPEAK—*See* Tell.

SPEAK *to*—accost′, address′; *with*, talk, converse′, discourse′, commune′. *See* Talk, Utter, Unspeakable.

SPEECH—lan′guage; ora′tion, philip′pic, harangue′, address′, discourse′; sol′ecism. *See* Language, Speech, Talk, Interview.

SPEND—lay out, dispose of, part with • expend′, consume′, waste, squan′der, exhaust′, drain; pass; har′ass, fatigue′. *See* Expensive, Waste.

SPIR′IT—*See* Life, Lively, Active.

SPIR′ITUAL—immate′rial, incorpo′real; men′tal, intellect′ual; sa′cred, ecclesiast′ical; ethe′real, ghost′ly; god′ly, ho′ly. *See* Intellectual, Godly, Holy.

SPITE—ha′tred, spleen, ran′cor, mal′ice, malig′nity, malev′olence, gall; grudge, pique. *See* Malice, Hatred, Enmity, Envy.

SPLEEN—*See* Spite.

SPOIL—Plunder.

SPOKE—*See* Beam.

SPORT—what diverts and makes merry, play, game, diver′sion, fun, drol′lery, frol′ic, wag′gery, wag′gishness; pas′time, recrea′tion; amuse′ment, entertain′ment; mock, mock′ery, contemptuous mirth; diversion of the field, as fowl′ing, hunt′ing, fish′ing. *See* Mirth, Jest, Frolic, Pleasure, Amusing, Lively.

SPOT—*See* Stain, Blemish, Blameless.

SPREAD *abroad*—scat′ter, disperse′, distrib′ute, diffuse′, dispense′, cir′culate, prop′agate, divulge′, pub′lish, dissem′inate; *out*, open, expand′, unfold′, unfurl′. *See* Dispel, Publish, Open, Lay, Swell, Unfold.

SPRING—*See* Issue.

SPROUT—*See* Bud.

SPUR—*See* Stir.

SPU′RIOUS—not genuine, coun′terfeit, suppositi′ous, false, fictiti′ous, deceit′ful, adul′terate; illegit′imate, bast′ard. *See* Genuine *not*, Bastard, Vain, Law.

SPURN—*See* Despise.

SQUEAM′ISH—fastid′ious, over-nice′, over-scrup′ulous. *See* Nice.

SQUEEZE—press, gripe; oppress′, har′ass, crush; hug, embrace closely; *out*, extort′, express′, extract′. *See* Press, Compress.

STA′BLE—*See* Strong.

STAG′GER—walk unsteadily, reel, tot′ter, vac′illate; fail, hesitate. *See* Doubt, Wave, Stammer.

STAIN—discol′or, mac′ulate, blot, spot, foul, soil, pollute′, blem′ish, sul′ly, tarn′ish, taint; dye, tinge. *See* Blot, Blemish, Corrupt, Disgrace, Color.

STAIN *without*—immac′ulate, spot′less, pure, untaint′ed, in′nocent, unstain′ed, unblem′ished, unpollut′ed, irreproach′able, unsul′lied, untarn′ished. *See* Harmless, Disgrace.

STAM′MER—stut′ter, fal′ter, hesitate in speaking. *See* Stagger.

Stamp—Character. *See* Mark.
Stand—*See* Stay.
State—*in life,* conditi′on, cir′cumstances, situa′tion, sta′tion; political body, *or* body politic, body of men; rank, post, degree′, qual′ity, dig′nity, gran′deur. *See* Condition, Situation, Order, Grand.
Stat′ue—*See* Stand.
Stay—remain′, contin′ue, abide′; endure′, last; wait, attend′; rest, rely′, confide in, trust; stop, restrain′, withhold′, delay′, obstruct′, hin′der. *See* Abide, Dwell, Delay, Hinder.
Step—*See* Go, Pace, Mark.
Stick—*See* Follower, Attachment.
Stiff—*See* Formal.
Still—stop, check, restrain′, calm, allay′, assuage′, lull, pac′ify, compose′, appease′, qui′et; si′lence, suppress′, subdue′. *See* Settle, Calm, Ease, Peace, Allay, Silence.
Stink—*See* Rotten.
Stir—move, ag′itate; *up,* incite′, in′stigate, prompt, excite′, raise, an′imate, stim′ulate, provoke′, rouse, begin′, quick′en, enli′ven, disturb′. *See* Move, Animate, Awaken, Agitation, Anger.
Stock—stem, bod′y; fam′ily, lin′eage; fund, cap′ital, store, mag′azine, supply′, accumula′tion, hoard, provisi′on; *live stock,* as cattle *or* sheep. *See* Body, House, Race, Goods, Lay.
Stop—*See* Hinder.
Store—*See* Stock.
Sto′ry—tale, narra′tion, nar′rative, memoir′, his′tory, recit′al, rela′tion; fic′tion, fa′ble; in′cident, an′ecdote; floor, loft. *See* Memoir, History, Chronicle, Falsehood.
Strange—*See* Odd, Outward.
Strat′agem—*See* Plan, Trick.
Stray—wan′der, de′viate, err, swerve, rove, ram′ble. *See* Ramble, Wander.
Stream—cur′rent, course, tide; riv′er, riv′ulet, brook, stream′let, rill; drift. *See* Course.
Strength—*See* Strong, Power.
Strength′en—make strong *or* stronger, for′tify, invig′orate, an′imate, encour′age; enforce′; estab′lish, confirm′, corrob′orate. *See* Encourage, Animate, Strong.
Strict—*See* Severe.
Strife—*See* Quarrel.
Strike—*See* Beat.
Strong—pow′erful, vig′orous, robust′, stout, sturd′y, hard′y, firm, sol′id, sin′ewy, mus′cular, a′ble; might′y, po′tent, co′gent, for′cible, effica′cious; ar′dent, e′ager, zeal′ous; vi′olent, ve′hement, earn′est; bright, glar′ing, viv′id. *See* **Powerful,** Firm, Solid, Able, Lusty, Bright, Zealous.
Stud′y—*See* Think, Attention.
Srrug′gle—*See* Unwilling.
Stup′id—*See* Blockhead.
Sub′ject—placed *or* situate under; expos′ed, li′able, obnox′ious; prone, dispos′ed. *See* Accountable.
Subside′—sink *or* fall to the bottom, set′tle; abate′, intermit′, assuage′, allay′, become tranquil. *See* Calm, Ease, Quiet, Settle.
Success′—*See* Prosper, Lucky.
Suc′kle—*See* Nourish.
Sud′den—without notice, abrupt′, unexpect′ed, unlooked for, unantic′ipated; emer′gent. *See* Abrupt.
Suf′fer—undergo′, feel *or* bear pain, endure′, support′, sustain′; allow′, tol′erate, permit′. *See* Support, Allow.
Suf′ferance — bear′ing, endur′ance, pa′tience, modera′tion; tolera′tion, permissi′on, suf′fering, allow′ance. *See* Bear, Suffer, Allow, Passive.
Suit′able—fit′ting, accord′ant, agree′able, conform′able, adapt′ed, conve′nient, prop′er, befit′ting, becom′ing, ad′equate. *See* Agreeable, Becoming, Fit.
Superfici′al—being on the surface; shal′low, flim′sy, not deep *or* profound, slight, cur′sory, de′sultory.
Support′—bear, sustain′, uphold′, stay, prop, sec′ond, for′ward, assist′, coun′tenance, fa′vor, pat′ronize, promote′, encour′age, nur′ture, nour′ish, cher′ish, fos′ter; maintain′, protect′, shield, defend′; ver′ify, make good, substan′tiate, vin′dicate. *See* Bear, Suffer, Stay, Assist, Favor, Encourage, Nourish, Foster, Protect.
Sure—cer′tain, unfail′ing, infal′lible, indub′itable; safe, secure′, firm. *See* Certain, Doubted *not to be,* Firm, Security.
Surround′—encom′pass, com′pass, envi′ron, inclose on all sides; inclose′, encir′cle, invest′, besiege′.
Survey′—*See* Look.
Swal′low *up*—take into the stomach; engulf′, absorb′, engross′, engage wholly; imbibe′, exhaust′, consume′, devour′. *See* Engross.
Sweet—*See* Amiable.
Sweet-smel′ling—odorif′erous, o′dorous, fra′grant, perfum′ed, sweet-scent′ed, ambro′sial.
Swell *out*—dilate′, distend′, expand′, extend′. *See* Lay, Spread
Swift—*See* Quick.
Swing—*See* Stagger.
Sys′tem—meth′od, or′der, mode, man′ner. *See* Manner, Order, Formality.

T.

TAKE—receive′, accept′; *from*, deprive of, deduct′, subtract′; detract′, der′ogate; *to* or *upon one's self*, appro′priate, assume′, adopt′, undertake′; ar′rogate, usurp′. *See* Seize, Embrace, Catching.

TAL′ENT—*See* Ability.

TALK—*See* Speak.

TALK—converse′, speak, confer′, discourse′, commune′, hold intercourse, chat, confab′ulate. *See* Speak.

TALK—con′verse, conversa′tion, col′loquy, di′alogue, discourse′, con′ference, confabula′tion, chat. *See* Speech, Hearsay.

TALK′ATIVE—speaking much, loqua′cious, gar′rulous.

TAME—*See* Overcome.

TART—*See* Sour.

TASTE—gusta′tion, sa′vor, rel′ish, fla′vor, pal′ate; judg′ment, ge′nius, discern′ment, percep′tion, sensibil′ity. *See* Palate, Flat, Judgment.

TAX—im′post, trib′ute, dut′y, contribu′tion, cus′tom, toll, rate, sum imposed, assess′ment; bur′den; charge, cen′sure; task. *See* Custom, Rate.

TEACH—*See* Instruct.

TEASE—*See* Trouble, Incommode.

TELL—*See* Relate, Declare.

TEM′PER—*See* Abstaining, Cool, Cross, Ill-tempered, Sourness, Qualify.

TEMPT—allure′, entice′, attract′, solic′it, incite′, provoke′, decoy′, seduce′, invei′gle, coax, persuade′, induce′, draw; *in Scripture*, try, prove, put to trial for proof. *See* Allure, Induce, Lead, Try.

TEND—*See* Lean.

TER′RIFY—fright′en, appal′, alarm′, intim′idate, dismay′. *See* Fright, Fear.

TEST—crite′rion; stand′ard; tri′al. *See* Trial.

THICK—dense, not thin, compact′, close, sol′id; gross, coarse; tur′bid, mud′dy, fec′ulent; inspis′sated; fre′quent; *make thick*, incras′sate; consol′idate. *See* Dense, Close, Solid, Gross.

THIN—rare, atten′uated, not dense, not close; slim, small, slen′der, lean, me′agre, slight. *See* Rare, Small, Lean.

THING *done*—fact; act, ac′tion, deed; feat, exploit′, achieve′ment. *See* Performance.

THINK—judge, conclude′, imag′ine, suppose′, conceive′, opine′, fan′cy, muse, rum′inate, med′itate, reflect′, call to mind, cog′itate, consid′er, delib′erate, contem′plate, pon′der; believe′, deem; guess, conject′ure, surmise′, divine′. *See* Fancy, Count.

THOUGHT—ide′a, concep′tion, imagina′tion, percep′tion, no′tion, fan′cy, conceit′; reflec′tion, considera′tion, contempla′tion, medita′tion, cogita′tion, delibera′tion, opin′ion, judg′ment, suppositi′on; design′, pur′pose; solic′itude, care, concern′. *See* Conceit, Judgment, Opinion, Care, Whim.

THOUGHT′FUL—full of thought, contemp′lative, med′itative, reflect′ive, mind′ful, consid′erate, delib′erate, delib′erative, attent′ive, care′ful, cir′cumspect, wa′ry, advis′ed, discreet′. *See* Careful, Watchful, Mind.

THROW—*See* Cast, Send.

THRUST—*See* Intrude.

TI′DINGS—*See* News.

TIE—*See* Gird, Band, Knot.

TIME—pe′riod, age, date; dura′tion, se′ason, e′ra, ep′och; repetiti′on, doub′ling.

TIME′LY—se′asonable, opportune′. *See* Untimely.

TIRE—*See* Weary.

TIR′ED—fatig′ued, wear′ied, har′assed, exhaust′ed. *See* Weary.

TONGUE—*See* Language, Speech.

TOOL—*See* Instrument.

TOP—*See* Height.

TRACE—*See* Mark.

TRADE—bus′iness, traf′fic, bar′ter, com′merce, merch′andise, deal′ing, exchange′, truck′age; occupa′tion. *See* Business, Interchange, Merchandise, Change.

TRANS′ITORY—pass′ing, fleet′ing, tem′porary, tran′sient, evanes′cent, mo′mentary, speedily vanishing, quickly passing away, fad′ing. *See* Time, Vanish, Mortal.

TRANSPAR′ENT—per′vious, pellu′cid, diaph′anous, translu′cent, transpic′uous, lim′pid. *See* Clear, Bright.

TRAV′EL—*See* Go.

TREAT′MENT—man′agement, manipula′tion; u′sage; entertain′ment. *See* Use.

TREM′BLE—*See* Shake, Fear.

TREM′BLING—tre′mor, trepida′tion, quak′ing, shaking with fear, shiv′ering. *See* Shake, Fear.

TRI′AL—exper′iment; expe′rience; test. *See* Test, Attempt, Proof, Try.

TRICK—*See* ENTANGLE.

TRICK—art′ifice, chicane′, strat′agem, cheat, cheat′ing, wile, fraud, cozen′age, jug′gle, finesse′, sleight, leger-demain′, decep′tion. *See* Cheat, Cunning, Shift, Jest.

TRIF′LING—triv′ial, pet′ty, friv′olous, fu′tile, unimpor′tant, insignif′icant immate′rial, use′less, inept′, unfit′, inconsid′erable, light, slight, worth′-less. *See* Idle, Vain.

TROUB′LE—*See* Grieve, Hurt.

TROUB′LE, TROUB′LES—disturb′ance, agita′tion, commo′tion, perplex′ity, distress′, afflic′tion, suf′fering, advers′ity, calam′ity, misfor′tune; molesta′tion, inconve′nience, annoy′ance, une′asiness, vexa′tion; dif′ficulties, embar′rassments, perplex′ities, vexa′tions, cares, anxi′eties, disqui′etudes; sor′row, mis′ery. *See* Agitation, Misfortune, Care, Difficulty, Pain, Vexation, Darkness.

TROUB′LESOME—molest′ing, annoy′ing, irk′some, disqui′eting, disturb′ing, har′assing, perplex′ing, afflict′ive, vexa′tious. *See* Wearisome.

TRUE—*See* Sincere.

TRUNK—*See* Body.

TRUST—*See* Belief, Confidence.

TRUTH—verac′ity; hon′esty, vir′tue, faith′fulness, fidel′ity, con′stancy; fact, real′ty, conform′ity. *See* Faithfulness, Honesty, Maxim, Doctrine.

TRY—*See* Trial, Attempt, Tempt.

TUM′BLE—roll, fall, roll down, drop, sink.

TU′MULT—commo′tion, disturb′ance, agita′tion, riot, broil, row, affray′, up′roar, confu′sion, bus′tle, stir, convul′sion. *See* Insurrection, Quarrel, Trouble.

TUMULT′UOUS—disor′derly, tumult′uary, ag′itated, rest′less, unqui′et, irreg′ular, nois′y, disturb′ed, confu′sed, promis′cuous, unru′ly, ungov′ernable, turb′ulent, vi′olent; sediti′ous, mu′tinous, rebel′lious, insur′gent, ri′otous. *See* Insurrection, Rebellious, Confused, Loud, Hasty.

TURN—*See* Change, Shift.

TWIG—*See* Shoot.

TWIST—contort′, writhe; wreathe, wind, encir′cle, twine, twirl, form, weave, bend, turn, wrest, wrench, swing; pervert′, distort′. *See* Entangle, Move *round*, Crooked.

TYPE—*See* Mark, Letter.

U.

UM′PIRE—*See* Judge.

UNBELIEF′—incredul′ty, infidel′ity, disbelief′, distrust′. *See* Belief.

UNBOUND′ED—bound′less, in′finite, unlim′ited, interm′inable, uncheck′ed, uncontrol′led, unrestrain′ed. *See* End *without*.

UNBUR′Y—exhume′, exhu′mate, disinter′. *See* Rise, Bury.

UNCER′TAIN *be*—wav′er, fluct′uate, un′dulate, os′cillate, vac′illate; doubt, hes′itate. *See* Wave, Doubted *not to be*.

UNCOM′MON—not com′mon, not u′sual, rare, scarce, unique′, choice, sin′gular. *See* Rare.

UNDERSTAND′—comprehend′, know, conceive′, apprehend′, appre′ciate. *See* Know.

UNDERSTAND′ING—in′tellect, intel′ligence, judg′ment, fac′ulty, comprehen′sion, knowl′edge, apprehen′sion, concep′tion, percep′tion. *See* Judgment, Knowledge, Sense.

UNDETERM′INED—not determ′ined, unset′tled, undecid′ed, indeterm′inate, irres′olute, unresolv′ed, unstead′y, wav′ering, fluc′tuating, doubt′ful, hes′itating. *See* Changeable, Uncertain *be*.

UNE′ASINESS—rest′lessness, want of ease, disqui′et, disqui′etude; solic′itude, anxi′ety, care. *See* Care, Trouble.

UNE′QUAL—*See* Equal.

UNFAITH′FUL—faith′less, perfid′ious, treach′erous; undut′iful, disloy′al; neglect′ful. *See* Faithless, Neglect.

UNFOLD′—open folds, unrav′el, expand′, spread out; devel′ope; disclose′, reveal′, divulge′, declare′, tell. *See* Explain, Spread, Declare.

UNHAP′PY—wretch′ed, mis′erable, unfor′tunate, unluck′y, calam′itous, e′vil, distress′ed, afflict′ed. *See* Pitiable.

UNIMPORT′ANT—immate′rial, insignif′icant. *See* Trifling.

UNIVERS′AL—*See* Whole, All.

UNJUST′—not just, ineq′uitable, unfair′, dishon′est, iniq′uitous, knav′ish, rog′uish, wrong′ful. *See* Iniquity, Wicked, Honesty, Justice.

UNLIKE′—not like, dissim′ilar; dif′ferent, di′verse; sep′arate, distinct′. *See* Separate.

UNRELENT′ING—relent′less, impla′cable, inex′orable, hard, cru′el. *See* Appeased *not to be*, Cruel, Deadly.

UNSET′TLE—unfix′, unhinge′, make uncertain *or* fluctuating, disconcert. *See* Order *put out of*.

UNSPEAK′ABLE—that cannot be uttered *or* expressed, inef′fable, inexpres′sible, unut′terable. *See* Speak.

UNTIME′LY—premature′, inopportune′, unse′asonable, ill-timed. *See* Timely, Time.

UNWIL′LING—not wil′ling, loth, disinclin′ed, reluct′ant, back′ward, averse′. *See* Averse, Obstinate.

UP′RIGHT—*See* Right.

UP′RIGHTNESS—perpendic′ular erection; rect′itude, integ′rity, hon′esty. *See* Honesty, Justice.

USE—use′fulness, util′ity, advan′tage, ben′efit, prof′it, avail′, ser′vice, ser′viceableness; employ′ment, prac′tice, cus′tom, u′sage. *See* Benefit, Profitable, Custom, Treatment, Apply.

USURP′—*See* Assume *falsely*, Take.

UT′TER—speak, pronounce′, artic′ulate, express′; disclose′, discov′er, divulge′, pub′lish. *See* Speak, Publish, Call *out*.

UT′TERED—spo′ken, pronounc′ed; disclos′ed, pub′lished; *by mouth* or *voice*, o′ral, ver′bal, vo′cal.

V.

VAIN—em′pty, unre′al; worth′less, i′dle, use′less, abort′ive, fruit′less, ineffect′ual; conceit′ed, proud, self-conceit′ed, opin′ionative, opin′iated, opin′ioned, self-opin′ioned, egotist′ical; show′y, ostenta′tious; light, incon′stant; unsat′isfying; false, deceit′ful, spu′rious. *See* Idle, Proud, Empty, Foolish, Conceit, Showy, Spurious.

VALE—val′ley, dale, dell, din′gle.

VAL′OR—*See* Courage.

VAL′UE—worth, price, rate; estima′tion, account′, import′ance, ef′ficacy, apprecia′tion; appraise′ment, *or* apprize′ment, valua′tion, assess′ment. *See* Rate, Worth.

VAL′UE—es′timate, rate, apprize′ *or* appraise′, assess′, compute′, cal′culate; esteem′, respect′, regard′, prize, appre′ciate. *See* Rate, Respect.

VAL′UABLE—having value *or* worth, preci′ous, cost′ly, es′timable, worth′y. *See* Worthy.

VAN′ISH—disappear′, pass away from sight; flit. *See* Transitory.

VAN′QUISH—*See* Overcome.

VAUNT′ING—boast′ing, glo′rying, vainglo′ry, ostenta′tion, display′, parade′, va′por, van′ity, ar′rogance, rodomontade′. *See* Boaster.

VEIL—*See* Hide.

VEN′GEANCE—*See* Punish, Assert.

VEST—*See* Covering.

VET′ERAN—*See* Old.

VEX—*See* Incommode.

VEXA′TION—chagrin′, mortifica′tion, teas′ing, troub′le, une′asiness. *See* Trouble, Wearisome.

VI′BRATE—*See* Shake.

VICE—*See* Crime.

VICT′UALS—*See* Food.

VIE—*See* Emulous.

VIEW—*See* Look, See, Glance.

VIG′OROUS—*See* Active, Strong.

VIL′LAGE—*See* Countryman, House.

VIL′LAIN—vas′sal, ser′vant, sub′ject, depend′ant; wretch, scoun′drel, ras′cal. *See* Follower, Blockhead.

VIOLA′TION—law-breaking, infringe′ment, infrac′tion, transgres′sion, tres′pass; rape. *See* Sin, Injury.

VI′OLENT—for′cible, ve′hement, outra′geous, bois′terous, turb′ulent, fierce, fu′rious, impet′uous, passi′onate, assail′ant. *See* Cruel, Hot, Force.

VI′PER—*See* Serpent.

VISI′ON—sight; appear′ance, appariti′on, phant′om, spec′tre, ghost. *See* Ghost, Ghostly.

VOICE—*See* Uttered.

VOID—*See* Empty *space*.

VOTE—suf′frage, voice.

VOW—*See* Pray.

VOW′EL—*See* Letter.

W.

WA′GES—*See* Pay, Reward.

WAIL—*See* Mourn, Grieve.

WALK—*See* Go.

WAN′DER—rove, ram′ble, stroll, roam, range; leave home, depart′, mi′grate; digress′, diverge′, de′viate, err, stray; be delir′ious. *See* Ramble, Go, Eccentric, Joint *out of*.

WANT—defici′ency, defect′; need, lack, neces′sity; pov′erty, pen′ury, in′digence. *See* Scarcity, Necessity; Poorness, Poor.

WAN′TON—*See* Lust, Loose.

WARM—*See* Heat.

WARM—cord′ial, heart′y, sincere′, zeal′ous, ar′dent, ferv′ent, intense′; keen, ir′ritable. *See* Affectionate, Hearty, Zealous, Keen, Hot, Enthusiast.

WARMTH—warm′ness, gentle heat, ferv′ency, ferv′or, zeal, ar′dor, intens′ity, cordial′ity, ve′hemence, heat, glow; earn′estness, e′agerness; excite′ment, anima′tion. *See* Heat, Eagerness, Life.

WARN′ING—previous notice, moniti′on, admoniti′on, cau′tion. *See* Caution.

WAR′RANT—*See* Answerable *for*, Promise.

WA′RY—cau′tious, cir′cumspect, watch′ful, guard′ed, scrup′ulous, timorously prudent. *See* Watchful, Careful, Aware.

WASTE—devasta′tion, spoil, rav′age, desola′tion, hav′oc, destruc′tion; squan′dering, dissipa′tion; consump′tion, loss, useless expense; desolate or uncultivated country; ground or space unoccupied. *See* Plunder, Loss, Destruction.

WASTE—cause to be lost, expend uselessly, squan′der, dis′sipate, lav′ish, consume′, spend, use; destroy′, des′olate; wear out, exhaust′. *See* Lavish, Spend, Destroy, Desolate, Corrupt.

WAST′ING—lav′ishing, dis′sipating, des′olating, laying waste; decay′, consump′tion, decline′, phthi′sis; per′ishing, fad′ing, deca′dence.

WATCH′FUL—vig′ilant, attent′ive, care′ful, heed′ful, observ′ant, cau′tious, cir′cumspect, wake′ful. *See* Careful, Thoughtful, Wary, Aware.

Wa'ter—*See* Soak.
Wave, Wa'ver—*See* Uncertain *be,* Pause.
Wave—bil'low, surge, break'er. *See* Sea.
Way—pas'sing; pas'sage, road, high'way, lane, street; meth'od, sys'tem, mode, course, means, man'ner, form, fash'ion. *See* System, Gap, Opening, Means, Course, Custom.
Weak—fee'ble, infirm', pip'ing, weak'ly, enfee'bled, debil'itated, enerv'ated, flac'cid, lim'ber, lax; easily broken; soft, pli'ant; low, small. *See* Broken *easily,* Foolish, Low.
Weak'en—debil'itate, enfee'ble, enerv'ate, effem'inate, inval'idate. *See* Droop.
Weak'ness—fee'bleness, debil'ity, lan'guor, infirm'ity, unhealthi'ness, imbecil'ity, frail'ty, frail'ness; fool'ishness; *in the plural,* defeat', fail'ing, fault, foi'ble. *See* Power *want of,* Fault, Folly.
Weap'on—*See* Arm, Covering.
We'arisome—causing weariness, tire'some, te'dious, prolix', fatig'uing, exhaust'ing, reduc'ing, troub'lesome, annoy'ing, vexa'tious. *See* Troublesome.
We'ary—reduce', exhaust', fatigue', tire, har'ass, dispir'it, jade, wear out, subdue'; annoy', vex. *See* Worry.
Weep—*See* Mourn.
Weigh—*See* Think.
Weight — *See* Burden, Importance, Heavy.
Well—*See* Good.
Wet—*See* Moist, Soak.
Wheat—*See* Food.
Whim—sudden turn *or* start of the mind, freak, fan'cy, mag'got, caprice', prank. *See* Conceit, Thought, Frolic, Lightness.
White—*See* Pale.
Whit'en—bleach, blanch.
Whole—all, to'tal, in'tegral; complete', entire', per'fect, sound, well, undivid'ed; full. *See* All, Holy.
Whol'ly—to'tally, complete'ly, entire'ly, per'fectly, ful'ly.
Wick'ed—e'vil, sin'ful, immor'al, im'pious, profane', irreligi'ous, deprav'ed, unjust', iniq'uitous, nefa'rious; *in a high degree,* atro'cious, hein'ous, fla'grant, flagiti'ous, facin'orous, vil'lanous, enor'mous, mon'strous. *See* Abandoned, Corrupt, Unjust, Iniquity, Sin.
Wide—*See* Large.
Wife—*See* Marriage.
Wild—*See* Cruel.
Will—*See* Disposition, Pleasure, Choice, Kindness, Malice.
Will—test'ament; cod'icil.
Wind'ing—*See* Crooked.
Wipe—*See* Clean.
Wise—having knowledge, sage, saga'cious, sa'pient, discern'ing; discreet', judici'ous pru'dent; learn'ed, know'ing, skil'ful, dex'terous; god'ly, pi'ous. *See* Godly, Ignorant.
Wise'ly—pru'dently, judici'ously, discreet'ly, with wisdom, sage'ly, saga'ciously, skil'fully, cau'tiously, cir'cumspectly.
Wish—*See* Hope, Choose.
Wish *for*—desire', cov'et, long for, hanker after, sigh for; request', entreat', soli'cit, beg, ask; aspire to. *See* Beg, Aim.
Wit'ty—*See* Odd.
Won'der—surprise', amaze'ment, aston'ishment, admira'tion; mir'acle, mar'vel, prod'igy, strange thing, mon'ster.
Wont—*See* Custom.
Work—employ'ment, occupa'tion, la'bor, toil, drud'gery, opera'tion; fab'ric, manufac'ture; ac'tion, deed, feat, achieve'ment; compositi'on, book. *See* Operation, Accomplishment, Performance, Pain.
Wor'ry—bore, tease, troub'le, vex, har'ass, perplex', distract', disturb', annoy', confuse', confound'; fatigue', tear, man'gle; taunt, tant'alize, torment'. *See* Trouble, Mangle, Displease, Plague.
Worse *make*—dete'riorate, impair', in'jure, dam'age. *See* Corrupt, Injure.
Worth—val'ue, ex'cellence, perfec'tion; mer'it, desert', good'ness, use'fulness; vir'tue, moral'ity. *See* Value, Morals.
Worth'y—*See* Valuable, Praiseworthy.
Wrath—*See* Anger.
Wretch—*See* Miser, Unhappy.
Wri'ter—pen'man, scribe, clerk, co'pyist, transcrib'er, sec'retary, amanuen'sis; law'yer; au'thor, clas'sic, ed'itor.
Writhe—*See* Twist.
Wrong—*See* Wicked, Ill.

Y.

Year—*See* Time.
Yield—*See* Give *up.*
Yield'ing—produc'ing, afford'ing; conced'ing, resign'ing, surren'dering, allow'ing; flex'ible, accom'modating; compli'ance, submissi'on, def'erence.
Young—youth'ful, juv'enile, in'fantile, in'fantine; pu'erile, boy'ish, child'ish.
Youth—juvenil'ity, adoles'cence, pueril'ity; boy'hood, child'hood, in'fancy.

Z.

Zeal—ar'dor, heat, ferv'ency, ferv'or, warmth, ear'nestness, intens'ity, e'agerness, avid'ity, enthu'siasm. *See* Warmth, Eagerness, Heat.
Zeal'ous—ar'dent, ear'nest, warm, ferv'ent, solic'itous, an'xious, intense'. *See* Warm, Affectionate.

A KEY

TO THE

LATIN, GREEK, AND OTHER ROOTS.

THE following key has been prepared to assist the pupil in analyzing the compound words, and in ascertaining the etymology of others, in which the form is very unlike that of its root. All the *leading* words are here alphabetically arranged, and the roots from which they are derived placed opposite to them. By *leading* words we mean those from which others are formed by the addition of ordinary terminations. Thus, *secure* is given, while *securely*, *security*, &c., are omitted; and if *accumulation* or *accumulative* is sought, *accumulate* alone will be found in the key. Those only, however, have been omitted, which are very obviously formed from those included in the key. The roots in parentheses are a few not found in the general collection, but which are necessary to the complete analysis of the words with which they are placed.

Abalienate. *Ab; alius.*
Abbreviate. *Ab; brevis.*
Abdicate. *Ab; dico.*
Abditive, abditory, abdomen. *Ab; do.*
Abduce, abduction. *Ab; duco.*
Aberr, aberration. *Ab; erro.*
Abhor, abhorrent. *Ab; horreo.*
Ability. *Habeo.*
Abject. *Ab; jacio.*
Abjure. *Ab; juro.*
Ablactate. *Ab; lac.*
Ablation. *Ab; latum.*
Able. *Habeo.*
Ablepsy. *A; blepo.*
Abligate. *Ab; ligo.*
Ablocate. *Ab; locus.*
Abluent, ablution. *Ab; luo.*
Abnegate. *Ab; nego.*
Abnormous. *Ab; norma.*
Abolish, abolition. *Ab; oleo.*
Abominable, abominate. *Ab; omen.*
Aboriginal. *Aborigines.*
Abortion. *Ab; orior.*
Abound. *Ab; undo.*
Abrade, abrasion. *Ab; rado.*
Abridge. *Ab; brevis.*
Abrogate, abrogable. *Ab; rogo.*
Abrupt. *Ab; ruptum.*
Abscind, absciss. *Ab; scindo.*
Abscond. *Abs; con; do.*
Absent, absentaneous. *Abs; ens.*
Absist. *Ab; sisto.*
Absolute, absolution, absolutory, absolve, absolvatory. *Ab; solvo.*
Absonant. *Ab; sonus.*
Absorb, absorption. *Ab; sorbeo.*
Abstain, abstemious. *Abs; teneo.*
Absterge, abstersion. *Abs; tergeo.*
Abstinent. *Abs; teneo.*
Abstract, abstractitious. *Abs; traho.*
Abstrude, abstruse. *Abs; trudo.*
Absurd. *Ab; surdus.*
Abundant. *Ab; undo.*

Abuse, abusive. *Ab; utor.*
Academy. *Academia.*
Acatalectic. *A; cata; lego.*
Acatalepsia. *A, cata; lepsis.*
Accede. *Ac; cedo.*
Accelerate. *Ac; celer.*
Accend, accension. *Ac; candeo.*
Accent, accentuate. *Ac; cano.*
Accept, acceptation. *Ac; capio.*
Access, accessary, accessory, accessible. *Ac; cedo.*
Accident. *Ac; cado.*
Accipient. *Ac; capio.*
Accite. *Ac; cito.*
Acclaim, acclamate. *Ac; clamo.*
Acclive, acclivity. *Ac; clivus.*
Accolent. *Ac; colo.*
Accommodate. *Ac; com; modus.*
Accompany. *Ac; com; pannus.*
Accomplice. *Ac; com; plico.*
Accomplish. *Ac; com; pleo.*
Accord. *Ac; cor.*
Accorporate. *Ac; corpus.*
Account. *Ac; con; puto.*
Accredited. *Ac; credo.*
Accrescent, accretion, accrue. *Ac; cresco.*
Accubation, accumb. *Ac; cubo.*
Accumulate. *Ac; cumulo.*
Accuracy, accurate. *Ac; cura.*
Accusable, accusation, accuse. *Ac; causa.*
Accustom. *Ac; coutume.*
Acephalous. *A; cephale.*
Acerbate, acerbity. *Acerbus.*
Acervate. *Acervus.*
Acescent, acetous, acetose. *Aceo.*
Ache. *Achos.*
Acid, acidulæ, acidulate. *Acidus.*
Acknowledge. *Ac; nosco.*
Acme. *Acme.*
Acoustics. *Acouo.*
Acquest. *Ac; quæro.*
Acquiesce. *Ac; quies.*
Acquire, acquisition. *Ac; quæro.*

Acrid, acrimony, acritude. *Acris.*
Acridophagus. (*Acris*, a locust); *phago.*
Acronic. *Acron; nyx.*
Acropolis. *Acron; polis.*
Acrospire. *Acron; sperma.*
Acrostic. *Acron; stichos.*
Act, action, actual, actuary, actuate. *Ago.*
Acuate, aculeate, acumen, acuminated, acute. *Acuo.*
Adacted. *Ad; ago.*
Adamant. *A; damao.*
Adapt, adaptation. *Ad; aptus.*
Add. *Ad; do.*
Adcorporate. *Ad; corpus.*
Addecimate. *Ad; deca.*
Addendum. *Ad; do.*
Addict. *Ad; dico.*
Additament, addition. *Ad; do.*
Adduce, adduction. *Ad; duco.*
Addulce. *Ad; dulcis.*
Adenography. *Aden; grapho.*
Adenology. *Aden; logos.*
Adequacy, adequate. *Ad; equus.*
Adhere. *Ad; hæreo.*
Adiaphory. *A; dia; phero.*
Adit. *Ad; eo.*
Adjacent. *Ad; jaceo.*
Adject, adjectitious. *Ad; jacio.*
Adjoin. *Ad; jungo.*
Adjourn. *Ad; jour.*
Adjudge, adjudicate. *Ad; judico.*
Adjugate. *Ad; jugum.*
Adjument. *Ad; juvo.*
Adjunct. *Ad; jungo.*
Adjure. *Ad; juro.*
Adjust. *Ad; justus.*
Adjutant, adjutor, adjuvant, adjuvate. *Ad; juvo.*
Admeasurement, admensuration, admetiate. *Ad; mensura.*
Adminicle, adminicular. *Ad; manus.*
Administer, administrate. *Ad; minister.*
Admirable, admiration, admire. *Ad; mirus.*
Admissible, admission, admit, admittance. *Ad; mitto.*
Admix. *Ad; misceo.*
Admonish, admonition, admonitory. *Ad; moneo.*
Admove. *Ad; moveo.*
Adnascent, adnate. *Ad; nascor.*
Adolescent. *Ad; oleo.*
Adopt. *Ad; opto.*
Adorable, adoration, adore. *Ad; oro.*
Adorn. *Ad; orno.*
Adulation, adulator. *Adulatum.*
Adult. *Ad; oleo.*
Adulterate, adultery. *Ad; alter.*
Adumbrant. *Ad; umbra.*
Adust, adustible, adustion. *Ad; ustum.*
Advance, advantage. *Avant.*
Advene, advenient, advent, adventitious, adventual, adventure. *Ad; venio.*
Adverb, adverbial. *Ad; verbum.*
Adversary, adverse, adversity, advert, advertize. *Ad; verto.*
Advice, advisable, advise, advisory. *Ad; video.*
Advocacy, advocate. *Ad; voco.*
Aerial, aerie. *Aer.*
Aeriform. *Aer; forma.*
Aerography. *Aer; grapho.*
Aerolite. *Aer; lithos.*
Aerology. *Aer; logos.*
Aeromancy. *Aer; mancia.*
Aerometry. *Aer; metrum.*
Aeronaut. *Aer; nauta.*
Aeroscope. *Aer; scopeo.*
Affable. *Af; fari.*
Affabrous. *Af; fabrico.*
Affamish. *Af; fames.*
Affect, affectation, affection, affectuous *Af; facio.*
Affiance, affidation, affidavit. *Af; fides.*
Affiliate. *Af; filius.*
Affinity. *Af; finis.*
Affirm, affirmative. *Af; firmus.*
Affix. *Af; fixus.*
Afflation, afflatus. *Af; flatus.*
Afflict. *Af; fligo.*
Affluent, afflux. *Af; fluo.*
Affranchise. *Af; franc.*
Affriction. *Af; frico.*
Affront. *Af; frons.*
Affuse. *Af; fundo.*
Affy. *Af; fides.*
Agalaxy, *A; galax.*
Agamist. *A; gameo.*
Agent. *Ago.*
Aggelation. *Ag; gelu.*
Aggeneration. *Ag; genus.*
Agglomerate. *Ag; glomus.*
Agglutinate. *Ag; gluten.*
Aggrandize. *Ag; grandis.*
Aggravate. *Ag; gravis.*
Aggregate. *Ag; grex.*
Aggress. *Ag; gradior.*
Aggrieve. *Ag; gravis.*
Agile. *Agilis.*
Agitate. *Agito.*
Agminal. *Agmen.*
Agnate. *Ag; nascor.*
Agnition, agnize. *Ag; nosco.*
Agnominate. *Ag; nomen.*
Agonistic, agony. *Agon.*
Agrammatist. *A; grapho.*
Agrarian. *Ager.*
Agree. *A; gratia.*
Agrestic. *Ager.*
Agricolation, agriculture. *Ager; colo.*
Aid. *Ad; juvo.*
Aide-de-camp. *Ad; juvo;* (*de*, of); *campus.*
Air. *Aer.*
Albification. (*Albus*, white); *facio.*
Alchymy. *Al; chymos.*
Alectryomachy. *Alectryon; machomai.*
Alectryomancy. *Alectryon; mancia.*
Alexander, Alexandrine. *Alexeo; aner.*
Alexipharmic. *Alexeo; pharmacon.*
Alexiteric. *Alexeo;* (*deleterion*, poison.)
Algebra. *Algebra.*
Algid. *Algeo.*
Algific. *Algeo; facio.*
Alias. *Alius.*
Alibi. *Alius; ibi.*
Alible. *Alo.*
Alien. *Alius.*
Aliferous. *Ala; fero.*
Aligerous. *Ala; gero.*
Aliment, alimony. *Alo.*
Aliquant. *Alius; quantus.*
Aliquot. *Alius; quot.*
Alkalescent, alkali, alkalizate. *Alkali.*
Allege, allegiance. *Al; lego.*
Allegoric, allegorist, allegory. *Allos; egorea.*
Alleviate. *Al; levo.*
Allicient. *Al; licio.*
Alligate. *Al; ligo.*
Allision. *Al; lido.*
Alliteration. *Al; litera.*
Allocation. *Al; locus.*
Allocution, alloquy. *Al; loquor.*
Allow. *Al; laus.*
Allude. *Al; ludo.*
Alluminor. *Al; lumen.*

Allure. *Al; lure.*
Allusive, allusory. *Al; ludo.*
Alluvial, allusion. *Al; luo.*
Almanac. *Al; men.*
Almoner, alms. *Alo.*
Alphabet. *Alpha; beta.*
Alpine. *Alpes.*
Alter. *Alter.*
Altercation, altern. *Alternus.*
Altigrade. *Altus; gradior.*
Altiloquence. *Altus; loquor.*
Altimetry. *Altus; metrum.*
Altisonant. *Altus; sonus.*
Altitude. *Altus.*
Altivolant. *Altus; volo.*
Amain. *A; magnus.*
Amalgam. (*Hama*, together); *gamco.*
Amanuensis. *A; manus.*
Amateur, amatorial. *Amo.*
Ambages. *Am; ago.*
Ambidexter, ambidextrous. *Ambo; dexter.*
Ambient. *Am; eo.*
Ambiguity, ambiguous. *Am; ago.*
Ambilogy. *Ambo; logos.*
Ambit, ambition. *Am; eo.*
Amble. *Ambulo.*
Ambrosia. *Ambrosia.*
Ambulant, ambulation. *Ambulo.*
Ambustion. *Am; ustum.*
Ameliorate. *A; melior.*
Amend. *A; menda.*
Amethodical. *A; meta; odos.*
Amiable. *Amo.*
Amicable. *Amicus.*
Amission, amit. *A; mitto.*
Amity. *Amicus.*
Ammunition. *Am; munio.*
Amnesty. *A; mneo.*
Amorist, amorous. *Amo.*
Amorphous, amorphy. *A; morphe.*
Amort, amortize. *A; mors.*
Amotion. *A; moveo.*
Amour. *Amo.*
Amove. *A; moveo.*
Amphibious. *Amphi; bios.*
Amphibology. *Amphi; boleo; logos.*
Amphibolous. *Amphi; boleo.*
Amphiscii. *Amphi; scia.*
Amphitheatre, amphitheatrical. *Amphi; theatrum*
Ample, ampliate. *Amplus.*
Amplificate. *Amplus; facio.*
Amplify, amplitude. *Amplus.*
Amputate. *Am; puto.*
Amuse. *A; musa.*
Anabaptist. *Ana; bapto.*
Anacamptic. *Ana; campto.*
Anachoret. *Ana; choreo.*
Anachronism. *Ana; chronos.*
Anaglyph. *Ana; glypho.*
Anagram, anagrammatical, anagrammatize. *Ana; grapho.*
Analepsis, analeptic *Ana; lepsis.*
Analogical, analogize, analogy. *Ana; logos.*
Analysis, analytical, analyze. *Ana; lysis.*
Anamorphosis. *Ana; morphe.*
Anaphora. *Ana; phero.*
Anaplerotic. *Ana; pleo.*
Anarch. *An; arche.*
Anasarca, anasarcous. *Ana; sarx.*
Anastrophe. *Ana; strophe.*
Anathema, anathematical, anathematize. *Ana; thesis.*
Anatiferous. *Anas; fero.*
Anatomical, anatomize, anatomy. *Ana; tomos.*
Ancestor. *Antiquus.*
Anchorite. *Ana; choreo.*
Ancient. *Antiquus.*
Andranatomy. *Aner; tomos.*
Andrew. *Aner.*
Androgynus. *Aner; gyne.*
Andronicus. *Aner; nice.*
Androphagi. *Aner; phago.*
Androtomy. *Aner; tomos.*
Anecdote. *An; ec; dotos.*
Anemography. *Anemos; grapho.*
Anemometer. *Anemos; metrum.*
Anemone. *Anemos.*
Anemoscope. *Anemos; scopeo.*
Angel. *Angello.*
Anger. *Ango.*
Angiography. *Angion; grapho.*
Angiology. *Angion; logos.*
Angiomonospermous. *Angion; monos, sperma.*
Angiosperm. *Angion; sperma.*
Angiotomy. *Angion; tomos.*
Angle. *Angulus.*
Angry. *Ango.*
Anguilliform. (*Anguilla*, a serpent); *forma.*
Anguish. *Ango.*
Angular, angulosity, angulous. *Angulus.*
Anhelation, anhelose. *Am; halo.*
Anile. *Anus.*
Animable. *Anima.*
Animadversion, animadvert. *Animus; verto.*
Animal, animate. *Anima.*
Animosity. *Animus.*
Annalist, annals. *Annus.*
Annex, annexation. *An; necto.*
Annihilate. *An; nihil.*
Anniversary. *Annus; verto.*
Anno Domini. *Annus; dominus.*
Annotate. *An; nota.*
Announce. *An; nuncio.*
Annual, annuity. *Annus.*
Annul. *An; nullus.*
Annular, annulet. *Annulus.*
Annumerate. *An; numerus.*
Annunciate. *An; nuncio.*
Anoint. *An; unguo.*
Anomaliped. *A; omalos; pes.*
Anomalistic, anomalous, anomaly. *An omalos.*
Anomy. *A; nomos.*
Anonymous. *A; onoma.*
Ansated. *Ansa.*
Antagonize. *Anti; agon.*
Antalgic. *Anti; algos.*
Antaphroditic. *Anti; aphrodite.*
Antapoplectic. *Anti; apo; plectos.*
Antarctic. *Anti; arctos.*
Antasthmatic. *Anti; asthma.*
Anteact. *Ante; ago.*
Antecede, antecessor. *Ante; cedo.*
Antecursor. *Ante; curro.*
Antedate. *Ante; do.*
Antediluvian. *Ante; diluvium.*
Antelucan. *Ante; luceo.*
Antemeridian. *Ante; meridies.*
Antemundane. *Ante; mundus.*
Antepaschal. *Ante; pascha.*
Antepast. *Ante; pasco.*
Antepenult, antepenultimate. *Ante; pene, ultimus.*
Antepileptic. *Anti; epi; lepsis.*
Antepone. *Ante; pono.*
Antepredicament. *Ante; pre; dico.*
Antevert. *Ante; verto.*
Anthelminthic. *Anti helmins.*
Anther. *Anthos.*
Anthology. *Anthos; logos.*

Anthophyllite. *Anthos; phyllon.*
Anthropology. *Anthropos; logos.*
Anthropomorphite. *Anthropos; morphe.*
Anthropopathy. *Anthropos; pathos.*
Anthropophagi. *Anthropos; phago.*
Anthroposophy. *Anthropos; sophia.*
Anthypochondriac. *Anti; hypo; chondros.*
Antiacid. *Anti; acidus.*
Antiapostle. *Anti; apo; stello.*
Antibilious. *Anti; bilis.*
Antic. *Antiquus.*
Anticachectic. *Anti; cacos; exis.*
Antichrist. *Anti; christos.*
Antichronism. *Anti; chronos.*
Anticipate. *Anti; capio.*
Anticlimax. *Anti; climax.*
Anticonstitutional. *Anti; con; sto.*
Anticonvulsive. *Anti; con; vello.*
Anticor. *Anti; cor.*
Antidote. *Anti; dotos.*
Antidysenteric. *Anti; dys, enteron.*
Antiepiscopal. *Anti; epi; scopeo.*
Antifanatic. *Anti; fanum.*
Antifebrile. *Anti; febris.*
Antihypnotic. *Anti; hypnos.*
Antilogarithm. *Anti; logos; arithmos.*
Antilogy. *Anti; logos.*
Antiloquy. *Anti; loquor.*
Antimagisterial. *Anti; magister.*
Antimaniacal. *Anti; mania.*
Antimonarchical. *Anti; monos; arche.*
Antimoralist. *Anti; mos.*
Antinomy, antinomian. *Anti; nomos.*
Antipapal. *Anti; papas.*
Antiparalytic. *Anti; para; lysis.*
Antipathetic, antipathy. *Anti; pathos.*
Antipas. *Anti; pas.*
Antipatriotic. *Anti; pater.*
Antiperistasis, antiperistatic. *Anti; peri; stasis.*
Antipestilential. *Anti; pestis.*
Antiphlogistic. *Anti; phlegma.*
Antiphon. *Anti; phone.*
Antiphrasis, antiphrastic. *Anti; phrasis.*
Antipode. *Anti; pous.*
Antiposition. *Anti; pono.*
Antiprelatic. *Anti; pre; latum.*
Antiprinciple. *Anti; primus; capio.*
Antiprophet. *Anti; pro; phano.*
Antiptosis. *Anti; ptoma.*
Antipuritan. *Anti; purus.*
Antiquary, antiquate, antique, antiquity. *Antiquus.*
Antireformer. *Anti; re; forma.*
Antirevolutionary. *Anti; re; volvo.*
Antisabbatarian. *Anti; sabbatum.*
Antisacerdotal. *Anti; sacer; dos.*
Antiscii. *Anti; scia.*
Antiscorbutic. *Anti; scorbutum.*
Antiscripturist. *Anti; scribo.*
Antispasis, antispasmodic, antispastic. *Anti; spasma.*
Antisplenetic. *Anti; splen.*
Antistrophe, antistrophon. *Anti; strophe.*
Antithesis, antithetic. *Anti; thesis.*
Antitrinitarian. *Anti; tres; unus.*
Antitype. *Anti; typus.*
Antivariolus. *Anti; variolæ.*
Antivenereal. *Anti; venus.*
Antœci. *Anti; eceo.*
Antonomasy. *Anti; onoma.*
Anxiety, anxious. *Ango.*
Apagogical. *Apo; agogeus.*
Apart. *A; pars.*
Apathetic, apathy. *A; pathos.*
Apepsy. *A; peptos.*
Aperient, aperative, apert, aperture. *Aperio.*
Apetalous. *A; petalon.*
Aphelion. *Apo; helios*
Aphæresis. *Apo; aeresis.*
Aphilanthropy. *A; philos; anthropos.*
Aphony. *A; phone.*
Aphorism, aphoristical. *Apo; horos.*
Aphrodisiac. *Aphrodite.*
Apiary. *Apis.*
Apocalypse, apocalyptical. *Apo; calypto.*
Apocope. *Apo; cope.*
Apocrypha. *Apo; crypto.*
Apodictic, apodixis. *Apo; dico.*
Apodosis. *Apo; dotis.*
Apogee. *Apo; ge.*
Apograph. *Apo; grapho.*
Apologetic, apology, apologue. *Apo; logos.*
Aponeurosy. *Apo; neuron.*
Apophasis. *Apo; phano.*
Apophlegmatic. *Apo; phlegma.*
Apophthegm. *Apo; phthegma.*
Apophysis. *Apo; physis.*
Apoplectic, apoplexy. *Apo; plectos.*
Apostasy, apostate, apostatize. *Apo; stasis.*
Apostemate, apostematous, aposteme. *Apo; stasis.*
Apostle, apostolate, apostolic. *Apo; stello.*
Apostrophe, apostrophic, apostrophize. *Apo; strophe.*
Apothegm, apothegmatic, apothem. *Apo; phthegma.*
Apotheosis. *Apo; theos.*
Apothesis. *Apo; thesis.*
Apotome. *Apo; tomos.*
Apozem. *Apo; zelos.*
Apparatus, apparel *Ap; paro.*
Apparent, apparition, apparitor. *Ap; pareo.*
Appeal. *Ap; pello.*
Appear. *Ap; pareo.*
Appeasable, appease. *Ap; pax.*
Appellant, appellation, appellee, appellor. *Ap; pello.*
Append, appendicle, appendix. *Ap; pendeo.*
Appertain, appertenence, appertinent. *Ap; per; teneo.*
Appetent, appetible, appetite, appetitious. *Ap; peto.*
Applaud, applause. *Ap; plaudo.*
Appliable, appliance, applicable, applicant, application. *Ap; plico.*
Apportion. *Ap; pars.*
Appose, apposition. *Ap; pono.*
Appraise. *Ap; precium.*
Apprecation. *Ap; precor.*
Appreciate. *Ap; precium.*
Apprehend, apprehensible, apprehension, apprentice, apprize. *Ap; prehendo.*
Approach. *Ap; prope.*
Approbation. *Ap; probo.*
Appropinquation. *Ap; prope.*
Appropriable, appropriate, appropriatary. *Ap; proprius.*
Approve. *Ap; probo.*
Approximate. *Ap; prope.*
Appulse. *Ap; pello.*
Appurtenant. *Ap; per; teneo.*
Apropos. *Ap; pro; pono.*
Apt, aptitude. *Aptus.*
Aptote. *A; ptoma.*
Aqua fortis. *Aqua; fortis.*
Aqua marina. *Aqua; mare.*
Aqua vitæ. *Aqua; vivo.*
Aquatic. *Aqua.*
Aqueduct. *Aqua; duco.*
Aqueous. *Aqua.*

Aquiline. *Aquila.*
Aquosity. *Aqua.*
Arable. *Aro.*
Araneous. *Araneus.*
Aration. *Aro.*
Arbiter, arbitrament, arbitrary, arbitrate. [*Arbiter.*
Arbor, arbuscle. *Arbor.*
Arch. *Arcus.*
Arch, archaism. *Arche.*
Archangel. *Arche; angello.*
Archaiology. *Arche; logos.*
Archapostate. *Arche; apo; stasis.*
Archapostle. *Arche; apo; stello.*
Archarchitect. *Arche; tecton.*
Archbishop. *Arche; epi; scopeo.*
Archchanter. *Arche; cano.*
Archconspirator. *Arche; con; spiro.*
Archdeacon. *Arche; dia; coneo.*
Archduchess, archduke. *Arche; duco.*
Archelaus. *Arche; laos.*
Archer. *Arcus.*
Archetype. *Arche; typus.*
Archflamen. *Arche; flamen.*
Archheresy, archheretic. *Arche; heresis.*
Archidiaconal. *Arche; dia; coneo.*
Archiepiscopal. *Arche; epi; scopeo.*
Archippus. *Arche; hippos.*
Architect, architectonic, architecture. *Arche; tecton.*
Architrave. *Arche;* (*trabs*, a beam).
Architype. *Arche; typus.*
Archives. *Arche.*
Archmagician. *Arche; magus.*
Archpastor. *Arche; pasco.*
Archphilosopher. *Arche; philos; sophia.*
Archpoet. *Arche; poieo.*
Archpolitician. *Arche; polis.*
Archprelate. *Arche; pre; latum.*
Archpresbyter. *Arche; presbyteros.*
Archprimate. *Arche; primus.*
Archprophet. *Arche; pro; phano.*
Archprotestant. *Arche; pro; testis.*
Archpublican. *Arche; populus.*
Archtraitor. *Arche; trado.*
Arctic. *Arctos.*
Arcturus. *Arctos;* (*oura*, the tail).
Arcuate. *Arcus.*
Arcubalister. *Arcus; boleo*
Ardent, ardor. *Ardeo.*
Arduous. *Arduus.*
Arefaction. *Areo; facio.*
Arefy. *Areo.*
Arenaceous, arenose, arenulous. *Arena.*
Areometer. *Areo; metrum.*
Areopagite, areopagus. *Ares; pagos.*
Areotics. *Areos.*
Aretology. (*Arete*, virtue); *logos.*
Argent. *Argentum.*
Argil, argillaceous. *Argilla.*
Argue, argument. *Arguo.*
Arid. *Aridus.*
Arietate. *Aries.*
Aristarchus. *Aristos; arche.*
Aristocracy, aristocrat. *Aristos; cratos.*
Arithmancy. *Arithmos; mancia.*
Arithmetic. *Arithmos.*
Arm, armada, armadillo, armament. *Arma.*
Armental. *Armentum.*
Armigerous. *Arma; gero.*
Armillary. *Armilla.*
Armipotent. *Arma; posse; ens.*
Armisonous. *Arma; sonus.*
Armistice. *Arma; sto.*
Armor, arms, army. *Arma.*
Aromatic, aromatize. *Aromata.*
Arrange. *Ar; rang.*
Arrant. *Erro.*
Arrect. *Ar; rego.*
Arreptitious. *Ar; reptum.*
Arrest, arrestation, arret. *Ar; re; sto*
Arride, arrision. *Ar; rideo.*
Arrive. *Ar; rivus.*
Arrode. *Ar; rodo.*
Arrogant, arrogate. *Ar; rogo.*
Arrosion. *Ar; rodo.*
Arsenic, arsenious. *Arsen; nice.*
Arson. *Ardeo.*
Art. *Ars.*
Arteriotomy. *Arteria; tomos.*
Artery. *Arteria.*
Arthritic. *Arthritis.*
Article, articulate. *Articulus.*
Artifice, artificial. *Ars; facio.*
Artisan, artist. *Ars.*
Artocarpus. *Articulus; carpus.*
Arundinaceous. *Arundo.*
Ascend, ascension, ascent. *A; scando.*
Ascertain. *As; certus.*
Ascetic. *Asceo.*
Ascii. *A; scia.*
Ascites, ascitic. *Ascites.*
Ascribe, ascription, ascriptitious. *A; scribo*
Asinine. *Asinus.*
Asomatous. *A; soma.*
Aspect. *A; specto.*
Asperate. *Asper.*
Asperifolious. *Asper; folium.*
Asperse, aspersion. *A; spargo.*
Aspirant, aspirate, aspiration, aspire. *A, spiro.*
Ass. *Asinus.*
Assail, assault. *As; salio.*
Assecution. *As; sequor.*
Assent. *As; sentio.*
Assert. *As; sertum.*
Assess, assessionary. *As; sedeo.*
Assiduity, assiduous. *As; sedeo.*
Assign, assignation. *As; signum.*
Assimilable, assimilate. *As; similis.*
Assist. *As; sisto.*
Assize. *As; sedeo.*
Associable, associate. *As; socio.*
Assoil. *Ab; solvo.*
Assonant. *As; sonus.*
Assort. *As; sors.*
Assuage, assuasive. *As; suadeo.*
Assubjugate. *As; sub; jugum.*
Assuefaction. *As; sueo; facio.*
Assuetude. *As; sueo.*
Assume, assumpsit, assumption. *As; sumo.*
Assurgent. *As; surgo.*
Asterisk, asterism. *Astron.*
Asthenic. *A; sthenos.*
Asthenology. *A; sthenos; logos.*
Asthma, asthmatic. *Asthma.*
Astonish, astound. *As; tonos.*
Astral. *Astron.*
Astrict. *A; stringo.*
Astriferous. *Astron; fero.*
Astrigerous. *Astron; gero.*
Astringe. *A; stringo.*
Astrography. *Astron; grapho.*
Astrolabe. *Astron; labo.*
Astrology. *Astron; logos.*
Astronomy. *Astron; nomos.*
Astroscope. *Astron; scopeo.*
Astrotheology. *Astron; theos; logos.*
Asylum. *A; syle.*
Asymmetry. *A; sym; metrum.*
Asymptote. *A; sym; ptoma.*
Atheism, atheistic, atheize. *A; theos*
Atheologian, atheology. *A; theos; logos*
Athletic. *Athlos.*

Atlantic. *Atlas.*
Atmosphere. *Atmos; sphæra.*
Atom. *A; tomos.*
Atony *A; tonos.*
Atrabilarious. *Atra; bilis.*
Atramental. *Atra.*
Atrocious, atrocity. *Atrox.*
Atrophy. *A; trophe.*
Attain. *At; tango.*
Attainder, attaint. *At; tingo*
Attempt. *At; tento.*
Attend, attention. *At; tendo.*
Attenuate. *At; tenuis.*
Atterate. *At; tero.*
Attest, attestation. *At; testis*
Attollent. *At; tollo.*
Attract, attrahent. *At; traho.*
Attribute. *At; tributum.*
Attrite, attrition. *At; tero.*
Attune. *At; tonos.*
Auction. *Augeo.*
Audacious, audacity. *Audax.*
Audible, audience, audit. *Audio.*
Augment, augmentation. *Augeo.*
Augur, auguration. *Augur.*
August. *Augustus.*
Auletic. *Aulos.*
Aulic. *Aula.*
Aurelia. *Aurum.*
Auricle, auricular. *Auris.*
Auriferous. *Aurum; fero.*
Aurist. *Auris.*
Auscultation. *Auris; colo.*
Auspice, auspicious. *Avis; specio.*
Austere, austerity. *Austerus.*
Austral. *Auster.*
Australasia. *Auster;* (*Asia.*)
Authentic. *Authenteo.*
Author, authoritative, authorization. *Augeo.*
Autobiography. *Autos; bios; grapho.*
Autocrat. *Autos; cratos.*
Autogeneal. *Autos; genea.*
Autograph. *Autos; grapho.*
Automatical, automaton. *Autos; matos.*
Autonomy. *Autos; nomos.*
Autopsy, autoptical. *Autos; opto.*
Autumn. *Autumnus.*
Auxiliar, auxiliation. *Auxilium.*
Avail. *A; valeo.*
Avantguard. *Avant; guarder.*
Avarice, avaricious. *Avaritia.*
Avenge. *A, vindex.*
Aventure, avenue. *A; venio.*
Aver. *A; verus.*
Averruncate. *A; verrunco.*
Aversation, averse, avert. *A; verto.*
Aviary. *Avis.*
Avidity. *Avidus.*
Avocation. *A; voco.*
Avoid. *A; viduo.*
Avouch. *A; voco.*
Avow. *A; votum.*
Avulsion. *A; vello.*
Axillar. *Axilla.*
Axiom *Axioma.*

B.

Babel, Babylon. *Babel.*
Baccated. *Bacca.*
Bacchanal, bacchantes. *Bacchus.*
Bacciferous. *Bacca; fero.*
Baccivorous. *Bacca; voro.*
Baculometry. (*Baculus*, a staff); *metrum.*
Balm *Balsamon.*
Balneary, balneation. *Balneum.*
Balsam. *Balsamon.*
Bankrupt. (*Abacus*, a bench); *ruptum*
Baptist, baptize. *Bapto.*
Bar. *Barre.*
Barb. *Barba.*
Barbaric, barbarity, barbarous. *Barbarus.*
Barjesus. *Bar; Jesus.*
Barjonas. *Bar;* (*iona*, a dove).
Barnabas. *Bar;* (*naba*, to prophesy).
Barometer, barometrical. *Baros; metrum.*
Baroscope. *Baros; scopeo.*
Barrator, barricade, barrier, barrister. *Barre.*
Barsabas. *Bar;* (*saba*, rest).
Bartholomew. *Bar;* (*tala*, to raise; *mim*, waters).
Bartimeus. *Bar; time.*
Barytone. *Baros; tonos.*
Base. *Basis.*
Basilic, basilisk. *Basileus.*
Battology. (*Battos*, a silly poet); *logos.*
Beast. *Bestia.*
Beatification. *Beatus; facio.*
Beatify, beatitude. *Beatus.*
Beau. *Beau.*
Beaumonde. *Beau;* (*monde*, the world.)
Beauteous, beautify, beauty, belle. *Beau.*
Belles-lettres. *Beau;* (*lettres*, letters).
Belligerent. *Bellum; gero.*
Bellipotent. *Bellum; posse; ens.*
Belluine. *Bellua.*
Belomancy. (*Belos*, an arrow); *mancia*
Benedict. *Bene; dico.*
Benefaction, benefice, beneficent, benefit *Bene; facio.*
Benevolent. *Bene; volo.*
Benign, benignity. *Benignus.*
Benison. *Bene.*
Berea. *Baros.*
Besiege. *Be; sedeo.*
Bestial. *Bestia.*
Betray. *Be; traho.*
Bibacious, bibber. *Bibo.*
Bible, biblical. *Biblos.*
Bibliography. *Biblos; grapho.*
Bibliomania. *Biblos; mania.*
Bibliopolist. *Biblos; poleo.*
Bibliothecal, bibliothece. *Biblos; thece.*
Bibulous. *Bibo.*
Bicapsular. *Bini; capsula.*
Bicephalus. *Bini; cephale.*
Bicipital. *Bini; caput.*
Bicornous. *Bini; cornu.*
Bicorporal. *Bini; corpus.*
Bidental. *Bini; dens.*
Biennial. *Bini; annus.*
Bifarious. *Bini; fari.*
Biferous. *Bini; fero.*
Bifid. *Bini; findo.*
Biflorous. *Bini; flos.*
Bifold. *Bini;* (fold).
Biform. *Bini; forma.*
Bifronted. *Bini; frons.*
Bifurcated, bifurcous. *Bini; furca.*
Bigam. *Bini; gameo.*
Biliary. *Bilis.*
Bilinguous. *Bini; lingua.*
Bilious. *Bilis.*
Binary. *Bini.*
Binocle, binocular. *Bini; oculus.*
Binominal, binominous. *Bini; nomen.*
Binotonous. *Bini; tonos.*
Biography. *Bios; grapho.*
Biparous. *Bini; pario.*
Bipartite, bipartible, bipartient, bipartile. *Bini; pars.*
Biped. *Bini; pes*

Bipennate. *Bini; penna.*
Bipetalous. *Bini; petalon.*
Biquadrate. *Bini; quadra.*
Biradiate. *Bini; radius.*
Birhomboidal. *Bini; rhombos; oidos.*
Birostrate. *Bini; rostrum.*
Biscuit. *Bini; coquo.*
Bisect, bisegment. *Bini; seco.*
Bisexous. *Bini; sexus.*
Bishop. *Epi; scopeo.*
Bivalve. *Bini; valvæ.*
Biventral. *Bini; venter.*
Bivious. *Bini; via.*
Blame. *Blamer.*
Bland. *Blandus.*
Blaspheme. *Blapto; phano.*
Boil. *Bulla.*
Bolis, bolt, bolus. *Boleo.*
Bona fide. *Bonus; fides.*
Boreas. *Boreas.*
Botanic. *Botane.*
Botanology. *Botane; logos.*
Botany. *Botane.*
Bounty, bounteous. *Bonus.*
Brachial. *Brachium.*
Brachygraphy. *Brachys; grapho.*
Breviary, breviat, brevity, brief. *Brevis.*
Brilliant. *Briller.*
Bronchial. *Bronchos.*
Bronchocele. *Bronchos; cele.*
Bronchotomy. *Bronchos; tomos.*
Brumal. *Bruma.*
Brutal, brute, brutify, brutish. *Brutus.*
Bubo. *Bubon.*
Bubonocele. *Bubon; cele.*
Bucephalus. (*Bous*, an ox); *cephale.*
Bucolic. *Bucolos.*
Bulb, bulbaceous. *Bulbus.*
Bullition. *Bulla.*
Butyraceous *Butyrum.*

C.

Cabal, cabalistical. *Cabal.*
Cabin, cabinet. *Cabin.*
Cachectic, cachexy. *Cacos; exis.*
Cacochymy. *Cacos; chymos.*
Cacodæmon. *Cacos; dæmon.*
Cacophony. *Cacos; phone.*
Cacuminate. *Cacumen.*
Cadaverous. *Cadaver.*
Cadent, caducity. *Cado.*
Calamitous, calamity. *Calamitas.*
Calcination, calcine. *Calx.*
Calculable, calculate, calcule, calculus. *Calculus.*
Caldron. *Caleo.*
Calefaction. *Caleo; facio.*
Calefy. *Caleo.*
Caleidoscope. *Calos; scopeo.*
Calenture, calid. *Caleo.*
Caliduct. *Caleo; duco.*
Caligation, caliginous. *Caligo.*
Caligraphy. *Calos; grapho.*
Callosity, callus. *Callus.*
Caloric *Caleo.*
Calorific. *Caleo; facio.*
Calumniate, calumnious, calumny. *Calumnia.*
Calx. *Calx.*
Camp, campaign, campestral. *Campus.*
Cancer, cancrine. *Cancer.*
Candent, candicant, candid, candidate, candify, candle, candor. *Candeo.*
Candlemas. *Candeo;* (*mæssa*, a feast).
Canker. *Cancer.*
Canon, canonical, canonization. *Canon.*
Canorous, cant, canticle. *Cano.*
Cap. *Caput.*
Cap-a-pie. *Caput; a; pes.*
Capable, capacious, capacitate, capacity *Capio.*
Capillacious, capillament, capillary. *Capillus.*
Capital, capitation, capitulate. *Caput.*
Capsular, capsule. *Capsula.*
Captain. *Caput.*
Captation, caption, captivate, captive, captor, capture. *Capio.*
Carbonado, carbonarism, carbonic. *Carbo.*
Carboniferous. *Carbo; fero.*
Carbuncle, carbuncular. *Carbo.*
Carcelage. *Carcer.*
Cardiac. *Cardia.*
Cardialgia. *Cardia; algos.*
Cardinal. *Cardo.*
Care. *Cura.*
Career. *Curro.*
Caress. *Carus.*
Caries, cariosity, carious. *Caries.*
Carnage, carnal, carnation, carnelion, carnify. *Caro.*
Carnival. *Caro; valeo.*
Carnivorous. *Caro; voro.*
Carnosity. *Caro.*
Carp. *Carpo.*
Carriage, carry. Curro.
Cartilage, cartilaginous. *Cartilago.*
Caruncle. *Caro.*
Carve. *Carpo.*
Cascade, case. *Cado.*
Castigate. *Castigo.*
Casual, casuist. *Cado.*
Catalepsy, cataleptic. *Cata; lepsis.*
Catalogue. *Cata; logos.*
Catalysis. *Cata; lysis.*
Cataplasm. *Cata; plasso.*
Cataphonics. *Cata; phone.*
Catarrh. *Cata; rheo.*
Catastrophe. *Cata; strophe.*
Catechectic, catechise, catechistic, catechumen. *Cata; echeo.*
Categorical, category. *Cata; egora.*
Catenarian, catenate. *Catena.*
Cathedral. *Cata; edra.*
Catholic. *Cata; holos.*
Catoptric. *Cata; opto.*
Catoptromancy. *Cata; opto; mancia.*
Cauliferous. *Caulis; fero.*
Cauliflower. *Caulis; flos.*
Causal, causation, cause. *Causa.*
Caustic. *Causticos.*
Cautel. *Cautio.*
Cauterize, cautery. *Causticos.*
Caution. *Cautio.*
Cavalcade, cavalier, cavalry. *Cavallo.*
Cavate, cave, cavern. *Cavus.*
Cavil, cavillation. *Cavilla.*
Cavity. *Cavus.*
Cease, cede. *Cedo.*
Celebrate, celebrious, celebrity. *Celebris.*
Celerity. *Celer.*
Celestial, celestify. *Cœlestis.*
Celibacy, celibate. *Cœlebs.*
Cell, cellar, cellule. *Cella.*
Celsitude. *Celsus*
Cenobite. (*Coinos*, common); *bios.*
Cenotaph. (*Cenos*, empty); *taphos.*
Cense, censorious, censure, census. *Censeo*
Cent. *Centum.*
Centenary. *Centum.*
Centennial. *Centum; annus.*
Centesimal. *Centum.*

Centifolious. *Centum; folium.*
Centiloquy. *Centum; loquor.*
Centipede. *Centum; pes.*
Central, center. *Centrum.*
Centrifugal. *Centrum; fugio.*
Centripetal. *Centrum; peto.*
Centuple, centuplicate. *Centum; plico.*
Centuriate, centurion, century. *Centum.*
Cephalalgia. *Cephale; algos.*
Cephalic. *Cephale.*
Cephalology. *Cephale; logos.*
Cerastes. *Ceras.*
Cerate, cere. *Cera.*
Cerealious. *Ceres.*
Cerebel, cerebrum. *Cerebrum.*
Ceremonious, ceremony. *Ceremonia.*
Certain, certes. *Certus.*
Certificate. *Certus; facio.*
Certify, certitude. *Certus.*
Cerulean. *Ceruleus.*
Cerulific. *Ceruleus; facio.*
Cerumen. *Cera.*
Cervical. *Cervix.*
Cespititious. *Cæspes.*
Cess. *Censeo.*
Cessation, cessavit, cession. *Cedo.*
Cetaceous. *Cetus.*
Chagrin. *Chagrin.*
Chalcography. *Chalcos; grapho.*
Chalybian. *Chalybs.*
Champagne, champaign. *Campus.*
Chandelier, chandler. *Candeo.*
Chant. *Cano.*
Chanticleer. *Cano; clarus.*
Chaos, chaotic. *Chaos.*
Chapiter, chapter. *Caput.*
Character, characteristic. *Character.*
Charity. *Charis.*
Charm. *Cano.*
Charnel. *Caro.*
Chaste. *Castus.*
Chasten, chastise. *Castigo.*
Chastity. *Castus.*
Chemist. *Chymos.*
Cherish. *Carus.*
Cherub. *Cherub.*
Chevalier. *Cheval.*
Chicane. *Chicane.*
Chiliad. *Chilioi.*
Chiliaedron. *Chilioi; edra.*
Chiliarch. *Chilioi; arche.*
Chiliast. *Chilioi.*
Chimera, chimerical. *Chimæra.*
Chiragra. *Chir;* (*agra*, a catching).
Chirograph. *Chir; grapho.*
Chirology. *Chir; logos.*
Chiromancy. *Chir; mancia.*
Chirosophist. *Chir; sophia.*
Chirurgery, chirurgical. *Chir; ergon.*
Chivalry. *Cheval.*
Choir. *Chorus.*
Cholagogue. *Chole; agogeus.*
Choler. *Chole.*
Cholera-morbus. *Chole; morbus*
Cholic. *Chole.*
Choragus. *Chorus; agogeus.*
Choral. *Chorus.*
Chord. *Chorda.*
Chorepiscopus. *Chorus; epi; scopeo.*
Chorist. *Chorus.*
Chorography. *Choros; grapho.*
Chorus. *Chorus.*
Chrism, chrisom, Christ, Christianize, Christianity. *Christos.*
Christianography. *Christos; grapho.*
Christmas. *Christos;* (*mæssa*, a feast).
Chronic, chronicle, chronique. *Chronos.*
Chronogram, chronogrammatical, chronography. *Chronos; grapho.*
Chronological, chronology. *Chronos; logos.*
Chronometer. *Chronos; metrum.*
Chrysalis. *Chrysos.*
Chrysanthemum. *Chrysos; anthos.*
Chrysoberyl. *Chrysos;* (*beryllos*, a precious stone).
Chrysography. *Chrysos; grapho.*
Chrysolite. *Chrysos; lithos.*
Church. *Eceo;* (*Curios*, the Lord).
Chylaceous, chyle. *Chylos.*
Chylifaction. *Chylos; facio.*
Chylopoetic. *Chylos; poieo.*
Chylous. *Chylos.*
Chymic, chymist. *Chymos.*
Cibarious. *Cibus.*
Cicatrisive, cicatrix, cicatrize. *Cicatrix.*
Cichoraceous. *Cichoreum.*
Cicurate. *Cicur.*
Ciliary. *Cilium.*
Cilicious. *Cilicium.*
Cincture. *Cingo.*
Cinder, cineration, cinerous, cineritious, cinerulent. *Cinis.*
Cingle. *Cingo.*
Circle. *Circulus.*
Circuit. *Circum; eo.*
Circular, circulate. *Circulus.*
Circumambient. *Circum; am; eo.*
Circumambulate. *Circum; ambulo.*
Circumcise. *Circum; cædo.*
Circumcursation. *Circum; curro.*
Circumduct. *Circum; duco.*
Circumference, circumferential. *Circum; fero.*
Circumflect, circumflex. *Circum; flecto.*
Circumfluent. *Circum; fluo.*
Circumforanean. *Circum; forum.*
Circumfuse. *Circum; fundo.*
Circumgyrate. *Circum; gyrus.*
Circumition. *Circum; eo.*
Circumjacent. *Circum; jaceo*
Circumligation. *Circum; ligo.*
Circumlocution. *Circum; loquor*
Circummure. *Circum; murus.*
Circumnavigable, circumnavigate. *Circum; navis; ago.*
Circumplication. *Circum; plico.*
Circumpolar. *Circum; polus.*
Circumposition. *Circum; pono.*
Circumrasion. *Circum; rado.*
Circumrotary, circumrotation. *Circum; rota.*
Circumscribe, circumscription. *Circum; scribo.*
Circumspect. *Circum; specio.*
Circumstant, circumstantial, circumstantiate. *Circum; sto.*
Circumterraneous. *Circum; terra.*
Circumvallate. *Circum; vallum.*
Circumvection. *Circum; veho.*
Circumvent. *Circum; venio.*
Circumvest. *Circum; vestis.*
Circumvolation. *Circum; volo.*
Circumvolution, circumvolve. *Circum, volvo.*
Cisalpine. *Cis; Alpes.*
Citation, cite. *Cito.*
Citizen, city, civic, civil, civilization. *Civis.*
Claim, clamor. *Clamo.*
Clancular, clandestine. *Clandestinus.*
Clang. *Clungo.*
Clarichord. *Clarus; chorda.*
Clarification. *Clarus; facio.*
Clarify, clarinet, clarion. *Clarus.*

Class, classic. *Classici.*
Classification. *Classici; facio.*
Classis. *Classici.*
Claudent. *Claudo.*
Claudicate. *Claudus.*
Clause, claustral, clausure. *Claudo.*
Clear. *Clarus.*
Clement. *Clemens.*
Clepsydra. (*Clepto,* to steal); *hydor.*
Clergy, clerical, clerk. *Cleros.*
Client. *Cliens.*
Cliff. *Clivus.*
Climax. *Climax.*
Clinic. *Clino.*
Cloister, close, closure. *Claudo.*
Coacervate. *Co; acervus.*
Coact. *Co; ago.*
Coadjument, coadjutant, coadjutor. *Co; ad; juvo.*
Coadunate, coadunition. *Co; ad; unus.*
Coalesce, coalition. *Co; alo.*
Coaptation. *Co; aptus.*
Coassume. *Co; as; sumo.*
Coast. *Costa.*
Cochleary, cochleated, cockle. *Cochlea.*
Coctile, coction. *Coquo.*
Code, codicil, codicillary. *Codex.*
Coefficacy, coefficient. *Co; ef; facio.*
Coequal. *Co; equus.*
Coerce, coercion. *Co; erceo.*
Coessential. *Co; ens.*
Coetaneous. *Co; evum.*
Coeternal. *Co; eternus.*
Coeval. *Co; evum.*
Coexist. *Co; ex; sisto.*
Coextend, co-extension. *Co; ex; tendo.*
Cogenial. *Co; genus.*
Cogent. *Co; ago.*
Cogitate. *Co; agito.*
Cognate. *Cog; nascor.*
Cognition, cognizance. *Cog; nosco.*
Cohabit. *Co; habeo.*
Coheir. *Co; hæres.*
Cohere, cohesion. *Co; hæreo.*
Cohibit. *Co; habeo.*
Coincide. *Co; in; cado.*
Coition. *Co; eo.*
Colic. *Colon.*
Collapse. *Col; labor.*
Collate. *Col; latum.*
Collateral. *Col; latus.*
Collaud. *Col; laudo.*
Colleague. *Col; lego.*
College, collegiate. *Col; lego.*
Colliquable, colliquate. *Col; liqueo.*
Colliquefaction. *Col; liqueo; facio.*
Collision. *Col; lido.*
Collocate. *Col; locus.*
Collocution, colloquy. *Col; loquor.*
Colluctation. *Col; luctor.*
Collude, collusion, collusory. *Col; ludo.*
Colon. *Colon.*
Colonize, colony. *Colo.*
Color, colorate. *Color.*
Colorific. *Color; facio.*
Colossus. *Colossus.*
Colubrine. *Coluber.*
Columbary. *Columba.*
Column, columnar. *Columna.*
Combine. *Com; bini.*
Combust, combustible, combustion. *Com; ustum.*
Comedy. *Comos; ode.*
Comfort. *Com; fortis.*
Comic. *Comos.*
Command. *Com; mando.*
Commaterial. *Com; materia.*
Commeasurable. *Com; mensura.*
Commemorate. *Com; memor.*
Commend. *Com; mando.*
Commensal, commensation. *Com; mensa*
Commensurate. *Com; mensura.*
Comment, commentate, commentitious [*Com; mens*
Commerce. *Com; mercor.*
Commigrate. *Com; migro.*
Commination, comminatory. *Com; minæ.*
Commingle. *Com; misceo.*
Comminuate, comminute. *Com; minuo.*
Commiserable, commiserate. *Com; miser.*
Commissarial, commissary, commission, commissure, commit. *Com; mitto.*
Commix. *Com; misceo.*
Commode, commodious, commodity. *Com; modus.*
Commons, commonalty, commons. *Com;* [*munus.*
Commorient. *Com; mors.*
Commotion. *Com; moveo.*
Commune, communicable, communicate, communion, community. *Com; munus.*
Commutable, commutation, commute. *Com; muto.*
Commutual. *Com; mutuus.*
Compact, compages, compagination. *Com; pactus.*
Companion, company. *Com; pannus.*
Comparative, compare, comparison. *Com; par.*
Compart, compartner. *Com; pars*
Compass. *Com; passus.*
Compassion. *Com; patior.*
Compaternity. *Com; pater.*
Compatible. *Com; peto.*
Compatient. *Com; patior.*
Compatriot. *Com; pater.*
Compeer. *Com; par.*
Compel, compellation. *Com; pello.*
Compend, compendium, compendiosity, compensable, compensate. *Com; pendo.*
Compete, competible, competition. *Com, peto.*
Compile. *Com; pilo.*
Complacent. *Com; placeo.*
Complain. *Com; plango.*
Complaisant. *Com; placeo.*
Complanate, complane. *Com; planus.*
Complement, complete. *Com; pleo.*
Complex, compliant, complicate, complice, complied. *Com; plico.*
Compliment. *Com; pleo.*
Comply. *Com; plico.*
Component. *Com; pono.*
Comport. *Com; porto.*
Compose, composite, composition, compost, composure. *Com; pono.*
Compotation. *Com; poto.*
Compound. *Com; pono.*
Comprecation. *Com; precor.*
Comprehend, comprehensible, comprehension. *Com; prehendo.*
Compresbyterial. *Com; presbyteros.*
Compress, comprint. *Com; premo.*
Comprise. *Com; prehendo.*
Comprobate. *Com; probo.*
Compromise, compromissorial, compromit *Com; pro; mitto.*
Compulsative, compulsion, compulsory *Com; pello.*
Compunction. *Com; pungo.*
Compurgation. *Com; purgo.*
Computable, computation, compute. *Com; puto.*
Concatenate. *Con; catena.*
Concavation, concave, concavo-concave. *Con; cavus.*

Concavo-convex. *Con; cavus—con; veho.*
Conceal. *Con; celo.*
Concede. *Con; cedo.*
Conceit, conceive. *Con; capio.*
Concelebrate. *Con; celebris.*
Concentrate, concentre, concentric. *Con; centrum.*
Conception. *Con; capio.*
Concern. *Con; cerno.*
Concert, concertation, concerto. *Con; certo.*
Concession. *Con; cedo.*
Conch, conchilious. *Concha.*
Conchology. *Concha; logos.*
Conciliar, conciliate. *Concilio.*
Concise. *Con; cædo.*
Concitation. *Con; cito.*
Conclamation. *Con; clamo.*
Conclude, conclusion. *Con; claudo.*
Concoct. *Con; coquo.*
Concolor. *Con; color.*
Concomitant, concomitate. *Con; comes.*
Concord. *Con; cor.*
Concorporate. *Con; corpus.*
Concourse. *Con; curro.*
Concredit. *Con; credo.*
Concremation. *Con; cremo.*
Concrement, concrescence, concrete. *Con; cresco.*
Concubinate, concubine. *Con; cubo.*
Conculcate. *Con; culco.*
Concur. *Con; curro.*
Concussation, concussion. *Con; cutio.*
Condemn. *Con; damnum.*
Condense. *Con; densus.*
Condescend,condescension. *Con; de; scando.*
Condign *Con; dignus.*
Condition. *Con; do.*
Condole. *Con; doleo.*
Condonation. *Con; donum.*
Conduce, conduct, conduit. *Con; duco.*
Conduplicate. *Con; duo; plico.*
Confabulate. *Con; fabula.*
Confamiliar. *Con; familia.*
Confarreation. *Con; farina.*
Confect, confectionary. *Con; facio.*
Confederacy, confederate. *Con; fedus.*
Confer. *Con; fero.*
Confess, confessional, confest. *Con; fessum.*
Confide, confidential. *Con; fides.*
Configurate, configure. *Con; figura.*
Confine. *Con; finis.*
Confirm. *Con; firmus.*
Confiscable, confiscate. *Con; fiscus.*
Confissure. *Con; findo.*
Confitent. *Con; fessum.*
Confiture. *Con; facio.*
Confix. *Con; fixus.*
Conflagrant, conflagration. *Con; flagro.*
Conflation. *Con; flatus.*
Conflexure. *Con; flecto.*
Conflict. *Con; fligo.*
Confluent, conflux. *Con; fluo.*
Conform. *Con; forma.*
Confound. *Con; fundo.*
Confraternity. *Con; frater.*
Confrication. *Con; frico.*
Confront. *Con; frons.*
Confuse. *Con; fundo.*
Confutable, confute. *Con; futo.*
Congeal, congelation. *Con; gelu.*
Congemination. *Con; geminus.*
Congener, congenial, congenite. *Con; genus.*
Congeries, congest. *Con; gero.*
Conglaciate. *Con; glacies.*
Conglobate, conglobe, conglobulate. *Con; globus.*
Conglomerate. *Con; glomus*
Conglutinate. *Con; gluten.*
Congratulate. *Con; gratia.*
Congregate. *Con; grex.*
Congress. *Con; gradior.*
Congruent, congruity. *Con; grus*
Conic. *Conos.*
Conic-sections. *Conos; seco.*
Coniferous. *Conos; fero.*
Conject, conjectural. *Con; jacio.*
Conjoin. *Con; jungo.*
Conjugal, conjugate. *Con; jugum.*
Conjunct. *Con; jungo.*
Conjuration, conjūre. *Con; juro.*
Connascence, connate, connatural. *Con; nascor.*
Connect, connex. *Con; necto.*
Connivance, connive. *Con; niveo.*
Connoisseur. *Con; nosco.*
Connotate, connote. *Con; nota.*
Connubial. *Con; nubo.*
Connumeration. *Con; numerus.*
Conoid. *Conos; oidos.*
Conquassate. *Con; quatio.*
Conquer, conquest. *Con; quæro.*
Consanguinity. *Con; sanguis.*
Conscience, conscientious, conscionable, conscious. *Con; scio.*
Conscript. *Con; scribo.*
Consecrate. *Con; sacer.*
Consectary, consecution. *Con; sequor.*
Conseminate. *Con; semen.*
Consenescence. *Con; senex.*
Consension, consent, consentaneous, consentient. *Con; sentio.*
Consequent, consequential. *Con; sequor.*
Conservant, conservation, conserve. *Con; servo.*
Consession, consider. *Con; sedeo,* or *sidus.*
Consign, consignature. *Con; signum.*
Consignification. *Con; signum; facio.*
Consignment. *Con; signum.*
Consimilar, consimilitude. *Con; similis.*
Consist. *Con; sisto.*
Consociate. *Con; socio.*
Consol. *Con; solidus.*
Consolable, consolation, console. *Con; solor.*
Consolidate. *Con; solidus.*
Consonant. *Con; sonus.*
Consopiate. *Con; sopor.*
Consort. *Con; sors.*
Conspicuity, conspicuous. *Con; specio.*
Conspiracy, conspirant, conspirator, conspire. *Con; spiro.*
Conspissation. *Con; spissus.*
Constable, constant. *Con; sto.*
Constantinople. (*Constantine*); *polis.*
Constellate. *Con; stella.*
Consternation. *Con; sterno.*
Constipate. *Con; stipo.*
Constituent, constitution. *Con; sto.*
Constraint, constrict, constringe. *Con; stringo.*
Construct, construe. *Con; struo.*
Consubstantial, consubstantiate. *Con; sub; sto.*
Consul, consult. *Con; salio.*
Consumable, consume. *Con; sumo.*
Consummate. *Con; summa.*
Consumption. *Con; sumo.*
Contabulate. *Con; tabula.*
Contact, contagion. *Con; tango.*
Contain. *Con; teneo.*
Contemn. *Con; temno.*
Contemper. *Con; tempero.*
Contemplate. *Con; templum.*

Contemporaneous, contemporary, contemporize. *Con; tempus.*
Contempt. *Con; temno.*
Contend. *Con; tendo.*
Contenement, content. *Con; teneo.*
Conterminable, conterminate. *Con; terminus.*
Conterraneous. *Con; terra.*
Contest. *Con; testis.*
Context. *Con; textus.*
Contiguity, contiguous. *Con; tango.*
Continent. *Con; teneo.*
Contingent. *Con; tango.*
Continual, continuance, continuation, continue. *Con; teneo.*
Contort, contorsion. *Con; tortum.*
Contract. *Con; traho.*
Contradict. *Contra; dico.*
Contradistinct, contradistinguish. *Contra; di; stinguo.*
Contraindicate. *Contra; in; dico.*
Contramure. *Contra; murus.*
Contraregularity. *Contra; rego.*
Contrariety, contrarious, contrary. *Contra.*
Contrast. *Contra; sto.*
Contravallation. *Contra; vallum.*
Contravene, contravention. *Contra; venio.*
Contraversion. *Contra; verto.*
Contributary, contribute. *Con; tributum.*
Contrite, contrition. *Con; tero.*
Contrivance, contrive. *Con; trouver.*
Controversary, controverse, controvert. *Contra; verto.*
Contumacious, contumacy, contumelious, contumely. *Con; tumeo.*
Contund, contuse. *Con; tundo.*
Convalescent. *Con; valeo.*
Convene, convenient, convent, conventicle. *Con; venio.*
Converge. *Con; vergo.*
Conversable, conversation, conversazione, converse, convert. *Con; verto.*
Convex. *Con; veho.*
Convexo-concave. *Con; veho—con; cavus.*
Convexo-convex, convey. *Con; veho.*
Convicinity. *Con; vicinus.*
Convict, convince. *Con; vinco.*
Convivial. *Con; vivo.*
Convocate, convoke. *Con; voco.*
Convolute, convolve. *Con; volvo.*
Convoy. *Con; via.*
Convulse. *Con; vello.*
Cook. *Coquo.*
Co-operate. *Co; opera.*
Co-optate. *Co; opto.*
Co-ordinate. *Co; ordo.*
Co-parcener, co-partner. *Co; pars.*
Copious. *Copia.*
Copper, copperas. *Cuprum.*
Copula, copulate. *Copula.*
Cord, cordelier. *Chorda.*
Cordial, core. *Cor.*
Coriaceous. *Corium.*
Co-rival. *Co; rivus.*
Cork. *Cortex.*
Cornific. *Cornu; facio.*
Cornea, corneous, cornel, cornicle, corniculate. *Cornu.*
Cornigerous. *Cornu; gero.*
Cornu-copiæ. *Cornu; copia.*
Cornute, corny. *Cornu.*
Corollary, corona, coronation, coronet. *Corona.*
Corporal, corporate, corporeal, corporeity. *Corpus.*
Corporification. *Corpus; facio.*
Corporify, corps, corpulent, corpuscle, corpuscular. *Corpus.*

Corradiation. *Cor; radius.*
Correct. *Cor; rego.*
Correlate. *Cor; re; latum.*
Correption. *Cor; rapio.*
Correspond. *Cor; re; spondeo.*
Corrigible. *Cor; rego.*
Corrival, corrivate. *Cor; rivus.*
Corroborant, corroborate. *Cor; robur.*
Corrode, corrodible, corrosion. *Cor; rodo.*
Corrugate. *Cor; ruga.*
Corrupt. *Cor; ruptum.*
Cortex, cortical, corticose. *Cortex.*
Coruscate. *Coruscus.*
Corymbiated. *Corymbus.*
Corymbiferous. *Corymbus; fero.*
Coscinomancy. *Coscinon; mancia.*
Cosecant. *Co; seco.*
Cosmetic, cosmical. *Cosmos.*
Cosmogony. *Cosmos; genea.*
Cosmography. *Cosmos; grapho.*
Cosmoplastic. *Cosmos; plasso.*
Cosmopolite. *Cosmos; polis.*
Cosmorama. *Cosmos; orama.*
Cost. *Costa.*
Costive. *Con; stipo.*
Council. *Concilio.*
Co-unite. *Co; unus.*
Counsel. *Con; salio.*
Count. *Con; puto.*
Countenance. *Con; teneo.*
Counter. *Contra.*
Counteract. *Counter; ago.*
Counterevidence. *Counter; e; video*
Counterfeit. *Counter; facio.*
Counterfort. *Counter; fortis.*
Counterinfluence. *Counter; in; fluo.*
Countermand. *Counter; mando.*
Countermure. *Counter; murus.*
Counterpart. *Counter; pars.*
Counterpoise. *Counter; pondus.*
Countervail. *Counter; valeo.*
County. *Con; eo.*
Couple. *Copula*
Courage. *Cor.*
Courant, courier, course. *Curro.*
Covenant. *Co; venio.*
Cover, coverlet, covert. *Couvrir.*
Coy. *Quies.*
Craniology. *Cranium; logos.*
Cranioscopy. *Cranium; scopeo.*
Cranium. *Cranium.*
Crasse, crassitude. *Crassus.*
Crastination. *Cras.*
Create, creature. *Creo.*
Credenda, credent, credible, credit, credulity, creed. *Credo.*
Cremation. *Cremo.*
Crepitate. *Crepo.*
Crepuscule. *Crepusculum.*
Crescent, crescive. *Cresco.*
Cretaceous, cretated. *Creta.*
Crevice. *Crepo.*
Crime, criminal, criminate. *Crimen.*
Crinigerous. *Crinis; gero.*
Crinite, crinose. *Crinis.*
Crisis, criterion, critic, criticise, critique *Crites.*
Croceus. *Crocus.*
Crocodile. *Crocus; (deilos,* fearful).
Crocus. *Crocus.*
Crosier, croslet, cross. *Crux.*
Crown. *Corona.*
Crucial, crucible. *Crux.*
Cruciferous. *Crux; fero.*
Crucifix. *Crux; fixus.*
Cruciform. *Crux; forma.*
Crucify. *Crux.*

Crucigerous. *Crux; gero.*
Crude, cruel. *Crudus.*
Cruentous. *Cruor.*
Crural. *Crus.*
Crust, crustaceous, crustation. *Crusta.*
Crux. *Crux.*
Crypt. *Crypto.*
Cryptogamy. *Crypto; gameo.*
Cryptography. *Crypto; grapho.*
Cryptology. *Crypto; logos.*
Crystal, crystallization. *Crystallus.*
Cub, cubation. *Cubo.*
Culinary. *Culina.*
Culmen. *Culmus.*
Culmiferous. *Culmus; fero.*
Culminate. *Culmus.*
Culpable. *Culpa.*
Cultivate, culture. *Colo.*
Cumbent. *Cubo.*
Cumulate. *Cumulo.*
Cuneal, cuneated. *Cuneus.*
Cuneiform. *Cuneus; forma.*
Cupidity. *Cupio.*
Cupreous. *Cuprum.*
Curacy, curate, cure, curious. *Cura.*
Current, curricle. *Curro.*
Currier, curry. *Corium.*
Cursitor, cursory. *Curro.*
Curt. *Curtus.*
Curtail. *Curtus; tailler.*
Curtal, curtate. *Curtus.*
Curule. *Curro.*
Curvated, curve. *Curvus.*
Curvilinear. *Curvus; linea.*
Cusp, cuspidate. *Cuspis.*
Custody. *Custodia.*
Custom. *Coutume.*
Cutaneous, cuticle, cuticular. *Cutis.*
Cycle. *Cyclus.*
Cycloid. *Cyclus; oidos.*
Cyclometry. *Cyclus; metrum.*
Cyclopedia. *Cyclus; pedia.*
Cylinder, cylindric. *Cylindros.*
Cylindroid. *Cylindros; oidos.*
Cynanthropy. *Cyon; anthropos.*
Cynegetics. *Cyon; egesis.*
Cynic. *Cyon.*
Cynosure. *Cyon;* (*oura*, the tail).
Cyst. *Cystus.*
Cystotomy. *Cystis; tomos.*

D.

Dactyl. *Dactylus.*
Dactylology. *Dactylus; logos.*
Damage, damn, damnation, damnify. *Damnum.*
Date, datum. *Do.*
Daunt. *Domo.*
Deacon. *Dia; coneo.*
Deambulation. *De; ambulo*
Dean. *Deca.*
Dearticulate. *De; articulus.*
Debase. *De; basis.*
Debauch. *De; Bacchus.*
Debel. *De; bellum.*
Debile, debilitate. *Debilis.*
Debit, debt. *Debitus.*
Decachord. *Deca; chorda.*
Decade. *Deca.*
Decadency. *De; cado.*
Decagon. *Deca; gonia.*
Decalogue. *Deca; logos.*
Decamp. *De; campus.*
Decanal. *Deca.*
Decant. *De; cano.*
Decapitate. *De; caput.*
Decapolis. *Deca; polis.*
Decastich. *Deca; stichos.*
Decay. *De; cado.*
Decease. *De; cedo.*
Deceit, deceive. *De; capio.*
December. *Deca.*
Decempedal. *Deca; pes.*
Decemvir. *Deca; vir.*
Decency. *Decens.*
Decennial. *Deca; annus.*
Decent. *Decens.*
Deceptible, deception. *De; capio.*
Decern. *De; cerno.*
Decerpt. *De; carpo.*
Decession. *De; cedo.*
Decharm. *De; cano.*
Decide, deciduous. *De; cædo.*
Decimal, decimate. *Deca.*
Decision. *De; cædo.*
Declaim, declamation. *De; clamo.*
Declaration, declare. *De; clarus.*
Declension, declination, decline. *De; clin*
Declivity, declivous. *De; clivus.*
Decoct. *De; coquo.*
Decompose, decomposition, decompound *De; com; pono.*
Decorate, decorous. *Decor*
Decorticate. *De; cortex.*
Decorum. *Decor.*
Decrease. *De; cresco.*
Decree. *De; cerno.*
Decrement. *De; cresco.*
Decrepit. *De; crepo.*
Decrescent. *De; cresco.*
Decretal. *De; cerno.*
Decretion. *De; cresco.*
Decretory. *De; cerno.*
Decrown. *De; corona.*
Decubation, decumbent, decumbiture. *De cubo.*
Decuple. *Deca; plico.*
Decurion. *Deca.*
Decursion. *De; curro.*
Decurt. *De; curtus.*
Dedecorate. *De; decor.*
Dedicate. *De; dico.*
Dedition. *De; do.*
Deduce, deduct. *De; duco.*
Deface. *De; facio.*
Defalcate. *De; falcatus.*
Defamation, defame. *De; fama.*
Defatigate. *De; fatigo.*
Defeasible, defeat. *De; facio.*
Defecate. *De; fæx.*
Defect, defectuous. *De; facio.*
Defend, defensative, defense. *De; fendo.*
Defer, deference. *De; fero.*
Defiance. *De; fides.*
Deficient, deficit. *De; facio.*
Defigure. *De; figura.*
Definable, define, definite, definition. *De; finis.*
Deflagrable, deflagrate. *De; flagro.*
Deflect, deflexure. *De; flecto.*
Deflorate, deflour. *De; flos.*
Deflow, defluous, deflux. *De; fluo.*
Deforce. *De; fortis.*
Deform. *De; forma.*
Defraud. *De; fraus.*
Defunct. *De; functus.*
Defy. *De; fides.*
Degeneracy, degenerate. *De; genus.*
Deglutition. *De; glutio.*
Degradation, degrade, degree. *De; gradior.*
Degustation. *De; gustus*

Dehort. *De; hortor.*
Deicide. *Deus; cædo.*
Deification. *Deus; facio.*
Deiform. *Deus; forma.*
Deify, deity. *Deus.*
Deign. *Dignus.*
Deiparous. *Deus; pario.*
Deism, deistical. *Deus.*
Deject. *De; jacio.*
Delacerate. *De; lacer.*
Delachrymation. *De; lachryma.*
Delactation. *De; lac.*
Delapse. *De; labor.*
Deleble. *De; leo.*
Delegacy, delegate. *De; lego.*
Delete, deleterious, deletory. *De; leo.*
Delibate. *De; libo.*
Deliberate. *De; liber.*
Delicacy, delicate, deliciate, delicious. *Deliciæ.*
Deligation. *De; ligo.*
Delineament, delineate. *De; linea.*
Delinquent. *De; linquo.*
Deliquate. *De; liqueo.*
Delirament, deliriate, delirium. *De; lira.*
Delitigate. *De; lis; ago.*
Deliver. *De; livrer.*
Delude. *De; ludo.*
Deluge. *Diluvium.*
Delusion. *De; ludo.*
Deluviate. *Diluvium.*
Demagogue. *Demos; agogeus.*
Demand. *De; mando.*
Dementate. *De; mens.*
Demerit. *De; meritum.*
Demersed. *De; mergo.*
Demi. *Demi.*
Demirep. *Demi; re; puto.*
Demise, demission, demit. *De; mitto.*
Democracy, democrat. *Demos; cratos.*
Demolish, demolition. *De; molior.*
Demon. *Demon.*
Demonocracy. *Demon; cratos.*
Demonolatry. *Demon; latria.*
Demonology. *Demon; logos.*
Demonomy. *Demon; nomos.*
Demonstrable, demonstrate. *De; monstro.*
Demoralize. *De; mos.*
Demy. *Demi.*
Denationalize. *De; nascor.*
Dendretic, dendrotic. *Dendron.*
Denegate, denial. *De; nego.*
Denigrate. *De; niger.*
Denominate. *De; nomen.*
Denotate, denote. *De; nota.*
Denounce. *De; nuncio.*
Dense. *Densus.*
Dental, dentist, denticulation. *Dens.*
Dentifrice. *Dens; frico.*
Dentition. *Dens.*
Denude. *De; nudus.*
Denunciate. *De; nuncio.*
Deny. *De; nego.*
Deobstruct, deobstruent. *De; ob; struo.*
Deodand. *Deus; do.*
Depaint. *De; pingo.*
Depart. *De; pars.*
Depascent, depasture. *De; pasco.*
Depauperate. *De; pauper.*
Depectible. *De; pecto.*
Depend. *De; pendeo.*
Deperdit. *De; per; do.*
Dephlegmate, dephlogisticate. *De; phlegma.*
Depict. *De; pingo.*
Depilate. *De; pilus.*
Deplantation. *De; planta.*
Depletion. *De; pleo*
Deplorable, deplore. *De, ploro.*
Deplumation, deplume. *De; pluma.*
Depone. *De; pono.*
Depopulate. *De; populus.*
Deport. *De; porto.*
Depose, deposit, depot. *De; pono.*
Deprave. *De; pravus.*
Deprecate. *De; precor.*
Depreciate. *De; precium.*
Depredate. *De; preda.*
Deprehend, deprehension. *De; prehendo.*
Depress. *De; premo.*
Deprivation, deprive. *De; privus.*
Depulsion. *De; pello.*
Depurate. *De; pus.*
Deputation, depute, deputize, deputy. *De; puto.*
Derange. *De; rang.*
Derelict. *De; re; linquo.*
Deride, derision. *De; rideo.*
Derivation, derive. *De; rivus.*
Derogate. *De; rogo.*
Descant. *De; cano.*
Descend, descension, descent. *De; scando.*
Describable, describe, description. *De, scribo.*
Desecrate. *De; sacer.*
Desert. *De; sertum.*
Desert. *De; servo.*
Deserve. *De; servio.*
Desiccate. *De; sicco.*
Desiderate. *De; sidus.*
Design, designate. *De; signum.*
Desirable, desire. *De; sidus.*
Desist. *De; sisto.*
Desolate. *De; solus.*
Despair, desperado, desperate. *De; spero*
Despicable, despisable, despise, despite *De; specio.*
Despoil, despoliation. *De; spolium.*
Despond. *De; spondeo.*
Despot. *Despotes.*
Despumate. *De; spuma.*
Desquamation. *De; squama.*
Destinate, destine. *De; stino.*
Destitute. *De; sto.*
Destroy, destructible, destruction. *De; struo*
Desudation. *De; sudo.*
Desuetude. *De; sueo.*
Desultory. *De; salio.*
Desume. *De; sumo.*
Detail. *De; tailler.*
Detain. *De; teneo.*
Detect. *De; tego.*
Detent. *De; teneo.*
Deter. *De; terreo.*
Deterge. *De; tergeo.*
Deteriorate. *Deterior.*
Determinable, determinate, determine. *De terminus.*
Deterration. *De; terra.*
Detersion. *De; tergeo.*
Detest. *De; testis.*
Dethrone. *De; thronus.*
Detinue. *De; teneo.*
Detonate, detonize. *De; tonos.*
Detorsion, detort. *De; tortum.*
Detract. *De; traho.*
Detriment, detrition, detritus. *De; tero.*
Detrude. *De; trudo.*
Detruncate. *De; trunco.*
Detrusion. *De; trudo.*
Deuce. *Duo.*
Deuterogamy. *Deuteros; gameo.*
Deuteronomy. *Deuteros; nomos.*
Deuteroscopy. *Deuteros; scopeo.*
Devast. *De; vastus.*

Develope. *De; velo.*
Devest. *De; vestis.*
Devex. *De; veho.*
Deviate. *De; via.*
Device. *De; viduo*
Devious. *De; via.*
Devise. *De; viduo.*
Devoid. *De; viduo.*
Devolution, devolve. *De; volvo.*
Devote. *De; votum.*
Devour. *De; voro.*
Devout. *De; votum.*
Dexter. *Dexter.*
Diabolic, diabolify. *Dia; boleo.*
Diaconal. *Dia; coneo.*
Diacoustics. *Dia; acouo.*
Diacritic. *Dia; crites.*
Diadem. *Dia; deo.*
Diadrom. *Dia; dromos.*
Diæresis. *Dia; aeresis.*
Diagonal. *Dia; gonia.*
Diagram, diagraphic. *Dia; grapho.*
Dialect. *Dia; lego.* [*logos.*
Dialogistic, dialogize, dialogue. *Dia;*
Dialysis. *Dia; lysis.*
Diamantine. *A; damao.*
Diameter, diametrical. *Dia; metrum.*
Diamond. *A; damao.*
Diaphanic, diaphanous. *Dia; phano.*
Diarrhea. *Dia; rheo.*
Diary. *Dies.*
Diastole. *Dia; stello.*
Diatessaron. *Dia; tetra.*
Dichotomize, dichotomy. *Dicha; tomos.*
Dictate, dictatorial, diction, dictum. *Dico.*
Diet, dietetic. *Dieta.*
Diffarreation. *Dif; farina*
Differ. *Dif; fero.*
Difficult. *Dif; facilis.*
Diffide. *Dif; fides.*
Diffind. *Dif; findo.*
Diffinitive. *Dif; finis.*
Diffision. *Dif; findo.*
Difflation. *Dif; flatus.*
Diffluent. *Dif; fluo.*
Difform. *Dif; forma.*
Diffuse. *Dif; fundo.*
Digamy. *Dis; gameo.*
Digastric. *Dis; gaster.*
Digerent, digest. *Di; gero.*
Digit. *Digitus.*
Digladiate. *Di; gladius.*
Dignification. *Dignus; facio.*
Dignify, dignitary, dignity. *Dignus.*
Digress. *Di; gradior.*
Dijudicate. *Di; judico.*
Dilacerate. *Di; lacer.*
Dilaniate. *Di; lanius.*
Dilapidate. *Di; lapis.*
Dilate. *Di; latus.*
Dilatory. *Di; latum.*
Dilemma. *Dis; lepsis.*
Diligent. *Di; lego.*
Diluent, dilute. *Di; luo.*
Diluvian. *Diluvium.*
Dimension, dimensity. *Di; mensura.*
Dimeter. *Dis; metrum.*
Dimidiate. *Dis; medius.*
Diminish, diminuent, diminute. *Di; minuo.*
Dimission, dimit. *Di; mitto.*
Diocese. *Dia; eceo.*
Dioptrics. *Dia; opto.*
Diorama. *Dia; orama.*
Diorism, dioristic. *Dia; horos.*
Diorthosis. *Dia; orthos.*
Dipetalous. *Dis; petalon.*
Diphthong *Dis; phthegma*
Diploma, diplomatic. ***Diploma.***
Diptote. *Dis; ptoma.*
Direct. *Di; rego.*
Direption. *Di; rapio.*
Disable. *Dis; habeo.*
Disadvantage. *Dis; ad; avant.*
Disaffect. *Dis; af; facio.*
Disaffirm. *Dis; af; firmus.*
Disagree. *Dis; a; gratia.*
Disannul. *Dis; an; nullus.*
Disappear. *Dis; ap; pareo.*
Disapprobation. *Dis; ap; probo.*
Disappropriate. *Dis; ap; proprius.*
Disapprove. *Dis; ap; probo.*
Disarrange. *Dis; ar; rang.*
Disaster. *Dis; astron.*
Discern. *Dis; cerno.*
Discerp. *Dis; carpo.*
Dischurch. *Dis; eceo;* (*Curios,* the Lord).
Disciple, disciplinarian, discipline. *Discipulus.*
Disclaim. *Dis; clamo.*
Disclose, disclusion. *Dis; claudo.*
Discoast. *Dis; costa.*
Discolor. *Dis; color.*
Discomfort. *Dis; com; fortis.*
Discommend. *Dis; com; mando.*
Discommission. *Dis; com; mitto.*
Discommodate, discommode. *Dis; com, modus.*
Discompose, discomposition. *Dis; com; pono.*
Disconcert. *Dis; con; certo.*
Disconformity. *Dis; con; forma.*
Discongruity. *Dis; con; grus.*
Disconnect. *Dis; con; necto.*
Disconsent. *Dis; con; sentio.*
Disconsolate. *Dis; con; solor.*
Discontent, discontinue, discontinuance. *Dis; con; teneo.*
Disconvenient. *Dis; con; venio.*
Discord. *Dis; cor.*
Discount. *Dis; con; puto.*
Discountenance. *Dis; con; teneo.*
Discourage. *Dis; cor.*
Discourse. *Dis; curro.*
Discover. *Dis; couvrir.*
Discredit. *Dis; credo.*
Discreet. *Dis; cerno.*
Discrepant. *Dis; crepo.*
Discrete, discretion, discriminate. *Dis; cerno.*
Discubitory, discumbency. *Dis; cubo.*
Discursive. *Dis; curro.*
Discuss, discutient. *Dis; cutio.*
Disdain. *Dis; dignus.*
Disease. *Dis; otium.*
Disembarrass. *Dis; em; barre.*
Disenterre. *Dis; en; terra.*
Disenthrone. *Dis; en; thronus.*
Disentitle. *Dis; in; titulus.*
Disexercise. *Dis; ex; erceo.*
Disfavor. *Dis; faveo.*
Disfiguration, disfigure. *Dis; figura.*
Disfranchise. *Dis; franc.*
Disglorify. *Dis; gloria.*
Disgrace. *Dis; gratia.*
Disgust. *Dis; gustus.*
Dishabilitate, dishabille, dishabit. *Dis. habeo.*
Disharmony. *Dis; harmonia.*
Disheir, disherison, disherit. *Dis; hæres*
Dishonest, dishonor. *Dis; honor.*
Dishumor. *Dis; humeo.*
Disincarcerate. *Dis; in; carcer.*
Disinclination. *Dis; in; clino.*
Disincorporation. *Dis; in; corpus.*

Disingenuous. *Dis; in; genu*
Disinhabited. *Dis; in; habeo.*
Disinherison. *Dis; in; hæres.*
Disinter. *Dis; in; terra.*
Disinterest. *Dis; inter; ens.*
Disinvite. *Dis; invito.*
Disinvolve. *Dis; in; volvo.*
Disjection. *Dis; jacio.*
Disjoin, disjunct. *Dis; jungo.*
Dislocate. *Dis; locus.*
Disloyalty. *Dis; loy.*
Dismal. *Dies; male.*
Dismiss. *Dis; mitto.*
Dismortgage. *Dis; mors; (gage).*
Dismount. *Dis; mons.*
Disnatured. *Dis; nascor.*
Disobedience, disobey. *Dis; ob; audio.*
Disobligation, disoblige. *Dis; ob; ligo.*
Disorbed. *Dis; orbis.*
Disorder, disordinate. *Dis; ordo.*
Disorganize. *Dis; organum.*
Dispair. *Dis; par.*
Dispand. dispansion. *Dis; pando.*
Disparadised. *Dis; paradisos.*
Disparage, disparity. *Dis; par.*
Dispart. *Dis; pars.*
Dispassion. *Dis; patior.*
Dispauper. *Dis; pauper.*
Dispel. *Dis; pello.*
Dispend, dispensary, dispensation, dispense. *Dis; pendo.*
Dispeople. *Dis; populus.*
Disperge. *Di; spargo.*
Dispermous. *Dis; sperma.*
Disperse. *Di; spargo.*
Dispirit. *Di; spiro.*
Displant. *Dis; planta.*
Display. *Dis; plico.*
Displease. *Dis; placeo.*
Displode, displosion. *Dis; plaudo.*
Dispose, disposition. *Dis; pono.*
Dispossess. *Dis; posse.*
Disposure. *Dis; pono.*
Disproof. *Dis; probo.*
Disproportion. *Dis; pro; pars.*
Disprove. *Dis; probo.*
Dispunishable. *Dis; punio.*
Disputable, disputant, disputatious, dispute. *Dis; puto.*
Disqualification. *Dis; qualis; facio.*
Disqualify. *Dis; qualis.*
Disquiet. *Dis; quies.*
Disquisition. *Dis; quæro.*
Disreputable, disrepute. *Dis; re; puto.*
Disrespect. *Dis; re; specio.*
Disrupt. *Dis; ruptum.*
Dissatisfaction. *Dis; satis; facio.*
Dissatisfy. *Dis; satis.*
Dissect. *Dis; seco.*
Dissemble. *Dis; similis.*
Disseminate. *Dis; semen.*
Dissension, dissent, dissentaneous, dissentient. *Dis; sentio.*
Dissert. *Dis; sertum.*
Disserve, disservice. *Dis; servio.*
Dissever. *Dis; se; paro.*
Dissilient, dissilition. *Dis; salio.*
Dissimilar, dissimilitude, dissimulation. *Dis; similis.*
Dissipate. *Dis; sipo.*
Dissociable, dissociate. *Dis; socius.*
Dissoluble, dissolute, dissolvable, dissolve. *Dis; solvo.*
Dissonant. *Dis; sonus.*
Dissuade, dissuasion. *Dis; suadeo.*
Dissyllable. *Dis; syl; labo.*
Distant. *Di; sto.*
Distaste. *Dis; taster.*
Distemper, distemperature. *Dis; tempero.*
Distend, distension. *Dis; tendo.*
Distich. *Dis; stichos.*
Distil. *Di; stilla.*
Distinct, distinguish. *Di; stinguo.*
Distitle. *Dis; titulus.*
Distort. *Dis; tortum.*
Distract. *Dis; traho.*
Distributable, distribute. *Dis; tributum.*
Disturb. *Dis; turba.*
Disuniform. *Dis; unus; forma.*
Disunion, disunite. *Dis; unus.*
Disusage, disuse. *Dis; utor.*
Disvalidity, disvaluation, disvalue. *Dis; valeo.*
Diuretic. *Dia; urina.*
Diurnal. *Dies.*
Diuturnal. *Diuturnus.*
Divaricate. *Di; varico.*
Divellant, divellicate. *Di; vello.*
Diverge. *Di; vergo.*
Diversification. *Di; verto; facio.*
Diversify, diversion, diversity, divert, divertizement. *Di; verto.*
Divest. *Di; vestis.*
Dividable, divide, dividend, dividual. *Di; viduo.*
Divination, divine, divinified. *Divus.*
Division. *Di; viduo.*
Divorce. *Di; verto.*
Divulgate, divulge. *Di; vulgus.*
Divulsion. *Di; vello.*
Docile, doctor, doctrine, document. *Doceo.*
Dodecagon. *Duo; deca; gonia.*
Dodecaedron. *Duo; deca; edra.*
Dogma, dogmatize. *Dogma.*
Dole, dolor. *Doleo.*
Doloriferous. *Doleo; fero.*
Dolorific. *Doleo; facio.*
Dolorigerous. *Doleo; gero.*
Dom. *Domus.*
Domain. *Dominus.*
Domestic, domicile. *Domus.*
Domify. *Domo.*
Dominate, domineer, dominical, dominion, don. *Dominus.*
Donary, donation, donee, donor. *Do.*
Dormant, dormitory, dormouse. *Dormio.*
Dorsal. *Dorsum.*
Dorsiferous. *Dorsum; fero.*
Dorsiparous. *Dorsum; pario.*
Dorture. *Dorsum.*
Dose, dosis. *Dotos.*
Dotal. *Dos.*
Double. *Duo; plico.*
Doubt. *Dubius.*
Doxology. *Doxa; logos.*
Drag, drail. *Traho.*
Drama, dramatize. *Drama.*
Draw. *Traho.*
Dromedary. *Dromos.*
Dropsical, dropsy. *Hydor; opto.*
Druid, dryad. *Drus.*
Dual. *Duo.*
Dubiety, dubious, dubitation. *Dubius.*
Ducal, ducat, duct. *Duco.*
Duel, duet. *Duo.*
Duke. *Duco.*
Dulcet. *Dulcis.*
Dulcification. *Dulcis; facio.*
Dulcify, dulcor *Dulcis.*
Duo. *Duo.*

Duodecagon. *Duo; deca; gonia.*
Duodecimo. *Duo; deca.*
Duodecuple. *Duo; deca; plico.*
Duple, duplicate, duplicity. *Duo; plico.*
Durable, durance, dure. *Durus.*
Dutchy, duke. *Duco.*
Dynamics. *Dynastia.*
Dynamometer. *Dynastia; metrum.*
Dynasty. *Dynastia.*
Dyscrasy. *Dys; cratos.*
Dysentery. *Dys; enteron.*
Dysnomy. *Dys; nomos.*
Dyspepsy. *Dys; peptos.*
Dysphony. *Dys; phone.*
Dyspnœa. *Dys; pneuma*
Dysury. *Dys; urina.*

E.

Ease. *Otium.*
Ebriety, ebriosity. *Ebrius.*
Ebullition. *E; bulla.*
Eccentric. *Ec; centrum.*
Ecclesiastic. *Ec; clesis.*
Echo. *Echeo.*
Echometer. *Echeo; metrum.*
Eclectic. *Ec; lego.*
Eclipse, ecliptic. *Ec; lipo.*
Eclogue. *Ec; logos.*
Economics, economize, economy. *Eceo; nomos.*
Ecphonesis. *Ec; phone.*
Ecstasy, ecstatic. *Ec; sto.*
Ectype. *Ec; typus.*
Ecumenical. *Eceo.*
Edacious, edacity. *Edo.*
Edematous. *Edema.*
Edentated. *E; dens.*
Edible. *Edo.*
Edificant, edification, edifice. *Edes; facio.*
Edify, edible. *Edes.*
Edit, editorial. *E; do.*
Educate, educe, eduction. *E; duco.*
Edulcorate. *E; dulcis.*
Edulious. *Edo.*
Effable. *Ef; fari.*
Efface. *Ef; facies.*
Effascinate. *Ef; fascinum.*
Effect, effectual. *Ef; facio.*
Effeminacy, effeminate. *Ef; femina.*
Effervesce. *Ef; ferveo.*
Effete. *Ef; fetus.*
Efficacy, efficient. *Ef; facio.*
Effigiate, effigy. *Ef; figura.*
Efflate. *Ef; flatus.*
Efflorescent. *Ef; flos.*
Effluent, effluvium, efflux. *Ef; fluo.*
Effort. *Ef; fortis.*
Effossion. *Ef; fossa.*
Effrontery. *Ef; frons.*
Effulge. *Ef; fulgeo.*
Effume. *Ef; fumus.*
Effuse. *Ef; fundo.*
Egerminate. *E; germen.*
Egest. *E; gero.*
Egoist, egotist. *Ego.*
Egregious. *E; grex.*
Egress. *E; gradior.*
Ejaculate, eject. *E; jacio.*
Elaborate. *E; labor.*
Elapse. *E · labor.*
Elastic. *Elao.*
Elate. *E; latum.*
Elect, *E; lego.*
Electre, electric. *Electrum.*
Electrification. *Electrum; facio.*
Electrify, electrise. *Electrum.*
Electrometer. *Electrum; metrum.*
Eleemosynary. *Eleemosyne.*
Elegant. *Elegans.*
Elegiac. *Elegia.*
Elegit. *E; lego.*
Elegy. *Elegia.*
Element. *Elementum.*
Elevate. *E; levo.*
Elicit. *E; licio.*
Elide. *E; lido.*
Eligible. *E; lego.*
Eliminate. *E; limen.*
Eliquation. *E; liqueo.*
Elision. *E; lido.*
Elixate. *Elixus.*
Ellipsis, elliptic. *El; lipo.*
Elocation. *E; locus.*
Elocution. *E; loquor.*
Eloge. *E; logos.*
Elong, elongation. *E; longus.*
Eloquent. *E; loquor.*
Elucidate. *E; luceo.*
Eluctation. *E; luctor.*
Elude, elusion. *E; ludo.*
Elute, elutriate. *E; luo.*
Elysium. *Elysium.*
Emaciate. *E; maceo.*
Emaculate. *E; macula.*
Emanate. *E; mano.*
Emancipate. *E; manus; capio.*
Emasculate. *E; masculus.*
Embalm. *Em; balsamon.*
Embarrass. *Em; barre.*
Embase. *Em; basis.*
Embellish. *Em; beau.*
Emblem, embolism, embolus. *Em; boleo*
Embrocate. *Em; broche.*
Embryo. *Em; bryo.*
Emend. *E; menda.*
Emendicate. *E; mendicus.*
Emerge. *E; mergo.*
Emeroids. *Hema; rheo.*
Emersion. *E; mergo.*
Emetic. *Emeo.*
Emication. *E; mica.*
Emigrate. *E; migro.*
Eminent. *E; mineo.*
Emissary, emission, emissitious, emit. *E mitto.*
Emmenagogue. *En; men; agogeus.*
Emollescence, emolliate, emollient. *E, mollis.*
Emotion. *E; moveo.*
Empassion. *Em; patior.*
Empeople. *Em; populus.*
Emperor. *Em; paro;* or *Impero.*
Emphasis, emphatic. *Em; phano.*
Empire. *Em; paro;* or *Impero.*
Empiric. *Em; pirates.*
Emplaster, emplastic, *Em; plasso.*
Emporetic, emporium. *Em; poros.*
Empoverish. *Em; pauper.*
Empress. *Em; paro.*
Empyrean, empyreuma, empyrical, empyrosis. *Em; pyr.*
Emulate, emulous. *Emulus.*
Enable. *En; habeo.*
Enact. *En; ago.*
Enamor. *En; amo.*
Encamp. *En; campus.*
Encave. *En; cavus.*
Enchant. *En; cano.*
Encircle. *En; circulus.*
Enclitic. *En; clino.*

Encloister, enclose. *En; claudo.*
Encomiastic, encomium. *En; comos.*
Encompass. *En; com; passus.*
Encourage. *En; cor.*
Encrease. *En; cresco.*
Encyclical. *En; cyclus.*
Encyclopedia. *En; cyclus; pedia.*
Encysted. *En; cystis.*
Endamage. *En; damnum.*
Endecagon. *En; deca; gonia.*
Endemic, endemial. *En; demos.*
Endict, endite. *En; dico.*
Endorse, *En; dorsum.*
Endow. *En; dos.*
Endue. *En; duo.*
Endure. *En; durus.*
Enemy. *In; amicus.*
Energetic, energic, energize, energy. *En; ergon.*
Enervate, enerve. *E; neuron.*
Enfeoff. *En; feof.*
Enfever. *En; febris.*
Enforce. *En; fortis.*
Enform. *En; forma.*
Enfranchise. *En; franc.*
Engender. *En; genus.*
Engrave. *En; grapho.*
Enigma. *Enigma.*
Enjoin. *En; jungo.*
Enlarge. *En; largus.*
Enmity. *In; amicus.*
Enneagon. *Ennea; gonia.*
Enneatical. *Ennea.*
Enormity, enormous. *E; norma.*
Enrapture, enravish. *En; rapio.*
Ens. *Ens.*
Ensanguine. *En; sanguis.*
Ensiform. *Ensis; forma.*
Ensphere. *En; sphæra.*
Ensue. *En; sequor.*
Entail. *En; tailler.*
Enterocele. *Enteron; cele.*
Enterology. *Enteron; logos.*
Enterprise *Inter; prehendo.*
Entertain. *Inter; teneo.*
Entheastic. *In; theos.*
Enthrone. *En; thronus.*
Enthusiasm, enthusiastic. *En; theos.*
Enthymematical, enthymeme. *En; thymos.*
Entire. *In; tango.*
Entitle. *In; titulus.*
Entity. *Ens.*
Entomb. *En; tumeo.*
Entomolite. *En; tomos; lithos.*
Entomology. *Entomon; logos.*
Enubilate. *E; nubes.*
Enucleate. *E; nux.*
Enumerate. *E; numerus.*
Enunciate. *E; nuncio.*
Envelope. *En; velo.*
Envenom. *En; venenum.*
Enviable, envious. *In; video.*
Envoy. *En; via.*
Envy. *In; video.*
Epenthesy, epenthetic. *Epi; thesis.*
Ephemera, ephemeris, ephemerous. *Epi; hemera.*
Epic. *Epos.*
Epicure. *Epicurus.*
Epicycle. *Epi; cyclus.*
Epicycloid. *Epi; cyclus; oidos.*
Epidemic. *Epi; demos.*
Epiglottis. *Epi; glossa.*
Epigram, epigraph. *Epi; grapho.*
Epilepsy, epileptic. *Epi; lepsis.*
Epilogue. *Epi; logos.*
Epinicion. *Epi; nice.*
Epiphany. *Epi; phano.*
Epiphonem. *Epi; phone.*
Epiphora. *Epi; phero.*
Epiphyllospermous. *Epi; phyllon; sperma.*
Epiphysis. *Epi; physis.*
Episcopacy, episcopal. *Epi; scopeo.*
Episode. *Epi; odos.*
Epispastic. *Epi; spasma.*
Epistle, epistolary, epistolic. *Epi; stello.*
Epistolography. *Epi; stello; grapho.*
Epistrophe. *Epi; strophe.*
Epitaph. *Epi; taphos.*
Epithem, epithet. *Epi; thesis.*
Epitome, epitomize. *Epi; tomos.*
Epoch. *Epi; exis.*
Epode. *Epi; ode.*
Epopee. *Epos; poieo.*
Epulary, epulation. *Epulæ.*
Equable, equal. *Equus.*
Equangular. *Equus; angulus.*
Equanimity. *Equus; animus.*
Equator. *Equus.*
Equery, equestrian. *Eques.*
Equiangular. *Equus; angulus.*
Equicrural. *Equus; crus.*
Equidistant. *Equus; di; sto.*
Equiformity. *Equus; forma.*
Equilateral. *Equus; latus.*
Equilibrate, equilibrium. *Equus; libra*
Equinal. *Eques.*
Equinecessary. *Equus; necesse.*
Equinoctial, equinox. *Equus; nox.*
Equinumerant. *Equus; numerus.*
Equip. *Eques.*
Equipendency. *Equus; pendeo.*
Equipoise. *Equus; pondus.*
Equipollent. *Equus; pollens.*
Equiponderant, equiponderate, equipondious. *Equus; pondus.*
Equitable, equity. *Equus.*
Equivalent. *Equus; valeo.*
Equivocal. *Equus; vox.*
Equivorous. *Equus; voro.*
Eradiate. *E; radius.*
Eradicate. *E; radix.*
Erase, erasion. *E; rado.*
Erect. *E; rego.*
Eremitage, eremite. *Eremos.*
Ereption. *E; rapio.*
Erode. *E; rodo.*
Erogate. *E; rogo.*
Erose, erosion. *E; rodo.*
Err, erratic, erratum, erroneous, error. *Error.*
Erubescent. *E; ruber.*
Eruct. *E; ructus.*
Erudite. *E; rudis.*
Eruginous. *Erugo.*
Erupt. *E; ruptum.*
Escalade. *E; scala.*
Escritoir. *Scribo.*
Esculent. *Esca.*
Escutcheon. *Scutum.*
Esotery. *Eso.*
Especial. *Specio.*
Espousal, espouse. *E; spondeo*
Espy. *Specio.*
Essence, essential. *Ens.*
Establish. *E; sto.*
Esteem, estimable, estimate. *Estimo.*
Estival. *Estiva.*
Estrange. *Exterus.*
Estuary, estuate. *Estu*
Esurient, esurine. *Esurio.*
Etern, eternal, eternize. *Eternus.*
Ether. *Ether.*

Ethic. *Ethos.*
Ethnic. *Ethnos.*
Ethnography. *Ethnos; grapho.*
Ethnology. *Ethnos; logos.*
Etymology. *Etymon; logos.*
Etymon. *Etymon.*
Eucharist. *Eu; charis.*
Euchology. *Euche; logos.*
Eucrasy. *Eu;* (*crasis*, temperament).
Euctical. *Euche.*
Eudiometer. *Eudios; metrum.*
Eulogium, eulogy. *Eu; logos.*
Eupathy. *Eu; pathos.*
Eupepsy, eupeptic. *Eu; peptos.*
Euphemism. *Eu; phano.*
Euphony. *Eu; phone.*
Euroclydon. *Eurus;* (*clydon*, a wave).
Europe. *Europe.*
Eurus. *Eurus.*
Eutaxy. *Eu; tactos.*
Euthanasy. *Eu; thanatos.*
Evacate, evacuate. *E; vaco.*
Evade. *E; vado.*
Evagation. *E; vagus.*
Eval. *Evum.*
Evanescent. *E; vanus.*
Evangelic, evangelist. *Eu; angello.*
Evanid, evanish. *E; vanus.*
Evaporable, evaporate. *E; vapor.*
Evaporometer. *E; vapor; metrum.*
Evasion. *E; vado.*
Even. *Equus.*
Event. *E; venio.*
Eventerate. *E; venter.*
Eventilate. *E; ventus.*
Eventual, eventuate. *E; venio*
Ever. *Evum.*
Evict. *E; vinco.*
Evident. *E; video.*
Evigilation. *E; vigil.*
Evince. *E; vinco.*
Eviscerate. *E; viscus.*
Evitable, evitate. *E; vito.*
Eviternal, eviternity. *Evum.*
Evocate, evoke. *E; voco.*
Evolation. *E; volo.*
Evolution, evolve. *E; volvo.*
Evomition. *E; vomito.*
Exacerbate. *Ex; acerbus.*
Exacervation. *Ex; acervus.*
Exact. *Ex; ago.*
Exaggerate. *Ex; agger.*
Exagitate. *Ex; agito.*
Exalt. *Ex; altus.*
Examen, examine. *Examen.*
Example. *Exemplum.*
Exanimate. *Ex; anima.*
Exanthemata. *Ex; anthos.*
Exantlate. *Ex; antlos.*
Exarticulation. *Ex; articulus.*
Exasperate. *Ex; asper.*
Excandescence. *Ex; candeo.*
Excantation. *Ex; cano.*
Excarnate. *Ex; caro.*
Excarnification. *Ex; caro; facio.*
Excavate. *Ex; cavus.*
Exceed. *Ex; cedo.*
Excel, excellent. *Ex; celsus.*
Except. *Ex; capio.*
Excern. *Ex; cerno.*
Excerp, excerption. *Ex; carpo.*
Excess. *Ex; cedo.*
Excise. *Ex; cædo.*
Excitate, excite. *Ex; cito.*
Exclaim, exclamation. *Ex; clamo.*
Exclude, exclusion. *Ex; claudo.*
Excoct. *Ex; coquo.*
Excogitate. *Ex; co; agito.*
Excommunicate. *Ex; com; munus.*
Excoriate. *Ex; corium.*
Excortication. *Ex; cortex.*
Excrement, excretion. *Ex; cerno.*
Excrescent. *Ex cresco.*
Excruciate. *Ex; crux.*
Excubation. *Ex; cubo.*
Exculpate. *Ex; culpa.*
Excursion. *Ex; curro.*
Excusable, excusation, excuse. *Ex; causa.*
Excuss. *Ex; cutio.*
Execrable, execrate. *Ex; sacer.*
Execute. *Ex; sequor.*
Exegesis, exegetical. *Ex; egesis.*
Exemplar. *Exemplum.*
Exemplification. *Exemplum; facio,*
Exemplify. *Exemplum.*
Exempt. *Ex; emo.*
Exenterate. *Ex; enteron.*
Exequies. *Ex; sequor.*
Exercise, exercitation. *Ex; erceo.*
Exert. *Ex; sertum.*
Exesion. *Ex; edo.*
Exestuation. *Ex; estuo.*
Exfoliate. *Ex; folium.*
Exhale. *Ex; halo.*
Exhaust. *Ex; haustum.*
Exheredate. *Ex; hæres.*
Exhibit. *Ex; habeo.*
Exhort. *Ex; hortor.*
Exhumation, exhume. *Ex; humus.*
Exiccate. *Ex; sicco.*
Exigent, exiguity. *Ex; ago.*
Exile. *Exilium.*
Exist. *Ex; sisto.*
Exit. *Ex; eo.*
Exodus. *Ex; odos.*
Exomphalos. *Ex; omphalos.*
Exonerate. *Ex; onus.*
Exorable. *Ex; oro.*
Exorbitant, exorbitate. *Ex; orbis.*
Exorcised. *Ex; orcos.*
Exordium, exordial. *Ex; ordior.*
Exornation. *Ex; orno.*
Exortive. *Ex; orior.*
Exossated, exosseous. *Ex; os.*
Exoteric, exotery, exotic. *Exterus.*
Expand, expanse. *Ex; pando.*
Expatiate. *Ex; spatium.*
Expatriate. *Ex; pater.*
Expect. *Ex; specio.*
Expectorate. *Ex; pectus.*
Expedient, expeditate, expedite, expedition. *Ex; pes.*
Expel. *Ex; pello.*
Expend, expenditure, expense. *Ex; pendo.*
Experience, experiment, expert. *Ex; perior.*
Expiable, expiate. *Ex; pio.*
Expirable, expiration, expire. *Ex; spiro.*
Explain, explanation. *Ex; planus.*
Expletion. *Ex; pleo.*
Explicable, explicate, explicit. *Ex; plico.*
Explode. *Ex; plaudo.*
Exploration, explore. *Ex; ploro.*
Explosion. *Ex; plaudo.*
Expolish. *Ex; polis.*
Export. *Ex; porto.*
Expose, exposition. *Ex; pono.*
Expostulate. *Ex; postulo.*
Exposure, expound. *Ex; pono.*
Express. *Ex; premo.*
Exprobate. *Ex; probrum.*
Expropriate. *Ex; proprius.*
Expugn, expugnable. *Ex; pugna.*
Expuition. *Ex; sputo.*
Expulse. *Ex; pello*

Expunction, expunge. *Ex; pungo.*
Expurgate, expurge. *Ex; purgo.*
Exquisite. *Ex; quæro.*
Exsanguious. *Ex; sanguis.*
Exscind. *Ex; scindo.*
Exscribe, exscript. *Ex; scribo.*
Exsiccant, exsiccate. *Ex; sicco.*
Expoliation. *Ex; spolium.*
Exspuition. *Ex; sputo.*
Exstipulate. *Ex; stipula.*
Exsuction. *Ex; sugo.*
Exsudation, exsude. *Ex; sudo.*
Exsufflation. *Ex; suf; flatus.*
Exsuscitation. *Ex; sus; cito.*
Extancy, extant. *Ex; sto.*
Extacy. *Ex; stasis.*
Extemporal, extemporaneous, extemporary, extempore, extemporize. *Ex; tempus.*
Extend, extensible, extension, extent. *Ex; tendo.*
Extenuate. *Ex; tenuis.*
Exterior. *Exterus.*
Exterminate, extermine. *Ex; terminus.*
Extern. *Exterus.*
Exterraneous. *Ex; terra.*
Extimulate. *Ex; stimulus.*
Extinct, extinguish. *Ex; stinguo.*
Extirp, extirpation. *Ex; stirps.*
Extol. *Ex; tollo.*
Extort. *Ex; tortum.*
Extract. *Ex; traho.*
Extramission. *Extra; mitto.*
Extramundane. *Extra; mundus.*
Extraneous. *Exterus.*
Extraordinary. *Extra; ordo.*
Extraparochial. *Extra; para; eceo.*
Extraprovincial. *Extra; pro; vinco.*
Extraregular. *Extra; rego.*
Extravagant, extravagate. *Extra; vagus.*
Extravasated. *Extra; vas.*
Extreme. *Exterus.*
Extricable, extricate. *Ex; tricæ.*
Extrinsic. *Exterus.*
Extruct. *Ex; struo.*
Extrude, extrusion. *Ex; trudo.*
Extuberant, extuberate. *Ex; tuber.*
Extumescence. *Ex; tumeo.*
Exuberant. *Ex; uber.*
Exuccous. *Ex; sugo.*
Exudate, exude. *Ex; sudo.*
Exulcerate. *Ex; ulcus.*
Exult. *Ex; salio.*
Exundate. *Ex; undo.*

F.

Fabaceous. *Faba.*
Fable. *Fabula.*
Fabric. *Fabrico.*
Fabulous. *Fabula.*
Facade, face. *Facies.*
Facete, facetious. *Facetus.*
Facile, facilitate. *Facilis.*
Facinerious, facinorous. *Facinus.*
Fac-simile. *Facio; similis.*
Fact, faction, factitious, factor. *Facio.*
Factotum. *Facio; totus.*
Facture. *Facio.*
Faculty. *Facilis.*
Facund. *Facundus.*
Fæcal, fæces. *Fæx.*
Fair. *Forum.*
Faith *Fides.*
Falcade, falcon. *Falcatus*
Fallacy, fallency, fallible, false. *Fallo.*
Falsification. *Fallo; facio.*
Falsify. *Fallo.*
Fame. *Fama.*
Familiar, familism, family. *Familia*
Famine, famish. *Fames.*
Fanatic. *Fanum.*
Fancy. *Fantasia.*
Fane. *Fanum.*
Fantasm, fantastic, fantasy. *Fantasia.*
Fantom. *Phano.*
Farinaceous, farrago, farraginous, farreation. *Farina.*
Farrier. *Ferrum.*
Fasces, fascia, fascicle, fascicular. *Fascia.*
Fascinate. *Fascinum.*
Fashion. *Facies.*
Fastidious, fastuous. *Fastidium.*
Fatal, fate. *Fatum.*
Fatidical. *Fatum; dico.*
Fatiferous. *Fatum; fero.*
Fatigate, fatigue. *Fatigo*
Fatuus. *Fatuus.*
Faun. *Faunus.*
Fautor, favor. *Faveo.*
Favillous. *Favilla.*
Feasible. *Facio.*
Feast. *Festum.*
Feat, feateous. *Facio.*
Feature. *Facies.*
Febriciate. *Febris.*
Febrific. *Febris; facio.*
Febrifuge. *Febris; fugio.*
Febrile. *Febris.*
February. *Februo.*
Fecal, feces, feculent. *Fæx.*
Fecund, fecundity. *Fecundus.*
Federal, federate. *Fedus.*
Felicitate, felicity. *Felix.*
Feline. *Feles.*
Fellifluous. *Fel; fluo.*
Felon, felonious. *Felon.*
Female, feminine. *Femina.*
Femoral. *Femur.*
Fence, fend. *Fendo.*
Fenestral. *Fenestra.*
Feod. *Feudum.*
Feof. *Feof.*
Feracious, feracity. *Fero.*
Feral. *Feralis.*
Ferine, ferity. *Fera.*
Ferment. *Fermentum.*
Ferocious. *Fera.*
Ferrier. *Ferrum.*
Ferruginous. *Ferrum.*
Ferrule. *Ferrum.*
Ferry, fertile. *Fero.*
Ferule. *Ferula.*
Fervent, fervid, fervor. *Ferveo.*
Festal, festive. *Festum.*
Festucine, festucous. *Festuca.*
Fetid, fetor, fetus. *Fetus.*
Feud, feudalism, feudatory. *Feudum.*
Fever. *Febris.*
Fiat. *Facio.*
Fib. *Fabula.*
Fibre, fibril, fibrous. *Fibra.*
Fickle. *Vacillo.*
Fictile, fiction, fictitious. *Fingo.*
Fidelity, fiducial, fiduciary. *Fides.*
Fief. *Feof.*
Fierce. *Fera.*
Figure. *Figura.*
Filaceous, filament, file. *Filum.*
Filial *Filius.*
Filicide. *Filius; cædo.*

Filter, filtrate. *Filum.*
Final. *Finis.*
Finance. *Finance.* [*Finis.*
Fine, finery, finis, finish, finite, finitude.
Firm, firmament. *Firmus.*
Fisc. *Fiscus.*
Fissile, fissure. *Findo.*
Fistula. *Fistula.*
Fix, fixture. *Fixus.*
Flabby. *Flaccidus.*
Flabile. *Flatus.*
Flaccid. *Flaccidus.*
Flagitious. *Flagitium.*
Flagrant, flagrate. *Flagro.*
Flambeau. *Flamma; beau.*
Flame. *Flamma.*
Flamen, flaminical. *Flamen.*
Flammiferous. *Flamma; fero.*
Flammivorous. *Flamma; voro.*
Flatulent, flatuous. *Flatus.*
Flegm. *Phlegma.*
Flexanimous. *Flecto; animus.*
Flexile, flexion. *Flecto.* [*Flos.*
Flora, Florence, Florentine, floriage, florid.
Floriferous. *Flos; fero.*
Florin, florist, florulent, flosculous, flourish, flower. *Flos.*
Fluctuate. *Fluctuo.* [*Fluo.*
Fluent, fluid, fluor, fluviatic, flux, fluxility.
Fluviatic. *Fluvius.*
Focal, focus. *Focus.*
Fœtus. *Fœtus.*
Foible. *Foible.*
Foliaceous, foliage, foliate, folio. *Folium.*
Foment. *Fomentum.*
Font. *Fons.*
Forage. *Foris.*
Foraminous. *Foro.*
Force. *Fortis.*
Forceps, forcipated. *Forceps.*
Foreign. *Foris.*
Foreknow, foreknowledge. *Fore; nosco.*
Forensic. *Forum.*
Forfeit. *Foris; facio.*
Forinsical. *Foris;* (*secus*, by).
Fork. *Furca.*
Form, formal, formation. *Forma.*
Formidable. *Formido.*
Formosity, formula. *Forma.*
Fornicate. *Fornix.*
Fort, forte. *Fortis.*
Fortification. *Fortis; facio.*
Fortify, fortitude. *Fortis.*
Fortuitous, fortunate, fortune. *Fors.*
Forum. *Forum.*
Fosse, fossil. *Fossa.*
Found, foundation, foundling. *Fundus.*
Fountain. *Fons.* [*Frango.*
Fract, fractious, fragile, fragment, fragor.
Fragrant. *Fragro.*
Frail. *Frango.*
Franchise. *Franc.*
Frangible. *Frango.*
Frank. *Franc.*
Frankincense. *Franc; in; candio.*
Franklin. *Franc.*
Frantic. *Phren.*
Fraternal. *Frater.*
Fratricide. *Frater; cœdo.*
Fraud, fraudulent. *Fraus.*
French, frenchify. *Franc.*
Frenetic, frensical, frenzied. *Phren.*
Frequent, frequentation. *Frequens.*
Friable. *Frio.*
Frication, friction. *Frico.*
Frigefaction. *Frigus; facio.*
Frigid. *Frigus.*
Frigorific. *Frigus; facio.*
Frivolity, frivolous. *Frivolus*
Front, frontal. *Frons.*
Frugal. *Fruges.*
Frugiferous. *Fruges; fero.*
Frumentaceous. *Frumentum.*
Fructify, fruit, fruition. *Fructus.*
Frustrate. *Frustra.*
Fugitive. *Fugio.*
Fulgent, fulgid, fulgor, fulgurate. *Fulgeo.*
Fuliginous. *Fuligo.*
Fulminate, fulmine. *Fulmen.*
Fumado, fumatory, fume, fumid, fumigate *Fumus.* [*bulo.*
Funambulatory, funambulist. *Funis; am-*
Function. *Functus.*
Fund. *Funda.*
Fundament. *Fundus.*
Funebrial, funeral. *Funus.*
Fungus, fungosity. *Fungus.*
Funicle, funicular. *Funis.*
Furacious. *Fur.*
Furcation. *Furca.*
Furfur, furfuraceous. *Furfur.*
Furious. *Furia.*
Furtive, furuncle. *Fur.*
Fury. *Furia.*
Fuse, fusil. *Fundo.*
Fustigation. *Fustis.*
Futile. *Futilis.*
Future, futurition. *Futurus.*

G.

Gælic, galic. *Gallia.*
Gala. *Gala.*
Galaxy. *Galax.*
Galeated. *Galea.*
Gallant. *Gala.*
Gallic, gallicism. *Gallia.*
Gallinaceous. *Gallina.*
Galvanic. *Galvani.*
Galvanometer. *Galvani; metrum.*
Gangrene. *Gangrena.*
Garrulity, garrulous. *Garrio.*
Gasometer. (*Gas*)*; metrum.*
Gastric. *Gaster.*
Gastriloquist. *Gaster; loquor.*
Gastroraphy. *Gaster; rapto.*
Gastrotomy. *Gaster; tomos.*
Gaul. *Gallia.*
Gazet, gazette. *Gazetta.*
Gelable, gelatin, gelly. *Gelu.*
Gem. *Gemma.*
Gemelliparous. *Geminus; pario.*
Geminate, gemini. *Geminus.*
Gemmary. *Gemma.*
Gemmiferous. *Gemma; fero.*
Gemmosity. *Gemma.*
Gender. *Genus.*
Genealogy. *Genea; logos.*
General, generalissimo, generalize, generate, generic, generous. *Genus.*
Genesis. *Genea.*
Genethliacs. *Genea.*
Genethlialogy. *Genea; logos.*
Genial. *Genus.*
Geniculate. *Genu.*
Geneo, genitals, genitive, genius, genteel, Gentile, gentle, gentry. *Genus.*
Genuflection. *Genu; flecto.*
Genuine, genus. *Genus.*
Geocentric. *Ge; centrum.* [vide.)
Geodesy, geodetical. *Ge;* (*daio*, to di-
Geography. *Ge; grapho.*
Geology. *Ge; logos.*

Geomancy. *Ge; mancia.*
Geometry. *Ge; metrum.*
Geoponics. *Ge; ponos.*
George, georgic. *Ge; ergon.*
Geoscopy. *Ge; scopeo.*
Geotic. *Ge.*
Gerent. *Gero.*
Germ, german, germinate. *Germen.*
Gerocomy. *Geron;* (*comeo*, to take care of).
Gerund, gest, gestation, gesticulate, gesture. *Gero.*
Giant. *Gigas.*
Gibbosity, gibbous. *Gibbus.*
Gigantic. *Gigas.*
Gingival. *Gingiva.*
Glacial, glaciate. *Glacies.*
Gladiator. *Gladius.*
Gland. *Glans.*
Glandiform. *Glans; forma.*
Glandule. *Glans.*
Glebe. *Gleba.*
Glew. *Gluten.*
Globe, globose, globule. *Globus.*
Glomerate. *Glomus.*
Gloriation. *Gloria.*
Glorification. *Gloria; facio.*
Glorify, glorious, glory. *Gloria.*
Gloss. *Glossa.*
Glossography. *Glossa; grapho.*
Glossy, glottis. *Glossa.*
Glue. *Gluten.*
Glut. *Glutio.*
Glutinate, glutinosity. *Gluten*
Glutton. *Glutio.*
Glyph. *Glypho.*
Glyptography. *Glypho; grapho.*
Gnome. *Gnomon.*
Gnomology. *Gnomon; logos.*
Gnomon, gnostic. *Gnomon.*
Goniometer. *Gonia; metrum.*
Gordian. *Gordius.*
Gorgon, gorgonian. *Gorgon.*
Gormand. *Gourmand.*
Gospel. *Angello.*
Gothic, gothicise. *Gotthi.*
Gourmand. *Gourmand.*
Govern. *Guberno.*
Grace. *Gratia.*
Gracile. *Gracilis.*
Gracious. *Gratia.*
Grade, gradient, gradual, graduate. *Gradior.*
Grain. *Granum.*
Gramineous. *Gramen.*
Graminivorous. *Gramen; voro.*
Grammar, grammatic, grammatist. *Grapho.*
Granary, granate. *Granum.*
Grand, grandeur. *Grandis.*
Grandevity. *Grandis; evum.*
Grandific. *Grandis; facio.*
Grandiloquence. *Grandis; loquor.*
Grandinous *Grando.*
Granite. *Granum.*
Granivorous. *Granum; voro.*
Granulate, granule. *Granum.*
Graphic. *Grapho.*
Graphometer. *Grapho; metrum.*
Grateful. *Gratia.*
Gratification. *Gratia; facio.*
Gratify, gratis, gratuitous. *Gratia.*
Grave. *Grapho.*
Grave, gravid. *Gravis.*
Gravimeter. *Gravis; metrum.*
Gravitate. *Gravis.*
Grecism Greece, Greek. *Grecia.*
Greet. *Gratia.*
Gregal, gregarious. *Grex.*
Gremial. *Gremium.*
Grenade. *Granum.*
Grief, grievance, grieve, grievous. *Gravis.*
Guarantee, guaranty. *Guarantir.*
Guard. *Guarder.*
Gubernate. *Guberno.*
Gurge. *Gurges.*
Gust, gustation, gusto. *Gustus.*
Guttated, guttulous. *Gutta.*
Gutter, guttural. *Guttur.*
Gymnastic, gymnic. *Gymnos.*
Gymnosophist. *Gynos; sophia.*
Gymnospermous. *Gymnos; sperma.*
Gynæcian. *Gyne.*
Gynaeocracy. *Gyne; cratos.*
Gynarchy. *Gyne; arche.*
Gynecocracy. *Gyne; cratos.*
Gyration, gyre. *Gyrus.*
Gyromancy. *Gyrus; mancia.*

H.

Habiliment, habit, habitant, habitation, habituate, habitude. *Habeo.*
Hagiography. *Hagios; grapho.*
Halcyon. *Halcyon.*
Halituous. *Halo.*
Halleluiah. *Halleluia.*
Hallucinate. *Hallucino.*
Harmony. *Harmonia.*
Hebdomad, hebdomatical. *Hebdomas.*
Hebetate, hebetude. *Hebes.*
Hebraist, Hebrew, hebrician. *Hebræus*
Hecatomb. *Hecaton;* (*bous*, an ox).
Hederaceous. *Hedera.*
Heir. *Hæres.*
Heliacle. *Helios.*
Heliocentric. *Helios; centrum.*
Heliometer. *Helios; metrum.*
Heliopolis. *Helios; polis.*
Helioscope. *Helios; scopeo.*
Heliotrope. *Helios; tropos.*
Hellenic, hellenist. *Hellen.*
Helminthic. *Helmins.*
Helminthology. *Helmins; logos.*
Hemicrany. *Hemisus; cranium.*
Hemicycle. *Hemisus; cyclus.*
Hemiplegy. *Hemisus; plectos.*
Hemisphere. *Himisus; sphæra.*
Hemistich. *Hemisus; stichos.*
Hemoptysis. *Hema; ptyo.*
Hemorrhage, hemorrhoids. *Hema; rheo.*
Hepatic. *Hepar.*
Heptacapsula. *Hepta; capsula.*
Heptachord. *Hepta; chorda.*
Heptagon. *Hepta; gonia.*
Heptander. *Hepta; aner.*
Heptarchy. *Hepta; arche.*
Heptateuch. *Hepta; teuchos.*
Herb, herbescent, herbid. *Herba.*
Herbivorous. *Herba; voro.*
Herborization, herbulent. *Herba.*
Herculean. *Hercules.*
Hereditary. *Hæres.*
Heresiarch. *Heresis; arche.*
Heresy, heretic. *Heresis.*
Heritage. *Hæres.*
Hermaphrodite. *Hermes; aphrodite.*
Hermetic. *Hermes.*
Hermit, hermitage. *Eremos.*
Hero, heroical. *Heros.*
Heroicomic. *Heros; comos.*
Heroism. *Heros.*
Hesitant, hesitate. *Hæreo.*
Heterarchy. *Heteros; arche.*

Heteroclite. *Heteros; clino.*
Heterodox. *Heteros; doxa.*
Heterogeneal. *Heteros; genea.*
Heteroscian. *Heteros; scia.*
Hexagon. *Hex; gonia.*
Hexaedron. *Hex; edra.*
Hexameter. *Hex; metrum.*
Hexander. *Hex; aner.*
Hexangular. *Hex; angulus.*
Hexaped. *Hex; pes.*
Hexastich. *Hex; stichos.*
Hexastyle. *Hex; stylos.*
Hexdecagon. *Hex; deca; gonia.*
Hiation, hiatus. *Hiatus.*
Hibernal. *Hibernus.*
Hibernian, hibernicism. *Hibernia.*
Hierarch. *Hieros; arche.*
Hieroglyph. *Hieros; glypho.*
Hierogram, hierography. *Hieros; grapho.*
Hierology. *Hieros; logos.*
Hieromancy. *Hieros; mancia.*
Hierophant. *Hieros; phano.*
Hieropolis. *Hieros; polis.*
Hilarate, hilarity. *Hilaris.*
Hippocentaur. *Hippos;* (*centeo*, to spur); *taurus.*
Hippodrome. *Hippos; dromos.*
Hippogriff. *Hippos;* (*gryps*, a fabulous bird).
Hippopotamus. *Hippos; potamos.*
Historian, historify. *Historia.*
Historiography. *Historia; grapho.*
Historiology. *Historia; logos.*
History. *Historia.*
Histrion. *Histrio.*
Hodiernal. *Hodie.*
Holocaust. *Holos; causticos.*
Holograph. *Holos; grapho.*
Homicide. *Homo; cædo.*
Homiletical, homily. *Homilos.*
Homogeneal. *Homos; genea.*
Homologous. *Homos; logos.*
Homonymous, homonymy. *Homos; onoma.*
Homotonous. *Homos; tonos.*
Honest, honor, honorary. *Honor.*
Horal. *Hora.*
Horizon. *Horos.*
Horography. *Hora; grapho.*
Horologe. *Hora; logos.*
Horologiography. *Hora; logos; grapho.*
Horology. *Hora; logos.*
Horometry. *Hora; metrum.*
Horoscope. *Hora; scopeo.*
Horrent, horrible, horrid. *Horreo.*
Horrific. *Horreo; facio.*
Horrisonous. *Horreo; sonus.*
Horror. *Horreo.*
Hortation. *Hortor.*
Hortensial. *Hortus.*
Horticulture. *Hortus; cultus.*
Hortulan. *Hortus.*
Hortus-siccus. *Hortus; siccus.*
Hospitable, hospital, host. *Hospes.*
Host. *Hostis.*
Hostile, hostility. *Hostis.*
Hostler, hotel. *Hospes.*
Hour. *Hora.*
Human. *Homo.*
Humation, humble. *Humus.*
Humect. *Humeo.*
Humeral. *Humerus.*
Humicubation. *Humus; cubo.*
Humid. *Humeo.*
Humiliate. *Humus.*
Humor. *Humeo.*
Hyads. *Hydor.*
Hyaline. *Hyalos.*
Hydra. *Hydor.*
Hydragogue. *Hydor; agogeus.*
Hydraulic. *Hydor; aulos.*
Hydrocele. *Hydor; cele.*
Hydrocephalus. *Hydor; cephale.*
Hydrodynamics. *Hydor; dynastia.*
Hydrogen. *Hydor; genea.*
Hydrography. *Hydor; grapho.*
Hydromel. *Hydor; mel.*
Hydrometer. *Hydor; metrum.*
Hydrophobia. *Hydor; phobos.*
Hydropic. *Hydor; opto.*
Hydrostatic. *Hydor; stasis.*
Hydrotic. *Hydor.*
Hyemal. *Hyems.*
Hygrometer. *Hygros; metrum.*
Hygroscope. *Hygros; scopeo.*
Hymen, hymenean. *Hymen.*
Hymnology. (*Hymnos*, a hymn); *logos.*
Hyperbole. *Hyper; boleo.*
Hyperboliform. *Hyper; boleo; forma.*
Hyperborean. *Hyper; boreas.*
Hypercritic. *Hyper; crites.*
Hypermeter. *Hyper; metrum*
Hyperphysical. *Hyper; physis.*
Hypersarcous. *Hyper; sarx.*
Hypnotic. *Hypnos.*
Hypochondria. *Hypo; chondros.*
Hypocrisy, hypocrite. *Hypo; crites.*
Hypogastric. *Hypo; gaster.*
Hypogeum. *Hypo; ge.*
Hypostasy, hypostatic. *Hypo; stasis.*
Hypoteneuse. *Hypo; tonos.*
Hypothecate, hypothesis, hypothetic. *Hypo; thesis.*
Hysteric. *Hysteros.*

I

Iambic. *Iambus.*
Ichneumon. *Ichneumon.*
Ichnography. *Ichneumon; grapho.*
Ichthyology. *Ichthys; logos.*
Ichthyophagy. *Ichthys; phago.*
Icon. *Icon.*
Iconoclast. *Icon;* (*clazo*, to break).
Iconography. *Icon; grapho.*
Iconolater. *Icon; latria.*
Iconology. *Icon; logos.*
Icteric. *Icterus.*
Idea, idealize. *Idea.*
Identic. *Idem.*
Identification. *Idem; facio.*
Identify, identity. *Idem.*
Idiocrasy. *Idios;* (*crasis*, temperament).
Idiocy, idiom, idiomatic. *Idios.*
Idiopathy. *Idios; pathos.*
Idiosyncrasy. *Idios; syn;* (*crasis*, temperament).
Idiot. *Idios.*
Idol. *Idolum.*
Idolater, idolatry. *Idolum; latria*
Igneus, ignify. *Ignis.*
Ignifluous. *Ignis; fluo.*
Ignisfatuus. *Ignis; fatuus.*
Ignite. *Ignis.*
Ignivomous. *Ignis; vomito.*
Ignoble. *Ig; nosco.*
Ignominious, ignominy. *Ig; nomen.*
Ignoramus, ignorant. *Ig; gnorus.*
Iliad. (*Ilion*, Troy); *ode*
Illachrymable. *Il; lachryma.*
Illapse. *Il; labor.*
Illaqueate. *Il; laqueus.*
Illation. *Il; latum*

Illaudable; Il; *laus.*
Illegal. *Il; lex.*
Illegible. *Il; lego.*
Illegitimate. *Il; lex.*
Illeviable. *Il; levo.*
Illiberal. *Il; liber.*
Illicit. *Il; liceo.*
Illimited. *Il; limes.*
Illiterate. *Il; litera.*
Illogical. *Il; logos.*
Illude. *Il; ludo.*
Illume, illuminate. *Il; lumen.*
Illusion, illusory. *Il; ludo.*
Illustrate, illustrious. *Il; lustrum*
Illuxurious. *Il; luxuria.*
Image, imagine. *Imago.*
Imbecile. *Imbecillis.*
Imbibe, imbibition. *Im; bibo.*
Imbrute. *Im; brutus.*
Imitate. *Imitor.*
Immaculate. *Im; macula.*
Immalleable. *Im; malleus.*
Immanacle. *Im; manus.*
Immanent. *Im; mano.*
Immartial. *Im; mars.*
Immaterial. *Im; materia.*
Immature. *Im; maturus.*
Immeability. *Im; meo.*
Immeasured. *Im; mensura.*
Immechanical. *Im; mechanao.*
Immediate. *Im; medius.*
Immedicable. *Im; medeor.*
Immelodious. *Im; melos; ode.*
Immemorial. *Im; memor.*
Immense, immensurable. *Im; mensura.*
Immerge. *Im; mergo.*
Immerit. *Im; meritum.*
Immerse. *Im; mergo.*
Immethodical. *Im; meta; odos.*
Immigrate. *Im; migro.*
Imminent. *Im; mineo.*
Immingle. *Im; misceo.*
Imminution. *Im; minuo.*
Immiscible. *Im; misceo.*
Immission, immit. *Im; mitto.*
Immitigable. *Im; mitis.*
Immix. *Im; misceo.*
Immoderate, immodest. *Im; modus.*
Immolate. *Im; mola.*
Immoment. *Im; momentum.*
Immoral. *Im; mos.*
Immorigerous. *Im; mos; gero.*
Immortal. *Im; mors.*
Immortification. *Im; mors; facio.*
Immovable. *Im; moveo.*
Immund, immundicity. *Im; mundus.*
Immunity. *Im; munus.*
Immure. *Im; murus.*
Immusical. *Im; musa.*
Immutable, immutate, immute. *Im; muto.*
Impacable. *Im; pax.*
Impact. *Im; pactus.*
Impallid. *Im; palleo.*
Impalm. *Im; palma.*
Impanate. *Im; panis.*
Impannel. *Im; pannus.*
Imparadise. *Im; paradisos.*
Impardonable. *Im; pardonner.*
Imparity. *Im; par.*
Imparl. *Im; parler.*
Impart, impartial. *Im; pars.*
Impassible, impassion, impassive, impatient. *Im; patior.*
Impeccancy, impeccable. *Im; pecco.*
Impede, impediment. *Im; pes.*
Impel. *Im; pello.*
Impenetrable. *Im; penetro.*
Impend. *Im; pendeo.*
Impenitent. *Im; peniteo.*
Impennous. *Im; penna.*
Impeople. *Im; populus.*
Imperative. *Impero*, or *Im; paro.*
Imperceptible. *Im; per; capio.*
Imperfect. *Im; per; facio.*
Imperforate. *Im; per; foro.*
Imperial. *Impero*, or *Im; paro.*
Imperishable. *Im; per; eo.*
Impermanence. *Im; per; maneo.*
Impermeable. *Im; per; meo.*
Impersonal, impersonate. *Im; persona.*
Imperspicuity, imperspicuous. *Im; per; specio.*
Impersuasible. *Im; per; suadeo.*
Impertinent. *Im; per; teneo.*
Imperturbation, imperturbed. *Im; per; turba.*
Impervious. *Im; per; via.*
Impetus. *Im; peto.*
Impictured. *Im; pingo.*
Impiety. *Im; pius.*
Impignorate. *Im; pignus.*
Impious. *Im; pius.*
Implacable. *Im; placo.*
Implant. *Im; planta.*
Implausible. *Im; plaudo.*
Implement, impletion. *Im; pleo.*
Implex, implicit. *Im; plico.*
Implore. *Im; ploro.*
Implumed. *Im; pluma.*
Imply. *Im; plico.*
Impolicy, impolished, impolite, impolitic. *Im; polis.*
Imponderable, imponderous. *Im; pondus.*
Imporosity, imporous. *Im; poros.*
Import, important, importunate, importune. *Im; porto.*
Impose. *Im; pono.*
Impossible. *Im; posse.*
Impost, imposture. *Im; pono.*
Impotent. *Im; posse.*
Impoverish. *Im; pauper.*
Impracticable. *Im; practos.*
Imprecate. *Im; precor.*
Impregn, impregnable, impregnate. *Im; pregnans.*
Imprescriptible. *Im; pre; scribo.*
Impress. *Im; premo.*
Imprevalence. *Im; pre; valeo.*
Imprimatur, imprint. *Im; premo.*
Imprison. *Im; prehendo.*
Improbable, improbate, improbity. *Im; probo.*
Improlific. *Im; proles; facio.*
Improper. *Im; proprius.*
Improportionate. *Im; pro; pars.*
Impropriate, impropriety. *Im; proprius.*
Improsperity, improsperous. *Im; prosper.*
Improvable, improve. *Im; probo.*
Improvident, improvision, imprudent. *Im; pro; video.*
Impudent, impudicity. *Im; pudeo.*
Impugn. *Im; pugna.*
Impuissance. *Im; posse.*
Impulse. *Im; pello.*
Impunity. *Im; punio.*
Impure. *Im; purus.*
Imputation, impute. *Im; puto.*
Imputrescible. *Im; putris.*
Inable. *In; habeo.*
Inaccessible. *In; ac; cedo.*
Inaccuracy, inaccurate. *In; ac; cura.*
Inaction. *In; ago.*
Inadequacy, inadequate. *In; ad; equus.*
Inadmissible. *In; ad; mitto.*

Inadvertent. *In; ad; verto.*
Inaffable. *In; af; fari.*
Inaffectation. *In; af; facio.*
Inalienable. *In; alius.*
Inalimental. *In; alo.*
Inamissible. *In; a; mitto.*
Inanimate. *In; anima.*
Inanity. *Inanis.*
Inappetence. *In; ap; peto.*
Inapplicable. *In; ap; plico.*
Inapposite. *In; ap; pono.*
Inapprehensive. *In; ap; prehendo.*
Inaptitude. *In; aptus.*
Inarable. *In; aro.*
Inarticulate. *In; articulus.*
Inartificial. *In; ars; facio.*
Inattentive. *In; at; tendo.*
Inaudible. *In; audio.*
Inaugurate. *In; augur.*
Inauration. *In; aurum.*
Inauspicious. *In; avis; specio.*
Incalculable. *In; calculus.*
Incalescence. *In; caleo.*
Incandescence. *In; candeo.*
Incantation. *In; cano.*
Incapable, incapacity. *In; capio.*
Incarcerate. *In; carcer.*
Incarnate. *In; caro.*
Incautious. *In; cautio.*
Incendiary, incense, incentive. *In; candeo.*
Inception. *In; capio.*
Inceration. *In; cera.*
Incertain. *In; certus.*
Incessible, incessant. *In; cedo.*
Incest, incestuous. *In; castus.*
Inchoate. *Inchoo.*
Incide, incident. *In; cado.*
Incinerate. *In; cinis.*
Incirclet. *In; circulus.*
Incircumscriptible. *In; circum; scribo.*
Incised. *In; cædo.*
Incite. *In; cito.*
Incivil. *In; civis.*
Inclement. *In; clemens.*
Inclination, incline. *In; clino.*
Inclose, inclosure, include, inclusion. *In; claudo.*
Incogitancy, incogitative. *In; co; agito.*
Incoherent. *In; co; hæreo.*
Incombustible. *In; com; ustum.*
Incommensurate. *In; com; mensura.*
Incommixture. *In; com; misceo.*
Incommodate, incommode. *In; com; modus.*
Incommunicable, incommunicative. *In; com; munus.*
Incompact. *In; com; pactus.*
Incomparable, incompared. *In; com; par.*
Incompassion. *In; com; patior.*
Incompatible, incompetence. *In; com; peto.*
Incomplete. *In; com; pleo.*
Incomplex, incompliant. *In; com; plico.*
Incomposed, incomposite. *In; com; pono.*
Incomprehensive. *In; com; prehendo.*
Inconcealable. *In; con; celo.*
Inconceivable, inconceptible. *In; con; capio.*
Inconcludent, inconclusive. *In; con; claudo.*
Inconcoct. *In; con; coquo.*
Inconcurring. *In; con; curro.*
Inconcussible. *In; con; cutio.*
Incondite, inconditional. *In; con; do.*
Inconformity. *In; con; forma.*
Inconfused. *In; con; fundo.*
Incongelable. *In; con; gelu.*
Incongruent, incongruous. *In; con, grus*
Inconnection. *In; con; necto.*
Inconscionable. *In; con; scio.*
Inconsequent. *In; con; sequor.*
Inconsiderable, inconsiderate. *In; con; sedeo.*
Inconsistent. *In; con; sisto.*
Inconsolable. *In; con; solor.*
Inconsonancy. *In; con; sonus.*
Inconspicuous. *In; con; specio.*
Inconstant. *In; con; sto.*
Inconsumable. *In; con; sumo.*
Inconsummate. *In; con; summa.*
Inconsumptible. *In; con; sumo.*
Incontestable. *In; con; testis.*
Incontiguous. *In; con; tango.*
Incontinent. *In; con; teneo.*
Incontracted. *In; con; traho.*
Incontrovertible. *In; contra; verto.*
Inconvenient. *In; con; venio.*
Inconversable. *In; con; verto*
Inconvincible. *In; con; vinco.*
Incorporal, incorporate. *In; corpus.*
Incorrect, incorrigible. *In; cor; rego*
Incorrupt. *In; cor; ruptum.*
Incrassate. *In; crassus.*
Increase. *In; cresco.*
Increate. *In; creo.*
Incredible, incredulous. *In; credo.*
Incremable. *In; cremo.*
Increment. *In; cresco.*
Increpate. *In; crepo.*
Increscent. *In; cresco.*
Incruental. *In; cruor.*
Incrust. *In; crusta.*
Incubate, incubiture, incubus. *In; cubo*
Inculcate. *In; culco.*
Inculpable. *In; culpa.*
Incumbent. *In; cubo.*
Incur. *In; curro.*
Incurious. *In; cura.*
Incursion. *In; curro.*
Incurvate. *In; curvus.*
Indamage. *In; damnum.*
Indebt. *In; debitus.*
Indecent. *In; decens.*
Indeciduous. *In; de; cado.*
Indecimable. *In; deca.*
Indecision. *In; de; cædo.*
Indeclinable. *In; de; clino.*
Indecorous. *In; decor.*
Indefatigable. *In; de; fatigo.*
Indefeasible, indefective. *In; de; facio.*
Indefensive. *In; de; fendo.*
Indeficient. *In; de; facio.*
Indefinable, indefinite. *In; de; finis.*
Indeliberate. *In; de; liber.*
Indelible. *In; de; leo.*
Indelicate. *In; deliciæ.*
Indemnification. *In; damnum; facio.*
Indemnify, indemnity. *In; damnum.*
Indent. *In; dens.*
Independent. *In; de; pendeo.*
Indeprecable. *In; de; precor.*
Indeprehensible. *In; de; prehendo.*
Indeprivable. *In; de; privus.*
Indescribable, indescriptive. *In; de; scribo.*
Indestructible. *In; de; struo.*
Indeterminable, indetermined. *In; de, terminus.*
Indevotion, indevout. *In; de; votum.*
Index. *In; dico.*
Indexterity. *In; dexter.*
Indicate, indice. *In; dico.*
Indict. *In; dico.*
Indifferent. *In; dif; fero.*
Indigent. *In; egeo.*

Indigest. *In; di; gero.*
Indigitate. *In; digitus.*
Indign, indignant, indignify. *In; dignus.*
Indilatory. *In; di; latum*
Indiligent. *In; di; lego.*
Indiminishable. *In; di; minuo.*
Indirect. *In; di; rego.*
Indiscernible. *In; dis; cerno.*
Indiscerpible, indiscerptible. *In; dis; carpo.*
Indiscreet, indiscrete. *In; dis; cerno.*
Indiscriminate. *In; dis; cerno.*
Indispensable. *In; dis; pendo.*
Indispersed. *In; di; spargo.*
Indispose. *In; dis; pono.*
Indisputable. *In; dis; puto.*
Indissoluble, indissolvable. *In; dis; solvo.*
Indistinct, indistinguishable. *In; di; stinguo.*
Individable, individual, indivisible. *In; di; viduo.*
Indocible, indocile, indoctrinate. *In; doceo.*
Indolent. *In; doleo.*
Indomable, indomite. *In; domo.*
Indubious, indubitate. *In; dubius.*
Induce, induct. *In; duco.*
Indulge. *Indulgeo.*
Indurate. *In; durus.*
Industrious. *Industria.*
Inebriate, inebriety. *In; ebrius.*
Inedited. *In; e; do.*
Ineffable. *In; ef; fari.*
Ineffectual, inefficacy, inefficient. *In; ef; facio.*
Inelaborate. *In; e; labor.*
Inelegant. *In; elegans.*
Ineluctable. *In; e; luctor.*
Ineludible. *In; e; ludo.*
Inept. *In; aptus.*
Inequal. *In; equus.*
Inerrable, inerringly. *In; err.*
Inert. *In; ars.*
Inescate. *In; esca.*
Inestimable. *In; estimo.*
Inevident. *In; e; video.*
Inevitable. *In; e; vito.*
Inexcusable. *In; ex; causa.*
Inexecution. *In; ex; sequor.*
Inexhalable. *In; ex; halo.*
Inexhausted. *In; ex; haustum*
Inexistent. *In; ex; sisto.*
Inexorable. *In; ex; oro.*
Inexpectation, inexpected. *In; ex; specio.*
Inexpedient. *In; ex; pes.*
Inexpiable. *In; ex; pio.*
Inexplainable. *In; ex; planus.*
Inexplicable. *In; ex; plico.*
Inexplorable. *In; ex; ploro.*
Inexpressive. *In; ex; premo.*
Inexpugnable. *In; ex; pugna.*
Inextinct, inextinguishable. *In; ex; stinguo.*
Inextricable. *In; ex; tricæ.*
Inexuperable. *In; ex; super.*
Infallible. *In; fallo.*
Infamy. *In; fama.*
Infandous, infant. *In; fari.*
Infanticide. *In; fari; cædo.*
Infatuate. *In; fatuus.*
Infeasible, infect, infectious. *In; facio.*
Infecund. *In; fecundus.*
Infelicity. *In; felix.*
Infer. *In; fero.*
Inferior, infernal. *Inferus.*
Infertile. *In; fero.*
Infestive. *In; festum.*
Infeudation. *In; feudum.*
Infidel. *In; fides.* [*In, finis.*
Infinite, infinitesimal, infinitive, infinity.
Infirm. *In; firmus.*
Infix. *In; fixus.*
Inflame, inflammation. *In; flamma.*
Inflate. *In; flatus.*
Inflect, inflexed, inflexible. *In; flecto*
Inflict. *In; fligo.*
Influent, influx. *In; fluo.*
Infoliate. *In; folium.*
Inform. *In; forma.*
Informidable. *In; formido.*
Infortunate. *In; fors.*
Infract, infrangible. *In; frango.*
Infrequent. *In; frequens.*
Infrigidate. *In; frigus.*
Infringe. *In; frango.*
Infrugal. *In; fruges.*
Infumed. *In; fumus.*
Infuriate. *In; furia.*
Infuscation. *In; fuscus.*
Infuse. *In; fundo.*
Ingelable. *In; gelu.*
Ingeminate. *In; geminus.*
Ingender, ingenerate, ingenious, ingenite, ingenuous. *In; genus.*
Ingest *In; gero.*
Ingrained. *In; granum.*
Ingrate, ingratiate, ingratitude. *In; gratia*
Ingravidate. *In; gravis.*
Ingredient, ingress. *In; gradior.*
Inguinal. *Inguen.*
Ingurgitate. *In; gurges.*
Ingustable. *In; gustus.*
Inhabile, inhabit. *In; habeo.*
Inhale. *In; halo.*
Inharmonical. *In; harmonia.*
Inhere. *In; hæreo.*
Inherit. *In; hæres.*
Inhesion. *In; hæreo.*
Inhiation. *In; hiatus.*
Inhibit. *In; habeo.*
Inhospitable, inhospitality. *In; hospes*
Inhostile. *In; hostis.*
Inhuman. *In; homo.*
Inhumate, inhume. *In; humus.*
Inimaginable. *In; imago.*
Inimical. *In; amicus.*
Inimitable. *In; imitor.*
Iniquity. *In; equus.*
Initial, initiate. *Initium.*
Inject. *In; jacio.*
Injoin. *In; jungo.*
Injudicious. *In; judico.*
Injunction. *In; jungo.*
Injure. *In; jus.*
Injustice. *In; justus.*
Inlapidate. *In; lapis.*
Inlimine. *In; limen.*
Innate. *In; nascor.*
Innavigable. *In; navis; ago.*
Innocent, innocuous. *In; noceo.*
Innominable, innominate. *In; nomen.*
Innovate. *In; novus.*
Innoxious. *In; noceo.*
Innuendo, innuent. *In; nuo*
Innumerable, innumerous. *In; numerus*
Innutrition. *In; nutrio.*
Inobservable, inobservant. *In; ob; servo*
Inoculate. *In; oculus.*
Inodiate. *In; odi.*
Inodorous. *In; odor.*
Inoffensive. *In; of; fendo.*
Inofficious. *In; of; facio.*
Inoperative. *In; opera.*
Inopinate. *In, opinor.*
Inopportune. *In; op; porto.*

Inoppressive. *In; op; premo.*
Inopulent. *In; opulentus.*
Inordinacy, inordinate. *In; ordo.*
Inorganic, inorganized. *In; organum.*
Inosculate. *In; oro.*
Inquest. *In; quæro.*
Inquietude. *In; quies.*
Inquinate. *Inquino.*
Inquire, inquisition, inquisitorial. *In, quæro.*
Insafety, insalubrious, insalutary. *In; salus.*
Insanable, insane. *In; sanus.*
Insapory. *In; sapio.*
Insatiable, insatiate, insatiety, insaturable. *In; satis.*
Inscience. *In; scio.*
Inscribe, inscription. *In; scribo.*
Inscrutable. *In; scrutor.*
Insculp, insculpture. *In; sculpo.*
Insecable, insect. *In; seco.*
Insectator. *In; sequor.*
Insectile, insection. *In; seco*
Insectivorous. *In; seco; voro.*
Insectologer. *In; seco; logos.*
Insecure. *In; se; cura.*
Inseminate. *In; semen.*
Insensate, insensible, insentient. *In; sentio.*
Inseparable, inseparate. *In; se; paro.*
Insert. *In; sertum.*
Inservient. *In; servio.*
Insidiate, insidious. *In; sedeo.*
Insignia. *In; signum.*
Insignificant. *In; signum; facio.*
Insincere. *In; sine; cera.*
Insinuate. *In; sinus.*
Insipid, insipience. *In; sapio.*
Insist. *In; sisto.*
Insobriety. *In; sine; ebrius.*
Insocial. *In; socio.*
Insolate. *In; sol.*
Insolent. *In; soleo.*
Insolidity. *In; solidus.*
Insoluble, insolvable, insolvent. *In; solvo.*
Insomnious. *In; somnus.*
Inspect, inspectorate. *In; specto.*
Inspersion. *In; spargo.*
Insphere. *In; sphæra.*
Inspirable, inspiration, inspire, inspirit. *In; spiro.*
Inspissate. *In; spissus.*
Instability, instable, instant, instantaneous, instead. *In; sto.*
Instigate. *In; stigo.*
Instill. *In; stilla.*
Instimulate. *In; stimulus.*
Instinct. *In; stinguo.*
Institute. *In; sto.*
Instratified. *In; sterno.*
Instruct, instrument. *In; struo.*
Insuavity. *In; suavis.*
Insubjection. *In; sub; jacio.*
Insubordinate. *In; sub; ordo.*
Insubstantial. *In; sub; sto.*
Insufferable. *In; suf; fero.*
Insufficient. *In; suf; facio.*
Insular. *Insula.*
Insult. *In; salio.*
Insume. *In; sumo.*
Insuperable. *In; super.*
Insupportable. *In; sup; porto.*
Insuppressive. *In; sup; premo.*
Insurgent, insurrection. *In; surgo.*
Intactible, intangible. *In; tango.*
Intastable. *In; taster.*
Integer, integral, integrate, integrity. *Integer.*
Integumation, integument. *In; tego.*

Intellect, intellectual, intelligent, intelligible. *Inter; lego.*
Intemperance, intemperate, intemperature. *In; tempero.*
Intempestive. *In; tempus.*
Intend, intense, intent. *In; tendo.*
Inter. *In; terra.*
Intercede. *Inter; cedo*
Intercept. *Inter; capio*
Intercession. *Inter; cedo.*
Intercipient. *Inter; capio.*
Intercision. *Inter; cædo.*
Interclude, interclusion. *Inter; claudo.*
Intercourse, intercur. *Inter; curro.*
Intercutaneous. *Inter; cutis.*
Interdict. *Inter; dico.*
Interest. *Inter; ens.*
Interfere. *Inter; ferio.*
Interfluent. *Inter; fluo.*
Interfoliate. *Inter; folium.*
Interfulgent. *Inter; fulgeo.*
Interfused. *Inter; fundo.*
Interior. *Intus.*
Interjacent. *Inter; jaceo.*
Interject. *Inter; jacio.*
Interlapse. *Inter; labor.*
Interline, interlinear. *Inter; linea.*
Interlocation. *Inter; locus.*
Interlocution. *Inter; loquor.*
Interlucent. *Inter; luceo.*
Interluency. *Inter; luo.*
Interlunar. *Inter; luna.*
Intermediate. *Inter; medius.*
Intermention. *Inter; memor.*
Intermigration. *Inter; migro.*
Interminable, interminate. *In; terminus.*
Intermission, intermit. *Inter; mitto.*
Intermix. *Inter; misceo.*
Intermundane. *Inter; mundus.*
Intermural. *Inter; murus.*
Intermuscular. *Inter; musculus.*
Intermutation. *Inter; muto.*
Intermutual. *Inter; mutuus.*
Intern. *Intus.*
Internuncio. *Inter; nuncio.*
Interosseal. *Inter; os.*
Interpel. *Inter; pello.*
Interpolate, interpolish. *Inter; polis.*
Interpose. *Inter; pono.*
Interpret. *Interpretor.*
Interregnum, interreign, interrex. *Inter; rego.*
Interrogate. *Inter; rogo.*
Interrupt. *Inter; ruptum.*
Interscapular. *Inter; scapula.*
Interscind. *Inter; scindo.*
Interscribe. *Inter; scribo.*
Intersecant, intersect. *Inter; seco.*
Intersert. *Inter; sertum.*
Intersperse. *Inter; spargo.*
Interstellar. *Inter; stella.*
Interstice. *Inter; sto.*
Interstinctive. *Inter; stinguo.*
Interstitial. *Inter; sto.*
Interstratified. *Inter; sterno.*
Intertexture. *Inter; textus.*
Intertropical. *Inter; tropos.*
Interval. *Inter; vallum.*
Interveined. *Inter; vena.*
Intervene, intervention. *Inter; venio*
Intervert. *Inter; verto.*
Intervolve. *Inter; volvo.*
Intestable, intestacy, intestate. *In; testis.*
Intestine. *Intestina.*
Inthrone, inthronize. *In; thronus.*
Intimacy, intimate. *Intus.*
Intimidate. *In; timeo.*
Intire. *In; tango*

Intitle. *In; titulus.*
Intolerable, intolerant, intoleration. *In; tolero.*
Intonate, intone. *In; tonos.*
Intorsion, intort. *In; torqueo.*
Intoxicate. *In; toxicum.*
Intractable. *In; traho.*
Intransient, intransitive. *In; trans; eo.*
Intransmutable. *In; trans; muto.*
Intrepid. *In; trepidus.*
Intricable, intricacy, intricate, intrigue. *In; tricæ.*
Intrinsic. *Intus.*
Introduce, introduction. *Intro; duco.*
Introgression. *Intro; gradior.*
Intromission, intromit. *Intro; mitto.*
Introspect. *Intro; specio.*
Introsume. *Intro; sumo.*
Introvenient. *Intro; venio.*
Introversion, introvert. *Intro; verto.*
Intrude, intrusion. *In; trudo.*
Intuition. *In; tueor.*
Intumesce. *In; tumeo.*
Inturgescence. *In; turgeo.*
Inumbrate. *In; umbra.*
Inundate. *In; undo.*
Inurbanity. *In; urbs.*
Inure. *In; ustum.*
Inusitation. *In; utor.*
Inustion. *In; ustum.*
Inutile, inutility. *In; utor.*
Invade. *In; vado.*
Invalescence, invaletudinary, invalid, invaluable. *In; valeo.*
Invariable, invaried. *In; varius.*
Invasion. *In; vado.*
Invection, inveigh. *In; veho.*
Inveiled. *In; velo.*
Invent. *In; venio.*
Inverse, invert. *In; verto.*
Invest. *In; vestis.*
Investigable, investigate. *In; vestigium.*
Investiture. *In; vestis.*
Inveteracy, inveterate. *In; vetus.*
Invidious. *In; video.*
Invigilance. *In; vigil.*
Invigorate. *In; vigor.*
Invillaged. *In; villa.*
Invincible. *In; vinco.*
Inviolable, inviolate. *In; violo.*
Invious. *In; via.*
Inviscate. *In; viscum.*
Invisible, invision. *In; video.*
Invitation, invite. *Invito.*
Invocate. *In; voco.*
Invoice. *In; via.*
Invoke. *In; voco.*
Involuntary. *In; volo.*
Involute, involve. *In; volvo.*
Invulnerable. *In; vulnus.*
Iota. *Iota.*
Irascible, ire. *Ira.*
Irenarch. *Irene; arche.*
Irenical. *Irene.*
Iris. *Iris.*
Ironic, ironist, irony. *Ironia.*
Irradiate, irradiance. *Ir; radius.*
Irrational. *Ir; ratus.*
Irreclaimable. *Ir; re; clamo.*
Irreconcilable, irreconcile. *Ir; re; concilio.*
Irreducible. *Ir; re; duco.*
Irrefragable. *Ir; re; frango.*
Irrefutable. *Ir; re; futo.*
Irregular, irregulate. *Ir, rego.*
Irrelative. *Ir; re; latum.*
Irrelevant. *Ir; re; levo.*
Irreligion. *Ir; re; ligo.*
Irremeable. *Ir; re; meo.*
Irremediable. *Ir; re; medeor*
Irremissible. *Ir; re; mitto.*
Irremovable. *Ir; re; moveo.*
Irremunerable. *Ir; re; munus.*
Irreparable. *Ir; re; paro.*
Irrepealable. *Ir; re; pello.*
Irrepentance. *Ir; re; peniteo.*
Irreprehensible. *Ir; re; prehendo.*
Irrepresentable. *Ir; re; pre; ens.*
Irrepressible. *Ir; re; premo.*
Irreproachable. *Ir; re; prope.*
Irreprovable. *Ir; re; probo.*
Irreptitious. *Ir; reptum.*
Irresistance, irresistible. *Ir; re; sisto.*
Irresoluble, irresolute. *Ir; re; solvo.*
Irrespective. *Ir; re; specio.*
Irrespirable. *Ir; re; spiro.*
Irretentive. *Ir; re; teneo.*
Irretrievable. *Ir; re; trouver.*
Irreverent. *Ir; re; vereor.*
Irreversible. *Ir; re; verto.*
Irrevocable. *Ir; re; voco.*
Irrevoluble. *Ir; re; volvo.*
Irrigate, irriguous. *Ir; rigo.*
Irrision. *Ir; rideo.*
Irritate, irritable. *Ira.*
Irruption. *Ir; ruptum.*
Ischuretic, ischury. *Ischo.*
Island, isle. *Insula.*
Isochronal. *Isos; chronos.*
Isolated. *Insula.*
Isoperimetrical. *Isos; peri; metrum.*
Isosceles. *Isos; scelos.*
Isothermal. *Isos; thermos.*
Isotonic. *Isos; tonos.*
Israelite. *Israel.*
Isthmus. *Isthmus.*
Italian, italic. *Italia.*
Iterate. *Iter.*
Itinerant, itinerate. *Iter.*

J.

Jacobin, jacobite, jacobus. *Jacobus*
Jactitation, jaculate. *Jacio.*
Janitor. *Janua.*
January. *Januarius.*
Jealous. *Jaloux.*
Jejune. *Jejunus.*
Jelly. *Gelu.*
Jest. *Gero.*
Jesuit. *Jesus.*
Jew. *Judah.*
Jocose, jocular, jocund. *Jocus.*
Join. *Jungo.*
Joke. *Jocus.*
Jolly. *Jupiter.*
Jot. *Iota.*
Journal, journey. *Jour.*
Jovial. *Jupiter.*
Jubilant, jubilee. *Jubilum.*
Jucundity. *Jucundus.*
Jadaism. *Judah.*
Judge, judicial, judiciary, judicious *Jus; dico.*
Jugular. *Jugulum.*
Juncous. *Juncus.*
Junction, juncture. *Jungo.*
Junior. *Juvenis.*
Junto. *Jungo.*
Jurat. *Juro.*
Juridical. *Jus.*
Jurisconsult. *Jus; con; salio.*
Jurisdiction. *Jus; dico.*
Jurisprudence. *Jus; pro; video.*

Jurist. *Jus.*
Just, justice. *Justus.*
Justification. *Justus; facio.*
Justify. *Justus.*
Juvenile. *Juvenis.*

K.

Know, knowledge. *Nosco.*

L.

Labent. *Labor.*
Labiodental. *Labium; dens.*
Labor, laboratory, laborious. *Labor.*
Labyrinth. *Labyrinthus.*
Lacerate. *Lacer.*
Lachrymal, lachrymation. *Lachryma.*
Laconic. *Laconia.*
Lactary, lactean, lactescent. *Lac.*
Lactiferous. *Lac; fero.*
Laic, laity. *Laos.*
Lamellar. *Lamina.*
Lament. *Lamentor.*
Lamina. *Lamina.*
Lance, lancinate. *Lancea.*
Language, languet. *Lingua.*
Languid, languish, languor. *Langueo.*
Laniary, laniate. *Lanius.*
Lanifice. *Lana; facio.*
Lanigerous. *Lana; gero.*
Lanuginous. *Lanugo.*
Laodicea. *Laos.*
Lapicide. *Lapis; cædo.*
Lapidary, lapideous, lapidescent. *Lapis.*
Lapidific. *Lapis; facio.*
Lapidist, lapis. *Lapis.*
Lapse. *Labor.*
Lard. *Lardum.*
Large, largess, largition. *Largus.*
Lascivious. *Lascivus.*
Lassitude. *Lassus.*
Latent. *Lateo.*
Lateral. *Latus.*
Lateritious. *Later.*
Latin. *Latinus.*
Latirostrous. *Latus; rostrum.*
Latitant. *Lateo.*
Latitude, latitudinarian. *Latus.*
Latria. *Latria.*
Laud, laudanum. *Laus.*
Launder, laundry. *Lavo.*
Laureate, laurel. *Laurus.*
Lava, lavatory. *Lavo.*
Law. *Lex.*
Lax. *Laxus.*
Lay. *Laos.*
League. *Ligo.*
Leaven *Levo.*
Lecher, lecherous. *Lecher.*
Lection, lecture. *Lego.*
Legacy. *Lego.*
Legal. *Lex.*
Legate. *Lego.*
Legends, legible, legion. *Lego.*
Legislate. *Lex; latum.*
Legist, legitimate. *Lex.*
Leisure. *Leisure.*
Lemma. *Lepsis.*
Lenient, lenify, leniment, lenity *Lenis.*
Lens, lenticular. *Lens.*
Lentiform. *Lens; forma*
Lentiginous, lentigo. *Lentigo*
Lentil. *Lens.*
Leo, leonine. *Leo.*
Leper. *Lepra.*
Leporine. *Lepus.*
Leprosy, leprous. *Lepra.*
Lesson. *Lego.*
Lethal. *Lethum.*
Lethargy. *Lethe; argos.*
Lethe. *Lethe.*
Lethiferous. *Lethe; fero.*
Letter. *Litera.*
Leucophlegmacy, leucophlegmatic. *Leucos; phlegma.*
Levant, levator, levee, lever, leviable, levigate. *Levo.*
Levite, levitical. *Levi.*
Levity, levy. *Levo.*
Lexicographer. *Lego; grapho.*
Lexicon. *Lego.*
Liable. *Ligo.*
Libation. *Libo.*
Libel. *Liber.*
Liberal, liberate, libertine, liberty. *Liber.*
Libidinous. *Libido.*
Libra. *Libra.*
Library. *Liber.*
Librate. *Libra.*
License, licentiate, licentious, licit. *Liceo.*
Lector. *Lego.*
Lictor. *Lictor.*
Liege. *Ligo.*
Lienteric. *Lios.*
Lieu. *Lieu.*
Lieutenant. *Lieu; teneo.*
Lift. *Levo.*
Ligament, ligature. *Ligo.*
Lignaloes. *Lignum;* (*aloe*, the aloe)
Ligneous. *Lignum.*
Lignum vitæ. *Lignum; vivo.*
Limbo. *Limbus.*
Limit. *Limes.*
Limpid. *Limpidus.*
Line, lineal, lineage, lineament. *Linea.*
Lingo, linguacious. *Lingua.*
Linguadental. *Lingua; dens.*
Linguist. *Lingua.*
Lion. *Leo.*
Lipothymy. *Lipo; thymos.*
Liquate. *Liqueo.*
Liquefaction. *Liqueo; facio.*
Liquefy. *Liqueo.*
Liquescent, liquid, liquidate, liquor. *Liqueo.*
Litany. *Litania.*
Literal, literary, literati. *Litera.*
Litharge. *Lithos;* (*argyros*, silver).
Lithic. *Lithos.*
Lithography. *Lithos; grapho.*
Lithomancy. *Lithos; mancia.*
Lithontriptic. *Lithos;* (*tripsis*, a breaking.)
Lithotomy. *Lithos; tomos.*
Lithoxyle. *Lithos; xylon.*
Litigate, litigious. *Lis; ago.*
Littoral. *Littus.*
Liturgy. *Litos; ergon.*
Livery. *Livrer.*
Livid. *Lividus.*
Lixiviate, lixivium. *Lixivium.*
Local, locate. *Locus.*
Locomotion. *Locus; moveo.*
Locust. *Locusta.*
Locution. *Loquor.*
Logarithm. *Logos; arithmos.*
Logic. *Logos.*
Logogriphe. *Logos; griphos.*

Logomachy. *Logos; machomai.*
Long. *Longus.*
Longanimity. *Longus; animus.*
Longeval, longevity. *Longus; evum.*
Longimanous. *Longus; manus.*
Longimetry. *Longus; metrum.*
Longinquity. *Longus.*
Longitude. *Longus.*
Loquacity. *Loquor.*
Loricate. *Lorica.*
Lotion. *Lavo.*
Loxodromic. *Loxos; dromos.*
Lubric, lubricate. *Lubricus.*
Lubrifaction, lubrification. *Lubricus; facio.*
Lucent, lucid. *Luceo.*
Lucifer. *Luceo; fero.*
Lucific. *Luceo; facio.*
Luciform. *Luceo; forma.*
Lucrative, lucre. *Lucrum.*
Lucriferous. *Lucrum; fero.*
Lucrific. *Lucrum; facio.*
Luctation. *Luctor.*
Luctual. *Lugubris.*
Lucubrate. *Lucubro.*
Luculent. *Luceo.*
Ludibrious, ludicrous. *Ludo.*
Ludification. *Ludo; facio.*
Lugubrious. *Lugubris.*
Lumbago, lumbar. *Lumbus.*
Lumbrical. *Lumbricus.*
Luminary, lumine. *Lumen.*
Lunacy, lunar, lunatic, lune, lunette. *Luna.*
Lunisolar. *Luna; sol.*
Lupine. *Lupus.*
Lure. *Lure.*
Luscious. *Luxuria.*
Lusorious. *Ludo.*
Lustrate, lustre, lustrous, lustrum. *Lustrum.*
Lutarious, lute. *Lutum.*
Lutheran. *Luther.*
Lutulent. *Lutum.*
Luxuriant, luxurious, luxury. *Luxuria.*
Lycanthropy. *Lycos; anthropos.*
Lymph, lymphatic. *Lympha.*
Lympheduct. *Lympha; duco.*
Lyre, lyric, lyrist. *Lyra.*

M.

Macerate. *Maceo.*
Machinate, machine. *Machina.*
Macrocosm. *Macros; cosmos.*
Macrology. *Macros; logos.*
Maculate, maculæ. *Macula.*
Magazine. *Magazin.*
Magi, magic, magical. *Magus.*
Magisterial, magistracy, magistral, magistrate. *Magister.*
Magna-charta. *Magnus;* (*charta*, paper).
Magnanimity, magnanimous. *Magnus; animus.*
Magnet. *Magnes.*
Magnific, magnificent. *Magnus; facio.*
Magnify. *Magnus.*
Magniloquence. *Magnus; loquor.*
Magnitude. *Magnus.*
Mahometan. *Mahomet.*
Maintain, maintenance. *Manus; teneo.*
Majestic, majesty, major, majority. *Magnus.*
Maladministration. *Male; ad; minister.*
Malapropos. *Male; a; pro; pono.*
Malcontent. *Male; con; teneo.*
Male. *Masculus*
Maledicent, malediction. *Male; dico.*
Malefaction, malefic, malefique, maleficient. *Male; facio.*
Malevolent. *Male; volo.*
Malice, malicious. *Malitia.*
Malign, malignancy, malignant. *Malignus.*
Malleate, mallet. *Malleus.*
Malvaceous. *Malva.*
Malversation. *Male; verto.*
Mamma. *Mamma.*
Mammiferous. *Mamma; fero.*
Mammiform. *Mamma; forma.*
Mammillary. *Mamma.*
Mammon. *Mammon.*
Manacle, manage. *Manus.*
Manation. *Mano.*
Mancipate, manciple. *Manus.*
Mandamus, mandate. *Mando.*
Mandible, mandibular, manducate. *Mando.*
Maniac. *Mania.*
Manichean, manichee. *Manes.*
Manifest. *Manifestus.*
Maniple, manipular, manipulation. *Manus; plico.*
Manœuvre. *Manus; opera.*
Manometer. *Manus; metrum.*
Manoscope. *Manos; scopeo.*
Manse, mansion. *Maneo.*
Mantology. *Mancia; logos.*
Manual, manubial, manubrium. *Manus.*
Manuduction. *Manus; duco.*
Manufacture. *Manus; facio.*
Manumise, manumit. *Manus; mitto.*
Manure. *Manus; opera.*
Manuscript. *Manus; scribo.*
March. *Mars.*
Margin. *Margo.*
Marine. *Mare.*
Marinorama. *Mare; orama.*
Marital. *Maritus.*
Mariticide. *Maritus; cædo.*
Maritime. *Mare.*
Market. *Mercor.*
Marriage, marry. *Maritus.*
Martial. *Mars.*
Martyr, martyrdom. *Martyr.*
Martyrology. *Martyr; logos.*
Masculate, masculine. *Masculus.*
Massacre. *Massacre.*
Master. *Magister.*
Masticate. *Mando.*
Material, materiate. *Materia.*
Maternal, maternity. *Mater.*
Mathematic, mathesis. *Mathema.*
Matrice. *Mater.*
Matricide. *Mater; cædo.*
Matriculate, matrimony, matrix, matron. *Mater.*
Maturate, mature. *Maturus.*
Matutine. *Matutinum.*
Mausoleum. *Mausoleum.*
Maxillar. *Maxilla.*
Maxim, maximum. *Maximum.*
M. D. *Medeor; doceo.*
Meager. *Maceo.*
Measure. *Mensura.*
Meander. *Meo.*
Mechanic. *Mechanao.*
Mediate. *Medius.*
Medicate, medicament, medicine. *Medeor.*
Mediocrity. *Medius.*
Meditate. *Meditor.*
Mediterranean. *Medius; terra.*
Medium. *Medius.*

Medullar, medullin. *Medulla.*
Megacosm. *Megas; cosmos.*
Melanagogue. *Melan; agogeus.*
Melanite, melanteri, melasses. *Melan.*
Melicerous. *Mel.*
Meliorate. *Melior.*
Mell, mellate. *Mel.*
Mellification. *Mel; facio.*
Mellifluence, mellifluent. *Mel; fluo.*
Mellit. *Mel.*
Melodrama. *Melos; drama.*
Melody. *Melos; ode.*
Membrane. *Membrana.*
Membraniform. *Membrana; forma.*
Memento, memoir, memorable, memorandum, memorial, memory. *Memor.*
Menace. *Minæ.*
Menage, menagery. *Menage.*
Mend. *Menda.*
Mendacious. *Mendax.*
Mendicant, mendicity. *Mendicus*
Menial. *Menage.*
Meniscus. *Men.*
Menology. *Men; logos.*
Mensal. *Mensa.*
Menstrual, menstruum. *Mensis.*
Mensurate. *Mensura.*
Mental. *Mens.*
Mention. *Memor.*
Mercantile, mercature, mercenary, mercer, merchand, merchant. *Mercor.*
Mercify. *Mercy.*
Mercurial. *Mercor.*
Mercurification. *Mercor; facio.*
Mercurify, mercury. *Mercor.*
Mercy. *Merci.*
Merge. *Mergo.*
Meridian, meridional. *Meridies.*
Merit, meritorious. *Meritum.*
Mersion. *Mergo.*
Mesaraic, mesentery. *Mesos; enteron.*
Mesoleucys. *Mesos; leucos.*
Mesolite. *Mesos; lithos.*
Mesologarithm. *Mesos; logos; arithmos.*
Mesomelas. *Mesos; melan.*
Mesotype. *Mesos; typus.*
Messiah. *Messiah.*
Messieurs. *Messieurs.*
Metabola. *Meta; boleo.*
Metacarpus. *Meta; carpus.*
Metachronism. *Meta; chronos.*
Metagrammatism. *Meta; grapho.*
Metal. *Metallum.*
Metalepsis, metaleptic. *Meta; lepsis.*
Metalliferous. *Metallum; fero.*
Metalliform. *Metallum; forma.*
Metallize. *Metallum.*
Metallography. *Metallum; grapho.*
Metalloid. *Metallum; oidos.*
Metallurgy. *Metallum; ergon.*
Metamorphic. *Meta; morphe.*
Metaphor. *Meta; phero.*
Metaphrase, metaphrastic. *Meta; phrasis.*
Metaphysic, metaphysician. *Meta; physis.*
Metastasis. *Meta; stasis.*
Metathesis. *Meta; thesis.*
Mete. *Mensura.*
Metempsychosis. *Meta; psyche.*
Metemptosis. *Meta; ptoma.*
Meteor. *Meteora.*
Meteorolite. *Meteora; lithos.*
Meteorology. *Meteora; logos.*
Meteoromancy. *Meteora; mancia*
Meterolite. *Meteora; lithos.*
Meteromancy. *Meteora; mancia.*
Meteoroscopy. *Meteora; scopeo.*
Method. *Meta, odos.*
Metonymical, metonymy. *Meta; onoma.*
Metoposcopy *Metopon; scopeo.*
Metre, metrical. *Metrum.*
Metropolis, metropolitan. *Meter; polis.*
Mezzo. *Mesos.*
Mezzorelievo. *Mesos; re; levo.*
Mezzotinto. *Mesos; tingo.*
Miasm, miasmatic. *Miasma.*
Mica, micaceous. *Mica.*
Microcosm. *Micros; cosmos.*
Microcoustic. *Micros; acouo.*
Micrography. *Micros; grapho.*
Micrometer. *Micros; metrum.*
Microphone. *Micros; phone.*
Microscope. *Micros; scopeo.*
Migrate. *Migro.*
Milfoil. *Mille; folium.*
Miliary. *Milium.*
Military, militate, militia. *Miles.*
Millenarian, millenist, millenium. *Mille; annus.*
Milleped. *Mille; pes.*
Millesimal, milliary. *Mille*
Milligram. *Mille; grapho.*
Milliter. *Mille.*
Millimeter. *Mille; metrum.*
Mime, mimetic, mimic. *Mimus.*
Mimographer. *Mimus; grapho.*
Minaceous, minatory. *Minæ.*
Mineral. *Mineral.*
Mineralogy. *Mineral; logos.*
Mingle. *Misceo.*
Miniature, minikin, minim, minimum, minion, minish. *Minuo.*
Minister, ministration. *Minister.*
Minor, minuend, minum, minute, minutiæ. *Minuo.*
Mirable, miracle, miraculous, mirror. *Mirus.*
Misacceptation. *Mis; ac; capio.*
Misadventure. *Mis; ad; venio.*
Misadvised. *Mis; ad; video.*
Misallege. *Mis; al; lego.*
Misanthropy. *Misos; anthropos.*
Misapplication, misapply. *Mis; ap; plico.*
Misapprehend, misapprehension. *Mis; ap, prehendo.*
Misascribe. *Mis; a; scribo.*
Misattend. *Mis; at; tendo.*
Miscalculate. *Mis; calculus.*
Miscellany, miscible. *Misceo.*
Miscitation, miscite. *Mis; cito.*
Misclaim. *Mis; clamo.*
Misconceit, misconception. *Mis; con; capio.*
Misconduct. *Mis; con; duco.*
Misconjecture. *Mis; con; jacio.*
Misconstruction, misconstrue. *Mis; con, struo.*
Miscreate. *Mis; creo.*
Misdirect. *Mis; di; rego.*
Miser, misery. *Miser.*
Misfortune. *Mis; fors.*
Misgovernment. *Mis; guberno.*
Misinfer. *Mis; in; fero.*
Misinform. *Mis; in; forma.*
Misinstruct. *Mis; in; struo.*
Misinterpret. *Mis; interpretor.*
Misjoin. *Mis; jungo.*
Misjudge. *Mis; judico.*
Mismanage. *Mis; manus.*
Mismeasure. *Mis; mensura.*
Misogamist. *Misos; gameo*
Misogyny. *Misos; gyne.*
Misopinion. *Mis; opinor.*
Mispersuade, mispersuasion. *Mis; per, suadeo*
Mispronounce. *Mis; pro; nuncio.*
Misproportion. *Mis; pro; pars*

Misquote. *Mis; ito.*
Misrelate. *Mis; re; latum.*
Misremember. *Mis; re; memor.*
Misrepresent. *Mis; re; pre; ens*
Misserve. *Mis; servio.*
Missile, mission. *Mitto.*
Mistemper. *Mis; tempero.*
Mistion. *Misceo.*
Misusage, misuse. *Mis; utor.*
Misvouch. *Mis; voco.*
Miszealous. *Mis; zealos.*
Mitigable, mitigate. *Mitis.*
Mittent, mittimus. *Mitto.*
Mix. *Misceo.*
Mixtilineal. *Misceo; linea.*
Mixture. *Misceo.*
Mnemonic. *Mneo.*
Mob, mobile. *Moveo.*
Modal, mode, model, moderate, modern, modest, modicum. *Modus.*
Modification. *Modus; facio.*
Modify, modish, modulate, module, modus. *Modus.*
Mole. *Molior.*
Molecule. *Mola.*
Molest. *Molestus.*
Mollient. *Mollis.*
Mollification. *Mollis; facio.*
Mollify. *Mollis.*
Moment, momentaneous, momentum. *Momentum.*
Monachal, monachism, monad. *Monos.*
Monadelph. *Monos; adelphos.*
Monarch. *Monos; arche.*
Monastic. *Monos.*
Monecian. *Monos; eceo.*
Monish, monition, monitor. *Moneo.*
Monk. *Monos.*
Monoceros. *Monos; ceras.*
Monochord. *Monos; chorda.*
Monocule. *Monos; oculus.*
Monodist. *Monos; ode.*
Monodon. *Monos; odoys.*
Monody. *Monos; ode.*
Monogamy. *Monos; gameo.*
Monogram. *Monos; grapho.*
Monogyn. *Monos; gyne.*
Monologue. *Monos; logos.*
Monomachy. *Monos; machomai.*
Monomial. *Monos; nomen.*
Monopathy. *Monos; pathos.*
Monopetalous. *Monos; petalon.*
Monophthong. *Monos; phthegma.*
Monophyllous. *Monos; phyllon.*
Monophysite. *Monos; physis.*
Monopolist, monopolize, monopoly. *Monos; polis.*
Monoptote. *Monos; ptoma.*
Monospermous. *Monos; sperma.*
Monostich. *Monos; stichos.*
Monostrophic. *Monos; strophe.*
Monosyllable. *Monos; syl; labo.*
Monotheism. *Monos; theos.*
Monothelite. *Monos; (thelesis,* will).
Monotone. *Monos; tonos.*
Monster, monstrosity, monstrous. *Monstro.*
Montanic, montanist. *Montanus.*
Monument. *Moneo.*
Moon. *Men.*
Moral. *Mos.*
Moravian. *Moravia.*
Morbid. *Morbus.*
Morbific. *Morbus; facio.*
Morbose. *Morbus.*
Mordacious, mordicant. *Mordeo.*
Morigerous. *Mos; gero.*
Morose, morosity. *Morosus.*
Morsel, morsure. *Mordeo.*
Mort, mortal. *Mors.*
Mortgage. *Mors; (gage,* a pledge).
Mortiferous. *Mors; fero.*
Mortification. *Mors; facio.*
Mortify, mortise. *Mors.*
Mortmain. *Mors; manus.*
Mortuary. *Mors.*
Motion, motive. *Moveo.*
Mound, mount, mountain. *Mons.*
Mountebank. *Mons; (abacus,* a bench.)
Mouse. *Musculus.*
Movable, move. *Moveo.*
Mucic, mucid, mucilage, mucilaginous, mucite, muck. *Mucus.*
Mucoso-saccharine. *Mucus; saccharum.*
Mucous, muculent, mucus. *Mucus.*
Mugient. *Mugio.*
Mulct, mulctuary. *Mulcta.*
Multangular. *Multus; angulus.*
Multicapsular. *Multus; capsula.*
Multicavous. *Multus; cavus.*
Multifarious. *Multus; fari.*
Multifid. *Multus; findo.*
Multiflorous. *Multus; flos.*
Multiform. *Multus; forma.*
Multigenerous. *Multus; genus.*
Multijugous. *Multus; jugum.*
Multilateral. *Multus; latus.*
Multilineal. *Multus; linea.*
Multilocular. *Multus; (loculus,* a cell).
Multiloquous. *Multus; loquor.*
Multinomial, multinominal. *Multus; nomen.*
Multiparous. *Multus; pario.*
Multipartite. *Multus; pars.*
Multiped. *Multus; pes.*
Multiple, multiplex, multipliable, multiplicand, multiplicate, multiplicity, multiply. *Multus; plico.*
Multipotent. *Multus; posse; ens.*
Multipresence. *Multus; pre; ens.*
Multisiliquous. *Multus; siliqua.*
Multisonous. *Multus; sonus.*
Multisyllable. *Multus; syl; labo.*
Multitude, multitudinous. *Multus.*
Multivagant. *Multus; vagus.*
Multivalve. *Multus; valvæ.*
Multiversant. *Multus; verto.*
Multivious. *Multus; via.*
Multocular. *Multus; oculus.*
Mundane. *Mundus.*
Mundation, mundic. *Mundus.*
Mundification. *Mundus; facio.*
Mundify. *Mundus.*
Mundivagant. *Mundus; vagus.*
Munerary. *Munus.*
Municipal. *Municipium.*
Munificent. *Munus; facio.*
Muniment, munite. *Munio.*
Murage, mural. *Murus.*
Murder. *Mors.*
Muriate, muriatic. *Muria.*
Muriatiferous. *Muria; fero.*
Murine. *Musculus.*
Murmur, murmuration. *Murmur.*
Muscle, muscular, musculite. *Musculus.*
Muse, museum, music, musician. *Musa.*
Musteline. *Mustela.*
Muster. *Monstro.*
Mutable, mutation. *Muto.*
Mute. *Mutus.*
Mutilate. *Mutilus.*
Mutinous, mutiny. *Muto.*
Mutual, mutuatitious, mutuation. *Mutuus.*
Myography. *Mys; grapho.*
Myology. *Mys; logos.*

Myope. *Myo; opto.*
Myriad. *Myrias.*
Myriameter. *Myrias; metrum.*
Myriarch. *Myrias; arche.*
Myriare. *Myrias.*
Myrioliter. *Myrias;* (*litra*, a part of a pound).
Myriorama. *Myrias; orama.*
Myropolist. *Myron; poleo.*
Myrtiform. (*Myrtus*, the myrtle); *forma.*
Mystagogue. *Mystes; agogeus.*
Mysteriarch. *Mystes; arche.*
Mystery, mystic, mysticism. *Mystes.*
Mythic. *Mythos.*
Mythographer. *Mythos; grapho.*
Mythology. *Mythos; logos.*

N.

Name. *Nomen.*
Narcissus, narcosis, narcotic. *Narce.*
Nard, nardine. *Nardus.*
Narrable, narrate. *Narro.*
Nasal, nascal. *Nasus.*
Nascent. *Nascor.*
Nasicornus. *Nasus; cornu.*
Nasute. *Nasus.*
Natal, natalitial, nation, native, natural, nature. *Nascor.*
Naufrage. *Navis; frango.*
Naulage. *Navis.*
Naumachy. *Navis; machomai.*
Nauscopy. *Navis; scopeo.*
Nausea, nauseous. *Nausea.*
Nautic, nautilus. *Nauta.*
Navarch. *Navis; arche.*
Navicular. *Navis.*
Navigable, navigate. *Navis; ago.*
Navy. *Navis.*
Nay. *Nego.*
Nazarine, nazarite. *Nazareth.*
Neapolitan. *Neos; polis.*
Nebula, nebulosity, nebulous. *Nebula.*
Necessary, necessitate, necessity. *Necesse.*
Necrologist, necrology. *Necros; logos.*
Necromancy, necromantic. *Necros; mancia.*
Necronite, necrosis. *Necros.*
Nectar, nectarean. *Nectar.*
Nectariferous. *Nectar; fero.*
Nefandous, nefarious. *Ne; fari.*
Negation, negative. *Nego.*
Neglect, negligent. *Neg; lego.*
Negotiable, negotiate. *Neg; otium.*
Negro. *Niger.*
Nemolite. *Nemus; lithos.*
Nemoral. *Nemus.*
Neogamist. *Neos; gameo.*
Neologism, neology. *Neos; logos.*
Neonomian. *Neos; nomos.*
Neophyte. *Neos; physis.*
Neoteric. *Neos.*
Nerve, nervine, nervous. *Neuron.*
Nescience. *Ne; scio.*
Neurology. *Neuron; logos.*
Neuropter. *Neuron; opto.*
Neurospast. *Neuron; spasma.*
Neurotic. *Neuron.*
Neurotomy. *Neuron; tomos.*
Neuter, neutral. *Neuter.*
New, news. *Novus.*
Nicanor. *Nice.*
Nicopolis. *Nice; polis.*
Nicodemus. *Nice; demos.*
Nicolas, Nicolaitans. *Nice; laos.*
Nicotian, nicotin. *Nicot.*
Nictate. *Nicto.*
Nide. *Nidus.*
Nidor, nidorosity. *Nidor.*
Nidulant, nidulate, nidus. *Nidus.*
Niger. *Niger.*
Night. *Nox.*
Nigrescent. *Niger.*
Nigrification. *Niger; facio.*
Nigrin. *Niger.*
Nihility. *Nihil.*
Nitre, niter, nitrate, nitric. *Nitrum.*
Nitrifaction. *Nitrum; facio.*
Nitrify, nitrite. *Nitrum.*
Nitrogen, nitrogenous. *Nitrum; genea.*
Nitroleucic. *Nitrum;* (*leucos*, white).
Nitrometer. *Nitrum; metrum.*
Nitromuriatic. *Nitrum; muria.*
Nitrous. *Nitrum.*
Nival, niveous. *Nix.*
Nobilitate, nobility, noble. *Nosco.*
Nocent, nocive. *Noceo.*
Noctambulation. *Nox; ambulo.*
Noctidial. *Nox; dies.*
Noctiferous. *Nox; fero.*
Noctiluca. *Nox; luceo.*
Noctivagant. *Nox; vagus.*
Noctuary, noctule, nocturnal. *Nox.*
Nocuous. *Noceo.*
Nodation, node, nodosity, nodosous, nodous, nodule. *Nodus.*
Noetic. *Noos.*
Nolens-volens. *Non; volo.*
Nolition. *Non; volo.*
Nomad. *Nomas.*
Nomenclature. *Nomen;* (*calo*, to call).
Nomial, nominal, nominate, nominee. *Nomen.*
Nomothetic. *Nomos; thesis.*
Nonage. *Non;* (*age*).
Nonagesimal. *Novem.*
Nonagon. *Novem; gonia.*
Nonappearance. *Non; ap; pareo.*
Nonappointment. *Non; ap; pungo*
Nonattendance. *Non; at; tendo.*
Noncompliance. *Non; com; plico.*
Nonconductor. *Non; con; duco.*
Nonconforming, nonconformist, nonconformity. *Non; con; forma.*
Noncontagious. *Non; con; tango.*
Nondescript. *Non; de; scribo.*
None. *Ne;* (*one*).
Nonelect. *Non; e; lego.*
Nonelectric. *Non; electrum.*
Nonemphatic. *Non; em; phano.*
Nonentity. *Non; ens.*
Nonepiscopal. *Non; epi; scopeo.*
Nones. *Novem.*
Nonexistence. *Non; ex; sisto.*
Nonillion. *Novem; mille.*
Nonjuring, nonjuror. *Non; juro.*
Nonmetallic. *Non; metallum.*
Nonnaturals. *Non; nascor.*
Nonpareil. *Non; par.*
Nonplus. *Non; plus.*
Nonproduction. *Non; pro; duco.*
Nonproficient. *Non; pro; facio.*
Nonresident. *Non; re; sedeo.*
Nonresistant. *Non; re; sisto.*
Nonsense, nonsensical, nonsensitive. *Non, sentio.*
Nonsolution, nonsolvent. *Non; solvo.*
Nonsparing. *Non;* (*sparing*).
Nonsuit. *Non; sequor.*
Normal. *Norma*

Norman, Norwegian. *Norway.*
Nosology. *Nosos ; logos.*
Nosopoetic, nosopoietic. *Nosos ; poieo.*
Note. *Nota.*
Notice. *Nosco.*
Notification. *Nosco ; facio.*
Notify, notion, notoriety, notorious. *Nosco.*
Notus. *Notus.*
Noun. *Nomen.*
Nourish. *Nutrio.*
Novation, novel, novelist. *Novus.*
November, novenary. *Novem.*
Novennial. *Novem ; annus.*
Novercal. *Noverca.*
Novice, novitiate. *Novus.*
Noxious. *Noceo.*
Nubiferous. *Nubes ; fero.*
Nubilate. *Nubes.*
Nubile. *Nubo.*
Nuciferous. *Nux ; fero.*
Nucleus. *Nux.*
Nudation, nude, nudity. *Nudus.*
Nugacity, nugation. *Nugæ.*
Nuisance. *Noceo.*
Nullibiety. *Nullus ; ibi.*
Nullifidian. *Nullus ; fides.*
Nullify. *Nullus.*
Number, numbers, numeral, numerate, numeric, numerist, numerous. *Numerus.*
Numismatic. *Nummus.*
Numismatology. *Nummus ; logos.*
Nummary, nummular, nummilite. *Nummus.*
Nunciature, nuncio, nuncupate. *Nuncio.*
Nundinal, Nundinate. *Nundinæ.*
Nuptials. *Nubo.*
Nurse, nurture, nutrient. *Nutrio.*
Nutrification. *Nutrio ; facio.*
Nutriment. *Nutrio.*
Nyctalops, nyctalopy. *Nyx ; ops.*

O.

Obambulation. *Ob ; ambulo.*
Obdormition. *Ob ; dormio.*
Obduce, obduction. *Ob ; duco.*
Obduracy, obdurate. *Ob ; durus.*
Obedience. *Ob ; audio.*
Obeliscal, obelisk. *Obeliscus.*
Obequitation. *Ob ; eques.*
Oberration. *Ob ; erro.*
Obey. *Ob ; audio.*
Obit, obituary. *Ob ; eo.*
Object. *Ob ; jacio.*
Oblate. *Ob ; latum.*
Oblatrate. *Ob ; latro.*
Oblectate. *Ob ; lac.*
Obligate, obligato, oblige. *Ob ; ligo.*
Oblique, oblike, obliquity. *Obliquus.*
Obliterate. *Ob ; litera.*
Oblivion. *Oblivio.*
Oblong. *Ob ; longus.*
Obloquy. *Ob ; loquor.*
Obluctation. *Ob ; luctor.*
Obnoxious. *Ob ; noceo.*
Obnubilate. *Ob ; nubes.*
Obreption, obreptitious. *Ob ; reptum.*
Obscene, obscenity. *Obscœnus.*
Obscuration, obscure. *Obscurus.*
Obsecrate. *Ob ; sacer.*
Obsequent, obsequies, obsequious. *Ob ; sequor.*
Observanda, observation, observatory, observe. *Ob ; servo.*
Obsess, obsidional. *Ob ; sedeo.*
Obsignate. *Ob ; signum.*
Obsolescent, obsolete. *Ob ; oleo.*
Obstacle, obstancy. *Ob ; sto.*
Obstetric. *Obstetrix.*
Obstinacy, obstinate. *Ob ; sto.*
Obstreperous. *Ob ; strepo.*
Obstriction. *Ob ; stringo.*
Obstruct, obstruent. *Ob ; struo.*
Obstupefaction. *Ob ; stupeo ; facio.*
Obtain. *Ob ; teneo.*
Obtemperate. *Ob ; tempero.*
Obtend. *Ob ; tendo.*
Obtenebration. *Ob ; tenebræ.*
Obtension. *Ob ; tendo.*
Obtest, obtestation. *Ob ; testis.*
Obtrectation. *Ob ; traho.*
Obtrude. *Ob ; trudo.*
Obtruncate. *Ob ; trunco.*
Obtrusion. *Ob ; trudo.*
Obtund. *Ob ; tundo.*
Obtusangular. *Ob ; tundo ; angulus*
Obtuse. *Ob ; tundo.*
Obumbrate. *Ob ; umbra.*
Obverse, obvert. *Ob ; verto.*
Obviate, obvious. *Ob ; via.*
Obvolute. *Ob ; volvo.*
Occasion, occident, occiduous. *Oc ; cado.*
Occipital, occiput. *Oc ; caput.*
Occision. *Oc ; cædo.*
Occlude, occlusion. *Oc ; claudo.*
Occult, occultation. *Occultus.*
Occupant, occupy. *Oc ; capio.*
Occur, occurrent, occursion. *Oc ; curro.*
Ocean. *Oceanus.*
Ocellated. *Oculus.*
Ochlocracy. *Ochlos ; cratos.*
Ochre, ocher. *Ochra.*
Octachord. *Octo ; chorda.*
Octagon. *Octo ; gonia.*
Octaedron. *Octo ; edra.*
Octander. *Octo ; aner.*
Octangular. *Octo ; angulus.*
Octateuch. *Octo ; teuchos.*
Octant, octavo. *Octo.*
Octennial. *Octo ; annus.*
Octile, October. *Octo.*
Octodecimal. *Octo ; decem.*
Octodentate. *Octo ; dens.*
Octofid. *Octo ; findo.*
Octogenary. *Octo ; genus.*
Octolocular. *Octo ;* (*loculus*, a little place).
Octonary. *Octo.*
Octonocular. *Octo ; oculus.*
Octopetalous. *Octo ; petalon.*
Octoradiated. *Octo ; radius.*
Octospermous. *Octo ; sperma.*
Octostyle. *Octo ; stylos.*
Octosyllable. *Octo ; syl ; labo*
Octuple. *Octo ; plico.*
Ocular, oculate. *Oculus.*
Oculiform. *Oculus ; forma.*
Oculist. *Oculus.*
Ode. *Ode.*
Odious, odium. *Odi.*
Odontalgy. *Odoys ; algos.*
Odor, odorament, odorate. *Odor.*
Odoriferous. *Odor ; fero.*
Odorous. *Odor.*
Œconomical. *Eceo ; nomos.*
Offend, offence, offensive. *Of ; fendo.*
Offer. *Of ; fero.*
Office, official, officious. *Of ; facio.*
Oil. *Oliva.*
Oint. *Unguo.*
Oleaginous, oleaster, oleate. *Oliva.*
Olefiant. *Oleo ; facio.*

Oleic. *Oliva.*
Oleosaccharum. *Oliva; saccharum.*
Oleose. *Oliva.*
Oleraceous. *Olus.*
Olfact. *Oleo; facio.*
Olid. *Oleo.*
Oligarchy. *Oligos; arche.*
Oligist. *Oligos.*
Olitory. *Olus.*
Olivaceous, olivaster, olive. *Oliva.*
Olympiad, olympic. *Olympus.*
Ombrometer. *Ombros; metrum.*
Omega. *Omega.*
Omen, ominate, ominous. *Omen.*
Omission, omit. *Ob; mitto.*
Omnifarious. *Omnis; fari.*
Omniferous. *Omnis; fero.*
Omnific. *Omnis; facio.*
Omniform. *Omnis; forma.*
Omnigenous. *Omnis; genus.*
Omniparity. *Omnis; par.*
Omnipercipient. *Omnis; per; capio.*
Omnipotent. *Omnis; posse; ens.*
Omnipresent. *Omnis; pre; ens.*
Omniscient. *Omnis; scio.*
Omnium. *Omnis.*
Omnivorous. *Omnis; voro.*
Omphalic. *Omphalos.*
Omphalocele. *Omphalos; cele.*
Omphalopter. *Omphalos; opto.*
Omphalotomy. *Omphalos; tomos.*
Oneirocritic. *Oneiros; crites.*
Oneiromancy. *Oneiros; mancia.*
Onerary, onerate. *Onus.*
Onkotomy. (*Onkos*, a swelling); *tomos.*
Onomancy, onomantic. *Onoma; mancia.*
Onomatopy. *Onoma; opto.*
Ontologic, ontology. *Onta; logos.*
Opacate, opacity. *Opacus.*
Opal, opalescent, opaline, opalize. *Opalus.*
Opaque, opake. *Opacus.*
Opera. *Opera.*
Operate, operose. *Opera.*
Ophidion. *Ophis.*
Ophiology. *Ophis; logos.*
Ophiomancy. *Ophis; mancia.*
Ophiomorphous. *Ophis; morphe.*
Ophiophagous. *Ophis; phago.*
Ophite. *Ophis.*
Ophiuchus. *Ophis;* (*echo*, to have).
Ophthalmic. *Ophthalmos.*
Ophthalmoscopy. *Ophthalmos; scopeo.*
Ophthalmy. *Ophthalmos.*
Opiate. *Opium.*
Opine, opiniate, opiniative, opinion, opinionate. *Opinor.*
Opium. *Opium.*
Oppidam. *Oppidum.*
Oppignorate. *Op; pignus.*
Oppone. *Op; pono.*
Opportune. *Op; porto.*
Oppose. opposition. *Op; pono.*
Oppress. *Op; premo.*
Opprobrious. *Op; probrum.*
Oppugn, oppugnant, oppugnation. *Op; pugna.*
Opsimathy. (*Opse*, late); *mathema.*
Optable, optative. *Opto.*
Optic, optician. *Opto.*
Option. *Opto.*
Opulent. *Opulentus.*
Opuscule. *Opera.*
Oracle, oracular, oraison, oral, oration, orator, oratorio, oratrix. *Oro.*
Orb, orbicular, orbit, orby. *Orbis.*
Orchard. *Hortus.*
Orchestre, orchestral. *Orchestra.*
Ordain, ordeal, order, ordinal, ordinance. ordinary, ordination, ordnance, ordonnance. *Ordo.*
Oread. *Oros.*
Organ, organize. *Organum.*
Organography. *Organum; grapho.*
Orient, orientalist. *Orior.*
Orifice. *Oro; facio.*
Origin, originality, originate. *Orior.*
Orison. *Oro.*
Ornament, ornate, ornature. *Orno.*
Orniscopics. *Ornis; scopeo.*
Ornitholite. *Ornis; lithos.*
Ornithology. *Ornis; logos.*
Ornithomancy. *Ornis; mancia.*
Orology. *Oros; logos.*
Orphan. *Orphanos.*
Orphanotrophy. *Orphanos; trophe.*
Orthodoxy. *Orthos; doxa.*
Orthodromics. *Orthos; dromos.*
Orthoepy. *Orthos; epos.*
Orthogon. *Orthos; gonia.*
Orthography. *Orthos; grapho.*
Orthology. *Orthos; logos.*
Orthometry. *Orthos; metrum.*
Orthopny. *Orthos; pneuma.*
Ortive. *Orior.*
Oryctognostic, oryctognosy. *Oryctos; gnostos.*
Oryctography. *Oryctos; grapho.*
Oryctology. *Oryctos; logos.*
Oscillate. *Oscillum.*
Oscitant, oscitation. *Oscito.*
Ospray. *Os; frango.*
Osselet. osseous, ossicle. *Os.*
Ossiferous. *Os; fero.*
Ossific, ossification. *Os; facio*
Ossifrage. *Os; frango.*
Ossify. *Os.*
Ossivorous. *Os; voro.*
Ossuary. *Os.*
Ostensible, ostensive, ostent, ostentation, ostentatious. *Os; tendo.*
Osteocol. *Osteon;* (*colla*, glue).
Osteocope. *Osteon; cope.*
Osteology. *Osteon; logos.*
Ostler. *Hospes.*
Ostracite, ostracize. *Ostracon.*
Otacoustic. *Ous; acouo.*
Otalgia. *Ous; algos.*
Ouranography. *Ouranos; grapho.*
Outrage. *Ultra.*
Oval, ovarious, ovate. *Ovum.*
Ovation. *Ovis.*
Overt, overture. *Ob; pario.*
Ovicular. *Ovum.*
Oviduct. *Ovum; duco.*
Oviform. *Ovum; forma.*
Ovine. *Ovis.*
Oviparous. *Ovum; pario.*
Ovoid. *Ovum; oidos.*
Oxalic. *Oxys.*
Oxycrate. *Oxys;* (*cerao*, to mix)
Oxyd, oxydate, oxydize. *Oxys.*
Oxygen. *Oxys; genea.*
Oxygon *Oxys; gonia.*
Oxyiodine. *Oxys;* (*iodes*, violet colored).
Oxymel. *Oxys; mel.*
Oxymoron. *Oxys;* (*moros*, foolish).
Oxyrhodine. *Oxys;* (*rodon*, rose).
Oxytone. *Oxys; tonos.*

P.

Pacate. *Pax.*
Pace. *Passus.*
Pacific, pacification. *Pax; facio.*
Pacify. *Pax.*
Pact, paction, pactitious. *Pactus.*
Pagan. *Pagus.*
Paginal. *Pagina.*
Pain. *Peniteo.*
Paint. *Pingo.*
Pair. *Par.*
Palace. *Palatium.*
Palatable, palatal, palate, palatial. *Palatum.*
Palatial, palatine. *Palatium.*
Pale. *Palleo.*
Pale. *Palus.*
Paleography. *Paleos; grapho.*
Paleology. *Paleos; logos.*
Paleous. *Palea.*
Palestric. *Palæstra.*
Palification. *Palus; facio.*
Palindrome. *Palin; dromos.*
Palinode. *Palin; ode.*
Palisade. *Palus.*
Pall. *Pallium.*
Palladium. *Pallas.*
Pallet. *Palea.*
Palliament, palliate. *Pallium.*
Pallid, pallor. *Palleo.*
Palm, palmated, palmetto. *Palma.*
Palmiferous. *Palma; fero.*
Palmiped. *Palma; pes.*
Palmistry. *Palma.*
Palpable, palpation, palpitate. *Palpo.*
Palsical, palsy. *Para; lysis.*
Pan, panic. *Pan.*
Panacea. *Pas;* (*acesis*, a cure).
Panada. *Panis.*
Pancratic. *Pas; cratos.*
Pancreas, pancreatic. *Pas;* (*creas*, flesh).
Pandect. *Pas; dechomai.*
Pandemic. *Pas; demos.*
Pandiculation. *Pando.*
Panegyric. *Pas; egora.*
Panicle, paniculate. *Pannus.*
Pannage, pannier. *Panis.*
Pannicle. *Pannus.*
Panoply. *Pas; oplon.*
Panorama. *Pas; orama.*
Pansophical, pansophy. *Pas; sophia.*
Pantheism, pantheistic, pantheon. *Pas; theos.*
Pantograph. *Pas; grapho.*
Pantometer, pantometric. *Pas; metrum.*
Pantomime, pantomimic. *Pas; mimus.*
Pantry. *Panis.*
Panurgy. *Pas; ergon.*
Pap. *Papilla.*
Papa, papacy, papal. *Papas.*
Papaverous. *Papaver.*
Paper. *Papyrus.*
Papescent. *Papilla.*
Papil, papillate, papillose, papillary *Papilla.*
Papilonaceous. *Papilio.*
Pappous. *Pappus.*
Pappy, papulæ, papulose. *Papilla.*
Papyrus. *Papyrus.*
Par *Par.*
Parable, parabola. *Para; boleo.*
Paraboliform. *Para; boleo; forma.*
Paraboloid. *Para; boleo; oidos.*
Paracentric. *Para; centrum.*
Parade. *Paro.*
Paradigm, paradigmatic, paradigmatize. *Paradigma.*
Paradise. *Paradisos.*
Paradox. *Para; doxa.*
Paradoxology. *Para; doxa; logos.*
Paragoge. *Para; agogeus.*
Paragraph. *Para; grapho.*
Parallax. *Para; allaxis.*
Parallel. *Para; allelon.*
Parallelogram. *Para; allelon; grapho.*
Parallelopiped. *Para; allelon; epi;* (*pedon*, a plain).
Paralogy. *Para; logos.*
Paralysis, paralytic. *Para; lysis.*
Parapet. *Per; pectus.*
Paraphernalia. *Para; pherne.*
Paraphrase, paraphrast. *Para; phrasis.*
Paraphrenitis. *Para; phren.*
Paraselene. *Para; selene.*
Parasite. *Para; sitos.*
Parathesis. *Para; thesis.*
Parcel, parcener. *Pars.*
Pardon. *Pardonner.*
Parenchyma. *Para; en; chymos.*
Parent, parentage. *Pario.*
Parenthesis, parenthetic. *Para; en; thesis.*
Parenticide. *Pario; cædo.*
Parhelion. *Para; helios.*
Parietal. *Paries.*
Parish. *Para; eceo.*
Parisyllabic. *Par; syl; labo.*
Parity. *Par.*
Parlance, parle, parl, parley, parliament, parlor, parlous. *Parler.*
Parochial. *Para; eceo.*
Parody. *Para; ode.*
Parol. *Parler.*
Paronomasia, paronomastic, paronymous. *Para; onoma.*
Parotid, parotis. *Para; ous.*
Paroxysm. *Para; oxys.*
Parricide. *Pater; cædo.*
Parse. *Pars.*
Parsimonious, parsimony. *Parsimonia.*
Part. *Pars.*
Partake. *Pars;* (*take*).
Partial, partible. *Pars.*
Participate, participle. *Pars; capio.*
Particle, particular, partisan, partite, partition, partner. *Pars.*
Parturiate, parturition. *Pario.*
Party. *Pars.*
Paschal. *Pascha.*
Pasigraphy. *Pas; grapho.*
Pass, passage, passenger, passible. *Passus.*
Passerine. *Passer.*
Passion, passive. *Patior.*
Passover. *Passus;* (*over*).
Passport. *Passus; porto.*
Past. *Passus.*
Pastime. *Passus; tempus.*
Pastor, pasturage, pasture. *Pasco.*
Patefaction. *Pateo; facio.*
Patelliform. *Patella; forma.*
Patellite. *Patella.*
Patent. *Pateo.*
Paternal, paternity. *Pater.*
Paternoster. *Pater;* (*noster*, our).
Pathetic. *Pathos.*
Pathognomonic, pathognomy. *Pathos; gnomon.*
Pathology. *Pathos; logos.*
Pathopoiea. *Pathos; poieo.*
Pathos. *Pathos.*
Patible, patient. *Patior.*
Patibulary. *Patibulum.*
Patriarch. *Pater; arche.*
Patrician, patrimony, patriot, patristic *Pater.*

Patroll. *Pateo.*
Patron, patronize. *Pater.*
Patronymic. *Pater; onoma.*
Patulous. *Pateo.*
Pauciloquy. *Pauci; loquor.*
Paucity. *Pauci.*
Pauper. *Pauper.*
Pavo, pavonine. *Pavo.*
Pawn. *Pignus.*
Peace. *Pax.*
Peasant. *Pais.*
Peccable, peccadillo, peccant. *Pecco.*
Pectinal, pectinate, pectinite. *Pecto.*
Pectoral. *Pectus.*
Peculate. *Peculor.*
Peculiar, peculiarity, peculiarize. *Peculium.*
Pecuniary. *Pecunia.*
Pedagogue, pedagoge. *Pedia; agogeus.*
Pedal, pedaneous, pedate. *Pes.*
Pedantic, pedantry. *Pedia.*
Pedatifid. *Pes; findo.*
Pedestal, pedestrian, pedicle, pedicular, pedicellate. *Pes.*
Pedigree. *Pes; gradior.*
Pediment. *Pes.*
Pedobaptist. *Pes; bapto.*
Pedometer. *Pes; metrum.*
Peduncle. *Pes.*
Peer. *Par.*
Pelagian, pelagic. *Pelagus.*
Pelican. *Pelecan.*
Pelisse, pell, pellicle. *Pellis.*
Pellucid. *Per; luceo.*
Peloponnesus. (*Pelops*); *nesos.*
Pelvimeter. *Pelvis; metrum.*
Pelvis. *Pelvis.*
Pen. *Penna.*
Penal, penance. *Peniteo.*
Pendant, pendent, pendule, pendulosity, pendulum. *Pendeo.*
Penetrant, penetrate. *Penetro.*
Peninsula. *Pene; insula.*
Penitent, penitentiary. *Peniteo.*
Pennant. *Pendeo.*
Pennate. *Penna.*
Penniform. *Penna; forma.*
Pensile. *Pendeo.*
Pension, pensive. *Pendo.*
Pentacapsular. *Pente; capsula.*
Pentachord. *Pente; chorda.*
Pentacoccous. *Pente;* (*coccus*, a berry).
Pentacrostic. *Pente; acron; stichos.*
Pentadactyl. *Pente; dactylus.*
Pentagon. *Pente; gonia.*
Pentagraph. *Pente; grapho.*
Pentagyn. *Pente; gyne.*
Pentaedrous. *Pente; edra.*
Pentameter. *Pente; metrum.*
Pentander. *Pente; aner.*
Pentangular. *Pente; angulus.*
Pentapetalous. *Pente; petalon.*
Pentaphyllous. *Pente; phyllon.*
Pentarchy. *Pente; arche.*
Pentaspast. *Pente; spasma.*
Pentaspermous. *Pente; sperma.*
Pentastich. *Pente; stichos.*
Pentastyle. *Pente; stylos.*
Pentateuch. *Pente; teuchos.*
Pentecost. *Pente.*
Penult, penultimate. *Pene; ultimus.*
Penumbra. *Pene; umbra.*
Penurious, penury. *Penuria.*
People. *Populus.*
Peptic. *Peptos.*
Peradventure. *Per; ad; venio.*
Perambulate. *Per; ambulo.*
Perceive, perception, percipient. *Per; capio.*
Percuss, percutient. *Per; cutio.*
Perdition, perdulous. *Per; do.*
Peregrinate, peregrine. *Per; ager.*
Peremptory. *Per; emo.*
Perennial. *Per; annus.*
Pererration. *Per; erro.*
Perfect. *Per; facio.*
Perfidy. *Per; fides.*
Perflate. *Per; flatus.*
Perforate. *Per; foro.*
Perform. *Per; forma.*
Perfricate. *Per; frico.*
Perfunctory. *Per; functus.*
Pericardium. *Peri; cardia.*
Pericarpium. *Peri; carpus.*
Pericranium. *Peri; cranium.*
Periculous. *Periculum.*
Perihelion. *Peri; helios.*
Peril. *Periculum.*
Perimeter. *Peri; metrum.*
Periœci. *Peri; eceo.*
Period. *Peri; odos.*
Peripatetic. *Peri; pateo.*
Peripheric, periphery. *Peri; phero.*
Periphrase, periphrastic. *Peri; phrasis.*
Peripneumony. *Peri; pneuma.*
Peripolygonal. *Peri; poly; gonia.*
Periscii. *Peri; scia.*
Perish. *Per; eo.*
Perispheric. *Peri; sphæra.*
Perissology. *Perissos; logos.*
Peristaltic. *Peri; stello.*
Perisystole. *Peri; syn; stello.*
Peritoneum. *Peri; tonos.*
Perjure. *Per; juro.*
Perlustration. *Per; lustrum.*
Permanent, permansion. *Per; maneo.*
Permeable,permeant,permeation. *Per; meo.*
Permiscible, permission. *Per; mitto.*
Permission. *Per; misceo.*
Permit. *Per; mitto.*
Permixtion. *Per; misceo.*
Permute. *Per; muto.*
Pernicious. *Per; nex.*
Pernoctation. *Per; nox.*
Peroration. *Per; oro*
Perpend. *Per; pendo*
Perpendicle, perpendicular. *Per; pendeo.*
Perpension. *Per; pendo.*
Perpetrate. *Per; petro.*
Perpetual, perpetuate, perpetuity. *Perpes.*
Perplex. *Per; plico.*
Perpotation. *Per; poto.*
Perquisite. *Per; quæro.*
Persecute. *Per; sequor.*
Persevere. *Persevero.*
Persist. *Per; sisto.*
Person, personage, personate. *Persona.*
Personification. *Persona; facio.*
Personify. *Persona.*
Perspective. *Per; specio.*
Perspicacious, perspicacity, perspicacy, perspicil, perspicuity, perspicuous. *Per; specio.*
Perspirable, perspiration, perspire. *Per; spiro.*
Persuadable, persuade, persuasible, persuasion, persuasory. *Per; suadeo.*
Pertain. *Per; teneo.*
Perterebration. *Per; terebra.*
Pertinacious, pertinacity, pertinent. *Per; teneo.*
Pertingent. *Per; tango.*
Pertransient. *Per; trans; eo.*
Perturb, perturbate. *Per; turba.*
Pertuse, pertusion. *Per; tundo.*
Peruse. *Per; utor.*

Pervade, pervasion. *Per; vado.*
Perverse, perversion, perversity, pervert. *Per; verto*
Pervestigate. *Per; vestigium.*
Pervicacious, pervicacity *Per; vinco.*
Pervious. *Per; via.*
Pest. *Pestis.*
Pestiduct. *Pestis; duco.*
Pestiferous. *Pestis; fero.*
Pestilent. *Pestis.*
Petal, petalite. *Petalon.*
Petaloid. *Petalon; oidos.*
Petiolar, petiole. *Pes.*
Petition, petitionary, petitory. *Peto.*
Petre, Peter, petrescent. *Petra.*
Petrifaction, petrification. *Petra; facio.*
Petrify. *Petra.*
Petrol. *Petra; oliva.*
Petrology. *Petra; logos.*
Petrosilex, petrosilicious. *Petra; silex.*
Petrous. *Petra.*
Petticoat. *Petit;* (*cotte*, a coat).
Pettifogger. *Petit;* (*voguer*, to row).
Petulant. *Petulans.*
Phæton. *Phano.*
Phagedenic. *Phago.*
Phalangite, phalanx. *Phalanx.*
Phantasm, phantom. *Phano.*
Pharisaic, pharisee. *Pharisees.*
Pharmaceutic. *Pharmacon.*
Pharmacology. *Pharmacon; logos.*
Pharmacopæia, pharmacopy. *Pharmacon; poieo.*
Pharmacopolist. *Pharmacon; polis.*
Pharmacy. *Pharmacon.*
Pharyngotomy. *Pharynx; tomos.*
Pharynx. *Pharynx.*
Phase, phasis. *Phano.*
Phenicia, phenix. *Phenix.*
Phenogamian. *Phano; gameo.*
Phenomenology. *Phano; logos.*
Phenomenon. *Phano.*
Philadelphian. *Philos; adelphos.*
Philanthropy. *Philos; anthropos.*
Philippic. *Philippus.*
Philologic, philology. *Philos; logos.*
Philomath. *Philos; mathema.*
Philomela. *Philos; melos.*
Philopolemic. *Philos; polemos.*
Philosophize, philosophy. *Philos; sophia.*
Philter. *Philos.*
Phlebotomy. *Phleps; tomos.*
Phlem, phlegmatic, phlegmon. *Phlegma.*
Phlogisticate, phlogiston. *Phlegma.*
Phonics. *Phone.*
Phonocamptic. *Phone; campto.*
Phonolite. *Phonos; lithos.*
Phonology. *Phone; logos.*
Phosphate, phosphite. *Phos.*
Phosphor, phosphorate, phosphorescent, phosphorite, phosphuret. *Phos; phero.*
Photometer. *Phos; metrum.*
Photonomics. *Phos; nomos.*
Phrase. *Phrasis.*
Phraseology. *Phrasis; logos.*
Phrenetic, phrenic, phrenitis. *Phren.*
Phrenology. *Phren; logos.*
Phrensy. *Phren.*
Phrontistery. *Phren.*
Phthisis. *Phthisis.*
Phylacter. *Phylacterion.*
Phyllite. *Phyllon.*
Phyllophorous. *Phyllon; phero.*
Physianthropy. *Physis; anthropos.*
Physic, physician. *Physis.*
Physicologic. *Physis; logos.*
Physicotheology. *Physis; theos; logos.*
Physiognomy. *Physis; gnomon.*
Physiography. *Physis; grapho.*
Physiology. *Physis; logos.*
Phytivorous. *Phyton; voro.*
Phytography. *Phyton; grapho.*
Phytolite. *Phyton; lithos.*
Phytology. *Phyton; logos.*
Piacular. *Pio.*
Picts, pictorial, picture, picturesque. *Pingo.*
Piety. *Pius.*
Pigment. *Pingo.*
Pignoration. *Pignus.*
Pilage. *Pilus.*
Pilfer. *Pilo.*
Pilgrim. *Pilgrim* (*per; ager*).
Pillage. *Pilo.*
Pilose, pilous. *Pilus.*
Pious. *Pius.*
Piracy, pirate, piratical. *Pirates.*
Piscatory, pisces, piscine. *Piscis.*
Piscivorous. *Piscis; voro.*
Pistil, pistillaceous, pistillate. *Pistilum*
Pistilliferous. *Pistillum; fero.*
Pituitary, pituite, pituitous. *Pituita.*
Placable. *Placeo.*
Plagiarist, plagiary. *Plagium.*
Plague, plaint, plaintiff. *Plango.*
Plane. *Planus.*
Planet. *Plane.*
Planifolious. *Planus; folium.*
Planimetry. *Planus; metrum.*
Planipetalous. *Planus; petalon.*
Planish. *Planus.*
Planisphere. *Planus; sphæra.*
Planoconical. *Planus; conos.*
Planoconvex. *Planus; con; veho.*
Planohorizontal. *Planus; horos.*
Plant. *Planta.*
Plasm, plasmatic, plaster, plastic. *Plasso.*
Platonic, platonist. *Plato.*
Plaudit, plausible, plausive. *Plaudo.*
Pleasant, please, pleasure. *Placeo.*
Plebeian. *Plebs.*
Plenal, plenary. *Plenus.*
Plenipotent, plenipotentiary. *Plenus; pos se; ens.*
Plenist, plenitude, plenteous, plenty, plenum. *Plenus.*
Pleonasm, pleonastic. *Pleo.*
Plerophory. *Pleo; phero.*
Plethoric, plethory. *Pleo.*
Pleura, pleurisy, pleuritic. *Pleura.*
Plexiform. *Plico; forma.*
Plexus, pliable, pliant, plicate, plicature pliers. *Plico.*
Plumage. *Pluma.*
Plumbaginous, plumbago. *Plumbum.*
Plumbiferous. *Plumbum; fero.*
Pluma. *Pluma.*
Plumigerous. *Pluma; gero.*
Plumiped. *Pluma; pes.*
Plummet. *Plumbum.*
Pluperfect. *Plus; per; facio*
Plural. *Plus.*
Pluriliteral. *Plus; litera.*
Plus. *Plus.*
Plutonic. *Pluto.*
Pluvial. *Pluvia.*
Pluviameter, pluviametrical. *Pluvia; metrum.*
Ply. *Plico.*
Pneumatic. *Pneuma.*
Pneumatocele. *Pneuma; cele.*
Pneumatology. *Pneuma; logos.*
Pneumony. *Pneuma.*
Poculent. *Poto.*

Podagric. ***Pous;*** (*agra*, a catching).
Poem. *Poieo.*
Poise. *Pondus.*
Polar, polarize, pole. *Polus.*
Polemic. *Polemos.*
Polemoscope. *Polemos; scopeo.*
Police, policy, polish, polite, politic. *Polis.*
Pollute. *Per; luo.*
Polyacoustic. *Poly; acouo.*
Polyadelph. *Poly; adelphos.*
Polyander. *Poly; aner.*
Polyanthos. *Poly; anthos.*
Polyautography. *Poly; autos; grapho.*
Polychord. *Poly; chorda.*
Polycotyledon. *Poly;* (*cotyle*, a cavity).
Polygam, polygamy. *Poly; gameo.*
Polygenous. *Poly; genea.*
Polyglot. *Poly; glossa.*
Polygon. *Poly; gonia.*
Polygram, polygraphy. *Poly; grapho*
Polygyn. *Poly; gyne.*
Polyedron. *Poly; edra.*
Polylogy. *Poly; logos.*
Polymathy. *Poly; mathema.*
Polymorphous. *Poly; morphe.*
Polynesia. *Poly; nesos.*
Polynome. *Poly; nomen.*
Polyoptrum. *Poly; opto.*
Polypetalous. *Poly; petalon.*
Polyphony. *Poly; phone.*
Polyphyllous. *Poly; phyllon.*
Polypode, polypous, polype. *Poly; pous.*
Polyscope. *Poly; scopeo.*
Polyspast. *Poly; spasma.*
Polysperm. *Poly; sperma.*
Polysyllable. *Poly; syl; labo.*
Polysyndeton. *Poly;* (*syndetos*, connecting).
Polytechnic. *Poly; techne.*
Polytheist. *Poly; theos.*
Pomace, pome. *Pomum.*
Pomecitron. *Pomum;* (*citrus*, a citron).
Pomegranate. *Pomum; granum.*
Pomeroy. *Pomum; roy.*
Pomiferous. *Pomum; fero.*
Pommel. *Pomum.*
Pomp, pomposity. *Pompa.*
Ponder, ponderosity. *Pondus.*
Ponent. *Pono.*
Poniard. *Pungo.*
Pontage. *Pons.*
Pontifex, pontiff, pontific. *Pons; facio.*
Pontoon. *Pons.*
Poor. *Pauper.*
Pope. *Papas.*
Popliteal, poplitic. *Poples.*
Populace, popular, populate. *Populus.*
Porch. *Porto.*
Porcine, porcupine. *Porcus.*
Pore, porism, poristic. *Poros.*
Pork. *Porcus.*
Porosity, porous. *Poros.*
Porphyritic, porphyry. *Porphyra.*
Porpoise, porpus. *Porcus.*
Porraceous. *Porrum.*
Porrection. *Porro.*
Porret, porridge, porringer. *Porrum.*
Port, portable, portal. *Porto.*
Portcullis. *Porto;* (*coulir*, to slip down).
Porte. *Porto.*
Portend, portension, portent. *Porro; tendo.*
Porter. *Porto.*
Portfolio. *Porto; folium.*
Portico. *Porto.*
Portion. *Pars*
Portmanteau, *Porto; manus.*
Portrait, portraiture, portray. *Pro; traho*
Pose, position, positive. *Pono.*
Posology. *Posos; logos.*
Posse, possess, possible. *Posse.*
Post. *Pono.*
Postdiluvian. *Post; diluvium.*
Posterior, postern. *Posterus.*
Postfix. *Post; fixus.*
Posthume, posthumous. *Post; humus.*
Postmeridian. *Post; meridies.*
Postmundane. *Post; mundus.*
Postnate. *Post; nascor.*
Postobit. *Post; ob; eo.*
Postpone. *Post; pono.*
Postulate, postulatum. *Postulo.*
Posture. *Pono.*
Potable. *Poto.*
Potamology. *Potamos; logos.*
Potation. *Poto.*
Potent, potential, potestative. *Posse; ens.*
Potion, potulent. *Poto.*
Potvaliant. *Poto; valeo.*
Poult, poultry. *Pullus.*
Pounce. *Pungo.*
Pound. *Pondus.*
Poverty. *Pauper.*
Powder. *Pulvis.*
Power. *Posse.*
Practicable, practice, practitioner. *Practos.*
Præcognita. *Præ; cog; nosco.*
Præmunire. *Præ; munio.*
Pragmatic. *Practos.*
Praise. *Precium.*
Pravity. *Pravus.*
Praxis. *Practos.*
Pray, preach. *Precor.*
Preadministration. *Pre; ad; minister.*
Preadmonish. *Pre; ad; monio.*
Preantepenultimate. *Pre; ante; pene; ultimus.*
Precarious, precative. *Precor.*
Precaution. *Pre; cautio.*
Precedaneous, precede, precedent. *Pre; cedo.*
Precentor. *Pre; cano.*
Precept. *Pre; capio.*
Precession. *Pre; cedo.*
Precinct. *Pre; cingo.*
Precious. *Precium.*
Precipice, precipitate. *Pre; capio.*
Precise, precisian, precision. *Pre; cædo.*
Preclude, preclusion. *Pre; claudo.*
Precognita. *Pre; cog; nosco.*
Precompose. *Pre; com; pono.* [*Pre; con; capio.*
Preconceit, preconceive, preconception.
Preconcerted. *Pre; con; certo.*
Preconsign. *Pre; con; signum.*
Preconstitute. *Pre; con; sto.*
Precontract. *Pre; con; traho.*
Precurse. *Pre; curro.*
Predaceous, predal, predatory. *Preda.*
Predeceased, predecessor. *Pre; de; cedo.*
Predelineation. *Pre; de; linea.*
Predesign. *Pre; de; signum.*
Predestinarian, predestinate, predestine. *Pre; de; stino.*
Predeterminate, predetermine. *Pre; de; terminus.*
Predial. *Predium.*
Predicable, predicament, predicate, predict. *Pre; dico.*
Predigestion. *Pre; di; gero.*
Predilection. *Pre; di; lego.*
Predisponent, predispose. *Pre; dis; pono*

Predominant, predominate. *Pre; dominus.*
Pre-elect. *Pre; e; lego.*
Pre-eminent. *Pre; e; mineo.*
Pre-emption. *Pre; emo.*
Pre-exist. *Pre; ex; sisto.*
Preface, prefatory. *Pre; fari.*
Prefect. *Pre; facio.*
Prefer. *Pre; fero.*
Prefigure. *Pre; figura.*
Prefix. *Pre; fixus.*
Pregnable, pregnant. *Pregnans.*
Pregustation. *Pre; gustus.*
Prehensile. *Prehendo.*
Preinstruct. *Pre; in; struo.*
Prejudge, prejudicate, prejudice. *Pre; judico.*
Prelacy, prelate. *Pre; latum.*
Prelect. *Pre; lego.*
Preliminary. *Pre; limen.*
Prelude, prelusory. *Pre; ludo.*
Premature. *Pre; maturus.*
Premeditate. *Pre; meditor.*
Premerit. *Pre; meritum.*
Premise. *Pre; mitto.*
Premonish, premonition, premonitory. *Pre; moneo.*
Premonstrate. *Pre; monstro.*
Premunire. *Pre; munio.*
Prenominate. *Pre; nomen.*
Prenotion. *Pre; nosco.*
Prensation. *Prehendo.*
Prenunciation. *Pre; nuncio.*
Preobtain. *Pre; ob; teneo.*
Preoccupate, preoccupy. *Pre; oc; capio.*
Preominate. *Pre; omen.*
Preoption. *Pre; opto.*
Preordain, preordinate. *Pre; ordo.*
Preparable, preparatory, prepared. *Pre; paro.*
Prepense. *Pre; pendeo.*
Prepollent. *Pre; pollens.*
Preponder. *Pre; pondus.*
Prepose, preposition. *Pre; pono.*
Prepossess. *Pre; posse.*
Preposterous. *Pre; posterus.*
Prepotent. *Pre; posse; ens.*
Prerequire, prerequisite. *Pre; re; quæro.*
Preresolve. *Pre; re; solvo.*
Prerogative. *Pre; rogo.*
Prerupt. *Pre; ruptum.*
Presage. *Pre; sagax.*
Presbyter, presbyterian. *Presbyteros.*
Prescient. *Pre; scio.*
Prescind. *Pre; scindo.*
Prescribe, prescript, prescription. *Pre; scribo.*
Presence. *Pre; ens.*
Presensation, presension. *Pre; sentio.*
Present, presential. *Pre; ens.*
Presentific. *Pre; ens; facio.*
Presentiment. *Pre; sentio.*
Preservation, preserve. *Pre; servo.*
Preside, president, presidial. *Pre; sedeo.*
Presignification. *Pre; signum; facio.*
Presignify. *Pre; signum.*
Press. *Premo.*
Prestiges, prestigiation. *Prestigiæ.*
Presume, presumption, presumptuous. *Pre; sumo.*
Presuppose, presupposition. *Pre; sup; pono.*
Pretend, pretense, pretension. *Pre; tendo.*
Pretentative. *Pre; tento.*
Preterimperfect. *Preter; im; per; facio.*
Preterite. *Preter; eo.*
Preterlapsed. *Preter; labor.*
Pretermission, pretermit. *Preter; mitto.*
Preternatural. *Preter; nascor.*
Preterperfect. *Preter; per; facio.*
Preterpluperfect. *Preter; plus; per; facio.*
Pretext. *Pre; textus.*
Pretor. *Pre; eo.*
Pretypify. *Pre; typus.*
Prevail, prevalent. *Pre; valeo.*
Prevaricate. *Pre; varico.*
Prevenient, prevent, prevention. *Pre; venio*
Previous. *Pre; via.*
Prevision. *Pre; video.*
Prey. *Preda.*
Price. *Precium.*
Priest. *Pre; sto.*
Prim, primacy, primary, primate, prime *Primus.*
Primeval. *Primus; evum.*
Primigenial, primigenous. *Primus; genus.*
Primitive. *Primus.*
Primogenial, primogeniture. *Primus; genus*
Primordial. *Primus; ordo.*
Prince, principal, principia, principle *Primus; capio.*
Print. *Premo.*
Prior. *Primus.*
Prism, prismatic. *Prisma.*
Prismatoidal, prismoid. *Prisma; oidos.*
Prison. *Prehendo.*
Privacy, private, privateer. *Privus.*
Privilege. *Privus; lex.*
Privity, privy. *Privus.*
Prize. *Prehendo.*
Prize. *Precium.*
Probable, probate, probation. *Probo.*
Probatum-est. *Probo; (est,* it is).
Probe, probity. *Probo.*
Problem. *Pro; boleo.*
Procacious, procacity. *Procax.*
Procatarctic, procatarxis. *Pro; cata; arche*
Procedure, proceed, process, procession *Pro; cedo.*
Proclaim, proclamation. *Pro; clamo.*
Proclive, proclivity, proclivous. *Pro; clivus.*
Proconsul. *Pro; con; salio.*
Procrastinate. *Pro; cras.*
Procreant, procreate. *Pro; creo.*
Proctor. *Pro; cura.*
Procumbent. *Pro; cubo.*
Procurable, procurator, procure. *Pro; cura.*
Prodigal, prodigious, prodigy. *Prodigium*
Prodrome. *Pro; dromos.*
Produce, product, production. *Pro; duco.*
Proem. *Proemium.*
Proemptosis. *Proemium; ptoma.*
Profanation, profane. *Pro; fanum.*
Profection. *Pro; facio.*
Profess, profession. *Pro; fessum.*
Proffer. *Pro; fero.*
Proficient, profit. *Pro; facio.*
Profluent. *Pro; fluo.*
Profound, profundity. *Pro; fundus.*
Profuse. *Pro; fundo.*
Progeneration, progenitor, progeny *Pro; genus.*
Prognostic, prognosticate. *Pro; gnomon*
Progress. *Pro; gradior.*
Prohibit. *Pro; habeo.*
Project, projectile, projecture. *Pro; jacio.*
Prolate. *Pro; latum.*
Prolegomena. *Pro; lego.*
Prolepsis, proleptic. *Pro; lepsis.*
Proliferous. *Proles; fero.*
Prolific. *Proles; facio.*
Prolix. *Pro; laxus.*
Prolocutor. *Pro; loquor.*
Prologue. *Pro; logos.*

Prolong. *Pro; longus.*
Prolusion. *Pro; ludo.*
Promerit. *Pro; meritum.*
Prominent. *Pro; mineo.*
Promiscuous. *Pro; misceo.*
Promise, promissory. *Pro; mitto.*
Promontory. *Pro; mons.*
Promote. *Pro; moveo.*
Promp, promptitude, promptuary. *Pro; emo.*
Promulgate, promulge. *Pro; vulgus.*
Pronation, prone. *Pronus.*
Pronoun. *Pro; nomen.*
Pronounce, pronunciation. *Pro; nuncio.*
Proof. *Probo.*
Propagable, propagandist, propagate. *Pro; ago.*
Propel. *Pro; pello.*
Propend, propense, propensity. *Pro; pendeo.*
Proper, property. *Proprius.*
Prophasis, prophecy, prophesy, prophet. *Pro; phano.*
Prophylactic. *Pro; phylacterion.*
Propinquate. *Prope.*
Propitiable, propitiate, propitious. *Prope.*
Proplasm, proplastic. *Pro; plasso.*
Proponent. *Pro; pono.*
Proportion. *Pro; pars.*
Propose, proposition, propound. *Pro; pono.*
Proprietary, propriety. *Proprius.*
Propugn, propugnation. *Pro; pugna.*
Propulsation, propulse. *Pro; pello.*
Prorogation, prorogue. *Pro; rogo.*
Proruption. *Pro; ruptum.*
Prosaic, prosal. *Prosa.*
Proscribe, proscription. *Pro; scribo.*
Prose. *Prosa.*
Prosecute. *Pro; sequor.*
Proselyte. *Proselytos.*
Prosemination. *Pro; semen.*
Prosody. (*Pros*, to); *ode.*
Prosopolepsy. *Prosopon; lepsis.*
Prosopopœia, prosopopy. *Prosopon; poieo.*
Prospect, prospective, prospectus. *Pro; specio.*
Prosper, prosperity. *Prosper.*
Prospicience. *Pro; specio.*
Prosternation. *Pro; sterno.*
Prosthesis, prosthetic. *Pro; thesis.*
Prostitute. *Pro; sto.*
Prostrate. *Pro; sterno.*
Prosyllogysm. *Pro; syl; logos.*
Protect, protectorate. *Pro; tego.*
Protend. *Pro; tendo.*
Protest. *Pro; testis.*
Proteus. *Proteus.*
Prothesis. *Pro; thesis.*
Prothonotary. *Protos; nosco.*
Protocol. *Protos*; (*colla*, glue).
Protomartyr. *Protos; martyr.*
Protoplast. *Protos; plasso.*
Protopope. *Protos; papas.*
Prototype. *Protos; typus.*
Protoxyd. *Protos; oxys.*
Protract. *Pro; traho.*
Protrude, protrusion. *Pro; trudo.*
Protuberance, protuberate, protuberous. *Pro; tuber.*
Prove. *Probo.*
Proveditor, provedore, provender. *Pro; video.*
Proverb. *Pro; verbum.*
Provide, providential. *Pro; video.*
Province, provincial. *Pro; vinco.*
Provision, proviso. *Pro; video.*
Provocation, provoke. *Pro; voco.*
Provost. *Pro; pono.*
Proximal, proximity. *Prope.*
Proxy. *Pro; cura.*
Prudent. *Pro; video.*
Prurient, prurigo, prurigenous. *Prurio*
Psalm. *Psalma.*
Psalmody. *Psalma; ode.*
Psalmography. *Psalma; grapho.*
Psalter. *Psalma.*
Pseudo-apostle. *Pseudos; apo; stello.*
Pseudography. *Pseudos; grapho.*
Pseudology. *Pseudos; logos.*
Pseudometallic. *Pseudos; metallum.*
Pseudomorphous. *Pseudos; morphe.*
Pseudo-prophet. *Pseudos; pro; phano.*
Pseudo-volcano. *Pseudos; vulcanus.*
Psyche. *Psyche.*
Psychology. *Psyche; logos.*
Psychomachy. *Psyche; machomai.*
Psychomancy. *Psyche; mancia.*
Ptyalism. *Ptyo.*
Ptysmagogue. *Ptyo; agogeus.*
Puberty, pubescent. *Puber.*
Public, publican, publish. *Populus.*
Pudency, pudical, pudicity. *Pudeo.*
Puerile, puerperal. *Puer.*
Pugilism, pugnacious, pugnacity. *Pugna.*
Puissant. *Posse.*
Puke. *Sputo.*
Pulicose. *Pulex.*
Pullet, pullulate. *Pullus.*
Pulmonary, pulmonic. *Pulmo*
Pulp. *Pulpa.*
Pulpit. *Pulpitum.*
Pulpous. *Pulpa.*
Pulsation, pulse. *Pello.*
Pulsific. *Pello; facio.*
Pulsion. *Pello.*
Pulverin, pulverize, pulverous, pulverulent, pulvic. *Pulvis.*
Punch, punctate. *Pungo.*
Punctiform. *Pungo; forma.*
Punctilio, puncto, punctual, punctuate, punctulate, puncture, pungent. *Pungo.*
Punic. *Punicus.*
Punish, punition. *Punio.*
Pup, pupa, pupil, pupilage. *Pupa.*
Pupivorous. *Pupa; voro.*
Puppet, puppy. *Pupa.*
Pure. *Purus.*
Purgation, purgatory, purge. *Purgo.*
Purification. *Purus; facio.*
Puriform. *Purus; forma.*
Purify, purist, puritan, purity. *Purus.*
Purlieu. *Purus; lieu.*
Purloin. *Purloin.*
Purport. *Pro; porto.*
Purpose. *Pro; pono.*
Pursuant, pursue, pursuit, pursuivant. *Per; sequor.*
Purtenance. *Per; teneo.*
Purulent. *Pus.*
Purvey. *Pro; video.*
Pus. *Pus.*
Pusillanimity, pusillanimous. *Pusillus; animus.*
Pustule. *Pus.*
Putative. *Puto.*
Putredinous. *Putris.*
Putrefaction. *Putris; facio*
Putrefy, putrescent, putrid. *Putris*
Putrification. *Putris; facio.*
Pygmean, pygmy. *Pygme.*
Pylorus. *Pylorus.*
Pyramid, pyre. *Pyr.*
Pyretology. *Pyr; logos.*
Pyritaceous, pyrite. *Pyr.*

Pyritiferous. *Pyr; fero.*
Pyritology. *Pyr; logos.*
Pyrolatry. *Pyr; latria.*
Pyroligneous. *Pyr; lignum.*
Pyrology. *Pyr; logos.*
Pyromancy. *Pyr; mancia.*
Pyrometer. *Pyr; metrum.*
Pyronomics. *Pyr; nomos.*
Pyrophanous. *Pyr; phano.*
Pyrophorus. *Pyr; phero.*
Pyroscope. *Pyr; scopeo.*
Pyrotechnic *Pyr; techne.*
Pyrotic. *Pyr.*
Pyrrhonic, pyrrhonism. *Pyrrho.*
Pythagoric, pythagorism. *Pythagoras.*
Pythian, pythonic. *Python.*

Q.

Quadragene. *Quadra; genea.*
Quadragesima. *Quadra.*
Quadrangle. *Quadra; angulus.*
Quadrant, quadrat. *Quadra.*
Quadrennial. *Quadra; annus.*
Quadrible. *Quadra.*
Quadricapsular. *Quadra; capsula.*
Quadridecimal. *Quadra; decem.*
Quadridentate. *Quadra; dens.*
Quadrifid. *Quadra; findo.*
Quadrijugous. *Quadra; jugum.*
Quadrilateral. *Quadra; latus.*
Quadrille. *Quadra.*
Quadrilobed. *Quadra;* (*lobos*, a lobe).
Quadrilocular. *Quadra;* (*loculus*, a little place).
Quadrinomial. *Quadra; nomen.*
Quadripartite. *Quadra; pars.*
Quadriphyllous. *Quadra; phyllon.*
Quadrireme. *Quadra; remus.*
Quadrisyllable. *Quadra; syl; labo.*
Quadrivalve. *Quadra; valvæ.*
Quadrivial. *Quadra; via.*
Quadroon. *Quadra.*
Quadruman. *Quadra; manus.*
Quadruped. *Quadra; pes.*
Quadruple, quadruplicate. *Quadra; plico.*
Qualification. *Qualis; facio.*
Qualify, quality. *Qualis.*
Quantitative, quantity, quantum. *Quantus.*
Quarantine. *Quadra.*
Quarrel. *Queror.*
Quart, quarter, quartern, quarto. *Quadra.*
Quash. *Quatio.*
Quatern, quaternion, quatrain. *Quadra.*
Querent, querimonious. *Queror.*
Querry. *Eques.*
Querulous. *Queror.*
Query, quest, question, questor, questuary. *Quæro.*
Quidnunc. *Quid;* (*nunc*, now).
Quiesce, quiet, quietus. *Quies.*
Quinary, quinate, quincuncial, quincunx. *Quinque.*
Quindecagon. *Quinque; deca; gonia.*
Quindecemvir. *Quinque; deca; vir.*
Quinquagesima. *Quinque.*
Quinquangular. *Quinque; angulus.*
Quinquecapsular. *Quinque; capsula.*
Quinquefarious. *Quinque; fari.*
Quinquefid. *Quinque; findo.*
Quinquefoliated. *Quinque; folium.*
Quinqueliteral. *Quinque; litera.*
Quinquelobed. *Quinque;* (*lobos*, a lobe).
Quinquelocular. *Quinque;* (*loculus*, a little place)
Quinquennial. *Quinque; annus.*
Quinquepartite. *Quinque; pars.*
Quinquereme. *Quinque; remus.*
Quinquevalve. *Quinque; valvæ.*
Quinquevir. *Quinque; vir.*
Quinquisyllable. *Quinque; syl; labo.*
Quint. *Quinque.*
Quintessence. *Quinque; ens.*
Quintillion. *Quinque; mille.*
Quintuple. *Quinque; plico.*
Quodlibet. *Quid;* (*libet*, it pleases).
Quorum, quota. *Quot.*
Quote. *Cito.*
Quotidian. *Quot; dies.*
Quotient. *Quot.*

R.

Rabbi, rabbin. *Rabbi*
Rabdology. *Rabdos.*
Rabid. *Rabies.*
Racemation. *Racemus.*
Racemiferous. *Racemus; fero.*
Racemous. *Racemus.*
Radial, radiant, radiate. *Radius.*
Radical, radicate, radicle. *Radix.*
Radiometer. *Radius; metrum.*
Radius. *Radius.*
Radix. *Radix.*
Ramage, rameous, ramous. *Ramus.*
Ramification. *Ramus; facio.*
Ramify, ramous. *Ramus.*
Rancescent, rancid, rancor, rank, rankle *Ranceo.*
Rank. *Rang.*
Rap, rape, rapid, rapier, rapine, rapture. *Rapio.*
Rare. *Rarus.*
Rarefaction. *Rarus; facio.*
Rarefy, rarity. *Rarus.*
Rase, rash. *Rado.*
Rate. *Ratus.*
Ratification. *Ratus; facio.*
Ratify, ratio, ratiocinate, ration, rationality. *Ratus.*
Raucity, raucous. *Raucus.*
Ravage, rave, ravish. *Rapio.*
Ray. *Radius.*
Raze, razor. *Rado.*
React. *Re; ago.*
Readmission, readmit. *Re; ad; mitto.*
Readopt. *Re; ad; opto.*
Readorn. *Re; ad; orno.*
Real, realize. *Res.*
Reanimate. *Re; anima.*
Reannex. *Re; an; necto.*
Reascend, reascension, reascent. *Re; a scando.*
Reason. *Ratus.*
Reassert. *Re; as; sertum.*
Reassimilate. *Re; as; similis.*
Reassume, reassumption. *Re; as; sumo.*
Reattempt. *Re; at; tento.*
Rebaptize. *Re; bapto.*
Rebel. *Re; bellum.*
Recant. *Re; cano.*
Recapitulate. *Re; caput.*
Recede. *Re; cedo.*
Receipt, receive, receit. *Re; capio*
Recelebrate. *Re; celebris.*
Recension. *Re; censeo.*
Recent. *Recens.*
Receptacle, reception. *Re; capio.*
Recess. *Re; cedo.*
Recidivation. *Re; cado.*

Recipe, recipient. *Re; capio.*
Reciprocal, reciprocate, reciprocity. *Reciprocus.*
Recision. *Re; cædo.*
Recitation, recite. *Re; cito.*
Reclaim, reclamation. *Re; clamo.*
Recline. *Re; clino.*
Reclose, reclude, recluse. *Re; claudo.*
Recoct. *Re; coquo.*
Recognition, recognize. *Re; cog; nosco.*
Recollect. *Re; col; lego.*
Recomfort. *Re; com; fortis.*
Recommend. *Re; com; mando.*
Recommission, recommit. *Re; com; mitto.*
Recompact. *Re; com; pactus.*
Recompense. *Re; com; pendo.*
Recompilement. *Re; com; pilo.*
Recompose, recomposition. *Re; com; pono.*
Reconcile, reconciliation. *Re; concilio.*
Recondense, *Re; con; densus.*
Recondite. *Re; con; do.*
Reconduct. *Re; con; duco.*
Reconjoin. *Re; con; jungo.*
Reconnoiter. *Re; con; nosco.*
Reconquer. *Re; con; quæro.*
Reconsecrate. *Re; con; sacer.*
Reconsolate. *Re; con; solor.*
Reconvene. *Re; con; venio.*
Reconversion, reconvert. *Re; con; verto.*
Reconvey. *Re; con; veho.*
Record. *Re; cor.*
Recount. *Re; con; puto.*
Recourse. *Re; curro.*
Recreant, recreate. *Re; creo*
Recrement, recrementitious. *Re; cerno.*
Recriminate. *Re; crimen.*
Recrudency, recrudescent. *Re; crudus.*
Recruit. *Re; cresco.*
Rectangle. *Rego; angulus.*
Rectification. *Rego; facio.*
Rectify. *Rego.*
Rectilinear. *Rego; linea.*
Rectitude, rector. *Rego.*
Recubation, recumbent. *Re; cubo.*
Recuperation. *Re; capio.*
Recur, recurrent. *Re; curro.*
Recurvation, recurve. *Re; curvus.*
Recusant, recuse. *Re; causa.*
Reddition. *Re; do.*
Redeem. *Re; emo.*
Redeliberate, redeliver. *Re; de; liber.*
Redemand. *Re; de; mando.*
Redemption. *Re; emo.*
Redescend. *Re; de; scando.*
Redintegrate. *Re; in; tango.*
Redispose. *Re; dis; pono.*
Redissolve. *Re; dis; solvo.*
Redistribute. *Re; dis; tribuo.*
Redolent. *Re; olio.*
Redouble. *Re; duo; plico.*
Redound. *Re; undo.*
Reduce, reduction. *Re; duco.*
Redundant. *Re; undo.*
Reduplicate. *Re; duo; plico*
Re-echo *Re; echeo.*
Re-edify *Re; edes.*
Re-elect. *Re; e; lego.*
Re-enact. *Re; en; ago.*
Re-enforce. *Re; en; fortis.*
Re-enthrone. *Re; en; thronus.*
Re-establish. *Re; sto.*
Re-examine. *Re; examen.*
Re-export. *Re; ex; porto.*
Refect. *Re; facio.*
Refel. *Re; fallo.*
Refer, reference. *Re; fero.*
Refine *Re; finis.*
Refit. *Re; facio.*
Reflect, reflex. *Re; flecto.*
Reflourish. *Re; flos.*
Reflow, refluent, reflux. *Re; fluo.*
Reformed. *Re; fomentum.*
Reform. *Re; forma.*
Refossion. *Re; fossa.*
Refound. *Re; fundus.*
Refract, refragable. *Re; frango.*
Refrain. *Re; frenum.*
Refrangible. *Re; frango.*
Refrenation. *Re; frenum.*
Refresh, refrigerate. *Re; frigus.*
Refuge. *Re; fugio.*
Refulgent. *Re; fulgeo.*
Refund, refuse. *Re; fundo.*
Refute. *Re; futo.*
Regal, regalia. *Rego.*
Regenerate. *Re; genus.*
Regent. *Rego.*
Regermination. *Re; germen.*
Regible. *Rego.*
Regicide. *Rego; cædo.*
Regimen, regiment, region, regnant. *Rego.*
Regress. *Re; gradior.*
Regular, regulate, regulus, reign. *Rego.*
Reimplant. *Re; im; planta.*
Reimportune. *Re; im; porto.*
Reimpregnate. *Re; im; pregnans.*
Reimpress, reimprint. *Re; im; premo.*
Reinquire. *Re; in; quæro.*
Reins. *Renes.*
Reinsert. *Re; in; sertum.*
Reinspect. *Re; in; specio.*
Reinspire. *Re; in; spiro.*
Reinstate. *Re; in; sto.*
Reinterrogate. *Re; inter; rogo.*
Reinthrone. *Re; in; thronus.*
Reinvest. *Re; in; vestis.*
Reinvigorate. *Re; in; vigor.*
Reiterate. *Re; iter.*
Reject, rejectaneous, rejectitious. *Re; jacio*
Rejoin, rejoinder. *Re; jungo.*
Rejourn. *Re; jour.*
Rejudge. *Re; judico.*
Rejuvenescence. *Re; juvenis.*
Relapse. *Re; labor.*
Relate. *Re; latum.*
Relax. *Re; laxus.*
Relegate. *Re; lego.*
Relevant. *Re; levo.*
Relict. *Re; linquo.*
Relief, relieve. *Re; levo*
Religion. *Re; ligo.*
Relinquish. *Re; linquo.*
Relish. *Re; lecher.*
Relucent. *Re; luceo.*
Reluct, reluctant. *Re; luctor.*
Relume, relumine. *Re; lumen.*
Remain. *Re; maneo.*
Remand. *Re; mando.*
Remarry. *Re; maritus.*
Remediate, remedy. *Re; medeor.*
Remember, remembrance. *Re; memor.*
Remigrate. *Re; migro.*
Reminiscence. *Re; memor.*
Remise, remiss, remit. *Re; mitto.*
Remnant. *Re; maneo.*
Remodel. *Re; modus.*
Remonstrance, remonstrate. *Re; monstro*
Remord, remorse. *Re; mordeo.*
Remote. *Re, moveo.*
Remount. *Re; mons*
Remove. *Re; moveo.*
Remugient. *Re; mugio.*
Remunerate. *Re; munus*
Remurmur. *Re; murmur*

Remus. *Rome.*
Renal. *Renes.*
Renascent. *Re; nascor.*
Renavigate. *Re; navis; ago.*
Render, rendezvous, rendible, rendition. *Re; do.*
Renegade, renege. *Re; nego.*
Renew. *Re; novus.*
Renitent. *Re; nitor.*
Renounce. *Re; nuncio.*
Renovate. *Re; novus.*
Renunciation. *Re; nuncio.*
Reobtain. *Re; ob; teneo.*
Reoppose. *Re; op; pono.*
Reordain. *Re; ordo.*
Repacify. *Re; pax.*
Repair, reparable, reparation. *Re; paro.*
Repartee. *Re; pars.*
Repass. *Re; passus.*
Repast, repasture. *Re; pasco.*
Repeal. *Re; pello.*
Repeat. *Re; peto.*
Repel. *Re; pello.*
Repent. *Reptum.*
Repent. *Re; peniteo.*
Repeople. *Re; populus.*
Repercuss. *Re; per; cutio.*
Repetend, repetition. *Re; peto.*
Replant. *Re; planta.*
Replication, reply. *Re; plico.*
Repolish. *Re; polis.*
Report. *Re; porto.*
Repose, reposit. *Re; pono.*
Repossess. *Re; posse.*
Reprehend, reprehensible, reprehensory. *Re; prehendo.*
Represent. *Re; pre; ens.*
Repress. *Re; premo.*
Reprieve. *Re; prehendo.*
Reprimand, reprint. *Re; premo.*
Reprisal. *Re; prehendo.*
Reproach. *Re; prope.*
Reprobate. *Re; probo.*
Reproduce, reproduction. *Re; pro; duco.*
Reproof, reprove. *Re; probo.*
Reptile. *Reptum.*
Republic, republication, republish. *Re; populus.*
Repudiate. *Re; pudeo.*
Repugnant. *Re; pugna.*
Repullulate. *Re; pullus.*
Repulse. *Re; pello.*
Reputable, repute. *Re; puto.*
Request. *Re; quæro.*
Requiem. *Re; quies.*
Require, requisite, requisition. *Re; quæro.*
Resalute. *Re; salus.*
Rescind, rescission, rescissory *Re; scindo.*
Rescribe, rescript. *Re; scribo.*
Resection. *Re; seco.*
Resent, resentiment. *Re; sentio.*
Reservation, reserve, reservoir. *Re; servo.*
Reside, resident, residentiary, residue, residuum. *Re; sedeo.*
Resign, resignation. *Re; signum.*
Resile, resilient, resilition. *Re; salio.*
Resin. *Rheo.*
Resiniferous, *Rheo; foro.*
Resiniform. *Rheo; forma.*
Resino-electric. *Rheo; electrum.*
Resino-extractive. *Rheo; ex; traho.*
Resinous. *Rheo.*
Resipience *Re; sapio.*
Resist. *Re; sisto.*
Resoluble, resolute, resolvable, resolve. *Re; solvo.*
Resonant. *Re; sonus.*
Resorb. *Re; sorbeo.*
Resort. *Re; sors.*
Resound. *Re; sonus.*
Respect, respectability. *Re; specio*
Resperse. *Re; spargo.*
Respiration, respiratory, respire. *Re; spiro.*
Resplendent. *Re; splendeo.*
Respond, response, responsible. *Re; spondeo.*
Rest. *Re; sto.*
Restagnate. *Re; stagnum.*
Restauration. *Re; storo.*
Restif. *Re; sto.*
Restinction, restinguish. *Re; stinguo.*
Restitute. *Re; sto.*
Restoration, restore. *Re; storo.*
Restrain, restraint, restrict, restringe. *Re; stringo.*
Resudation. *Re; sudo.*
Result. *Re; salio.*
Resume, resumption. *Re; sumo.*
Resupinate, resupine. *Re; supinus.*
Resurrection. *Re; surgo.*
Resurvey. *Re; super; video.*
Resuscitation. *Re; sus; cito.*
Retail. *Re; tailler.*
Retain. *Re; teneo.*
Retaliate. *Re; talis.*
Retard. *Re; tardus.*
Retection. *Re; tego.*
Retention. *Re; teneo.*
Reticence. *Re; taceo.*
Reticle, reticular. *Rete.*
Retiform. *Rete; forma.*
Retina. *Rete.*
Retinue. *Re; teneo.*
Retort. *Re; tortum.*
Retract, retraxit. *Re; traho.*
Retribute. *Re; tribuo.*
Retrieve. *Re; trouver.*
Retrocede. *Retro; cedo.*
Retrograde, retrogression. *Retro; gradior*
Retrospect. *Retro; specio.*
Retroversion, retrovert. *Retro; verto.*
Retrude, retruse. *Re; trudo.*
Retund, retuse. *Re; tundo.*
Reveal. *Re; velo.*
Revel. *Re; vello.*
Revel. *Rabies.*
Revelation. *Re; velo.*
Revenge. *Re; vindex.*
Revenue. *Re; venio.*
Reverb, reverberate. *Re; verbum.*
Reverence, reverend, reverential. *Re; vereor.*
Reverse, reversion, revert. *Re; verto.*
Revest, revestiary, revestment. *Re; vestis.*
Revibrate. *Re; vibro.*
Revictual. *Re; vivo.*
Review. *Re; video.*
Revile. *Re; vilis.*
Revindicate. *Re; vindex.*
Revise, revision, revisit. *Re; video.*
Revival, revive. *Re; vivo.*
Revivificate. *Re; vivo; facio.*
Revivify, reviviscent. *Re; vivo.*
Revocation, revoke. *Re; voco.*
Revolt, revoluble, revolution, revolve. *Re; volvo.*
Revomit. *Re; vomito.*
Revulsion. *Re; vello.*
Rex. *Rego.*
Rhabdology. *Rabdos; logos.*
Rhabdomancy. *Rabdos; mancia.*
Rhapsody. *Rhapto; ode.*
Rhetoric, rhetorize. *Rheo.*
Rheum, rheumatic. *Rheo.*

Rhime. *Rhythmus.*
Rhine. *Rheo.*
Rhinoceros. *Rhin; ceras.*
Rhomb. *Rhombos.*
Rhomboid. *Rhombos; oidos.*
Rhyme, rhymist, rhythm, rhythmical. *Rhythmos.*
Ridicule, ridiculous. *Rideo.*
Right, righteous. *Rego.*
Rigid, rigor. *Rigeo.*
Rill. *Rivus.*
Risible. *Rideo.*
Rite, ritual. *Ritus.*
Rival, river, rivulet. *Rivus.*
Roborant, robust. *Robur.*
Rogation. *Rogo.*
Roman, Rome, romish, Romulus. *Rome.*
Ropalic. *Ropalon.*
Roral, roration, rorid. *Ros.*
Roriferous. *Ros; fero.*
Rorifluent. *Ros; fluo.*
Rosaceous, rosary. *Rosa.*
Roscid. *Ros.*
Rose, roseate. *Rosa.*
Rostrate, rostrum. *Rostrum.*
Rosy. *Rosa.*
Rota, rotary, rotate, rote, rotund. *Rota.*
Rotundifolious. *Rota; folium.*
Routine. *Rota.*
Royal. *Roy.*
Rubefacient. *Ruber; facio.*
Rubescent, rubican, rubicund. *Ruber.*
Rubific. *Ruber; facio.*
Rubify, rubric, ruby. *Ruber.*
Ructation. *Ructus.*
Rude, rudiment. *Rudis.*
Rufescent, rufous. *Rufus.*
Rugose. *Ruga.*
Ruin. *Ruina.*
Ruiniform. *Ruina; forma.*
Rule. *Rego.*
Ruminant, ruminate. *Rumen.*
Rumor. *Rumor.*
Runcinate. *Runcina.*
Ruption, rupture. *Ruptum.*
Rural. *Rus.*
Ruricolist. *Rus; colo.*
Rurigenous. *Rus.*
Russet. *Russus.*
Rustic, rusticate. *Rus.*

S.

Sabbattarian, sabbath, sabbatic, sabbatism. *Sabbatum.*
Sabellian. *Sabellius.*
Sabulosity, sabulous. *Sabulum.*
Sacchariferous. *Saccharum; fero.*
Saccharine. *Saccharum.*
Saccholactic. *Saccharum; lac.*
Sacerdotal. *Sacer; dos.*
Sacrament, sacred. *Sacer.*
Sacrific. sacrifice. *Sacer; facio*
Sacrilege, sacrilegious. *Sacer; lex.*
Sacris· *Sacer.*
Sacrosanct. *Sacer; sanctus.*
Sadducean, sadducism. *Sadducees.*
Safe. *Salus.*
Sagacious, sagacity, sage. *Sagax.*
Sagittal, sagittarius. *Sagitta.*
Saint. *Sanctus.*
Sal, salacious, salacity, salad, salary. *Sal.*
Salebrosity, salebrous. *Salebræ.*
Salient. *Sal.*
Saliferous. *Sal; fero.*
Salification. *Sal; facio.*
Salify, saline. *Sal.*
Saliniferous. *Sal; fero.*
Saliform. *Sal; forma.*
Salino-terrene. *Sal; terra.*
Salite. *Sal.*
Saliva, salivate, salivous. *Saliva.*
Sally, salmon. *Salio.*
Salso-acid. *Sal; acidus.*
Salsuginous. *Sal.*
Salt. *Sal.*
Saltant. *Salio.*
Saltpetre. *Sal; petra.*
Salubrious, salutary, salutation, salute. *Salus.*
Salutiferous. *Salus; fero.*
Salvage, salvation, salve, salvo. *Salus.*
Samaritan. *Samaria.*
Sample. *Exemplum.*
Sanable, sanative. *Sanus.*
Sanctification. *Sanctus; facio.*
Sanctify, sanctimony, sanction, sanctitude, sanctity, sanctuary. *Sanctus.*
Sane. *Sanus.*
Sanguiferous. *Sanguis; fero.*
Sanguification. *Sanguis; facio.*
Sanguifluous. *Sanguis; fluo.*
Sanguify, sanguinary, sanguine. *Sanguis*
Sanguinivorous. *Sanguis; voro.*
Sanguisuge. *Sanguis; sugo*
Sanity. *Sanus.*
Sapid, sapient. *Sapio.*
Saponaceous, saponary. *Sapo.*
Saponification. *Sapo; facio*
Saponify. *Sapo.*
Sapor. *Sapio.*
Saporific. *Sapio; facio.*
Saraband, Saracens. *Sara.*
Sarcasm, sarcastic. *Sarx.*
Sarcocele. *Sarx; cele.*
Sarcocolla. *Sarx;* (*colla*, glue).
Sarcology. *Sarx; logos.*
Sarcoma. *Sarx.*
Sarcophagus. *Sarx; phago.*
Sarcotic. *Sarx.*
Satan. *Satan.*
Sate. *Satis.*
Satellite, satellitious. *Satellus.*
Satiate, satiety. *Satis.*
Satire, satirical, satirize. *Satira.*
Satisfaction. *Satis; facio.*
Satisfy. *Satis.*
Satrap. *Satrap.*
Saturable, saturate. *Satis.*
Saturday, Saturn, saturnalian, saturnine. *Saturnus.*
Sauce, sausage. *Sal.*
Savage. *Sylva.*
Save, savior. *Salus.*
Savor. *Sapio.*
Saw. *Seco.*
Saxatile. *Saxum.*
Saxifrage, saxifragous. *Saxum; frango.*
Saxon. *Saxon.*
Scalable, scalade, scalary. *Scala.*
Scald. *Caleo.*
Scale. *Scala.*
Scalene, scalenous. *Scalenos.*
Scan. *Scando.*
Scandal. *Scandalon.*
Scandent, scansion. *Scando.*
Scapula. *Scapula.*
Scarificator, scarify. *Scariphos.*
Scatebrous, scaturient. *Scaturio.*
Scaturiginous. *Scaturio.*
Scene, scenic. *Scena.*

Scenography. *Scena; grapho.*
Scent. *Sentio.*
Sceptic, scepticism. *Sceptomai.*
Sceptre. *Sceptrum.*
Schedule. *Schedula.*
Scheme, schemist. *Schema.*
Schism, schismatic, schismatize. *Schisma.*
Scholar, scholastic, scholiast, scholium, school. *Schola.*
Sciagraphy. *Scia; grapho.*
Sciatheric. *Scia;* (*thera*, a hunting).
Sciatic. *Sciatica.*
Science. *Scio.*
Scientific. *Scio; facio.*
Scintillate. *Scintilla.*
Sciomachy. *Scia; machomai.*
Scioptic. *Scia; opto.*
Scissible, scissile, scission, scissors, scissure. *Scindo.*
Sclavonian, sclavonic. *Sclavi.*
Sclerotic. *Scleros.*
Scobiform. *Scobs; forma.*
Scobs. *Scobs.*
Scoff. *Scopto.*
Scope. *Scopeo.*
Scopiform. *Scopæ; forma.*
Scoptic. *Scopto.*
Scorbutic. *Scorbutum.*
Scoria, scoriaceous. *Scoria.*
Scorification. *Scoria; facio.*
Scoriform. *Scoria; forma.*
Scorify. *Scoria.*
Scot, scotch, scotticism. *Scotus.*
Scribble, scribe, scrip, scripture. *Scribo.*
Scrofula. *Scrofula.*
Scruple, scrupulize, scrupulosity, scrupulous. *Scrupulus.*
Scrutable, scrutation, scrutinize, scrutiny. *Scrutor.*
Scrutoir. *Scribo.*
Sculp, sculpture. *Sculpo.*
Scurrile, scurrility, scurrilous *Scurra.*
Scurvy. *Scorbutum.*
Scutage. *Scutum.*
Scutiform. *Scutum; forma.*
Scythian. *Scythia.*
Season. *Saison.*
Sebaceous, sebacic. *Sebum.*
Secant. *Seco.*
Secede. *Se; cedo.*
Secern. *Se; cerno.*
Secession. *Se; cedo.*
Seclude, seclusion. *Se; claudo.*
Second, secondary. *Secundus.*
Secrecy, secret, secretary, secrete, secretitious. *Secretus.*
Sect, sectarian, sectary, sectile, section. *Seco.*
Secular, secularize. *Seculum.*
Secure. *Se; cura.*
Securiform. *Securis; forma.*
Sedan, sedate, sedation, sedentary, sediment, sedition. *Sedeo.*
Seduce, seduction. *Se; duco.*
Sedulity, sedulous. *Sedeo.*
Segment. *Seco.*
Segregate. *Se; grex.*
Seignior. *Senex.*
Select. *Se; lego.*
Selenic, selenite, selenium, selenuret. *Selene.*
Selenography. *Selene; grapho.*
Selenuret. *Selene.*
Semiannual. *Semi; annus.*
Semiannular. *Semi; annulus.*
Semibarbarian. *Semi; barbarus.*
Semibreve. *Semi; brevis.*
Semicircle. *Semi; circulus.*
Semicolon. *Semi; colon.*
Semicolumnar. *Semi; columna.*
Semicrustaceous. *Semi; crusta.*
Semicylindric. *Semi; cylindros.*
Semideistical. *Semi; deus.*
Semidiameter. *Semi; dia; metrum.*
Semidiaphanous. *Semi; dia; phano.*
Semiflosculous. *Semi; flos.*
Semifluid. *Semi; fluo.*
Semilunar. *Semi; luna.*
Semimetal. *Semi; metallum.*
Seminal, seminary, seminate. *Semen.*
Seminiferous. *Semen; fero.*
Seminific. *Semen; facio.*
Semiopacous. *Semi; opacus.*
Semiorbicular. *Semi; orbis.*
Semiordinate. *Semi; ordo.*
Semiosseous. *Semi; os.*
Semiovate. *Semi; ovum.*
Semiped. *Semi; pes.*
Semipellucid. *Semi; per; luceo.*
Semiperspicuous. *Semi; per; specio.*
Semiprimigenous. *Semi; primus; genus.*
Semiquaver. *Semi;* (*quiebro*, a musical shake).
Semispherical. *Semi; sphæra.*
Semispheroidal. *Semi; sphæra; oidos.*
Semitertian. *Semi; ternus.*
Semitone. *Semi; tonos.*
Semitransparent. *Semi; trans; pareo.*
Semivitreous. *Semi; vitrum.*
Semivocal, semivowel. *Semi; vox.*
Sempervirent. *Semper; virgo.*
Sempiternal. *Semper; æternum.*
Senary. *Sex.*
Senate, senator, senescence, senile. senior. *Senex.*
Senocular. *Sex; oculus.*
Sense, sensible, sensitive, sensorium, sensual, sentence, sententious, sentient, sentiment, sentinel, sentry. *Sentio.*
Separable, separate. *Se; paro.*
Sepose, seposition. *Se; pono.*
Septangular. *Septem; angulus.*
September. *Septem.*
Septempartite. *Septem; pars.*
Septenary. *Septem.*
Septennial. *Septem; annus.*
Septentrion. *Septentrio.*
Septic. *Sepo.*
Septilateral. *Septem; latus.*
Septinsular. *Septem; insula.*
Septuagenary. *Septem.*
Septuagesima, septuagint. *Septem.*
Septuple. *Septem; plico.*
Sepulchre, sepulture. *Sepulchrum.*
Sequacious, sequel, sequent. *Sequor.*
Seraph. *Seraph.*
Serenade, serene, serenitude, serenity *Serenus.*
Sergeant. *Servio.*
Sericeous. *Sericum.*
Series. *Sertum.*
Serious. *Serius.*
Sermocination. *Sertum; cano.*
Sermon. *Sertum.*
Serpent, serpentarius, serpentine. *Serpo.*
Serpiginous, serpigo. *Serpo.*
Serrate, serration, serrature, serrous, serrulate. *Serra.*
Servant, serve, service, servile, servitor, servitude. *Servio.*
Sess, sessile, session. *Sedeo.*
Setaceous. *Seta.*
Setiform. *Seta; forma.*
Seton, setous. *Seta.*

Seven. *Septem.*
Sever, several. *Se; paro.*
Severe. *Severus.*
Sex. *Sexus.*
Sexagenary, sexagesima. *Sex.*
Sexangular. *Sex; angulus.*
Sexennial. *Sex; annus.*
Sexfid. *Sex; findo.*
Sexisyllable. *Sex; syl; labo.*
Sexlocular. *Sex;* (*loculus,* a little place).
Sextain, sextary, sextile. *Sex.*
Sextuple. *Sex; plico.*
Sexual. *Sexus.*
Sibilant, sibilation. *Sibilus.*
Siccate. *Sicco.*
Siccific. *Sicco; facio.*
Siccity. *Sicco.*
Sideral, sideration. *Sidus.*
Siderite. *Sideros.*
Siderography. *Sideros; grapho.*
Sideroscope. *Sideros; scopeo.*
Siege. *Sedeo.*
Sigil, sigillative, sign, signal, signature signet. *Signum.*
Significant. *Signum; facio.*
Signify. *Signum.*
Silence, silentiary. *Sileo.*
Silex. *Silex.*
Siliciferous. *Silex; fero.*
Silicify, silicious, silicicarious. *Silex.*
Siliculous, silicle, siliqua, siliquose. *Siliqua.*
Silvan. *Silva.*
Simile, similitude, similitudinary. *Similis.*
Simoniac, simonious, simony. *Simonia.*
Simple, simplicity. *Sine; plico.*
Simplification. *Sine; plico; facio.*
Simplify. *Sine; plico.*
Simulate. *Similis.*
Simultaneous. *Simul.*
Sincere. *Sine; cera.*
Sinecure. *Sine; cura.*
Single, singular. *Singulus.*
Sinister, sinistrorsal, sinistrous. *Sinister.*
Sinuate, sinuosity, sinuous, sinus. *Sinus.*
Siphon. *Syphon.*
Sire. *Senex.*
Siren. *Siren.*
Site, situation *Situs.*
Six. *Sex.*
Soap. *Sapo*
Sober, sobriety. *Sine; ebrius.*
Sociable, social, society. *Socio.*
Socinian. *Socinus.*
Socratic, socratist. *Socrates.*
Sojourn. *Jour;* (perhaps) *sub.*
Solace. *Solor.*
Solar. *Sol.*
Solder, soldier. *Solidus.*
Sole. *Solum.*
Solecism, solecistical. *Solecos.*
Solemn, solemnity. *Solemnis.*
Solicit, solicitation, solicitude. *Solicitus.*
Solid. *Solidus.*
Solidification. *Solidus; facio.*
Solidify. *Solidus.*
Solidungulous. *Solidus; unguis.*
Solifidian. *Solus; fides.*
Soliloquy. *Solus; loquor.*
Soliped. *Solus; pes.*
Solitaire, solitary, solitude. *Solus.*
Solivagant. *Solus; vagus.*
Solo. *Solus.*
Solstice, solstitial. *Sol; sto.* [*Solvo.*
Soluble, solution, solvable, solve, solvent.
Somatic. *Soma.*
Somatology. *Soma; logos.*
Somnambulist. *Somnus; ambulo.*
Somniferous. *Somnus; fero.*
Somnific. *Somnus; facio.*
Sonata. *Sonus.*
Soniferous. *Sonus; fero.*
Sonnet. *Sonus.*
Sonometer. *Sonus; metrum.*
Sonoriferous. *Sonus; fero.*
Sonorific. *Sonus; facio.*
Sonorous. *Sonus.*
Sophical, sophism, sophistic, sophisticate, sophistry. *Sophia.*
Sopite, soporate. *Sopor.*
Soporiferous. *Sopor; fero.*
Soporific. *Sopor; facio.*
Sorbent, sorbic, sorbile, sorbition. *Sorbeo*
Sordid. *Sordidus.*
Sororicide. *Soror; cædo.*
Sort, sortable. *Sors.*
Sortilege. *Sors; lex.*
Sortition. *Sors.*
Sound. *Sonus.*
Sound. *Sanus.*
Source. *Surgo.*
Souter. *Sutus.*
Sovereign. *Super.*
Space, spacious. *Spatium.*
Sparse. *Spargo.*
Spasm, spasmodic. *Spasma.*
Spatiate. *Spatium.*
Special, specie, species. *Specio.*
Specific. *Specio; facio.*
Specify, specimen, specious, spectacle, spectator, spectatrix, spectre, spectrum, specular, speculate, speculum. *Specio.*
Sperable, sperate. *Spero.*
Sperm, spermatic. *Sperma.*
Spermatocele. *Sperma; cele.*
Spew. *Sputo.*
Sphacelate, sphacelus. *Sphacelos.*
Sphagnous. *Sphagnos.*
Sphenoid. *Sphen.*
Sphere, spherical, sphericity. *Sphæra.*
Spheroid. *Sphæra; oidos.*
Spherule, sphery. *Sphæra.*
Spicate, spicular, spiculate, spike. *Spica.*
Spikenard. *Spica; nardus.*
Spine, spinescent, spinet. *Spina.*
Spiniferous. *Spina; fero.*
Spinosity, spinous, spiny. *Spina.*
Spiracle, spire, spirit, spiritual, spirituous. *Spiro.*
Spissitude. *Spissus.*
Splanchnology. *Splanchna; logos.*
Spleen. *Splen.*
Splendid, splendor. *Splendeo.*
Splenetic, splenic, splenitive. *Splen.*
Spoil, spoliation. *Spolium.*
Spondaic, spondee. *Spondæus.*
Sponge. *Spongia.*
Sponsal, sponsible, sponsion. *Spondeo.*
Spontaneity, spontaneous. *Spontaneus.*
Spousal, spouse. *Spondeo.*
Sprite, spright, sprightly. *Spiro.*
Spume, spumous, spumy. *Spuma.*
Spunge. *Spongia.*
Spungiform. *Spongia; forma.*
Spungy. *Spongia.*
Spurious. *Spurius.*
Sputation, sputter. *Sputo.*
Spy. *Specio.*
Squadron. *Quadra.*
Squalid, squalor. *Squaleo.*
Squamiform. *Squama; forma.*
Squamigerous. *Squama; gero.*
Squamous. *Squama.*
Square. *Quadra.*

Squash. *Quatio.*
Stab. *Sto.*
Stabilitate, stability, stable, establish. *Sto.*
Stagnant, stagnate. *Stagnum.*
Staid. *Sto.*
Stamen, staminal, staminate, stamineous. *Sto.*
Staminiferous. *Sto; fero.*
Stanch, stanchion, stand. *Sto.*
Stannary, stannic. *Stannum.*
Stanza. *Sto.*
Statary, state, statics, station, statistic, statuary, statue, stature, statutable, statute, stay, stead. *Sto.*
Steganography. *Steganos; grapho.*
Stellar, stellate. *Stella.*
Stelliferous. *Stella; fero.*
Stelliform. *Stella; forma.*
Stellify. *Stella.*
Stelography. *Stele; grapho.*
Stenography. *Stenos; grapho.*
Stephan. *Stephanos.*
Stercoraceous, stercorary, stercoration. *Stercus.*
Stereography. *Stereos; grapho.*
Stereometry. *Stereos; metrum.*
Stereotomy. *Stereos; tomos.*
Stereotype. *Stereos; typus.*
Stereotypography. *Stereos; typus; grapho.*
Sterile, sterility, sterilize. *Sterilis.*
Sternutation, sternutatory. *Sternuto.*
Stethoscope. *Stethos; scopeo.*
Stich. *Stichos.*
Stichometry. *Stichos; metrum.*
Stigma. *Stigma.*
Still, stillatitious. *Stilla.*
Stillicide. *Stilla; cado.*
Stimulate, stimulus. *Stimulus.*
Stipend, stipendiary. *Stipendium.*
Stipula, stipulaceous, stipulate. *Stipula.*
Stoic, stoical, stoicism. *Stoa.*
Stomach. *Stomachus.*
Story. *Historia.*
Straight, strain, strait. *Stringo.*
Stramineous. *Sterno.*
Strange. *Exterus.*
Strangle, strangulation. *Strangulo.*
Strangurious, stranguary. *Strangos; urina.*
Strata. *Sterno.*
Stratagem, strategus. *Stratos; ago.*
Stratification. *Sterno; facio.*
Stratify. *Sterno.*
Stratocracy. *Stratos; cratos.*
Stratography. *Stratos; grapho.*
Stratum, straw. *Sterno.*
Strenuous. *Strenus.*
Strepent, streperous. *Strepo.*
Strict, stricture. *Stringo.*
Stridor, stridulous. *Strideo.*
Strophe. *Strophe.*
Structure. *Struo.*
Stubble. *Stipula.*
Student, studious, study. *Studeo.*
Stultify. *Stultus.*
Stultiloquy. *Stultus; loquor.*
Stupefaction. *Stupeo; facio.*
Stupefy, stupendous, stupid, stupor. *Stupeo.*
Stygian. *Styx.*
Style. *Stylos.*
Styliform. *Stylos; forma.*
Styloid. *Stylos; oidos.*
Styptic, stypticity. *Stypho.*
Styx. *Styx.*
Suasible, suasion, suasory. *Suadeo.*
Suavity. *Suavis.*
Subacid. *Sub; acidus.*
Subaction. *Sub; ago.*
Subaqueous. *Sub; aqua.*
Subastringent. *Sub; a; stringo.*
Subcelestial. *Sub; cœlestis.*
Subchanter. *Sub; cano.*
Subcommittee. *Sub; com; mitto.*
Subconstellation. *Sub; con; stella.*
Subcontrary. *Sub; contra.*
Subcutaneous. *Sub; cutis.*
Subdecuple. *Sub; deca; plico.*
Subdititious. *Sub; do.*
Subdiversify. *Sub; di; verto.*
Subdivide, subdivision. *Sub; di; viduo.*
Subduce, subduct. *Sub; duco.*
Subdue. *Sub; do* or *jugum.*
Subduple, subduplicate. *Sub; duo; plico.*
Suberic, suberous. *Suber.*
Subindication. *Sub; in; dico.*
Subingression. *Sub; in; gradior.*
Subjacent. *Sub; jaceo.*
Subject. *Sub; jacio.*
Subjoin. *Sub; jungo.*
Subjugate. *Sub; jugum.*
Subjunction. *Sub; jungo.*
Sublapsarian. *Sub; labor.*
Sublation. *Sub; latum.*
Sublevation. *Sub; levo.*
Sublimate, sublime, sublimity. *Sublimis.*
Sublineation. *Sub; linea.*
Sublingual. *Sub; lingua.*
Sublunar. *Sub; luna.*
Submarine. *Sub; mare.*
Submerge, submerse. *Sub; mergo.*
Subminister. *Sub; minister.*
Submiss, submission, submit. *Sub; mitto.*
Submonish, submonition. *Sub; moneo.*
Subnascent. *Sub; nascor.*
Suboctave. *Sub; octo.*
Suboctuple. *Sub; octo; plico.*
Subordinancy, subordinate. *Sub; ordo.*
Suborn, subornation. *Sub; orno.*
Subpœna. *Sub; peniteo.*
Subprior. *Sub; primus.*
Subrector. *Sub; rego.*
Subreption, subreptitious. *Sub; reptum.*
Subscribe, subscription. *Sub; scribo.*
Subsection. *Sub; seco.*
Subsecutive. *Sub; sequor.*
Subseptuple. *Sub; septum; plico.*
Subsequent. *Sub; sequor.*
Subserve, subservient. *Sub; servio.*
Subsextuple. *Sub; sex; plico.*
Subside, subsidence, subsidiary, subsidize subsidy. *Sub; sedeo.*
Subsign. *Sub; signum.*
Subsist. *Sub; sisto.*
Substance, substantial, substantiate, substantive, substitute. *Sub; sto.*
Substratum. *Sub; sterno.*
Substruction, substructure. *Sub; struo.*
Substyle. *Sub; stylos.*
Subsultory, subsultus. *Sub; salio.*
Subsume. *Sub; sumo.*
Subtend, subtense. *Sub; tendo.*
Subterfluent. *Subter; fluo.*
Subterfuge. *Subter; fugio.*
Subterrane, subterraneous. *Sub; terra.*
Subtile, subtiliate, subtilize, subtle. *Subtilis*
Subtract, subtrahend. *Sub; traho.*
Suburb, suburban, suburbicarian. *Sub; urbs.*
Subvention. *Sub; venio.*
Subverse, subvert. *Sub; verto.*
Succedaneum, succeed, success. *Suc; cedo.*
Succiferous. *Sugo; fero.*
Succinate. *Succinum.*
Succinct. *Suc; cingo.*
Succinous. *Succinum.*
Succor. *Suc; curro.*

Succulent. ***Sugo.***
Succumb. ***Suc; cubo.***
Succussation, succussion. *Suc; cutio.*
Suck, suction. *Sugo.*
Sudary, sudation, sudorous. *Sudo.*
Sudorific. *Sudo; facio.*
Sue. *Sequor.*
Suffer, sufferance. *Suf; fero.*
Suffice, sufficient. *Suf; facio.*
Sufflation. *Suf; flatus.*
Suffocate. *Suf; foces.*
Suffossion. *Suf; fossa.*
Suffragan, suffragate, suffrage, suffraginous. *Suffragium.*
Suffumigation. *Suf; fumus.*
Suffuse. *Suf; fundo.*
Sugescent. *Sugo.*
Suggest. *Sug; gero.*
Suggil, suggilate. *Sugillo.*
Suicide. *Sui; cædo.*
Suit, suitable. *Sequor.*
Sulcate. *Sulcus.*
Sulphur, sulphuret, sulphureous. *Sulphur.*
Sultan. *Sultan.*
Sum, summary, summit. *Summa.*
Summon. *Sub; moneo.*
Sumption, sumptuary, sumptuosity, sumptuous. *Sumo.*
Superable. *Super.* [*undo.*
Superabound, superabundant. *Super; ab;*
Superadd. *Super; ad; do.*
Superadvenient. *Super; ad; venio.*
Superannuate. *Super; annus.*
Superb. *Super.*
Supercelestial. *Super; cælestis.*
Superciliary, supercilious. *Super; cilium.*
Superconception. *Super; con; capio.*
Superconsequence. *Super; con; sequor.*
Supercrescence. *Super; cresco.*
Supereminent. *Super; e; mineo.*
Supererogant, supererogate, supererogatory. *Super; rogo.*
Superexcellent. *Super; ex; celsus.*
Superexcrescence. *Super; ex; cresco.*
Superfetate. *Super; fœtus.*
Superficial. *Super; facies.*
Superfine. *Super; finis.*
Superfluitant, superfluous, superflux. *Super; fluo.*
Superimpose, superimposition. *Super; im; pona.*
Superimpregnation. *Super; im; pregnans.*
Superincumbent. *Super; in; cubo.*
Superinduce, superinduction. *Super; in; duco.*
Superinjection. *Super; in; jacio.*
Superinspect. *Super; in; specio.*
Superinstitution. *Super; in; sto.*
Superintend, superintendent. *Super; in; tendo.*
Superior. *Super.*
Superlative. *Super; latum.*
Superlunar. *Super; luna.*
Supernal. *Super.*
Supernatant, supernatation. *Super; nato.*
Supernatural. *Super; nascor.*
Superponderate. *Super; pondus.*
Superpose, superposition. *Super; pono.*
Superproportion. *Super; pro; pars.*
Superpurgation. *Super; purgo.*
Superreflection. *Super; re; flecto.*
Supersalient. *Super; salio.*
Supersaturate. *Super; satis.*
Superscribe, superscription. *Super; scribo.*
Supersecular. *Super; seculum.*
Supersede, supersedeas, supersedure. *Super; sedeo.*
Superserviceable. *Super; servio.*
Superstition. *Super; sto.*
Superstruct. *Super; struo.*
Supersubstantial. *Super; sub; sto.*
Supersubtle. *Super; subtilis.* [*sulphur.*
Supersulphate, supersulphuretted. *Super;*
Superterrene, superterrestrial. *Super; terra.*
Supertragical. *Super; tragœdia.*
Supervacaneous. *Sur; vaco.*
Supervene, supervenient, supervention. *Super; venio.*
Supervise. *Super; video.*
Supination, supine. *Supinus.*
Suppedaneous. *Sup; pes.*
Supplant, supplantation. *Sup; planta.*
Supplement, suppletory. *Sup; pleo.*
Suppliant, supplicate, supply. *Sup; plico.*
Support. *Sup; porto.*
Suppose, supposition, supposititious, suppositive. *Sup; pono.*
Suppress. *Sup; premo.*
Suppurate. *Sup; pus.*
Suppute. *Sup; puto.*
Supralapsarian. *Supra; labor.*
Supramundane. *Supra; mundus.*
Suprascapulary. *Supra; scapula.*
Supravulgar. *Supra; vulgus.*
Supremacy, supreme. *Super.*
Suraddition. *Sur; ad; do.*
Sural. *Sura.*
Surcease. *Sur; cedo.*
Surcle. *Surculus.*
Surd. *Surdus.*
Surface. *Sur; facies.*
Surfeit. *Sur; facio.*
Surge. *Surgo.*
Surgery. *Chir; ergon.*
Surmise. *Sur; mitto.*
Surmount. *Sur; mons.*
Surpass. *Sur; passus.*
Surplus. *Sur; plus.*
Surprise. *Sur; prehendo.*
Surrender. *Sur; re; do.*
Surrogate. *Sur; rogo.*
Sursolid. *Sur; solidus.*
Surtout. *Sur; totus.*
Survene. *Sur; venio.*
Survey. *Sur; video.*
Survive. *Sur; vivo.*
Susceptible, susception, suscipient. *Sus; capio.*
Suscitate. *Sus; cito.*
Suspect. *Sub; specto.*
Suspend, suspense, suspension. *Sus; pendeo*
Suspicion. *Sub; specio.*
Suspiral, suspiration, suspire. *Sub; spiro*
Sustain, sustenance, sustentation. *Sus; teneo.*
Susurration. *Susurrus.*
Sutile, suture. *Sutus.*
Suveran. *Super.*
Sweat. *Sudo.*
Sweet. *Suavis.*
Sybaritic. *Sybaris.*
Sycamore. *Sycos;* (*moron*, a mulberry).
Sycite. *Sycos.*
Sycophancy, sycophant. *Sycos; phano.*
Syllable, syllabus. *Syl; labo.*
Syllogism. *Syl; logos.*
Sylvan. *Sylva.*
Symbol. *Sym; boleo.*
Symmetrical, symmetry. *Sym; metrum.*
Sympathetic, sympathy. *Sym; pathos.*
Symphony. *Sym; phone.*
Symphysis. *Sym; physis.*
Symposium. *Sym; poto.*
Symptom, symptomatic. *Sym; ptoma.*

Symptomatology. *Sym; ptoma; logos.*
Synagogue. *Syn; agogeus.*
Syncronysm. *Syn; chronos.*
Synchysis. *Syn; chymos.*
Syncopate, syncope. *Syn; cope.*
Syncratist. *Syn; cratos.*
Syndrome. *Syn; dromos.*
Synecdoche. *Syn; ec; dechomai.*
Synergistic. *Syn; ergon.*
Synod, synodical. *Syn; odos.*
Synonyme, synonymous. *Syn; onoma.*
Synopsis, synoptical. *Syn; opto.*
Syntactic, syntax. *Syn; tactos.*
Synthesis, synthetic. *Syn; thesis.*
Syntonic. *Syn; tonos.*
Syphon. *Syphon.*
Syringe. *Syrigx.*
Syringotomy. *Syrigx; tomos.*
Syro-phenican. (*Syria*); *phenix.*
System, systematic, systematize. *Syn; stasis.*
Systole. *Syn; stello.*

T.

Tabefaction. *Tabes; facio.*
Tabefy. *Tabes.*
Tabernacle, tabernacular. *Taberna.*
Tabescent, tabid, tabitude. *Tabes.*
Tablature, table, tablet, tabular. *Tabula.*
Tace. *Taceo.*
Tachygraphy. *Tachys; grapho.*
Tacit, taciturn. *Taceo.*
Tact, tactic. *Tactos*
Tail, tailor. *Tailler.*
Taint. *Tingo.*
Talent. *Talentum.*
Talion, tally. *Talis.*
Talmud, talmudic. *Talmudist.*
Tangent, tangible. *Tango.*
Tantalize. *Tantalus.*
Tantamount. *Tantus; ad; mons.*
Tapestry. *Tapes.*
Tardation. *Tardus.*
Tardigrade. *Tardus; gradior.*
Tardify, tardy. *Tardus.*
Tare. *Tero.*
Targum. *Targum.*
Tartar, tartareous. *Tartarus.*
Tastable, taste, tasty. *Taster.*
Tauricornous. *Taurus; cornu.*
Tauriform. *Taurus; forma.*
Taurus. *Taurus.*
Tautologize, tautology. *Tautos; logos.*
Tautophony. *Tautos; phone.*
Tavern. *Taberna.*
Tax, taxable, taxation. *Taxo.*
Taxiarch. *Tactos; arche.*
Taxidermy. *Tactos;* (*derma*, the skin).
Taxonomy. *Tactos; nomos.*
Tear. *Tero.*
Technical, technics. *Techne.*
Technology. *Techne; logos.*
Tectonic. *Tecton.*
Te Deum. (*Tu*, thou); *Deus.*
Tedious, tedium. *Tedium.*
Tegular, tegument. *Tego.*
Telegraph. *Telos; grapho.*
Teleology. *Telos; logos.*
Telescope. *Telos; scopeo.*
Telestic. *Telos; stichos.*
Temerarious, temerity. *Temere.*
Temper, temperament, temperance, temperate, temperature. *Tempero.*
Tempest, tempestuous. *Tempus*
Temporal, temporaneous, temporary, temporize. *Tempus.*
Tempt, temptable, temptation. *Tento.*
Tenable, tenacious, tenacity, tenant. *Teneo.*
Tend, tendinous, tendon, tendril. *Tendo.*
Tenebrous, tenebrious, tenebrosity. *Tenebræ.*
Tenement. *Teneo.*
Tenesmus. *Tendo.*
Tenet, tennis, tenon. *Teneo.*
Tense. *Tempus.*
Tense, tension, tensor, tent. *Tendo.*
Tentation. *Tento.*
Tentory. *Tendo.*
Tenuifolious. *Tenuis; folium.*
Tenuity, tenuous. *Tenuis.*
Tenure. *Teneo.*
Tepefaction. *Tepeo; facio.*
Tepefy, tepid, tepor. *Tepeo.*
Terebinth. *Terebinthos.*
Terebrate. *Terebra.*
Tergeminate, tergeminous. *Tergeminus.*
Tergifetous. *Tergum; fetus.*
Tergiversate. *Tergum; verto.*
Term, terminable, terminal, terminate, termination, terminist. *Terminus.*
Terminology. *Terminus; logos.*
Tern, ternary, ternate. *Ternus.*
Terrace. *Terra.*
Terraqueous. *Terra; aqua.*
Terretenant, tertenant. *Terra; teneo.*
Terreous, terrestrial, terrestrify. *Terra.*
Terrible. *Terreo.*
Terrier. *Terra.*
Terrific. *Terreo; facio.*
Terrify. *Terreo.*
Territorial, territory. *Terra.*
Terrigenous. *Terra; genus.*
Terror. *Terreo.*
Terse. *Tergeo.*
Tertian, tertiary, tertiate. *Ternus.*
Tesselate, tesseraic. *Tetra.*
Test. *Testis.*
Test. *Testa.*
Testaceography. *Testa; grapho.*
Testaceology, testalogy. *Testa; logos.*
Testaceous. *Testa.*
Testament, testate, testator, testatrix. *Testis.*
Testification. *Testis; facio.*
Testify, testimony. *Testis.*
Testudinal, testudinated, testudo. *Testa.*
Tetrachord. *Tetra; chorda.*
Tetrad. *Tetra.*
Tetradactylous. *Tetra; dactylus.*
Tetradynamian. *Tetra; dynastia.*
Tetragon. *Tetra; gonia.*
Tetragyn. *Tetra; gyne.*
Tetrahedral. *Tetra; edra.*
Tetrameter. *Tetra; metrum.*
Tetrander. *Tetra; aner.*
Tetrapetalous. *Tetra; petalon.*
Tetraphyllous. *Tetra; phyllon.*
Tetraptote. *Tetra; ptoma.*
Tetrarch. *Tetra; arche.*
Tetraspermous. *Tetra; sperma.*
Tetrastich. *Tetra; stichos.*
Tetrastyle. *Tetra; stylos.*
Tetrasyllable, tetrasyllable. *Tetra; syl; labo.*
Teutonic. *Teutones.*
Text, textrine, textuary, texture. *Textus*
Thaumaturgic, thaumaturgy. *Thauma; ergon.*
Thearchy. *Theos; arche.*
Theatre, theatrical. *Theatrum.*
Theism, theistic. *Theos.*
Theme. *Thesis*

Theocracy, theocratic. *Theos; cratos.*
Theodicy. *Theos; dico.*
Theogony. *Theos; genea.*
Theologaster, theological, theologue, theology. *Theos; logos.*
Theomachy. *Theos; machomai.*
Theopathy. *Theos; pathos.*
Theophilanthropy. *Theos; philos; anthropos.*
Theorem, theorematic, theoretic, theorize, theory. *Theoros.*
Theosophic, theosophism, theosophy. *Theos; sophia.*
Therapeutic. *Therapeuo.*
Thermal. *Thermos.*
Thermolamp. *Thermos; (lamp).*
Thermometer, thermometrical. *Thermos; metrum.*
Thermoscope. *Thermos; scopeo.*
Thesis, thetical. *Thesis.*
Theurgy. *Theos; ergon.*
Third. *Ternus.*
Thoracic. *Thorax.*
Thoral. *Thorus.*
Thorax. *Thorax.*
Throne. *Thronus.*
Thunder. *Tonos.*
Thurible. *Thus.*
Thuriferous. *Thus; fero.*
Thurification. *Thus; facio.*
Thyroid. *Thyreos.*
Tibial. *Tibia.*
Tickle. *Titillo.*
Time. *Tempus.*
Timeus. *Time.*
Timid. *Timeo.*
Timocracy. *Time; cratos.*
Timon. *Time.*
Timorous. *Timeo.*
Timous. *Tempus.*
Timothy. *Time.*
Tinct, tincture, tinge, tint. *Tingo.*
Titillate. *Titillo.*
Title, titular. *Titulus.*
Titus. *Time.*
Tobacco. *Tobaco.*
Togated, toged. *Toga.*
Tolerable, tolerant, toleration. *Tolero.*
Toll. *Tollo.*
Tomb. *Tumeo.*
Tome. *Tomos.*
Tomentous. *Tomentum.*
Tone. Tonic. *Tonos.*
Toparch. *Topos; arche.*
Toph, tophaceous, tophus. *Tophus.*
Tophet. *Tophet.*
Topic. *Topos*
Topography. *Topos; grapho*
Toreumatology. *Toreuma; logos.*
Torment. *Tortum.*
Torpedo, torpent, torpescent, torpid, torpitude, torpor. *Torpeo.*
Torporific. *Torpeo; facio.*
Torrefaction. *Torreo; facio.*
Torrefy, torrent, torrid. *Torreo.*
Torse, torso, tort, tortious, tortoise, tortuosity, tortuous, torture, torvity, torvous. *Tortum.*
Total. *Totus.*
Toxical. *Toxicum.*
Toxicology. *Toxicum; logos.*
Trace. *Traho.*
Trachea. *Trachea.*
Tracheocele. *Tracheo; cele.*
Tracheotomy. *Trachea; tomos.*
Trachyte, trachytic. *Trachea.*
Track, tract, tractable, tractate, tractatrix, traction. *Traho.*

Trade. *Traho.*
Tradition. *Trado.*
Traduce, traduction. *Tra; duco.*
Tragedy, tragic. *Tragœdia.*
Tragicomedy. *Tragœdia; comos; ode.*
Tragicomical. *Tragœdia; comos.*
Trail, train, trait. *Traho.*
Traitor. *Trado.*
Traject. *Tra; jacio.*
Tralineate. *Tra; linea.*
Tramontane. *Tra; mons.*
Tranquil. *Tranquillus.*
Transact. *Trans; ago.*
Transalpine. *Trans; Alpes.*
Transanimation. *Trans; anima.*
Transcend. *Trans; scando.*
Transcribe, transcript. *Trans; scribo.*
Transcur. *Trans; curro.*
Transe. *Trans; eo.*
Transelementation. *Trans; elementum.*
Transfer. *Trans; fero.*
Transfiguration. *Trans; figura.*
Transfix. *Trans; fixus.*
Transform. *Trans; forma.*
Transfuse. *Trans; fundo.*
Transgress. *Trans; gradior.*
Transient. *Trans; eo.*
Transilience. *Trans; salio.*
Transit. *Trans; eo.*
Translate. *Trans; latum.*
Translocation. *Trans; locus.*
Translucent. *Trans; luceo.*
Transmarine. *Trans; mare.*
Transmigrate. *Trans; migro.*
Transmissible, transmission, transmit. *Trans; mitto.*
Transmute. *Trans; muto.*
Transparent. *Trans; pareo.*
Transpicuous. *Trans; specio.*
Transpirable, transpiration, transpire. *Trans; spiro.*
Transplant. *Trans; planta.*
Transplendent. *Trans; splendeo.*
Transportation. *Trans; porto.*
Transpose, transposition. *Trans; pono.*
Transubstantiate. *Trans; sub; sto.*
Transudation, transude. *Trans; sudo.*
Transume, transumption. *Trans; sumo.*
Transvection. *Trans; veho.*
Transverse. *Trans; verto.*
Trapezian. *Trapezium.*
Trapeziform. *Trapezium; forma.*
Trapezihedron. *Trapezium; edra.*
Trapezium. *Trapezium.*
Trapezoid. *Trapezium; oidos.*
Traumatic. *Trauma.*
Travail, travel. *Travail.*
Traversable, traverse. *Tra; verto.*
Treasure. *Treasurus.*
Treat, treatise, treaty. *Traho.*
Treble. *Tres; plico.*
Trefoil. *Tres; folium.*
Tremble, tremendous, tremor, tremulous. [*Tremo.*
Trepan, trephine. *Trepan.*
Trepid. *Trepidus.*
Trespass. *Trans; passus.*
Trevet, trey, triad. *Tres.*
Trialogue. *Tres; logos.*
Triander. *Tres; aner.*
Triangle. *Tres; angulus.*
Triarian. *Tres.*
Tribe. *Tribus.*
Tribometer. *Tribo; metrum.*
Tribrach. *Tres; brachys.*
Tribulation. *Tribo.*
Tribunal, tribune, tribunician, tribunitial. *Tribus.*

Tributary, tribute. *Tribuo.*
Tricapsular. *Tres; capsula.*
Trichotomy. *Tres; tomos.*
Trick. *Tricæ.*
Tricliniary. *Tres; clino.*
Tricoccous. *Tres;* (*coccus*, a berry).
Tricorporal. *Tres; corpus.*
Tricuspidate. *Tres; cuspis.*
Tridactylous. *Tres; dactylus.*
Trident. *Tres; dens.*
Triduan. *Tres; dies.*
Triennial. *Tres; annus.*
Trietrical. *Tres;* (*etos*, a year).
Trifallow. *Tres;* (*fallow*).
Trifid. *Tres; findo.*
Trifistulary. *Tres; fistula.*
Trifle. *Tres; via.*
Triflorous. *Tres; flos.*
Trifoliate. *Tres; folium.*
Triform. *Tres; forma.*
Trigamy. *Tres; gameo.*
Trigon. *Tres; gonia.*
Trigonometry. *Tres; gonia; metrum.*
Trigyn. *Tres; gyne.*
Trihedron. *Tres; edra.*
Trijugous. *Tres; jugum.*
Trilateral. *Tres; latus.*
Triliteral. *Tres; litera.*
Trillion. *Tres; mille.*
Trilobate. *Tres;* (*lobus*, a lobe).
Trilocular. *Tres;* (*loculus*, a little place).
Triluminar. *Tres; lumen.*
Trimeter. *Tres; metrum.*
Trine. *Tres.*
Trinitarian, trinity. *Tres; unus.*
Trinomial. *Tres; nomen.*
Trio. *Tres.*
Tripartite, tripartition. *Tres; pars.*
Tripedal. *Tres; pes*
Tripennate. *Tres; penna.*
Tripersonal. *Tres; persona.*
Triphthong. *Tres; phthegma.*
Triphyllous. *Tres; phyllon.*
Triple, triplicate, triplicity. *Tres; plico.*
Tripod, tripos. *Tres; pous.*
Triptote. *Tres; ptoma.*
Tripudiary, tripudiation. *Tripudium.*
Tripyramid. *Tres; pyr.*
Triradiated. *Tres; radius.*
Trireme. *Tres; remus.*
Trirhomboidal. *Tres; rhombus; oidos.*
Trisect. *Tres; seco.*
Trispast. *Tres; spasma.*
Trispermous. *Tres; sperma.*
Trisulc. *Tres; sulcus.*
Trisyllable. *Tres; syl; labo.*
Trite. *Tero.*
Triternate. *Tres; ternus.*
Tritheist. *Tres; theos.*
Tritical. *Tero.*
Triton, tritone. *Tres; tonos.*
Tritoxyd. *Tres; oxys.*
Triturable, triturate, triturium. *Tero.*
Triumph. *Triumphus.*
Triumvir, triumvirate. *Tres; vir.*
Triune, triunity. *Tres; unus.*
Trivalvular. *Tres; valvæ.*
Trivial. *Tres; via.*
Trochaic, trochee, trochilic, trochilus, trochite, trochlea, trochoid. *Trochaios.*
Trope. *Tropos.*
Trophimus. *Trophe.*
Trophy, tropist. *Tropos.*
Tropology. *Tropos; logos.*
Trouble. *Turba.*
Trover. *Trouver.*
Trucidation. *Trucido.*
Truck. *Trochaios.*
Truculent. *Trux.*
Trump. *Triumphus.*
Truncate, truncheon, trunk. *Trunco.*
Trusion. *Trudo.*
Truttaceous. *Trutta.*
Tuber, tubercle, tubercular, tuberculate. *Tuber.*
Tuberose. *Tuber; rosa.*
Tubular, tubule. *Tubus.*
Tubuliform. *Tubus; forma.*
Tubulous. *Tubus.*
Tuition. *Tueor.*
Tumble. *Tumeo.*
Tumefaction. *Tumeo; facio.*
Tumefy, tumid, tumor, tump, tumulate, tumulosity, tumult, tumultuary, tumultuous, tumultuate. *Tumeo.*
Tunable, tune. *Tonos.*
Tunic, tunicated, tunicle. *Tunica.*
Turbid. *Turba.*
Turbillion, turbinate, turbinite. *Turbo.*
Turbulent. *Turba.*
Turgent, turgesence, turgid. *Turgeo.*
Turioniferous. *Turio; fero.*
Turmoil. *Turba.*
Turpitude. *Turpis.*
Turret. *Turris.*
Tutelage, tutelar, tutor, tutrix. *Tueor.*
Type. *Typus.*
Typhoid. *Typho; oidos.*
Typhus. *Typho.*
Typic, typify. *Typus.*
Typocosmy. *Typus; cosmos.*
Typography. *Typus; grapho*
Typolite. *Typus; lithos.*
Tyrannicide. *Tyrannus; cædo.*
Tyrannize, tyranny, tyrant *Tyrannus*
Tyro. *Tyro*

U.

Uberous, uberty. *Uber.*
Ubication, ubiety, ubiquitary, ubiquity. *Ubi*
Ulcer, ulcusle. *Ulcus.*
Uliginous. *Uligo.*
Ulterior, ultimate, ultimatum, ultimity. *Ultimus.*
Ultramarine *Ultra; mare.*
Ultramontane. *Ultra; mons.*
Ultramundane. *Ultra; mundus.*
Ululate. *Ululo.*
Umbel, umbellar, umbellate, umbellicle *Umbella.*
Umbilliferous. *Umbella; fero.*
Umbilic. *Umbilicus.*
Umbrage, umbrate, umbratile, umbrel, umbrella, umbrosity. *Umbra.*
Unability, unable. *Un; habeo.*
Unabolished. *Un; ab; oleo.*
Unabrogated. *Un; ab; rogo.*
Unacceptable. *Un; ac; capio.*
Unaccessible. *Un; ac; cedo.*
Unaccommodated. *Un; ac; com; modus*
Unaccompanied. *Un; ac; com; pannus*
Unaccountable. *Un; ac; con; puto.*
Unaccustomed. *Un; ac; coutume.*
Unacknowledged. *Un; ac; nosco.*
Unacquired. *Un; ac; quæro.*
Unactive. *Un; ago.*
Unadmired. *Un; ad; mirus.*
Unadmonished. *Un; ad; moneo.*
Unadored. *Un; ad; oro.*
Unadulterated. *Un; ad; alter.*
Unadventurous. *Un; ad; venio*

Unadvisable, unadvised. *Un; ad; video.*
Unaffected. *Un; af; facio.*
Unalienable. *Un; alius.*
Unalterable. *Un; alter.*
Unambitious. *Un; am; eo.*
Unanalogical. *Un; ana; logos.*
Unanimity, unanimous. *Unus; animus.*
Unappealable. *Un; ap; pello.*
Unappeasable, unappeased. *Un; ap; pax.*
Unapposite. *Un; ap; pono.*
Unappreciated. *Un; ap; precium.*
Unapprehensive, unapprised. *Un; ap; prehendo.*
Unapproached. *Un; ap; prope.*
Unappropriated. *Un; ap; proprius.*
Unapproved. *Un; ap; probo.*
Unapt. *Un; aptus.*
Unargued. *Un; arguo.*
Unarmed. *Un; arma.*
Unarranged. *Un; ar; rang.*
Unarrested. *Un; ar; sto.*
Unarrived. *Un; ar; rivus.*
Unartful. *Un; ars.*
Unascendible. *Un; a; scando.*
Unaspective. *Un; a; specio.*
Unassailed, unassaulted. *Un; as; salio.*
Unasserted. *Un; as; sertum.*
Unassessed. *Un; as; sedeo.*
Unassimilated. *Un; as; similis.*
Unassisted. *Un; as; sisto.*
Unassociated. *Un; as; socio.*
Unassuming. *Un; as; sumo.*
Unatoned. *Un; atone.*
Unattempted. *Un; at; tento.*
Unattended. *Un; at; tendo.*
Unattested. *Un; at; testis.*
Unattracted. *Un; at; traho.*
Unauthorized. *Un; augeo.*
Unavailable. *Un; a; valeo.*
Unavenged. *Un; a; vindex.*
Unaverted. *Un; a; verto.*
Unbeneficed. *Un; bene; facio.*
Unbenevolent. *Un; bene; volo.*
Unbenign. *Un; benignus.*
Unbetrayed. *Un; be; traho.*
Unbishop. *Un; epi; scopeo.*
Unblamable. *Un; blamer.*
Uncalcined. *Un; calx.*
Uncanonical. *Un; canon.*
Uncarnate. *Un; caro.*
Uncautious. *Un; cautio.*
Uncertain. *Un; certus.*
Uncharitable. *Un; charis.*
Unchaste, unchastity. *Un; castus.*
Unchristian. *Un; christos.*
Uncircumcised. *Un; circum; cædo.*
Uncircumscribed. *Un; circum; scribo.*
Uncircumspect. *Un; circum; specio.*
Uncircumstantial. *Un; circum; sto.*
Uncivil. *Un; civis.*
Unclaimed. *Un; clamo.*
Unclarified. *Un; clarus.*
Unclassic. *Un; classici.*
Uncollected. *Un; col; lego.*
Uncollegiate. *Un; col; lego.*
Uncolored. *Un; color.*
Uncomfortable. *Un; com; fortis.*
Uncommanded, uncommended. *Un; commando.*
Uncommissioned, uncommitted. *Un; com; mitto.*
Uncommon, uncommunicated *Un; com; munus.*
Uncompact. *Un; com; pactus.*
Uncompelled. *Un; com; pello.*
Uncomplaining. *Un; com; plango.*
Uncomplaisant. *Un; com; placeo.*
Uncompounded. *Un; com; pono.*
Uncompressed. *Un; com; premo.*
Unconceived. *Un; con; capio.*
Unconcern. *Un; con; cerno.*
Unconcludent, unconclusive. *Un; con; claudo.*
Unconcocted. *Un; con; coquo.*
Unconditional. *Un; con; do.*
Unconducted. *Un; con; duco.*
Unconfidence. *Un; con; fides.*
Unconfined. *Un; con; finis.*
Unconnected. *Un; con; necto.*
Unconquerable, unconquered. *Un, con; quæro.*
Unconscientious, unconscionable, unconscious. *Un; con; scio.*
Unconsecrated. *Un; con; sacer.*
Unconsolidated. *Un; con; solidus.*
Unconsonant. *Un; con; sonus.*
Unconstitutional. *Un; con; sto.*
Unconstrained. *Un; con; stringo.*
Unconsulting. *Un; con; salio.*
Unconsumed. *Un; con; sumo.*
Unconsummate. *Un; con; summa.*
Uncontemned. *Un; con; temno.*
Uncontended. *Un; con; tendo.*
Uncontented. *Un; con; teneo.*
Uncontested. *Un; con; testis.*
Uncontrasted. *Un; contra; sto.*
Unconversable, unconversant, unconverted. *Un; con; verto.*
Unconvinced. *Un; con; vinco.*
Uncorrected, uncorrigible. *Un; cor; rego.*
Uncorrupt. *Un; cor; ruptum.*
Uncountable. *Un; con; puto.*
Uncounterfeit. *Un; contra; facio*
Uncreate. *Un; creo.*
Uncredited. *Un; credo.*
Uncrossed. *Un; crux.*
Uncrowned. *Un; corona.*
Unction, unctuosity, unctuous. *Unguo.*
Unculpable. *Un; culpa.*
Uncultivated. *Un; colo.*
Uncurrant. *Un; curro.*
Undamaged. *Un; damnum.*
Undaunted. *Un; domo.*
Undecagon. *Un; deca; gonia.*
Undeceive. *Un; de; capio.*
Undecent. *Un; decens.*
Undecided, undecisive. *Un, de, cædo.*
Undeclined. *Un; de; clino*
Undecomposed. *Un; de; com; pono.*
Undedicated. *Un; de, dico.*
Undefaced. *Un; de, facio.*
Undefeasible. *Un; de; facio.*
Undefended. *Un; de; fendo.*
Undefied. *Un; de; fides.*
Undefined. *Un; de; finis.*
Undeformed. *Un; de; forma.*
Undeliberated. *Un; de; liber.*
Undemolished. *Un; de; molior.*
Undemonstrable. *Un; de; monstro.*
Undeniable. *Un; de; nego.*
Undepending. *Un; de; pendeo.*
Undeplored. *Un; de; ploro.*
Undeposable. *Un; de; pono.*
Undepraved. *Un; de; pravus.*
Undeprecable. *Un; de; precor.*
Undepreciated. *Un; de; precium.*
Underanged. *Un; de; rang.*
Underived. *Un; de; rivus.*
Underogatory. *Un; de; rogo.*
Undescendible. *Un; de; scando*
Undescribed. *Un; de; scribo.*
Undeserved. *Un; de; servio.*
Undesigned. *Un; de; signum.*
Undestroyed. *Un; de; struo.*

Undetected. *Un; de; tego.*
Undeterminable, undeterminate, undetermined. *Un; de; terminus.*
Undeterred. *Un; de; terreo.*
Undetesting. *Un; de; testis.*
Undeveloped. *Un; de; velo.*
Undeviating. *Un; de; via.*
Undevoted, undevout. *Un; de; votum.*
Undiaphanous. *Un; dia; phano.*
Undiminished. *Un; di; minuo.*
Undirected. *Un; di; rego.*
Undiscerned. *Un; dis; cerno.*
Undisciplined. *Un; discipulus.*
Undiscovered. *Un; dis; couvrir.*
Undiscreet. *Un; dis; cerno.*
Undishonored. *Un; dis; honor.*
Undispensed. *Un; dis; pendo.*
Undispersed. *Un; dis; spargo.*
Undisposed. *Un; dis; pono.*
Undisputed. *Un; dis; puto.*
Undisquieted. *Un; dis; quies.*
Undissembled. *Un; dis; similis.*
Undissipated. *Un; dis; sipo.*
Undissolved. *Un; dis; solvo.*
Undistempered. *Un; dis; tempero.*
Undistended. *Un; dis; tendo.*
Undistilled. *Un; di; stilla.*
Undistinguished. *Un; di; stinguo.*
Undistorted. *Un; dis; tortum.*
Undistracted. *Un; dis; traho.*
Undistributed. *Un; dis; tribuo.*
Undisturbed. *Un; dis; turba.*
Undiversified, undiverted. *Un; di; verto.*
Undivided. *Un; di; viduo.*
Undivulged. *Un; di; vulgus.*
Undoubted, undubitable. *Un; dubius.*
Undulate. *Undo.*
Unedifying. *Un; edes.*
Uneducated. *Un; e; duco.*
Uneffectual. *Un; ef; facio.*
Unelected, uneligible. *Un; e; lego.*
Unembarrassed. *Un; em; barre.*
Unendowed. *Un; en; dos.*
Unenterprising. *Un; enter; prehendo.*
Unentertaining. *Un; enter; teneo.*
Unenvied. *Un; in; video.*
Unepitaphed. *Un; epi; taphos.*
Unequable, unequal. *Un; equus.*
Unequivocal. *Un; equus; voco.*
Uneradicated. *Un; e; radix.*
Unerrable, unerring. *Un; erro.*
Unessential. *Un; ens.*
Unestablish. *Un; sto.*
Unevitable. *Un; e; vito.*
Unexacted. *Un; ex; ago.*
Unexamined. *Un; examen.*
Unexampled. *Un; exemplum.*
Unexceptionable. *Un; ex; capio.*
Unexcised. *Un; ex; cædo.*
Unexecuted. *Un; ex; sequ'r.*
Unexemplified. *Un; exemplum.*
Unexempt. *Un; ex; emo.*
Unexercised. *Un; ex; erceo.*
Unexerted. *Un; ex; sertum.*
Unexhausted. *Un; ex; haustum.*
Unexisted. *Un; ex; sisto.*
Unexpanded. *Un; ex; pando.*
Unexpected. *Un; ex; specio.*
Unexpedient. *Un; ex; pes.*
Unexpended, unexpensive. *Un; ex; pendo.*
Unexperienced, unexpert. *Un; ex; perior.*
Unexplored. *Un; ex; ploro.*
Unexposed. *Un; ex; pono.*
Unexpressible, unexpressive. *Un; ex; premo.*
Unextended. *Un; ex; tendo.*
Unextinguished. *Un; ex; stinguo.*

Unfamiliar. *Un; familia.*
Unfatigued. *Un; fatigo.*
Unfavorable. *Un; faveo.*
Unfeasible. *Un; facio.*
Unfeigned. *Un; fingo.*
Unfenced. *Un; fendo.*
Unfermented. *Un; fermentum.*
Unfertile. *Un; fero.*
Unfinished. *Un; finis.*
Unfirm. *Un; firmus.*
Unfix. *Un; fixus.*
Unforced. *Un; fortis.*
Unformed. *Un; forma.*
Unfortified. *Un; fortis.*
Unfortunate. *Un; fors.*
Unfounded. *Un; fundus.*
Unfrequent. *Un; frequens.*
Unfrustrable. *Un; frustra.*
Unfumed. *Un; fumus.*
Ungallant. *Un; gala.*
Ungenerated, ungenerous, ungenial, ungenteel, ungentle. *Un; genus.*
Ungeometrical. *Un; ge; metrum.*
Unglorified. *Un; gloria.*
Unglue. *Un; gluten.*
Ungoverned. *Un; guberno.*
Ungracious, ungrateful. *Un; gratia.*
Unguarantied. *Un; guarantir.*
Unguarded. *Un; guarder.*
Unguent. *Unguo.*
Unquicular, unquiculate. *Unguis.*
Unguinous. *Unguo.*
Ungulate. *Unguis.*
Unhonored. *Un; honor.*
Unhostile. *Un; hostis.*
Unicapsular. *Unus; capsula.*
Unicorn. *Unus; cornu.*
Unideal. *Unus; idea.*
Uniflorous. *Unus; flos.*
Uniform. *Unus; forma.*
Unigeniture, unigenous. *Unus; genus.*
Unilabiate. *Unus; labium.*
Unilateral. *Unus; latus.*
Unilocular. *Unus; (loculus,* a little place).
Unimaginable. *Un; imago.*
Unimitable. *Un; imitor.*
Unimmortal. *Un; im; mors.*
Unimpassioned. *Un; im; patior.*
Unimplicated, unimplied. *Un; im; plico.*
Unimplored. *Un; im; ploro.*
Unimportant. *Un; im; porto.*
Unimposing. *Un; im; pono.*
Unimpregnated. *Un; im; pregnans.*
Unimpressive. *Un; im; premo.*
Unimproved. *Un; im; probo.*
Unincreasible. *Un; in; cresco.*
Unindifferent. *Un; in; dif; fero.*
Unindustrious. *Un; industria.*
Uninfected. *Un; in; facio.*
Uninflamed. *Un; in; flamma.*
Uninformed. *Un; in; forma.*
Uningenious, uningenuous. *Un; in; genus.*
Uninhabited. *Un; in; habeo.*
Uninitiated. *Un; initium.*
Uninjured. *Un; in; jus.*
Uninquisitive. *Un; in; quæro.*
Uninscribed. *Un; in; scribo.*
Uninstructed. *Un; in; struo.*
Unintelligent. *Un; inter; lego.*
Unintended, unintentional. *Un; in; tendo.*
Uninterested. *Un; inter; esse.*
Unintermission, unintermitted. *Un; inter; mitto.*
Unintermixed. *Un; inter; misceo*
Uninvented. *Un; in; venio.*
Uninvested. *Un; in; vestis*

Uninvestigable. *Un; in; vestigium.*
Uninvidious. *Un; in; video.*
Uninvited. *Un; invito.*
Union. *Unus.*
Uniparous. *Unus; pario.*
Unique. *Unus.*
Uniradiated. *Unus; radius.*
Unison, unisonant. *Unus; sonus.*
Unit, unitarian, unite, unity. *Unus.*
Univalve, univalvular. *Unus; valvæ.*
Universal, universe. *Unus; verto.*
Univocal, univocation, univoke, univoque. *Unus; voco.*
Unjealous. *Un; jaloux.*
Unjoint. *Un; jungo.*
Unjudged. *Un; judico.*
Unjust. *Un; justus.*
Unjustified. *Un; justus.*
Unknow. *Un; nosco.*
Unlabored. *Un; labor.*
Unlamented. *Un; lamentor.*
Unlectured. *Un; lego.*
Unlibinous. *Un; libido.*
Unlimited. *Un; limes.*
Unlineal. *Un; lineo.*
Unliquified. *Un; liqueo.*
Unmalleable. *Un; malleus.*
Unmanaged. *Un; manus.*
Unmasculate. *Un; masculus.*
Unmeasured. *Un; mensura.*
Unmeditated. *Un; meditor.*
Unmelodious. *Un; mel; ode.*
Unmentioned. *Un; memor.*
Unmercantile, unmercenary, unmerchantable. *Un; mercor.*
Unmerciful. *Un; merci.*
Unmerited. *Un; meritum.*
Unmetallic. *Un; metallum.*
Unmingle. *Un; misceo.*
Unmissed. *Un; mitto.*
Unmitigated. *Un; mitis.*
Unmixed. *Un; misceo.*
Unmolested. *Un; molestus.*
Unmonopolize. *Un; monos; polis.*
Unmoralized. *Un; mos.*
Unmortified. *Un; mors.*
Unmoved. *Un; moveo.*
Unmurmured. *Un; murmur.*
Unmusical. *Un; musa.*
Unmutilated. *Un; mutilus.*
Unnarrated. *Un; narro.*
Unnative, unnatural. *Un; nascor.*
Unnavigable. *Un; navis; ago.*
Unnecessary. *Un; necesse.*
Unnegotiated. *Un; neg; otium.*
Unnerve. *Un; neuron.*
Unneutral. *Un; neuter.*
Unnoble. *Un; nosco.*
Unnoted, unnoticed. *Un; nota.*
Unnurtured. *Un; nutrio.*
Unobjected. *Un; ob; jacio.*
Unobnoxious. *Un; ob; noceo.*
Unobscured. *Un; obscurus.*
Unobsequious. *Un; ob; sequor.*
Unobservant, unobserved. *Un; ob; servo.*
Unobstructed. *Un; ob; struo.*
Unobtained. *Un; ob; teneo.*
Unobtrusive. *Un; ob; trudo.*
Unobvious. *Un; ob; via.*
Unoccupied. *Un, oc; capio.*
Unoffended, unoffensive. *Un; of; fendo.*
Unoffered. *Un; of; fero.*
Unopposed. *Un; op; pono.*
Unoppressed. *Un; op; premo.*
Unorderly, unordinary. *Un; ordo.*
Unoriginal, unoriginated. *Un; orior.*
Unornamental. *Un; orno.*
Unorthodox. *Un; orthos; doxa.*
Unostentatious. *Un; os; tendo.*
Unoxygenated, unoxygenized. *Un; oxys; genea.*
Unpacific, unpacified. *Un; pax.*
Unpalatable. *Un; palatum.*
Unparalleled. *Un; para; allelon.*
Unpardonable. *Un; pardonner.*
Unparted, unpartial. *Un; pars.*
Unpassable. *Un; passus.*
Unpassionate. *Un; patior.*
Unpastoral. *Un; pasco.*
Unpathetic. *Un; pathos.*
Unpatronized. *Un; pater.*
Unpeaceable, unpeaceful. *Un; pax.*
Unpenetrable. *Un; penetro.*
Unpenitent. *Un; peniteo.*
Unpensioned. *Un; pendo.*
Unpeople. *Un; populus.*
Unperceived. *Un; per; capio.*
Unperfect. *Un; per; facio.*
Unperformed. *Un; per; forma.*
Unperished. *Un; per; eo.*
Unperjured. *Un; per; juro.*
Unperplex. *Un; per; plico.*
Unpersuadable. *Un; per; suadeo.*
Unperverted. *Un; per; verto.*
Unpetrified. *Un; petra.*
Unphilosophic, unphilosophize. *Un; philos; sophia.*
Unplacable. *Un; placo.*
Unplanted. *Un; planta.*
Unplausible. unplausive. *Un; plaudo.*
Unpleasant, unpleased. *Un; placeo.*
Unpliable, unpliant. *Un; plico.*
Unplumed. *Un; pluma.*
Unpoetic. *Un; poieo.*
Unpoised. *Un; pondus.*
Unpolicied, unpolished, unpolite. *Un; polis.*
Unpolluted. *Un; per; luo.*
Unpopular. *Un; populus.*
Unportable. *Un; porto.*
Unportioned. *Un; pars.*
Unpossessed. *Un; posse.*
Unpracticable, unpracticed. *Un; practos.*
Unpredict. *Un; pre; dico.*
Unpreferred. *Un; pre; fero.*
Unpregnant. *Un; pregnans.*
Unprejudiced. *Un; pre; judico.*
Unprelatical. *Un; pre; latum.*
Unpremeditated. *Un; pre; meditor.*
Unprepared. *Un; pre; paro.*
Unprepossessed. *Un; pre; posse.*
Unpressed. *Un; premo.*
Unpresumptuous. *Un; pre; sumo.*
Unpretending. *Un; pre; tendo.*
Unprevailing. *Un; pre; valeo.*
Unprevented. *Un; pre; venio.*
Unprincely, unprincipled. *Un; primus; capio.*
Unprisoned. *Un; prehendo.*
Unproclaimed. *Un; pro; clamo*
Unprofaned. *Un; pro; fanum.*
Unprofitable. *Un; pro; facio.*
Unprolific. *Un; proles; facio.*
Unprompted. *Un; pro; emo.*
Unpronounced. *Un; pro; nuncio.*
Unproper. *Un; proprius.*
Unpropitious. *Un; prope.*
Unproportionable, unproportioned. *Un; pro; pars.*
Unproposed. *Un; pro; pono.*
Unprosperous. *Un; prosper.*
Unprotected. *Un; pro; tego.*
Unprotracted. *Un; pro; traho.*
Unproved. *Un; probo.*

Unprovide, unprovisioned. *Un; pro; video.*
Unprovoked. *Un; pro; voco.*
Unprudential. *Un; pro; video.*
Unpublic. *Un; populus.*
Unpunctual, unpunctuated. *Un; pungo.*
Unpunished. *Un; punio.*
Unpurged. *Un; purgo.*
Unpurified. *Un; purus.*
Unpurposed. *Un; pro; pono.*
Unpursued. *Un; pro; sequor.*
Unputrified. *Un; putris.*
Unqualify. *Un; qualis.*
Unquestioned. *Un; quæro.*
Unquiet. *Un; quies.*
Unreasonable, unreasoned. *Un; ratus.*
Unreceived. *Un; re; capio.*
Unreclaimed. *Un; re; clamo.*
Unreconciled. *Un; re; concilio.*
Unrecorded. *Un; re; cor.*
Unrecounted. *Un; re; con; puto.*
Unrecruitable. *Un; re; creo.*
Unrectified. *Un; rego.*
Unreduced, unreducible. *Un; re; duco.*
Unrefined. *Un; re; finis.*
Unreformed. *Un; re; forma.*
Unregenerate. *Un; re; genus.*
Unrelative. *Un; re; latum.*
Unremedied. *Un; re; medeor.*
Unremembering. *Un; re; memor*
Unremitted. *Un; re; mitto.*
Unremoved. *Un; re; moveo.*
Unrenewed. *Un; re; novus.*
Unrepealed. *Un; re; pello.*
Unrepentant, unrepented. *Un; re; peniteo.*
Unreplenished. *Un; re; plenus.*
Unreprievable. *Un; re; prehendo.*
Unreproached. *Un; re; prope.*
Unreproved. *Un; re; probo.*
Unrepugnant. *Un; re; pugna*
Unreputable. *Un; re; puto.*
Unrequested. *Un; re; quæro.*
Unreserved. *Un; re; servo.*
Unresisted. *Un; re; sisto.*
Unresolvable, unresolved. *Un; re; solvo.*
Unrespectable, unrespective. *Un; re; specio.*
Unresponsible. *Un; re; spondeo.*
Unrestored. *Un; re; storo.*
Unrestrained, unrestricted. *Un; re; stringo.*
Unretracted. *Un; re; traho.*
Unrevealed. *Un; re; velo.*
Unrevenged. *Un; re; vindex.*
Unrevenued. *Un; re; venio.*
Unreverend, unreverent. *Un; re; vereor.*
Unreversed. *Un; re; verto.*
Unrevised. *Un; re; video.*
Unrevived. *Un; re; vivo.*
Unrevoked. *Un; re; voco.*
Unridiculous. *Un; rideo.*
Unrighteous. *Un; rego.*
Unrivalled. *Un; rivus.*
Unromanized. *Un; Rome.*
Unroyal. *Un; roy.*
Unsaint. *Un; sanctus.*
Unsaint, unsanctified, unsanctioned. *Un; sanctus.*
Unsated, unsatiable, unsatiate. *Un; satis.*
Unsatisfaction. *Un; satis; facio.*
Unsatisfied, unsatisfying, unsaturated. *Un; satis.*
Unsavory. *Un; sapio.*
Unscanned. *Un; scando.*
Unscientific. *Un; scio; facio.*
Unscriptural. *Un; scribo.*
Unscrupulous *Un; scrupulus.*
Unseasonable, unseasoned. *Un; saison.*
Unseconded. *Un; secundus.*
Unsecret. *Un; secretus.*
Unsecularize. *Un; seculum.*
Unsecure. *Un; se; cura.*
Unseduced. *Un; se; duco.*
Unseparable, unseparated. *Un; se; par*
Unserved, unserviceable. *Un; servio.*
Unsevered. *Un; se; paro.*
Unsignalized. *Un; signum.*
Unsincere. *Un; sine; cera.*
Unsociable, unsocial. *Un; socio.*
Unsolicited, unsolicitous. *Un; solicitus.*
Unsolid. *Un; solidus.*
Unsolvable, unsolved. *Un; solvo.*
Unsophisticated. *Un; sophia.*
Unsorted. *Un; sors.*
Unspecified, unspecious, unspeculative. *Un; specio.*
Unsphere. *Un; sphæra.*
Unspoiled. *Un; spolium.*
Unstaid, unstanched, unstate, unstatutable, unsteadfast, unsteady. *Un; sto.*
Unstimulated. *Un; stimulus.*
Unstrained. *Un; stringo.*
Unstratified. *Un; sterno.*
Unstudy, unstudious. *Un; studeo.*
Unsubject. *Un; sub; jacio.*
Unsubmissive, unsubmitting. *Un; sub, mitto.*
Unsubsidized. *Un; sub; sedeo.*
Unsubstantial. *Un; sub; sto.*
Unsucceeded, unsuccessful. *Un; suc; cedo.*
Unsufferable. *Un; suf; fero.*
Unsufficient. *Un; suf; facio.*
Unsuperfluous. *Un; super; fluo.*
Unsupplanted. *Un; sup; planta.*
Unsupplied. *Un; sup; plico.*
Unsupported. *Un; sup; porto.*
Unsuppressed. *Un; sup; premo.*
Unsurmountable. *Un; sur; mons.*
Unsusceptible. *Un; sus; capio.*
Unsuspected, unsuspicious. *Un; sus; specio.*
Unsustained. *Un; sus; teneo.*
Unsystematic, unsystematized. *Un; syn; stasis.*
Untainted. *Un; tingo.*
Untasted. *Un; taster.*
Untaxed. *Un; taxo.*
Untempered. *Un; tempero.*
Untempted. *Un; tento.*
Untenable, untenantable. *Un; teneo*
Untended, untent. *Un; tendo.*
Unterrified. *Un; terreo.*
Untested. *Un; testis.*
Unthrone. *Un; thronus.*
Untimely. *Un; tempus.*
Untinctured, untinged. *Un; tingo.*
Untractable. *Un; traho.*
Untransferable. *Un; trans; fero.*
Untranslated. *Un; trans; latum.*
Untransparent. *Un; trans; pareo.*
Untransposed. *Un; trans; pono.*
Untravelled. *Un; travail.*
Untraversed. *Un; trans; verto.*
Untreasured. *Un; treasurus.*
Untriumphed. *Un; triumphus.*
Untroubled. *Un; turba.*
Untune. *Un; tonos.*
Untutored. *Un; tueor.*
Ununiform. *Un; unus; forma.*
Unurged. *Un; urgeo.*
Unused, unuseful, unusual. *Un; utor*
Unvail. *Un; velo.*
Unvaluable. *Un; valeo.*

Unvanquished, unvanquishable. *Un; vinco.*
Unvariable, unvaried, unvariegated. *Un; varius.*
Unveil. *Un; velo.*
Unverdant. *Un; verdis.*
Unversed. *Un; verto.*
Unvexed. *Un; veho.*
Unviolated. *Un; violo.*
Unvirtuous. *Un; virtus.*
Unvisard, unvisited. *Un; video.*
Unvital. *Un; vivo.*
Unvitiated. *Un; vitium.*
Unvitrified. *Un; vitrum.*
Unvolatilized. *Un; volo.*
Unvote. *Un; votum.*
Unvulgar. *Un; vulgus.*
Unwarranted. *Un; guarantir.*
Upright. (*Up*); *rego.*
Uranology. *Uranus; logos.*
Urbane, urbanity, urbanize. *Urbs.*
Urea, ureter, urethra. *Urina.*
Urge, urgent. *Urgeo.*
Urinal, urinative, urine. *Urina.*
Uroscopy. *Urina; scopeo.*
Ursa. *Ursa.*
Ursiform. *Ursa; forma.*
Ursine. *Ursa.*
Usable, usage, use. *Utor.*
Ustion, ustorious, ustulation. *Ustum.*
Usual. *Utor.*
Usucaption. *Utor; capio.*
Usufruct, usufructuary. *Utor; fruor.*
Usuror, usurious, usurer, usury, utensil, utility, utilize. *Utor.*
Utopian. *Utopia.*
Utricle, utricular. *Uterus.*
Uveous. *Uva.*
Uxoricide. *Uxor; cædo.*
Uxorious. *Uxor.*

V.

Vacation. *Vaco.*
Vaccary. *Vacca.*
Vacillate. *Vacillo.*
Vaccinate, vaccine. *Vacca.*
Vacuate, vacuist, vacuity, vacuum. *Vaco.*
Vade-mecum. *Vado;* (*mecum*, with me).
Vagabond, vagary. *Vagus.*
Vaginal, vaginant. *Vagina.*
Vagino-pennous. *Vagina; penna.*
Vagrant, vague. *Vagus.*
Vail. *Velo.*
Vain. *Vanus.*
Vale. *Vallis.*
Valediction. *Valeo; dico.*
Valet, valetudinarian, valiant, valid. *Valeo.*
Vallation. *Vallum.*
Valley. *Vallis.*
Vallum. *Vallum.*
Valor, valuation, value. *Valeo.*
Valve, valvular. *Valvæ.*
Van. *Avant.*
Vancourier. *Avant; curro.*
Vandal. *Vandals.*
Vanguard. *Avant; guarder.*
Vanish, vanity. *Vanus.*
Vanquish. *Vinco.*
Vant. *Vanus.*
Vantageground. *Avant;* (*ground*).
Vapid, vapor. *Vapor.*
Variable, variance, variation, variegate, variety. *Varius.*
Variolous. *Variolæ.*
Varioloid. *Variolæ; oidos.*
Various, vary. *Varius.*
Vascular. *Vas.*
Vasculiferous. *Vas; fero.*
Vase. *Vas.*
Vast. *Vastus.*
Vaticide. *Vates; cædo.*
Vaticinate. *Vates; cano.*
Vaunt. *Vanus.*
Vection, vectitation, vecture. *Veho.*
Vedet, vedette. *Video.*
Veer. *Verto.*
Vegetable, vegetate, vegete, vegetive. *Vegeto.*
Vehement, vehicle. *Veho.*
Veil. *Velo.*
Vein. *Vena.*
Vellicate. *Vello.*
Vellum. *Velo.*
Velocity. *Velox.*
Venal. *Vena.*
Venal. *Vendo.*
Venary, venatic, venation. *Venor.*
Vend, vendible, vendition, vendue. *Vendo.*
Venefice, veneficious. *Venenum; facio.*
Venenate, venene, venenose. *Venenum.*
Venerable, venerate. *Veneror.*
Venereal, venereous, venery. *Venus.*
Venesection. *Vena; seco.*
Vengeance, vengeful. *Vindex.*
Veniable, venial. *Venia.*
Venison. *Venor.*
Venom. *Venenum.*
Venous. *Vena.*
Vent. *Venio. Vendo.*
Venter. *Venter.*
Ventiduct. *Ventus; duco.*
Ventilate. *Ventus; latum.*
Ventriloquism. *Venter; loquor.*
Venture. *Venio.*
Venus. *Venus.*
Veracious, veracity. *Verus.*
Verb, verbality, verbalize, verbatim. *Verbum.*
Verbiage, verbose, verbosity. *Verbum.*
Verdant, verderor. *Verdis.*
Verdict. *Verus; dico.*
Verdigris. *Verdis;* (*gris*, grey).
Verditer, verdure. *Verdis.*
Verecund. *Verus.*
Verge. *Vergo.*
Veridical. *Verus; dico.*
Verification. *Verus; facio.*
Verify, verily. *Verus.*
Verisimilar, verisimilitude. *Verus; similis*
Veritable, verity. *Verus.*
Vermeology. *Vermis; logos.*
Vermicelli, vermicular, vermiculate, vermicule. *Vermis.*
Vermiform. *Vermis; forma.*
Vermifuge. *Vermis; fugio.*
Vermilion, vermin. *Vermis.*
Vermiparous. *Vermis; pario.*
Vermivorous. *Vermis; voro.*
Vernacular. *Vernaculus.*
Vernal, vernant, vernation. *Ver.*
Verrucous. *Verruca.*
Versable, versatile, verse, versicle. *Verto*
Versicolor. *Verto; color.*
Versification. *Verto; facio.*
Versify, version. *Verto.*
Vertex, vertical, verticil, verticity, vertiginous, vertigo. *Verto.*
Very. *Verus.*
Vesicate, vesicle, vesicular, vesiculate. *Vesica.*
Vesper, vespertine. *Vesper*
Vessel. *Vas.*

Vest, vestal. *Vestis.*
Vestibule. *Vestibulum.*
Vestige. *Vestigium.*
Vestment, vestry, vesture. *Vestis.*
Veteran. *Vetus.*
Veterinary. *Veho.*
Veto. *Veto.*
Vex, vexatious. *Veho.*
Vexil, vexillary, vexillation. *Vexillum.*
Via. *Via.*
Viaduct. *Via; duco.*
Viand. *Via.*
Viatic, viaticum. *Via.*
Vibrate, vibratiuncle, vibratory. *Vibro.*
Vicar, vicarage, vicariate, vicarious. *Vicis.*
Vice. *Vitium.*
Vice-admiral. *Vicis;* (*amiral*, an admiral).
Vice-agent. *Vicis; ago.*
Vice-chamberlain. *Vicis;* (*camera*, a chamber).
Vice-chancellor. *Vicis;* (*cancelli*, cross bars).
Vice-consul. *Vicis; con; salio.*
Vicegerent. *Vicis; gero.*
Vicenary. *Vicis.*
Vice-president. *Vicis; pre; sedeo.*
Viceroy, viceroyalty. *Vicis; roy.*
Viciate. *Vitium.*
Vicinage, vicine, vicinity. *Vicinus.*
Viciosity, vicious. *Vitium.*
Vicissitude, vicissitudinary. *Vicis.*
Victim, victor, victorious. *Vinco.*
Vide. *Video.*
Videlicit. *Video; licet.*
Vidual. *Viduo.*
View. *Video.*
Vigesimation. *Viceni.*
Vigil, vigilant. *Vigil.*
Vigor. *Vigor.*
Vile, vilify. *Vilis.*
Vilipend. *Vilis; pendeo.*
Ville, villa, village. *Villa.*
Villain, villanage, villany. *Villanus.*
Villous. *Villus.*
Viminal, vimineous. *Vimen.*
Vincible. *Vinco.*
Vindemial. *Vinum.*
Vindicable, vindicate, vindictive. *Vindex.*
Vine, vinery, vinous. *Vinum.*
Vinegar. *Vinum;* (*aigre*, sour).
Vintage. *Vinum.*
Violate, violent. *Violo.*
Viper. *Vipera.*
Viraginian, virago. *Vir.*
Virent, virgin, virginal, virgo, viridity. *Virgo.*
Virility. *Vir.*
Virtu, virtue, virtuoso, virtuous. *Virtus.*
Virulent, virus. *Virus.*
Visage. *Video.*
Viscera, viscerate. *Viscus.*
Viscid, viscosity. *Viscus.*
Viscount. *Vicis; comes.*
Viscous. *Viscus.*
Visible, vision, visit, visitorial, visor, vista, visual. *Video.*
Vital. *Vivo.*
Vitiate, vitious. *Vitium.*
Vitreo-electric. *Vitrum; electrum.*
Vitreous, vitrescent, vitrescible. *Vitrum.*
Vitrifaction. *Vitrum; facio.*
Vitrifiable. *Vitrum.*
Vitrificate. *Vitrum; facio.*
Vitrify, vitriol, vitriolate, vitriolic, vitriolize. *Vitrum.*
Vituline. *Vitulus.*
Vituperable, vituperate. *Vitupero.*
Vivacious, vivacity, vivary. *Vivo.*
Vivavoce. *Vivo; voco.*
Vivid. *Vivo.*
Vivific, vivification. *Vivo; facio.*
Vivify. *Vivo.*
Viviparous. *Vivo; pario.*
Vocable, vocabulary, vocal, vocation. *Voco*
Vociferate. *Voco; fero.*
Voice. *Voco.*
Void. *Viduo.*
Volant, volatile, volatilize. *Volo.*
Volcanic, volcanize, volcano. *Vulcanus.*
Volitation. *Volo.*
Volition. *Volo.*
Volley. *Volo.*
Volt, volubilate, voluble, volume. *Volvo.*
Voluntary, volunteer. *Volo.*
Voluptuary, voluptuous. *Voluptas.*
Volutation, volute. *Volvo.*
Vomit, vomition, vomitory. *Vomito.*
Voracious, voracity, voraginous. *Voro.*
Vortex, vortical *Verto.*
Votary, vote. *Votum.*
Vouch. *Voco*
Vow. *Votum.*
Vowel. *Voco.*
Voyage. *Via.*
Vulgar, vulgate. *Vulgus.*
Vulnerable, vulnerary. *Vulnus*
Vulpine. *Vulpes.*
Vulture, vulturine. *Vultu.*

W.

Wade. *Vado.*
Wall. *Vallum*
Wallow. *Valvo.*
Ward. *Guarder.*
Warrant. *Guarantir.*
Waste *Vastus.*
Way. *Via.*
Weigh, weight. *Veho.*
Whistle. *Fistula.*
Widow. *Viduo.*
Wine-bibber. (*Wine*); *bibo.*
Wonder, wondrous. *Wonder.*
Worm. *Vermis.*

X.

Xerophagy. *Xeros; phago.*
Xerophthalmy. *Xeros; ophthalmos.*
Xiphias. *Xiphos.*
Xiphoid. *Xiphos; oidos.*
Xylography. *Xylon; grapho.*
Xyster. *Xyster.*

Y.

Yoke. *Jugum.*

Z.

Zeal, zealot. *Zelos.*
Zenith. *Zenith.*
Zeolite. *Zelos; lithos.*
Zeolitiform. *Zelos; lithos; forma.*
Zephyr. *Zephyrus.*
Zetetic. *Zeteo.*
Zimome. *Zume.*
Zodiac. *Zoon.*
Zone. *Zona.*
Zoography. *Zoon; grapho.*

Zoolite. *Zoon; lithos.*
Zoology. *Zoon; logos.*
Zoophite *Zoon; phyton.*
Zoophorus. *Zoon; phero.*
Zoophthalmy. *Zoon; ophthalmos.*
Zoophyte. *Zoon; phyton.*
Zoophytology. *Zoon; phyton; logos.*
Zootomy. *Zoon; tomos.*
Zumate, zumic. *Zume.*
Zumology. *Zume; logos.*
Zumosimeter. *Zume; metrum.*
Zygodactylus. *Zygoo; dactylus.*

THE END

www.ingramcontent.com/pod-product-compliance
Lightning Source LLC
LaVergne TN
LVHW010204110826
845151LV00002B/603

* 9 7 8 1 4 2 5 5 3 5 5 1 3 *